# P. P. RUBENS

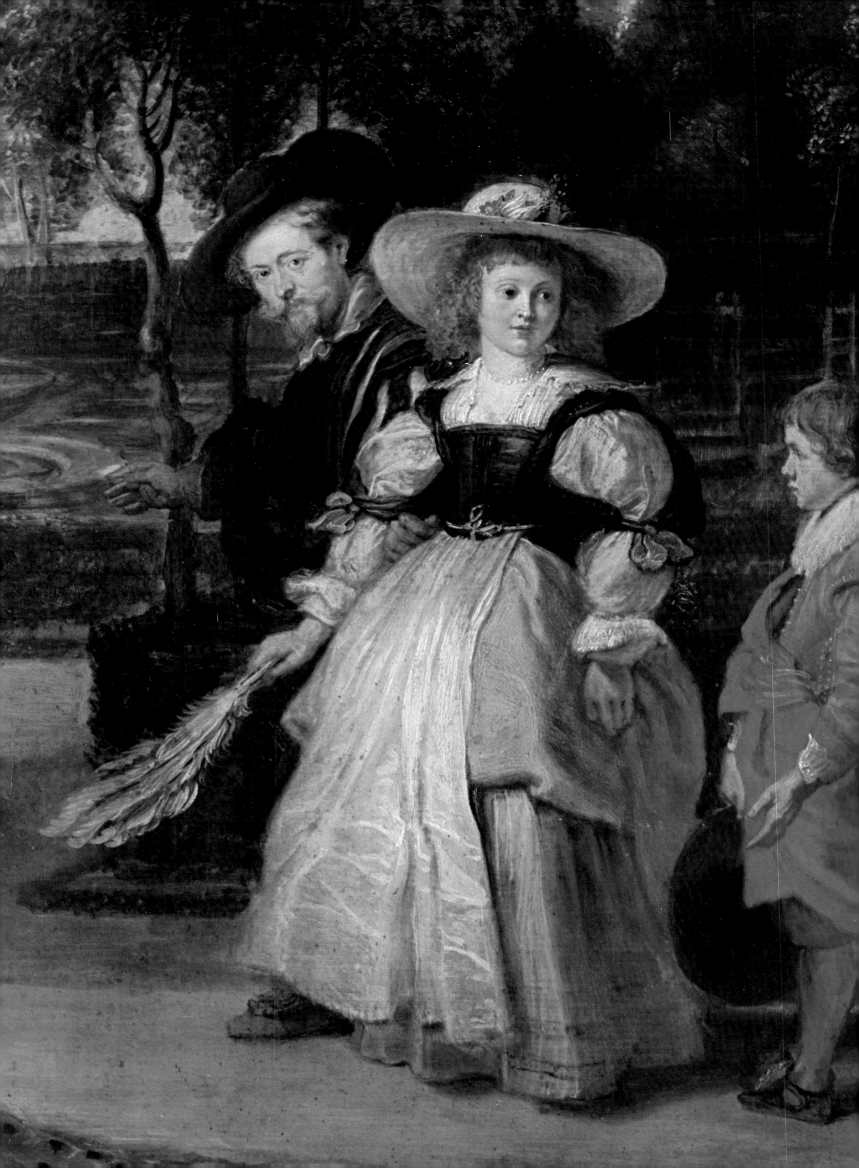

# Frans Baudouin

*Curator of the Rubens House*

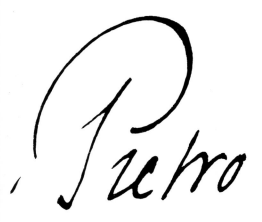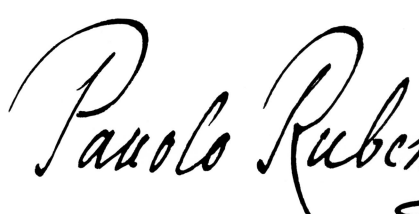

*Translated by Elsie Callander*

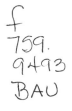

Harry N. Abrams, Inc., Publishers, New York

Library of Congress Catalogue Card Number: 77–82339
International Standard Book Number: 0–8109–1586–3

Copyright © in 1977 by Mercatorfonds, Antwerp
Published in 1977 by Harry N. Abrams, Incorporated, New York

Printed in Belgium. Bound in the Netherlands

# Contents

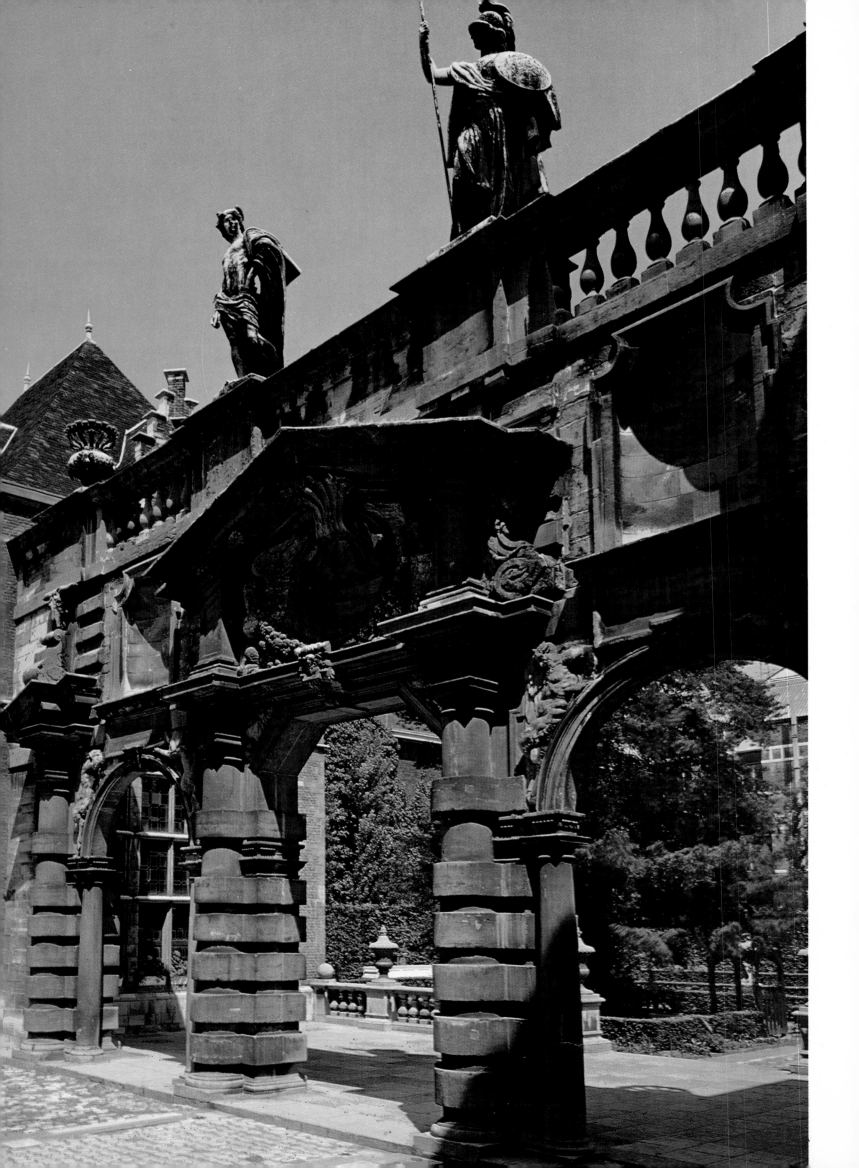

# Introduction to Rubens' Life and Work

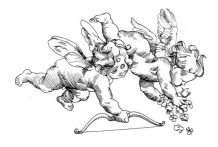

Plate 1
PORTICO OF RUBENS' HOUSE IN
ANTWERP

See Fig. 8

Ambrogio Spinola once declared that he saw so many brilliant talents in Rubens that the art of painting could be considered one of his lesser gifts. No doubt the statesman and soldier of Genoa was thinking at the time of Rubens' diplomatic activities, crowned by outstanding success. Another contemporary, the French humanist Nicolas-Claude Fabri de Peiresc, praised Rubens' honesty and "the charm of his society"; he added: "In the field of Antiquity, above all, his knowledge was the broadest and most excellent I have ever encountered." Peiresc, himself a great connoisseur of classical Antiquity, thus emphasized Rubens' competence in Greek and Roman literature and art, which would later stand the painter of mythological pictures in good stead. In another context the same author wrote that Rubens "had been born to give pleasure and charm in everything he said and did." But apart from this evidence, an acquaintance with Rubens' correspondence will prove the range of his knowledge, the diversity of his interests, and the charm of his personality.

If Rubens' art was "one of his lesser gifts" in Spinola's eyes, it is nevertheless thanks to that gift that Rubens is still acknowledged one of the most influential painters of his time, the European Baroque, and one of the most brilliant creative artists the world has ever known. He remains the unequaled colorist, the virtuoso for whom color was a principal means of expression; the "composer" whose imagination was inexhaustible but controlled; the rhapsodist of divine and human dramas, whom Eugène Delacroix and Jacob Burckhardt alike did not hesitate to compare to Homer; the artist whose work holds a rare balance between the sharp observation of reality and its transformation into idealized form.

Rubens did not attain this fullness of talent in one stroke. Unlike certain precocious artists, who reach their peak in early manhood and then die young or fall into repetition or sclerosis, Rubens had a rather modest beginning as an artist. His talent then matured for eight years in the warmth of the Italian sun, while he studied ancient statues and the paintings of the great Renaissance masters. Only after his return to Antwerp did his art suddenly blossom into a truly personal style. Rubens did not, however, become the prisoner of this style; a steady evolution continued right up to the very last years of his life, when his mastery became sovereign. Only death stopped the crescendo of this process.

Rubens was born in an epoch marked by the religious and political troubles of the Netherlands in the second half of the sixteenth century; these led to the rift between the Northern Netherlands—the United Provinces, which became independent—and the Southern Netherlands, which remained under the domination of the Spanish Habsburgs. Rubens' father, Jan, a lawyer and alderman of the city of Antwerp, was suspected of Calvinist sympathies (later he became a Lutheran) and had to flee in 1568 with his wife Maria Pijpelinckx and his older children, finding refuge in Cologne. There he soon was appointed legal adviser to Anne of Saxony, the second wife of William of Orange, the Silent. Convicted of adultery with this capricious woman, Jan Rubens was arrested in 1571 and, according to the law of the time, could have been sentenced to death. That he escaped this was owing above all to the pardon, the strength of character, and the persuasive powers of his admirable wife, and to the heavy financial sacrifices she made to obtain his release from prison.

Peter Paul Rubens was born in 1577, probably on June 28, at Siegen, the small Westphalian town where his father had been forced to reside since 1573, when his imprisonment had ended. Shortly after the birth the family was permitted to return to Cologne; Peter Paul, in his own words, lived there "until his tenth year."

Jan Rubens died in 1587, and his widow Maria Pijpelinckx then took the family back to Antwerp, their native city. There Peter Paul had his lessons with Rumoldus Verdonck at the Latin School of the

Figure 1
VIEW OF SIEGEN
Engraving in G. Braun and F. Hogenberg, *Civitates Orbis Terrarum*, Cologne, 1572
Brussels, Bibliothèque Royale Albert I$^{er}$, Réserve précieuse

*The town of Siegen, east of Cologne on the banks of the river Sieg, Westphalia. Jan Rubens, the artist's father, was required to live in this town after his release from the nearby prison at Dillenburg. Here Peter Paul Rubens was born in 1577.*

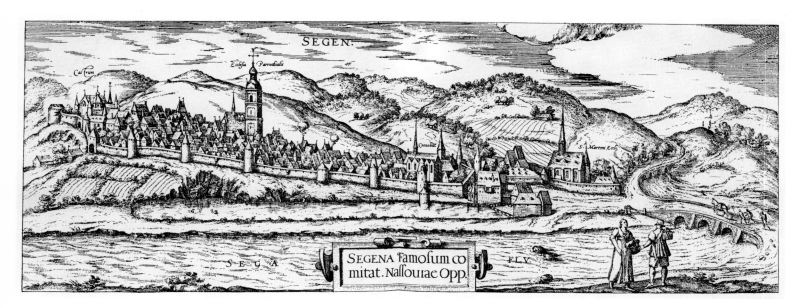

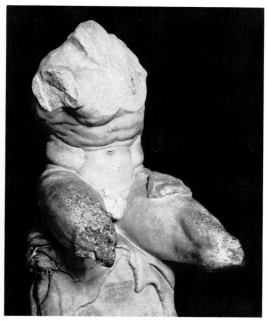

Figure 2
Apollonius of Athens
THE BELVEDERE TORSO
Vatican Museum

*This antique marble statue is one of the rare instances among those discovered at the time of the Renaissance in that it was not restored. The name of the sculptor, active in the first century B.C., is carved on the pedestal.*

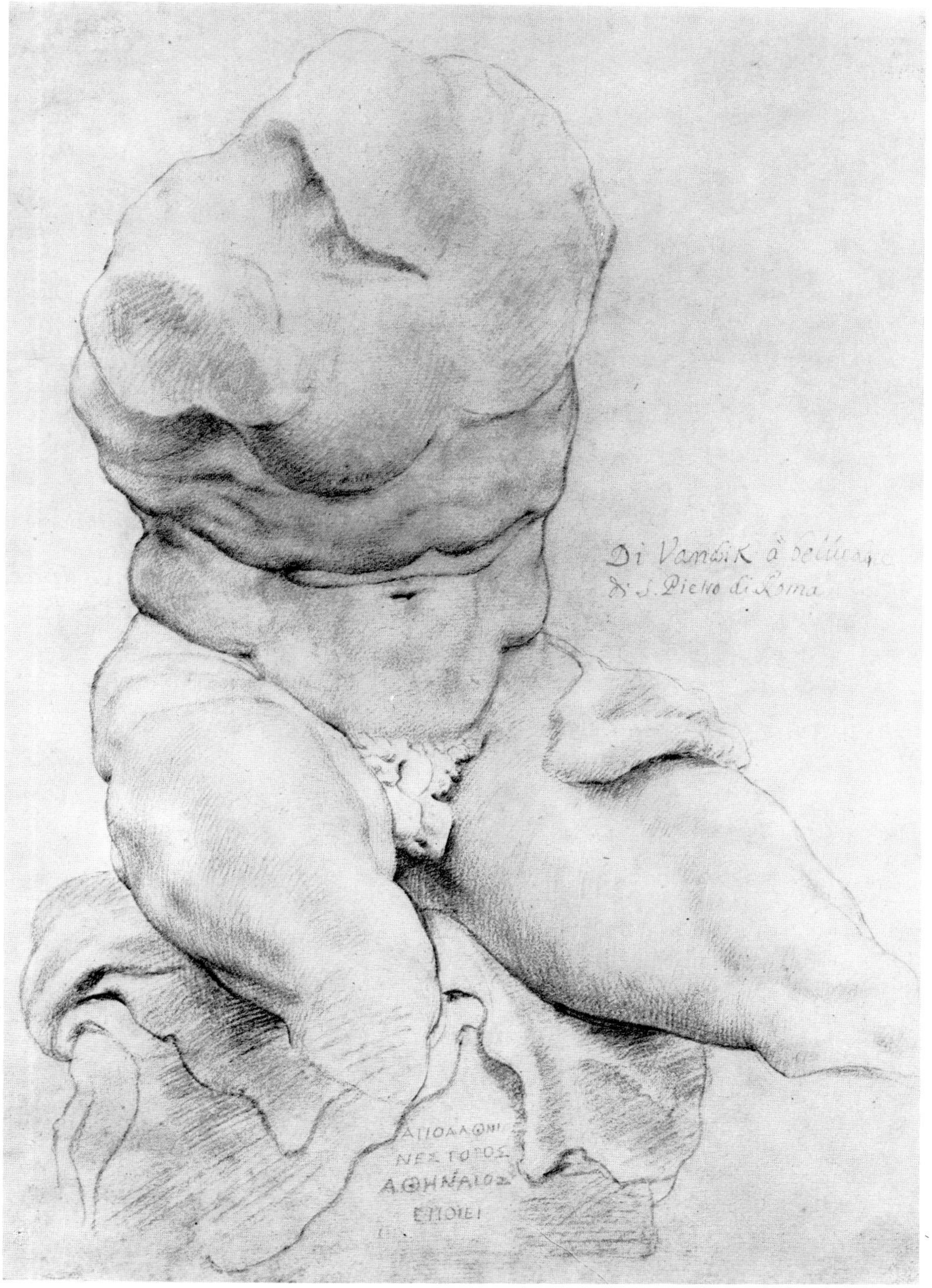

Figure 3
THE BELVEDERE TORSO
Drawing
Antwerp, Rubens House

*Rubens made this drawing in the Belvedere Gardens of the Vatican, where the statue then stood. It is one of the many drawings after antique statues that he made in Italy, particularly while he was in Rome. In the eighteenth century this drawing was wrongly attributed to Anthony van Dyck.*

chapter of the Cathedral of Notre-Dame, in the shadow of that beautiful church. He acquired a good knowledge of Greek and Latin, both in language and literature; throughout his life he was to broaden and deepen his knowledge of classical letters and culture.

Sometime during his fourteenth year he left school to become a page in the service of Marguerite de Ligne-Arenberg, the widow of Philippe, Count of Lalaing, who lived at Oudenarde, but he stayed only a few months in her service. Wishing ardently to become an artist, he returned to Antwerp to learn the art of painting.

11

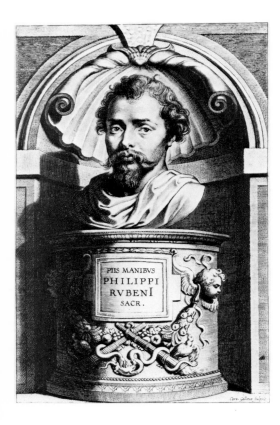

Figure 4
Cornelis Galle, after Rubens
PORTRAIT OF PHILIP RUBENS
Engraving in Philip Rubens, *S. Amaseae Homiliae*, Antwerp, 1615
Antwerp, Plantin-Moretus Museum

*Rubens was much attached to his brother Phillip, humanist and Secretary of Antwerp. He died in 1611, aged barely 37. Rubens' portrait of him, painted on panel, is now in the Detroit Institute of Arts.*

Already, on his own initiative, he had mastered the technique of drawing by copying prints by such artists as Jost Amman, Hans Weiditz, Hans Holbein, and Hendrik Goltzius. When we compare Rubens' copies that have come down to us with their models, it is surprising to find that the boy handled these characters and scenes with greater expression. One of Rubens' most striking features appeared very early: his aptitude for heightening the expressive power of his works by just a few strongly accentuated contours or two or three touches of color.

Rubens' apprenticeship in Antwerp led him successively to the workshops of Tobias Verhaecht, Adam van Noort, and Otto van Veen or Vaenius, the latter being certainly Rubens' most important master. *Adam and Eve in Paradise* (Plate 11), one of Rubens' rare early pictures still preserved, was painted when the artist was in his early twenties and shows clearly how much his art owed, before his departure to Italy, to the cold classicism of Otto van Veen. After some three years' apprenticeship with him, Rubens in 1598–99 was registered as a master in the Guild of St. Luke in Antwerp.

In May 1600, Rubens set off for Italy, "actuated by his desire to see the country, to admire at first hand the works of old and modern masters and, with the help of those models, to perfect his art," as his nephew, Philip Rubens, wrote in 1677.

Almost as soon as he arrived on Italian soil, Rubens was engaged as painter at the court of the reckless and luxury-loving Vincenzo Gonzaga, Duke of Mantua. But he was not to spend the eight years of his Italian visit confined to the Ducal Palace. During his first year he was for a short period in Florence with the Duke's retinue, and he settled in Rome for a few months in 1601–2. In March 1603, on the order of Vincenzo Gonzaga, he accompanied a large convoy bearing gifts to Spain for King Philip III, for his powerful minister, the Duke of Lerma, and for other court dignitaries. In Spain Rubens painted the impressive *Equestrian Portrait of the Duke of Lerma* (Fig. 33), a work showing an ease of movement which marks a turning point in the development of his art. On returning to Mantua in 1604 the Duke, who had thus far commissioned him only with minor works such as executing copies, now awarded him a task worthy of his talent. He was to paint three large canvases to decorate the choir of the church of the Jesuits in Mantua: *The Holy Trinity Worshiped by Vincenzo Gonzaga and His Family* (preserved in part in the Ducal Palace, Mantua), *The Baptism of Christ* (now in the Museum voor Schone Kunsten, Antwerp), and *The Transfiguration* (now in the Musée des Beaux-Arts, Nancy). After finishing these canvases he was called to Genoa in 1605 where he painted *The Circumcision of Christ* that still adorns the high altar in the church of the Jesuits. In 1606 and 1607 he probably spent another few months in Genoa, painting several portraits of members of the aristocracy; he also assembled some general plans and façade sketches of palaces which he later had engraved for a publication entitled *Palazzi di Genova* (Antwerp, 1622).

12

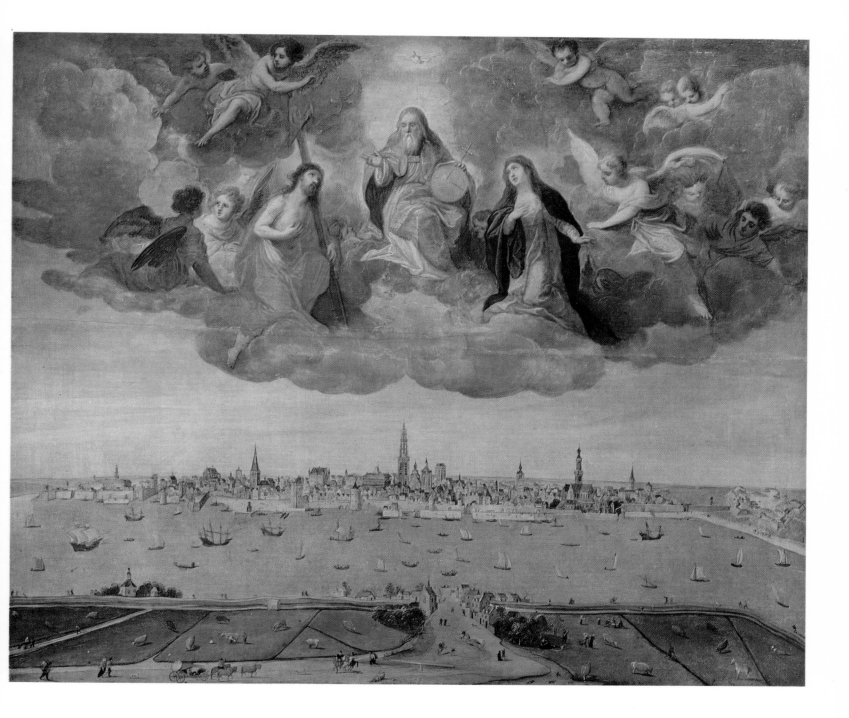

Plate 2
Abel Grimmer and Hendrik van Balen
THE RIVER SCHELDT AT ANTWERP
AND IN THE FOREGROUND A PART
OF THE "VLAAMS HOOFD" IN 1600
Antwerp, Koninklijk Museum voor
Schone Kunsten

*From about 1600, the separation between the
Northern and Southern Netherlands was an
accomplished fact. The Counter-Reformation triumphed in the South. In spite of its
economic regression, Antwerp remained the
center of thriving cultural activity in Rubens'
time.*

13

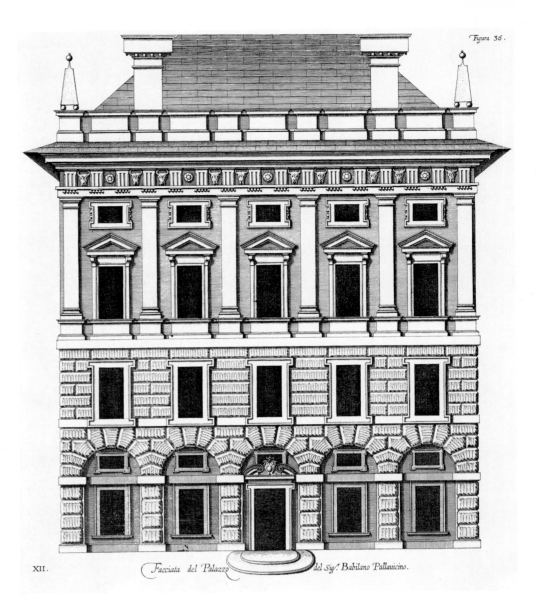

Figura 36.

XII.                    *Facciata del Palazzo* *del Sig.ᵗ Babilano Pallauicino.*

Figures 5, 6
TWO PALACES IN GENOA
Engravings in Peter Paul Rubens,
*Palazzi di Genova*, Antwerp, 1622 (figs.
36 and 39)
Antwerp, Rubens House

*During his eight-year stay in Italy, Rubens
went several times to the port city of
Genoa. He collected plans of houses and
drawings of façades which he later had engraved, and published them in the form of an
illustrated work intended to serve as a model-
book for architects.*

At the end of 1605 he went again to Rome, where his elder brother Philip, a favorite disciple of the humanist Justus Lipsius, had settled several months before as the librarian to Cardinal Ascanio Colonna. The two brothers lived there together and devoted their time to the study of Roman antiquities. Philip returned to Antwerp in 1607, but Peter Paul remained in Rome, devoting his best efforts to a work his influential patrons had obtained for him late in 1606: the paintings for the high altar of the church of Santa Maria in Vallicella, the "Chiesa Nuova" of the Oratorian Fathers. This was, as Rubens described it himself, "the finest and most splendid opportunity in all Rome [which] presented itself." He had to spend much more time on this commission than he expected. When the finished canvas (Plate 12) was placed on the high altar, the play of light reflections upon it made it scarcely visible. A man of less energetic temperament would have given up the work, but the ambitious young artist undertook to paint a new version executed this time on slate, a material less subject to reflec-

14

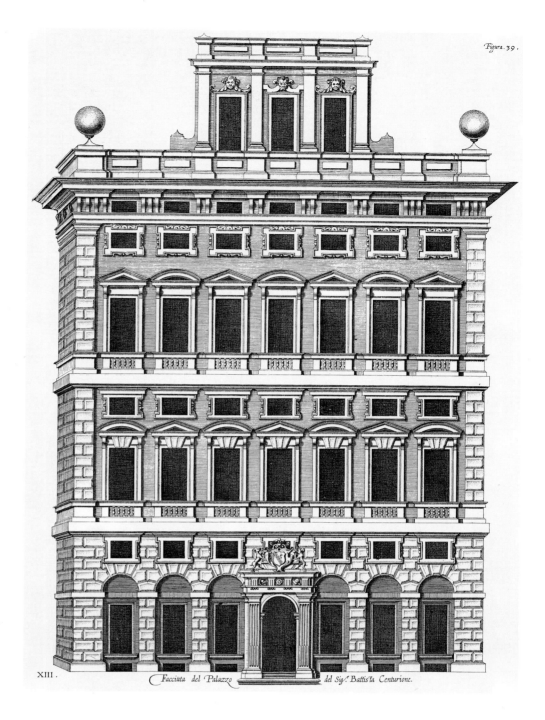

XIII.

Facciata del Palazzo del Sig.r Battista Centurione.

tions. The modified composition now covered three panels instead of one, and these can still be admired in the choir of the Roman church. No sooner was the work finished than he heard that his mother was seriously ill. In haste, he left Rome in October 1608. Although he wrote to Annibale Chieppio, the secretary of the Duke of Mantua, that he would not be absent for long, he was never to see Italy again.

Looking over the works Rubens painted in Italy, one finds the influence of Otto van Veen persisting in the first two years. Very soon, however, all sorts of innovations began to be grafted on, with the many and varied impressions he received from all that Italy had to offer in the way of artistic beauty. In the huge canvas *Assembly of the Gods on Olympus* (Fig. 29), doubtless painted in 1602 in Mantua, one can find, along with reminiscences of Van Veen, a certain number of borrowings from antique statues and sarcophagi as well as Venetian color effects.

*The Equestrian Portrait of the Duke of Lerma*, painted in 1603 during his first stay in Spain, marks a new stage in his development. The cold classicism of his apprentice years gives way to a greater freedom in his treatment of the forms and to a vibrant colorism, with more tones; the study of the glorious models of the Italian masters is beginning to bear fruit.

The eclecticism by which Rubens tried to assimilate the finest achievements of the Italians can be seen in the large canvases painted in 1604–5 for the church of the Jesuits in Mantua; they display numerous motifs and stylistic elements borrowed now from Michelangelo, now from Raphael or Tintoretto, but always bathed in soft, silver Venetian color. By 1606–8, in the altarpieces for Santa Maria in Vallicella, he had added the heroic monumentality which he owed to his attentive study of ancient sculpture during his second, longer stay in Rome.

During his stay in Italy, Rubens drew copies of Greek and Roman statues, some more than once and from different angles, in a hand both steady and sensitive. Dozens of such sheets have been preserved, but many more must have been lost. He also eagerly studied and made drawings after works by Michelangelo, Raphael, Titian, Giulio Romano, the Carracci, and many other great masters of the Renaissance. Years after he had left Italy, Rubens would reopen his sketchbooks and drawing portfolios whenever he wanted, for example, to paint gods and goddesses in an appropriate "classical" form, or when he needed an attitude, a gesture, or a personage for a religious painting. In addition there were his studies from nature and from a living model—a habit he kept up all his life. One sees the breadth of this repertory of forms that he started in Italy and never ceased to enrich, to use at will according to his needs.

Regarding studies after the antique, Rubens was well aware that there were dangers to a painter in copying classical marbles. He writes, in a treatise on the imitation of sculptures, that certain artists, "instead of rendering flesh, do nothing but reproduce marble, painted in different colors." Rubens, on the contrary, assimilated the classical forms so perfectly to his own genius that frequently we do not notice that a particular figure is derived from a Greek or Roman model.

When Rubens arrived in Antwerp at the end of 1608, Maria Pijpelinckx had already died. Upon her tomb in the abbey of St. Michael he placed his canvas first painted for the high altar of Santa Maria in Vallicella, which he had brought back because the reflections in the church were so unfortunate. Although he considered returning to Rome, where he could count on powerful patrons, he finally decided to settle in Antwerp. In September 1609 he became "painter to the Household of their Royal Highnesses," the Archduke Albert and the Infanta Isa-

Figure 7
THE CHURCH OF SANTA MARIA DI CARIGNANO IN GENOA
Engraving in Peter Paul Rubens, *Palazzi di Genova*, Antwerp, 1622 (fig. 63)
Antwerp, Rubens House

*This church was built according to the plans of Galeazzo Alessi (1522–72), the architect of many palaces in Genoa. The upper part of the towers served, without doubt, as a model for those on the corners of the church of St. Charles Borromeo, the former Jesuit Church in Antwerp (Fig. 80).*

Figura 63.

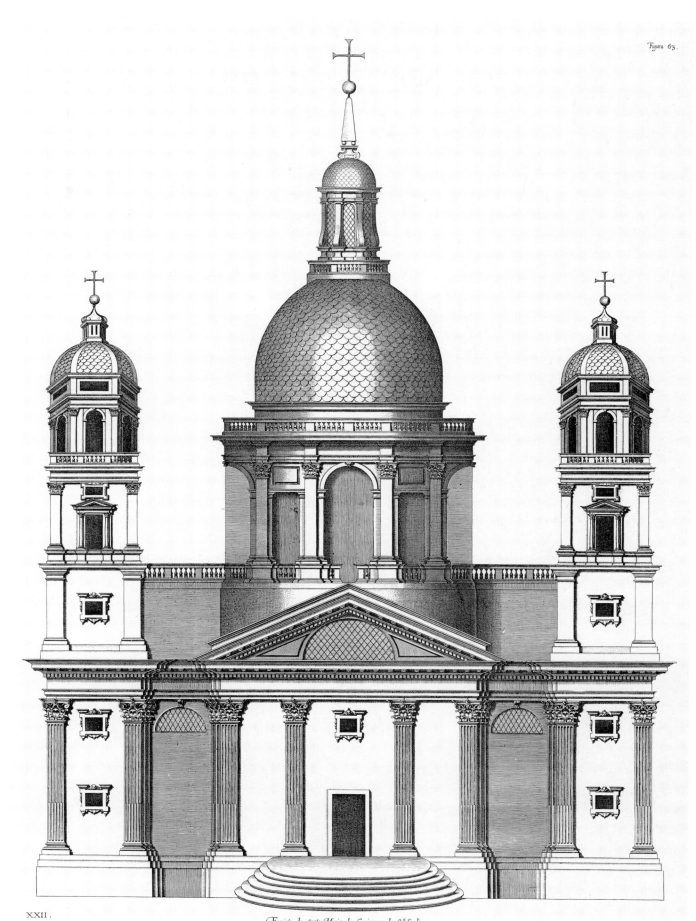

XXII.

Facciata de Santa Maria de Carignano de Sg.° Sauli.

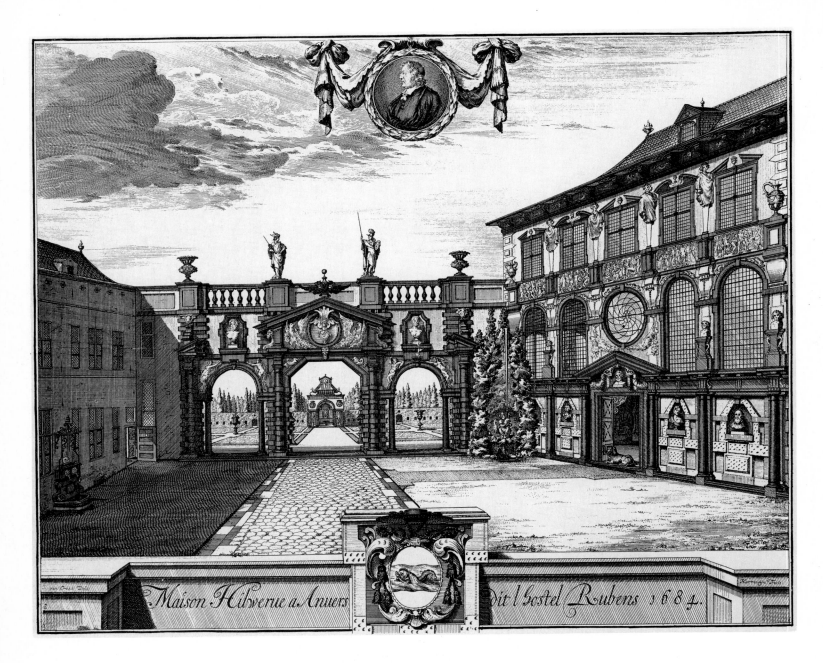

Figure 8
J. Harrewijn, after Jan van Croes
RUBENS' HOUSE IN 1684
Antwerp, Rubens House

*On the left the living quarters, on the right the studio. In the center the portico between the inner courtyard and the garden to which it also forms a triumphal entrance. The elegant pavilion is at the far end. In the medallion at the top is the portrait of Canon Hillewerve, who later lived in the house.*

Plate 3
STUDY OF HEADS AND HANDS (detail)
Drawing
Vienna, Graphische Sammlung Albertina

*These drawings of clasped hands are preliminary studies for the hands of the Virgin in the left wing of* The Raising of the Cross *(Antwerp Cathedral) painted in 1610 (see Fig. 37).*

bella. This appointment offered him financial advantages, but he accepted it on condition that he would not be obliged to live at their court in Brussels. In October he married the charming and intelligent Isabella Brant. On November 1, 1610, he bought a piece of land situated on the Wapper and proceeded to build on it his house and a large workshop; meanwhile he and his young wife lived with her parents in the Kloosterstraat, and he moved with his family into his new abode only about 1615.

Rubens had returned to Antwerp at a particularly favorable moment. At the end of 1608 the hopes were high for the conclusion of a peace treaty, and the Twelve-Years' Truce, putting an end to hostilities, was signed a few months later, in April 1609. Life settled down and the economy began to revive after the long period of insecurity

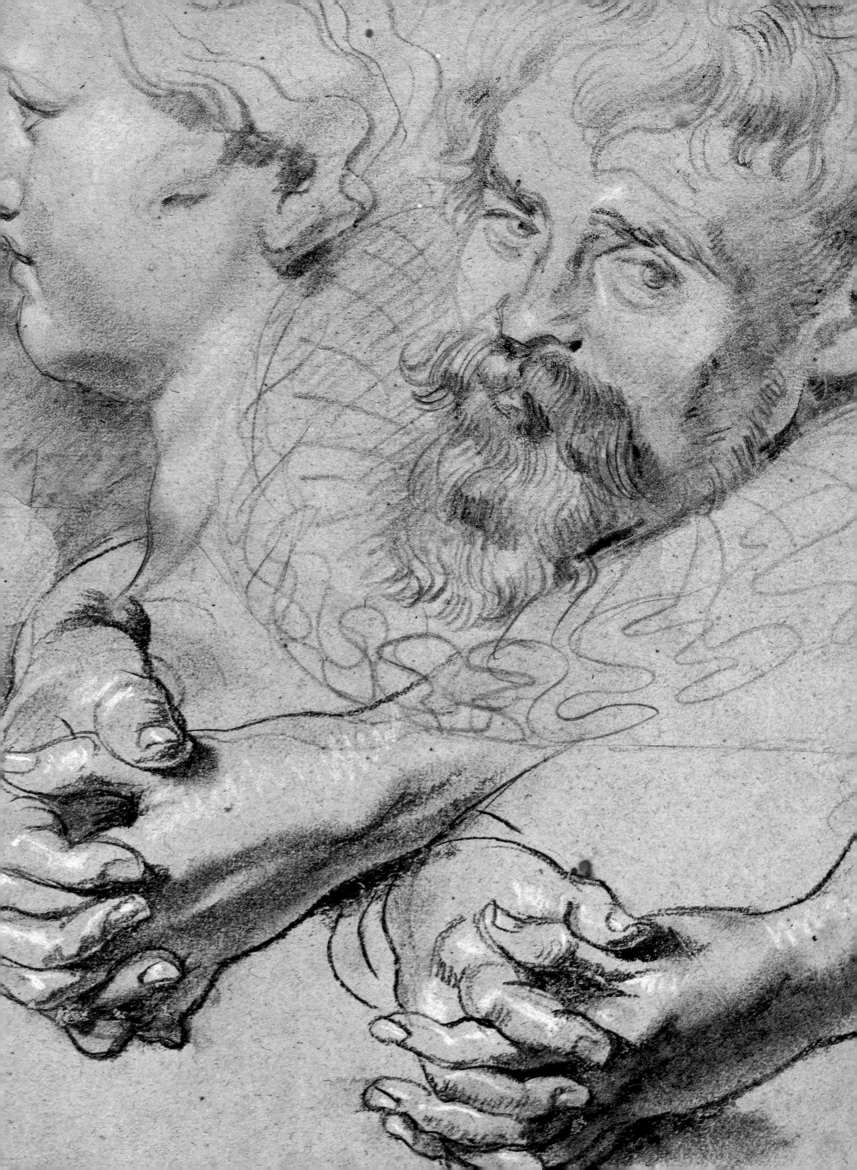

and misery. Damaged or abandoned churches and cloisters were rebuilt or restored, especially those stripped of their artistic treasures, and works of art had to be procured for new churches being built, as well as for the old ones; a great need for altarpieces and large-scale religious pictures was apparent. For Rubens, about to begin his career in Antwerp, conditions converged to give him important commissions that would permit him to display to the full his artistic gifts.

During his first years in Antwerp his work remained strongly influenced by Italian models. There is no break between his last productions in Rome and his new creations. *The Raising of the Cross* (Plate 15; Fig. 37), painted in 1610 for the high altar of the church of St. Walburga in Antwerp, is a powerful synthesis of what he had learned in Italy: the grandiose conception of composition, in this case recalling Tintoretto's paintings of the Passion; the strongly sculptural treatment of the anatomy, peculiar to Michelangelo, of the burly henchmen in the central panel; the vibrant Venetian colors in the right wing; the Caravaggesque women in the foreground of the left wing. But there also appears a boldness that is quite new; it characterizes these first years following his return. The sharp diagonal crossing the composition in the central panel, the twisting bodies leaning forward or backward, the pathos of certain gestures, the dazzling highlights in contrast to the darker tonalities of the garments, the nervous curls of the women's hair—all these features define the youthful period from 1609 to 1612, which has been called Rubens' *Sturm und Drang*.

This vehemence lasts only a few years. By 1611–12 the famous *Descent from the Cross* (Plate 16; Fig. 39) shows a greater mastery, both in the clarity and simplification of the whole and the serenity of the figures and attitudes. Here begins a stylistic phase which has been named "classical." The colors become lighter and certain local colors, clearly outlined, balance one another in the total composition. Rubens' style displays the same plasticity and linear treatment as before, but the drawing is less accentuated. A cold light, limpid and more uniformly spread, softly caresses the sculptural forms that often stand out as if in relief against the neutral background.

These characteristics are also found in the mythological and religious pictures of 1612–15. The *Rockox Altarpiece* triptych (Plate 18; Figs. 45, 46), painted between 1613 and 1615 for Nicolaas Rockox, Rubens' friend and patron, gives a good idea of the pictures with half-length figures that he created during these years.

After 1615 Rubens returned to the more dynamic style: the *Large Last Judgment* (Plate 22), impetuous hunting scenes, ecstatic Assumptions and impressive Adorations, the *Miracles of St. Ignatius of Loyola* (Fig. 85) and the *Miracles of St. Francis Xavier* (Fig. 88), among others. Although the forms preserve their modeling, the outlines become ever less pronounced, the movements more flexible, the tones of color more abundant. Between 1615 and 1620 Rubens is evidently using his stylistic methods, previously acquired, to fulfill the demands of the subject in hand. His pictorial resources, now considerably enriched, allowed him, so to speak, to utilize several registers simultaneously. Unlike

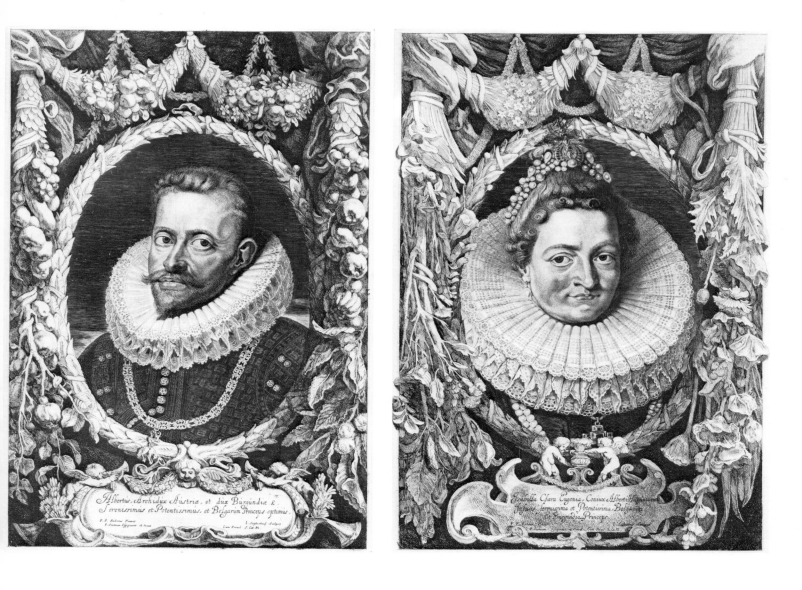

Figure 9
Jan Muller, after Rubens
THE ARCHDUKE ALBERT (1559–1621)
Engraving
Antwerp, Rubens House

*This print, dated 1615, was engraved after a portrait painted by Rubens in that year. In September 1609 Rubens had become "painter to the Household of their Highnesses."*

Figure 10
Jan Muller, after Rubens
THE INFANTA ISABELLA (1566–1633)
Engraving
Antwerp, Rubens House

*Also executed in 1615 after a portrait painted by Rubens the same year. Rubens had a high esteem for the Infanta, and after about 1623 he carried out numerous diplomatic missions for her.*

his methods in the first years after his return to Antwerp, he no longer has recourse to violent contrasts, nor to clearly outlined local colors as in the classical phase, but he now excels in the harmony of transitions and tones, sometimes light, sometimes darker, which he integrates into a whole that is well structured yet easily balanced.

Rubens was burdened with ever more numerous commissions; we know that he followed the example of the great Venetians, as well as of his compatriot Frans Floris, by increasingly calling upon collaborators to help him with the execution of large pictures. Between 1617 and 1620, the most famous of these was Anthony van Dyck; the contributions of the workshop assistants clearly vary from one work to another. Sometimes Rubens gave to specialists, such as Frans Snyders, Paul de Vos, or Jan Wildens, the task of painting particular elements of the picture: animals, still life, backgrounds. Sometimes a whole composition was carried out according to his sketches, Rubens

21

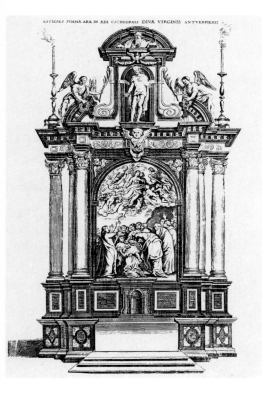

Figure 11
Adriaan Lommelin, after Rubens
HIGH ALTAR OF THE CATHEDRAL
OF OUR LADY OF ANTWERP
Engraving
Brussels, Bibliothèque Royale Albert
I<sup>er</sup>, Cabinet des Estampes

*Rubens not only painted* The Assumption of the Virgin *(Pl. 49), but also designed the altar on which his great altarpiece was placed. The subject of the picture is continued in the group of figures on the crest of the altar itself, where the Holy Trinity is awaiting the Virgin to crown her.*

keeping for himself only a few heads and other essential points. In some cases a picture was started by his assistants, but worked over by Rubens himself to such an extent that their contribution is scarcely perceptible. With his characteristic sense of organization he also delegated to his workshop all kinds of small practical tasks of secondary importance. This did not prevent him, even at times of great pressure, from executing with his own hand a large number of major works. We disregard, of course, the case of very popular paintings, as well as royal portraits; copies of these were made by collaborators in his workshop or from outside.

It should be mentioned that Rubens' artistic activity was not confined to painting. For his friend Balthasar Moretus, director of the Plantin Press, and occasionally also for other publishers, he designed title pages and illustrations which introduced the Baroque style into the printed book. He also commissioned a number of engravers to execute prints after his paintings under his guidance, with the necessary transpositions. Through cartoons or sketches for tapestries, sculpture, architectural decoration, and goldsmith's work he deeply influenced other artistic disciplines.

After about 1620, light colors come to dominate his pictures. Rubens no longer spreads his accents by means of chiaroscuro but multiplies the nuances and half-tints through the whole range of colors. Contour as well as local color more or less dissolves in the prodigal richness of his chromaticism. The new phase is seen both in the great *Christ on the Cross ("Le Coup de Lance")* of 1620 (Fig. 57), and in a few mythological pictures of smaller format, such as the *Battle of the Amazons* (Plate 78), possibly slightly earlier in date.

This new stylistic phase between about 1620 and 1628, when he left the Netherlands for two years, could be described as "the epoch of the great series." During this time Rubens received a significant number of commissions for large sequences of pictures and for tapestry cartoons. Those that deserve special mention are the thirty-nine canvases destined for the aisle ceilings of the new church of the Jesuits in Antwerp; these were completed in less than a year with the help of assistants, including Van Dyck, during 1620 and 1621. Unfortunately they were destroyed by fire in 1718, but we still have many of the oil sketches which served as models, and we can admire his bold foreshortening of the figures seen from below and the extraordinary suppleness with which the prophets and saints move toward the heavens.

This new phase coincides with the extension of Rubens' activity to other countries in Europe. He must have received a few commissions from abroad after 1615, but they were less numerous and important; now between 1622 and 1625 he had the cycle of the *Life of Maria de' Medici* (Plates 42–45, 60, 61; Figs. 93, 97) in twenty-five large canvases, dealing with the rather dull life of the queen-mother. Rubens elevates it into the realm of the Olympian gods and heroes, who seem to accompany her throughout the different episodes of her life. A

D. PETRVS PAVLVS RVBBENS EQVES.
REGI CATOLICO IN SANCTIORE CONSILIO A
SECRETIS ÆVI SVI APELLES ANTVERPIÆ

*Ant. van Dyck pinxit.*
*Paul. Pontius sculpsit.*

*Cum priuilegio.*

Figure 12
Paul Pontius, after Anthony van Dyck
PORTRAIT OF PETER PAUL RUBENS
Engraving
Antwerp, Osterrieth House

*Just as Rubens painted his pupil's portrait
(Fig. 149), so Anthony van Dyck painted
a portrait of his master. Pontius made this
engraving from it.*

second cycle, also commissioned by Maria de' Medici, was to have shown the life of Henry IV, but this was never finished. A number of oil sketches, however, and some unfinished canvases illustrate the grandiose vision which would have animated the work had not political circumstances prevented its realization.

In 1622, King Louis XIII of France commissioned Rubens to make cartoons for twelve wall tapestries of the *Life of the Emperor Constantine*. A few years later, this time for the Infanta Isabella, he designed cartoons for the *Triumph of the Eucharist*, a series of tapestries woven in Brussels; the princess wished to donate them to the convent of the "Descalzas Reales," the barefoot Carmelite nuns of Madrid with whom she had spent a part of her youth. This impressive sequence can be regarded as the exaltation of the Holy Eucharist and of the Catholic Church, newly reestablished and strengthened by the Counter-Reformation.

Apart from these great cycles, Rubens painted several altarpieces in this period. These are perhaps fewer than in the preceding decade, but some rank among the finest he ever created. They are characterized by greater unity of composition. The whole is no longer arranged along strongly marked diagonals; figures seem to be caught in a *perpetuum mobile* of movements and counter-movements that answer one another with intense joyousness, heightened by the richness of the pictorial values. Among these altarpieces some are striking by their huge dimensions and mark the summit of a fully expanded Baroque art which Rubens himself would never surpass: the *Adoration of the Magi* (Plate 46), the *Assumption of the Virgin* (Plate 49), and *The Virgin and Child Adored by Saints* (Plate 50).

From another point of view, what is striking in this period of altarpieces and great cycles is the frequency of Rubens' trips abroad. Whereas he had worked for ten years almost exclusively in Antwerp, his activity between 1622 and 1628 now became diversified. Apart from the important commission from Maria de' Medici which kept him in Paris for several months, the expiration of the Twelve-Years' Truce in 1621 brought him increasingly demanding diplomatic missions. His wife Isabella Brant died on June 20, 1626, possibly a victim of the plague, leaving him two sons, Albert and Nicolaas (the eldest child, Clara Serena, had died in 1624 at the age of twelve), and as a distraction from his grief Rubens now accepted more missions, such as a journey to Holland in 1627.

Rather accidentally, through two family contacts—one a Dutch nephew of his wife's, the other a high official at the Brussels court, related to the Rubens family—the artist became a political negotiator. Gradually Rubens began to sense the role he could play in this field and the contribution he could make to the conclusion of peace between the Northern and Southern Netherlands, a peace which was dear to his heart. On these missions he steadily enjoyed the complete confidence of the Infanta Isabella (now governor of the Netherlands, since the death of the regent, Archduke Albert, in 1621) and of her principal counsellor, Ambrogio Spinola. A meeting arranged in 1625

Plate 4
PORTRAIT OF NICOLAAS RUBENS
(detail)
Drawing, over-all dimensions
$11^1/_2$" × $9^1/_8$"
Vienna, Graphische Sammlung Albertina

*Nicolaas was the second son of Rubens and Isabella Brant, and was baptized in the church of St. Jacques in Antwerp on March 23, 1618. Here he is represented at the age of eight or nine.*

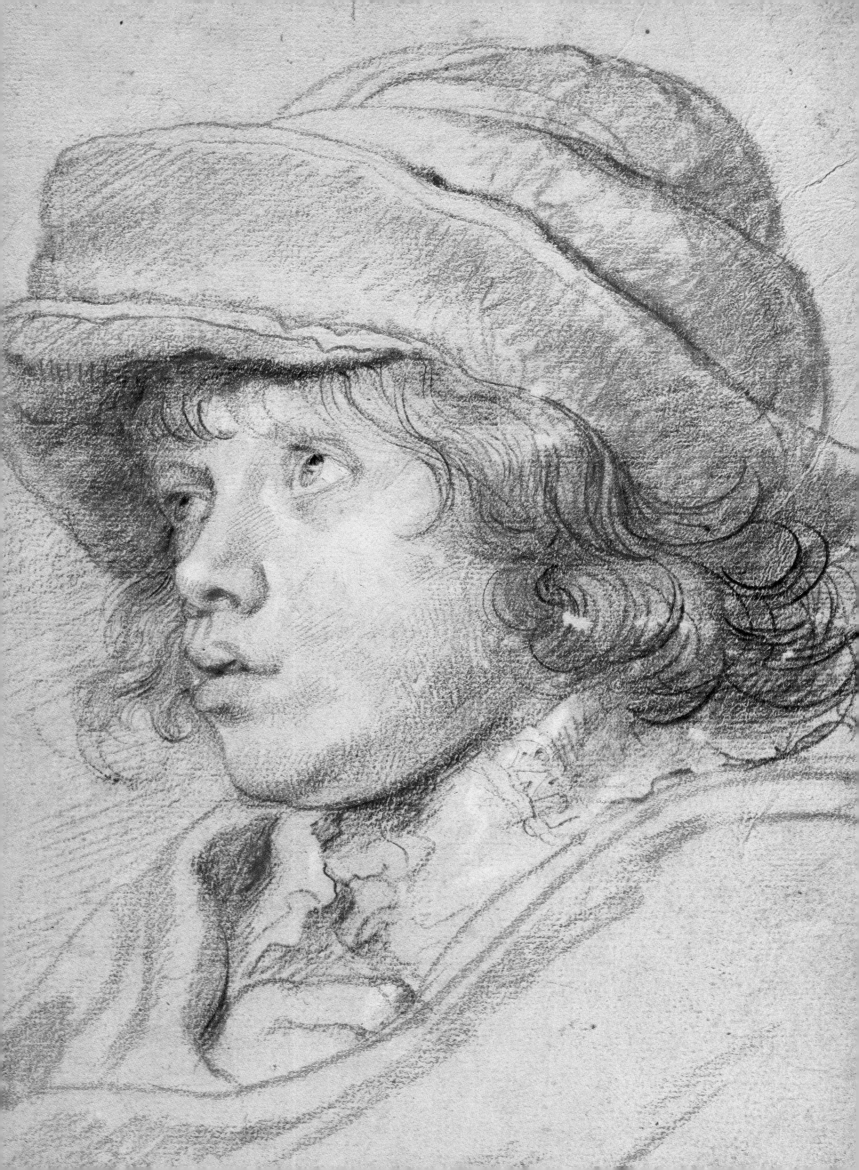

between Rubens and the English Duke of Buckingham (who commissioned a portrait) and his diplomatic agent, Balthasar Gerbier, himself a painter, was to add a European dimension to Rubens' activity. He occupied a key position in the negotiations then current between England and Spain. Finally, at the request of King Philip IV, he traveled to Madrid to report on his many contacts with Buckingham and his circle.

Leaving Antwerp in great haste at the end of August 1628, Rubens reached the Spanish capital within two weeks. Philip IV, Olivares, his powerful minister, and the king's other counsellors, all of whom had thus far maintained a cautious attitude toward him, were impressed by the good results of his negotiations and the soundness of his reasoning. After some eight months in Madrid—his stay unexpectedly extended by the assassination of Buckingham—Rubens left for London on April 29, 1629, charged with a mission by Philip IV in person. On the way he stopped in Brussels, where he met the Infanta, and briefly in Antwerp to see his sons.

In spite of many obstacles Rubens finally succeeded in laying the basis of a peace treaty between England and Spain. His discriminating judgment of people and events, his powers of persuasion, and his inventiveness and tact undoubtedly contributed much to the successful result; but he also possessed his reputation as a great painter, and Charles I of England, like Philip IV of Spain, was a keen lover of painting. Both welcomed the artist's presence at their courts.

These diplomatic journeys slowed his painting activities but were not without importance for his art. In Madrid he painted portraits of Philip IV and of members of the royal family. More essential was his renewed and deepened contact with Titian's paintings in the king's collection; he made free copies of several of them. From this moment on, the influence of the great Italian master would continue in his work until his death. In London he painted for Charles I *Minerva Defending the Peace* (Plate 63): Minerva, goddess of Peace, repulses Mars, god of War—an obvious allusion to the negotiations he conducted with Charles I, which led to the peace treaty between Spain and England.

In April 1630, Rubens was back in Antwerp, where he had long wished to return, and he resumed his activity as a painter. Before leaving England, he had accepted an important commission from Charles I: the painting of canvases to decorate the ceiling of the Banqueting Hall of the Palace of Whitehall, a task which occupied him until 1634–35.

An event of primary importance for his art was his marriage on December 6, 1630, to Helena Fourment, an Antwerp girl of barely seventeen years. Her great beauty was to inspire the artist to splendid portraits; she can also be recognized in biblical paintings and especially in mythological works of Rubens' last ten years.

It is striking that during this period he painted fewer altarpieces; generally speaking, they no longer pertain to the grandiose aesthetics

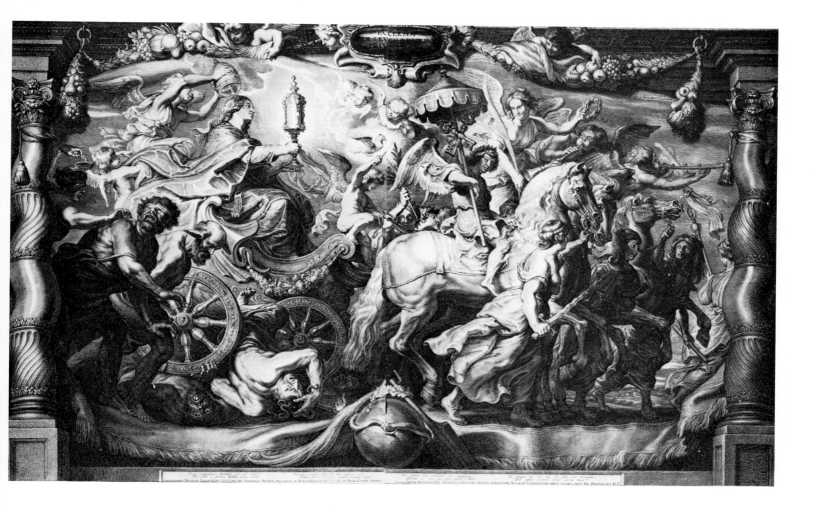

of the Baroque, and have a restricted number of figures. It seems indeed that the artist wished from now on to use his time freely, to choose the subjects he liked, and to paint them mostly on panels or canvases of relatively small size. The last ten years constitute his so-called lyrical period; it is also the most intimate. He devoted himself especially to mythological paintings which are like hymns in the celebration of the beauty of woman. His nudes, usually set in an Arcadian landscape, seem to be tender, pulsating with an inner warmth, and transparent as mother-of-pearl.

In 1634, as the city of Antwerp prepared for the Triumphal Entry of the Cardinal Infante Ferdinand, brother of Philip IV, who had been appointed governor of the Southern Provinces, the city magistrates asked Rubens to design the triumphal arches and stages. These festivities took place in April 1635 and gave Rubens his last opportunity to conceive grandiose architectural forms in an imposing Baroque style. To a galaxy of Antwerp painters was entrusted the task of executing from Rubens' designs the canvases which were used to decorate the arches.

In the same way he embarked between 1636 and 1638 on the more than sixty large pictures that were to decorate the Torre de la Parada,

Figure 14
Christoffel Jegher, after Rubens
THE GARDEN OF LOVE
Woodcut
Antwerp, Rubens House

*This woodcut reproduces in reverse two draw-ings by Rubens in the Metropolitan Museum in New York which together form a long frieze. Rubens executed these drawings for Jegher's woodcut of his painting entitled* The Garden of Love *(Pl. 88; Fig. 174).*

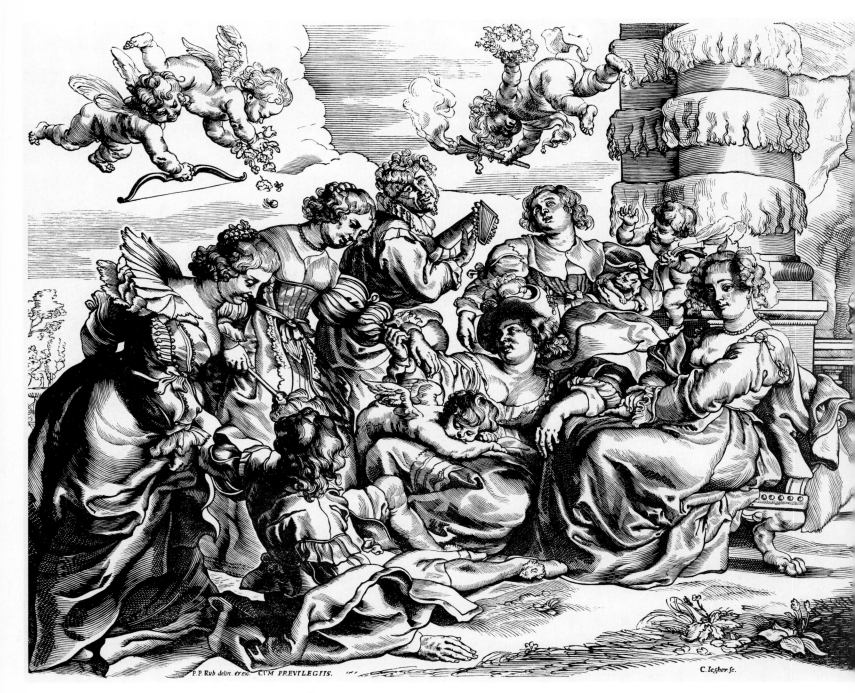

P.P. Rub delin. & ex. CVM PREVILEGIIS.

C. Iegher fc.

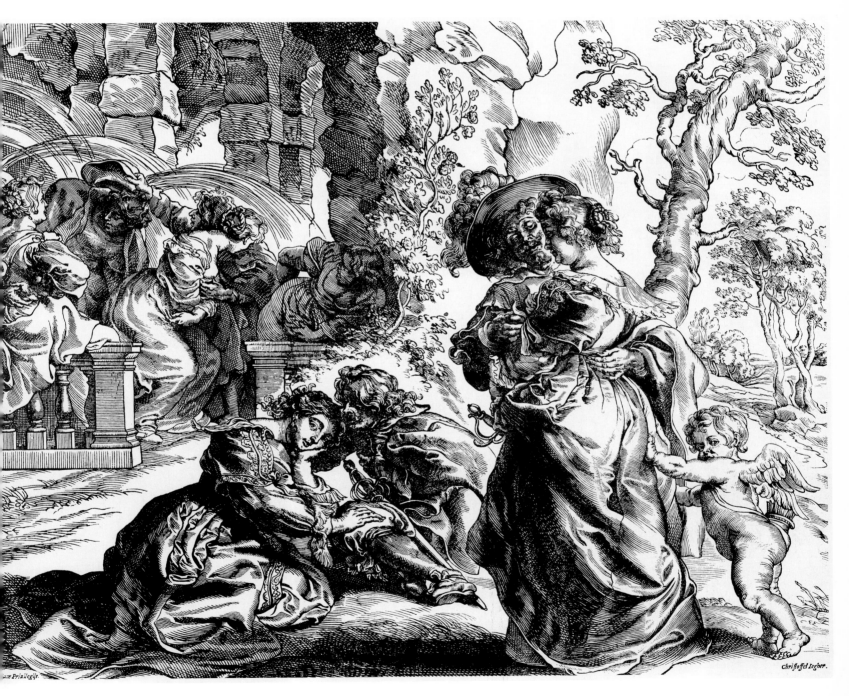

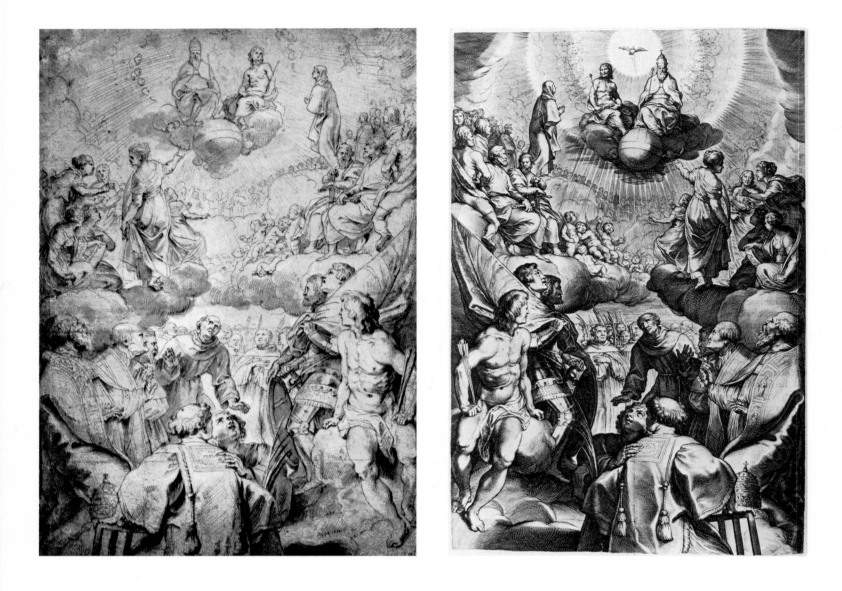

Figures 15, 16
ALL SAINTS
Drawing (left) and engraving (right)
Vienna, Graphische Sammlung Alber-
tina

*At the instance of Jan and Balthasar Mo-*
*retus I, Rubens made this sketch in 1612 for*
*one of the engraved illustrations in the* Breviarium Romanum, *published in 1614.*

the new hunting lodge of Philip IV, situated outside of Madrid.   Only
four canvases of this series—the most important series he ever accepted—were painted by his own hand; the others are the work of Jacob
Jordaens, Cornelis de Vos, Theodore van Thulden, Erasmus Quellin,
and other artists of his circle.   The oil sketches for this series rank
among his finest.   His hand was by now so expert that, drawing on
the store of forms which he had accumulated throughout his life and
giving play to his creative imagination, he had not the slightest difficulty in catching his vision with infallible virtuosity and sureness.   A
few strokes of the brush now suffice to suggest a figure, a few touches
of color give it relief and expression.

In 1635 Rubens bought a country house, the château of Steen, at
Elewijt, halfway between Malines and Brussels, where he was to spend
the summer months with his family.   The restrained mildness of the
Brabantian countryside, with its rows of trees lining the fields and
rivulets, impelled him to paint landscapes.   Not that he had neglected
this branch of painting hitherto, but at Elewijt the land showed the

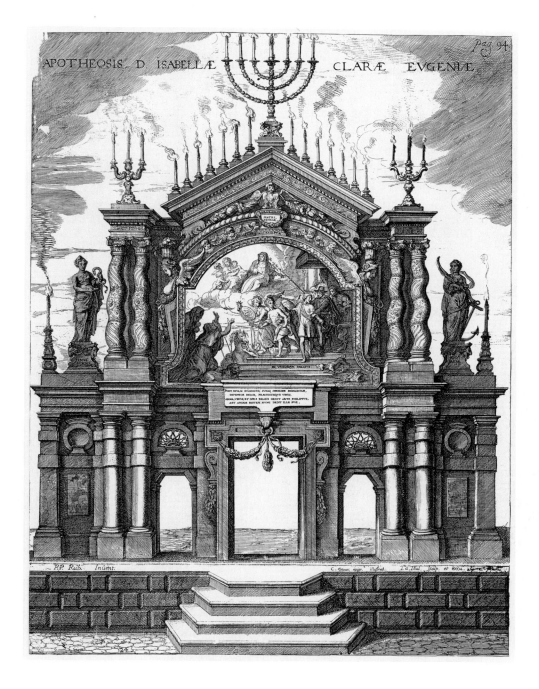

Figure 17
Theodore van Thulden, after Rubens
THE STAGE OF THE INFANTA ISA-
BELLA
Etching in *Pompa Introitus Ferdinandi*,
Antwerp, 1641

*It represents one of the decorated platforms
which, together with triumphal arches, were
built in 1635 in the streets of the city of
Antwerp on the occasion of the Entry of the
Cardinal Infante Ferdinand. The* Stage of
Isabella, *like nearly all of these constructions,
was built after a design by Rubens.*

lushness, the captivating diversity, and all the generous fruitfulness
that suited his temperament. Those familiar with the area know how
closely he observed nature, as well as how he painted it according
to his temperament, with a grandeur of vision and a cosmic animation
that reveals his almost pantheistic sense of life.

On May 30, 1640, Peter Paul Rubens died in his house in Antwerp.
He had already suffered for some time from gout; at the end, however,
he was not long confined to his sickbed. A few years after his death
one of his pictures, which he had chosen for that purpose himself,
was placed, according to his wishes, on the altar of the funeral chapel
of the church of St. Jacques, where he was buried. This was one

31

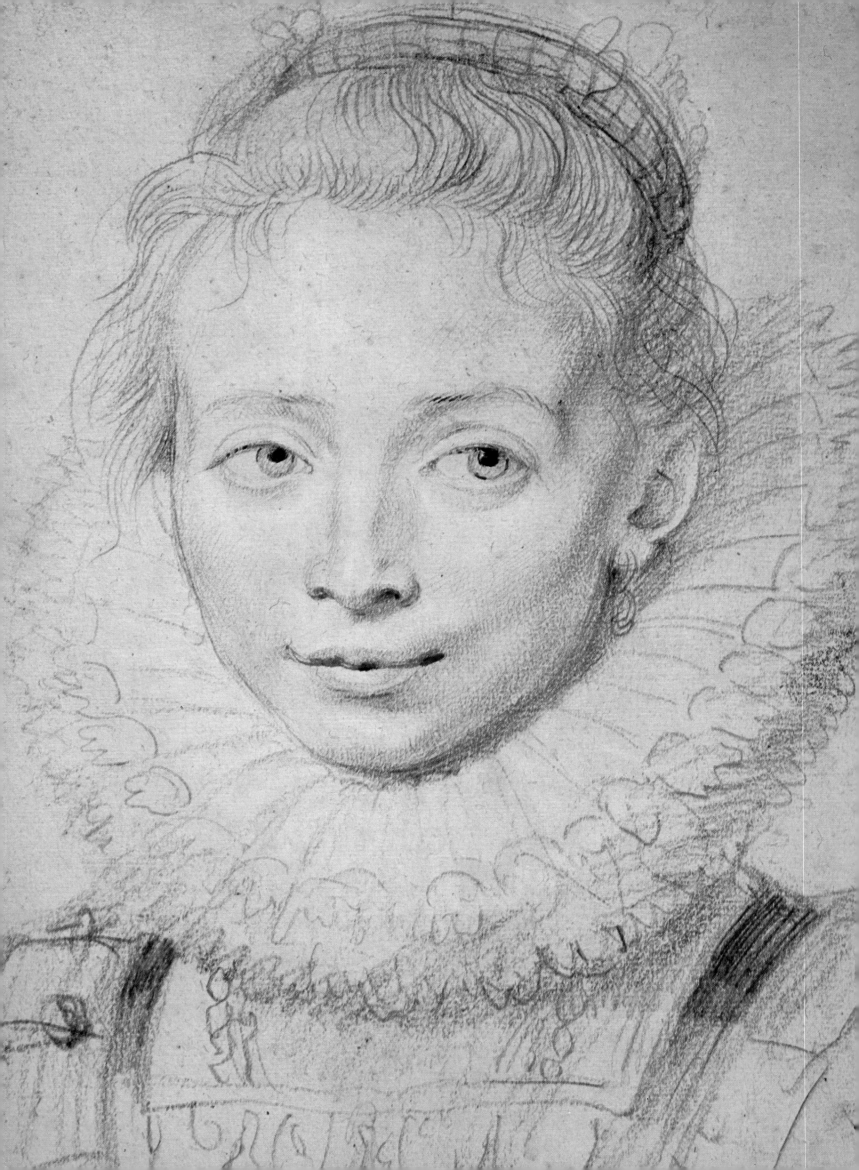

of his last pictures: *Virgin and Child with Saints* (Fig. 143). In this *sacra conversazione* there shines again the gentle light which gives a paradisiac touch to so many of his pictures. And again his unparalleled mastery is apparent, acquired in years of apprenticeship and consolidated and diversified throughout an unbroken stylistic development.

It has seemed appropriate to place this short biography of Rubens at the beginning of this book in which the main steps of his artistic development will be detailed. Thus the reader will be better able to see the context of the chapters, each dealing with a particular aspect of his work and art. In conclusion we add a few reflections on the judgments which Rubens' work has given rise to over the centuries, and on the relevance of his work to our time.

In his lifetime Rubens enjoyed a European renown, and this, to the present day, has suffered no eclipse; it now extends to all the continents, for one has only to think of the museums and private collections of the United States which house numerous masterpieces by his hand.

But this does not mean that Rubens knew only admirers. A few decades after his death a violent polemic broke out in France between partisans and adversaries of his art, the "Rubénistes" and the "Poussinistes." Later, when Watteau, Fragonard, and other leading artists of the Rococo regarded him as a master, the "classical" painters viewed him with a less favorable eye. But for the Romantics he became once again the great model. Thus Rubens' reputation has had its ups and downs, even in our own time. It should be noted, however, that in periods dominated by aesthetic values other than his, Rubens never lacked for enthusiastic admirers. Because he did not fall into oblivion, he never needed, like El Greco, Vermeer, and other great artists, to be "resuscitated."

Let us recognize, however, that a number of his works are less directly accessible to the present-day public than they were to his contemporaries. We need explanations to grasp the sense or to decipher the allegories in certain pictures that, in his time, were perfectly clear to the cultured observer. Our age is less familiar than previous ones with Greek and Latin mythology, which often prevents us from perceiving at once the dramatic tension and the human content of many scenes concerning gods, goddesses, and ancient heroes. It is paradoxical that Rubens' erudition, so often praised by his contemporaries, should form a barrier between us and his work. He seems nearest to us in the pictures whose content and style are the least closely linked with his time: subjects that belong to the common knowledge of Western culture.

Nevertheless, even when Rubens treats a theme unfamiliar to us, we are often caught up in the irresistible rhythm and expressiveness of the composition, particularly by the warmth and splendor of the color in its infinite richness. In these qualities he surpassed the artists of his own time and he still succeeds in delighting us today.

It is clear that our aesthetic enjoyment can be somehow deepened

Plate 5
PORTRAIT OF A LADY-IN-WAITING
TO THE INFANTA ISABELLA (detail)
Chalk drawing
Vienna, Graphische Sammlung Albertina

*The title given to this delicate head of a young girl has been deduced from an inscription in red chalk placed above the drawing: "Sael dochter van de Infante tot Brussel." It is a study from life for a captivating portrait, today in the Hermitage in Leningrad.*

33

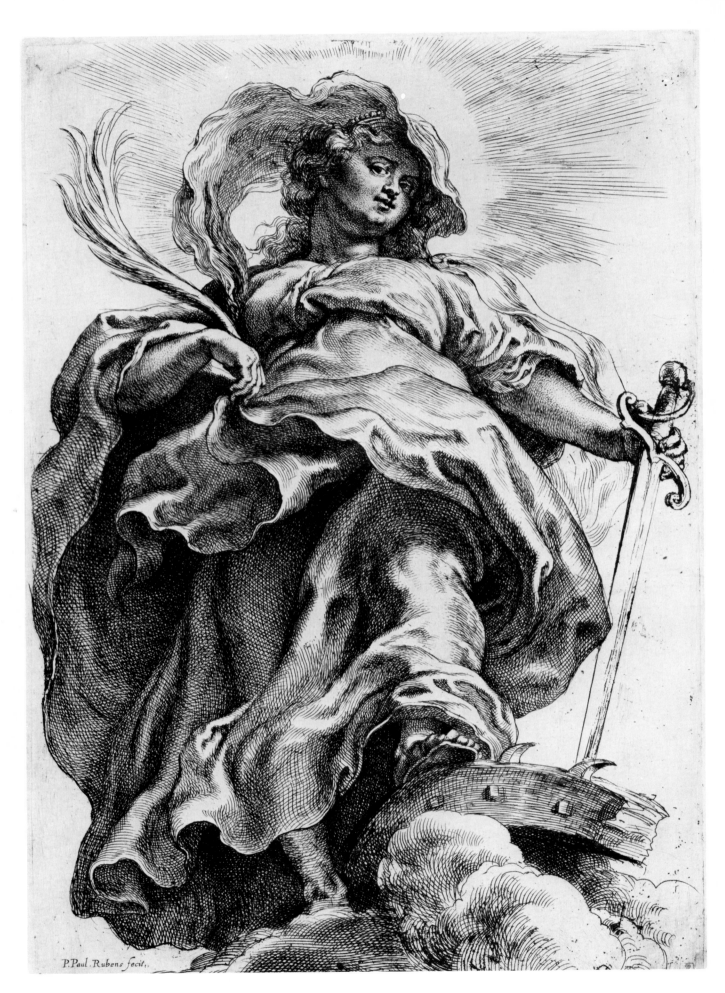

P.Paul.Rubens fecit.

34

by knowing more about the artist's personality, his methods, his subjects, his clientele, his social and cultural background—in short, about everything that links him to his period. The same is true of other arts. An oratorio can charm us by its harmonic richness and pathos, even if much of the text escapes us; an Oriental statue may strike us by its beauty, without our knowing what it represents or its cultural context; but for a better understanding of these works, as of Rubens', we are glad to accept the helping hand of the art historian. From personal experience I know that visitors are grateful for this help, provided, of course, that commentary does not replace or obstruct the contemplation of the work of art.

While contributing—at least, such is my hope—to a better knowledge of Rubens' art and personality, I must emphasize here that this book does not claim to be complete or to follow an elaborate plan. It brings together some published studies with others specially undertaken for this book, so as to cover the whole of Rubens' career from his youth to the end of his life. But if every aspect of Rubens' art and life has not been included, this plan offers the advantage of treating in greater depth the aspects to which each particular chapter is devoted. In trying to touch on all the problems, the author would have been obliged to reduce the matters actually treated to brief paragraphs; this solution enables him to give due importance to recent discoveries and points of view, his own as well as those of other scholars, some unpublished or published only in a form not easily accessible to most readers. We hope to have gained in originality and to have avoided the danger of covering yet again material already well known.

This book is published in 1977, declared the Rubens Year. May it contribute to the glory of the great Flemish artist, the four-hundredth anniversary of whose birth is being commemorated in his own country and abroad. May it above all lead to closer contact with the personality of the man and with his art.

Figure 18
ST. CATHERINE OF ALEXANDRIA
Etching
New York, The Metropolitan Museum of Art

*With slight differences, this etching reproduces one of the thirty-nine paintings for the ceiling of the Jesuit church in Antwerp, painted by Rubens and his assistants in 1620–21. Most authors attribute this print to Rubens himself. At all events, its quality is superior to that of the graphic productions of most artists in Rubens' circle. The possibility, however, should not be excluded that Anthony van Dyck, who was a distinguished etcher, may have made this print.*

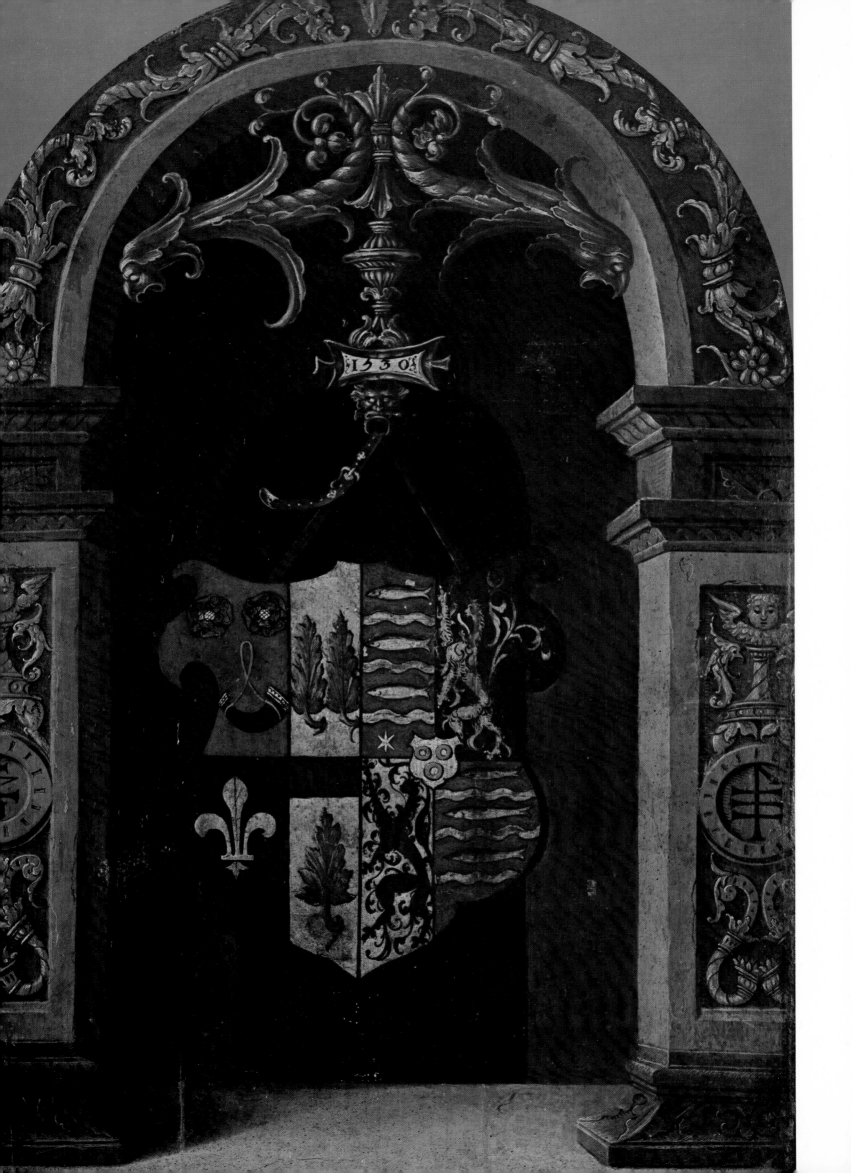

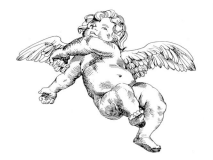

# CHAPTER I

# The Portraits of Rubens' Grandparents

Plate 6
Jacob Claesz. of Utrecht
MARRIAGE ESCUTCHEON OF
BARTHOLOMEUS RUBENS AND
BARBARA ARENTS, CALLED SPIE-
RINCK
Antwerp, Rubens House

*Reverse side of the portrait of Barbara Arents, called Spierinck (Pl. 8). The marriage escutcheon of the couple hangs in the arch before the niche. Above is the date, 1530. On the pilasters on left and right, house-marks can be seen, apparently those of the two families. The Renaissance ornament in the arch and on the archivolt and pilasters is noteworthy.*

In the Rubens House in Antwerp there now hang two sixteenth-century portraits which are important for the history of Peter Paul Rubens' family. They represent his paternal grandparents (Plates 7, 8).[1] The male portrait shows a rather young man with a lightly tanned face; he wears a black cap and a long black gown edged with fur, and with his right hand he absentmindedly fingers the lapel. On a little table in front of him is a pounding stone; he holds in his left hand an object which is probably a piece of gum resin. His coat of arms, framed by ornamental motifs, is seen in the middle of the arch at the top of the picture.

The pink-and-white complexion of the young woman has a soft bloom. She wears a little white coif, in the fashion of the time. Her dress with its deep square neckline edged with narrow fur bands is of the same dark color as the man's coat, and it contrasts with the lightness of her skin, coif, and blouse. Around her waist is a heavy gold chain; she holds in her left hand a coral-colored rosary, in her right hand two violets, flowers which have symbolized humility and modesty since the Middle Ages. At the top of this picture too is an escutcheon between decorative motifs similar to those in the male portrait. Behind both figures is a wall hanging of dark-green brocade with darker pomegranate motifs.

These fine portraits, full of charm, have all the features of the Antwerp School in the first decade of the sixteenth century. That they do in fact represent Rubens' grandparents was proved convincingly a few years ago by two Belgian experts in heraldry and genealogy, Viscount Fernand de Jonghe d'Ardoye and Louis Robyns de Schneidauer.[2] In 1960 the former identified the coats of arms in the portraits as those of Bartholomeus Rubens and his wife Barbara Arents called Spierinck. The back of the female portrait (Plate 6) bears the marriage escutcheon uniting the coats of arms which adorn the two pictures, and the date 1530.

In the light of these data the two authors have made a thorough study comparing the heraldic aspects of the two portraits, and their

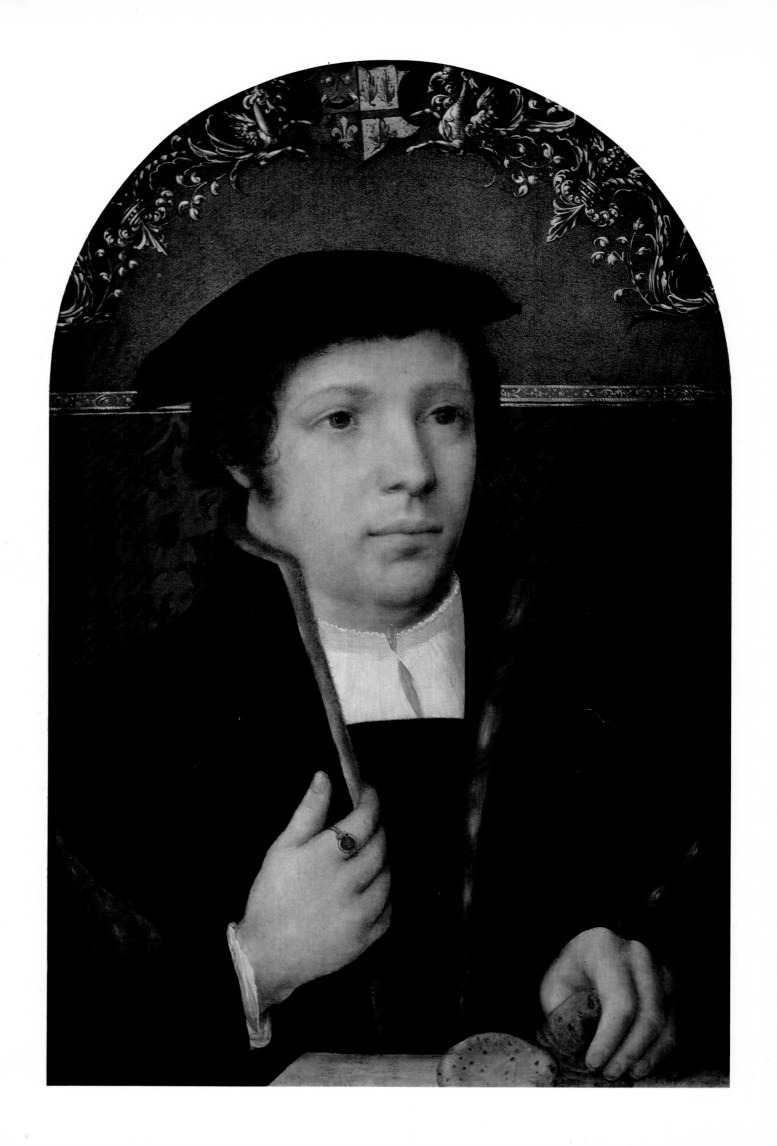

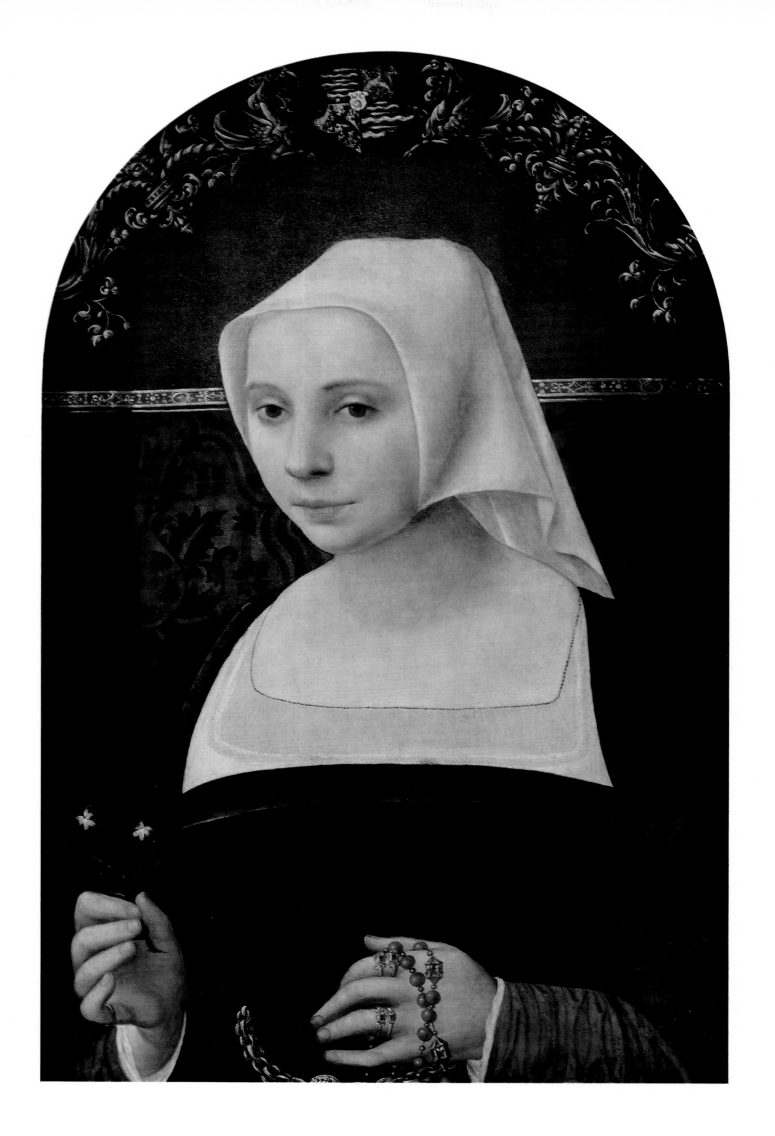

results have been published.[3]  We limit ourselves here to a few biographical and art-historical remarks concerning Rubens' grandparents and the presumed author of these portraits.

Who was Bartholomeus Rubens?  He was born in 1501, according to Frédéric Verachter, archivist of the city of Antwerp, who pursued detailed studies of the ancestors and descendants of Peter Paul Rubens, but gave no source for this assertion.[4]  Bartholomeus was the son of Pieter Rubens and Margareta van Looveren, married in 1499.[5]  The leaves (Dutch: "looveren") visible in the coat of arms in Bartholomeus' portrait form the canting arms of the Van Looveren family.

Pieter Rubens was a "drogist" or druggist by profession.  He lived in the house called "De Oude Ster" (The Old Star) in the Appelstraat, not far from the Grand Place.[6]  His wife Margareta was the daughter of Jan van Looveren, the landlord of the famous inn "In den Rhijn" which was incorporated in 1515 into the first stock exchange of Antwerp.[7]  They had five children: Bartholomeus, the eldest; Pieter II, who left one daughter, Maria; Constantijn, whose descendants lived in Herentals; Magdalena, who married Raphael Monicx in 1541; and Maria, about whom nothing more is known.[8]

When Pieter Rubens died in 1527 these children, except for Bartholomeus, were minors.  A municipal document dated December 5, 1527, contains this fact; Bartholomeus declares himself satisfied with the division of the patrimony by his brothers' and sisters' guardians.[9]  He inherited the druggist's shop and continued his father's business.  Two years later, in 1529, he married Barbara Arents called Spierinck, seventh child of Lambert Arents called Spierinck and Catherine Bisschot.[10]  On this occasion or soon afterward the portraits of the young couple were commissioned; her picture, as mentioned above, is dated 1530.  On March 13, 1530, was born Jan Rubens, who later became an alderman of Antwerp and married Maria Pijpelinckx; Peter Paul Rubens was born of this marriage.[11]  Batholomeus Rubens dies relatively young, a few years after his marriage; the date is not known, but in 1539 his widow married the widower Jan de Landmeter, another druggist.[12]

We have cited the statement that in 1527 Bartholomeus inherited his father's "druggist's shop"; Pieter Rubens, in a text dated 1499, is described as a "cruydenier" (grocer).[13]  In 1531 Bartholomeus is called "apothecaris" (apothecary).[14]  What precisely did these words mean at that time?  In his concise history of Antwerp apothecaries, Sergysels answers this question conclusively.[15]  Grocers sold colonial produce: herbs, spices, and foodstuffs.  This merchandise was also sold by druggists ("drogists"), who also occasionally sold medications, such as vermifuges, oils, and syrups.  In their shops could also be found "preserves, aromatic wines, sweetmeats, confectionery, pastry, spiced breads, honey, aniseed, marzipan, perfumes, cosmetics, wax, dry goods, circassian cloth, cotton thread, and pigments."[16]  Grocers and druggists who had studied the curative virtues of the herbs and medicinal plants in which they traded, and were thus engaged in the preparation

40

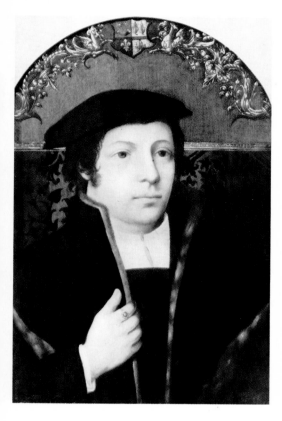

Figure 19
Jacob Claesz. van Utrecht
PORTRAIT OF BARTHOLOMEUS
RUBENS
Antwerp, Rubens House

*State before restoration; the left hand and
the attributes of the apothecary's trade are
still painted over.*

and sale of medications, were called "kruidenmenger" (herbalists) and
"apothecarii" or "apothecarissen" (apothecaries), and their shops had
the name "apotheek" (apothecary). They sold drugs and simples, con-
fections and mixtures, vermifuges, ointments, plasters, oils, pills,
powders, lozenges, and syrups. The first known Antwerp document
in which "apothecaryssen" are mentioned dates from 1499.[17]

Apothecaries, grocers, and druggists did not belong to an autonomous guild: all businessmen and shopkeepers who "wielded the ruler
and the scales" formed part of the main Guild of Clothiers (Meerseniers), founded in 1372. To be a member—taking the oath and pay-
ing an entry fee, annual subscription, and dues for the use of ruler
and balance—conferred the right to open and to operate an apothecary
shop. No courses or examinations were specified. Anyone willing
to accept the rules laid down by the guild and having the necessary
capital to stock his store with goods and merchandise could set up
as an apothecary without giving any proof of his competence in phar-
maceutics. Now and again, it is true, the shops were inspected by
the deans of the guild, but this check applied only to the condition
of the products for sale and the accuracy of the scales, weights, and
measures.

The profession of apothecary gradually became distinct during
Bartholomeus Rubens' time from that of grocer and druggist. A decree of the Magistrate of Antwerp, dated November 5, 1510, states that
the profession of apothecary would henceforth be restricted to "those
who would be promoted to this art after passing examinations."[18] On
August 17, 1517, it is expressly stipulated that to prevent abuses,
made-up medicines could be sold only by apothecaries, and that
grocers, druggists, peddlers, and clothiers were forbidden to sell such
remedies. About that time apothecary manuals appeared; and gardens
came increasingly to be arranged for the scientific study of botany.

Bartholomeus Rubens must have been aware of this development
while he was a young man helping his father, but it would be difficult
to find out whether he played an active role in the progressive
changes. His father was first a grocer, then no doubt a druggist;
Bartholomeus himself, after inheriting his father's business in 1531,
is always mentioned in the capacity of apothecary. To be recognized
by this title he must have passed the necessary examination, if the
decrees of 1510 and 1517 were indeed respected—and why doubt
this? The emancipation of the apothecary's profession was extended
from Antwerp to the whole country, and made final in a public notice
by Emperor Charles V, enacted in Brussels on October 8, 1540. After
this time candidates had to complete a course in a reputable office
and present themselves for examination by a competent jury. Two
or three times each year apothecary shops were to be inspected by
a committee of two or three doctors and as many apothecaries.[19]
Bartholomeus Rubens, who died before he was forty, never saw the
end of this rapid evolution.

Jan, his only offspring, was at the most eight years old when his
father died, and he did not follow in his father's footsteps. He became

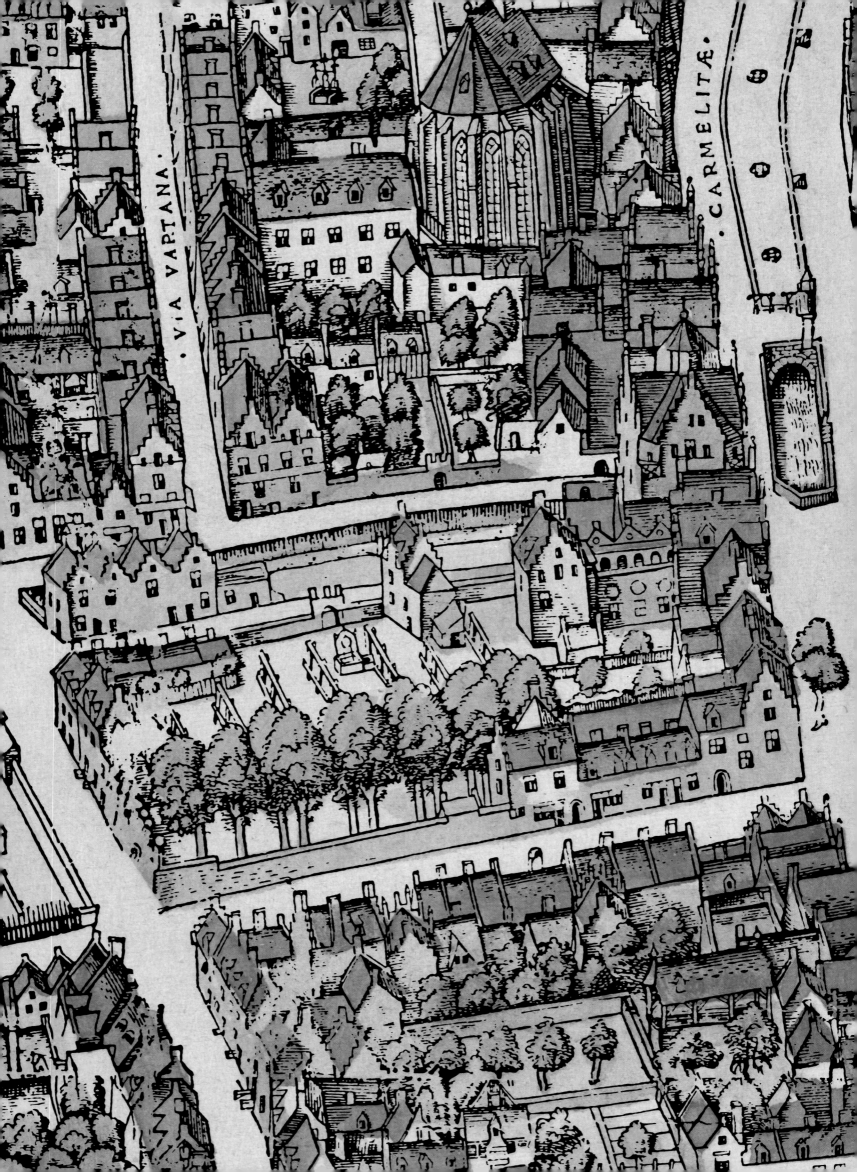

a lawyer and served as an alderman in Antwerp. Possibly the influence of his mother's family, which included numerous lawyers and high officials as well as churchmen, was decisive in his choice of career. It may be worth pointing out as well that one of his mother's elder brothers, Jan Arents called Spierinck, became young Jan Rubens' guardian.[20]

While the persons in the portraits we are discussing were identified through their coats of arms, no signature or monogram reveals the name of the painter. Max Friedländer, the eminent connoisseur of early Netherlandish painting, attributes them to Jacob Claesz. van Utrecht.[21] As the name indicates, this artist came from Holland and was probably trained there. He can, however, be identified with the Jacob van Utrecht who was received as master in 1506 by the Antwerp Guild of St. Luke, this identification resting mainly on the fact that most of his works show clearly the influence of the Antwerp School of painting. Like many artists in the early sixteenth century, the splendor of Antwerp, the flourishing metropolis—"Mercatorum Emporium"—doubtless tempted him to try his luck there. In any case, apprentices in his workshop were named in the 1511 and 1512 registers of the Antwerp guild of painters. Jacob van Utrecht soon left the banks of the Scheldt, however, and there is reason to believe that as early as 1517 he settled in Lübeck; he certainly lived in that Hanseatic city by 1519, for we know that he then lodged with the Bruskow family and belonged to the Brotherhood of St. Leonard. If Jacob van Utrecht had been in Antwerp no more than a good painter among others, in Lübeck he was considered the best.

Nevertheless he was in Antwerp again in 1520, and, according to Friedländer, must be acknowledged the "Jacob van Lübeck" whom Albrecht Dürer met in the metropolis in September of that year and whose portrait he drew. Was Jacob only back on a short visit? Whatever the circumstances, a document in which he is named "Mester Jacob van Utrecht" bears witness to his renewed presence in Lübeck in 1523. In 1524 he made a portrait of the bishop of that city, and portraits of several other persons belonging to Lübeck families must have been painted about that time; Friedländer thought it not improbable that Jacob van Utrecht ended his career in Lübeck. If, he wrote in 1941, the coats of arms in the portraits dated 1530 were those of Lübeck families, this would prove that the artist was still working there in that year.[22] But the portraits to which the historian was alluding were identified two decades later as representing Rubens' grandparents! It must therefore be accepted that Jacob van Utrecht returned to Antwerp by 1530, at the latest, but we do not know where he died, nor the date of his death.

Seven portraits are known that bear the signature *Jacobus Trajectensis*, the Latin translation of Jacob van Utrecht. Stylistic comparison permits us to attribute some fourteen other portraits to him. In addition, some signed religious pictures and triptychs have been discovered, several of them including donor portraits, and these make it possible

Plate 9
Virgilius Boloniensis
PLAN OF THE CITY OF ANTWERP,
1565 (detail)
Antwerp, Plantin-Moretus Museum

*Parallel to the right-hand margin, the broad Meir. When Maria Pijpelinckx returned to Antwerp she went to live with her children in a house (in the nineteenth century it was decorated with a bust of Rubens) situated between the Kalveniersstraat in the foreground, and, parallel to it, the Wapper. Behind it, a nearly empty space, bordered by a wall at the Wapper. Rubens bought this piece of land in 1610 and built his house and workshop there.*

43

to ascribe to him a certain number of other religious works, all of the latter attributions based on arguments of style. His known production thus numbers about forty works. Friedländer with characteristic conciseness defines the portraitist Jacob van Utrecht in these terms: "The portraitist has a predilection for half-length figures in half profile, the averted part of the face in shadow. In the lower part there is often a table or fence. Both hands are usually visible and in movement, holding a ring, a book, a rosary, or a flower (violet). Large heads, slender shoulders. The master tries to teach us something about the essence, the character, and the profession of the person, and he likes to embellish the picture by adding still-life motifs. The dark eyes, often without highlights, have a dull, surprised, or dreamy look. Innocence and modesty predominate in the expression... For the materials of the clothes, he likes brocades enhanced by large patterns."[23] These characteristics can be recognized in the portraits of Rubens' grandparents and their attribution to Jacob van Utrecht is made the more convincing.

Compared with other pictures by the master, in which the outlines are sometimes very pronounced, these two portraits seem to be executed with a certain softness. Friedländer did not miss this point, and sought the reason in the painter's artistic development. Indeed the portraits of Rubens' grandparents are dated 1530, and no known work by the painter bears a date later than 1524. Moreover, this circumstance is not unconnected with the fact that in Antwerp Jacob van Utrecht renewed his acquaintance with Quentin Matsys and Joos van Cleve; their influence is undeniable in these two portraits which the Dutch master painted at the close of his career.

To conclude with a few words on the provenance of these pictures. This can be traced back to 1913, when they were auctioned on October 7th or 8th at Helbing's in Munich with the Pickert Collection of Nuremberg. In the sale catalogue they are ascribed to a Middle-Rhenish master of the first half of the sixteenth century. According to a note by Friedländer, the portraits subsequently reappeared at Wildenstein's in Paris,[24] from which they passed into an English private collection. Later they were found again at Wildenstein's in London, where they were bought for the Rubens House in 1964.

In the reproduction of the man's portrait in the sale catalogue of 1913, as well as in a photograph taken shortly before restoration in the 1950s (Fig. 19), Bartholomeus Rubens' left hand is not to be seen. It had been painted over at some time, probably to hide the attributes of the apothecary's profession. It seems to us quite possible that Rubens' descendants, who belonged to the nobility, wished to suppress the emblems of a profession considered below their rank; indeed no one could attain to noble rank who exercised a gainful trade or profession. This hypothesis is not at all improbable when one remembers that in the eighteenth century Rubens' descendants and relatives tried to gain credence for the legend that the great artist came from an old aristocratic line that originated in Steiermark (Styria) and settled in Antwerp since the Middle Ages.[25] For whatever reason, the overpainting was not removed until shortly before 1960.[26] The hand and the attributes of the apothecary's profession then reappeared intact, and the balance of composition between the two portraits, broken by the overpainting, was reestablished.

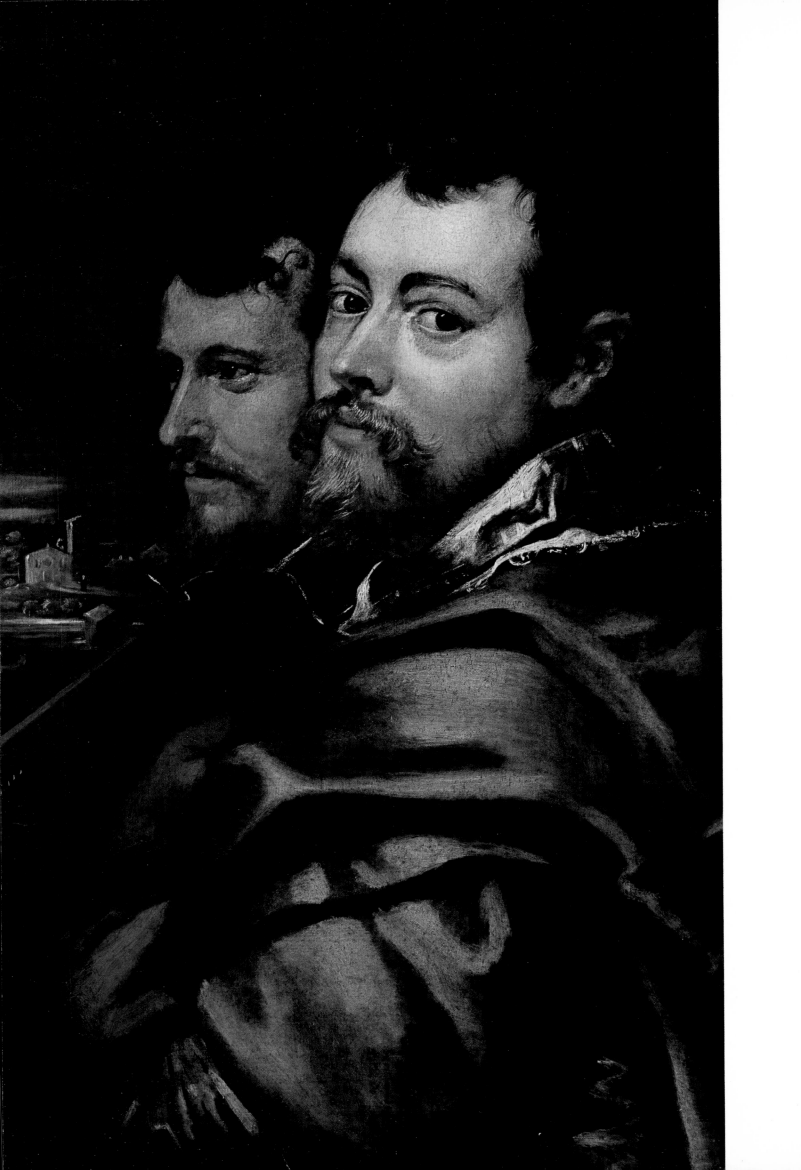

CHAPTER 2   An Early Work

# Adam and Eve in Paradise

## and the Relationship of Rubens and Otto van Veen

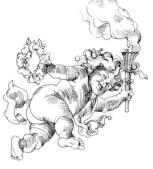

Rubens' apprenticeship in Antwerp was spent successively in the work-shops of Tobias Verhaecht, Adam van Noort, and Otto van Veen; of these masters, Van Veen was undoubtedly the most important.   His influence on the young artist is clearly seen in Rubens' early work *Adam and Eve in Paradise* (Plate 11),[1] acquired in London in 1967 for the Rubens House.   The style of this picture, however, shows—as we will demonstrate below—a more forceful temperament than that of Van Veen, and in it can already be found some features which are often characteristic of Rubens' great works.   Therefore this recently rediscovered work holds indisputable importance for the study of the relationship of Van Veen and Rubens, about which some new insights will be added.

But first let us look at a few details of the life of Otto van Veen, or Vaenius as he latinized his last name.[2]   He was born at Leyden in 1556 of an aristocratic family which boasted its descent from a bas-tard son of John III, Duke of Brabant (1300–1355).   After attending the Latin School in his native town, Otto, or Octavio, as he often preferred to call himself, became an apprentice with the painter Isaac Claesz. van Swanenburg.   But the whole Van Veen family left Leyden on October 20, 1572; although Otto's father was the mayor of Leyden, his loyalty to the Catholic faith and the king of Spain caused him to leave, and to settle in Antwerp.   But not for long: Antwerp, in turn, soon became dominated by supporters of the Reformation, and the family moved on to Liège.   There Otto studied with Dominicus Lampsonius and Jean de Ramey; the former was a distinguished artist, but more important, a humanist of refined tastes, cited with honor in the contemporary history of Latin letters.[3]

Lampsonius had a profound influence on the young Dutch painter: this can be seen in Van Veen's Latin writings, in his allegorical pictures, and in his emblem books.   The humanist education he received explains why the famous geographer Abraham Ortelius later compared the artist, in 1598, to the Greek painter Pamphilus: indeed we read in Otto van Veen's *Album Amicorum*, "Of you, Vaenius, I say the

Plate 10
RUBENS AND HIS MANTUAN
FRIENDS (detail; Fig. 162)
Canvas, over-all dimensions
30³/₄″ × 39³/₄″
Cologne, Wallraf-Richartz-Museum

*This group portrait, in which only the artist's head seems to have been completed, was painted during Rubens' stay in Italy (1600–1608).   His features are those of a man 25 to 29 years of age.*

47

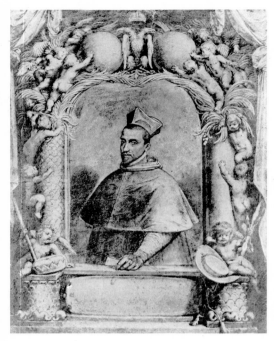

Figure 20
Otto van Veen (and Rubens?)
THE ARCHDUKE ALBERT AS CAR-
DINAL
Drawing
Vienna, Graphische Sammlung Alber-
tina

*The portrait was drawn by Otto van Veen,
while the putti appear to be by Rubens' hand.*

Plate 11
ADAM AND EVE IN PARADISE
Panel, 71″ × 62¼″
Antwerp, Rubens House

*Rubens painted this panel when he was barely
twenty, in any case before his departure for
Italy in 1600. The style of this youthful
work—the most important one known so
far—has a close affinity with the cold classicism of Otto van Veen; it testifies, however,
to Rubens' vigorous temperament which
would expand more fully in later works.*

same thing: you are the first on our globe who has reconciled painting and the liberal arts."[4]

After two years of assiduous work Otto van Veen left Liège for Rome, bearing recommendations to Cardinal Madruccio. He stayed there for five years and studied with the eclectic painter Federico Zuccari, whose classicizing influence remains still evident in some of Van Veen's much later works. On his way back he may have visited for some time in Munich, at the court of William IV of Bavaria. In any case, he was again in Liège in 1583, when he entered the service of Prince-Bishop Ernest of Bavaria. When the latter became cardinal of Cologne, Van Veen followed him but did not stay long on the banks of the Rhine. Soon after Antwerp was captured by Duke Alessandro Farnese in 1585, Van Veen was made painter to the duke's court in Brussels, and by 1590, at the latest, he was back in Antwerp. In 1594 he was made master in the Guild of St. Luke, and that year he married Maria Loets and settled in a house in the Vuylnis-straete—now Otto Vaenius Street—near the Meir, not far from where Rubens later built his house and workshop. Rubens probably joined Van Veen as an apprentice in 1594, at the latest in 1595. Roger de Piles tells us in his *Vie de Rubens*, published in Paris in 1677,[5] that Rubens stayed four years with Van Veen; other sources tell us that his apprenticeship did not end until 1598; thus we know that when Rubens came to perfect himself with Otto van Veen he can scarcely have acquired more than the rudiments of his trade from the landscape painter Tobias Verhaecht and from Adam van Noort; he was, in fact, about seventeen years old, and his new master was thirty-eight.

Roger de Piles obtained his information from Philip Rubens, the painter's nephew, and describes the relationship of master and pupil as follows: "The same penchant which they both had for literature having bound them in friendship, the Master did not fail to communicate everything he knew to his Disciple, disclosing to him liberally all the secrets of his art and teaching him above all how to arrange figures and distribute the highlights advantageously. Having caused him in a short time to make great progress, and the reputation of this illustrious Disciple having reached such a point that people were in doubt as to who was the more skillful, he or his master, Rubens resolved to go to Italy...."[6] This text tells us that their common taste for literature united master and disciple. As former Latin School pupils, both of them had conceived a passionate interest in the classics, so admired and idealized by the Renaissance. We have noted Ortelius' high praise for Otto van Veen in reconciling painting and the liberal arts; in 1607 Gaspard Scioppius speaks of Rubens in the same manner: "My friend Rubens, in whom I do not know what to praise most: his mastery in painting, an art, in which, according to the connoisseurs, he has reached perfection—as far as anyone has managed that in our age—or his knowledge of everything that concerns belles-lettres even more, or finally, that subtle judgment which goes along with such fascinating conversation."[7]

We have read what Roger de Piles wrote about Van Veen and

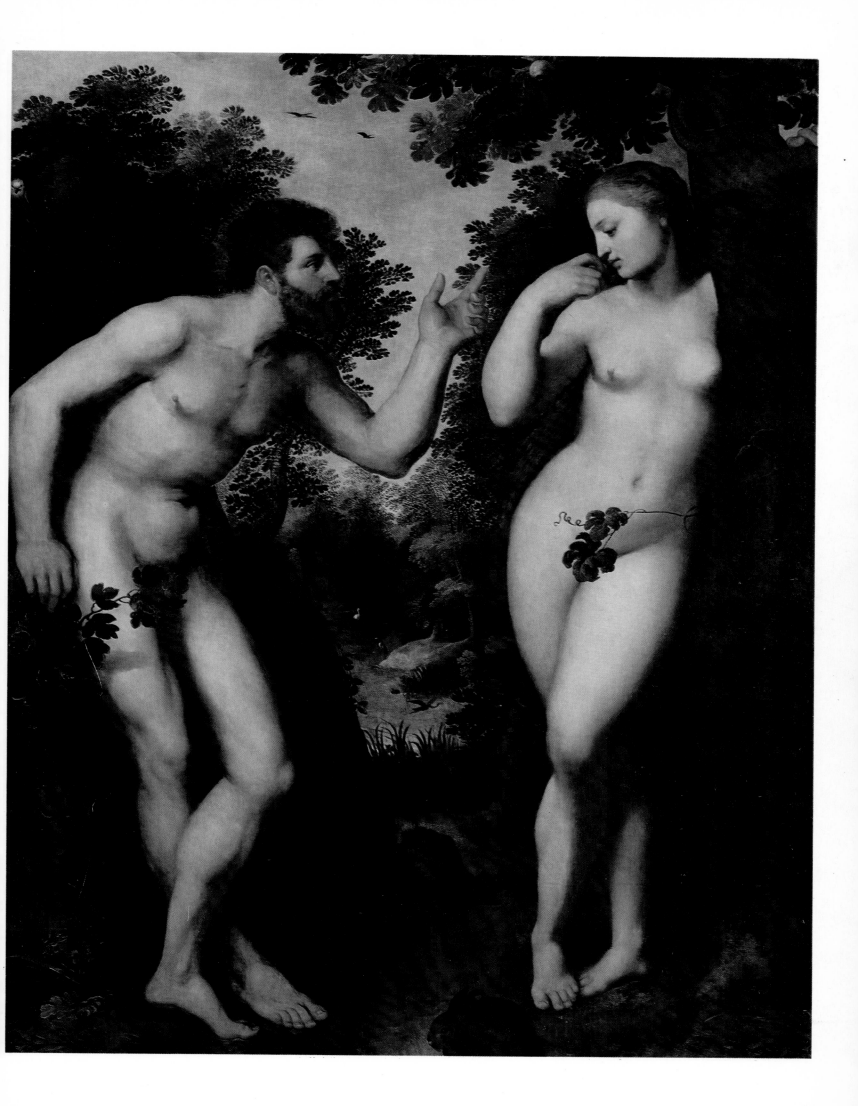

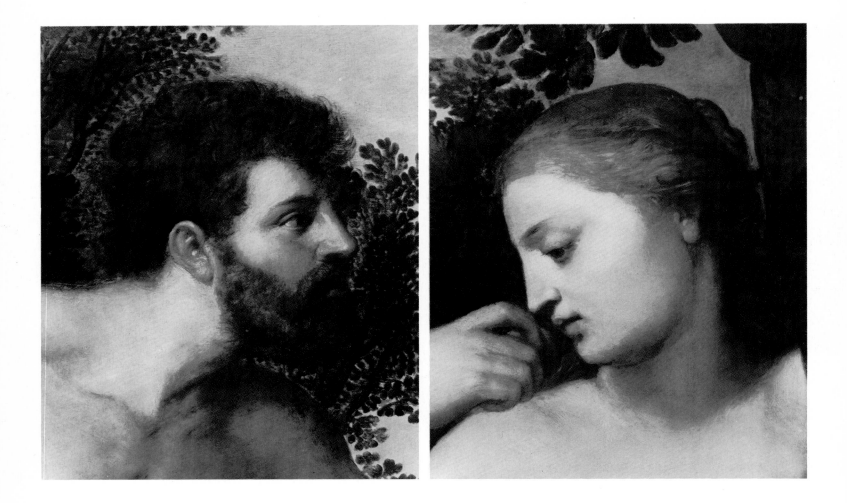

Rubens, the painter on the threshold of his career; to this testimony may be added Philip Rubens' statement in 1676 about his uncle's early pictures: "... before his journey to Italy, there was some resemblance between them and those of his master, Otto van Veen...."[8]

It is very probable that Rubens collaborated with his master according to the customs then prevailing in the workshops. A seventeenth-century document mentioned by Van den Branden seems even to prove this: it describes a certain picture as "A piece by Octavio and Breughel, first painted by Rubens, furnished with a frame, and representing Mount Parnassus."[9] This text, if we interpret it correctly, refers to a picture that was started by Rubens, executed in part by him, and then corrected(?) and completed by Van Veen and "Breughel." Although the text, alas, does not tell us which Breughel is meant here, we can suppose that it refers to Jan the Elder, "Velvet" Breughel, a friend of Rubens with whom he later worked on many occasions.

Other indications of the collaboration of master and pupil have been detected in a drawing in the Albertina in Vienna (Fig. 20). It is a study for an engraving by G. van Velden, in which Van Veen is named

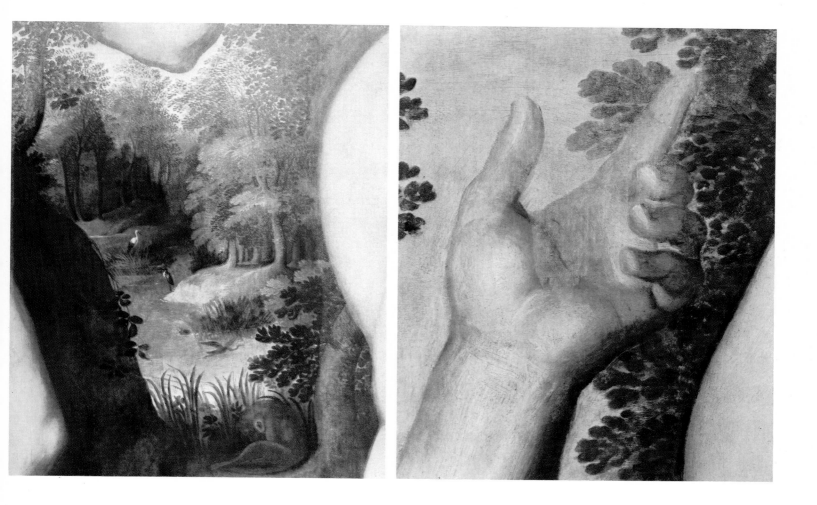

Figure 23
BACKGROUND OF LANDSCAPE WITH
POOL (detail; see Pl. 11)

Figure 24
ADAM'S LEFT HAND (detail; Pl. 11)

as the author of the composition; Archduke Albert is represented in half length, wearing the cardinal's robe. He is seen within an arch-shaped frame embellished by plants and a frolicsome crowd of plump putti. Christopher Norris has emphasized how these putti have greater liveliness in the strokes of both pencil and brush than has the portrait itself, and how this difference suggests another "hand";[10] he does not hesitate to attribute the putti to the young Peter Paul Rubens. Although Norris' hypothesis must be verified by a systematic and comparative study of Otto van Veen's drawings, it seems to us most probable that he will prove to be correct.

In *Adam and Eve in Paradise* (Plate 11) we can see the extent to which Rubens, before departing for Italy in May 1600, had built his style on that of Otto van Veen. Philip Rubens' statement about his uncle's first canvases is confirmed. Of Rubens' earliest works that we know, this painting is certainly the most important; some others have been attributed to the beginning of his career,[11] but none shows in so eloquent a fashion the standard he had already attained—a standard so high that, as Roger de Piles said, there was doubt as to whether master

51

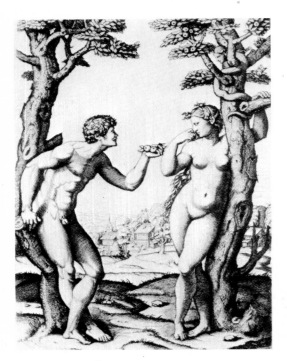

or pupil was the more skillful. No work by Otto van Veen makes so strong an impression as this one, as all will admit who are familiar with his art.

Against a delightful landscape of fresh green and blue, the earthly Paradise, the first human pair stands naked. Eve leans against a tree, her legs crossed, clinging to a branch with her left hand. Meditative and perhaps a bit hesitant, she looks down at the apple in her right hand (Fig. 22); above her the serpent twines around the tree trunk. On the left side Adam is leaning against a rock, his legs also crossed in a mannered way. He seems to gesture in reprimand with his left hand as he looks at Eve with surprised tenderness (Fig. 21). What is represented is the last moment of tension and uncertainty before the Fall.

Rubens borrowed the composition, as Jaffé has observed,[12] from an engraving by Marcantonio Raimondi after Raphael (Fig. 25).[13] His interpretation, however, is altogether personal. By turning Adam's face toward the spectator, he has given it a slightly more intense expression; Eve's face is more inscrutable. These modifications show Rubens' effort to achieve greater expressiveness within the limits of this classical composition. This appears most sharply in the vigorous movement given to Adam's left arm: contrary to the engraving, Adam does not present the apple with his left hand, but with his index finger seems both to reprove Eve and to point to the serpent hidden in the foliage. These variations on Raphael's composition prove that Rubens had modified the scene in order to emphasize the drama of the moment. His first efforts were not all fruitful; there are traces of repainting around Adam's face and, especially, changes in the raised left arm and hand. But in the corrections that the painter was willing to make, we can see better the efforts he made to express his vision more tellingly. One of Rubens' characteristics is already discernible, namely, his epic narration, praised by Eugène Delacroix and Jacob Burckhardt,[14] which he would later display much more spontaneously.

In comparing the picture with Marcantonio Raimondi's engraving, one certainly sees the greater monumentality of Rubens' figures, fuller, more sensual, more heroic. Leaning forward, Adam's bronzed torso is more thickset, more powerful; Eve's pale body, tinged here and there with pink, has a cold classical beauty. The graceful, taut contours make her slender beauty stand out admirably against the blue-green and brown landscape in the background.

As R.-A. d'Hulst[15] has observed, Eve's classical profile and Adam's bearded and idealized head comply with the classical canons of the sixteenth century, respected by Otto van Veen no less than by Raphael. The landscape, however, fits into the Flemish tradition (Fig. 22). The green and bluish tones of the thick forest are found in most of the Flemish landscape painters of the late sixteenth century. In certain places the feathery foliage recalls the small panels of Jan Breughel, Rubens' friend, while the "pointillism" in the background seems to be in a technique that Rubens could have learned from Tobias Verhaecht, his first teacher.

Figure 25
Marcantonio Raimondi, after Raphael
ADAM AND EVE
Engraving

*This print inspired Rubens' composition; his interpretation is nevertheless a personal one and he gives the figures a more monumental and sensual appearance.*

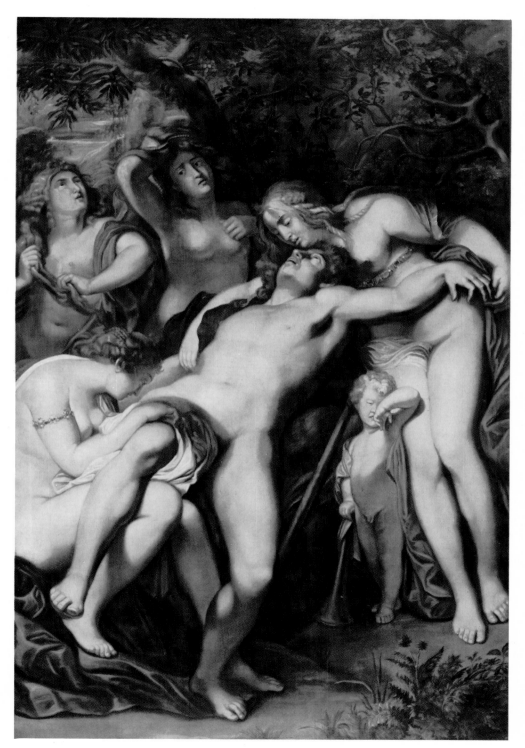

Figure 26
THE DEATH OF ADONIS
Canvas, 9′ × 6′
Paris, Private Collection

*Painted in 1601, this picture also shows some
of the characteristic features of the classicism
of Otto van Veen, Rubens' most important
teacher. The figure of Adonis, however, was
taken from an antique sarcophagus (Fig.
30).*

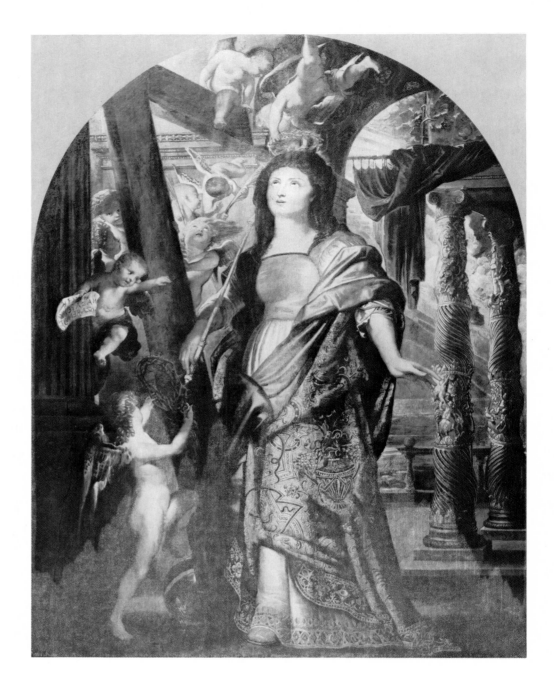

Figure 27
ST. HELEN
Panel, 8′3 × 6′2″
Grasse, Old Cathedral of Notre-Dame
(formerly in the Hospice)

*This picture was painted in Rome in 1601
for the church of Santa Croce in Gerusa-
lemme and commissioned by the Archduke
Albert. Many stylistic elements still recall
the years of Rubens' apprenticeship with Otto
van Veen.*

Rubens was not content with revising his landscape from Raimondi's; the glimpses we catch of birds and animals are also a personal
addition. In the foreground, at Eve's feet, a little rabbit crouches,
its ears raised as in Dürer's famous engraving of *Adam and Eve*.[16] A
small monkey hides in the reeds at the edge of the pond. Somewhat
farther back a stork can be seen on the left bank, a heron on the
right. A second heron flies over the pond; on the pond a duck swims,
and in the sky two ducks are flying. Far on the left, perched on a
branch above Adam, one glimpses the bright plumage of a bird which
has been identified as an Amazon parrot (*Amasona aestiva* Linn.).[17]

These creatures clearly illustrate the confidence between man and beast in the earthly Paradise, but some of them may have a symbolical meaning in addition, more in keeping with the subject: the Fall of Man. Thus the rabbit—like the hare—by reason of its extraordinary fertility, has always been a symbol not only of love, but also of lust.[18]   Since the Middle Ages, the monkey has symbolized vanity and lewdness, indeed all the lower instincts.[19] It seems less likely that symbolical value need be attributed to the birds.   The parrot frequently represents eloquence[20] and the stork the love of children,[21] but these qualities appear to have only remote connections with the subject.

Although *Adam and Eve in Paradise* recalls Otto van Veen's classicism in more than one respect, a force emanates from this work which one would seek in vain in the latter's canvases.   Is not this a definite indication in favor of attributing the picture to Rubens?   In the painter's wish to charge the scene with a degree of dramatic tension, we have already recognized that epic narration which is one of Rubens' major qualities.   Furthermore, we find here certain stylistic features which will reappear in the master's later work: note the remarkable touches of light at the fingertips of Adam's left hand (Fig. 24), which recur in many canvases, such as the small *Portrait of a Geographer* (Collection of Mr. and Mrs. Jack Linsky, New York), which Rubens painted at the outset of his career, in 1597.[22]   These accents of light seem to be a personal and precocious discovery by Rubens, since they are not seen in Otto van Veen's work.   Also typical of Rubens is the manner of encircling the foliage with a lighter stroke, finely delimiting the shape of the leaves: notice the hopvine and the branch of the vine-shoot[23] which safeguard the modesty of Adam and Eve.   Finally the modulation in long, bold strokes, giving sinuous relief to the bodies; this remains a constant quality of the great Antwerp master.   So there are many elements that make the attribution of this picture to Rubens entirely plausible.

Let us not forget, however, that Rubens was barely twenty when he painted this work.   We can see his point of departure: an art still closely linked with the classicism of the late sixteenth century, such as is found in Van Veen.   From this starting point Rubens was to develop gradually a more personal style, inaugurating with brilliance the Baroque era north of the Alps.   But before he reached this level he had to discover, to live with, and to study intensely for eight years the much-admired classical sculpture of Italy, and the famous models of the Renaissance in the South.

In Rubens' works of his first Italian years, the effects of his apprenticeship with Otto van Veen can still be detected, but many other influences begin to intermingle as he undergoes his first contacts with Italian art.   Rubens used again the smooth though already strongly modeled style of painting which characterizes Eve for the female figures in the *Death of Adonis* (Fig. 26).   He probably painted this picture in 1601 at the same time as its pendant, *Hercules and Omphale*, now in the Louvre.[24]

The *St. Helen* (Fig. 27), now in Grasse, one of the three works

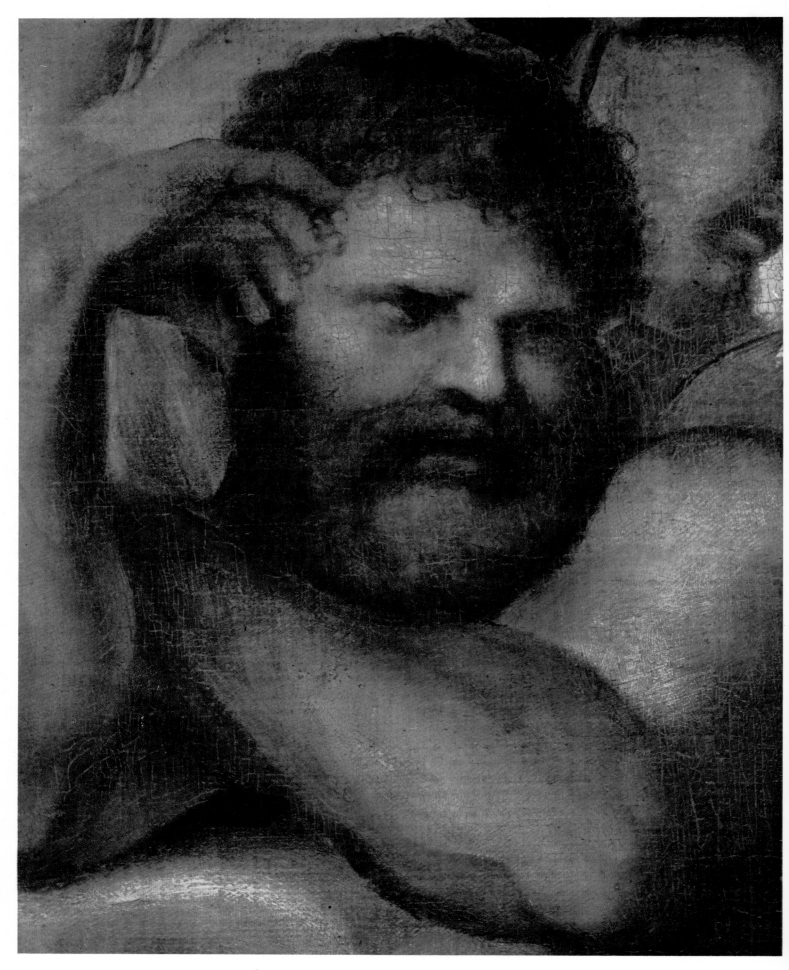

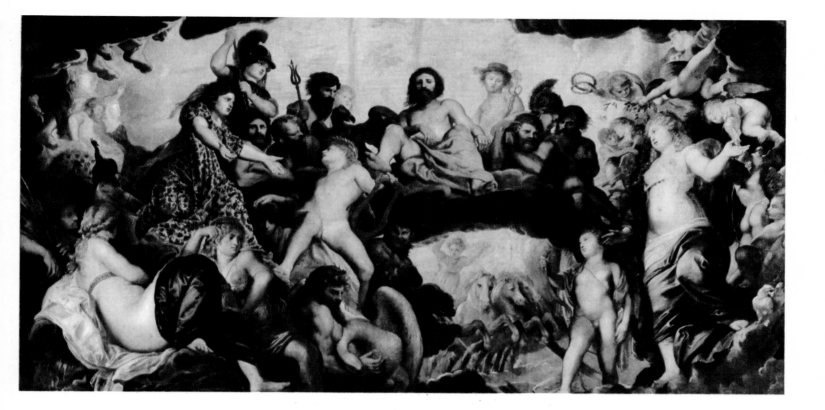

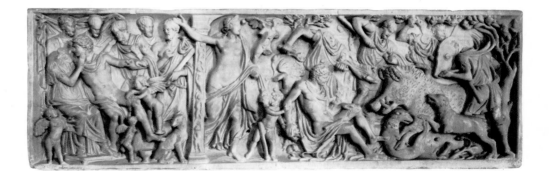

◀ Figure 28
HEAD OF A FIGURE TO THE RIGHT
OF JUPITER (detail; Fig. 29)

*This man leaning slightly forward on his arms recalls certain figures in the works of Otto van Veen.*

▲
Figure 29
THE ASSEMBLY OF THE GODS ON
OLYMPUS
Canvas, 6'8" × 12'5"
Prague, Hradsin (Castle)

*This huge canvas, probably painted in 1602 for the Mantuan court, was discovered about ten years ago in the Hradsin (Castle) of Prague. Along with numerous borrowings from antique sculpture, one can also observe elements recalling Rubens' years of apprenticeship with Otto van Veen.*

Figure 30
Roman Sarcophagus
THE DEATH OF ADONIS
Mantua, Palazzo Ducale

*As early as 1600, when Rubens became court painter to Vincenzo Gonzaga almost immediately on his arrival in Italy, he may have seen this sarcophagus in the Ducal Palace of Mantua. In several paintings from the first years of his stay in Italy there are motifs borrowed from this relief, some of them represented in reverse.*

carried out by Rubens in Rome that same year, also shows reminiscences of the training he had received with Otto van Veen.[25]   Jaffé has pointed out the resemblance of St. Helen's face to that of St. Cecilia in Raphael's famous painting in Bologna,[26] but we should not forget that Van Veen, too, liked to draw inspiration for his female figures from that High Renaissance master.   Even the technique in Rubens' picture accords with Van Veen's, in whose work we find, for example, the same rather stiff drapery folds as in Rubens' *St. Helen;* the angels hovering at the left of the cross, above the saint's head, recall Van Veen's putti and also those enframing the portrait drawing of Archduke Albert (Fig. 20)—but we remember that these have been attributed to Rubens.   We further note that the plump malicious-looking little putto at the lower right in that drawing looks like the twin of the cherub in the upper half of *St. Helen,*[27] at the left of the cross!

A large picture entitled *The Assembly of the Gods on Olympus* (Fig. 29), found a few years ago in the Castle of Prague, contains many elements recalling the style of Otto van Veen.[28]   This work was probably painted in 1602, and one notes especially the figures on either side of the enthroned Jupiter leaning forward on their arms as if at an open window (Fig. 28).   Such figures are often found in Otto van Veen: among many examples, St. Joseph in the *Mystic Marriage of St. Catherine,* a picture dating from 1585, now in the Musées Royaux des Beaux-Arts in Brussels;[29] St. Joseph in the *Adoration of the Shepherds* (Fig. 31);[30] and finally, St. Matthew in the *Calling of St. Matthew* (Fig. 32).[31]   Moreover, the flowing hair of Jupiter and the other gods reminds us of the head of St. Andrew in Van Veen's great *Martyrdom of St. Andrew,* painted for the church of St. Andrew in Antwerp during 1597–99, just when Rubens was his pupil;[32] and here the figures are piled up as in Rubens' Prague painting, where most of the gods have scarcely room to stretch their legs!   These few examples of his first Italian years clearly show the mark of Rubens' training with Van Veen, but many other currents mingled with this main one: certain color effects borrowed from the Venetians, certain models of great masters of the Italian Renaissance, and above all elements from the ancient sculpture which Rubens studied assiduously, as his drawings from classical examples testify.   Elsewhere it has been pointed out that the Venus and Apollo in the great Prague picture were inspired by motifs on a Roman sarcophagus (Fig. 30), still in the Ducal Palace in Mantua where Rubens admired it when he was court painter there.[33]

We must emphasize, however, that as the studious young artist built up new impressions, the memory of the Antwerp training gradually faded.   In the powerful *Equestrian Portrait of the Duke of Lerma* (Fig. 33), painted in 1603 during Rubens' first visit to Spain, this influence has become almost indiscernible.   A greater freedom of expression and a vibrant coloring with more chiaroscuro are evident, showing how far the artist has already gone over to Italian, in this case particularly Venetian, painting.[34]

While Rubens was sojourning beyond the Alps and developing his art in contact with Italian and antique examples, Otto van Veen was

Plate 12
ST. GREGORY THE GREAT AND OTHER SAINTS WORSHIPING THE MADONNA
Canvas, 15′7″ × 9′5″
Grenoble, Musée des Beaux-Arts

*Rubens painted this canvas in 1607–8 for the high altar of Santa Maria in Vallicella, the church of the Oratorian Fathers in Rome, but the artist took it back with him to Antwerp when he observed that it could scarcely be seen because of awkward reflections of light.   He later placed it above an altar in the abbey of St. Michael in Antwerp, in memory of his mother.*

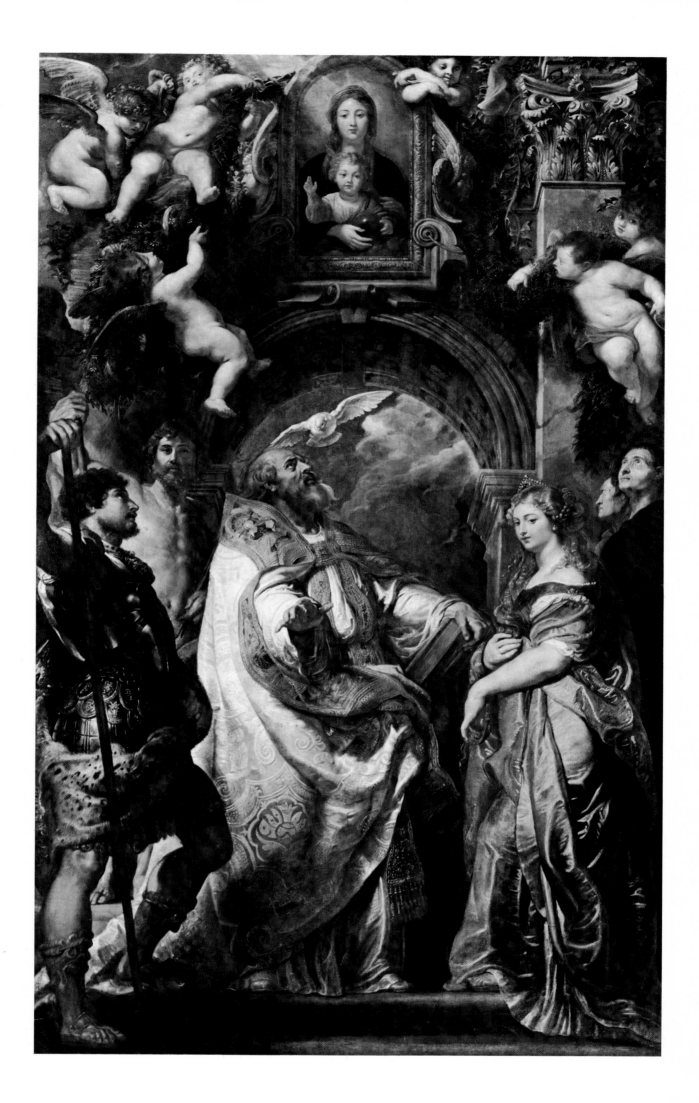

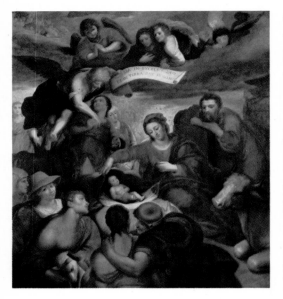

establishing himself more and more as the leading painter of Antwerp.  After the death of Marten de Vos in 1603, no one contested his supremacy, as clearly demonstrated by his appointment in 1603 to the rank of dean of the Guild of St. Luke.  After this he received very important commissions: the triptych of the *Adoration of the Shepherds*, in the Maagdenhuis (Fig. 31); this *Adoration of the Shepherds* was painted for the chapel of St. Anne, a building financed by the knight Simon Rodriguez Pretti de Evora, consecrated on May 16, 1601;[35] on June 21, 1602, the Antwerp city authorities paid Van Veen 300 florins for "the picture of the Assumption, which is here in this college,"[36] a work that had disappeared by the end of the eighteenth century;[37] in 1605 his altarpiece for the Clothiers Guild in the cathedral of Our Lady (central panel now in the Gemäldegalerie, Mainz);[38] finally, his *Raising of Lazarus*, painted in 1608 for the church of St. Bavo in Ghent.[39]  Critical analysis also leads to placing a number of other works by Van Veen between 1600 and 1608, the period when Rubens was in Italy.  Each of these pictures testifies to the artistic maturity Van Veen had then attained.

Late in 1608 Rubens returned to Antwerp,[40] and although he settled there definitely he continued to cherish for some time the hope of going back to Rome.[41]  The growing reputation that he enjoyed in Italy had brought him several important commissions that he carried out shortly before his departure.  But on September 23, 1609, he was appointed "painter to the Household of their Royal Highnesses,"[42] Archduke Albert and Infanta Isabella.  A month later he married Isabella Brant.  The young couple settled temporarily in the Kloosterstraat, in the vast dwellings of Rubens' father-in-law, the court-clerk and jurist, Jan Brant.[43]  Rubens, then aged thirty-two, soon bought a large piece of land in the Wapperstraat, to build a house and a spacious workshop.[44]  The land was very costly and the construction lasted for years, necessitating heavy expense.  But what was that!  Since his return from Italy, well-remunerated commissions for altarpieces and other works had not been slow in coming in; the young painter's success meant that Otto van Veen's primacy, uncontested until then, was soon challenged by his former pupil.  In 1611 a new high altar was proposed for the cathedral of Our Lady; both painters submitted designs for the picture that was to decorate it; the younger master won the commission.[45]

One can well imagine that it was a hard blow for Otto van Veen to see the sketches of his pupil, not long back from Italy, preferred to his own *modello*.  And the shock was all the more painful since this was no mean commission: to paint a large altarpiece for Antwerp Cathedral!  Van Veen must have understood that this was the end of his leading role in Antwerp's artistic life.  What could the aging master do, confronted with this young genius whom he had trained himself?  The drama has been well observed by De Maeyer: "In Antwerp, Vaenius, who has passed fifty, sees his prestige sinking.  Commissions are becoming scarcer, and doubtless he and his large family have their share of financial worries."[46]  When the city

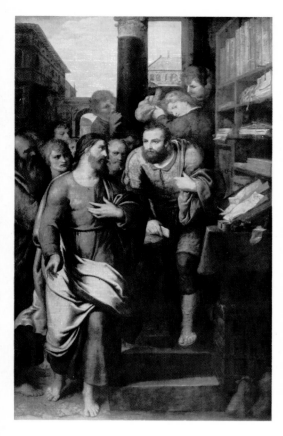

of Antwerp reduced his salary by one-third, he applied for the post of Director of the Mint as soon as it was created in Brussels. He postponed moving for some time, for it pained him to leave Antwerp, "where he felt at home and had a large circle of acquaintances." In September 1615, he at last settled in Brussels. "Thus Otto van Veen finally presents the rather distressing image of an artist whose prestige is in regression and whose artistic activity is gradually declining. His relations with the Archduke and his wife had not worsened, but his prestige as an artist nevertheless went down from the time that Rubens more and more occupied the first rank." The fact that Rubens was preferred over his master as early as 1611 for the execution of the large picture for the high altar of the cathedral shows clearly the decline of Van Veen.

It cannot be surprising that this new situation chilled the relationship of the two painters. On this point we must draw attention to a passage in a letter from Rubens to his former master's brother, Pieter van Veen, in The Hague. On June 19, 1622, he wrote: "I hear that M. Otto van Veen, your brother, has published a little anonymous work on the Universal Theory, or something of the sort. I should like very much to see this, and if it should be possible for you to lend it to me (for doubtless you have a copy), this would be very agreeable to me. I should accept it on my word of honor to keep this favor a complete secret, without speaking of it to a living soul, in case secrecy is necessary."[47] To see this publication, why did Rubens have to apply to Pieter van Veen, who lived in The Hague? Why not write to Otto van Veen, his master, who lived in Brussels and could have filled this request more easily? Commentators on the artist's correspondence, surprised at this unusual step, have concluded that the two painters had become so alienated from one another that Rubens did not dare to write directly to Van Veen—still less so because he thought, doubtless wrongly, that the booklet had appeared anonymously.

But however wide became the rift between Rubens and Van Veen, we must not forget the passage in Roger de Piles' biography of Rubens which tells us, on the basis of clear information received from Rubens' nephew Philip, that the memory of the old friendship with Van Veen remained much alive in the great artist's family. The gratitude which Rubens owed to his master was not forgotten. And from whom, but from Rubens himself, could his family have learned this?

Nothing prevents us from thinking that ultimately Otto van Veen felt satisfaction in having had the great chance of training so brilliant an artist as Rubens. When François Sweertius came to ask him questions about his life (for his biography, published in 1628), Van Veen did not omit to remind him that Peter Paul Rubens, whom he wished to describe as the "Apelles of the universe,"[48] had been his pupil.

What Rubens learned in Otto van Veen's workshop can be plainly seen in the *Adam and Eve in Paradise*, discussed above. The resemblance of his art to his master's, as Philip Rubens later wrote, is indeed striking in this early work, and confirms Roger de Piles' statement

61

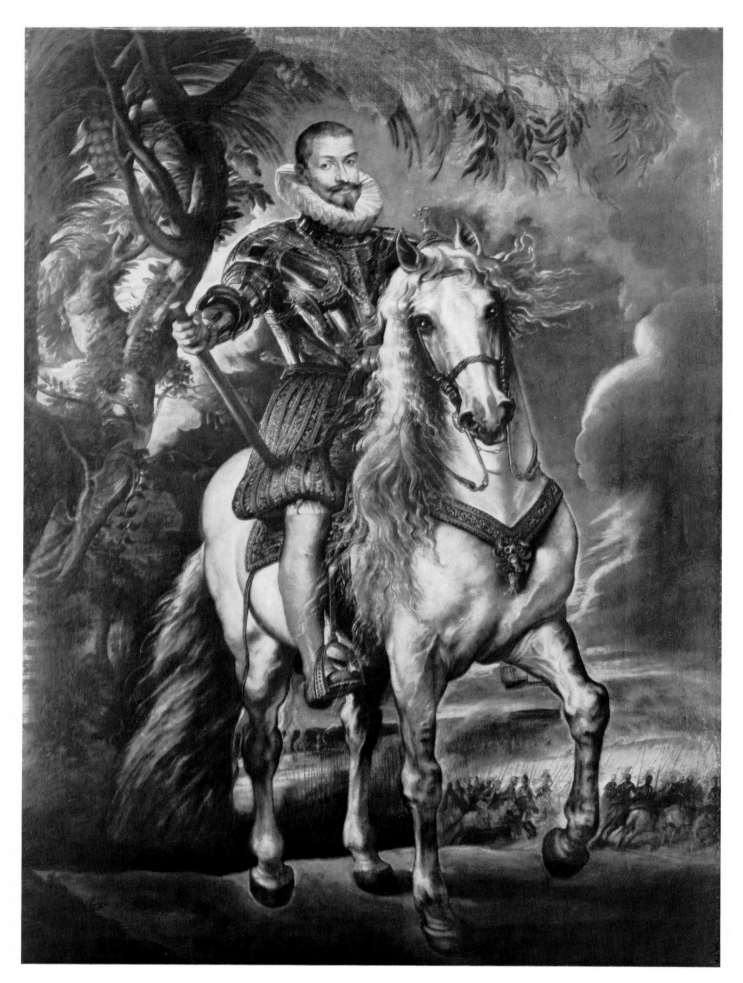

about the young painter's progress, so rapid that one soon asked whether master or disciple was the more skillful. Here a talent has been born; after ripening in the Italian sun it was gradually to open, and to become a completely individual style that would inaugurate a thrilling revival in the Southern Netherlands. In little more than ten years the art of the pupil so far surpassed the art of his master that the latter had to admit defeat. Otto van Veen's eclectic classicism gives way to the exuberant vitality of the Baroque, which celebrates its finest triumphs in the work of Rubens.

Figure 33
EQUESTRIAN PORTRAIT OF THE DUKE OF LERMA
Canvas, 9'5$^1/_2$" × 6'8$^1/_2$"
Madrid, Prado

*This large canvas was painted during Rubens' first stay in Spain, in 1603. A greater freedom of expression is evident, an indication that the artist has drawn largely upon Italian art, whose masterpieces he was studying. Here come to mind particularly the horsemen that figure in the Gonzaga series (now in the Alte Pinakothek, Munich) wich Tintoretto painted for the "appartamento maggiore" of the Castello of the Ducal Palace in Mantua.*

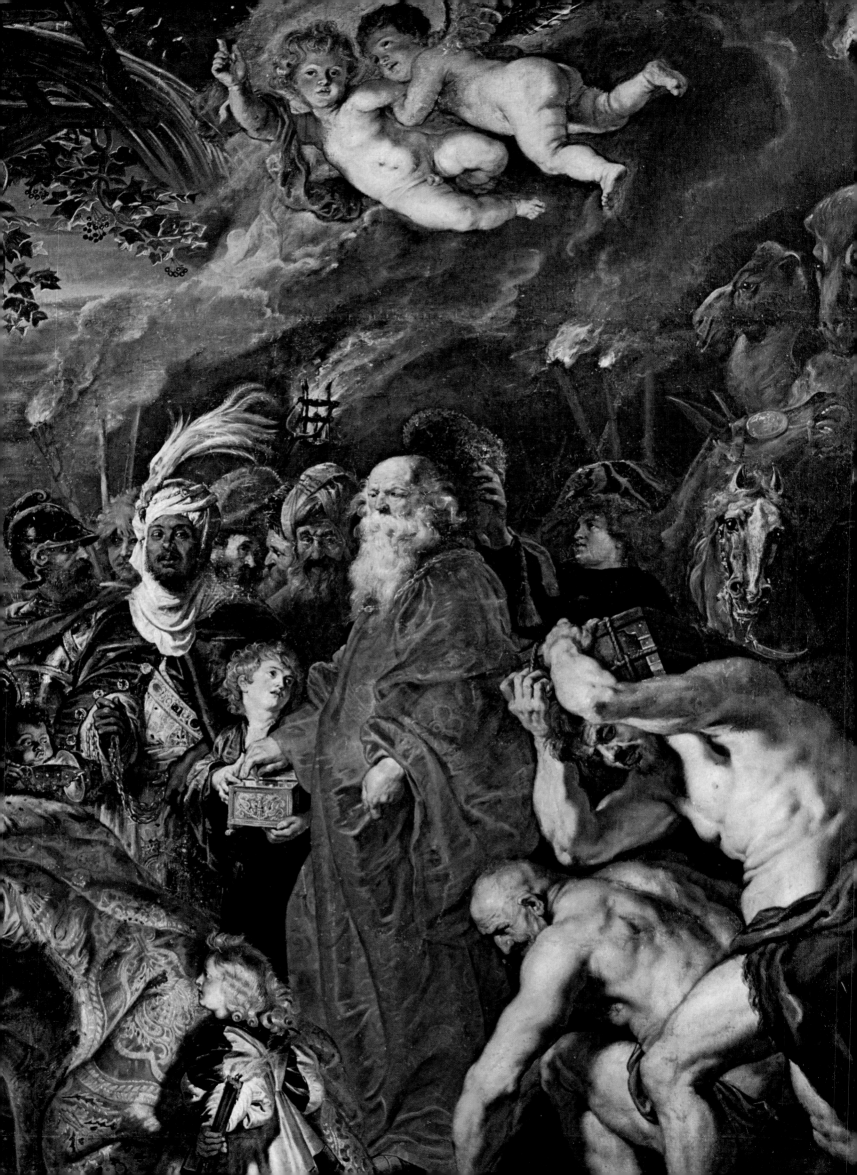

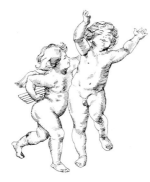

# CHAPTER 3   Altarpieces from the Period 1609 to 1620

The altarpieces that Rubens painted in the first ten or eleven years after his return to Antwerp surpass in their number and range those of all other periods in his career.   This should not surprise us, since it has frequently been emphasized that he returned to the Metropolis at a most opportune moment.   On his arrival, toward the end of 1608, hopes ran high for the early conclusion of a peace treaty, and a few months later, on April 9, 1609, the Twelve-Years' Truce was signed, finally suspending hostilities for that span of time.   Although the river Scheldt remained closed to free overseas shipping, this was clearly no obstacle to the economic revival which was so important, too, for the development of artistic life.[1]   Now that peace had finally returned, prosperity could be foreseen with the end of the long period of troubles and uncertainty.   It was possible to undertake the repair, or at least the restoring, of churches which had been damaged, neglected, or, most frequently, stripped of their artistic treasures during the hostilities and religious disturbances.   Work was resumed on certain buildings, such as the church of St. Jacques or that of the Dominicans (now St. Paul's), which had remained unfinished.   In 1611 the city counsellors, who had repeatedly provided subsidies for enterprises of building and repair, decided "that alms shall be collected during high masses and sermons for the purpose of restoring or repairing the churches."[2]   The religious orders which returned or indeed settled for the first time in the Metropolis could at last think seriously of building churches, in many cases replacements for the chapels they had been using and had now outgrown.

In 1611 the foundation stone was laid for the church of the Capuchin friars; in 1615, those of the "marble temple" of the Jesuits and of the church of the Augustinians; and a year later, of the convent of the "Annonciades."   Other buildings followed.   In all the new or restored churches, pictures and sculptures were needed.   The guilds, trades, and religious brotherhoods did not lag behind: they too wished to adorn their new altars with pictures corresponding in subject and dimension to the spirit of the Counter-Reformation, as well as to the taste for monumental and decorative exuberance in keeping with the

Plate 13
THE ADORATION OF THE MAGI (detail; Fig. 35)
Madrid, Prado

*One of the first works done by Rubens after his return from Italy, probably completed in January or February, 1609.*

65

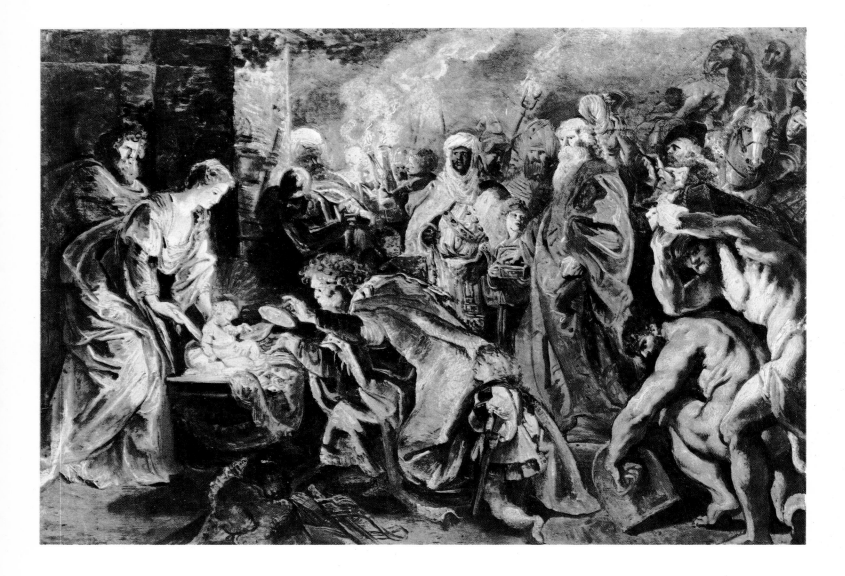

new artistic conceptions.[3]    All this resulted, immediately after the Twelve-Years' Truce, in a pressing demand for altarpieces and large religious paintings.

Rubens, his Antwerp career just beginning, could look forward to commissions which would give him a chance to display his artistic talents to the full in paintings of monumental dimensions.    Did he not write, some ten years later: "... I confess I am, by natural instinct, better fitted to execute very large works than curiosities"?[4]    For the time being, large paintings with mythological, allegorical, or historical subjects were in little demand in the Southern Netherlands.    The young painter had to be content with small- or medium-size works of this sort, intended for the dwellings of well-to-do Antwerp citizens, or for casual customers who sought him out in his workshop; later he would be asked—mainly by foreign courts—to treat these subjects in works of larger dimensions.    In the meantime numerous commis-

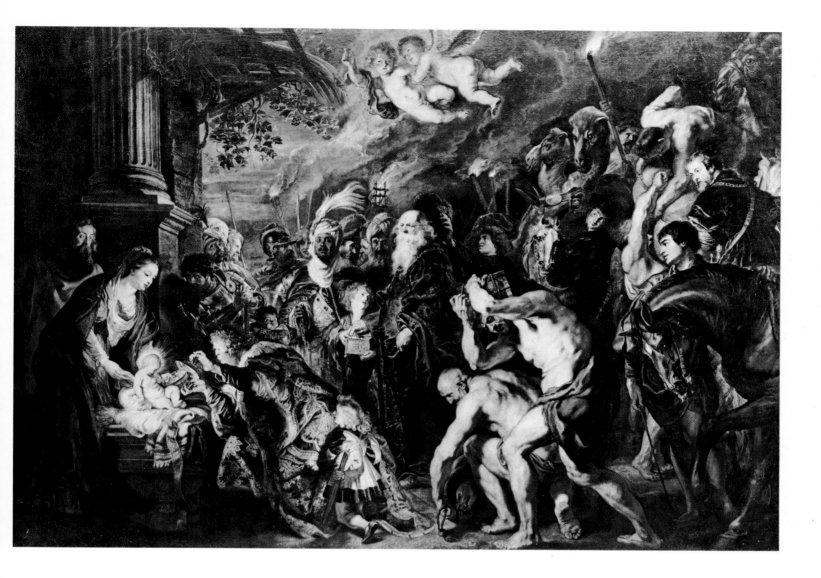

Figure 35
THE ADORATION OF THE MAGI (see
Pl. 13)
Canvas, 11′4″ × 16′
Madrid, Prado

*Painted in 1609 for the Town Hall of Antwerp. During Rubens' second stay in Madrid in 1628–29, where the picture had been since 1612, he enlarged this canvas on the right side and above. He portrayed himself as a man on horseback.*

sions for monumental altarpieces allowed him to prove his natural bent for "very large works."

These altarpieces were exceedingly important in launching the artist's career. In the churches, they could be admired by everybody, even casual travelers, for it is known that many foreigners visited the Southern Netherlands after peace was reestablished. Thus these pictures helped to spread Rubens' fame outside the country. The engravings that were made from them—in most cases several years later, however—also contributed greatly to his renown.

Since contemporary records and other reliable sources enable us to date a number of these altarpieces, they provide a useful basis both for establishing the development of Rubens' art, and then to fit into this chronology the works for which such documents are not available. It is necessary (as will be seen) that the effort be maintained to collect and correctly interpret every document that might possibly provide evidence.

67

In this outline of the altarpieces from the period 1609–20, we will try to be very precise about the dates of certain works, especially those painted soon after Rubens' return. This will give us a chance to describe the development of his art during this period. We cannot deal with all the altarpieces of those years; the choice is limited perforce to the most important, to those which have the fullest documentation and can thus be considered milestones in Rubens' art.

An exchange of letters beginning in 1611, published in 1965 by Monballieu,[5] proves that shortly after Rubens' return from Italy, he was already considered to be the most capable painter then active in Antwerp. When the governing authorities of the city and the castellany *(chatellenie)* of Bergues-St-Winoc (today in the Département du Nord, France) decided to provide an altarpiece of the *Last Supper* for the high altar of the local Benedictine abbey, they requested a merchant whom they knew in Dunkirk to find out who was "the best master" to be entrusted with this commission. On March 12, 1611—this date is not without importance, for Rubens then had been back from Rome only slightly more than two years—Jan Le Grand, an Antwerp merchant, replied: "We have here a good master who is called the god of painters, Peeter Rubbens, he is the painter of His Highness [Archduke Albert]." And to give more weight to his recommendation, Le Grand adds: "He has made here various pieces that are held in high esteem, as to wit, in the town hall, in Saint Michael's, at the Dominicans', and in the church of the Castle, and they are beautiful."[6] This information is interesting, since it enables us to fix the *terminus ad quem* of some pictures painted by Rubens shortly after he settled in Antwerp. It also confirms datings which hitherto had been made only a stylistic grounds.

It must, however, be pointed out that the picture which Jan Le Grand says is "in St. Michael's," that is, in the abbey of St. Michael (Plate 12), actually dates from before Rubens' return to Antwerp. He had painted it in Rome in 1607–8 for the high altar of the church of Santa Maria in Vallicella, but took it back when he found that it could scarcely be seen from the light reflections in the choir, and replaced it with three other pictures painted on slate which are still preserved in that church.[7] He had wanted to sell the picture to Vincenzo Gonzaga, duke of Mantua, whose official painter he was, but the latter did not accept his offer. When Rubens hurriedly left the Eternal City in October 1608, he brought the picture with him to Antwerp; there, in memory of his mother, Maria Pijpelinckx, who had died shortly before his return, he placed it near her tomb in the abbey of St. Michael on September 29, 1610, according to F. Sweertius' *Monumenta* (1613).[8] This picture, today in the Musée at Grenoble, was probably decisive in launching Rubens' career in Antwerp.

It may indeed appear astonishing that important commissions were given to a young artist only just returned from Italy when there were well-known masters who might have been called upon, whose important achievements could be admired in churches and in private collections. One thinks here of Otto van Veen, Adam van Noort—both of

Plate 14
THE ADORATION OF THE SHEPHERDS
Canvas, 13′1″ × 9′8″
Antwerp, Church of St. Paul

*This painting, whose composition recalls the altarpiece painted in Italy for the church of the Oratorian Fathers in Fermo (Fig. 68), was one of the first works Rubens executed upon his return from Italy.*

68

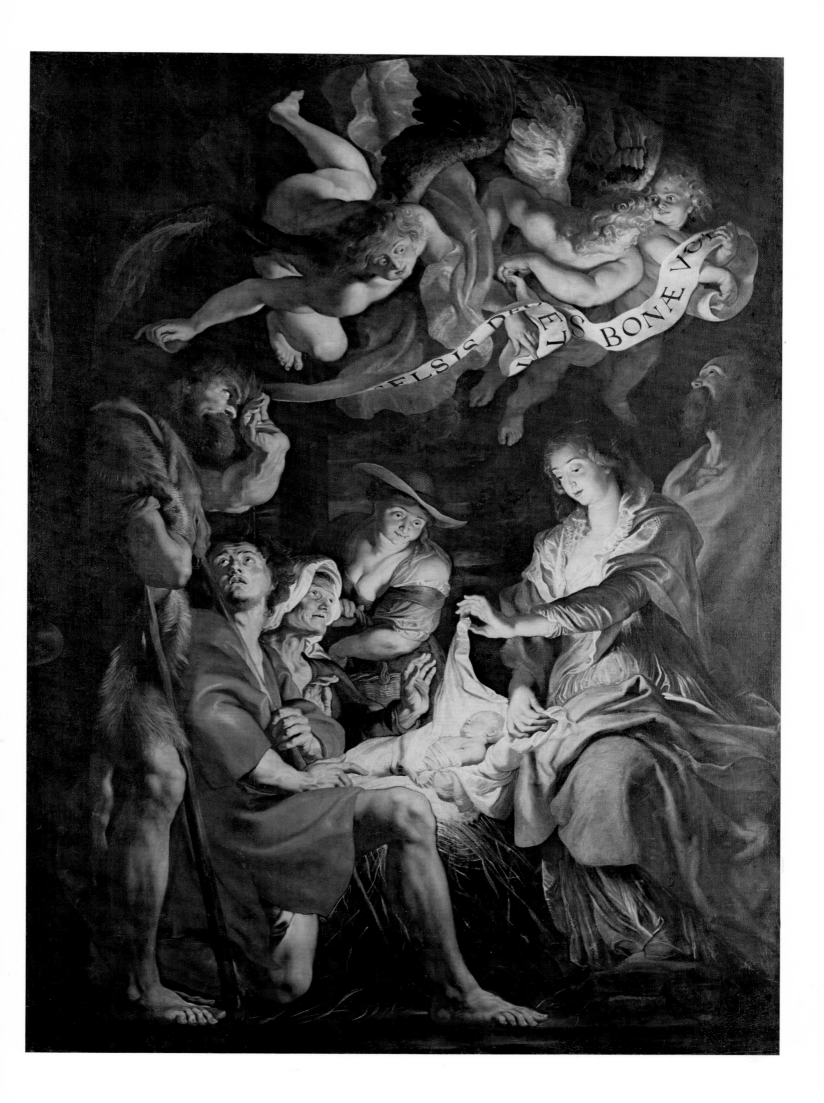

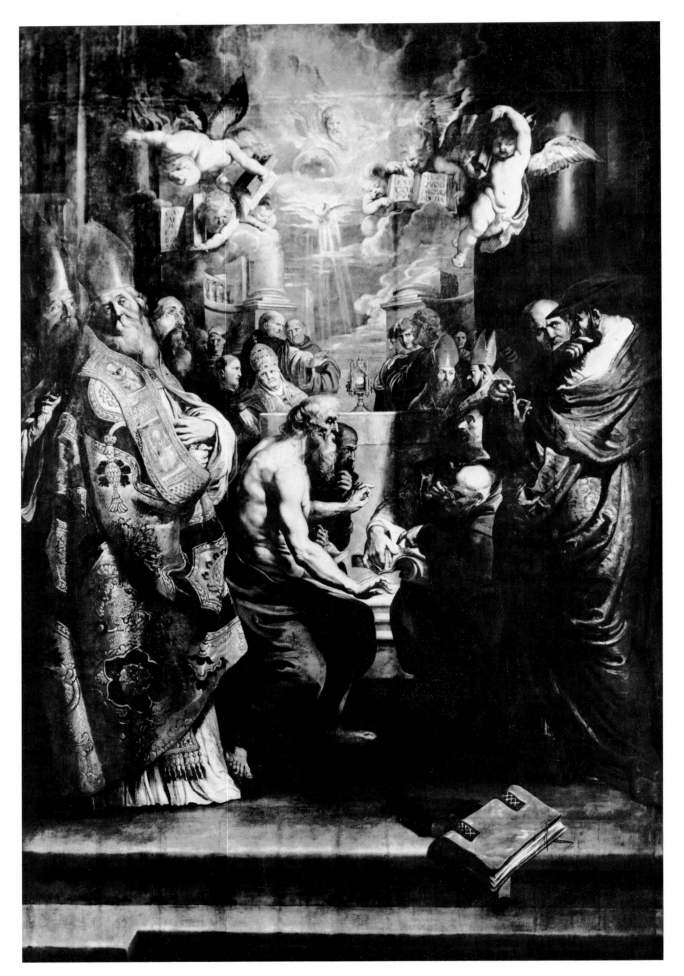

them former masters of Rubens—or Ambrosius Francken, or perhaps of younger contemporaries such as Abraham Janssens or Hendrik van Balen, who had already given proof of their talent.[9] Rooses and a number of authors after him have justifiably pointed out that Rubens, after his return, could count on the support of a fair number of influential persons, particularly his own brother Philip, who was soon to become Secretary of Antwerp; his father-in-law Jan Brant, who had long carried out the functions of city clerk; Nicolaas Rockox, several times alderman and mayor; and Cornelis van der Geest, a rich merchant. The word of these citizens would, however, have carried little weight if they had not been able to show an important work by their protégé. It is not impossible that some private collections in Antwerp included a number of paintings that Rubens had made before he left for Italy, but these only represented the work of a beginner and would hardly convince interested parties of the young artist's superiority over his Flemish contemporaries. He may have brought back sketches for works that he painted in Italy, but the finished altarpiece made in Rome surely had the most decisive effect.

The picture in the town hall to which Jan Le Grand alludes in his letter is without doubt *The Adoration of the Magi* (Plate 13; Fig. 35), which then adorned the Hall of the States.[10] The register of the Council of Aldermen mentions two orders of payment for this work, dated April 19 and August 4, 1610, amounting to 1800 florins. Another document, relating to the order of payment for the gilding of its frame, shows that the painting was completed in 1609. There are, in fact, good reasons to believe that it was finished early in 1609, and hence that Rubens had received the commission almost immediately after his return. This can be deduced from the circumstances in which the picture originated. When, in the course of 1609, the municipal authorities learned that the negotiations that were to lead to the conclusion of the Twelve-Years' Truce would be held in Antwerp, steps were taken to ensure that delegates would be welcomed in a setting suitable for the event. One room in the town hall, until then called the "Representation Room" *(Staetiekamer)*, was to be renamed Hall of the States *(Statenkamer;* now the marriage hall), and was reserved for this purpose. To decorate this room they proceeded to purchase a number of works of art, including the allegorical painting *Scaldis et Antverpia* by Abraham Janssens, as well as Rubens' *Adoration* under review.

A link can be established between the peace talks and the subject of both Abraham Janssens' work and Rubens' larger painting. *Scaldis et Antverpia* alludes to the hopes of the Metropolis that the river Scheldt might be reopened to free navigation, which would bring back its abundant prosperity to the city. *The Adoration of the Magi* expresses the desire for peace. The negotiators could more or less identify themselves, or their mostly royal mandators, with the Kings who came from the East with their offerings to the divine Child, the "Prince of Peace." Just as these magi came from their distant lands to adore Him, so the representatives of many European sovereigns had jour-

Figure 36
THE GLORIFICATION OF THE HOLY EUCHARIST
Panel, 12'1" × 7'11"
Antwerp, Church of St. Paul

*The slightly elongated figures in the foreground, the Venetian blue of the background, and the solid architectural accents of this work, painted around 1609–10, are still reminiscent of Rubens' style during the last years of his stay in Rome.*

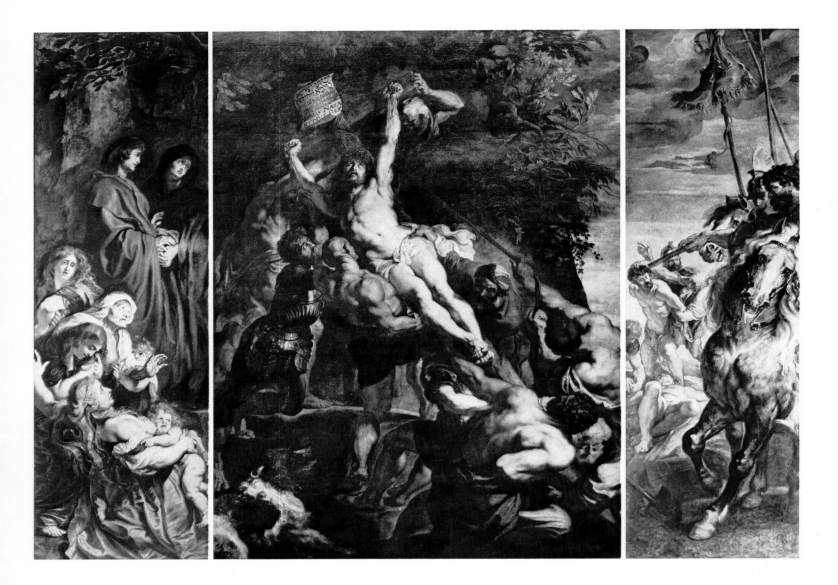

Figure 37
THE RAISING OF THE CROSS
Triptych; central panel 15′2″ × 11′2″,
wings each 15′2″ × 4′11″
Antwerp, Cathedral of Our Lady

*This triptych was painted in 1610 for the
high altar of St. Walburga's Church in
Antwerp, also called the church of the
Castle. The three panels together illustrate
one subject, for which Rubens invented a powerful and unified composition.*

Plate 15
THE RAISING OF THE CROSS
Central panel, 15′2″ × 11′2″
Antwerp, Cathedral of Our Lady

*All the features of the impetuous* Sturm und
Drang *style of the first years after Rubens'
return are found here: structure with forceful
diagonals, grandiose dynamics, contrasts of
light and shade. The forms are modeled in
a sculptural rather than pictorial language.*

neyed from their respective countries to Antwerp, to serve the cause
of peace. Such at least was the hope of the peace-loving Antwerp
citizens. The city fathers must certainly have insisted that both artists
finish their pictures in time for the opening of the negotiations. It
is known that the delegates arrived in Antwerp during January and
February 1609.[11] Thus it is altogether probable that Rubens' *Adoration of the Magi* was already completed by the early months of that
year, and that the powerful sketch made in preparation of the painting
(Fig. 34), at present in Groningen, was painted almost immediately
after his arrival from Italy late in 1608.

In the Dominican church also, writes Jan Le Grand, works by
Rubens could already be admired before March 1611. Unfortunately
he does not give particulars about them. Still to be seen in that
church, however, now St. Paul's, are two paintings which, on the basis
of stylistic analysis, can be placed among the first painted by Rubens
after his return. In one case, *The Adoration of the Shepherds* (Plate 14),
the absence of sources makes it impossible for us to know who ordered

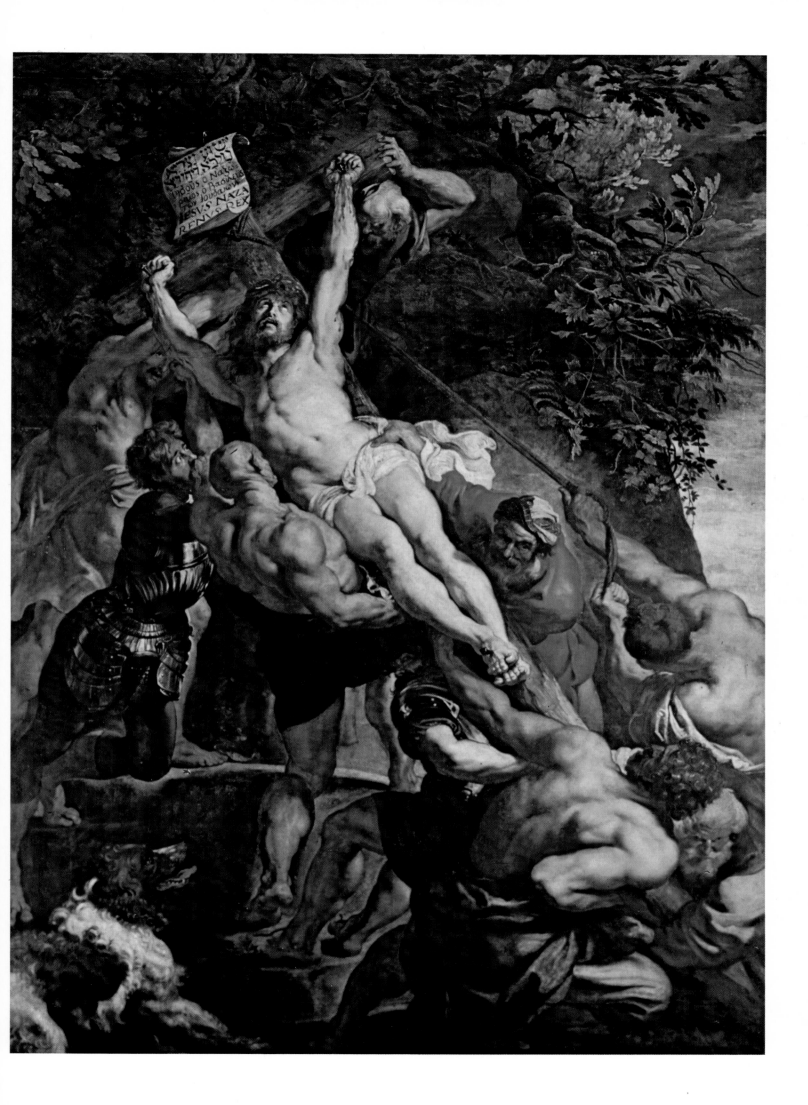

it and when it was placed in the church. In the eighteenth century it hung already in the transept, where it was when, on the night of April 3, 1969, fire broke out in the church. About 1748, Jacob de Wit described the painting as follows: "High up on the Wall, next to the Altar of the Rosary, hangs a beautiful painting, being a Christmas, or Birth of Christ, painted by P.P. Rubens, *very Capitally and Beautifully ordered*. The Figures are larger than Life."[12] But toward the end of that century Mols cast doubt on Rubens' authorship,[13] and after that the picture fell into oblivion until, in the last thirty years, it was reinstated by Burchard and Van Puyvelde.[14]

In this large picture, which has not yet received the attention it deserves, Rubens takes up again a composition he had designed in Italy for the altarpiece painted in 1608 for the church of the Oratorians in Fermo. To his second version of *The Adoration of the Shepherds*, however, he has given a more monumental character. The figures' poses and gestures have become freer and more pliant. Moreover the restoration since the fire of 1969 has revealed a splendor of unsuspected colors beneath the old layers of yellowish varnish. The radiant color, at the same time rich in contrasts, recalls Venetian painting and the art of Correggio, while both the figure types from the common people and the violent chiaroscuro seem to echo the art of Caravaggio. The gleaming brownish flesh tones and the flickering, palpitating touches of light are also characteristic of Rubens' art during the first few years after his homecoming.

A second painting in St. Paul's also presents the stylistic traits of the same years (Fig. 36). As early as 1672 Bellori described it as one of the artist's first works realized after his return from Italy.[15] It is often called *The Disputà*, but *The Glorification of the Holy Eucharist* would be more appropriate, unless one prefers *The Real Presence of the Holy Sacrament*, the title found in the inventory of the possessions of the Brotherhood of the "Holy Sweet Name of Jesus and of the Holy Sacrament," drawn up on July 24, 1616.[16] The latter title best renders the intentions of those who commissioned the picture. Indeed, in the work stand the Fathers of the Church and the theologians to "warrant," so to speak, this "reality": the real presence of Christ in the Holy Sacrament, an article of faith of the Roman Catholic Church which Protestants do not accept.

Were the costs of the picture covered by the subscriptions of the members of the Brotherhood of the Holy Sacrament? Or did a patron present the work to the Brotherhood? No documents seem to remain that would enable us to answer these questions. It is, however, significant that Cornelis van der Geest, a great admirer of Rubens, must have been in close relationship with the Brotherhood.[17] This does not necessarily mean that he paid for the work, but it makes it likely that he exerted some influence on the choice of the painter.

In this altarpiece, too, the links with Italy are clearly discernible. The slightly elongated figures in the foreground, the brownish tinge of their complexions, the Venetian blue-green in the background, the powerful architectural features which give the composition a stable

Figure 38
PROMETHEUS BOUND
Canvas, 7'11½" × 6'10½"
The Philadelphia Museum of Art (W.P. Wilstach Collection)

*In this mythological canvas, painted in 1611–12, the impetuosity of Rubens' art during the first year after his return from Italy is also evident. The writhing posture of the powerful foreshortened body accentuates the dynamic expressiveness of the scene. Rubens was inspired both by antique motifs and by Titian's* Tityus *in the Prado Museum, and Michelangelo's drawing of the same subject, now in Windsor. The eagle of Jupiter, piercing the breast with its beak to draw out the liver of this hero, who is being punished, is by the hand of the animal painter Frans Snyders.*

74

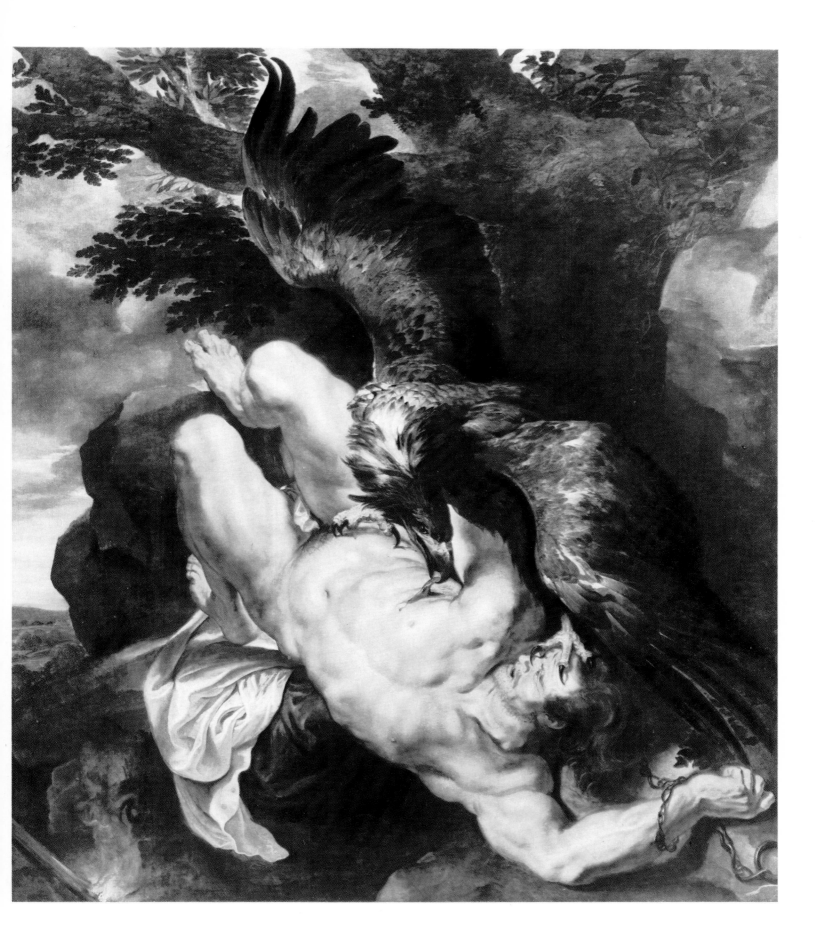

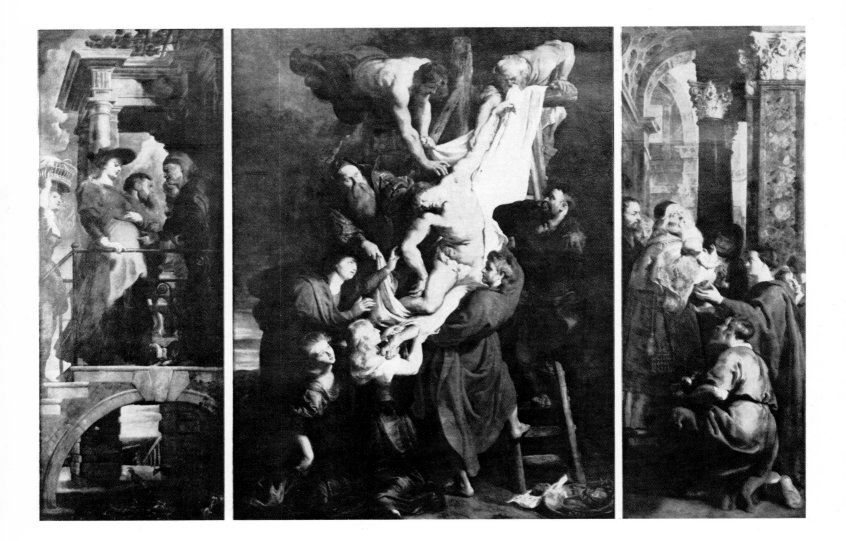

Figure 39
THE DESCENT FROM THE CROSS
Triptych; central panel, 13′9″ × 10′2″,
wings each 13′9″ × 4′11″
Antwerp, Cathedral of Our Lady

*This work was commissioned by the Guild
of the Arquebusiers of Antwerp for its
altar in the cathedral. The central panel
was completed in September, 1612, the side
panels in the spring of 1614. The three
panels each treat a different subject; they have,
however, a certain iconographic unity, since
all three represent "bearers of Christ."*

Plate 16
THE DESCENT FROM THE CROSS
Central panel, 13′9 × 10′2″
Antwerp, Cathedral of Our Lady

*The "classical" style which follows Rubens'
youthful and impetuous period is characterized by greater order and balance in composition as well as by a consummate mastery in
the poses and gestures of the characters.*

structure—all these are traits in common with the pictures Rubens had painted toward the end of his stay in Rome from 1606 to 1608. The putti swinging in the clouds above the groups of Fathers of the Church and theologians are the twins of those who fly about in the paintings at Grenoble and in the choir of Santa Maria in Vallicella in Rome.

The name of Cornelis van der Geest figures also in a record pertaining to another of Rubens' works, the famous *Raising of the Cross* (Fig. 37) painted for the church of the Castle or St. Walburga.[18] It was seen there above the high altar until the time of the French Revolution. Before the church was demolished at the beginning of the nineteenth century, the picture had been transferred to the cathedral, where it now forms a sort of pendant to the *Descent from the Cross*. Thanks to a copy, unfortunately incomplete, of the original church accounts which have disappeared, we know that on May 17, 1610, the vicar and the churchwardens took up a collection of donations "towards the decorating and painting of the High Altar." In June 1610, during a banquet at the "Klein Zeeland" inn, "an agreement was reached

76

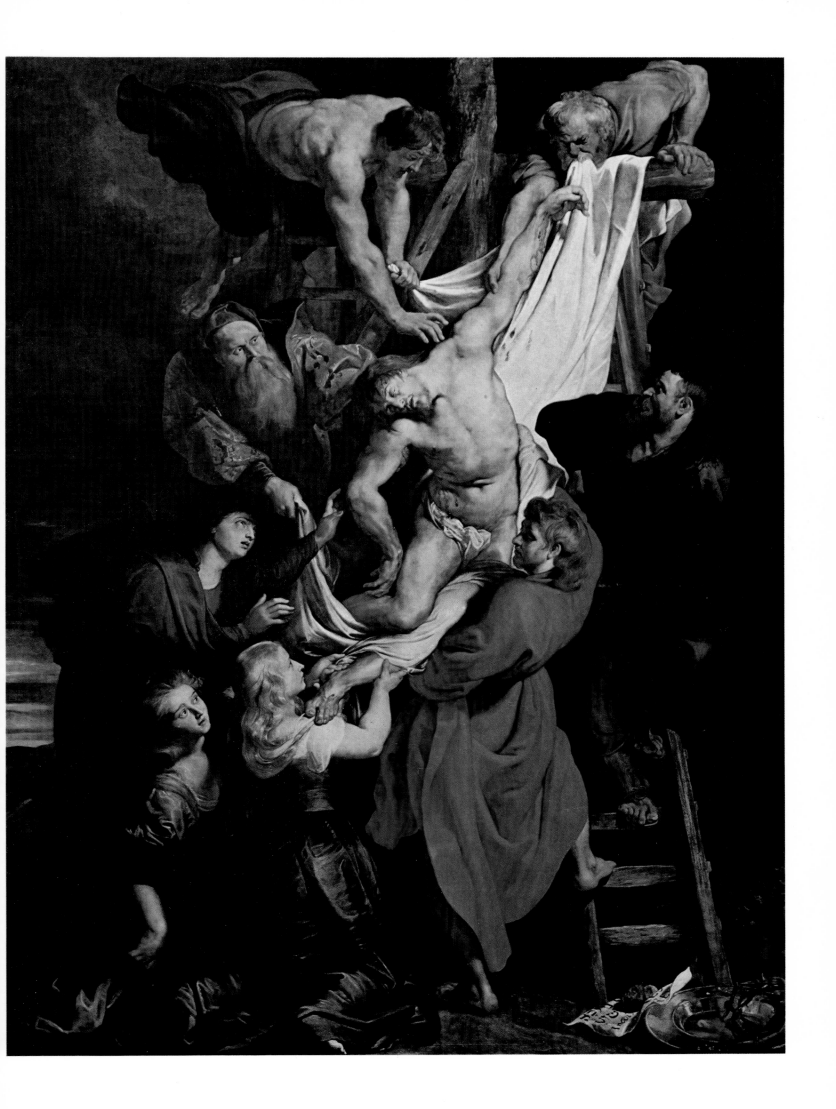

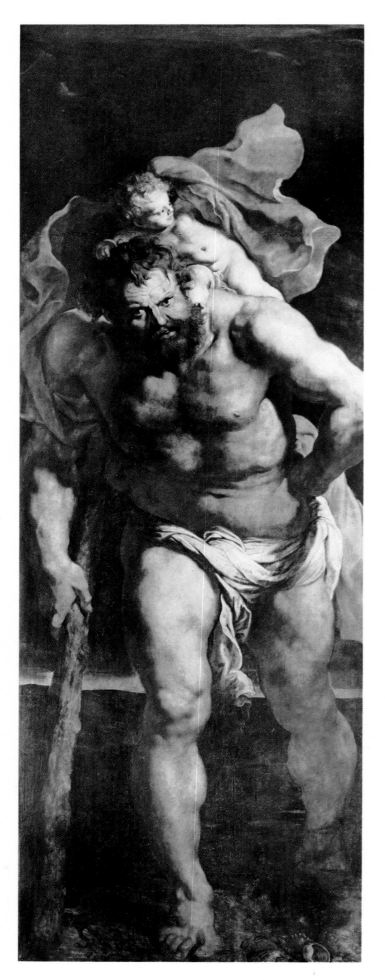

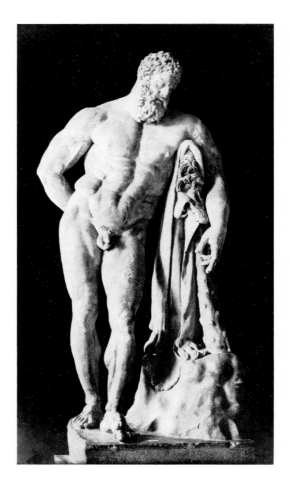

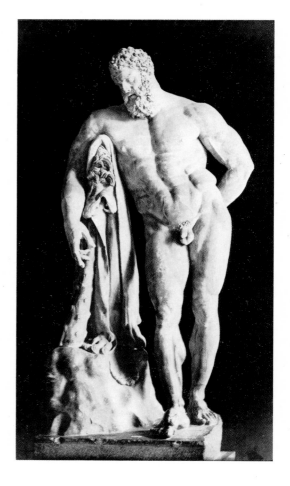

78

with Peeter Rubbens, painter, concerning the painting of the High Altar, in the presence of the vicar, Cornelis van der Geest, and the churchwardens."[19] It is certainly not a coincidence that a parishioner, outside the church administration, should be mentioned in this settlement. Clarification on this point is furnished in the legend beneath the large engraving made by Hans Witdoeck after the *Raising of the Cross*, published by Rubens in 1638 (Fig. 146), shortly after Cornelis van der Geest's death. The dedication, signed by Rubens, mentions Cornelis van der Geest as "the first to conceive" the painting in the church of St. Walburga, which he so zealously supported.[20] This testimony shows that the initiative to commission the painting came from Van der Geest; it also seems to indicate that the great patron must have disbursed a large sum for its execution.

On the other hand Jan Le Grand, in his letter dated March 12, 1611, mentions the triptych in the church of the Castle among Rubens' works "which are held in high esteem," so that we can assume it could already be seen in the church and was largely, if not completely, finished.

*The Raising of the Cross* (Plate 15; Fig. 37) united all the traits characteristic of Rubens' art in the first years after his homecoming and may be considered to synthesize them most perfectly. When the artist worked out the subject in a single composition divided across three panels, he quite probably had in mind Tintoretto's powerful paintings of the Passion (especially the three-panel *Crucifixion*) that he had seen in Venice. In Rubens' triptych one can identify a number of reminiscences of works of art that he had zealously studied in Italy. We find traces of Michelangelo in the muscular vigor of the executioner's servants, powerfully tensed in their combined efforts to set up the cross to which is nailed the noble body of Christ. Their glistening, bronzed bodies stand out in relief against the dark wall of rock in the background. Although it cannot be claimed that Rubens imitated Caravaggio directly, the common women in the foreground of the left wing and the strong lighting on them recall the style of that great realistic innovator whom Rubens might have met in Rome. And in the right wing, the clear daylight which gives a vibrant transparency to the bodies of the two thieves, as well as the greenish blue of the sky, recalls the color of certain Venetian masters. But it is not color that dominates this picture, it is the linearity of the style emphasized by the shadowed areas.

Yet the essentially plastic expression and the reminiscences of Italian art are not all that is to be seen here. Rubens' impetuous style in the first years after his return from Italy, what Oldenbourg called his youthful *Sturm und Drang* period,[21] is characterized by the pliant, fluid body forms, the twisting attitudes of the figures bending forward and back, the passionate gestures, the powerful chiaroscuro, the shimmering touches of light on rather dark garments, the luxuriant waves of the women's hair. It appears indeed that the young master, having now conquered all the lessons of his long years of apprenticeship, now gives full rein to his bravado, as if to demonstrate his facility.

Figure 40
ST. CHRISTOPHER
Exterior of left wing
(panel, 13′9″ × 4′11″),
THE DESCENT FROM THE CROSS
Antwerp, Cathedral of Our Lady

*St. Christopher is carrying the infant Jesus toward the opposite bank of the river. This figure recalls the classical statue of the Far-nese Hercules. The torso is reminiscent of one of Michelangelo's "ignudi" on the Sistine Ceiling. Rubens has interpreted the classi-cal motif in a totally personal way.*

Figures 41a, b
THE FARNESE HERCULES
Naples, Museo Nazionale

*Rubens made many drawings of this classical statue, which was then in the Farnese Palace in Rome, copying it from different angles. The statue is reproduced here also in reverse, to facilitate comparison.*

79

Looking at this work, its dynamic composition accentuated by the strong diagonal of the slanting, half-raised cross, the spectator is confronted with an action as yet unfinished, a movement which seems compelled to continue in crescendo. On the other hand, the *Descent from the Cross* (Plate 54; Fig. 39) in the cathedral in Antwerp strikes us with its controlled balance in sharp contrast with the "momentary situation," the dynamic suspense rendered in the earlier triptych. J.R. Martin writes: "It is not merely that the agony of the Crucified is over and that horror has been supplanted by grief: in addition, the suppression of receding diagonals and the consolidation of the figures into a composition lying essentially on one plane give to this work a quality of discipline and restraint that may properly be called 'classical.'"[22] This triptych heralds the beginning of a new evolution in Rubens' art, of what is called his "classical" period: discipline takes the place of youthful exuberance.

In *The Raising of the Cross* one subject is spread over three panels; *The Descent from the Cross* represents, by contrast, three subjects, according to the usual manner of triptychs in the Netherlands. But the three are connected: St. Christopher was the patron saint of the Guild of Arquebusiers which commissioned this masterpiece, and Rubens represented *St. Christopher and the Hermit* on the front of the closed panels (Fig. 40), the vigorous saint's figure inspired by the classical statue of the *Farnese Hercules* in Naples (Figs. 41a, b). On the central panel and on the opened side panels the artist, drawing his idea from the etymology of the name "Christophorus," has painted the "Bearers of Christ": in the center, the holy women and the disciples support the body of Christ as He is taken down from the cross; on the left, Mary bears the child in her womb when she visits St. Elizabeth; on the right the high priest holds the Child in his arms during the Presentation in the Temple.

Much has been written about *The Descent from the Cross*, and the accounts pertaining to it have repeatedly been published.[23] Further research in the archives, however, now makes it possible to add some significant data to our store of knowledge. The first hitherto-unpublished document to be mentioned is a request from the Guild of Arquebusiers to the magistrates of Antwerp:[24] the guild alleges that the Chapter of the Cathedral had repeatedly encouraged them to commission a new altar which would bear comparison with the altars recently erected in the cathedral by other guilds. As they were not in a position to afford such an altar, which was to cost an estimated 8,000 florins, they invoked a precedent that permitted other guilds to enroll a number of "wepelaers," persons exempted from certain public duties; these "wepelaers," in return for payment of a very large sum, would be granted "perpetual exemption from watch duty, as also from all duties within the same Guild, and also from the duties of churchwarden, borough-warden and dean of their craft, and further from all service under the Banners of the city militia." With a view toward covering the cost of the altar the Arquebusiers requested

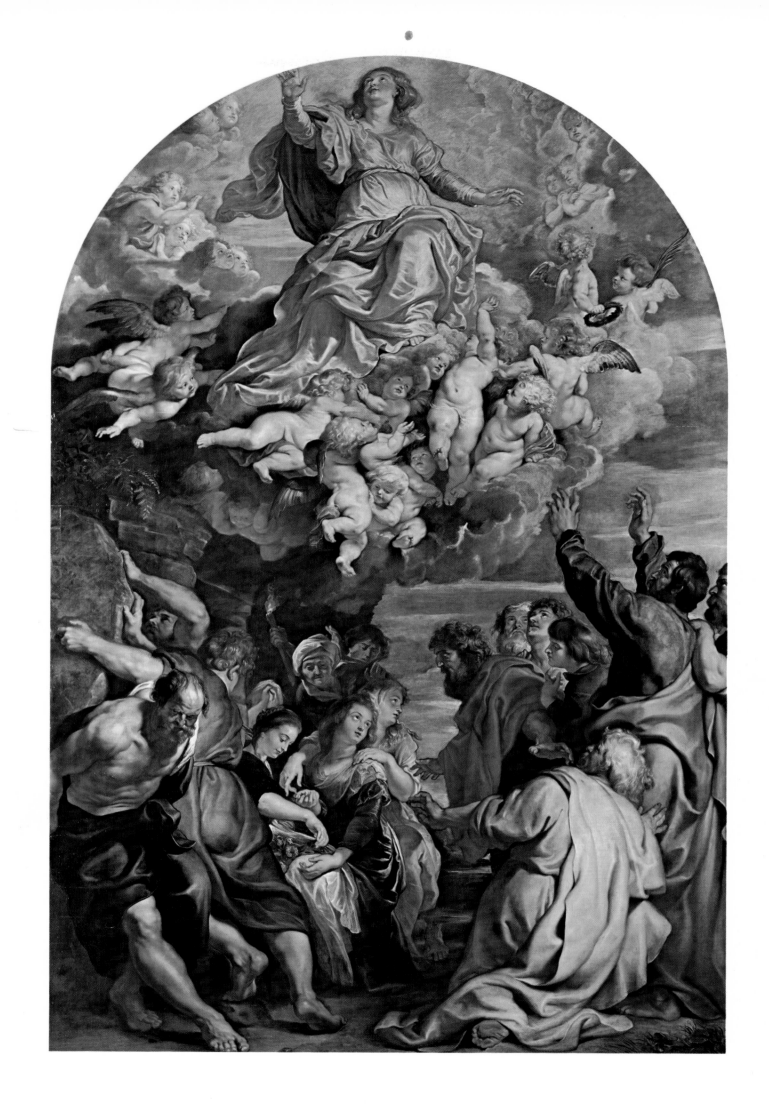

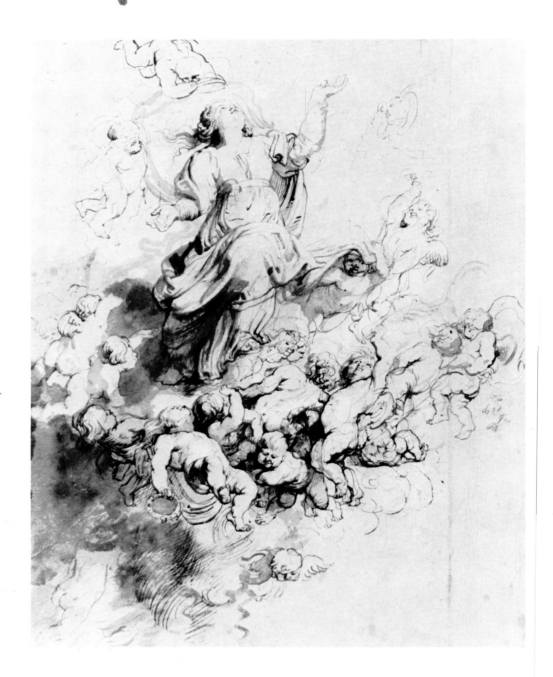

Figure 42
THE ASSUMPTION OF THE VIRGIN
Drawing, $11^3/_8'' \times 9''$
Vienna, Graphische Sammlung Albertina

*This drawing is perhaps a preparatory study for the second oil sketch—unknown today—which Rubens presented to the cathedral chapter in 1611 as an alternative for the one now preserved in Leningrad.*

permission to enroll twelve such "wepelaers," but on April 22, 1611, the Board of Mayor and Aldermen granted them only nine: four who did not yet belong to the guards, and five who were already enrolled but could now buy full exemption from all services. The Guild's accounts tell us that each such "ransomer" paid a lump sum of 400 florins on entering the guild and an annual payment of 3 or 4 florins.[25] Additional financial means came from the members' yearly subscriptions, annual subsidies from the city as compensation for service "under the Banners," occasional gifts, and the like.

Having received favorable promises of money, which would allow

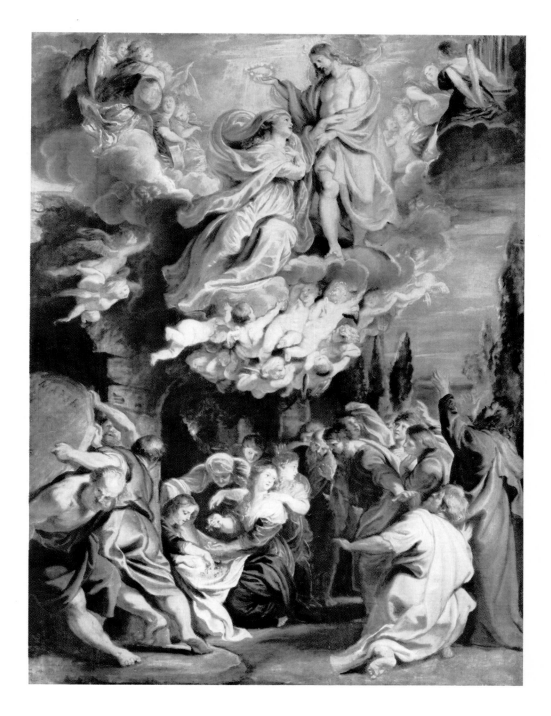

them to assume the risk of the undertaking, the deans of the guild arranged a meeting on September 7, 1611, "with the painter P. Rubbens, to whom, in the presence of the Chairman ["Hooftman"], the commission of the painting was offered."[26]   This head of the guild was none other than Nicolaas Rockox, a friend and great patron of Rubens whom he later entrusted with personal commissions.

It is known that a year after this agreement the central panel of the triptych was finished, because it was transferred to the cathedral no later than September 17, 1612, from Rubens' atelier, then still in the house of his father-in-law Jan Brant in the Kloosterstraat.[27]   The

83

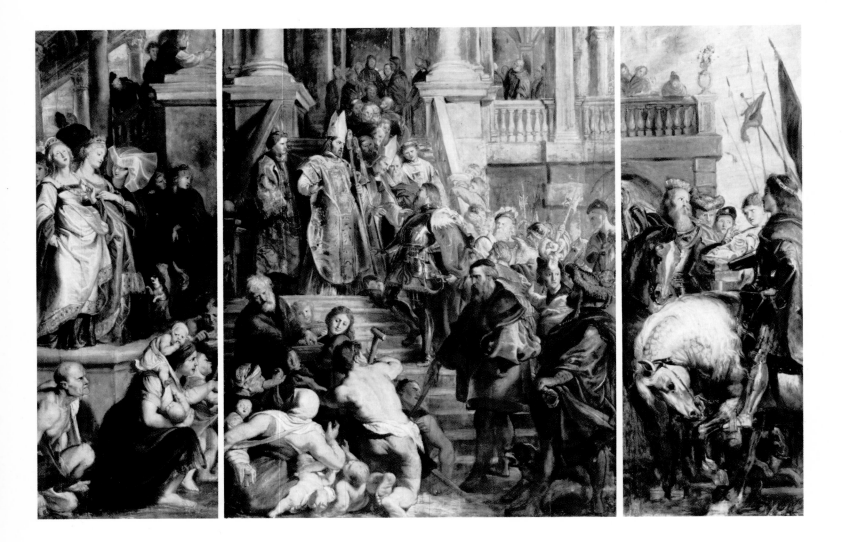

side panels did not leave the atelier until some eighteen months later, on February 8 and March 6, 1614, respectively.[28] Unless this delay came from difficulties in procuring suitable wood for making the panels,[29] it may have been caused by other commissions that Rubens had meanwhile received.

The literature concerning *The Descent from the Cross* mentions that Rubens first received 1,000 florins for his work, and four years later another 400 Flemish pounds. But attentive scrutiny of the relevant archives shows that he must have received a larger sum! Soon after the delivery of the central panel (certainly before December 25, 1612), a first installment was paid to him, the amount of which, however, cannot be determined; it was included under a hitherto unknown heading that comprised within one total the sums paid out not only to the painter, but also to the "image-carvers" (sculptors) and the "panel-maker."[30] In the course of 1615, that is, some time after the side panels were delivered, Rubens received the next 1,000 florins and his wife Isabella Brant was given a pair of gloves, the Arquebusiers wishing to show their satisfaction by this token present.[31] Rubens, however,

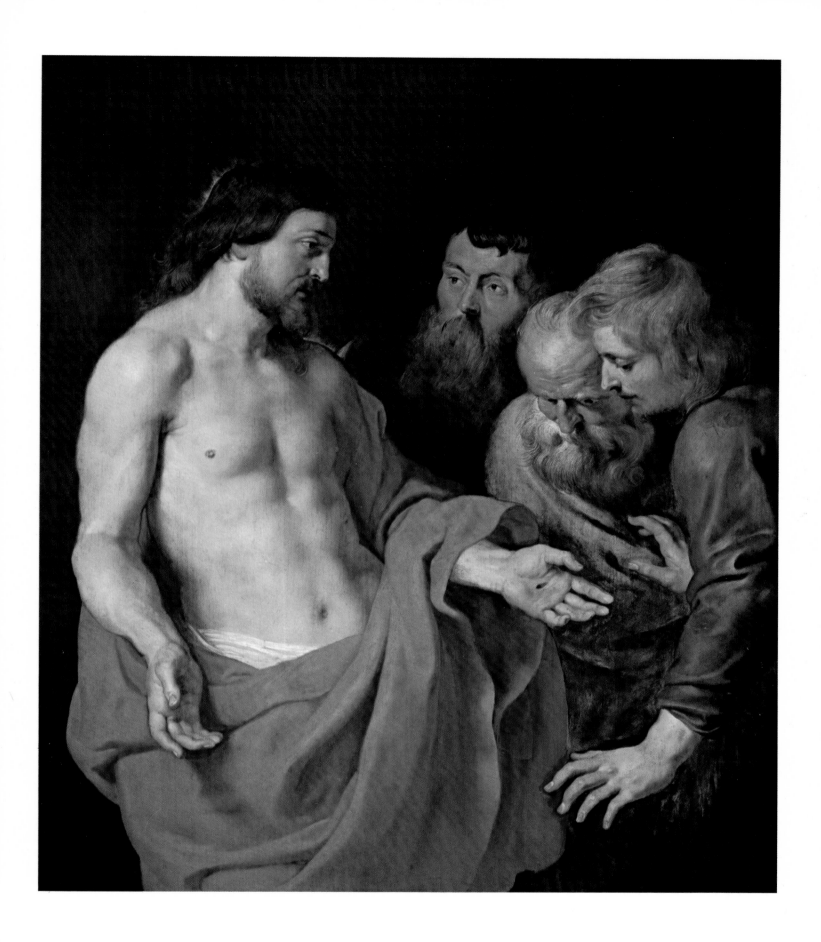

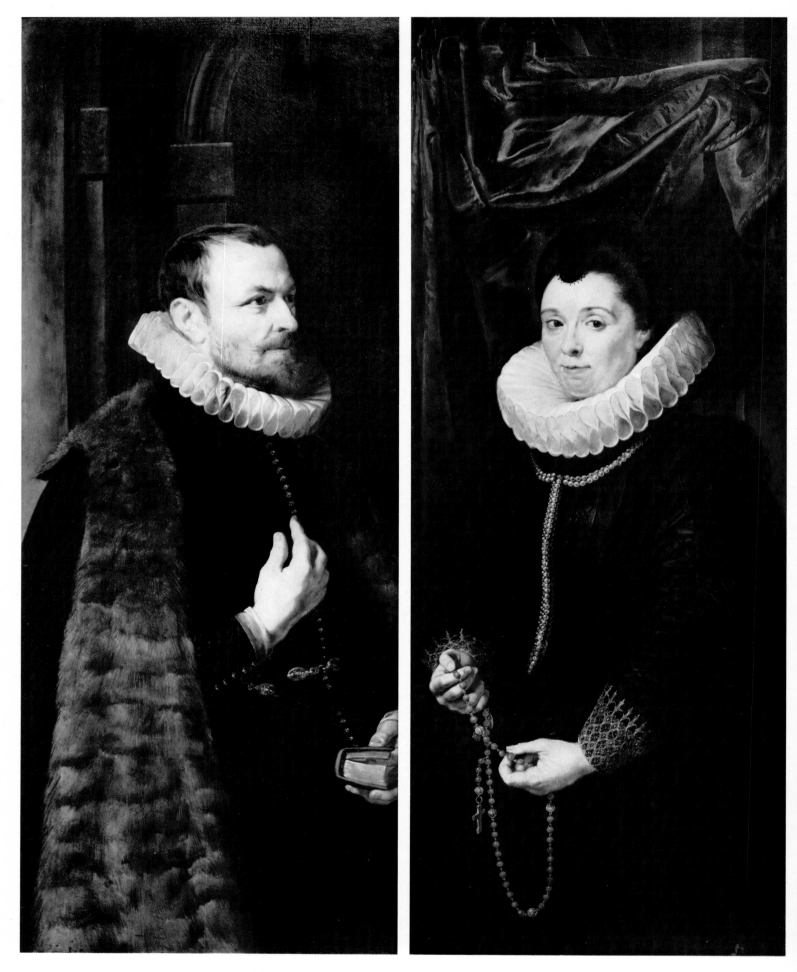

had to wait until February 13, 1621, another six years, before full payment was completed.[32]

The reference to the "panelmaker" in the account book of 1612 enables us to solve an important problem in dating the central panel. To grasp its full significance, one must realize that it was customary that the commissioner of a painting himself ordered the panels direct from the panelmaker, and thus had to pay the latter himself. In the accounts hitherto published about *The Descent from the Cross*, the only payments to be traced concerned the making and delivery of the two side panels, and from this fact some authors have somewhat rashly concluded that the central panel already existed as a separate painting, or that it had at least been already commenced when the Arquebusiers approached Rubens. Their commission would then have consisted merely of ordering two side panels to be affixed to an existing centerpiece, to make up a triptych. Some have even claimed to find a great difference in conception and execution between the central panel and the wings; it has also been asserted that Rubens was quite reluctant to enlarge his initial composition into a triptych.[33] But the recently discovered entry, dating from the end of 1612, shows that the panelmaker, as well as Rubens, was paid for making and delivering the central panel, proving that all these assumptions were unnecessary: indeed the *entire* triptych was well and truly painted on commission from the Guild of Arquebusiers.

We have followed the general practice in mentioning *The Descent from the Cross* in chronological order, immediately after *The Raising of the Cross*. It is indeed quite true that Rubens received the commission for the former shortly after completing the triptych for the church of St. Walburga. But it should be mentioned that between these two works he received another commission, though it was delivered only much later; this one for a painting for the high altar in the Church of Our Lady, or Antwerp Cathedral. Data concerning this altarpiece are to be found in certain documents which, although published some time ago, have thus far escaped the notice of Rubens scholars. The reports of the meetings of the Chapter of Notre-Dame state that on March 24, 1611, the canons received a painter named Octavio, who was none other than Octavio, or Otto, van Veen. He showed them a sketch for a painting of *Christ Inviting Mary to Her Coronation*, intended for the high altar. Although his way of representing the subject won the support of the Chapter, he did not receive the commission. It was decided to entrust the treasurer and the dean, Canon Joannes Del Rio, to reach agreement with the churchwardens on the choice of a painter for the high altar.[34] We may wonder whether, even at that early date, one of the Chapter members—possibly the dean himself—did not suggest that a better painter than Master Octavio could be found in Antwerp?

In any case, some four weeks later, on April 22, 1611, churchwarden Vriendt put before the Chapter on behalf of Rubens—who was later present at the meeting—two sketches of *The Assumption of the Virgin*

Figures 45, 46
PORTRAIT OF NICOLAAS ROCKOX
Left wing (panel, 57$^1$/$_2$″ × 21$^3$/$_4$″) of
*The Rockox Altarpiece*
Antwerp, Koninklijk Museum voor Schone Kunsten

*Nicolaas Rockox was repeatedly burgomaster and an alderman of Antwerp. Rubens called him his "friend and patron." The panel was first dated 1613, but the last figure has been painted over into a 5. The triptych seems to have been completed in 1615.*

PORTRAIT OF ADRIANA PEREZ
Right wing (panel, 57$^1$/$_2$″ × 21$^3$/$_4$″) of
*The Rockox Altarpiece*
Antwerp, Koninklijk Museum voor Schone Kunsten

*Adriana Perez was the wife of Nicolaas Rockox, and died in 1619. The triptych was later placed above the tomb of her and her husband in a chapel in the church of the Minorites (or Recollects) of Antwerp.*

in two different compositions. As the sketches "gave no offense to the faithful and were not opposed to the traditions of the Church," the canons liked them, but they did not make a choice between the two "excellent paintings."[35] We know nothing of what ensued, but there is no doubt that Otto van Veen's sketch was shelved: Rubens would be given the commission. Barely eighteen months after his return from Italy the brilliant former apprentice was being preferred to his master, now aging.

It seems that at least one of the two *modelli* that Rubens showed to the Chapter in April 1611 has survived: the *Assumption and Coronation of the Virgin* now in Leningrad (Fig. 43)[36] can safely be thus identified. This sketch has so far received only scant attention, but some twenty years ago Dobroklonsky showed by stylistic analysis that it was painted in the first years after Rubens' return from Italy.[37] Until now, however, the commission to which it was related could not be determined. That it was a preparatory design for a great altarpiece was never in doubt: its monumental character, the movement of the composition, and the large number of figures show that it was to cover a large area. Such a sketch would not have been painted without some hope of its serving as a model for a large altarpiece. Moreover, the subject corresponds with the theme set for the altarpiece in the cathedral of Notre-Dame: "Christ meeting his Mother in order to crown her." Such at least was the subject of the *modello* shown by Otto van Veen: "Sponsam de Libano provocantem ad coronam."[38]

From the Chapter's report of April 22, 1611, we know that Rubens showed a second sketch depicting the same subject in another man-

Figure 47
JUPITER AND CALLISTO
Panel, 49$\frac{1}{2}$" × 72$\frac{1}{2}$"
Kassel, Staatliche Gemäldegalerie

*The characteristics of the so-called classical period can be found in both religious and mythological works, as illustrated by this one, signed and dated 1613.*

Plate 19
VENUS BEFORE THE MIRROR (detail)
Panel, over-all dimensions
48$\frac{3}{4}$" × 38$\frac{1}{2}$"
Vaduz, Collection Prince of Liechtenstein

*This work dates from about the same time as the* Venus Shivering *(Pl. 20), that is to say, about 1614; its style is very similar to that Antwerp work.*

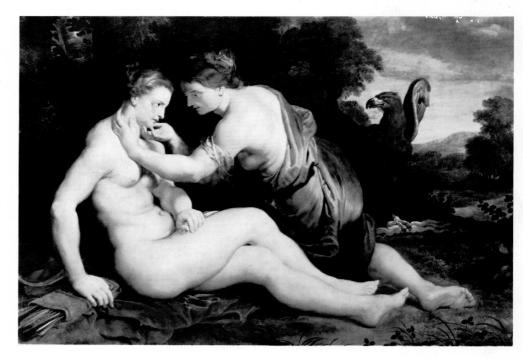

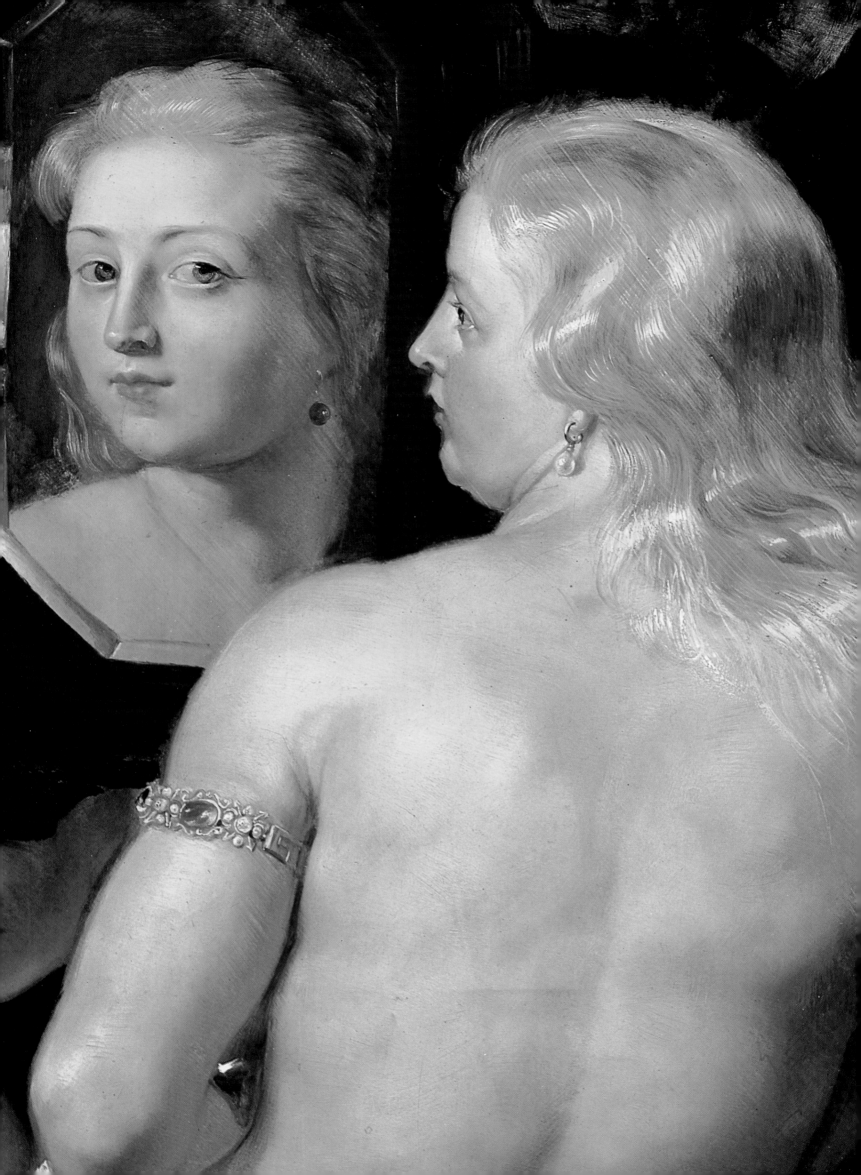

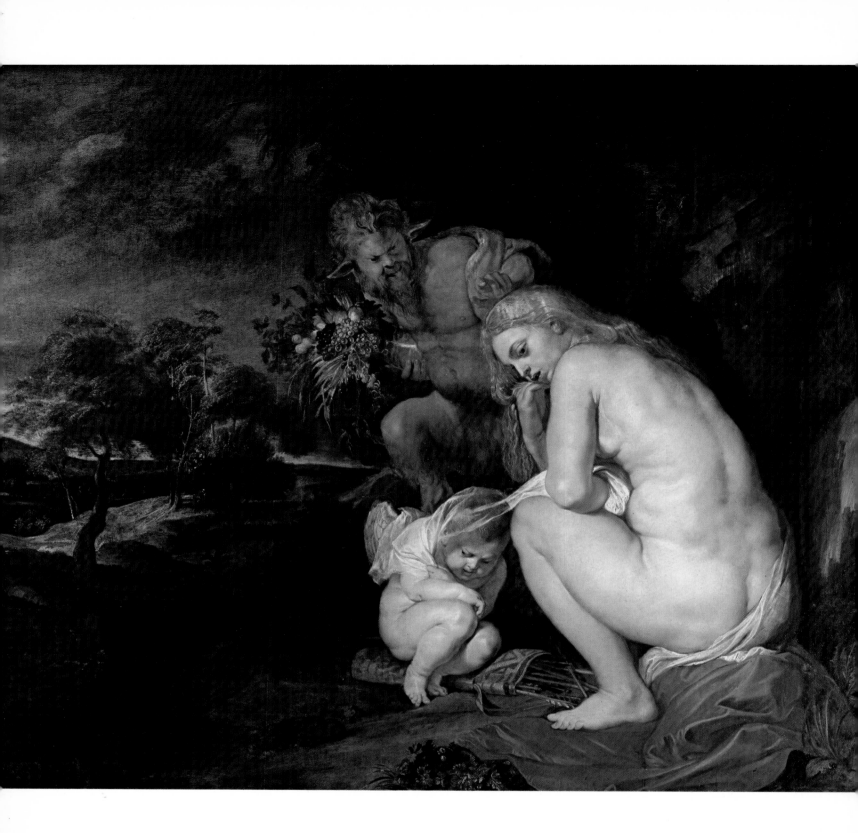

Plate 20
VENUS SHIVERING
Panel, 56″ × 72½″
Antwerp, Koninklijk Museum voor
Schone Kunsten

*This panel is signed and dated 1614. The
figure of Venus is drawn from a classical
statue, namely the* Crouching Venus *by
Doidalsas, a Greek sculptor of the mid-
third century B.C.*

ner.  It is not impossible that in this case he painted the Assumption of the Virgin as he later always represented this scene: the Virgin seated on a cloud surrounded by playful putti, her glance directed toward Heaven.

Vain attempts to find among Rubens' many sketches of the Assumption and Coronation of the Virgin a *modello* with the same stylistic traits as the Leningrad sketch have been made.  Was it lost during the centuries? or did Rubens only make a variant on the upper part of the Leningrad sketch?  The second hypothesis finds some support in a drawing in the Albertina, representing the ascending Virgin (Fig. 42).  The nervous touch, the chiaroscuro, and the rendering of the folds would justify dating it about the same time as the Leningrad sketch, that is, the spring of 1611.[39]  It is therefore not unlikely that this drawing may have been a preliminary study for an oil sketch of the upper half of the *Assumption of the Virgin*, the painting destined for the high altar of Notre-Dame Cathedral.  Further support is afforded by the existence of another *Assumption of the Virgin* by Rubens, also in Vienna (Plate 17),[40] the lower half of which is based on the composition of the Leningrad sketch while the soaring Virgin is represented in a way strongly reminiscent of the Albertina drawing.[41]  In the painting, however, the Virgin is admittedly shown reversed and slightly altered, whereas the group of angels supporting her in the clouds largely corresponds to that of the Albertina drawing.

Before the *Assumption* was taken to Vienna in 1776, it adorned the chapel of the Virgin (the so-called Houtappel chapel) in the church of the Jesuits in Antwerp.  Since this chapel was not built until after 1620,[42] most authors have given approximately that date to the altarpiece.[43]  Burchard's sharp eye discovered, however, that the style of the painting made this dating untenable.  He suggested a date of about 1614–15,[44] but it seems not impossible that the picture was painted even a few years earlier.  In any case, it must have been in existence long before the chapel was built, just as it may have been in Rubens' workshop for some time before it found a permanent home.  This hypothesis gives rise to a number of other suppositions.  Did Rubens settle down to the task of carrying out the full-scale altarpiece soon after showing his two oil sketches on April 22, 1611, convinced that a firm commission would soon follow?  Did he trust too much in the promised support of some of the canons or church-wardens?  There is no precise information on these points, but one fact may plead for our hypothesis: at the time when Van Veen and Rubens were offering their *modelli*, a painting by Frans Floris, the *Adoration of the Shepherds* now in the Museum voor Schone Kunsten in Antwerp, was above the high altar of the church.[45]  This work had originally adorned the altar in the chapel of the Guild of Gardeners; when the Antwerp Church of Our Lady was rearranged in 1585, after the capture of Antwerp by Duke Alessandro Farnese, it was transferred to the high altar, to replace an *Assumption of the Virgin* by Floris that had been lost in the troubled period.  The reports of the Chapter meetings show that on April 26, 1613, the leaders of the Guild of Gardeners had recently sent a request to the chapter to regain possession of their painting.[46]  From this we can conclude that it was anticipated that their painting would be replaced by a new altarpiece above the high altar.  This replacement was not then effected, probably owing to financial difficulties; indeed the altarpiece later delivered by Rubens was paid for neither by the Chapter nor the governors of the church as such, but out of the private purse of the dean, Canon Joannes Del Rio.

Rubens' contract, however, signed by the dean and the artist in person, is dated November 12, 1619,[47] over eight years after the painter had submitted his first *modelli*.  The previous year, on February 16, 1618, he had shown the churchwardens two sketches of the proposed altar on which his painting would be placed.[48]  Once again, the Guild of Gardeners followed the matter very attentively; probably as early as the end of 1617 or the beginning of 1618, they renewed their request for the return of their altarpiece.  On January 12, 1618, the Chapter, while not acknowledging in so many words that the painting belonged to the Guild of Gardeners, replied that a new high altar was going to be built and that Floris' painting would then be restored to its rightful owners.[49]

All of these facts prove that the intention to commission an altarpiece by Rubens had not been abandoned, but that certain difficulties had delayed its realization.  The later history of this commission is so well known[50] that it will suffice to mention that Rubens successfully completed the work only in 1626, fifteen years after first showing the *modelli*!  Rubens' art had meanwhile undergone a profound evolution, and the composition of the final altarpiece (Plate 49) no longer reflects that of the early Leningrad sketch.  Rubens made new sketches, more in keeping with his new vision and style.[51]  As mentioned above, he had in the interval given his first picture, now in Vienna, another destination.  He no doubt thought that this "old work" was only worthy of a side chapel in a church where several of his more recent paintings could now be admired.  But for the high altar of Antwerp Cathedral he would have made it a point of honor to paint an altarpiece—incidentally, of still larger size—in which he could show the full measure of his talents, matured and developed over the years.[52]

Until now we have limited our discussion to a few altarpieces painted by Rubens for Antwerp churches during the first years after his return.  But in 1611–12, while he was painting the central panel of *The Descent from the Cross*, commissions reached him from other towns in the Southern Netherlands.  *The Last Supper* for the abbey church of Bergues-St-Winoc, mentioned in Jan Le Grand's correspondence, was not followed by a definite order.  Rubens must surely have made a design—since lost—shortly before July 30, 1611, but the very high sum which the execution would have cost probably ended the matter.[53]  There were other disappointments.  At the request of Bishop Charles Maes of Ghent, probably in 1611 or, at the latest, early in 1612, Rubens painted a *modello* (Fig. 61) for a triptych representing

Plate 21
THE ASSUMPTION OF THE VIRGIN
Canvas, 16'4" × 11'2"
Brussels, Musées Royaux des Beaux-Arts de Belgique

*Rubens illustrated this subject several times.  Compared with his earlier versions, this canvas, executed around 1614 for the church of the Barefoot Carmelites of Brussels, is more balanced in composition, as indeed are the majority of his works painted between 1612 and 1615.*

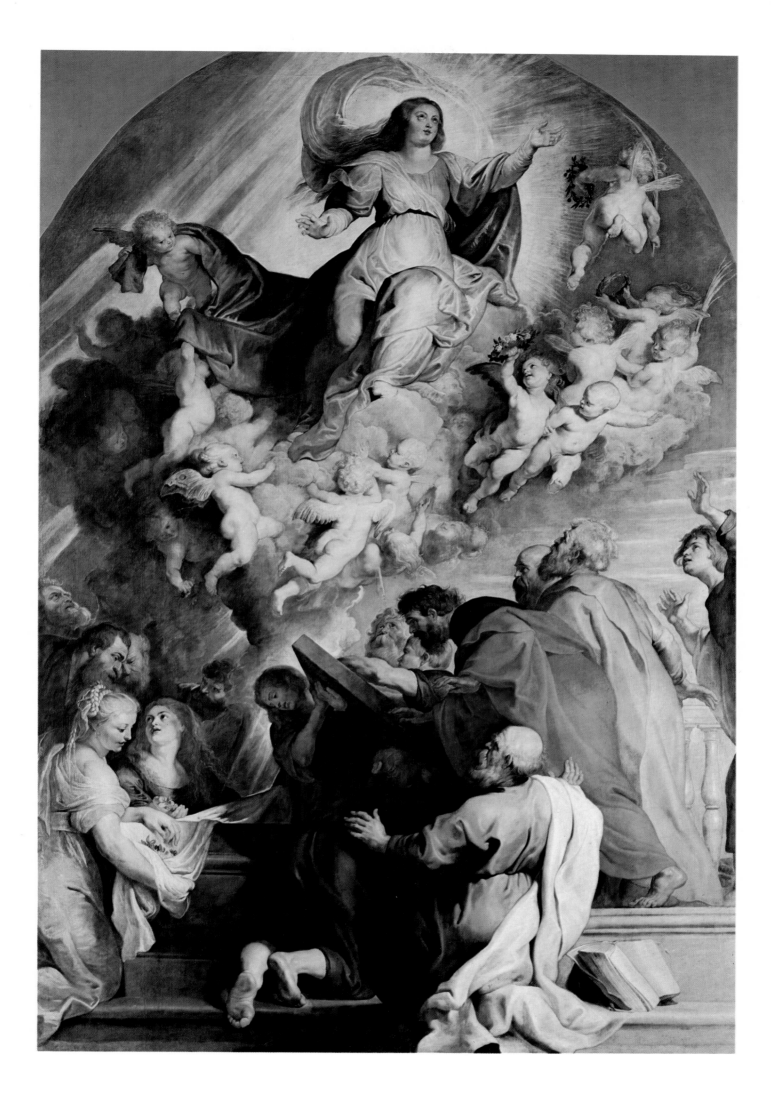

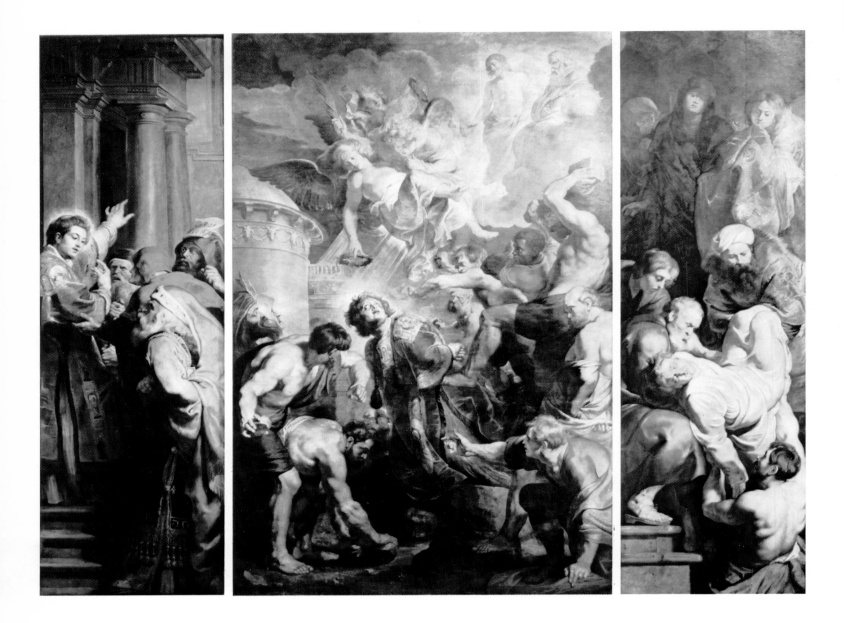

Figure 48

THE MARTYRDOM OF ST. STEPHEN
Triptych; central panel, 14'4" × 9'2",
wings each 13'1½" × 4'1½"
Valenciennes, Musée des Beaux-Arts

*Originally painted for the abbey church of
St-Amand, this important triptych is characteristic of the period 1612-15 in the plasticity of the figures and the balanced composition.*

Figure 49

ST. FRANCIS OF ASSISI RECEIVING
THE STIGMATA
Canvas, 12'4" × 7'10"
Cologne, Wallraf-Richartz-Museum

*This painting was executed in the years
1615-16 for the church of the Capuchin
Friars of Cologne. The landscape might
be by the hand of Jan Wildens.*

the history of St. Bavo;[54] the plans were modified by the bishop's
successors after he died in 1612, and Rubens had to wait to carry out
the order until 1622–24. As in the case of the *Assumption* for Antwerp
Cathedral, the composition had once again to yield to the evolution
of his art. In 1612, at the request of the Guild of Musicians in Brussels,
he painted a triptych of the biblical story of St. Job for their altar
in the church of St. Nicholas. This work, placed in position in 1613,[55]
was destroyed during the bombardment of Brussels in 1695, but some
preliminary drawings and prints give us an approximate idea of
it. Finally, it is not impossible that in 1612, the year he finished the
central panel of the *Descent from the Cross*, Rubens was also commissioned to paint a new version of the same subject for the church at
St.-Omer.[56] His fame had thus already reached other regions of the
Southern Netherlands.

94

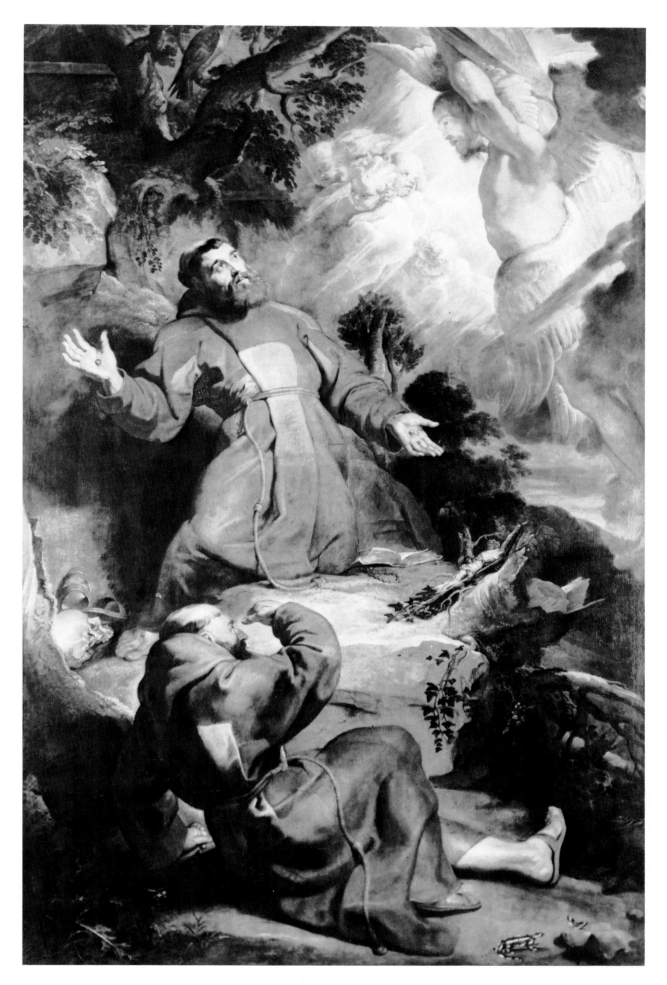

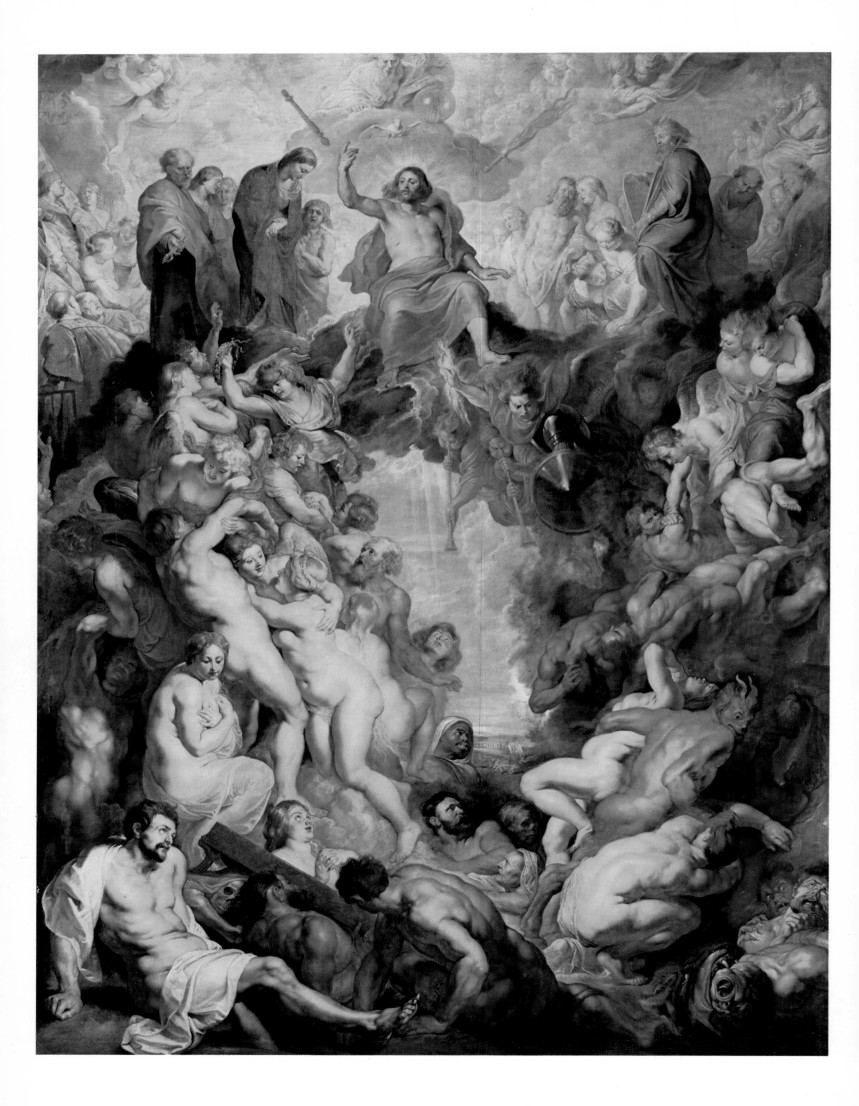

We noted above that *The Descent from the Cross* marks a turning point in Rubens' art, one that is already clear in the central panel, painted first. Apart from elements still linking this work in some ways to the previous period, there are a fair number of new features: the well-ordered and peaceful composition, which the eye takes in at a glance; the softer, more generous light shining on the figures; the partial revision of the palette: the light, vivid red of St. John's robe, replacing the red, sometimes a little grayish and soft, verging on purple, which the artist had used until now. But in other respects the coloring and certain chiaroscuros still recall the preceding period. The evolution is taking place gradually. It reaches its height in the side panels, which, as we stated above, were transferred to the cathedral a year and a half later. Although the compositions of these panels were based on oil sketches painted in 1611, with all the characteristic brushwork of that time,[57] the final execution marks a complete break with the first post-Italian years. Since the central panel was finished about September 1612, and the wings were transferred to the cathedral on February 8 and March 6, 1614, we can mark very clearly the extent of the development that they reveal.

The "classical" style which is now evident is characterized primarily by a more ordered and balanced composition, and a greater restraint in pose and gesture. The three-dimensional aspect of the figures is no longer marked by thick shading and violent chiaroscuro but rather by clear-cut contours. The nude figures are usually lit by a silvery or golden light, more evenly spread, in which there sometimes shines a glint of enamel. The particular local colors, now dominant and kept strictly within the well-defined contours of the garments, contribute to the clear, simple arrangement of the composition. These characteristics are best seen in some religious works of smaller format, made either for side altars or epitaphs or to be displayed in the houses of well-to-do citizens. Generally the figures in these compositions are half-length. As a typical example one might cite the small triptych with *The Doubting Thomas* in the central panel (Plate 18), and in the side panels the portraits of Nicolaas Rockox (Fig. 45) and his wife Adriana Perez (Fig. 46), who commissioned the work between 1613 and 1615.[58] These features are also found in certain smaller mythological pictures, such as *Jupiter and Callisto* (Fig. 47; signed and dated 1613),[59] and *Venus Shivering* (Plate 20; signed and dated 1614.)[60] But these same characteristics can be observed in some large altarpieces painted by Rubens about that time or a little later.

The work whose style is most akin to that of the wings of the Antwerp Cathedral *Descent from the Cross* and of the small-scale works of 1613 to 1614 seems to be the *Martyrdom of St. Stephen*, a triptych painted for the abbey church of St.-Amand-les-Eaux and now in the museum in Valenciennes (Fig. 48).[61] This work confirms the new direction of Rubens' art toward greater restraint and a more tangible plasticity of expression. Unfortunately we still do not have the documents enabling us to give a precise date to this work. The stylistic analogies mentioned above would suggest an approximate date of 1614.

Plate 22
THE LARGE LAST JUDGMENT
Canvas, 19'9³/₄" × 15'6¹/₄"
Munich, Alte Pinakothek

*This huge canvas, painted in 1615–16, had been commissioned by the Duke Wolfgang Wilhelm of Neuburg in January, 1615. It unites so to speak all the experience of the so-called classical period, and it brings together nearly all the figure types that Rubens had represented in his works up to this time. On the other hand it heralds a new phase in Rubens' stylistic development by its greater organization and more subtle nuances in the pictorial values.*

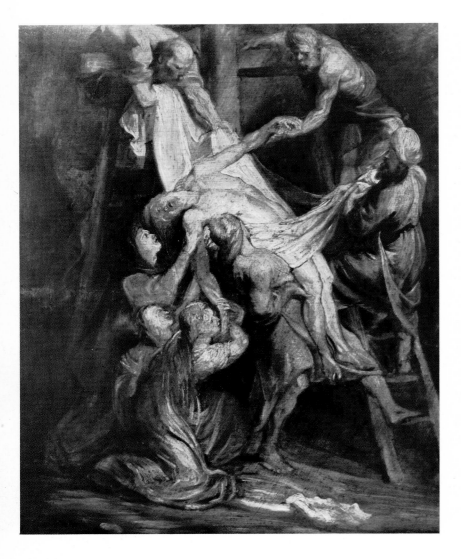

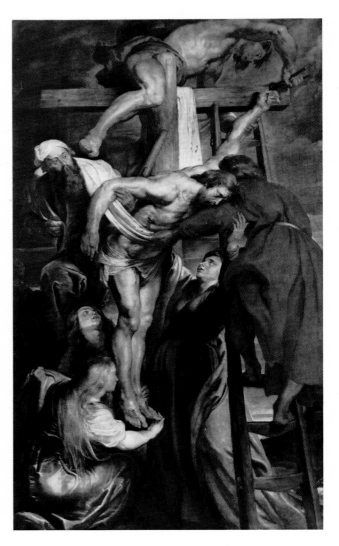

Figure 50

THE DESCENT FROM THE CROSS
Oil sketch on panel, $21\frac{1}{4}'' \times 16\frac{1}{8}''$
Lille, Musée des Beaux-Arts

*Sketch for the large canvas of that subject
preserved in the same museum. The altarpiece was commissioned for the church of
the Capuchin Friars in Lille.*

Figure 51

THE DESCENT FROM THE CROSS
Canvas, 10'6" × 6'5"
Valenciennes, Musée des Beaux-Arts

*Christ is represented with one hand still
nailed to the cross. The Virgin is raising
her arms as if to receive the body of her
Son.*

It is probable that about this time Rubens painted the *Assumption*
(Plate 21)[62] for the high altar of the church of the Barefoot Carmelites
in Brussels. The composition of this work seems to develop from
the Vienna *Assumption* (Plate 17), produced a few years earlier; the
Virgin's pose is a variant of that in the Vienna picture. In the Brussels
*Assumption* the flight of putti has taken on a triangular plan. The
artist has sought to give more balance to the arrangement, triangular
also, of the holy women on the left and the apostles on the right. The
poses and gestures are marked by great restraint. The earlier tomb
in a rock wall has been replaced by a sarcophagus, which Rubens will
use again in later representations of the subject.

Rooses' observation, that Rubens called on assistants for the execution
of this large canvas, seems to be true especially of the upper part. To
complete his numerous commissions the artist was obliged to make
use of assistants, in this respect imitating Tintoretto in Venice and
Frans Floris in Antwerp. On May 11, 1611, he wrote to the engraver

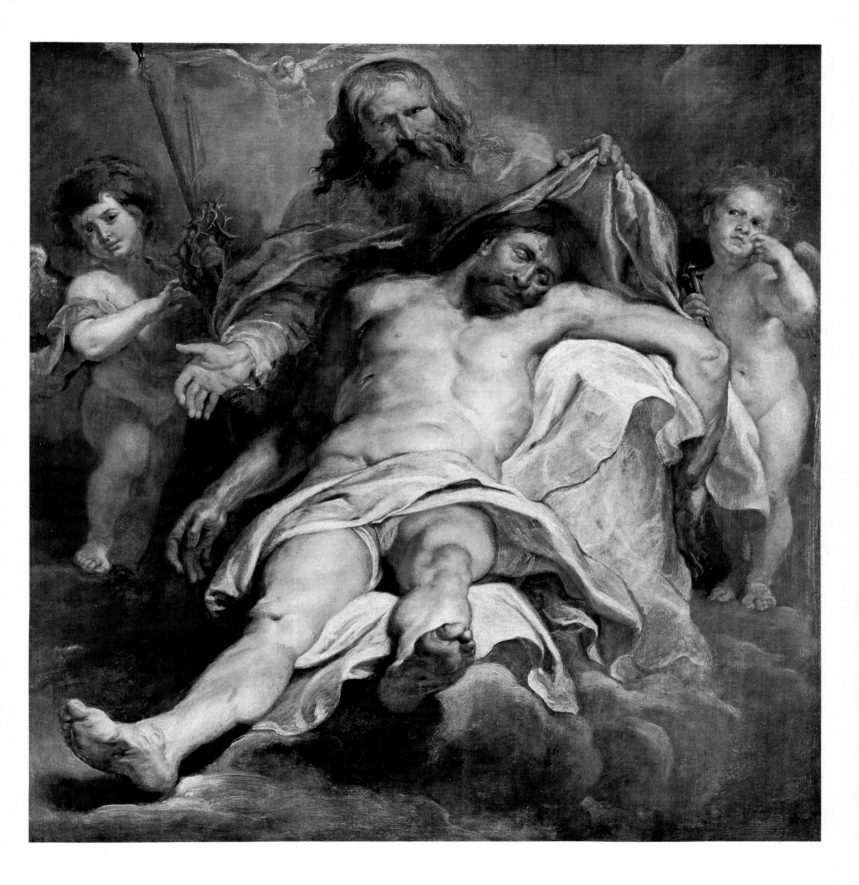

Plate 23
THE HOLY TRINITY
Panel, 62¼″ × 59¾″
Antwerp, Koninklijk Museum voor
Schone Kunsten

*Probably executed in 1617–18, this work
is comparable in its expression and harmonious composition to the painting entitled
Le Christ à la Paille (Fig. 52), also in
the Antwerp Museum, which dates from
about the same time.*

99

Jacob de Bie that he could not accept any more young beginners in his workshop,[63] but until about 1614 these assistants probably played only a minor role; later it seems to have become more important. The fact that Rubens signed some works of smaller dimensions precisely in 1613 and 1614, which otherwise he practically never did, is probably not a coincidence; did he intend by doing this to distinguish between works painted entirely by himself and others for which he had used collaborators in his workshop?;Collaboration is visible, for example, in the altarpiece *St. Francis of Assisi Receiving the Stigmata* (Fig. 49) for the high altar of the Capuchin Friars in Cologne, probably a little later than the Brussels *Assumption*. This Cologne picture is certainly one of the first commissions, if not the very first, which came to Rubens from outside the Netherlands. The church for which it was destined was built in 1615–16, and we know that the work adorned the high altar as early as October 1616.[64]

And Rubens certainly called on assistants for the execution of the huge canvas *The Last Judgment* in the Alte Pinakothek in Munich (Plate 22). Yet it is not very easy to determine their share in it. The master must have worked over the whole in a manner so personal that the assistants' part becomes in the end only subordinate. The commission for this large altarpiece probably came Rubens' way in January 1615, when Duke Wolfgang Wilhelm von Neuburg was a visitor in Antwerp.[65] The execution must have required a long preparation, and can be dated 1615–16. At all events, we know that in 1617 the canvas was in place on the high altar of the church of the Jesuits, which was also the chapel of the Court, at Neuburg on the Danube.[66]

All the features acquired in the "classical" period come together in this impressive canvas, just as all the types represented in the previous works are also found in it. We are struck with the sculptural forms of the figures, on whom shines a golden light, warm and fresh, accentuating their plasticity and throwing reflections of tender blue onto their milky white and rosy skin. The intertwined bodies of the blessed, raised to Heaven on the left, are modeled in so sculptural a manner that they involuntarily evoke the groups carved in ivory which Jörg Petel executed later after Rubens' models. The artist succeeds besides in giving such transparency and lightness to these floating forms that those in the upper zone are almost diaphanous. By contrast, he paints the bodies just emerging from the tombs in the left foreground in shades of pale gray. Thus the rising blessed are represented in graduated colors, while the descending damned on the right are in darker, more brownish tones. Despite the multitude of twisting figures, the structure of the composition remains clear. The scheme is triangular, corresponding more or less to a wedge,[67] the lower point discerned somewhere toward the bottom. The plasticity of the forms, the radiant luminosity, and the compositional clarity make us see in this great altarpiece the most perfect achievement of Rubens' "classical" period during the years 1612 to 1615/16. The large *Last Judgment* also heralds the next step in the development of his art. Rubens had to come to terms with the structural problems raised while realizing

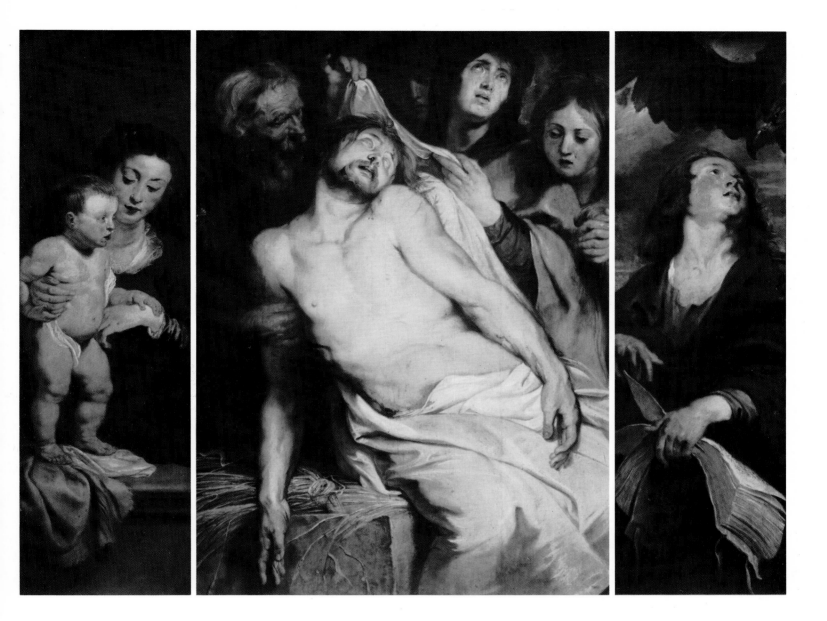

Figure 52
CHRIST IN THE TOMB ("LE CHRIST
À LA PAILLE")
Triptych; central panel $54\frac{1}{4}'' \times 38\frac{1}{2}''$,
wings each $54\frac{1}{4}'' \times 15\frac{3}{4}''$
Antwerp, Koninklijk Museum voor
Schone Kunsten
Left wing: VIRGIN AND CHILD
Right wing: ST. JOHN THE EVANGE-
LIST

*This triptych was painted in 1617–18 and
served as an epitaph to Jan Michielsen in
Antwerp Cathedral. The wings are probably by the hand of Anthony van Dyck, who
was then an assistant in Rubens' workshop.*

this picture by proposing solutions which in some degree would affect
the future. Thus the representation of the subject demanded a more
dynamic form; the vast surface necessitated a larger deployment of
colors; to bring out the values, tones had to be multiplied; the strength
of precision had to be set against the risk of monotony. The stylistic
implications of these new imperatives would be confirmed in the following years: "The sculptural character becomes less and less
severe. The contours become fainter, a generous warmth floods over
the stretched skin like a membrane and light envelops the forms from
all sides."[68]

We must not exaggerate these modifications, however: the development is progressive, following two parallel paths. Among the pictures
from the years 1616 to 1619/20, one group indeed continues the clear,

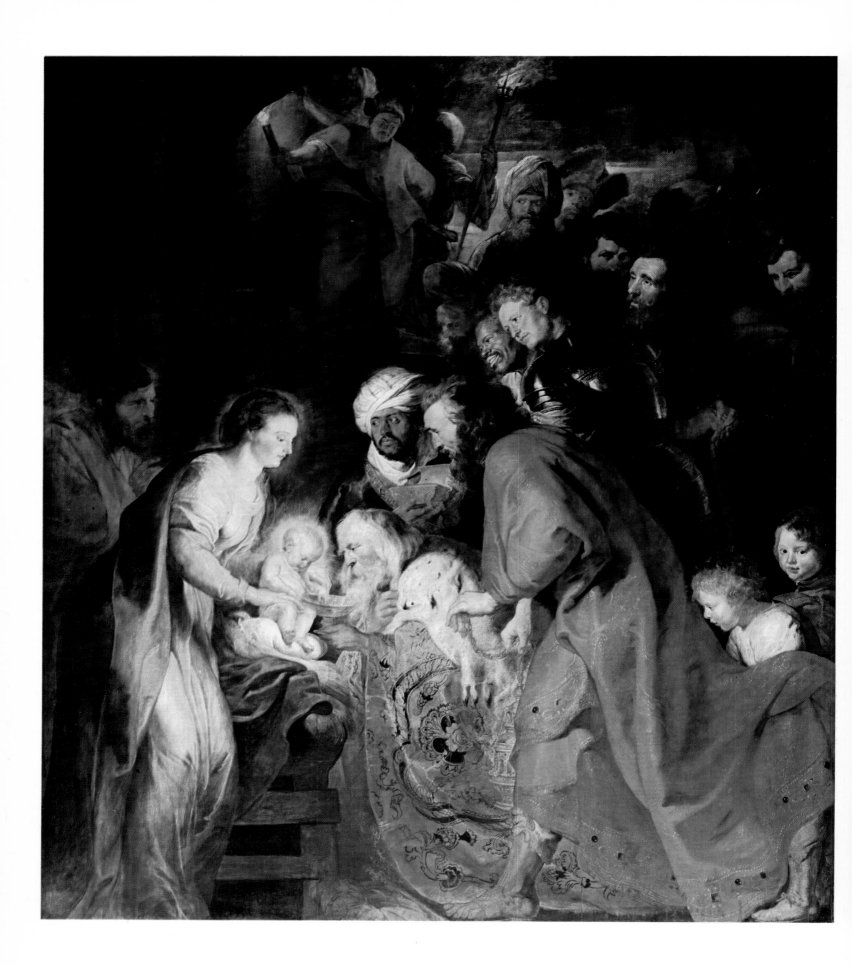

sculptural, "classical" style, but with subtler tonalities; in another group chiaroscuro again plays a more important part than during the first post-Italian years, although the passage from light to dark is now more gradual. We do not attribute to chance Rubens' renewal of interest in chiaroscuro in some altarpieces in which he returns to compositions conceived about 1611, among others the one that prepared the way for *The Descent from the Cross* in Antwerp Cathedral;[69] and in this connection Held has recently drawn attention to a most important work, namely, *The Entombment of Christ* in St-Géry in Cambrai,[70] which Canon Sebastian Briquet presented to the church of the Capuchin Friars in 1616.[71] Somewhat later Rubens must have painted *The Descent from the Cross* at Lille (see Fig. 50), which was not yet finished on March 10, 1617.[72] The composition takes up again an "idea" which Rubens had sketched roughly on a sheet of paper—preserved in Rennes—for the Antwerp *Descent from the Cross* for the Guild of the Arquebusiers.[73] Another *Descent from the Cross* in Valenciennes (Fig. 51), where the subject is treated in yet a different manner, could belong to this period.[74] In these last three works the body of Christ is illuminated by a very clear light, whose source is in front of the picture and high on the right. The same light touches gently the heads and shoulders of the figures grouped around Christ, but their shapes are absorbed in the penumbra of the background. An astonishing peculiarity must be noted, that in each of these works one kneeling figure is looking upward, her face lit from the front like Mary-Cleophas in *The Descent from the Cross* in Antwerp Cathedral. In the Cambrai picture this spot of light touches Mary's face; in the Lille altarpiece that of Mary-Cleophas; and in the Valenciennes altarpiece the face of St. John also, though less strongly. We mention too that the type of Christ in the Lille picture singularly recalls the *Christ in the Tomb ("Le Christ à la Paille")* in Antwerp (Fig. 52), which dates from about 1617–18.[75] *The Holy Trinity* (Plate 23) in the same museum was probably painted at the same time.[76]

The chiaroscuro is even more sensitive in *The Adoration of the Magi* in Malines (Plate 24), a triptych commissioned from Rubens on December 27, 1616; the side panels were delivered in 1617, the central panel on March 25, 1619.[77] Here the light radiates from a source that is not outside, but at the heart of the picture; it shines from the Child himself, the Light which dispels the darkness. It is reflected on the milky-white, diaphanous face of the Virgin, on her breast, on the head and shoulders of the Greek king who wears an ermine stole, on the snow-white turban and scarf of the Ethiopian king, and on the noble profile of the Assyrian king; and it brings out the heads of the children who hide in the darkness of the right foreground. Behind the front group the figures are gently touched by the light from the Child. Two torches cast a dull radish glow on the figures in the background; the forms of their bodies disappear slowly into the night. No violent contrasts, but soft transitions from light to dark, thanks to the gentleness of intermediate tones. What a difference from *The Last Judgment*, all plasticity and clarity,

Plate 24
THE ADORATION OF THE MAGI
Central panel, 10'5" × 9'1½"
Malines, Church of St. John

*Light radiates from the Child and is reflected on the transparent, milky-white face of the Virgin, on her chest and on the faces of the wise men; it also falls on the heads of the children in the right foreground.*

103

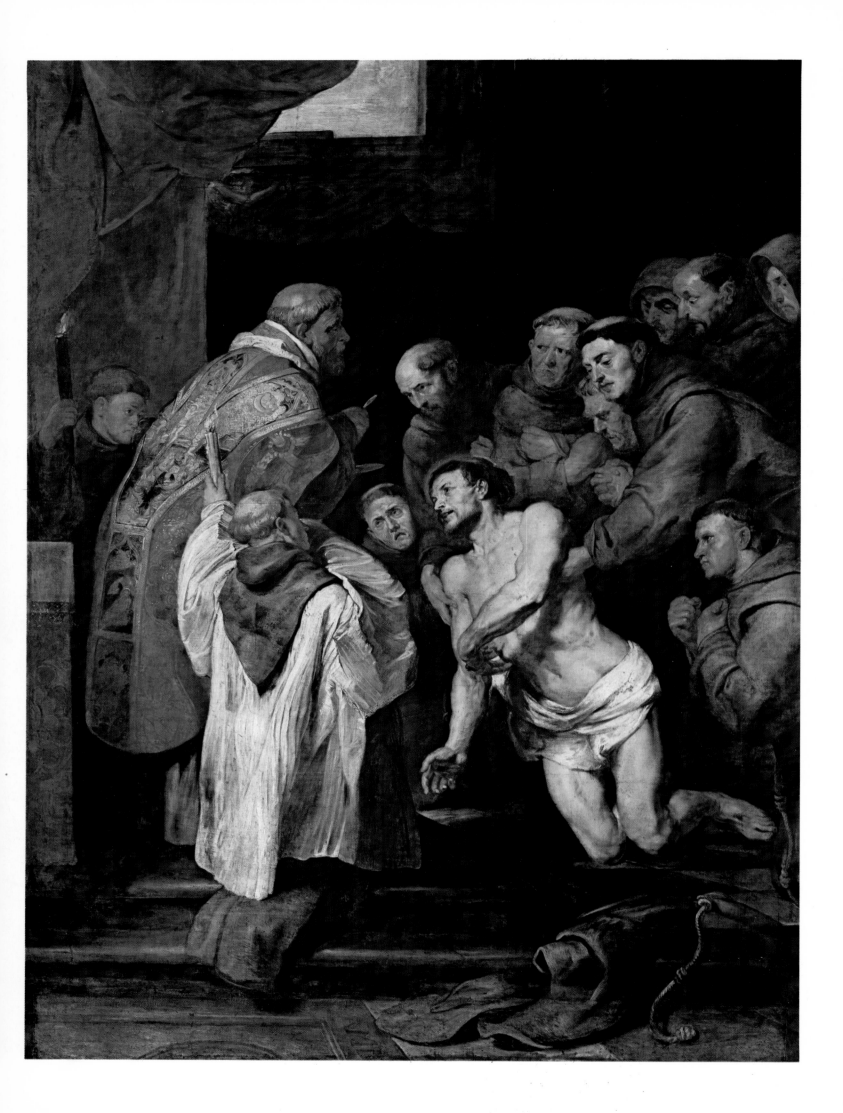

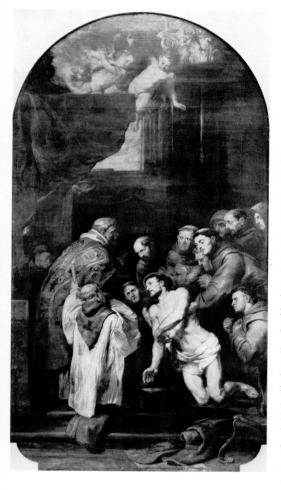

which was painted only a few years earlier! And yet what presence they have, these sculptural figures enveloped in darkness!

These emerge with growing clearness in another monumental work showing an event that takes place in the semidarkness of a church: *The Last Communion of St. Francis of Assisi* (Plate 25; Fig. 53), painted at the request of a wealthy merchant, Jaspar Charles, who intended it to hang on a side altar in the church of the Minorites in Antwerp. Since Rubens wrote a receipt for the payment of this work on May 19, 1619, it must have been finished shortly before.[78] From a handwritten note on one of the first sketches for this picture (now in the Wolfgang Burchard collection) we know that his first idea for the composition was a set of contrasts of light and shade: "The whole group in the shadow, and a fierce sunlight coming in through the window."[79] In the picture the window is about where it is indicated in the sketch, and St. Francis' disciples are around him in the semidarkness. But to make the main accent fall on the ivory-colored body of the dying man, Rubens has thought to cast a golden light from a source in front of the picture on the left, to suffuse the foreground.[80] On the other hand, he has partly covered the window with a red canopy, deflecting the angle of the incoming daylight. Thus the scene is bathed in an atmosphere of soft transitions between the light and dark areas, and the gentle thrill and blessed ecstasy of this encounter with the supernatural become tangible. By their restrained gestures and meditative expressions the monks show, each according to his character, the feelings inspired by the prodigious event taking place before their eyes.

The same play of forms evoked by subtle values of light and shade is seen in *The Adoration of the Shepherds*, a theme which Rubens made in several versions during this period.[81] In a few mythological pictures also, such as *"Sine Cerere et Baccho Friget Venus"* (Fig. 54), the reddish-brown reflections from Vulcan's furnace clothes the bodies of the goddesses with a soft light against the darkness of the forge.[82]

We have stated that some altarpieces from the same years, 1616–19, are characterized by more pronounced plastic expression and more even lighting. These link up with the preceding period, the "classical" phase, of which the large *Last Judgment* of 1615–16 can be taken as the most perfect example; and to this time belong also the two great paintings of 1617–18 for the high altar of the church of the Jesuits in Antwerp, which we will later discuss in greater detail;[83] another example is *The Assumption of the Virgin*, intended for the high altar of the church of Notre-Dame-de-la-Chapelle in Brussels, a work now in Düsseldorf (Fig. 55).[84] The date of this monumental work is probably slightly earlier than generally believed; indeed, according to a note in the archives in the church, the contract (since lost) formerly accompanied the accounts of 1616 and 1617. On the other hand, the chronicle of the church of the Chapel states that Rubens not only conceived the picture but also the altar on which it was placed, erected in 1618.[85] The date of 1616–18 thus becomes plausible. The composition can be regarded as a development of that of the *Assumption* of about 1614 (Plate 21), but the artist has achieved greater unity between the upper zone, where the Virgin is represented in greater movement, and the lower zone, where the figures are brought closer together and the light and dark areas balance one another better. The Virgin's flowing robe and the rays of light behind her emphasize her ascending movement; the gestures of the apostles' hands and their billowing draperies powerfully heighten the dynamism of the whole. Some of the apostles' heads may also be found in the Fishmongers' triptych in Malines, whose central panel is *The Miraculous Draft of Fishes* (Fig. 82).[86] Rubens has manifestly entrusted a large part of the execution to his workshop; in some areas we think we can recognize the hand of Anthony van Dyck, who is known to have been Rubens' main assistant after 1617.[87] On August 11, 1619, the triptych was sent to Malines, where it still hangs in the church of Our-Lady-beyond-the-Dyle. Striking in the central panel are the tones of light that vibrate around the sailors, and the reflections breaking on the tops of the waves. The plan of the composition has a certain analogy with *The Miracles of St. Francis Xavier*, formerly in the church of the Jesuits in Antwerp (Fig. 124); the main figure on the right stands in the same way as if on a dais, while the

Figure 54
SINE CERERE ET BACCHO FRIGET
VENUS
Panel, 5′11″ × 6′6½″
Brussels, Musées Royaux des Beaux-Arts de Belgique

*Among the mythological scenes of the years 1616–20 certain paintings also accentuate the contrasts of light and shade, but less violently than before, in 1609–12; the transitions from light to dark are now more softly graded.*

Plate 26
SINE CERERE ET BACCHO FRIGET
VENUS (detail)
Brussels, Musées Royaux des Beaux-Arts de Belgique

*A woman carrying on her shoulder a basket of fruit. This female type with big dark eyes appears frequently in Rubens' works.*

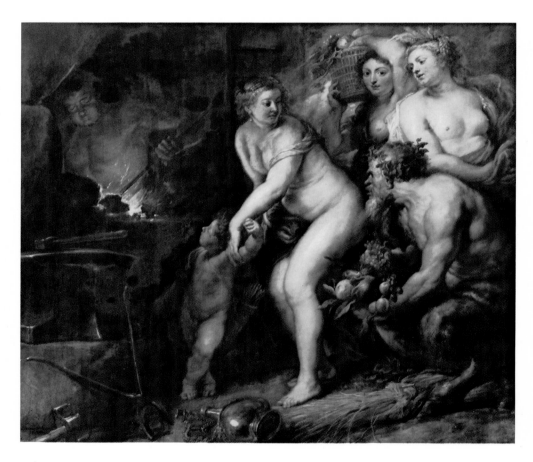

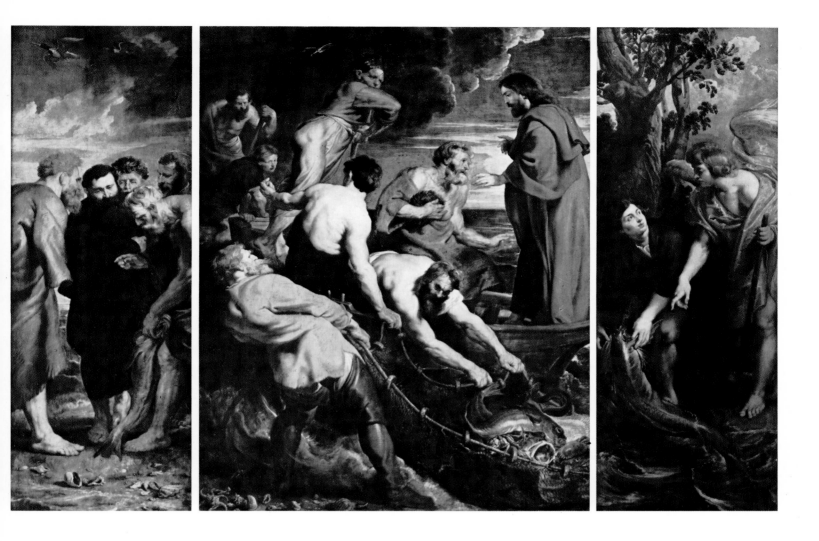

Figure 56
THE MIRACULOUS DRAFT OF
FISHES
Triptych; central panel 9'10" × 7'6",
wings each 9'10" × 3'6"
Malines, Church of Our-Lady-beyond-
the-Dyle
Left wing: THE TRIBUTE MONEY
Right wing: TOBIAS AND THE AN-
GEL

*The triptych commissioned by the Guild of
the Fishmongers was transported by boat
to Malines on August 11, 1619.*

other figures are grouped along a diagonal from the upper left to the lower right corner.

Let us emphasize this once again: the pictures showing the essentially plastic form of the figures and serene lighting, linked in some degree with the style of 1612–15, were painted during roughly the same period as those dominated by strong chiaroscuro and gradations. It could be said that from 1615 to 1619 Rubens made alternate use of earlier techniques according to the subject, and perhaps also to the light which the picture would receive on the altar of the church. As his choices increased during the decade after his return from Italy, he was now free to use several registers simultaneously and to obtain the desired tonalities for each subject. He prefers neither the violent contrasts of his first years nor the strong color and sharp contours of his "classical" period. What he seeks at this time are gradations of color that rise and fall, a harmonious transition toward a tonality that is now light, now dark, but always serves a composition that is at once balanced and full of *élan*.

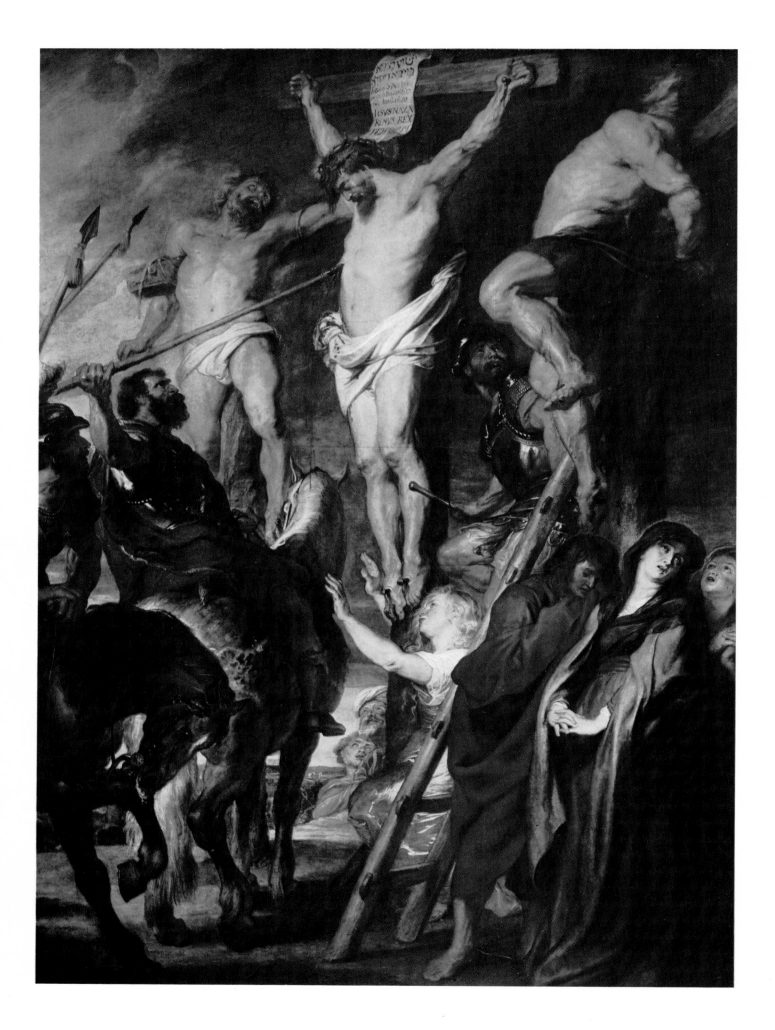

The synthesis of what might be called the "light" manner and the "dark" manner of these years takes place in the second version of *The Miracles of St. Ignatius of Loyola*, painted in 1619, which reached Genoa in 1620 where it is still in place on an altar in Sant' Ambrogio, the church of the Jesuits.[88]   Certain elements of the composition, as well as the effects of twilight and the subdued tones in the upper half of the canvas, recall strongly *The Last Communion of St. Francis of Assisi*.   In addition, the presentation of the figures in the lower half of the canvas has analogies with the altarpieces for the church of the Jesuits in Antwerp, except that the tones of light and color are more numerous here.   Eventually the "light" tonality prevails, when Rubens no longer uses contrasts of light and shade for accentuation but multiplies the tones and transitions in some way, choosing from among different registers.   Contours and local color tend to fuse more or less into the prodigious richness of his chromatic scale.   This new phase is heralded in the famous *Christ on the Cross* ("*Le Coup de Lance*"; Fig. 57).[89]   At the request of Nicolaas Rockox this canvas was placed, probably in 1620, on the high altar of the church of the Minorites in Antwerp.   But this leads us to the opening of a new development, which will take place after 1620.

Figure 57
CHRIST ON THE CROSS ("LE COUP DE LANCE")
Panel, 14' × 10'2"
Antwerp, Koninklijk Museum voor Schone Kunsten

*This impressive panel was commissioned by Nicolaas Rockox and was placed above the high altar of the church of the Minorites in Antwerp in 1620.*

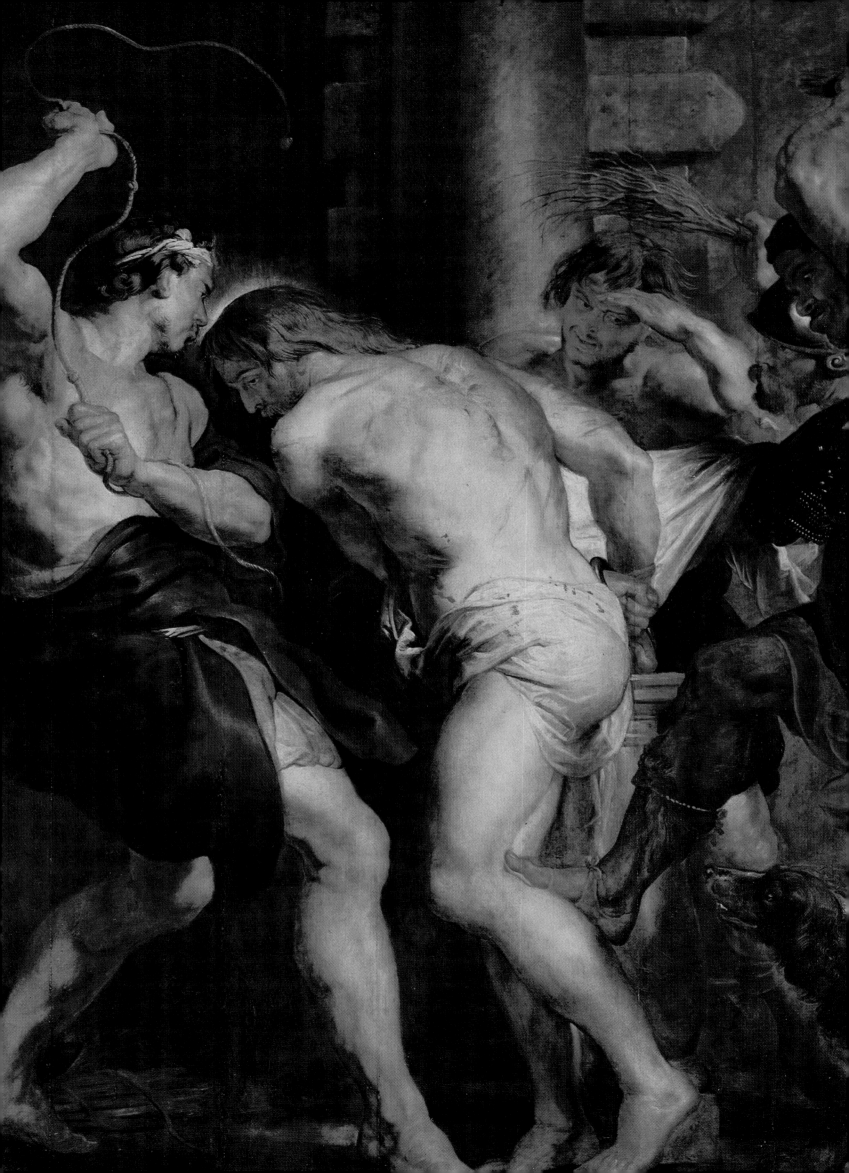

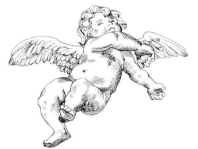

# CHAPTER 4

# The Flagellation of Christ

## in the Church of St. Paul in Antwerp

Plate 27
THE FLAGELLATION
Panel, 6'10" × 5'3"
Antwerp, Church of St. Paul

*This picture was probably completed in 1617. The active movement peculiar to the Baroque style is evident here. The supple contours harmonize and coil rhythmically, as they indicate poses and gestures. Here grace and strength go hand in hand. Subtle shades of chiaroscuro play on the forms.*

Together with Anthony van Dyck's *Christ Falling under the Cross* (Fig. 59) and Jacob Jordaens' *Christ on the Cross* (Fig. 60), the *Flagellation of Christ* by Rubens (Plate 27) ranks among the most remarkable pictures of the cycle of the Mysteries of the Rosary in St. Paul's Church in Antwerp, the former church of the Dominicans.[1] This impressive series consists of fifteen large panels, each representing one of the fifteen Mysteries: the five Joys (the Annunciation, the Visitation, the Nativity, the Presentation in the Temple, and Christ among the Doctors); the five Sufferings (Christ on the Mount of Olives, the Flagellation, the Crowning with Thorns, the Carrying of the Cross, and Christ on the Cross); and the five Glories (the Resurrection, the Ascension, the Descent of the Holy Spirit, the Assumption of the Virgin, and the Coronation of the Virgin).

The *Interior of the Church of the Antwerp Dominicans* (Fig. 58),[2] painted in 1636 by Pieter Neefs the Elder, shows the complete series of fifteen pictures fixed to the wall of the north aisle, from the doorway leading to the cloisters to the wrought-iron grille of Our Lady's Chapel. Between the eighth and ninth paintings hangs a larger picture, Caravaggio's famous *Madonna of the Rosary*, presented to the Antwerp Dominicans through the mediation of Rubens and other artists.[3] The Mysteries of the Rosary series has always occupied this wall; Caravaggio's picture, however, was placed on a special altar in Our Lady's Chapel sometime later in the seventeenth century. In 1786 it was replaced by a copy, at the order of the Emperor Joseph II, and the original was transferred to Vienna.[4] During the nineteenth century Rubens' *Flagellation of Christ* was taken out of the series and hung separately in the north transept; a few years ago it was fortunately put back in its original position.[5] It might be mentioned in passing that along the side walls of the church in Neefs' picture one does not see the confessionals which are admired there today; this superb ensemble was installed some twenty years after the picture was painted.[6]

The Dominicans were known for their great devotion to the Rosary,[7] so it is hardly surprising that, when they were furnishing their church early in the seventeenth century, they thought of a series of pictures representing the Mysteries of the Rosary. The project may have originated with the Fathers themselves, but again we must take note that only the generosity of the Antwerp citizens made its execution possible. A document of the seventeenth century, preserved in the archives of the church,[8] records for each item in the series the name of the donor, that of the painter, and the price. Two pictures were paid for "out of various charities,"[9] but usually one citizen undertook to pay for one item. In the case of Rubens' picture, this was none other than Louis Clarisse, one of the "wepelaars" (those exempted from military service) in the Guild of Arquebusiers whose gifts had contributed to the payment for Rubens' *Descent from the Cross* in St. Walburga.[10]

As no fewer than eleven artists worked on the series, this accounts for the flagrant differences in style and quality among the various works. Besides Rubens, Van Dyck, and Jordaens, one finds well-known masters such as Hendrik van Balen, Cornelis de Vos, Frans Francken the Younger, and David Teniers the Elder, as well as a few almost unknown painters from whom hardly any work has come down to us, apart from this series: Matthijs Voet, Antoni or Artus de Bruyn,[11] Arnout Vinkenborgh, and (Dirk?) Aertsen.

The date of the cycle poses a problem which has not yet been satisfactorily solved. No indications are found in the archive entries. The frame of Rubens' *Flagellation of Christ* bears the date 1617—an astonishing fact, since the frame is known to date from the nineteenth century, when Rubens' panel was replaced in the series by the copy by Van Ysendyck! But it is not impossible that the date was inscribed on the basis of information from certain documents (in the archives?) that have since disappeared.[12] In any case, the hypothesis that the series

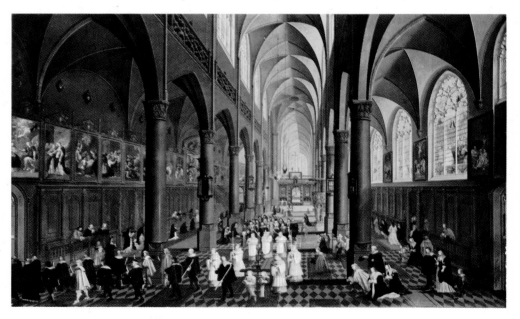

Figure 58
Peter Neefs the Elder
INTERIOR OF THE CHURCH OF THE
DOMINICANS IN ANTWERP IN 1636
Amsterdam, Rijksmuseum

*On the left wall, above the paneling, the series of pictures representing* The Fifteen Mysteries of the Rosary *can be seen.*

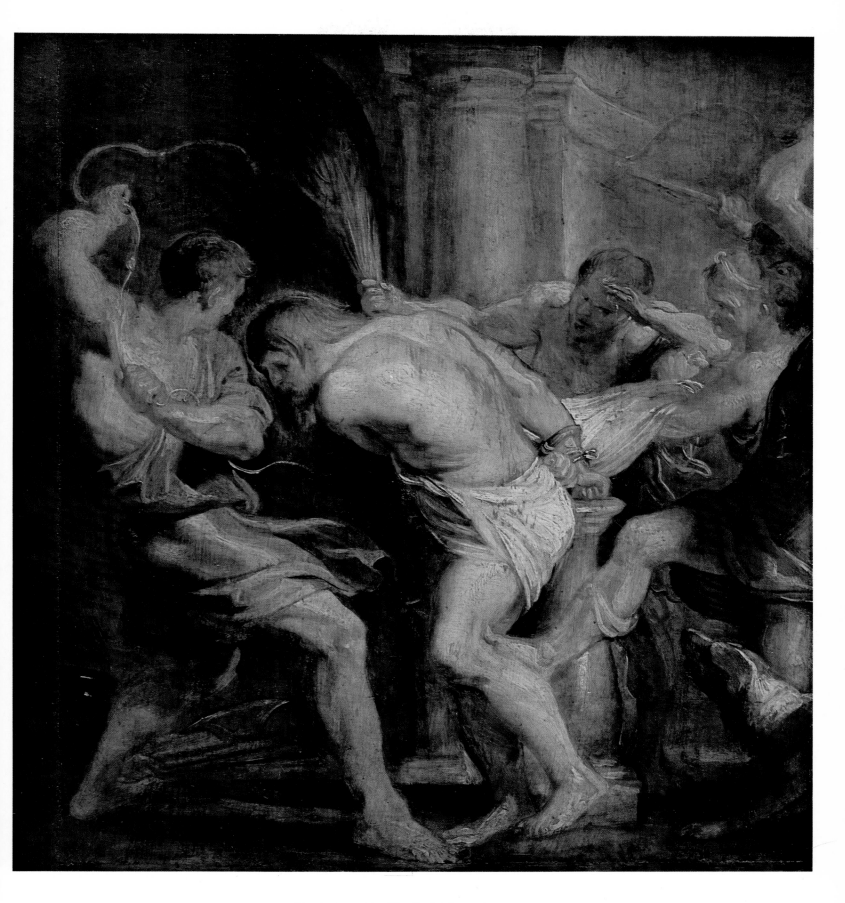

Plate 28
THE FLAGELLATION
Panel, $14\frac{1}{2}'' \times 13\frac{3}{4}''$
Ghent, Museum voor Schone Kunsten

*Already present in this oil sketch are the main stylistic features of the painting, today in St. Paul's Church in Antwerp. In particular, we see the convincing dynamic forces and the harmonious composition.*

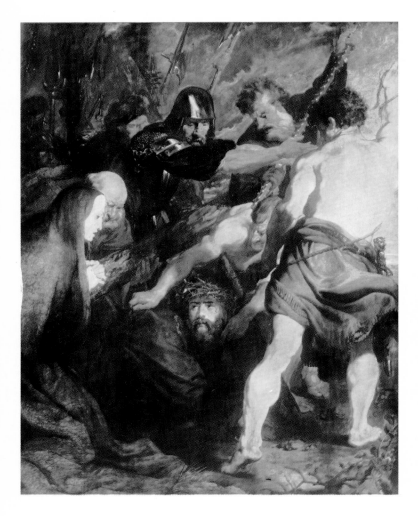 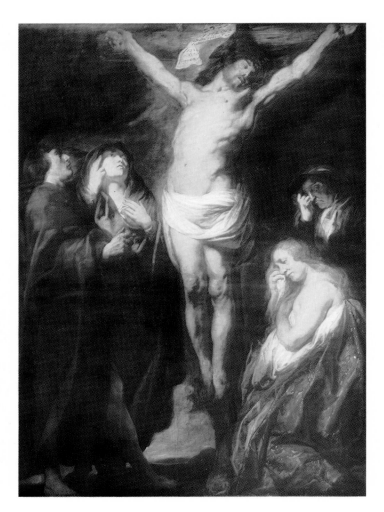

Figure 59
Anthony van Dyck
CHRIST FALLING UNDER THE
CROSS
Antwerp, Church of St. Paul

*A youthful work by Rubens' assistant in
the years 1617–20. Together with Rubens'
Flagellation, it forms part of the series
of The Fifteen Mysteries of the Rosary.*

Figure 60
Jacob Jordaens
THE CRUCIFIXION
Antwerp, Church of St. Paul

*An early work of the artist, in which, like
Van Dyck's Christ Falling under the
Cross, Jordaens draws inspiration from
Rubens' style while in other respects reflect-
ing his own personality.*

was painted about 1617 is not contradicted by stylistic analysis of other contemporary works by Rubens, or by the other artists with whose work the series can be compared.[13]

The pictures by Rubens, Van Dyck, and Jordaens in the series stand out in comparison with the others, which retain a fair number of "archaic" features of late sixteenth-century style. Their works share an undeniable sense of synthesis in the composition, a form which was rather daring for the time and consequently more "modern," and finally a more vigorous colorism. If, despite these differences, they integrate harmoniously into the series it is because all three painters complied with the general design governing the whole. In all fifteen panels all the figures are more or less life-size. Taking into account the height at which the pictures would be displayed, the compositions are designed on the front plane as much as possible; this produces a sculptural effect that is reinforced by moving the figures so far forward that they often rest or stand on the frame. In the *Flagellation of Christ* the composition virtually fills the whole foreground and the space

116

behind the figures has been narrowly limited to avoid any effect of depth. There are no striking perspectives here, no figures or columns or architectural motives arranged along impressive diagonals that cross deep in space like those so often found in Rubens' altarpieces. Rather this composition suggests a sculptured relief, the figures aligned on one plane against an almost flat background from which they seem to stand forward with increased volume.

The design does not prevent Rubens' *Flagellation of Christ* from being marked, like the rest of his work, by the undulating mobility of the Baroque. But the mobility shows itself in the particularly supple rhythm of sinuous contours which answer one another in attitude and gesture. Here grace and strength are united: the rope coils in the hand of the muscular tormentor on the left like a snake, and his athletic attitude has the balance and rhythm of a dancer. Christ's body, too, is in spiral movement. The legs are seen from the side, but the torso is twisted to show largely the back; at any moment the Saviour will turn his suffering face toward us, but his movements are hampered by the bonds that tie his hands to the short column. Brute force is unleashed in the movement of the two tormentors rushing at him from the right, a Negro and a bearded soldier in a helmet; they brandish small bundles of willow twigs and lash his back until they draw blood; one of them braces his foot against Christ's left calf to make him lose balance. A fourth observes the scene with a grimacing face and hateful look, his hand held above his eyes; his is the only face one sees from the front. The form of the picture shows at one and the same time a fiery movement and masterful composition.

In a small oil sketch Rubens established the broad lines of this composition (Plate 28),[14] and deviated from it only slightly in the large panel. The successful union of powerful movement with harmony of composition is already suggested in the sketch. When Rubens painted this *Flagellation of Christ*, about 1617, his art had undergone a complete evolution in a short time. After the impetuous effervescence of his first years home from Italy in 1608, the so-called classical period begins in 1612; his art, now mastered, has a serene balance in composition, restraint in its rounded form, and fiercely lighted figures. The *Flagellation of Christ* belongs to the subsequent period, beginning about 1615. The same control and plastic expression is still there, now used with less rigor. The painter again seeks for subtler movement, and his more flexible brush strokes and his greater use of intermediate shades in a more varied color scheme lead to a style that is more distinctly pictorial.

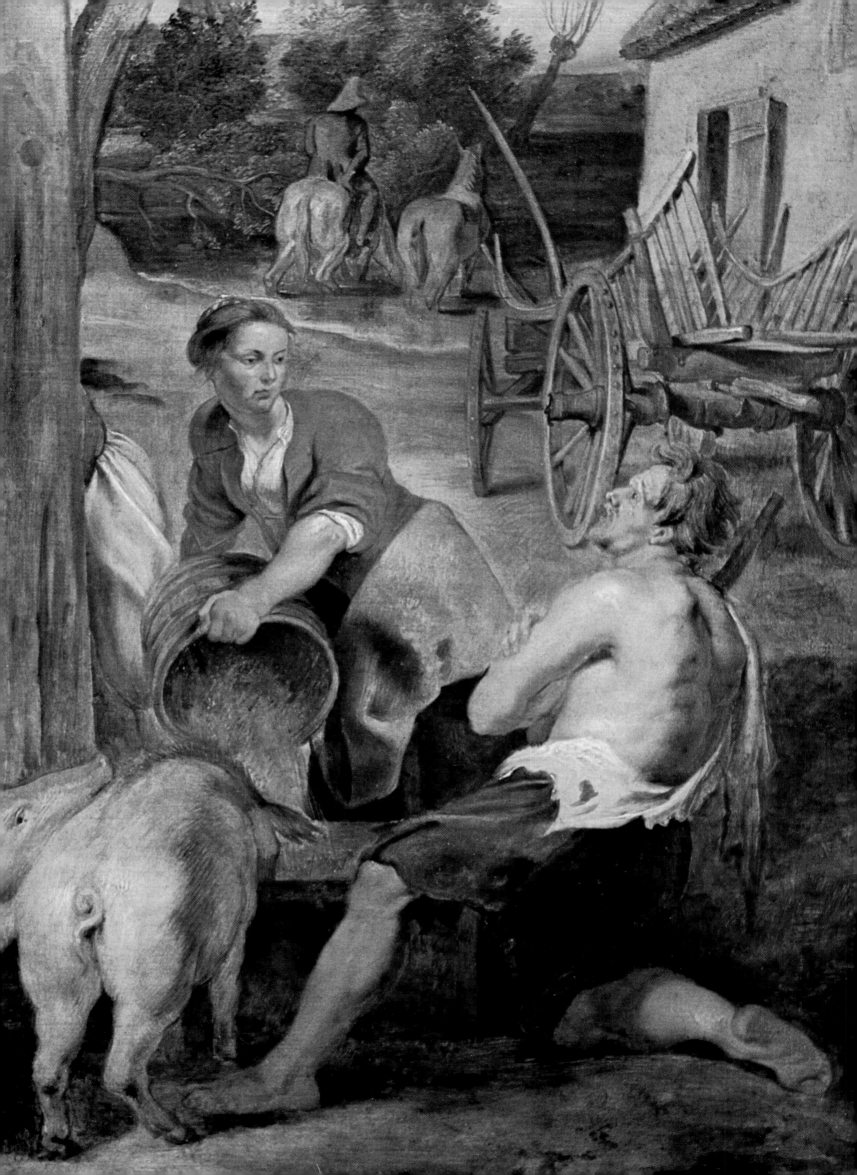

CHAPTER 5 # The Prodigal Son

### in the Koninklijk Museum voor Schone Kunsten in Antwerp

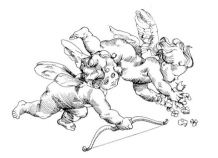

One of the finest rustic scenes Rubens ever painted is in the Koninklijk Museum voor Schone Kunsten in Antwerp (Plates 29, 30).[1] The museum catalogue gives the title of this panel as *The Prodigal Son*,[2] but we do not at first recognize the main person of the parable in the half-nude beggar in the lower right-hand corner, who kneels before the young peasant woman pouring mash for the pigs. The sows with their ravenous piglets, pursued by a dog, remind us that the Prodigal Son, having squandered his fortune, sought to become a swineherd. In the Gospel of St. Luke his situation is described thus (15 : 16): "And he would fain have filled his belly with the husks that the swine did eat: and no man gave unto him." The woman's rather kind face only expresses a slightly surprised indifference, however, while the farmer casts a glance of dark suspicion at the beggar.

Looking at this picture, the spectator's attention is captured first by the stable and the activity going on in there; the biblical theme clearly has only secondary importance. "Rubens has put into this work his great love of country life, and he has imbued the scene with golden light. It is the struggle between the dying day and the twilight which already fills the depths of the stable..."[3] In the center of the picture the oxen, home from their labors, rest in their stall and wait at their bars. On the floor above them we see a hayloft; a stableboy sleeps up there, for on the planking is his duffel bag, beside a winnowing-basket and a poultry carrier. Two horses, gray and brown, are stamping impatiently at the left. A farmhand is forking down hay to fill the rack, while a second stableboy has just unharnessed the gray horse and still attends to the animal. The flickering light of a candle on the wall casts a reddish glow on the faces of the two boys. At the back of the stable, in the narrow passage between the wall and the bars, a twisted little old woman struggles forward, trying to shield a candle flame with her hand and thereby producing the same effect of light.

The figures in the right foreground stand out, grouped around the Prodigal Son. Behind them stretches a landscape. Beside the farmhouse, surmounted by its dovecote, the unloaded cart stands in the

Plate 29
THE PRODIGAL SON (detail; Pl. 30)
Antwerp, Koninklijk Museum voor Schone Kunsten

*The Prodigal Son, a ragged, half-nude youth, kneels before the peasant woman who is throwing mash to the pigs. At the side of the house on the right, a cart is rendered with extraordinary accuracy.*

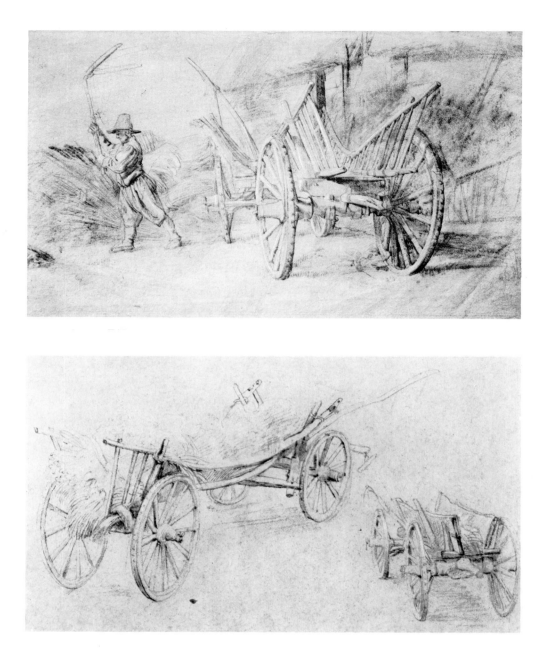

Figure 61
FARMYARD WITH FARMER
THRESHING AND HAY WAGON
Drawing, 10″ × 16³/₈″
Chatsworth, Collection Duke of Devonshire

*This study from life shows the cart which
Rubens used, after this drawing, in the picture entitled* The Prodigal Son. *The cart
also appears in the landscape of about that
time, now in Leningrad (Fig. 63).*

Figure 62
HAY WAGON AND CART
Drawing, 8³/₄″ × 14³/₄″
Berlin-Dahlem, Kupferstichkabinett
der Staatlichen Museen

*We see again how precisely Rubens observed
motifs of country life.*

farmyard; further back a stableboy leads two horses into a little pond
where they will drink before coming back to the stable. The evening
sun marks the horizon with a carmine streak; a golden light still quivers
behind the slender silhouette of the trees, but the sky is already turning
gray above the farmhouse roof. Evening is falling...

As far as it can be verified, Rubens must have been about forty when
he painted this scene and his first landscapes. *The Prodigal Son* looks
as if the artist, being accustomed to paint human figures, did not yet
dare to represent a country scene without adding a biblical subject
to it as a pretext.

One may wonder why Rubens, at this age, should set himself to
paint landscapes and rustic scenes as an autonomous subject. We

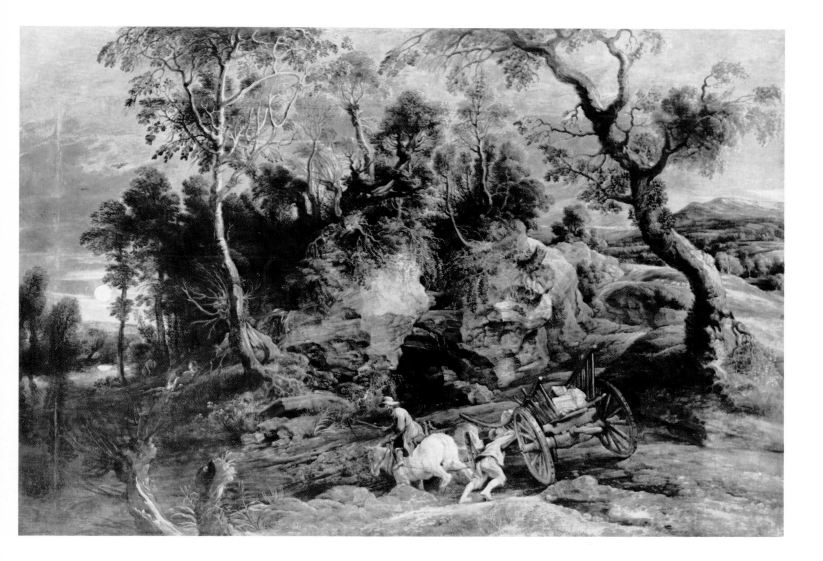

know that from 1617 to 1620, and perhaps even slightly earlier, Rubens executed a number of large altarpieces of the Adoration of the Shepherds. Upon being commissioned for pictures of this biblical subject, he no doubt went into the country looking for motifs suitable for the scenes that he was going to paint. Drawings by Rubens have been preserved which show farm girls and other country persons in various attitudes, and studies of trees, carts, and agricultural implements. The painter did not have to go far to find farms and barns: just beyond the ramparts of Antwerp (today's "leien" or avenues) he could see farm boys and girls at work and catch their poses and gestures in his sketchbook with an expert hand.

One of these studies of people and objects, taken from life on country walks, is the *Peasant Girl* (Fig. 64),[4] the drawing of a young girl carry-

121

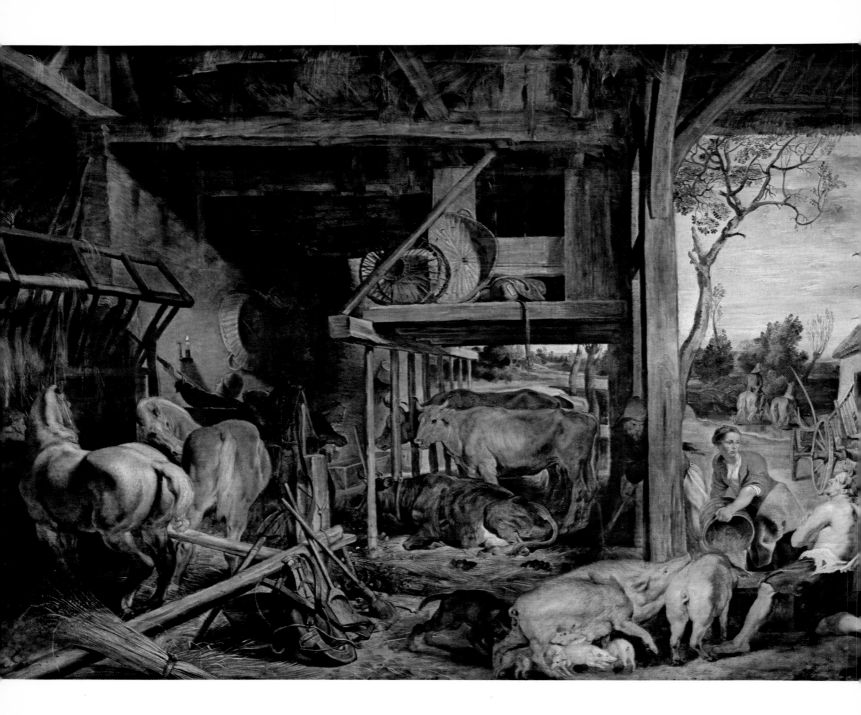

Plate 30
THE PRODIGAL SON
Panel, 42″ × 61″
Antwerp, Koninklijk Museum voor
Schone Kunsten

*One of Rubens' finest pictures of country
life, painted about 1617. Powerful horizontal lines and strict verticals define the
organization of the composition; diagonal
perspectives carry the spectator's gaze into
the distance, toward the sun setting on the
horizon.*

122

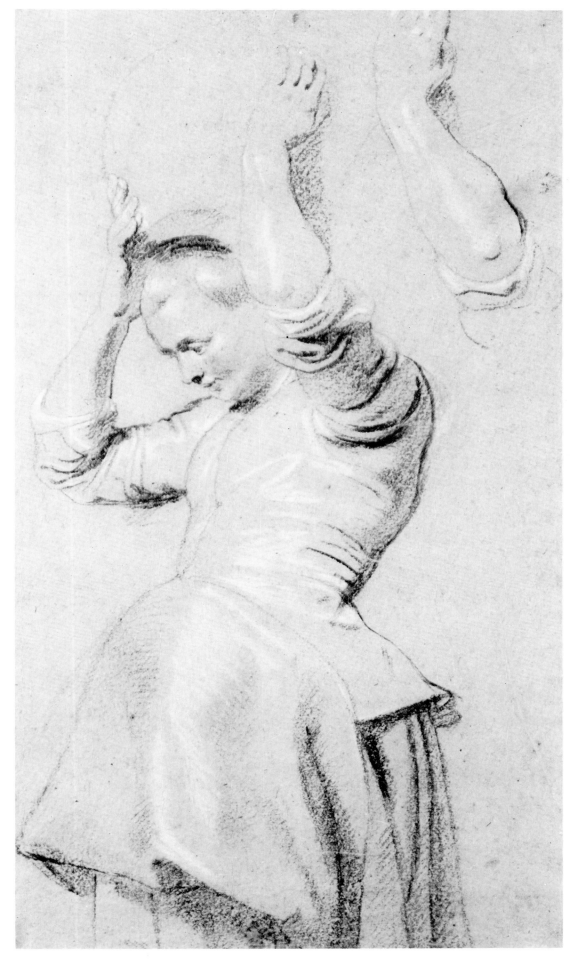

Figure 64
PEASANT GIRL
Drawing, $26^3/_4'' \times 10^1/_2''$
Berlin-Dahlem, Kupferstichkabinett
der Staatlichen Museen

*Preliminary study, taken from life, for* The
Adoration of the Shepherds *in Marseilles (Fig. 73), later reused in the* Landscape with Herd of Cows and Duck-
Shooters *(Fig. 65).*

123

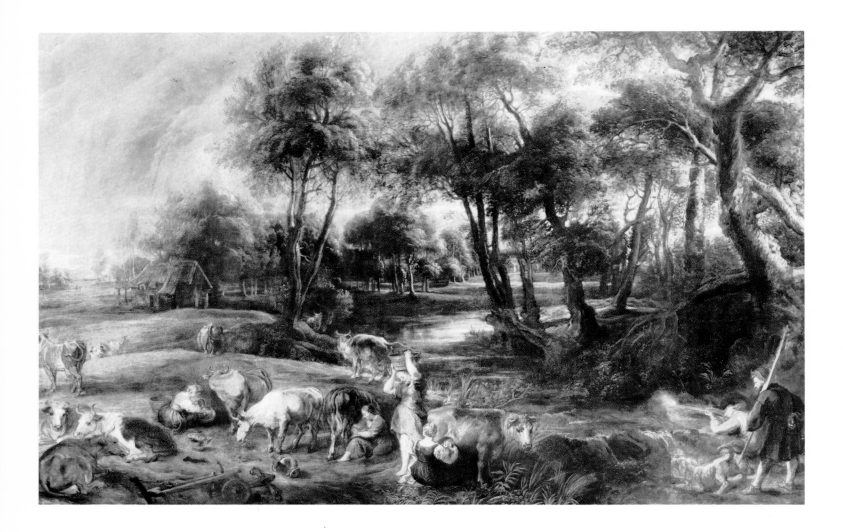

Figure 65
LANDSCAPE WITH HERD OF COWS
AND DUCK-SHOOTERS
Panel, 44½″ × 69¼″
Berlin-Dahlem, Gemäldegalerie der
Staatlichen Museen

*In the center of this landscape, painted
between 1620 and 1625, is again the girl
of whom Rubens had made the drawing which
is also in Berlin (Fig. 64); she had already
appeared in* The Dairy Farm at Laeken
*(Fig. 66), and again as a shepherdess in*
The Adoration of the Shepherds *(Fig.
73). Rubens constantly uses his repertory
of drawings which he never ceased to enrich
throughout his career.*

ing a jug on her head, made from nature when Rubens was preparing the *Adoration of the Shepherds* (Fig. 73)[5] now in the Marseilles Musée des Beaux-Arts (originally one of the predella panels of the *Adoration of the Magi* triptych in St. John's Church in Malines; Plate 24). Later the same sketch served for one of the girls' figures in *Landscape with Herd of Cows and Duck-Shooters* (Fig. 65).[6] Rubens probably made another study of the same young woman on that occasion, now in the Albertina in Vienna.[7] This second study was also made for the Marseilles picture, and he used it again for the famous *Dairy Farm at Laeken* (Fig. 66).[8]

Studies of rustic objects were made in the same way. In Chatsworth there is a sheet on which Rubens has drawn a cart and a peasant threshing wheat (Fig. 61).[9] We have seen this cart in *The Prodigal Son*, and before, in the *Landscape with Broken-Down Cart* (Fig. 63); it was used again in *Winter*, a painting of the 1620s, now in Windsor Castle.[10] A second page of studies of a cart is today in Berlin (Fig. 62).[11] Theuwissen has noted not long ago "the incredible accuracy" that Rubens applied to his observation and representation of these vehicles.[12]

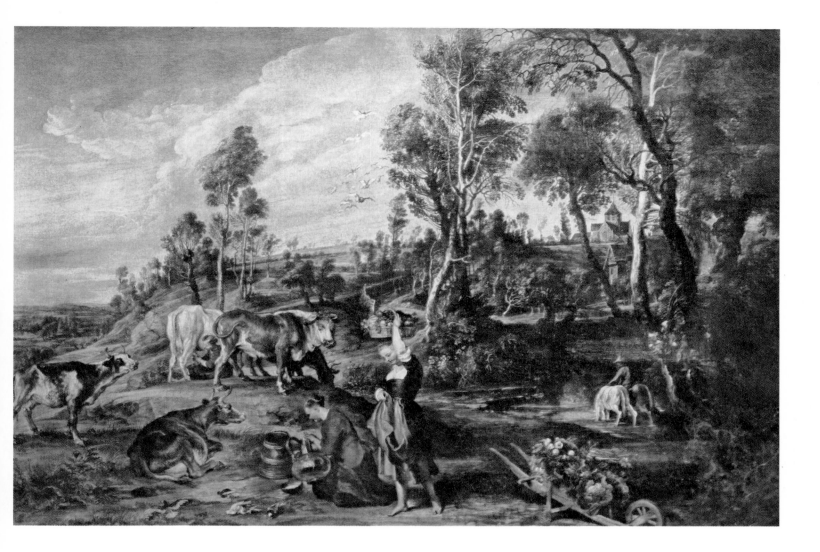

Figure 66
THE DAIRY FARM AT LAEKEN
Panel, 33½″ × 50½″
London, Buckingham Palace

*This landscape dates from about the same
time as* The Prodigal Son *(Pl. 30),
between 1617 and 1620.*

Possibly it was on these country outings that Rubens conceived the
idea to paint independent landscapes and rustic scenes. Or perhaps
he wanted to paint such works as a form of relaxation, to allow himself
a little respite between an altarpiece and a great mythological scene,
or to indulge occasionally in the pleasure of painting for his own enjoyment. It should be kept in mind that *The Prodigal Son* was still in
Rubens' possession in 1640, the year of his death.

The attentive observer cannot but be struck by the perfectly closed
structure of the composition of this picture. Powerful horizontals alternate with rigid verticals: the receding lines of the hayrack along
the wall, of the wooden barrier behind the horses, and of the beam
above the bars of the cow stalls are balanced by the sharp foreshortening of the wooden posts behind the crowding pigs, and, on the right,
the receding lines of the farmhouse roof. The asymmetry of this composition, so characteristic of Baroque art and heightened by the play
of colors, is emphasized by the barrier behind the gray horse. It estab-
lishes a diagonal in the foreground (actually starting in the area in
front of the picture) which extends through the whole stable, toward

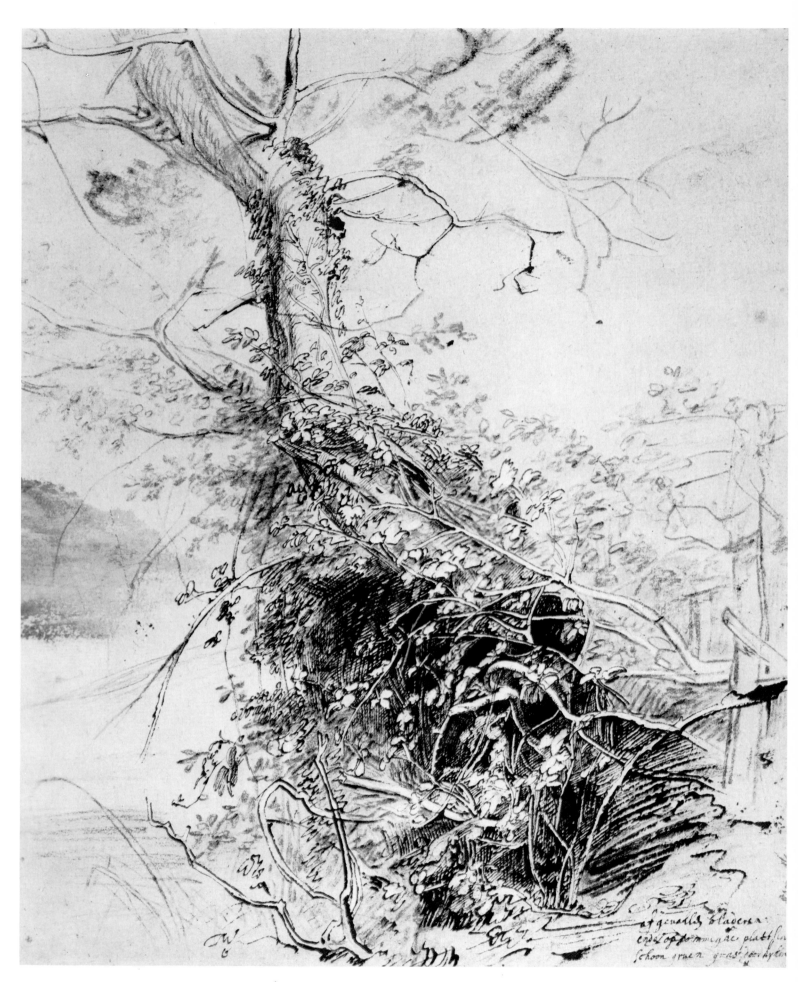

126

the landscape behind. Quite near the stableboy's little loft, the pole placed slantwise between the planking and the roof fulfills a similar optical function, this time drawing the gaze toward the top of the picture. If the oblique line of this pole were extended downward it would meet exactly the barrier behind the horse to form an acute angle. The predominant diagonals that cross the scene or move swiftly toward the background are balanced, one might say neutralized, by the accentuated vertical of the solid oak post at the right; this post also reinforces the separation between the stable, already partly taken over by darkness, and the perfect clarity of the landscape.

The severe structure of horizontals, verticals, and perspective diagonals is pleasantly broken by the broad zone which unites humans and animals as it winds around them like a scroll. Beginning at the level of the hayrack with its hanging wisps of hay, it moves to the foreground, coils upward from the piglets to the torso of the Prodigal Son, returns to the left along the peasant woman's chest and head, and finally goes off to the right, above the horses near the pond, to lose itself in the open sky. Various rounded forms make equally happy breaks in the linear structure of the picture: the baskets above the cattle, the wooden tub of pig mash, the winnowing-basket hanging on the wall, and the wheels of the cart near the farmhouse. The wayward silhouettes of slender branches soften the heavy linearity of the oak post.

It is obvious that this picture was not painted from nature in some stable. Rubens and his contemporaries did not proceed this way; not until the nineteenth century did painters set up their easels in front of a chosen landscape or building. Seventeenth-century landscape painters worked in their studios, using sketches taken from life, and one canvas could show figures, animals, trees, and details of buildings which the artist had previously sketched in his notebooks at different places and times. This technique allowed him much more freedom with his subject than if he painted it on the spot. The painter's creative memory, imagination, and sense of layout and composition thus played a larger part in his work than one might think at first sight.

Figure 67
TREE TRUNK AND BRAMBLES
Drawing
Chatsworth, Collection Duke of Devonshire

*Rubens was an accurate and sensitive observer of nature, as is evident in the fine drawing in pen and brown ink over black chalk, vivified by some red and blue chalk. In the lower right corner the artist has written some notes.*

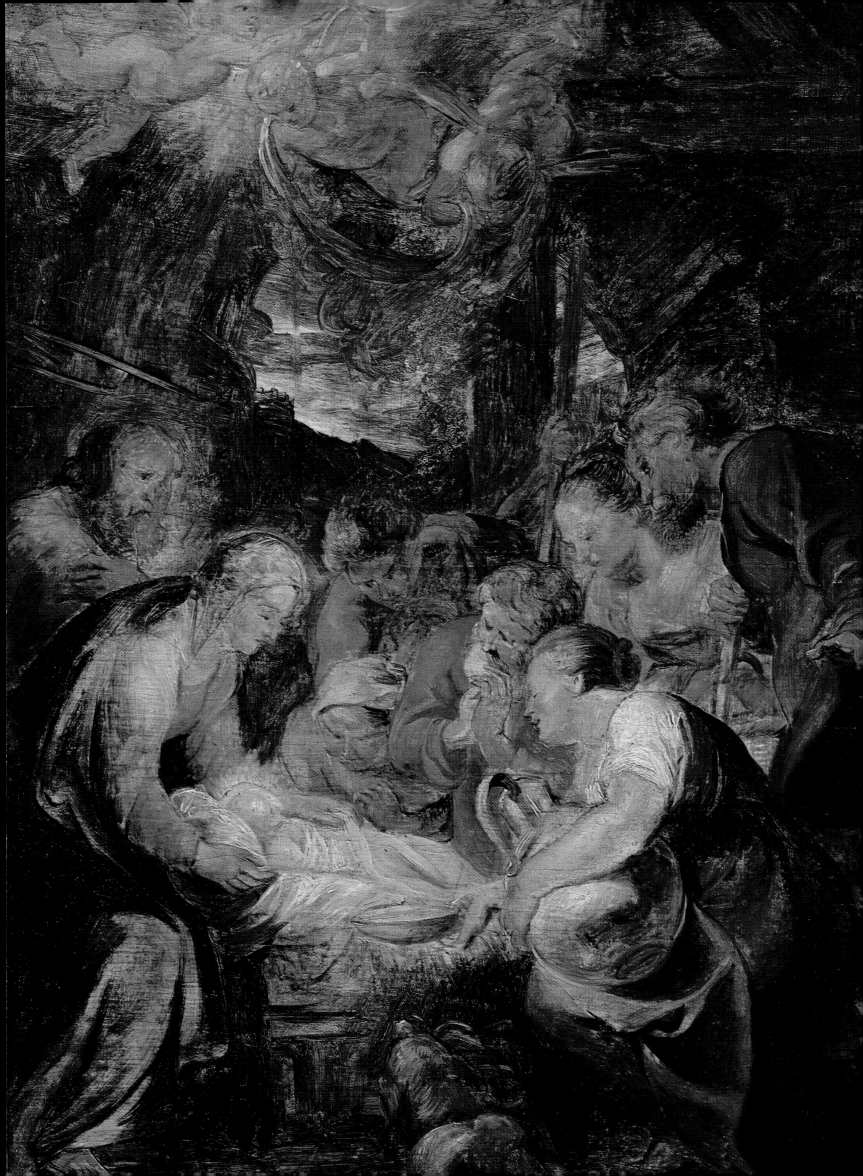

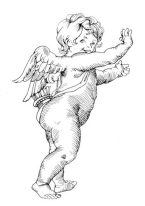

CHAPTER 6 # The Adoration of the Shepherds

an Oil Sketch by Rubens

In the Rubens House in Antwerp, the oil sketch of *The Adoration of the Shepherds*[1] (Plate 31) holds a special place: it was the museum's first acquisition of a work by Rubens. Publicly exhibited for the first time in Helsinki in 1952–53,[2] and shortly afterward in the Musées Royaux des Beaux-Arts de Belgique in Brussels,[3] this oil sketch had been almost unmentioned previously in the literature on Rubens, and it was a revelation for art historians when they first saw it. Held[4] described it as such, and we ourselves devoted a brief commentary to the small panel.[5] The exhibition *Olieverfschetsen van Rubens*[6] in the Boymans Museum in Rotterdam in 1953–54 made possible a comparison with the many admirable oil sketches assembled there, and confirmed that we had before us an important work painted by the master's own hand. When it was possible the following year to buy the piece for the Rubens House, we seized this opportunity with gratitude.

In *The Adoration of the Shepherds*, in the center of the lower half of the panel, the infant Jesus, wrapped in swaddling clothes, is lying in the manger. The Virgin leans slightly forward over Him, gently raising with her right hand the little pillow on which the Child's head is resting, and holding the simple coverlet with her left hand. Crossing his arms, the elderly Joseph behind her devoutly observes the scene with great restraint. A woman kneels on the right of the manger, holding a large brass jug; to the right of her a shepherd leans on his crook, and a young shepherdess and an old shepherd kneel behind. Less prominent is the figure of an old woman praying fervently over the Child, and a young shepherd with tousled hair also leans forward. A dog below the manger lifts its head toward the infant Jesus. The event is taking place in a stable which has rather the looks of a tumbledown barn. Through the large, wide-open doors there is a view to a fortress wall with low, crenelated towers. Above the nativity scene playful angels hover lightly in a resplendent glow.

Rubens represented the Adoration of the Shepherds several times; the first was in 1608 in Italy, for the church of the Oratorian Fathers in Fermo (Fig. 68).[7] The canvas reveals influences by Correggio and,

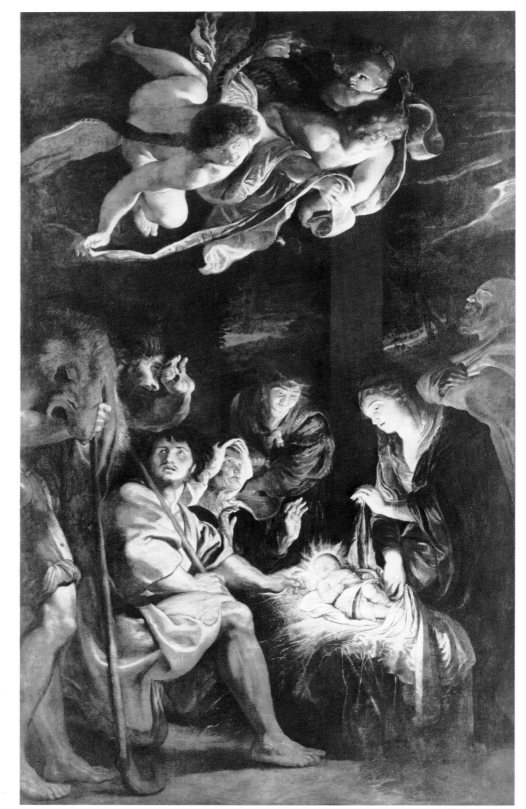

Figure 68
THE ADORATION OF THE
SHEPHERDS
Canvas, 9′10″ × 6′4″
Fermo, Museo Civico

*This work was executed in 1608 for San Filippo, the church of the Oratorian Fathers in Fermo. Rubens took up this composition again about 1609, shortly after his return from Italy, in a picture for the church of St. Paul in Antwerp (Pl. 14).*

in the use of light, of Caravaggio; the composition offers more than one point of comparison with Correggio's celebrated *Holy Night* now in Dresden, which in Rubens' day adorned the church of San Prospero in Reggio Emilia.[8]

Shortly after his return from Italy, Rubens again took up the composition of the Fermo picture in 1608–9, in a large canvas for St. Paul's Church in Antwerp (Plate 14).[9] In this work the handling already shows more strength and freedom. A few years later, the same theme inspired the artist to make a drawing for the engraving that appeared in 1614 in the *Breviarium Romanum* and the *Missale Romanum*, edited by Balthasar Moretus I (Figs. 69, 70).[10] Archival documents tell us that Rubens made his sketches for the illustrations in these liturgical books during the winters of 1612–13 and 1613–14.[11] In this drawing of the *Adoration*, and the engraving made from it, which of course reproduces the image in reverse, many elements recall the two *Adorations* in Fermo and Antwerp. The compositional scheme has remained about the same, although certain figures have been slightly modified. Thus the shepherd who stands in the left foreground in the two paintings has been replaced by a standing shepherdess carrying a large milk-jug on her head. Two male figures replace the kneeling shepherd and the old shepherdess at the left of the manger. The girl wearing the big felt hat remains, her attitude now slightly adapted to the grouping; the figure of the Virgin is almost identical, except for minor modifications, with her pose in the pictures at Fermo and St. Paul's. The angels are omitted from the upper part of the composition, and a dog has been added in the foreground, facing the manger and looking upward at the holy Child with an expression of wonder as great as the shepherds'. In both the drawing and the engraving there is an obvious effort to introduce more movement than there is in either of the two paintings.

When one compares the oil sketch in the Rubens House (Plate 31) with the drawing in the Burchard Collection or, better still, with the engraving for the *Breviarium*, one immediately notices certain points of resemblance: the general disposition of the figures, the attitude of the Virgin, the manner of representing the infant Jesus, the placing of the shepherds grouped around him, and the dog in the foreground. But in the oil sketch the shepherdess replaces the kneeling shepherd; encircling with her left arm a jug of glinting brass, she presents a bowl of milk in her right hand as her offering to the holy Child. Her figure is great and monumental, both in conception and execution. On the right hand side of the oil sketch the dairymaid of the engraving is replaced by a man who is strangely reminiscent of the Correggesque shepherd at the extreme left of the two altarpieces. Angels have returned to the upper part of the oil sketch—fresh, glowing putti instead of the earlier slim, graceful adolescents. And finally, the traces of retouching on Joseph's head show that Rubens' original intention was to pose the figure leaning slightly forward, as in the drawing and the engraving, but in making the oil sketch he has modified this attitude.

131

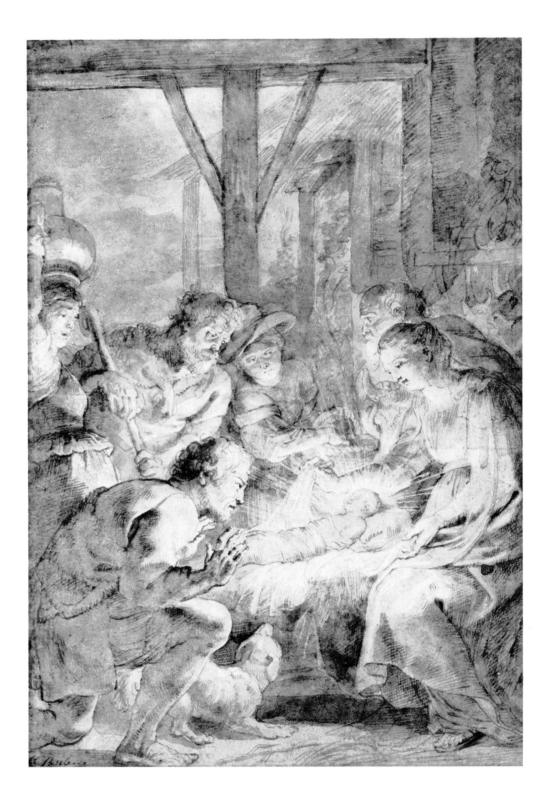

Figure 69
THE ADORATION OF THE
SHEPHERDS
Drawing
Farnham, Collection W. Burchard

*Design for an engraving in the* Breviarium
Romanum, *published in Antwerp in 1614
by Balthasar Moretus I.*

It seems to us that the composition of the oil sketch is derived from that conceived for the *Breviarium* and the *Missale Romanum*. Although richer and more elaborate, it has recourse to certain motifs previously used; it differs in having greater unity and cohesion, and every indication is that it was conceived later than the drawing and the print.

In their turn, certain elements of the oil sketch reappear in versions of the *Adoration of the Shepherds* executed between 1617 and 1620: the

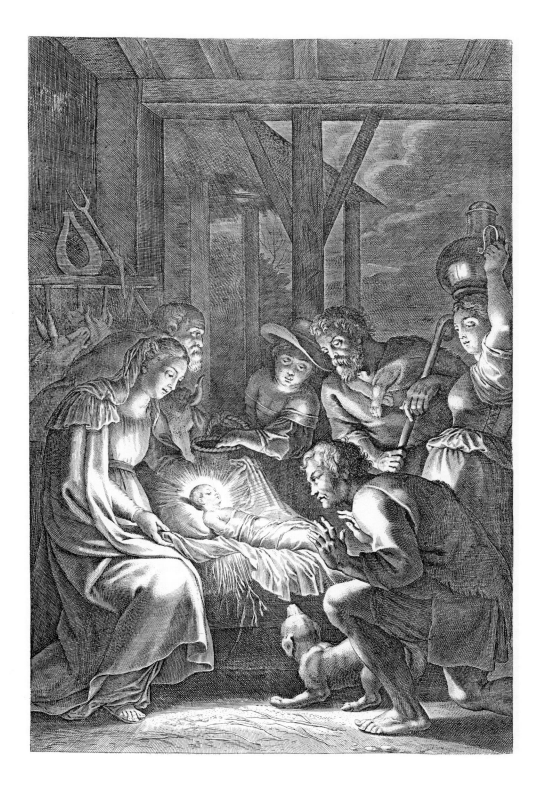

Figure 70
Cornelis Galle, after Rubens
THE ADORATION OF THE
SHEPHERDS
Engraving
Antwerp, Plantin-Moretus Museum

*This engraving is a later version of the original engraving by Theodore Galle in the 1614 Breviarium Romanum.*

panel from the former predella of the high altar of the church of St. John in Malines of 1617–18 (now in Marseilles; Fig. 73);[12] a large painting in the Musée des Beaux-Arts, Rouen;[13] and another *Nativity* painted in 1619 for the Duke Wolfgang Wilhelm von Neuburg, now in the Alte Pinakothek in Munich.[14]  We should also mention a drawing now in the Fondation Custodia (Collection Frits Lugt) in Paris (Fig. 72),[15] probably a design Rubens made for an engraving which

133

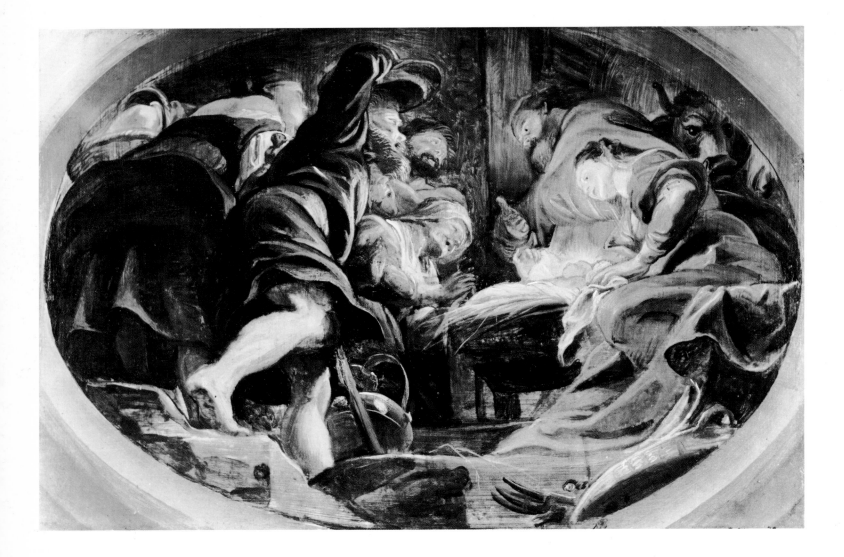

Figure 71
THE ADORATION OF THE
SHEPHERDS
Oil sketch on panel, $12^5/_8 \times 18^3/_4$"
Vienna, Gemäldegalerie, Akademie der
bildenden Künste

*Oil sketch for one of the ceiling paintings in the church of the Jesuits in Antwerp (1620; Pl. 32). The composition is adapted to the oval picture area and to the special perspective that was required for it to be seen from below.*

Plate 32
THE ADORATION OF THE
SHEPHERDS (detail)
Vienna, Gemäldegalerie, Akademie der
bildenden Künste

*An enlarged detail of the oil sketch for one of the thirty-nine ceiling paintings of the Jesuit Church in Antwerp (Fig. 71). It enables us to see how Rubens manages, with a few touches of color, to create forms and to suggest transitions.*

apparently was never executed; the young shepherdess in the foreground is represented in similar fashion to the girl in our oil sketch, except that she is shown in reverse and presents the bowl of milk with her left hand.    Another exemplar of this subject is the magnificent *modello* for one of the ceiling paintings of the church of the Jesuits in Antwerp and the painting itself (1620), both today in Vienna (Plate 32; Fig. 71).[16]    The composition in this case has been modified, however, and adapted to the oval shape of the painting and to the low viewpoint of the beholder.

After comparing these representations of the *Adoration of the Shepherds,* which we see as all elaborations and variants of the same pictorial idea, we conclude that the oil sketch under discussion can be assigned a date between the engraving in the 1614 *Breviarium* and the paintings of 1617 to 1620.

To determine the date of the oil sketch, however, it is also important to compare it with other works by Rubens.    It is immediately striking

134

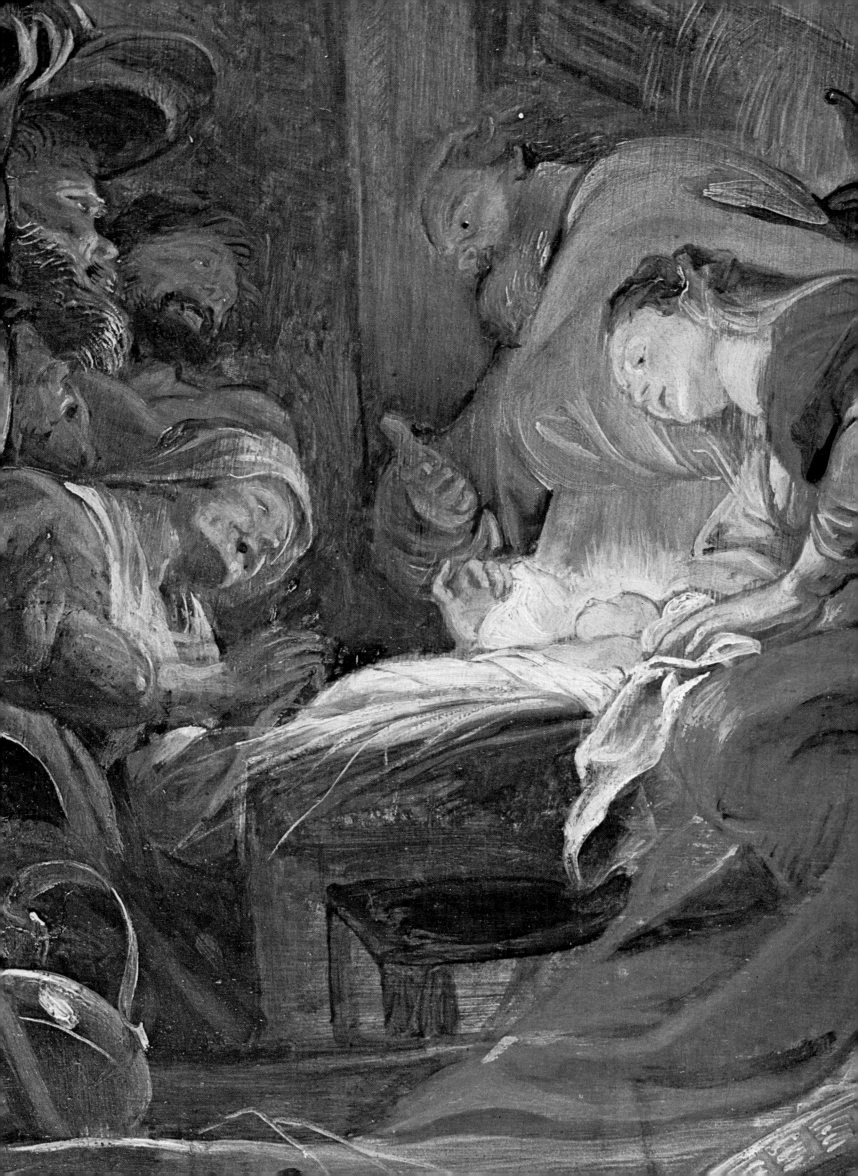

that the figure types are different from those in both the Fermo and Antwerp altarpieces, and in the drawing and the print. In the Rubens House *Adoration* one of the finest figures is certainly the shepherdess with the jug, in the right foreground. She reappears as a peasant woman carrying a basket of fruit on her head in the famous landscape *The Dairy Farm at Laeken* (Fig. 66);[17] we recognize her also as the woman kneeling with a child in the foreground of *The Meeting of Jacob and Esau* in the Alte Pinakothek, Munich,[18] and she recalls Diana in *The Return of Diana from the Hunt*, in the Gemäldegalerie, Dresden;[19] we think we can see her too in the figure at the extreme right of the painting *Lot and His Daughters Leaving Sodom*, in the John and Mable Ringling Museum of Art, Sarasota,[20] and as a shepherdess in the predella panel in Marseilles (Fig. 73), from the high altar in St. John's church in Malines.[21] In *The Adoration of the Magi* (1617–19), the major painting of that same altar (Plate 24), the figure of the Virgin has great affinity with that in the oil sketch we are discussing here.[22]

The oil sketch offers us the opportunity to make a final comparison of the figures it contains: the old woman in the oil sketch who bends over the infant Jesus in an attitude of devotion appears in *The Daughters of Cecrops* in the Liechtenstein Collection, Vaduz,[23] and in the *Drunken Silenus* in the Alte Pinakothek, Munich;[24] all of these pictures can be dated 1615–19. But other figures in the Rubens House *Adoration of the Shepherds* recall those in other works of about that time, which leads us to believe that the sketch was painted in the years 1615 to 1619, a conclusion in no way contradicted by its stylistic characteristics.

At first sight we have the impression that the oil sketch was painted at once, with no hesitation, with no laborious preliminaries, and in one outpouring, with that assurance so typical of Rubens' style. The few traces of repainting around Joseph's head and in a few other places are small immediate corrections, made in the process of execution. In our opinion this indicates that the picture cannot be the work either of an assistant or of a painstaking copyist. Besides, who in the master's circle could give, for example, such transparency to the arm of the milkmaid in the foreground, and catch at the same time the yellowish reflection from the brass jug—that tender gleam that is so distinctive of Rubens' way of working? Who but Rubens could have placed his accents with a hand so swift, light, and sure, accents made with little touches of white, pink, and yellow by which he gives relief to certain details? All that is so plainly Rubens-like that we have the feeling that the work itself can hardly proclaim its author more loudly.

The first impression that we receive from a work of art is often the most important one. The study of the composition and figures, and of the stylistic and historical elements, can only confirm this feeling by placing it on a rational basis. There is nothing more to do but find proof for this first impression, and this is like discovering in it a group of stylistic features which have become fixed in our memory by looking at other works by the artist. We recognize all these features like those of a friend's face, with intense pleasure.

Figure 72
THE ADORATION OF THE SHEPHERDS
Drawing
Paris, Fondation Custodia (Collection Frits Lugt)

*The young shepherdess represented here with a bowl of milk, is analogous to the girl holding a brass jug in the Rubens House sketch (Pl. 31), except that her image is reversed.*

136

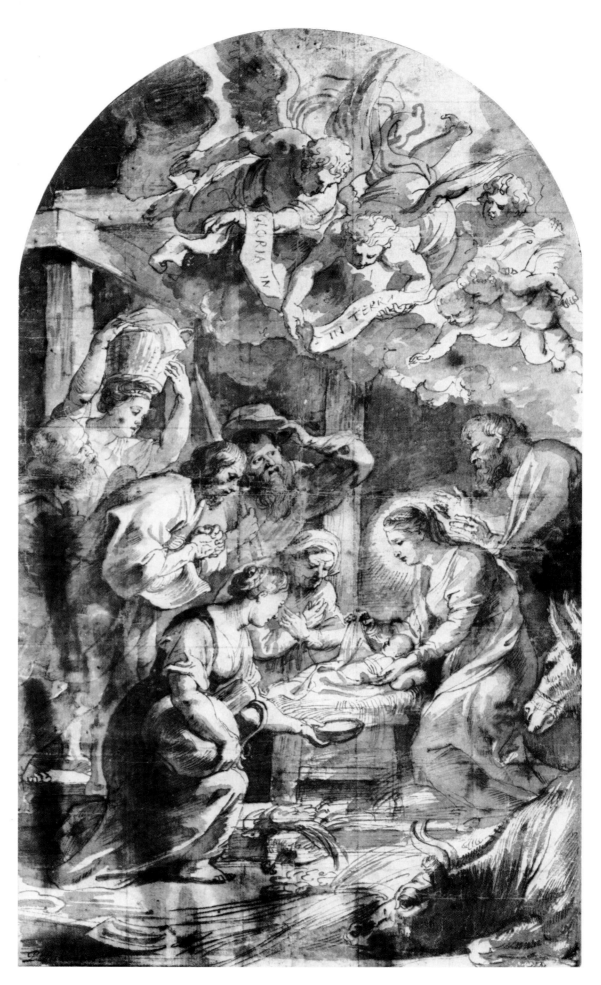

137

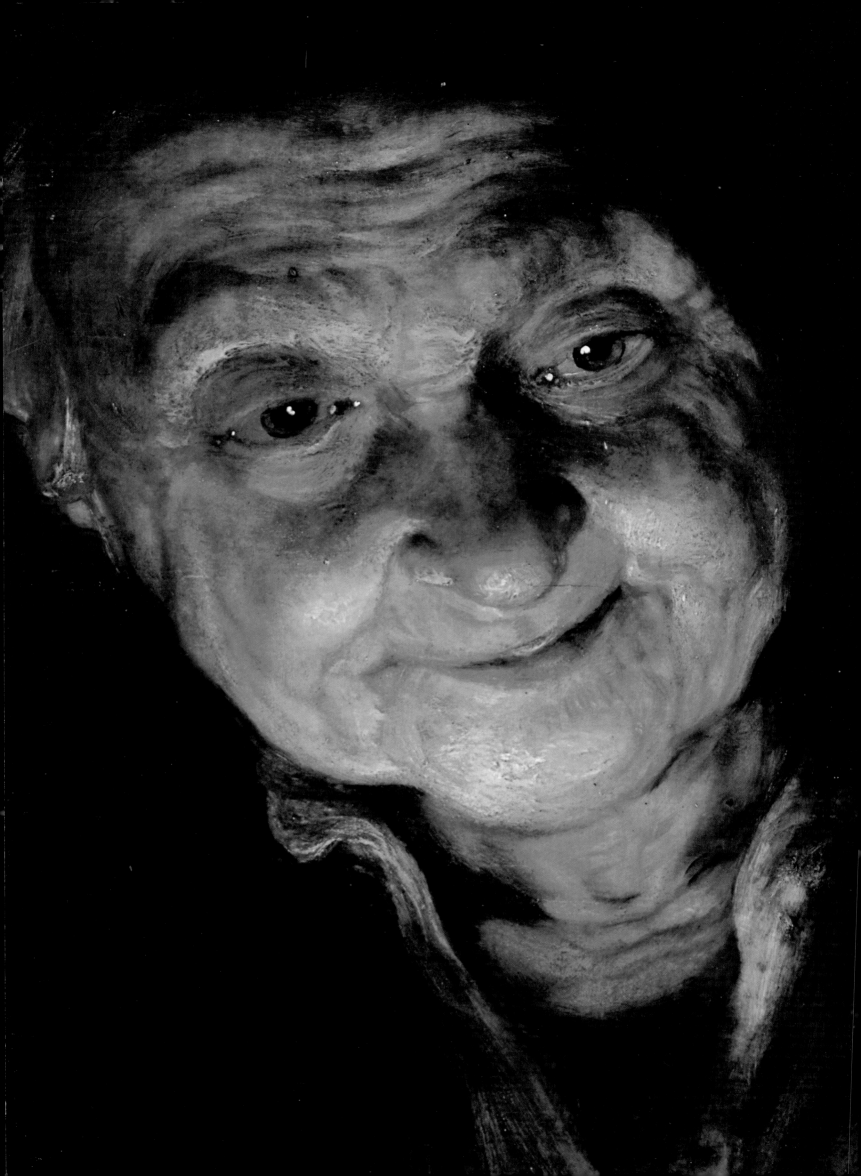

We know of no large picture by Rubens for which the Rubens House oil sketch could have served as a model. Was such a work destroyed, or lost over the centuries, as happened with other creations by him? Or was it never realized, the commission never executed for one or another reason? We do not know. We only know that in the eighteenth century the composition of the sketch was copied in oils by Fragonard,[25] that artist who greatly admired Rubens and copied other works by him. Nevertheless our sketch does seem to have been conceived as a *modello* for a picture of larger dimensions; the oil sketches that Rubens made for engravers were more detailed in execution, with indications of the hatching for reproduction. *The Adoration of the Shepherds* does not seem to belong to this type—and, moreover, no print based on this composition is known; therefore the oil sketch was in all probability painted to give a client an idea of the large-scale composition which the artist had in mind to execute. We should add that in the small oil sketch the composition is clearly indicated, though it is not complete in every detail and the colors in some places are only suggested.

Like most of Rubens' oil sketches, *The Adoration of the Shepherds* is painted on a white ground brushed over with a thin layer of ocher. The latter remains visible here and there. The elements of the composition are drawn with a very fine brush dipped in brown paint. Some figures are indicated only by these contours: the heads of Joseph, the young shepherd, and the old woman. Elsewhere the contours have disappeared under the paint, and it may be that certain parts were executed directly, in full color.

Here again we admire Rubens' great mastery of composition. As always, this is seen in the perfect balance that yet does not give the impression—as it so often does with, for example, Raphael—that the artist was following a deliberate plan. The infant Jesus occupies the center of the composition though his place is not exactly in the middle of the panel. Of the figures grouped around the manger, the Virgin and Joseph on the left and the milkmaid and the shepherd on the right are all in profile; the figures between these groups are in full-face or three-quarters, according to their positions relative to the manger. The pose of the Virgin, slightly leaning forward, is echoed in that of the kneeling milkmaid; the pose of Joseph is counterbalanced by the standing shepherd at the other side. The composition of the figures is linked by two imaginary diagonals. The first one, starting from the lower left-hand corner, crosses the Virgin's right leg and hand, and passes over the heads of the kneeling shepherd, the shepherdess, and the standing shepherd, ending at the right side of the panel. The second starts from the lower right-hand corner, goes over the heads of the kneeling old woman and of the Virgin and Joseph, and ends at the left side of the panel at about the level of the first diagonal. One notices how the position of the large brass jug accentuates the second diagonal. But it is striking—and typical of Rubens' style—that he does not follow his scheme rigidly, but uses it with spontaneity and flexibility. We should also notice that the line

139

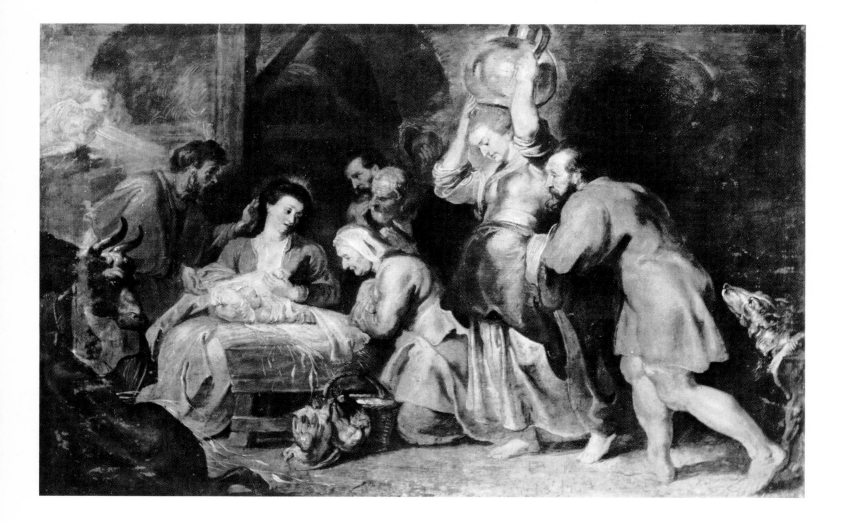

of the far horizon corresponds to the placing of Jesus' body, and that the artist has shifted the group of angels slightly toward the left in compensation for any slight heaviness of the right side of the composition. Making no concessions to a theoretical system and without laboring his points, Rubens creates a composition of perfect unity with a lively hand, as if it were child's play.

Rubens takes liberties with the color from time to time, yet he uses it with the same sense of balance and harmony. The dark areas in the garments of Mary and Joseph are repeated in value (although in different colors) in the gray-blue dress of the milkmaid and the gray-green coat of the standing shepherd. The white of the milkmaid's apron answers the white patch on the upper arm and shoulder of the Virgin. The pink, white, and yellowish tints of the infant Christ find their echo in the clear colors of the face and breast of the young standing shepherdess. One could point to a number of other "parallels" in this work that support the balance of colors.

And in this small panel Rubens is once again the great master of chiaroscuro. His is not the manner of Caravaggio, who contrives strongly accentuated contrasts, nor of Rembrandt, who aims at an intense expressiveness by mysterious alternations of light and dark. He follows a personal conception which does justice to all values. In the *Adoration of the Shepherds* the color has no less warmth than that in Rubens' other luminous works. From the infant Jesus there radiates a golden light which makes all the figures surrounding the manger loom out of the darkness as if by magic, and gives them light and color. This source of light in the center of the picture has a subdued echo in the brightness of the sky above the horizon, and another, more tender, in the rosy glow of the putti near the upper edge of the scene. And everywhere are seen these velvety transitions from one tone to another, from light to shadow.

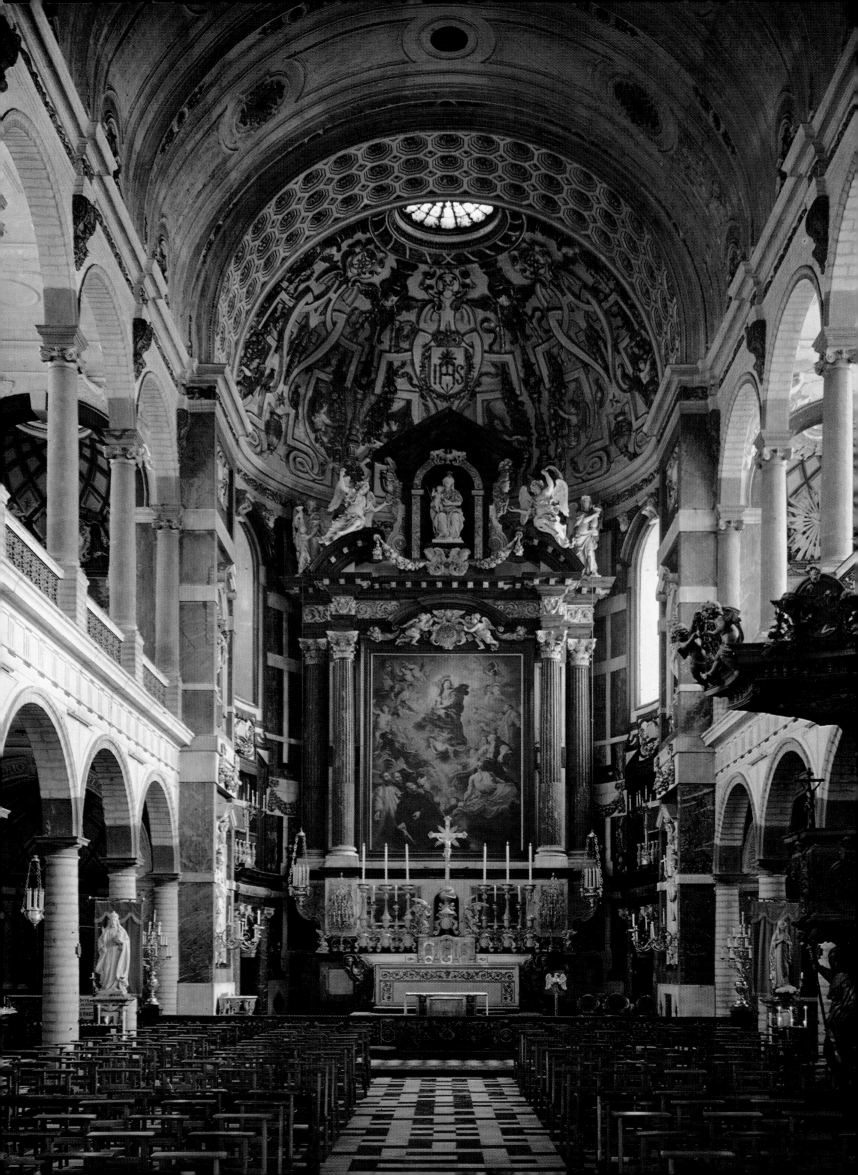

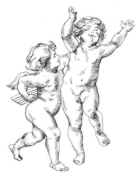

# CHAPTER 7

Rubens and the Church of the Jesuits
in Antwerp

On Sunday, September 12, 1621, a church that occupies an incomparable place in the history of the architecture of the Southern Netherlands was consecrated with great pomp and ceremony. Forming part of the Residence of the Jesuits, the church was dedicated to St. Ignatius, and was the first church in the world to have the founder of that order as its patron saint. In 1773, when the religious community was abolished, it became a parish church known as St. Charles Borromeo (Plate 34; Fig 79).

The origin of the church is closely connected with the history of the Antwerp Jesuits. The Jesuit order arrived in the Metropolis in 1562, but had to wait until 1585 before it had the strength to establish itself solidly there. The conventual community continuously developed after that time, and during the reign of the Archduke Albert and his wife the Infanta Isabella it became one of the principal centers of intellectual and scientific life in the Spanish Netherlands.[1] The idea was then born of building a large church to replace the former private chapel near the Korte Nieuwstraat, beside the College of the Jesuits—the future Residence of the Belgo-Flemish province in the Company. This church was to look so impressive that it would appear as the "symbol of triumphant Catholicism in Antwerp in the first half of the seventeenth century."[2] In 1613 the first plans were sent to Rome for the approval of the general of the order, but this superior expressed certain objections and new plans had to be submitted several times. Some of these are preserved in the Bibliothèque Nationale in Paris;[3] they tell us that a circular structure crowned with a huge dome was first considered, somewhat in the style of the pilgrimage church of Our Lady at Montaigu (Scherpenheuvel).[4] In due time a rectangular plan was adopted, and Rome finally accepted a relatively simple project which recalls in some ways the colonnaded basilicas of the Early Christian era.[5]

Meanwhile Father François Aguilon, rector of the Jesuit College, had already started to raise funds for the building, and had ordered blocks of marble from Italy. On April 15, 1615, the first stone was laid, although the authorization to build had still not arrived in Antwerp. But shortly thereafter it was possible to begin the construction with might and

Plate 34
INTERIOR OF THE ANTWERP JE-
SUIT CHURCH, NOW ST. CHARLES
BORROMEO

*With the exception of the richly decorated niche of the high altar, which escaped the fire of 1718, the interior decoration of this church now presents only a pale shadow of the former splendor of the "marble temple." The arcades were replaced after the fire by columns of white and blue stone. The painting on the altar is by Cornelis Schut.*

143

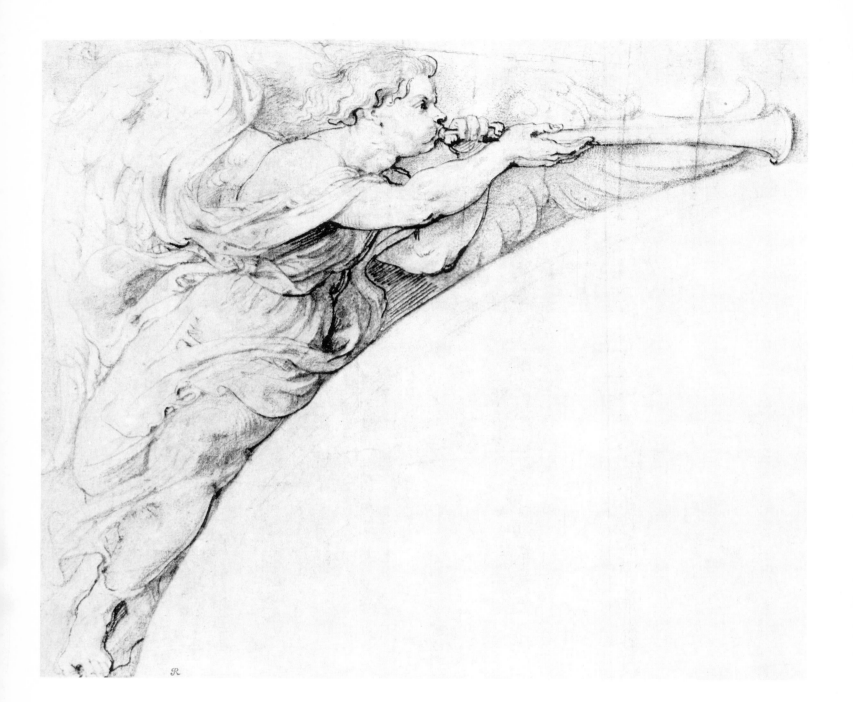

Figures 74, 75
TWO ANGELS BLOWING TRUMPETS
Drawings, $9^5/_8'' \times 11^1/_4''$ and
$9^7/_8'' \times 10^3/_4''$
New York, The Pierpont Morgan Library

*Designs for the spandrel reliefs at right and left above the arch of the main portal of the church.*

Figure 76
ARCH OF MAIN PORTAL, ANTWERP
JESUIT CHURCH,
NOW ST. CHARLES BORROMEO

*The trumpeting angels in the spandrels above the arch of the portal were probably carved by Hans van Mildert, after designs by Rubens.*

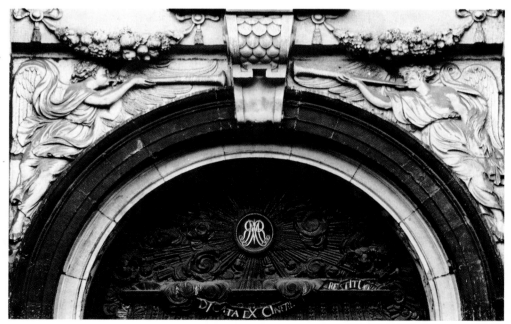

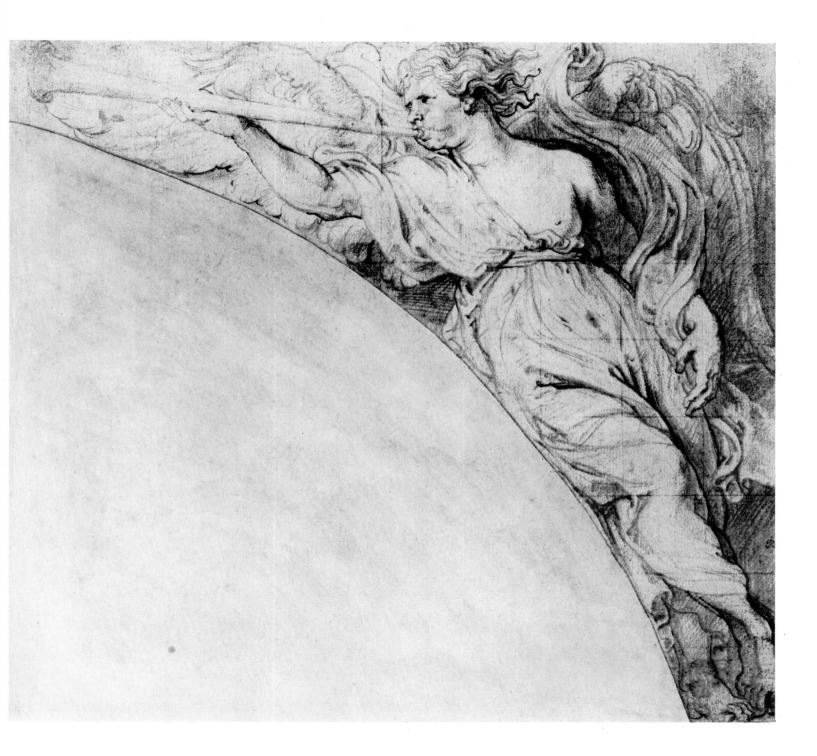

main. The church was finished six years later, in 1621, except for the two projecting side chapels, which were not part of the initial plan and were only added in 1622 and from 1625 onward, respectively.

The new church immediately made a deep impression on the contemporary public. Foreigners in accounts of their travels, Antwerp citizens in their descriptions, all agreed in celebrating the "marble temple." In his *Diary* John Evelyn praises it as a sumptuous, splendid, and glorious building inside and out.[6] Another author ends his description by remarking that these Jesuits truly possess their heaven

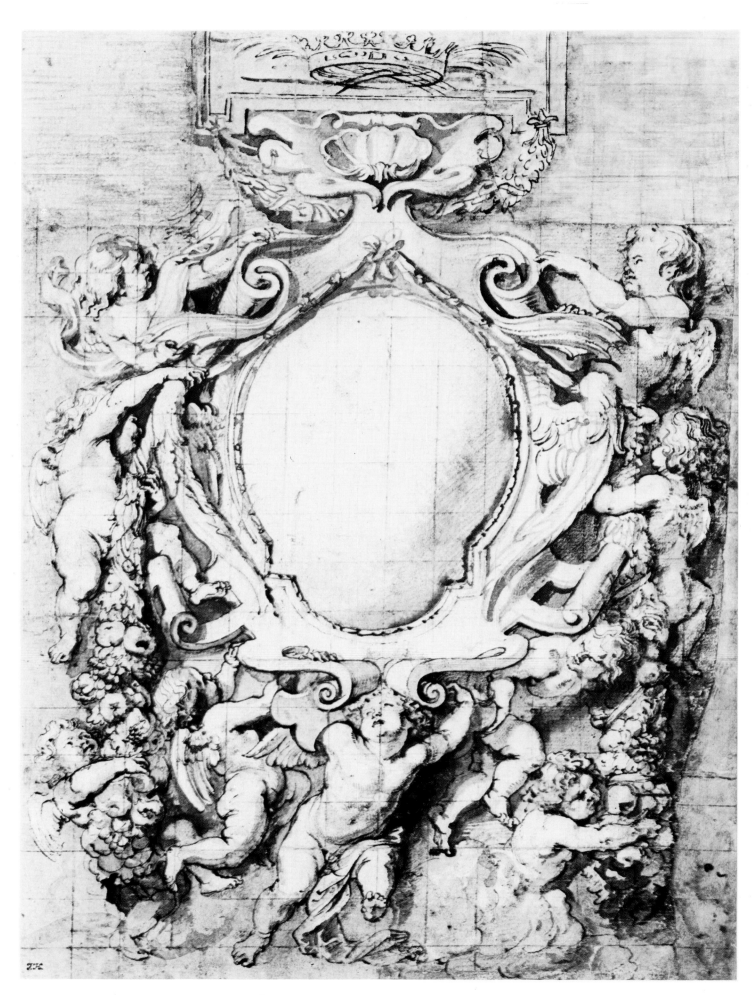

146

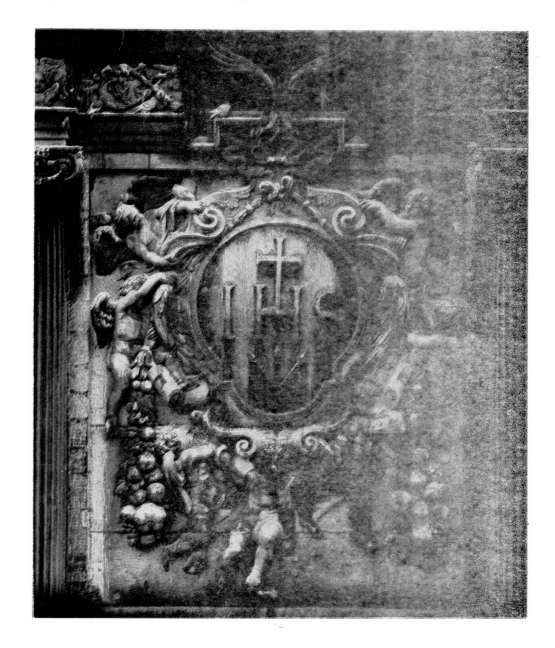

Figure 78

CARTOUCHE OVER MAIN PORTAL, ANTWERP JESUIT CHURCH

*This relief with the monogram of the Jesuit Order in the center was probably executed by Hans van Mildert after a design by Rubens.*

◀ Figure 77

CARTOUCHE SUPPORTED BY AN-GELS
Drawing
London, British Museum

*Design for the medallion in relief above the main entrance of the church (Fig. 78).*

on earth.[7] This effect certainly corresponded to the intentions of the Jesuit Fathers, who, in the spirit of the Counter-Reformation, wanted to make the church a reflection of the Heavenly Jerusalem. In this they flatly opposed the Calvinists, who maintained an extreme sobriety in their churches.

The splendor that so charmed visitors was, alas, largely destroyed on July 18, 1718, when fire ravaged the nave and the side aisles of the church. Jan Pieter van Baurscheit the Elder (1669–1728) immediately assumed direction of the reconstruction work and completed it in 1719, although he could not use materials as rich as those which had served a century earlier.[8] Today, despite the effects of time, the impressive façade, choir, and side chapels, which escaped destruction, still allow us to judge the richness of the original materials.

147

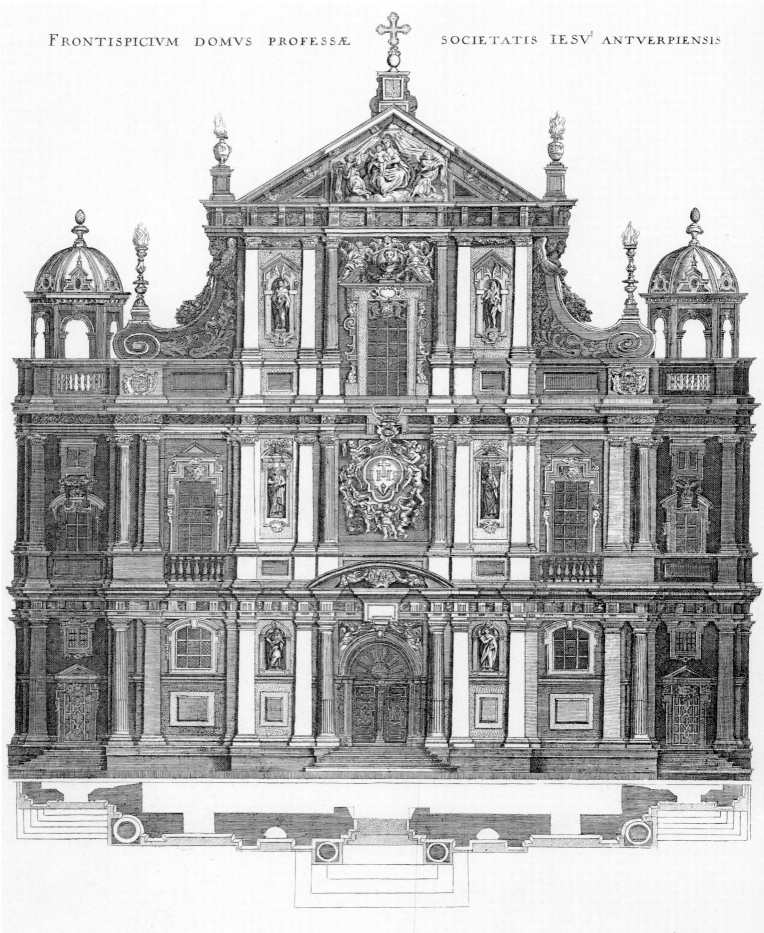

Figure 79
Jan de Labaer
THE FAÇADE OF THE ANTWERP JE-
SUIT CHURCH
Engraving
Antwerp, Stedelijk Prentenkabinet

*This church, today the church of St. Charles
Borromeo, was the first Jesuit church to be
dedicated to Ignatius of Loyola, the founder
of the order, before his canonization. The
exuberant sculptured decoration of the
façade, completed in 1621, is typically Baroque. Engraved about 1650.*

Figure 80
THE TOWER OF THE ANTWERP JE-
SUIT CHURCH

*One of the most charming Baroque towers
in the Southern Netherlands. It is adorned
with balustrades, columns, pilasters, and
sculptured elements, the architecture having
an outstanding degree of plasticity.*

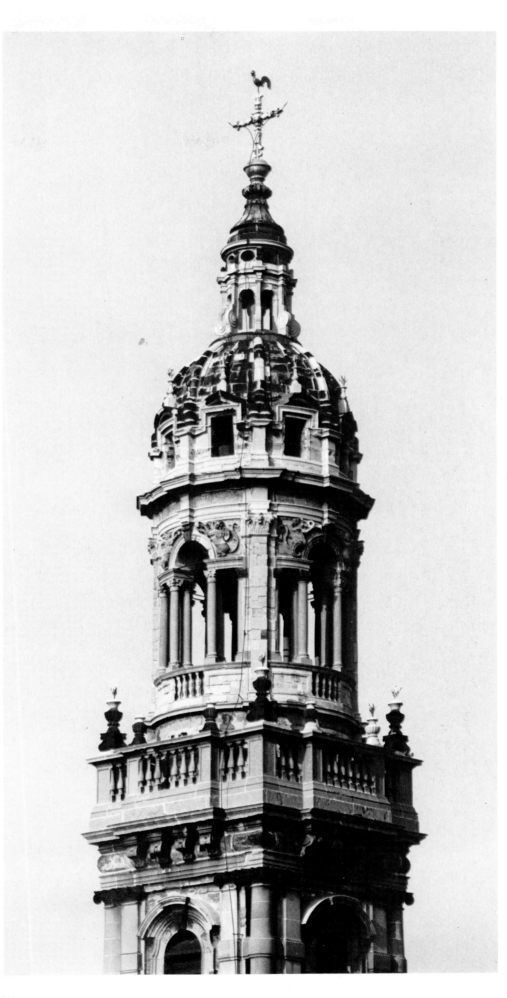

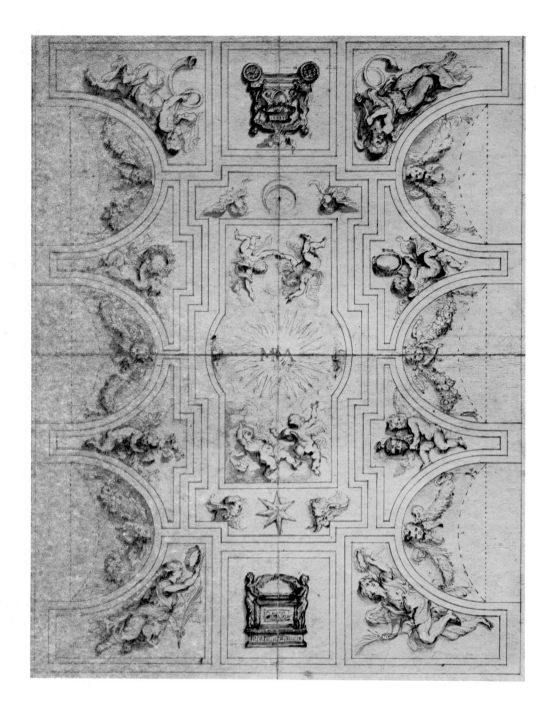

On entering the church, the visitor's eye is drawn to the arcades
with semicircular arches, resting on slender columns, that are seen in
the nave and in the galleries above the side aisles.   They lead the visitor
toward the conical, rather shallow choir, containing a monumental
portico-altar (Plate 34).   The Antwerp Jesuits certainly intended that
the altar should predominate, to remind the faithful that the Eucharist
represents an essential article of faith in the Roman Catholic
doctrine.   The choir is covered by a shell-shaped vault adorned with
stucco or carved plaster.   The barrel vault over the nave harmonizes
happily with the semicircles of the choir and the arcades; side aisles

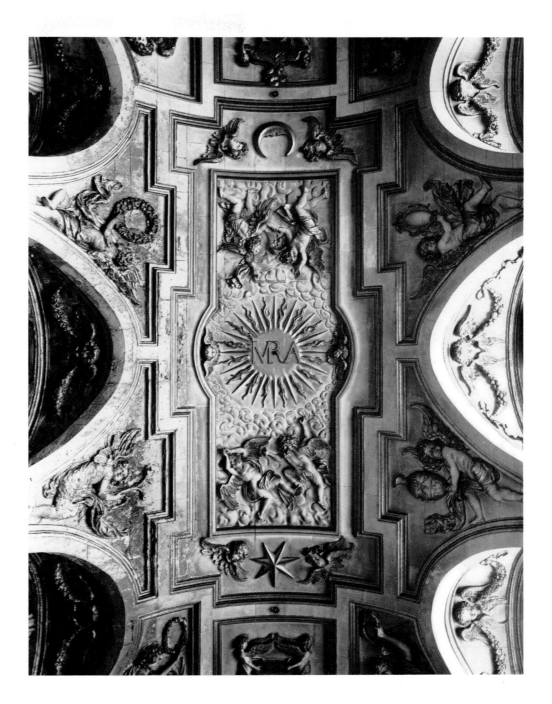

Figure 82
CEILING OF LADY CHAPEL;
ANTWERP JESUIT CHURCH

*The sculptural decoration was done after Rubens' design. Symbols of the Virgin make up the main part of the decoration.*

and galleries, however, have flat ceilings. Originally these were decorated with paintings executed in Rubens' workshop after sketches by the master; these canvases—there were thirty-nine—all burned in the fire of 1718.[9]

Apart from the richly ornamented choir, the inside of the church today has otherwise a rather sober appearance; this sobriety is in contrast with the ostentation of the west façade, an almost independent architectural and plastic unit that looks as if it had been attached to the building. The façade is articulated in three tiers: the lower section corresponds to the nave arcade, the middle to the gallery over

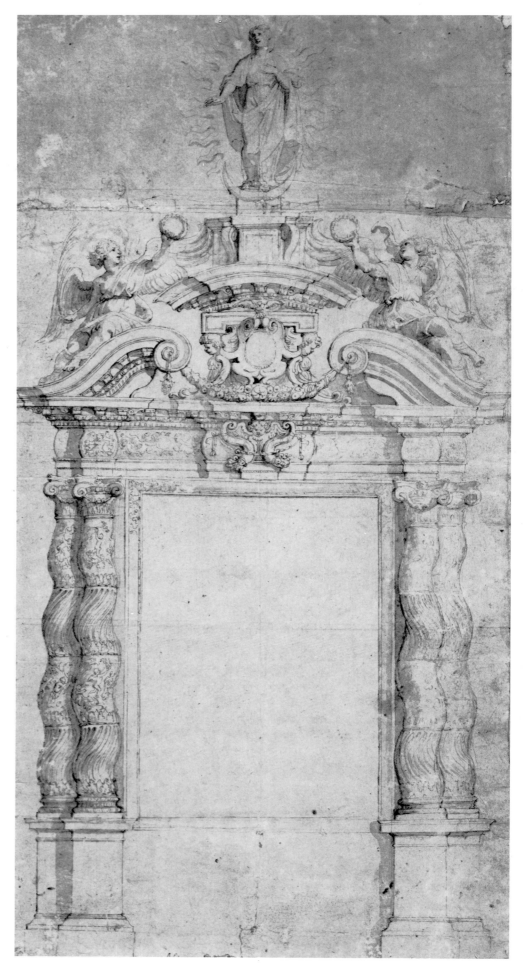

Figure 83
DESIGN FOR THE HIGH ALTAR,
ANTWERP JESUIT CHURCH
Drawing
Vienna, Graphische Sammlung Alber-
tina

*This is probably one of the first ideas for
the high altar. Twisted columns were originally planned, and the top was also modified
subsequently. The angels on the volutes correspond more or less to those represented in
this drawing. The rectangular shape of the
moldings around the picture was retained in
the final execution of the altar.*

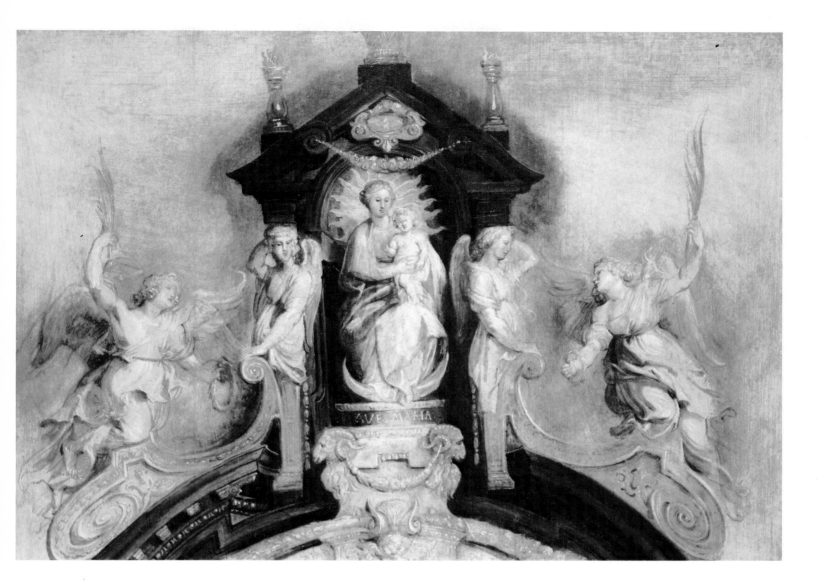

Figure 84
DESIGN FOR THE UPPER PART OF
THE HIGH ALTAR, ANTWERP JE-
SUIT CHURCH
Oil sketch on panel, $17^3/_8'' \times 25^1/_2''$
London, Private Collection

*Here one can observe various elements which
appear almost unaltered in the final execution. The two herms flanking the niche were
omitted, and the upper part of the frame
planned for the altarpieces is here still
arched.*

the side aisles, and the upper tier, for the most part, to the nave
vault. An impressive triangular pediment, rising higher than the top
of the building, crowns the central part of the façade. Although
crossed by horizontal elements, this central section constitutes a unit:
a large central bay flanked by two narrower bays. Above, elegant
volutes unite this central part on both sides with the lateral sections. Set slightly back from the elevation of the façade but nonetheless integrated with it are two corner turrets surmounted by small
domes of stone. Columns, pilasters, and entablatures mark the different parts of this majestic façade, but not to be omitted is its particularly
exuberant sculptural ornamentation, so typical of the Baroque. Here
sound the fanfares, honoring the entrance of the new style in the
Netherlands!

The tall, graceful tower that rises above the choir provided another
innovation. Leurs describes it well: "In spite of its modest dimensions, the tower of St. Charles is the most beautiful Baroque tower

153

in Flanders, and one of the finest in the world. Its architect demonstrates a remarkable plastic sense. It is charmingly crowned: the projections of the balustrade in the center of each side herald the cylindrical lantern laced with 'Venetian' openings and covered with an elegant dome of stone. The latter, by its slightly elliptical profile, by the beautiful lantern which crowns it, is the incarnation of refined dynamics."[10] And the author writes in conclusion that this tower could only have sprung from the indications of a brilliant master, "... who could hardly have been anyone else than Rubens."[11]

This phrase leads us to a most controversial question: who was the architect of the church of the Jesuits in Antwerp? In the eighteenth century and even later, Rubens was taken to be the author of the "marble temple." When the numerous plans, for the most part stored in the church archives, began to be studied at the beginning of this century, it was concluded that two Jesuits had been the authors. Indeed the rector, François Aguilon, seems himself to have conceived the general design, and perhaps even the architectural structure of the whole. On his death, in 1617, Brother Pieter Huyssens took over the direction of the proceedings and worked on the completion of the plans. It was suggested that Rubens' participation must have been very limited.

Since then, however, a certain number of drawings by Rubens have been found which show clearly that he did play an important part at least in the sculptural ornamentation of the church. There are two drawings for the trumpeting angels (Figs. 74, 75) in the spandrels above the central portal of the west façade (Fig. 76).[12] Another sheet (Fig. 77) bears a drawing manifestly for the shield with the monogram of Christ, surrounded by angels, in the section above this door (Fig. 78).[13] But Rubens' drawings are not limited to the façade decorations. Burchard has recognized in a drawing in Vienna (Fig. 83) a preliminary sketch for the high altar inside the church of the Jesuits;[14] this design was very much modified, however, when the altar was actually executed. Rubens made another oil sketch (Fig. 84) for the sculpture which crowns the altar;[15] the execution was given to Hans van Mildert, a friend of the painter. Probably this same artist was commissioned to decorate the main façade of the church[16] with statues and reliefs.

As we stated above, the projecting side chapels were not added until 1622 and 1625; Rubens made a drawing (Fig. 81) for the stucco decoration of the vault in the south chapel dedicated to the Virgin (Fig. 82).[17] Having divided the page into squares and angles, using compass and ruler, the artist decorated the central section with the monogram of Mary, and all around it he drew some playful angels, heads of winged putti, garlands, and symbols of the Virgin.

These examples of Rubens' share in the sculptural decoration of the church of the Jesuits could be multiplied. There is no doubt that a fair number of decorative motifs, both inside and outside the church, came from his fertile imagination. It is sufficient proof to mention the drawing in the Burchard Collection of a relief for the archivolt of the main entrance of the church, and that of an angel bearing a torch (Fig. 92), intended for a sculpture on the high altar, now in the Kupferstichkabinett in the Dahlem Museum, Berlin.[18]

It is less easy to determine whether Rubens also inspired the actual architecture of the building. Let us remember, however, that he had a close friendship with Aguilon, and drew the frontispieces and illustrations for the latter's books on optics.[19] It should not, therefore, be ruled out in any way that Aguilon discussed his plans with the painter, nor that he listened to the advice he received. Neither Aguilon nor his collaborator and successor, Huyssens, had ever visited Italy, and thus they had not seen the late Renaissance or early Baroque churches which nonetheless provided the inspiration for the Antwerp church of the Jesuits. Rubens, on the other hand, had spent eight years on the Italian peninsula and is known to have been interested in architecture. The question is open whether the church of the Jesuits, which in certain respects goes beyond its Italian models in the development of Baroque art, would have had this sumptuous grandeur, this decorative and plastic magnificence that assures its unique place in the history of Flemish architecture, without the collaboration of Rubens.

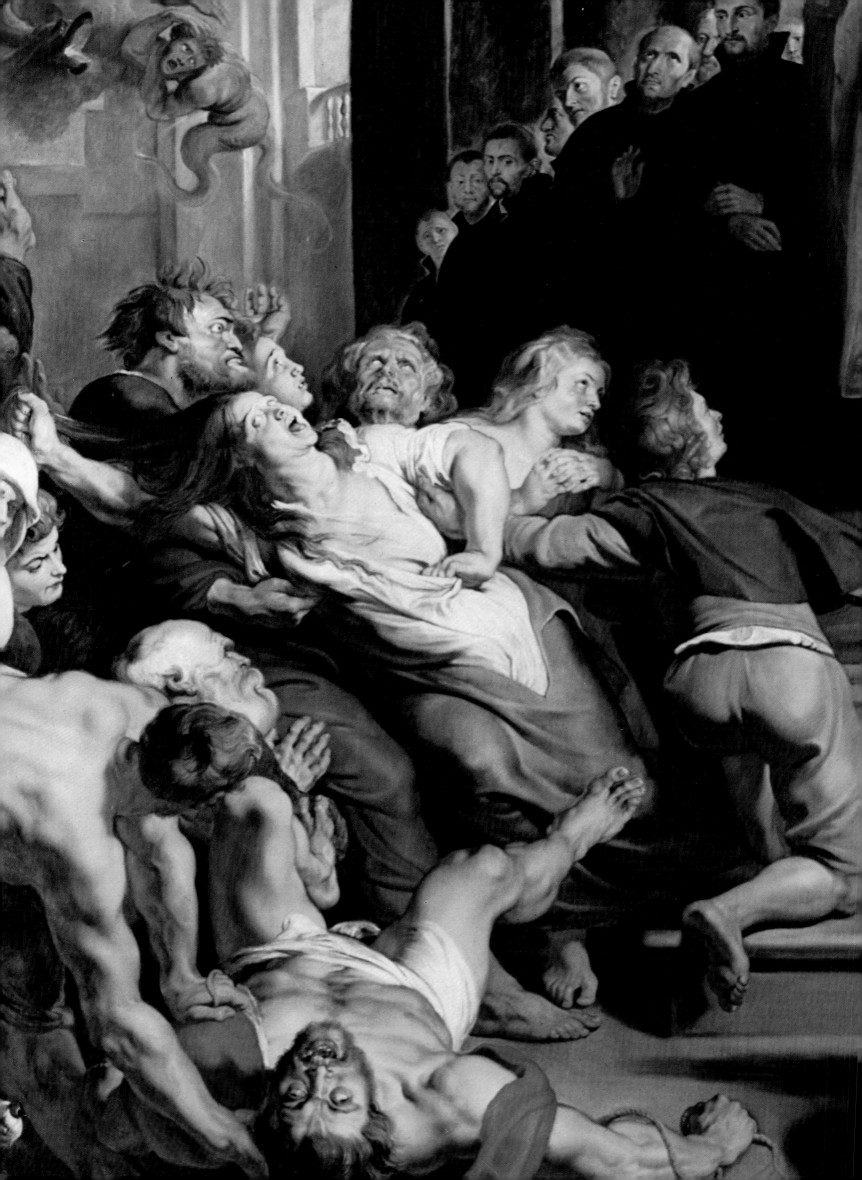

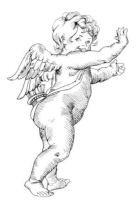

CHAPTER 8

# The Date of Two Pictures for the High Altar of the Church of the Jesuits in Antwerp

and Some Notes on Hans van Mildert

No fewer than four pictures were painted during the seventeenth century for the high altar of the church of the Jesuits in Antwerp; they were displayed there in turn, according to the various liturgical festivals. Rubens painted two of these pictures, *The Miracles of St. Ignatius of Loyola* (Fig. 85) and *The Miracles of St. Francis Xavier* (Fig. 88).[1] The other two were produced by two eminent artists in Rubens' circle: Cornelis Schut, whose *Coronation of the Virgin* can be considered one of his major works,[2] and Gerhard Seghers, whose *Descent from the Cross* recalls Rubens' triptych of the same subject in the Antwerp Cathedral.[3] The latter two pictures have never left the Jesuit Church, and continue up to this day to be exhibited alternately on the high altar of what is now the church of St. Charles Borromeo.[4] The two paintings by Rubens, however, were transferred to Austria in 1776, three years after the Society of Jesus was abolished in the Southern Netherlands. Today they are in the Kunsthistorisches Museum of Vienna,[5] as are the *modelli* for them (Plates 36, 37). These two oil sketches were also originally in the Antwerp church of the Jesuits, and were taken to Vienna together with the two large pictures.[6]

It is an interesting fact that Rubens received the commission for the two pictures even before Ignatius of Loyola and Francis Xavier had acceded to the honors of the altar.[7] Although Ignatius was beatified in 1609, Francis Xavier did not receive this favor until October 25, 1619[8]—by which time *The Miracles of St. Francis Xavier* was doubtless already finished. Thus these works for the world's first church dedicated to Ignatius of Loyola were planned even before the Roman Church had canonized him![9] Only on March 12, 1622, some six months after the inauguration of the "marble temple," did Ignatius and Francis Xavier take their places among the saints of the Church.[10]

We will not make here an exhaustive study of these works by Rubens. They are of great interest, notably from the iconographic point of view, but we propose to limit ourselves to certain considerations of their date, and to make use of a document that has hitherto been unexploited. This archival document will also furnish us with

Plate 35
THE MIRACLES OF ST. IGNATIUS
OF LOYOLA (detail, Fig. 85)
Vienna, Gemäldegalerie, Kunsthistorisches Museum

*Rubens' dramatic force is particularly evident in this detail of one of the two pictures that he painted for the high altar of the Antwerp Jesuit Church. It shows the founder of the order curing the possessed.*

157

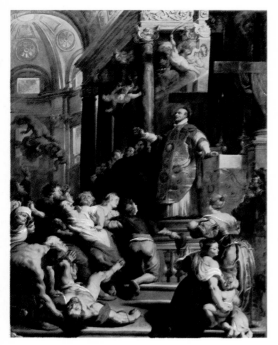

Figure 85
THE MIRACLES OF ST. IGNATIUS
OF LOYOLA
Canvas, 17'6½" × 12'11½"
Vienna, Gemäldegalerie, Kunsthisto-
risches Museum

*The first of the two large canvases which
alternately decorated the high altar of the
Antwerp Jesuit Church. Both had probably already been completed in 1618.*

Plate 36
THE MIRACLES OF ST. IGNATIUS
OF LOYOLA
Oil sketch on panel, 41³/₄" × 29¹/₈"
Vienna, Gemäldegalerie, Kunsthisto-
risches Museum

*This sketch for one of the large pictures
which alternately decorated the high altar
of the church of the Jesuits in Antwerp was
no doubt already executed in 1616–17, long
before the church was consecrated on September 12, 1621.*

some data on the sculptor who, in all probability, produced the high altar upon which the pictures by Rubens, Schut, and Seghers were seen alternatively for more than a century and a half.

Until now, two manuscript sources have been available for establishing the *terminus ad quem* of the original date of Rubens' altarpieces. First is the contract, drawn up on March 29, 1620, between Rubens and Father Jacobus Tirinus, provost of the Residence of the Antwerp Jesuits; the painter undertakes to deliver no fewer than thirty-nine ceiling pictures for the church. He was to receive 7,000 florins on delivery of these, and a further 3,000 florins for "two large pictures of our Holy Fathers Ignatius and Xavier, already completed by the said Mr. Rubens for the said church."[11]

On the basis of this text, Rooses initially asserted that the two pictures had been painted in 1619–20, and were complete in every respect by March 1620.[12] He later revised this opinion, proposing to date the pictures within 1618.[13] For this he relied on a second manuscript, namely, a letter by Rubens on January 23, 1619, addressed to Pieter van Veen in The Hague.[14] This letter is a follow-up to a previous one to the same correspondent on January 4, 1619, in which Rubens solicits Van Veen to obtain for him a privilege from the States General to distribute engravings after his compositions.[15] Pieter van Veen's reply is now lost, but presumably he promised to take the necessary steps, for Rubens furnished more information in his letter of January 23, including a list of copperplates already engraved and of others in preparation. In this list occur successively "A piece with the deeds of Ignatius" and "Another of Xavier,"[16] referring without any doubt to engravings after the two altarpieces in question. Rooses concluded that the pictures were already finished in early January, when Rubens was writing, and that therefore they had been painted in 1618.[17]

Whereas some art historians have neglected to take notice of Rooses' revision of the date,[18] others, such as Evers,[19] Van Puyvelde,[20] Gerson,[21] and finally Burchard and d'Hulst[22] have referred to Rubens' letter of January 23, 1619, and concluded from it that the pictures were either completed by that date or sufficiently advanced for Rubens to be thinking of having his compositions engraved. One author, Lewine, has proposed to date the pictures 1615–18 on the basis of stylistic criticism.[23] He supported his opinion on an oral communication from Burchard, quoted by Gerson, according to which the oil sketches for the pictures had been made even earlier, namely, about 1614–16;[24] he draws our attention particularly to the resemblance of the kneeling young man seen from the back in the center foreground of *The Miracles of St. Ignatius of Loyola* with a male figure in Rubens' *The Continence of Scipio*, a work now lost, but known through an engraving by Schelte à Bolswert.[25] Preliminary drawings for the Scipio composition have been dated stylistically by Held about 1615–17.[26] Although so early a date cannot be totally excluded for Rubens' two altarpieces, Lewine's arguments do not seem convincing to us. One must not forget that Rubens more than once reused motifs he had devised several years earlier, and that the affinity noted by this author

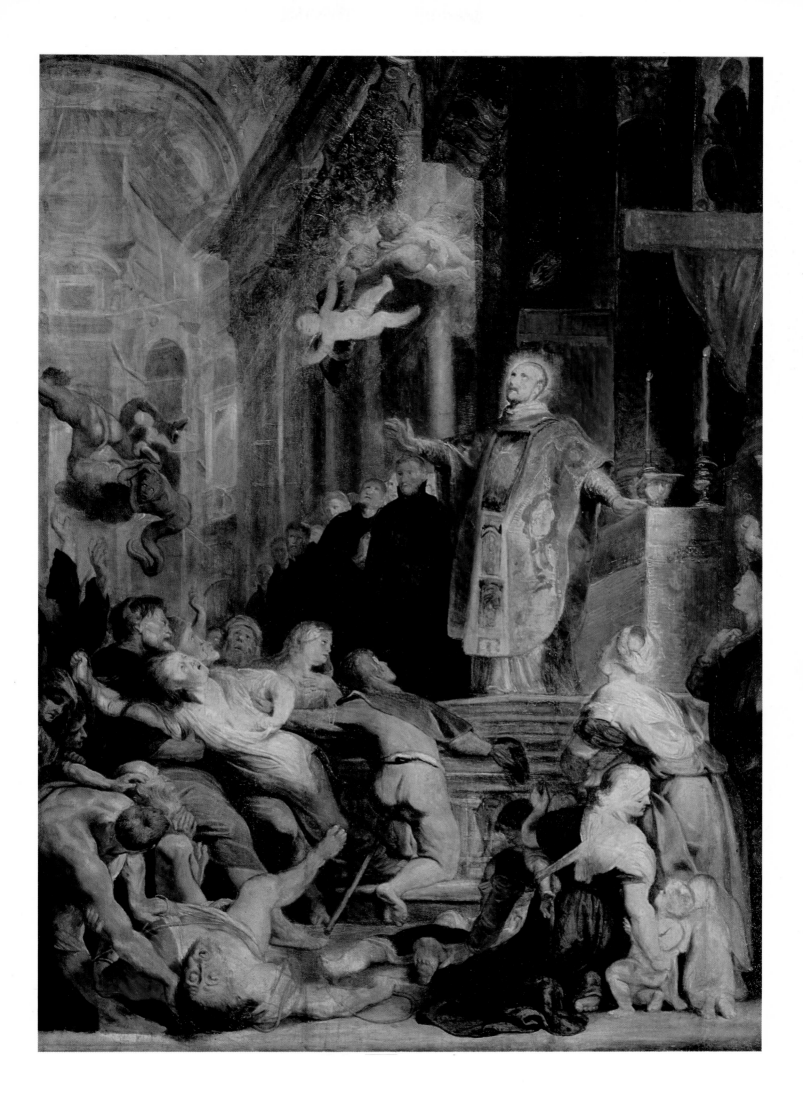

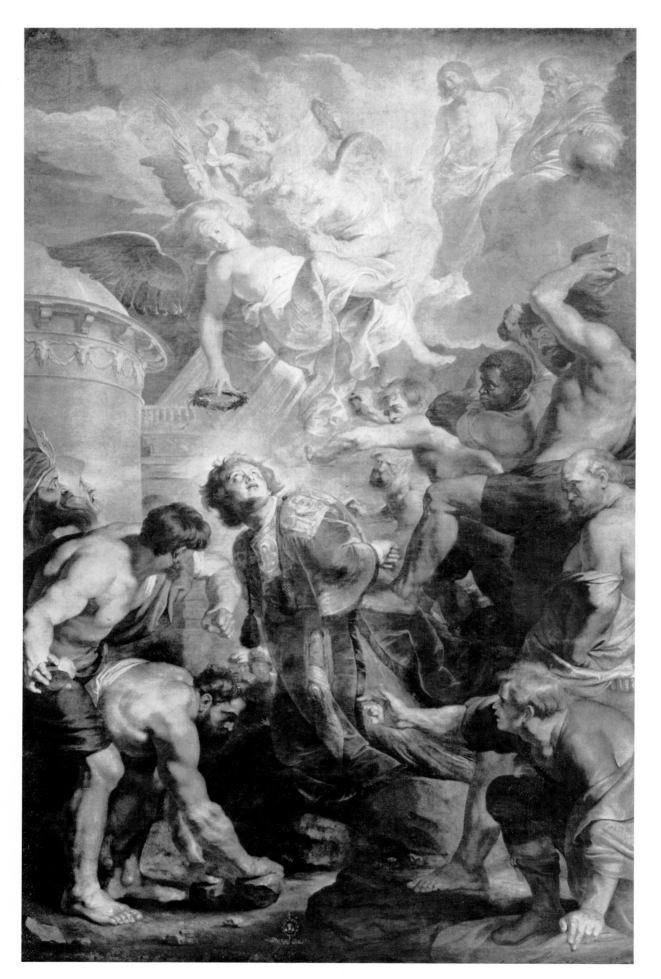

160

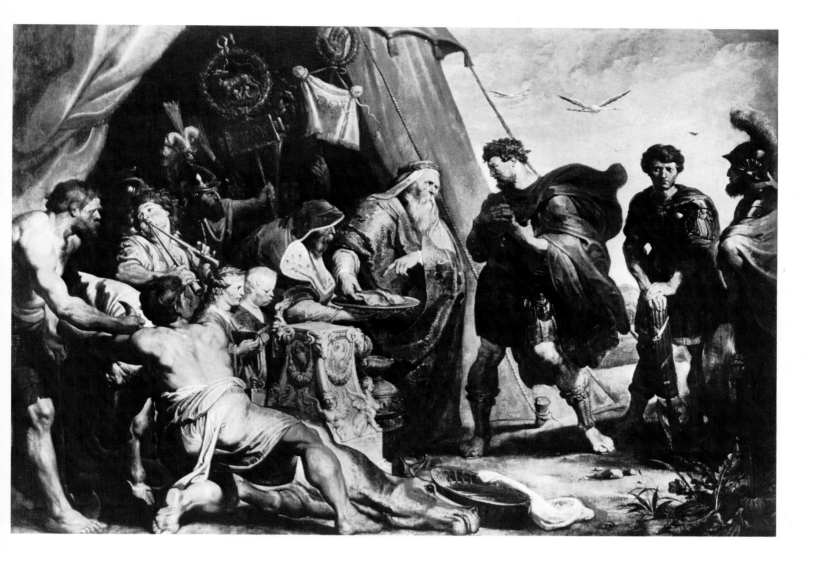

Figure 87
DECIUS MUS SERIES: THE
INTERPRETATION OF THE VICTIM
Canvas, 9'8" × 15'6"
Vaduz, Collection Prince of Liechten-
stein

*Before the tapestries were begun on the
looms, large canvases were made after
Rubens' oil sketches on panel. These canvases were painted with the help of Rubens'
assistants, among whom Anthony van Dyck
was the most prominent in this period.*

◀ Figure 86
THE MARTYRDOM OF ST. STEPHEN
Central panel of triptych, 14'4" × 9'2"
Valenciennes, Musée des Beaux-Arts

*The plasticity of the forms permits a date
before 1615–16 for this altarpiece.*

does not permit of the conclusion that the compositions of the *Scipio*
and *Ignatius* were conceived at the same moment.

For completeness we must mention Van Puyvelde's theory, which
holds that the two *Miracles* were not originally intended for the high
altar of the Jesuit Church. He sees evidence for this in the following
clause in the contract of March 29, 1620: "Sixthly, if a new painting
must be executed for the high altar of the aforesaid new church, the
Father Provost will not entrust this commission to any other than
Rubens, except under reasonable conditions and by mutual agreement."[27] According to Van Puyvelde, this painting was not executed,
and on the high altar were used the two large completed pictures
whose dimensions prevented their being placed on the walls or on
the two small side altars.[28] This interpretation is, however, erroneous,
for the contract expressly states "a new painting," not "a painting." The clause only means that the Jesuits were already thinking
of having a third painting made which they would place on the high
altar in alternation with Rubens' two completed works. If they had

161

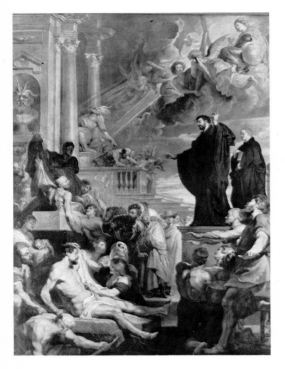

authorized the new commission, which their mounting financial difficulties probably did not permit at that time, they could have entrusted
it to no artist but Rubens. Later the third and even a fourth altarpiece were painted; since the Jesuits could no longer apply to Rubens,
they turned to Cornelis Schut and Gerard Seghers.[29]

There is a third manuscript source which throws interesting lights on
Rubens' two altarpieces, though it brings no surprising revelations. A
few years ago, the Rubens House bought from an antique dealer the
cash-book for the building of the Jesuit Residence in Antwerp.[30] It
recently became known that this document was still in the archives
of St. Charles Borromeo (the former church of the Jesuits) at the end
of the last century; we shall probably never know the circumstances
of its disappearance from there.

While it was still in the church a historian of the Antwerp Jesuits,
Father Charles Droeshout, S.J. (1824-1909), whose numerous manuscript works are stored in the archives of the Society,[31] took the trouble
to copy this register in its entirety—which is sufficient proof of its
importance. By his own statement, he did this in 1897, when the
register was put at his disposal by J.F. Corluy, the parish priest of
St. Charles Borromeo from 1890 to 1911.[32] Droeshout's copy was
consulted and quoted by Father Alfred Poncelet, S.J.,[33] another historian of the Society, but seems otherwise to have gone unnoticed.

The binding of the register in which Father Droeshout made his
copy bears on the back the following inscription: "Construction of
the Church of the Professed S.J. Antwerp/Expenditure Book
1614–1628."[34] This title is not found on the binding, admittedly
modern, of our original manuscript. Was it perhaps on the first page
of the manuscript and later obliterated (deliberately)?[35] Or did
Father Droeshout invent it himself?[36]

In this cash-book on the left monthly entries were made of income,
and on the right the expenses connected with the building of the
church. In several instances one finds references, without explanation,
to other more detailed account books, such as the "expenditures
book,"[37] the "memorial" book,[38] the "liber mutui,"[39] and once to
the "liber expositiorum."[40] All of these have disappeared. The cash-
book was therefore a recapitulary account book permitting the measure-
ment of credited and debited transactions. In addition, a general tally
was made from time to time, thanks to which the total difference
between the receipts and expenditures was calculated on a particular
date.[41] It is precisely this recapitulatory character of the cash-book
that often makes it difficult to determine which deliveries or services
were paid for out of the sums noted. For important purchases of marble and stone, which required large sums, one does find expense entries
such as the following: "To Cornelis Lanslodt, in payment of the bill
for marble ... 631.12½ (Fl)."[42] But mostly we must be content with
brief notes repeated almost every month, such as this one: "For various
materials and sundry other expenses as well as the wages of the workers,
as indicated in the expenditures book ... 2781.2 (Fl)."[43]

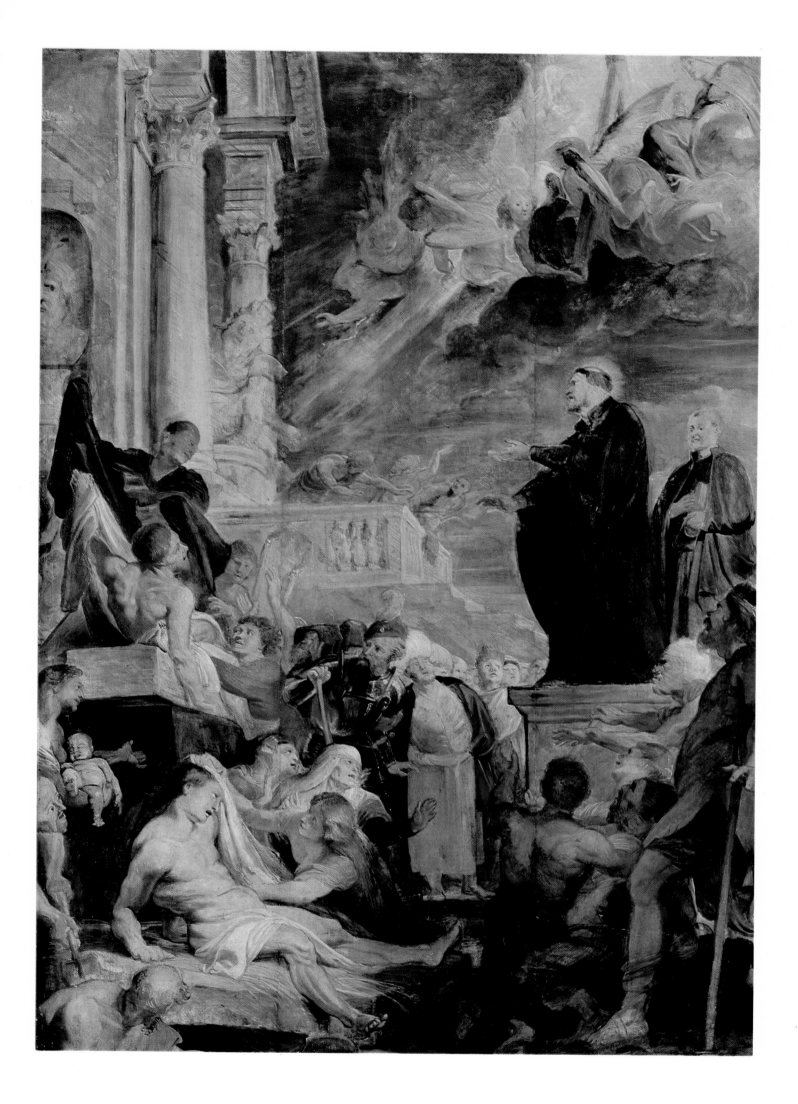

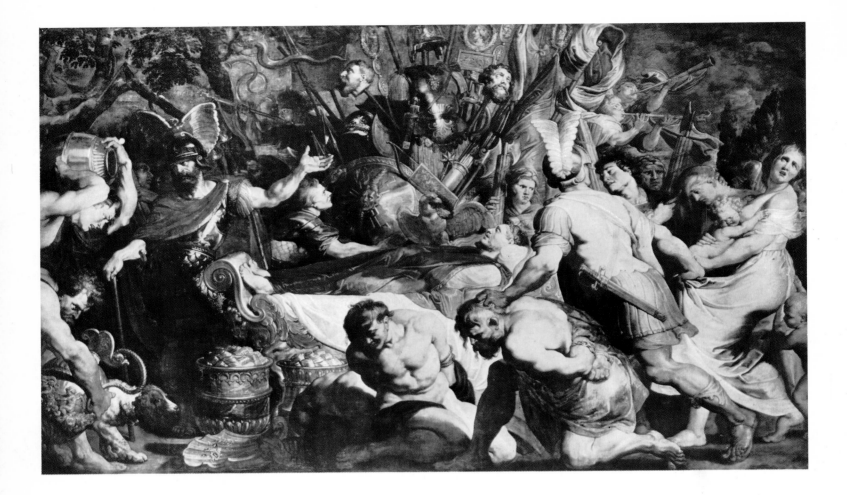

The first entry was made on April 15, 1614, when the Residence, of which the church formed part, had not yet been officially established. This took place on June 5, 1616,[44] and until shortly before that date the pages for credits and debits were always headed: "Cash owes to the Church" and "The Church owes to Cash," respectively.[45] "Cash" *(Cassa)* no doubt refers to the moneys of the Residence in the "House of Aachen."[46] After August 1616, the headings read: "Church Income" and "Church Outgo"; another change comes in January 1620: "Alms received to date" and "For materials, wages, etc., to date." The cash-book was closed on December 31, 1628, which in no way signifies that all debts had then been paid.[47]

It is evident that the cash-book was meant to furnish well-ordered and separate accounts concerned with the building of the church. But as a certain number of supplies and purchases, including houses and materials, were intended for the Residence as well as for the new church, a general balancing of accounts between the new church and the Residence was initiated on November 10, 1621.[48]

Father Droeshout tells us that the cash-book was kept by Father Andreas de Pretere, administrator of the Residence, assisted by Brother Paul van Mechelen,[49] whose name recurs several times in the register.[50]

164

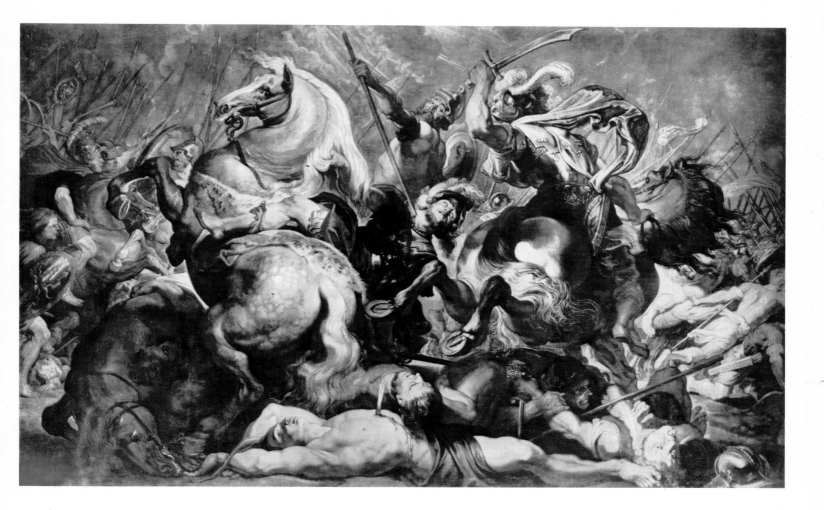

Figure 90
THE DEATH OF DECIUS MUS
Canvas, 9'5" × 17'
Vaduz, Collection Prince of
Liechtenstein

*Another large canvas preparatory to the
tapestry series illustrating the life of the
consul Decius Mus. The composition
reflects Rubens' sense of drama, so outstand-
ingly developed.*

These explanations about the cash-book are necessary if the reader
is to evaluate in its proper light the information this document furnishes
about Rubens. His name first appears in it on April 13, 1617, in the
first recapitulatory balance sheet of income and expenditures. The
heading "Debts charged to the new church" covers three subdivisions
entitled respectively "Loans without interest," "Loans with interest,"
and "To the persons named below,"[51] this last section being a short
list of sums owed for supplies of materials or services rendered. And
in the last line we read: "To Peter Rubens ... 3,000.–(Fl)."[52]

Unfortunately the reason is not specified for which the Antwerp
Jesuits owed Rubens this sum. Father Droeshout supposed it must
refer to remuneration for advice furnished by Rubens during the construction of the new church, and to fees for his designs for certain
decorative motifs.[53] Although 3,000 florins might seem to us a rather
large sum for services of this nature,[54] we nevertheless entertained that
hypothesis—until the day when we reread the contract of March 29,
1620. There we found the sum of 3,000 florins still owed to Rubens
by the Residence for the two altarpieces for the high altar, both completed some time before. These identical sums refer, without any
doubt, to the same commission. Thus it can be concluded that the

cash-book entry of April 13, 1617, relates to the fees for the two paintings of the miracles of the two Jesuit saints, Ignatius of Loyola and Francis Xavier, paintings for which Rubens was still awaiting payment on March 29, 1620.[55]

Must the inference from all this be that the two pictures were finished by April 13, 1617, and that they were being painted during 1616 and early in 1617? At first sight, the heading of the list that includes Rubens' name, that is, "Debts charged to the new church," would lead one to think so. We must not forget, however, that accountants in the seventeenth century customarily entered on the debit side not only actual debts but also future debts: those which they expected to have to pay according to agreements already signed.[56] Unfortunately no agreement of this kind is available to us, nor the "manual" in which we would find fuller information on this subject; consequently it is impossible to establish with certainty that the two pictures were indeed finished by April 13, 1617. Such was probably not the case, since the church itself was then far from completion; it was not consecrated until September 12, 1621. But what the cash-book reveals, at least, is that in 1617 Rubens had undertaken to execute the two works. So the entry of April 13, 1617, merely reinforces the hypothesis based on Rubens' letters to Pieter van Veen, namely, that the two pictures were finished in 1618.

Our arguments thus far rest solely on archival sources, and must be supported by stylistic criticism comparing the two *Miracles* altarpieces with other works by Rubens dated in the period 1616–20. To treat this problem in detail would lead us too far from our starting point, but it can be taken as agreed that nothing prevents us from believing that in their conception, at least, the two pictures go back to the years 1616–17. The rather sculptural style of these representations is still close to the large *Last Judgment* in Munich, of 1615–17 (Plate 22),[57] and also to *The Martyrdom of St. Stephen* in Valenciennes (Figs. 48, 86),[58] which cannot, according to recent analyses, have been painted later than 1615–16;[59] it is also akin to some scenes in the *Decius Mus* series (Figs. 87, 89, 90),[60] probably executed in 1616.[61] This confirms our opinion that the conception and probably also the execution of the two altarpieces for the church of the Jesuits cannot be placed much later.

On February 13, 1621, Rubens' name appears in the cash-book for the second time under the heading "Debts charged to the new church"; by that date the Antwerp Jesuits owed him 10,000 florins.[62] The sum evidently refers to the contract of March 12, 1620, which stipulated that on delivery of the thirty-nine ceiling paintings Rubens would receive 7,000 florins for that series (Plate 38) plus 3,000 florins for the two large canvases already completed, a total of 10,000 florins.[63]

On November 10, 1621, Rubens is named in an impressive list of "debts." Under the heading "To be paid to the persons named below, as annual rates" we read: "625– Pedro Paulo Rubens ... 10,000 (Fl)."[64] The number 625–, preceding the name, stands for the annual rate, calculated at 6.25 percent, which the Jesuits owed Rubens accord-

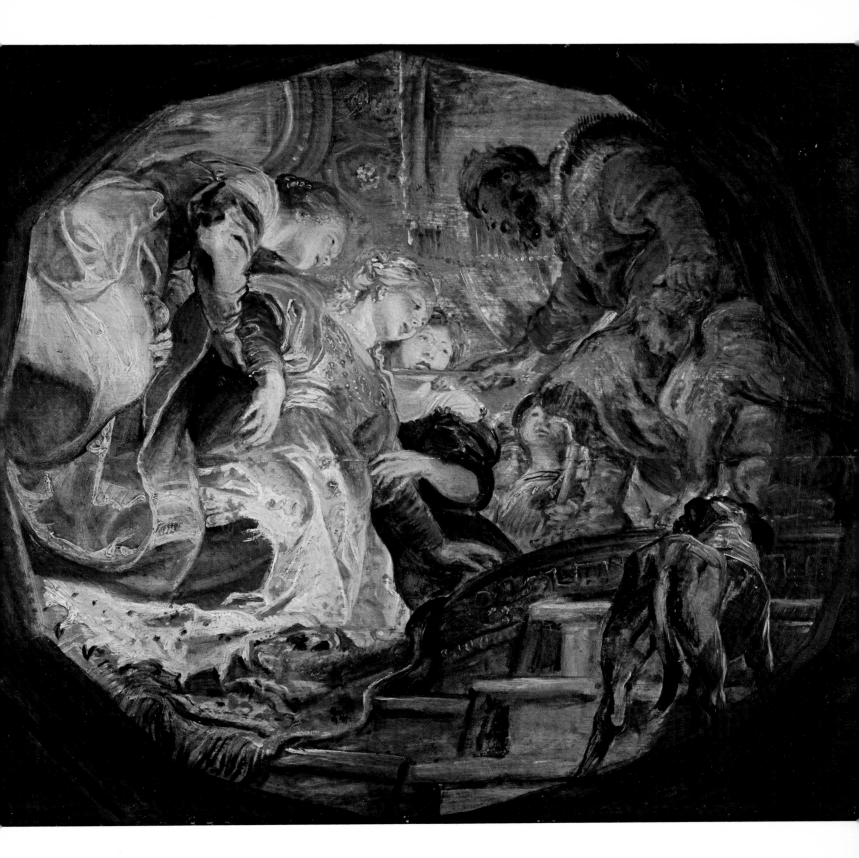

Plate 38
ESTHER BEFORE AHASUERUS
Oil sketch on panel, 19$\frac{1}{4}$" × 22$\frac{1}{2}$"
Vienna, Gemäldegalerie, Akademie der
bildenden Künste

*In 1620–21, thirty-nine canvases for the
ceilings of the Jesuit Church were executed
in Rubens' workshop after the master's
sketches, of which this is an example.*

167

ing to the contract of 1620, from the time the pictures were delivered until the Father Provost decided to pay the sum of 10,000 florins in whole or in part.[65]  The cash-book does not tell us when the debts to Rubens were completely cleared.  Under the dates April 15 and December 31, 1623, twice we find the total sum beside the artist's name.[66]  Other sources tell us that no decision was made until 1630 to take effective measures to liquidate the enormous pile of debts entailed by the building of the church; these were almost completely discharged only in 1634.[67]  Rubens may have had to exercise patience until that date before he received his full fee.

Rubens has long been known as the designer of the high altar (Fig. 83) where the pictures under discussion were displayed in turn,[68] but the identity of the sculptor who executed this impressive marble monument, and decorated it with statues (Fig. 91), has been less certain.

In 1853 Visschers atributed the statues of the high altar to Andreas Colijns de Nole the Younger,[69] but he named no sources.  Konrad, basing his statements on somewhat unconvincing stylistic criticism, wrote in 1923 that Hans van Mildert must be considered as the author of the statues.[70]  Both these names have since been constantly mentioned, together or separately, but the attributions have never been supported by really substantial arguments.[71]  No one has thus far cited Jacob van der Sanden, an author often demonstrably reliable, who wrote in his *Oud Konst-Toneel van Antwerpen* in 1775 that the superb high altar was probably carried out by Johannes van Mildert, after Rubens' designs.[72]

The Jesuit cash-book also contains interesting information concerning this problem.  Let us note immediately that Hans van Mildert's name is mentioned no fewer than five times, while that of Colijns de Nole is completely absent.

It should be pointed out at once, however, that here, as everywhere, an "argumentum ad silentium" has to be treated with the greatest caution!  We have already emphasized that the entries in the cash-book do not generally specify the deliveries or services to which they correspond, and works by one of the Colijns de Nole family may be hidden in the long lists of payments for "various materials and sundry other expenses as well as the workmen's wages"—payments,[73] it will be remembered, for which the cash-book refers to an "expenditures book" for more detailed specifications.  What a pity that this second register, which would have solved so many problems, seems to have disappeared!

In any case, let us simply state that "M. Hans van Mildert, sculptor" is first mentioned in a list of "Debts charged to the new church" on July 1, 1619, with the sum of 700 florins entered beside his name.[74]  The same artist appears a second time in another summary of debts dated February 12, 1621, the very list in which the sum of 10,000 florins appears by Rubens' name; the debt to Van Mildert is 2,688.10 (Fl).[75]

Nine months later his name reappears, on November 10, 1621; the

Plate 39
PORTRAIT OF A YOUNG GIRL
(CLARA SERENA RUBENS?) (detail)
Canvas, over-all dimensions
$14\frac{1}{2}'' \times 10\frac{1}{2}''$
Vaduz, Collection Prince of Liechtenstein

*This portrait is generally taken to represent Clara Serena Rubens, the eldest child of Rubens and Isabella Brant.  She was baptized on March 21, 1611, and she died in 1624, at the age of 12.  Her features, full of animation, resemble those of Rubens' eldest son, Albert.  A portrait of Clara Serena was listed in the estate of Jan Brant, Rubens' father-in-law.*

168

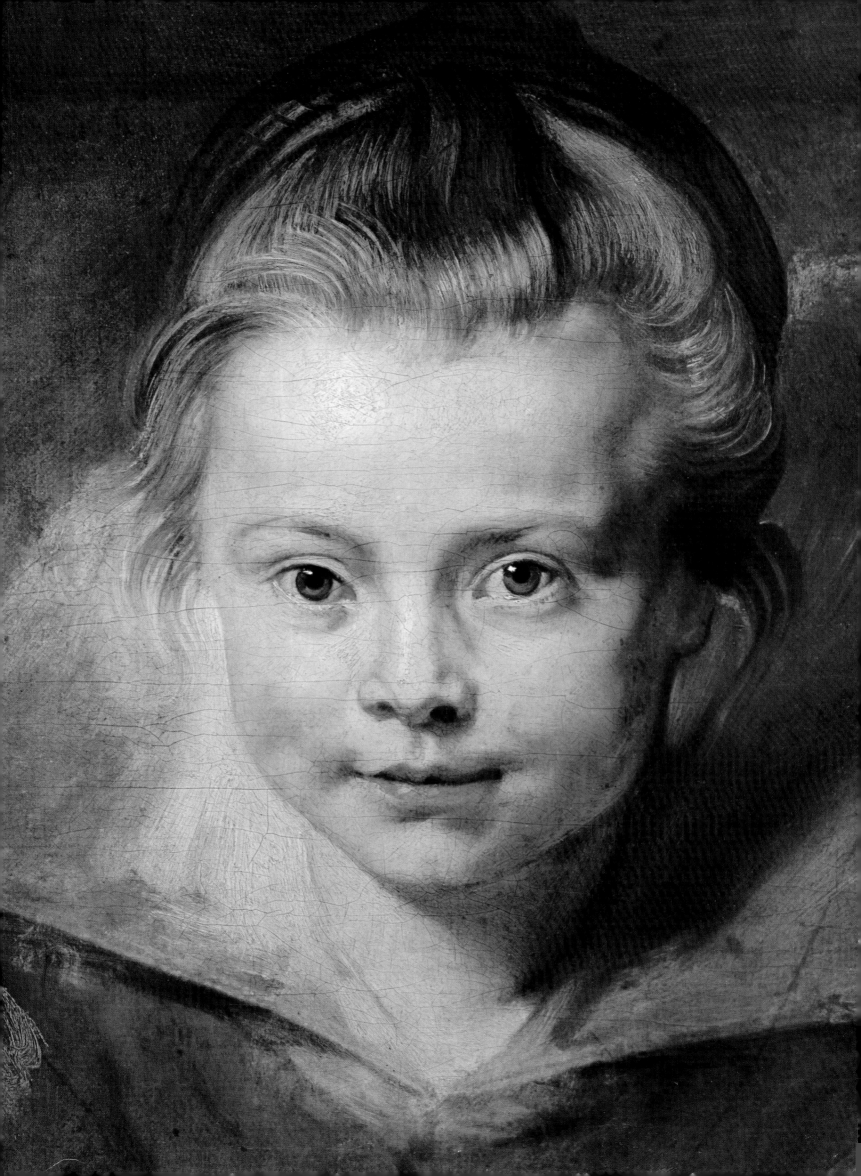

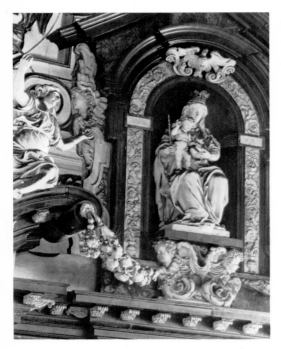

Jesuits' debt has reached 3,200 florins,[76] and on that date they also owe him another 4,234.10 florins, entered among "current debts."[77] Again we regret that the cash-book tells us only the sums, not the corresponding services. Do these payments refer to work on the high altar? Or to those sculptures in the interior and on the façade of the church, attributed sometimes to Robert or Andreas Colijns de Nole, sometimes to Hans van Mildert?[78] Other pieces of sculpture embellish the tower, and though we do not know the precise date of its building, it was finished by July 1622, at the latest.[79]

In our opinion, certain indications permit at least some of the quoted sums to be connected with the high altar. Before the altar could be erected, the exterior walls and the façade had to be completed and the church roofed over. One can reasonably assume that the high altar was finished after the façade and, moreover, that the façade was probably decorated with reliefs and statues while it was being erected. From the cash-book it emerges that the church was so far advanced by mid-1619 that the timbering of the roof was completed. A credit entry dated June 1, 1619, reads: "for the sale of the quantity of lumber bought in excess ... 1,249.10 (Fl.)."[80] The timbering was probably finished by the winter of that year, and the work could thus proceed on completing the interior and furnishing the church. If this reasoning is correct, the construction of the high altar took place about this time. On March 12, 1620, the contract was signed with Rubens to supply the ceiling pictures; the high altar was perhaps not finished then, for the contract mentions the two pictures as "already completed," not as "already delivered."[81] Granted the possibility of awkward wording, it might also be that delivery of the paintings was delayed; was there not some risk in storing them in an unfinished church where they might be damaged by work in progress? But in July 1620, more than a year before the church was consecrated, the interior was well on the way to completion; a letter to Thomas Howard, Earl of Arundel, in London, from his secretary in Antwerp, tells him that Lady Arundel visited the church on July 17, 1620, and admired it very much.[82]

The entry in the cash-book under the date February 13, 1621, for "van Baele, painter ... 500 (Fl.),"[83] offers great interest for the dating of the high altar. The said sum can refer to only one work, namely, the little scenes which Hendrik van Balen painted directly on the marble of the predella of the high altar.[84] For him to do this, the altar must have been set up; it is the cash-book that permits us to deduce that the monument was in the church by February 1621.[85] The significant fact that Hendrik van Balen's fee was entered in the same list with the 2,688 florins due to Hans van Mildert, as has been pointed out, indicates that the latter entry might refer both to the high altar and to the statues which were placed on it (Figs. 91, 92). Thus Jacob van der Sanden's statement that Hans van Mildert was probably the author of the high altar becomes the more plausible.

But there is more. We have already noted that on November 10, 1621, Hans van Mildert was entered twice as creditor for considerable

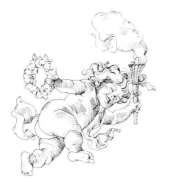

CHAPTER 9　An Outline of Works by Rubens
in the Period 1620 to 1628

In 1620 Rubens' career enters a new phase which could be called "the period of the great series." From this year onward he received commissions, in close succession, for several series of canvases and designs for tapestries. In addition to these, moreover, he continued to paint large altarpieces, some of them among the most impressive he ever executed; they are characterized by an increasing dynamism, an even more spontaneous style, and a palette so brilliant that they can be counted among the most accomplished achievements of the High Baroque. In this relatively short time Rubens also painted a considerable number of fascinating portraits. This extremely productive period closes at the end of August 1628 with the artist's departure for Madrid, where he was to carry out a diplomatic mission entrusted to him by the Infanta Isabella and King Philip IV of Spain.

Many other journeys preceded this one. Some of these were connected with an important royal commission for which Rubens visited Paris several times. After 1621, when the Twelve-Years' Truce expired, he intervened more and more frequently in diplomatic negotiations which obliged him to travel extensively. In the preceding decade he had scarcely left his workshop: from 1608, when he returned from Italy, until 1622 his traveling was limited, as far as we know, to Brussels, Malines, Louvain, and Bois-le-Duc, each occasion necessitating only a few days' absence.[1] According to Roger de Piles, he is supposed to have made in 1613 a slightly longer excursion to Haarlem, accompanied by Jan Breughel, Hendrik van Balen, and some other Flemings.[2]

But after 1622 he is constantly on the road, often for absences of several weeks. We find him in Paris a few times, in Brussels, Dunkirk, and at the German frontier.[3] When plague claimed numerous victims in Antwerp in 1625, he settled with his family for almost a year at an inn at Laeken, and, being then so near to the Brussels court, his interest in affairs of state seems to have grown. After Isabella Brant died on June 20, 1626, he devoted more and more time to diplomatic activities. These necessitated frequent journeys which distracted his mind from his wife's premature death.

Plate 40
Tapestry after a design by Rubens
THE TRIUMPH OF THE
EUCHARIST OVER IGNORANCE
AND BLINDNESS (detail)
Madrid, Descalzas Reales

*During 1620–28, the period of the great series, Rubens conceived, among other series, an impressive group of tapestries, The Triumph of the Eucharist, which the Infanta Isabella presented to the convent of the Barefoot Carmelites in Madrid. The tapestries were woven in Brussels in the workshops of Jan Raes and other tapestry makers.*

173

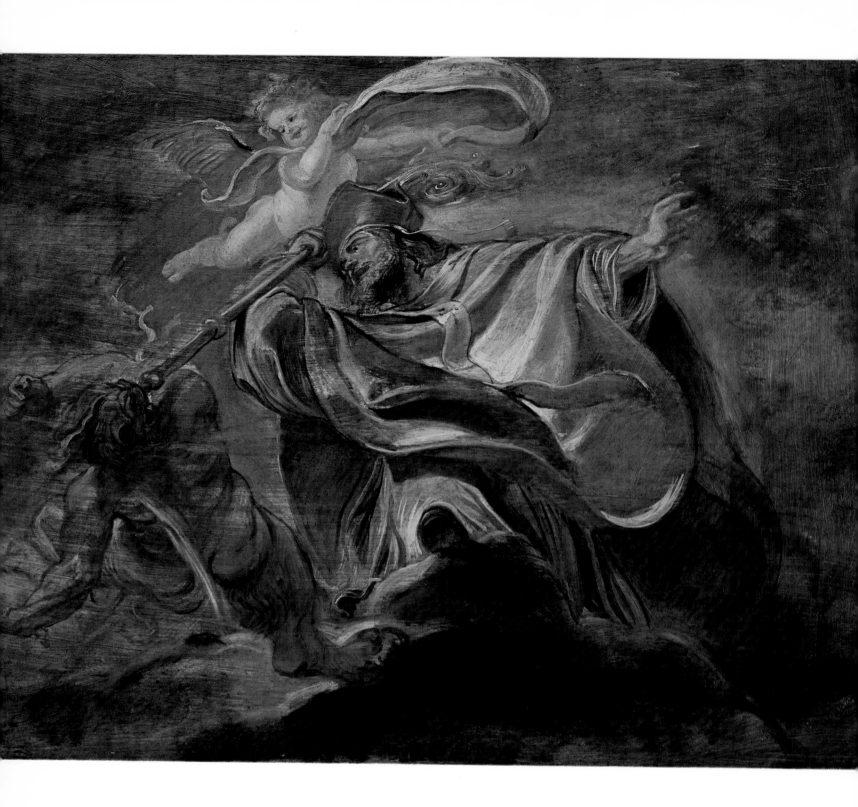

Plate 41
ST. GREGORY OF NAZIANZUS
Oil sketch on panel, 19³/₄″ × 25¹/₂″
Buffalo, Albright-Knox Art Gallery

*Brilliantly executed design, dating from
1620–21, for one of the thirty-nine ceiling
paintings for the Jesuit Church in Antwerp.*

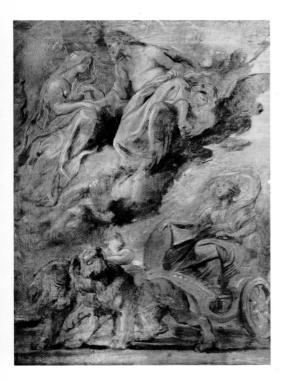

Busy with all these comings and goings, and with long negotiations and attendant correspondence, how did Rubens find time to paint so many brilliant canvases, which give evidence of his ever more pronounced mastery? Certainly his creative imagination and technical facility had developed strongly during the preceding decade, in years of intense labor devoted exclusively to his art. He now had a virtuosity which allowed him to conceive and to execute impressive pictures with unfailing facility.

Meanwhile, Rubens' workshop had probably now developed to a point where a better division of labor among well-trained collaborators was ensured; first among these was Anthony van Dyck, though he soon left his master's studio to build up an independent career abroad. Nevertheless we must point out that a good many large canvases from this period are still entirely, or for the most part, by Rubens' own hand. And the new pictorial conception manifested in these works allowed him to paint in freer strokes without touching up small details, which may also explain the great artistic productivity of these prodigiously active years.

The first large commission for an important series of pictures was awarded to Rubens by the Jesuits of Antwerp on March 29, 1620, with the contract signed by the prefect of the new Residence, Father Jacobus Tirinus. Rubens undertook to supply, in less than a year, thirty-nine ceiling paintings for the new church of the Jesuits (now St. Charles Borromeo);[4] for each one the painter was to submit a small sketch or *modello*; the execution of the large canvases after these models could be entrusted to the workshop. And the contract mentions the name of Anthony van Dyck "as well as some of his other pupils." But Rubens was obligated to "complete with his own hand whatever may be found to be lacking in them."[5]

The agreement from the outset, that the execution of the canvases could be entrusted to collaborators, was doubtless because the time allowed for completion was so short! Anthony van Dyck, as we have mentioned, is named explicitly in the contract, which shows that the patrons regarded his collaboration as a guarantee of succes. Other sources tell us that Rubens himself distinguished between work by "the best of his pupils," as he liked to call Van Dyck,[6] and that by other assistants who helped him in his workshop. We know that from about 1617 onward, Van Dyck collaborated on several works by Rubens. His name has already appeared in connection with *The Miraculous Draft of Fishes* (Fig. 56) in Our-Lady-beyond-the-Dyle at Malines;[7] it has been thought possible to recognize his hand in many other pictures too. But Rubens could not count on his help for long, because by November 20, 1620, Van Dyck was in London. He was already back in Antwerp in March 1621, but left again the following autumn for Italy, where he remained for six years.[8] The ceiling paintings for the church of the Jesuits in Antwerp must have been among the last important commissions he worked on under Rubens' direction.

The thirty-nine paintings were destroyed, as we related in Chapter

Figure 93
THE ENTRY INTO LYONS
Oil sketch on panel, $13\frac{1}{2}'' \times 9\frac{1}{2}''$
Leningrad, Hermitage

*This* bozzetto *or rapid sketch, executed by Rubens as a first draft for the picture of this subject in the cycle* The Life of Maria de' Medici, *was painted in 1622–25.*

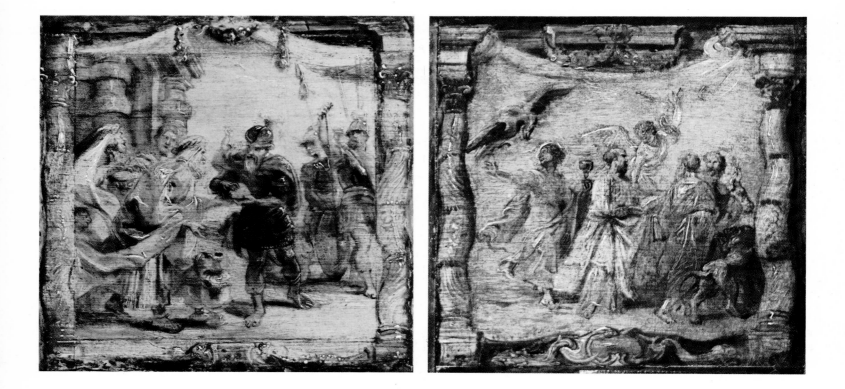

Figures 94, 95
THE MEETING OF ABRAHAM AND
MELCHIZEDEK (left)
THE FOUR EVANGELISTS (right)
Oil sketch on panel: (left)
$5^7/_8$" $\times$ $5^7/_8$"; (right) $6^3/_8$" $\times$ $6^3/_4$"
Cambridge, England, Fitzwilliam
Museum

*These are two of the seven small bozzetti
in the Eucharist series that are preserved
in this museum. Rubens had from the outset conceived the borders as an integral part
of the tapestries, even in the first stage of
his work on this series.*

7, in the fire of 1718. Thanks to some eighteenth-century drawings
and engravings made after these works, and also to the pictures of
W. von Ehrenberg and Anton Gheringh showing the interior of the
building, we can still gain an idea of their pictorial richness. The
gallery ceilings showed scenes from the New Testament, accompanied
by their prefiguration in the Old Testament. The ceilings of the side
aisles showed the lives of early Christian saints. Fortunately numerous
oil sketches, carried out to serve as models for the large canvases (Plate
41), have been preserved, scattered today in a number of museums
and private collections. While painting these *modelli* Rubens certainly
remembered the paintings by Titian, Tintoretto, and Veronese that
he had admired so much in Venice, for the oil sketches have that same
bold use of foreshortened figures and that same easy, elegant style
in the decoration. But Rubens' compositions are even more concentrated than his Italian models were. The touch of his brush
has such light vivacity and, at the same time, such sureness that it
looks as if painting these scenes, seen from below at a slant of some
forty degrees, did not cause him any technical problems. More surprising still is his virtuosity in adapting himself to the oval or octagonal
shapes of the ceilings, devising new compositions based on previous
ones, compressing the figures, and representing them from below as
if they were moving in the celestial spheres (Fig. 71).

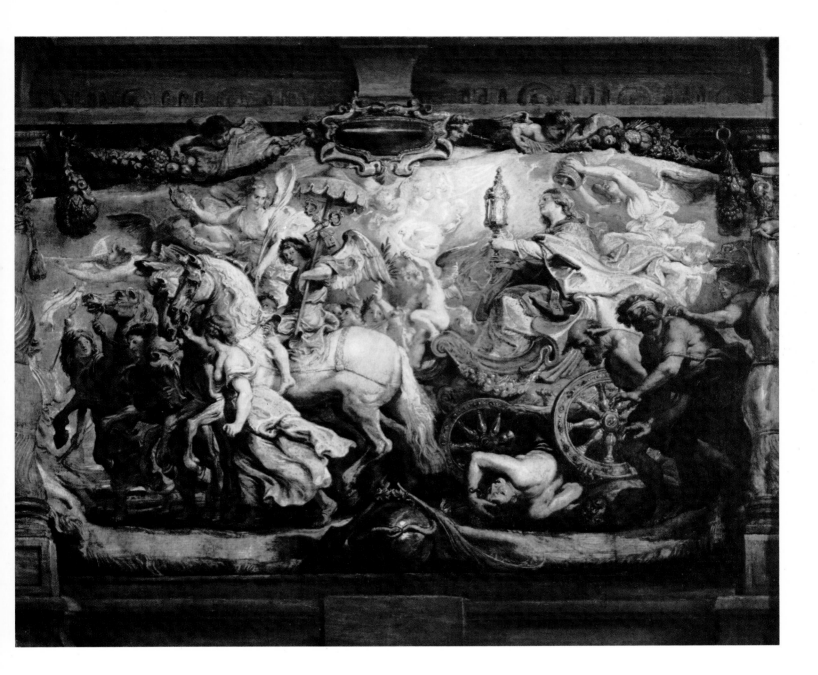

Figure 96
THE TRIUMPH OF THE
EUCHARIST OVER IGNORANCE
AND BLINDNESS
Oil sketch on panel, 33³/₄″ × 35³/₄″
Madrid, Prado

Modello *for one of the large tapestries in
the* Eucharist *series; large canvases were
executed after these* modelli; *most of them
are preserved in the John and Mable Ringling Museum of Art, Sarasota, Florida.*

The ceiling paintings for the Jesuit Church in Antwerp close a period
in Rubens' career that had taken place, after his return from Italy,
almost exclusively in his city and country. But they also open up
a new period, that of the great cycles, and these were executed in
nearly every case for foreign sovereigns. Rubens' fame appears to
have spread already far beyond the bounds of his own country.

Probably even before September 12, 1621, when the Antwerp church
of the Jesuits was consecrated, emissaries from King James I of England and his son, the future Charles I, a great friend of the arts, had
begun negotiating with Rubens to paint ceiling pieces for the newly
rebuilt Banqueting Hall in Whitehall Palace.[9] These plans, however, did not become definite until 1629, and in the meantime an impor-

177

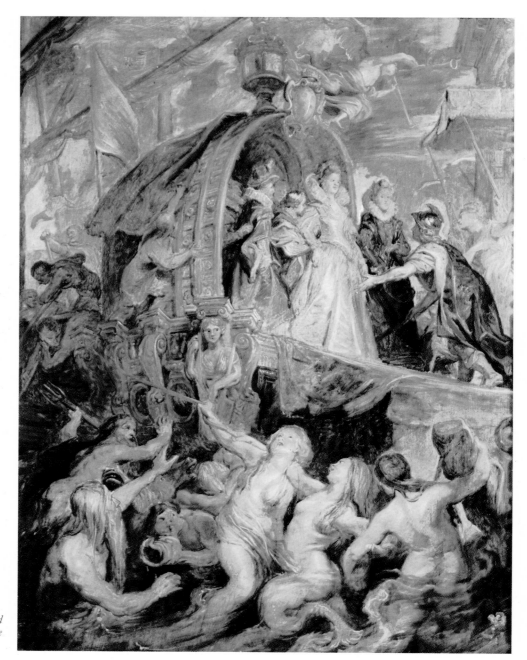

Figure 97
THE DEBARKATION AT
MARSEILLES
Oil sketch on panel, 25¼" × 19¾"
Munich, Alte Pinakothek

*Modello, or more elaborate sketch, painted in 1622–25 for one of the pictures in the series The Life of Maria de' Medici.*

Plate 42
THE DEBARKATION AT
MARSEILLES
Canvas, 12′11″ × 9′8″
Paris, Louvre

*Maria de' Medici is greeted by the personification of France as she disembarks at Marseilles, one stage in her journey to Lyons, where her marriage was to be celebrated. During the crossing the boat was favorably escorted by Neptune and the naiads, in the foreground.*

tant commission had come his way from Paris. In the first days of 1622 Rubens set out for the French capital, to discuss with the queen-mother Maria de' Medici and her chief counsellor Claude Maugis, the abbé de Saint-Ambroise, the plans for two cycles of pictures for the Palais du Luxembourg in Paris. On February 26 an agreement was signed between the painter and the sovereign;[10] it stipulated that Rubens would first execute a cycle of paintings representing events from the life of Maria de' Medici, and a second series, to follow, glorifying her deceased husband, King Henry IV. The day after his return to Antwerp Rubens began to paint the *bozzetti*, or first projects, mostly in grisaille on small panels (Fig. 93). He sent these to Paris as early

178

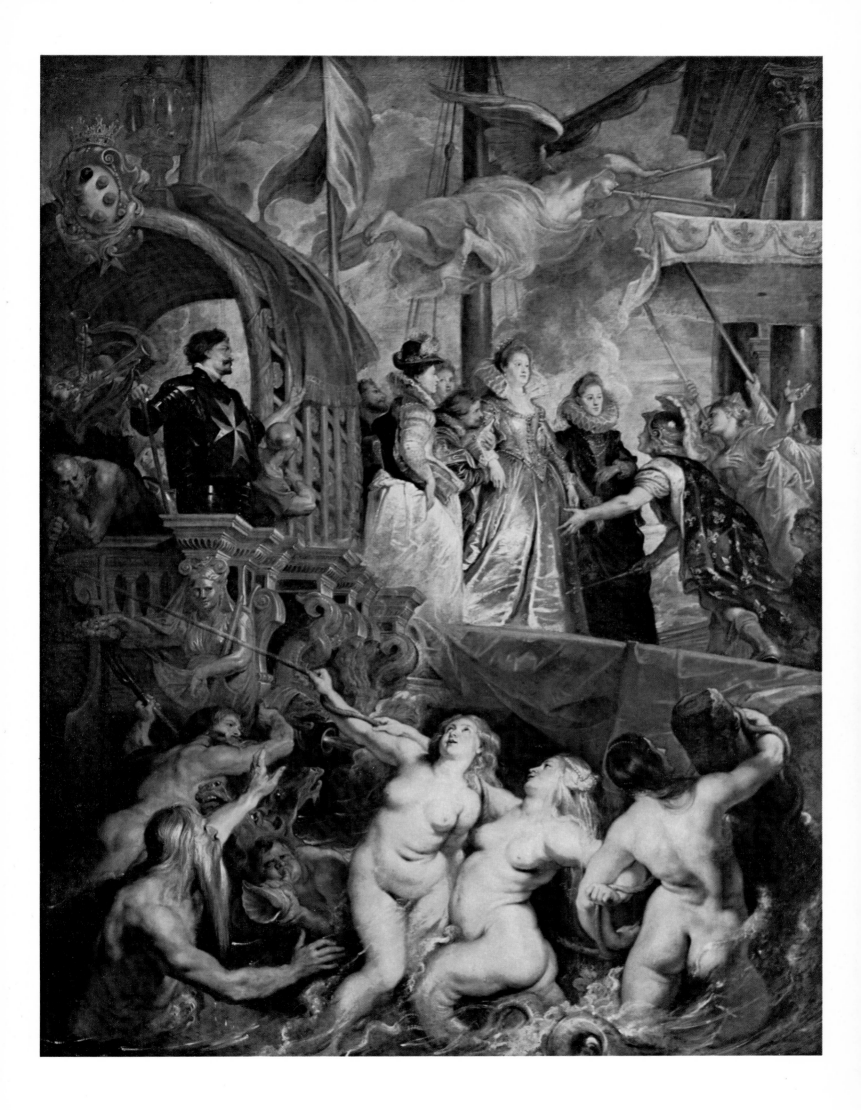

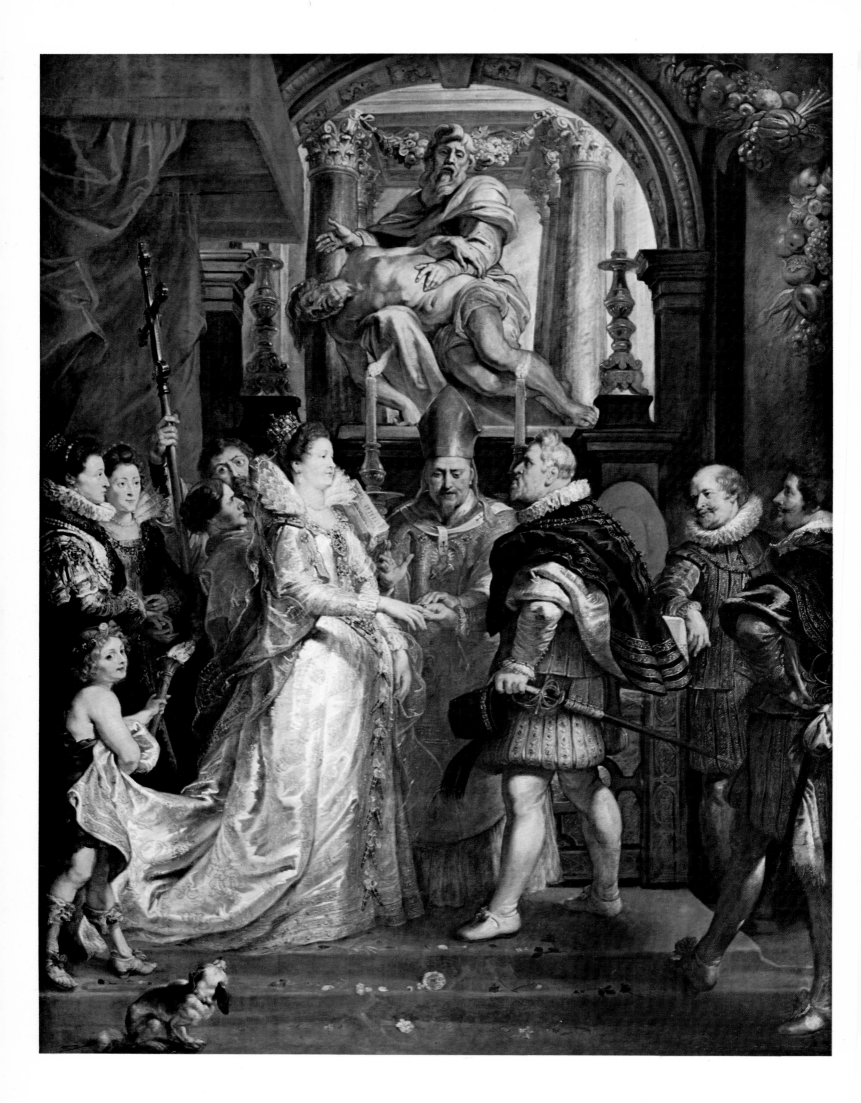

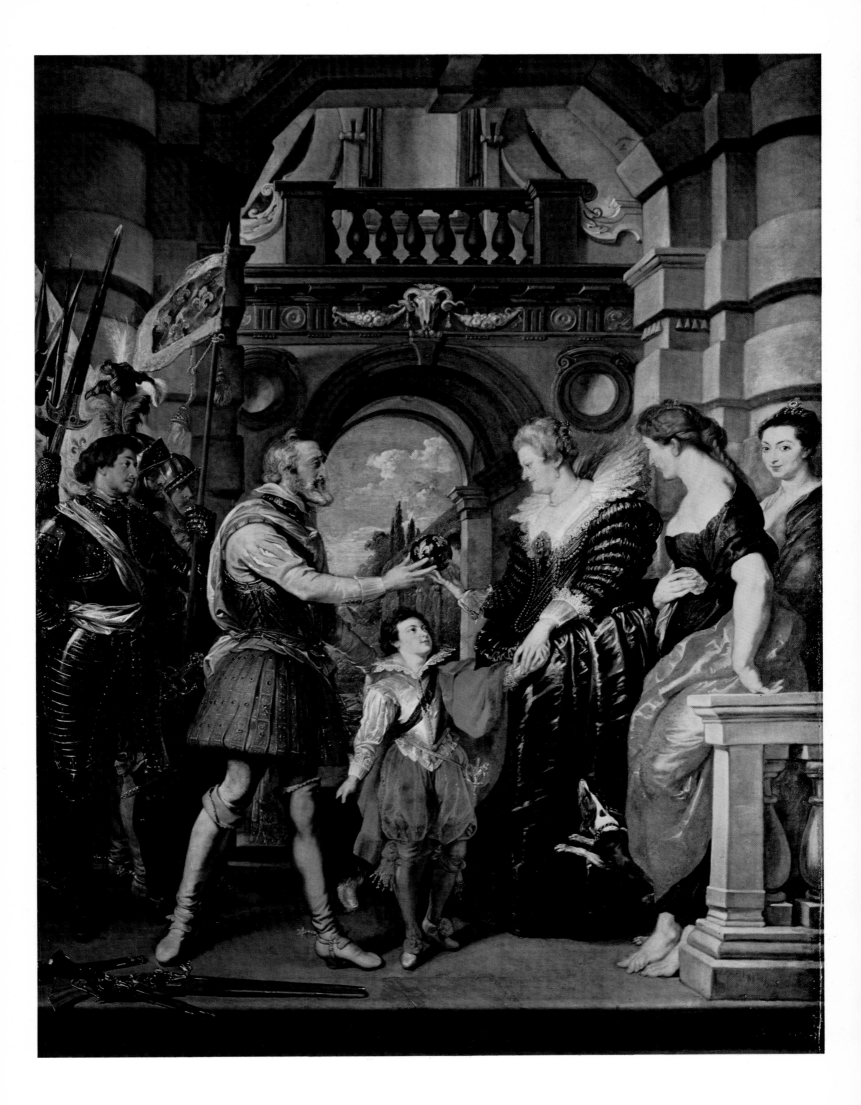

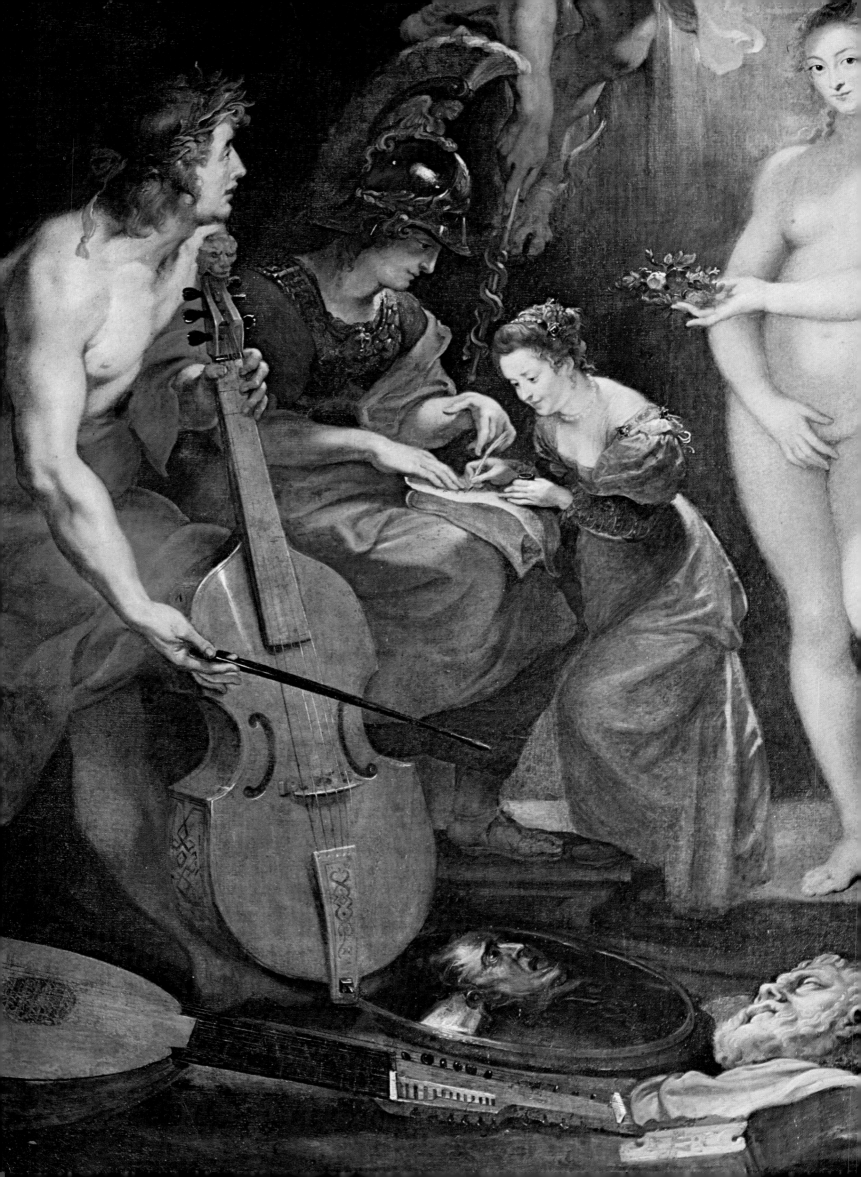

*Preceding pages*

Plate 43
THE MARRIAGE BY PROXY
Canvas, 12′11″ × 9′8″
Paris, Louvre

*Rubens could rely on his personal recollections when he painted the marriage by proxy of Maria de' Medici in Florence, on October 5, 1600, for he had been present at this festivity.*

Plate 44
THE CONSIGNMENT OF THE REGENCY
Canvas, 12′11″ × 9′8″
Paris, Louvre

*Before leaving for the war in Germany, Henry IV hands over power to Maria de' Medici. Between them is the Dauphin, the future Louis XIII. For the architectural elements, Rubens has used the central arch of the portico of his own house and the central arch of the pavilion in his garden (Pl. 1; Fig. 8); he represented the latter, however, as a second portico with a view onto the park.*

Plate 45
THE EDUCATION OF MARIA DE' MEDICI (detail)
Canvas, over-all dimensions 12′11″ × 9′8″
Paris, Louvre

*Minerva, goddess of wisdom, and Apollo, god of the arts, are instructing Princess Maria de' Medici. One of the three Graces stands nearby; Mercury, the messenger of the gods, inspires her from celestial heights. In the foreground lie attributes symbolizing the arts.*

as May 9 (today, most of them are in the Hermitage in Leningrad). New oil sketches, the *modelli*, were then painted in greater detail and with more color (nearly all are now in the Alte Pinakothek, Munich; Fig. 97). On May 24, 1623, Rubens arrived in Paris with nine canvases that he finished on the spot; the others were delivered in February 1625, and the artist remained in Paris until May to put the last touches on the whole cycle, which numbered no less than twenty-five large canvases (Plates 42–45).

The artist's task was made no easier by the fact that the life of the sovereign, a scheming and quarrelsome woman, had not always been glorious. It certainly needed a powerful imagination to confer an aura of triumph and heroism on the rather insignificant episodes of her life. Rubens therefore drew on his solid knowledge of ancient mythology and classical archaeology. Moreover he had to use a great deal of tact in representing the scenes showing the conflict between the queen and her son, the reigning monarch Louis XIII, in a manner that would offend no one. The gods, goddesses, and other allegorical figures who accompany the queen throughout the different events of her life raise her into a sort of empyrean situated somewhere between earth and sky (Fig. 93). These divine personages also appear in the scenes which are more faithful to history, lending the glamour of their presence. Thus rather humdrum facts take on the aspect of an apotheosis, in perfect accord with the idea of "royalty by divine grace." The bright colors are also striking, especially the royal blue which so often significantly dominates.

It may have been during his first stay in Paris in January and February of 1622 that Rubens received the order to design twelve tapestries depicting *The Life of the Emperor Constantine*.[11] In the oil sketches for this cycle of scenes from Roman history (Figs. 98-100), the painter had an opportunity to draw on his knowledge of classical archaeology. His acquaintance Nicolas-Claude Fabri de Peiresc, the French humanist and archaeologist whom he had met in Paris and with whom he was to remain in contact, certainly spurred him on to ever more frequent use of the many studies of ancient art he had made in Italy. The slightly solemn rhythm of several compositions in the *Constantine* series recalls the style of Roman sarcophagi and ancient reliefs.

The next step in the preparation of the tapestries was the painting, from Rubens' *modelli*, of cartoons having exactly the same size as the future tapestries. As early as November 1622, four of the twelve cartoons were already in the Parisian workshop of the tapestry weaver, Marc de Comans, and the complete series was apparently in position in February 1623.

Rubens had preferred not to include the borders of the tapestries in his designs.[12] He left the tapestry makers at liberty to execute them as they thought fit. The same was true for *The History of Decius Mus*, a set of tapestries produced in 1616-17 (Figs. 87, 89, 90). But henceforth Rubens himself designed the borders of the tapestries he created. These contained ornamental motifs and symbols relating to the subjects represented.

183

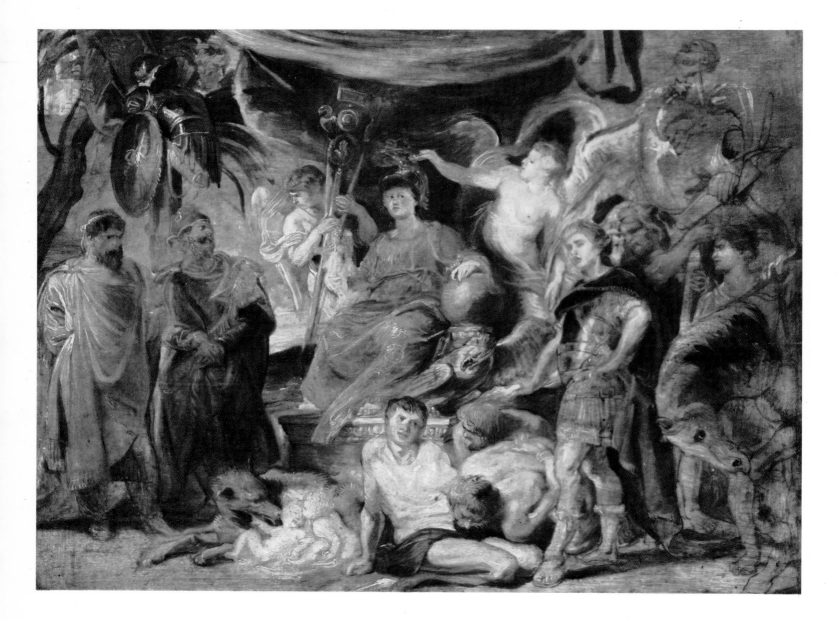

In the first place we must mention here the designs of the *Eucharist Series*, commissioned by the Infanta Isabella, which she intended for the Madrid convent of the Barefoot Carmelite order of the *Descalzas Reales.*[13] She had received part of her education there as a young girl and kept a deep attachment to that religious community all her life. By her gift of a sumptuous set of tapestries, she wished to contribute with royal magnificence toward enhancing the brilliance of the ceremonies in the convent church.

Rubens first painted a series of small oil sketches in grisaille on panel; today two are in the Musée Bonnat in Bayonne, and seven are in the Fitzwilliam Museum in Cambridge, England (Figs. 94, 95). The final compositions were already fixed in these sketches as they would ultimately be rendered in the tapestries. The painter certainly sketched these

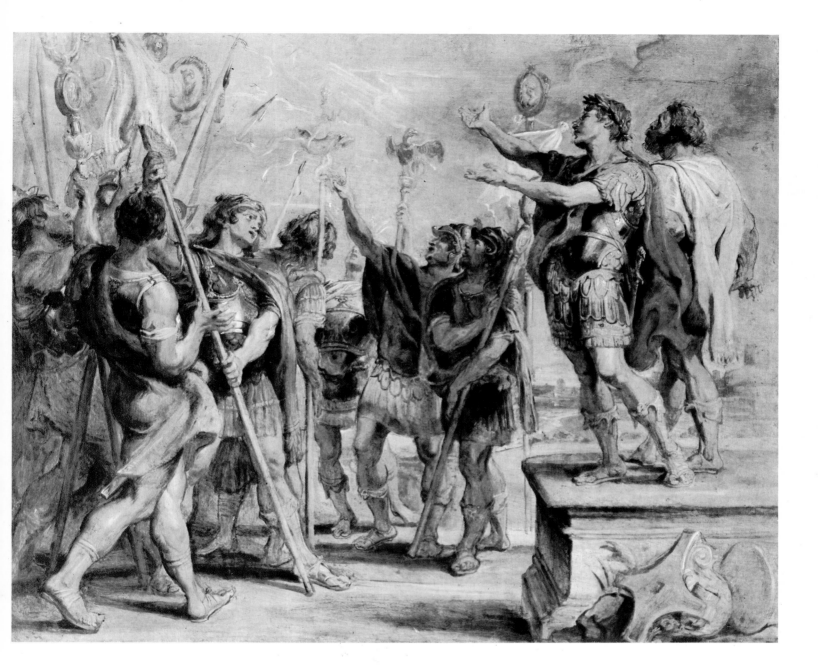

panels to submit them to the Infanta and possibly to her counsellors, and they had to show clearly how he intended to represent each scene. Later he repeated the compositions in reverse, modifying and elaborating here and there, in more highly colored oil sketches, painted on larger panels, averaging 33 by $35\frac{1}{2}$ inches; many of these are in the Prado in Madrid. Large canvases of the size envisaged for the tapestries were executed after these sketches in Rubens' workshop, four of them at present in the John and Mable Ringling Museum of Art at Sarasota, Florida. They were either meant to be followed directly by the weavers, or they served as models for large cartoons, now lost, that the weavers used as they worked. The compositions, woven from the back, appeared on the front in reverse of the models used, that is to say, the same as in the first small oil sketches. One might add

185

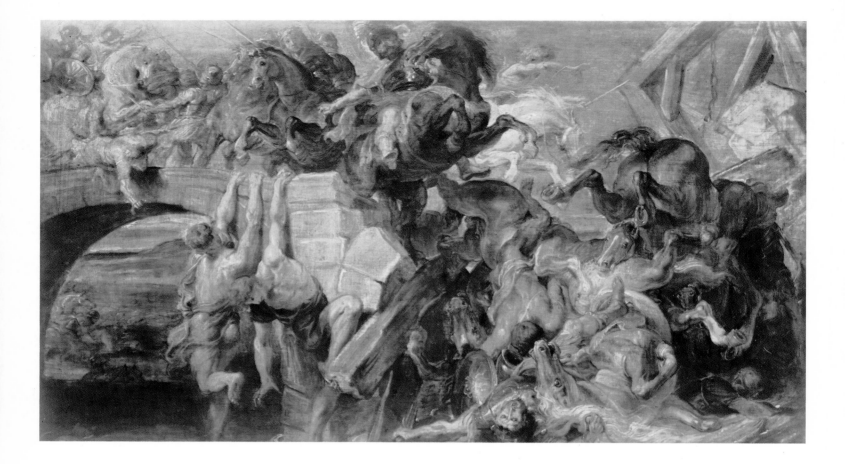

Figure 100
THE DEFEAT AND DEATH
OF MAXENTIUS
Oil sketch on panel, 14½″ × 25¼″
London, The Wallace Collection

*The series* The Life of the Emperor Constantine, *for which Rubens did the designs, was commissioned by King Louis XIII of France.*

that the first edition of the *Triumph of the Eucharist* tapestries was woven in Brussels, in the workshops of Jan Raes and his subcontractors, Geubels, Fobert, and Verwoert.

We do not know exactly when Rubens began the first sketches for this impressive series, but we are slightly better informed about the final phase of his work. On May 21, 1627, Philippe Chifflet, the Infanta's chaplain, wrote to the papal nuncio in Brussels that Rubens intended to leave for Rome in about September of that year, but wished first to finish the "pictures" for the Infanta. Other sources tell us that in January 1628 the Infanta presented Rubens with some pearls from her jewel box by way of remuneration for the tapestries for the *Descalzas Reales.* We can conclude that the work was finished in 1627, or by January 1628 at the latest.

In this series Rubens succeeded in masterly fashion to represent abstract ideas in allegorical form, in compositions with many figures. Four tapestries show prefigurations of the Eucharist in the Old Testament. Two show the propagation of the Holy Sacrament, one with the Evangelists and the other with the Fathers and the Doctors of the Church. Two tapestries exalt the victories of the Holy Sacrament over paganism and heresy. The cycle then presents three triumphs: of Faith over worldly wisdom, science, and nature; of the Church over ignorance and blindness; and the triumph of Divine

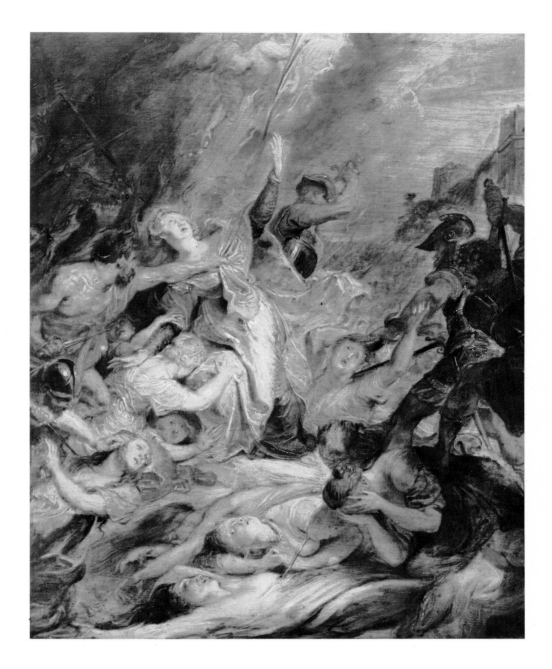

Figure 101

THE MARTYRDOM OF ST. URSULA
AND HER COMPANIONS
Oil sketch on panel, 19¼″ × 15⅜″
Brussels, Musées Royaux des Beaux-
Arts de Belgique

*The artist renders the violence of the scene
with incomparable dramatic vigor in this oil
sketch of about 1620. The multiplicity of
bodies, whirling and falling, forms a moving
whole.*

Love. In addition Rubens produced a large composition, divided into
separate sections, for a "velum" to be hung in front of the retable
of the convent church during certain liturgical ceremonies. For technical reasons this composition was executed in the form of a number
of smaller tapestries.

This impressive series can be considered a triumphant exaltation both
of the Eucharist and of the Roman Church, reestablished and consolidated by the Counter-Reformation, for which the Holy Sacrament is
one of the foundations of the Faith.

In one of the large oil sketches in the Prado (Fig. 96) Rubens' creative
power is revealed as well as his sense of allegory and his dynamic
and impetuous mode of expression, so characteristic of the High Ba-

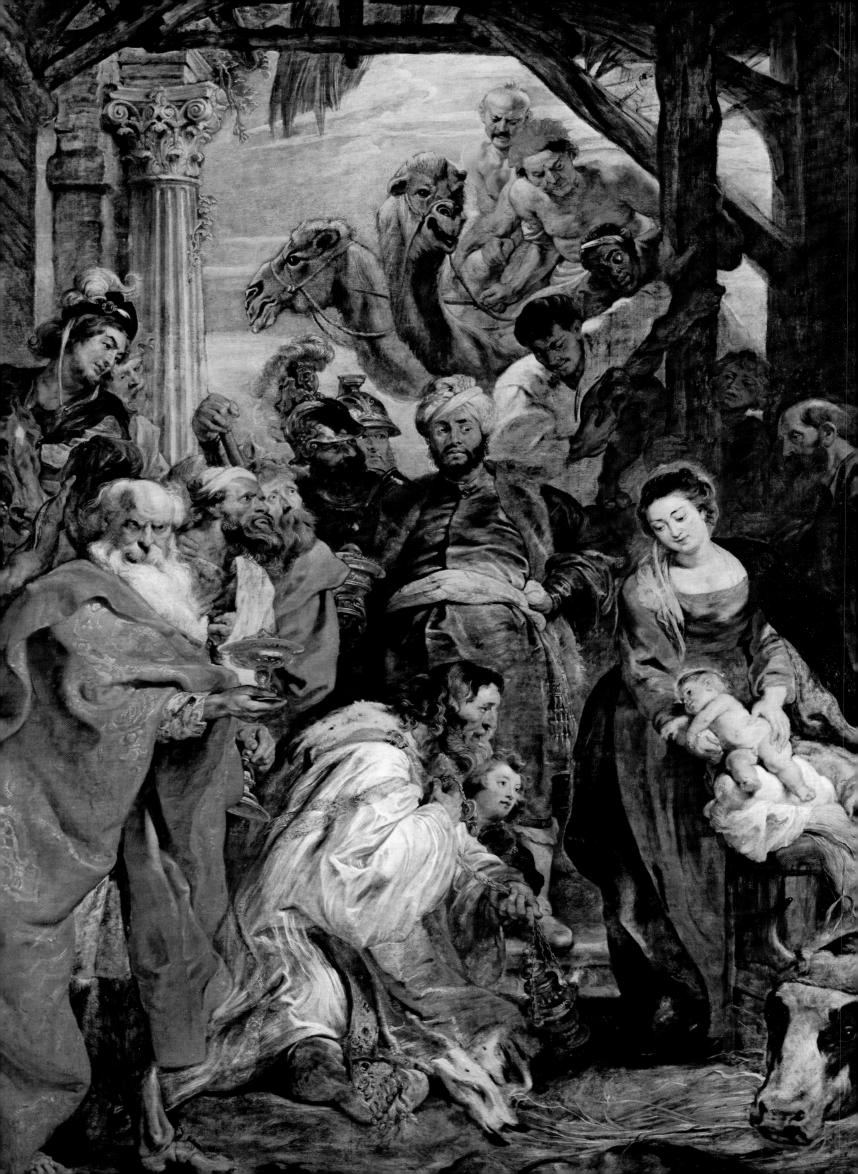

roque. Sabbe has written that the *Fides Catholica* triumphs here over "the Hatred and Discord which it crushes, in spite of the helpless violence of their Rubensian musculature, under the powerful hoofs of the chargers and the wheels of their chariot. It also triumphs over the Blindness and Ignorance which are henceforth illuminated by the light of Catholic doctrine shining forth from the sacramental Chalice, which *Fides Catholica* causes to light the world like a sun."[14] We also reproduce a portion of the tapestry in the convent of the *Descalzas Reales* (Plate 40), whose composition is the reverse of that on the finished oil sketch.

Meanwhile, in 1628, Rubens had not yet started on the series of the life of Henry IV which had been in the contract of February 1622 with Maria de' Medici. It is known that Rubens had to wait a long time for his fee for the first series on the queen-mother's life, and he was doubtless in no hurry to commence the second series. And there were so many other works to be finished! When we think of the number of large pictures and oil sketches he painted during those years, we well understand the artist when he wrote on January 10, 1625, before finishing the Maria de' Medici series, "I am the busiest and most harassed man in the world."[15] In the following years it would be the same, for in addition he was involved in diplomatic negotiations that became increasingly strenuous. Not until he had put the finishing touches to the *Eucharist* cycle did he start the projects for the episodes of the life of Henry IV,[16] as we can deduce from his letter of January 27, 1628 (he had just been remunerated for that series by the few pearls from the Infanta's jewel box), which tells us that he had begun with enthusiasm to paint the first sketches. Repeatedly his work was held back by modifications in the general scheme, or because the desired measurements for the pictures did not reach him. In spite of the resultant delays and the discouragement which his correspondence shows, Rubens was continuing the work even after the end of his diplomatic missions in Madrid and England. But when Maria de' Medici was obliged to flee from France in 1631, there was no longer any question of executing the series, though Rubens had prepared a certain number of oil sketches and even completed a few large canvases, among them *The Battle of Ivry* and the *Entry of Henry IV into Paris*, today in the Uffizi Gallery in Florence.[17]

Apart from the great series, Rubens continued to paint very important altarpieces during the period 1620 to 1628, although fewer, it is true, than during the previous decade. But some of them are among the finest he ever painted; and they reveal, moreover, a new stage in the development of his art. The compositions of these often monumental creations display greater cohesion. Constructions are no longer articulated along sharply defined diagonals; on the contrary, the figures are now caught, as if in perpetual motion, in graceful swinging movements which finally merge in a majestic synthesis. His palette grows more opulent, its ever-brighter pictorial values contributing to the cohesion,

189

Plate 47
THE ADORATION OF THE MAGI (detail; Pl. 46)
Antwerp, Koninklijk Museum voor
Schone Kunsten

*In this detail we can observe how brilliantly the artist succeeded, with just a few strokes of his brush, in giving shape and fullness to the face.*

*Following page*
Plate 48
THE ADORATION OF THE MAGI
Canvas, 12'7" × 9'2"
Brussels, Musées Royaux des Beaux-Arts de Belgique

*Rubens painted this altarpiece in 1618-20 in collaboration with Anthony van Dyck. He introduced a wooden staircase, which enabled him to place some figures in the upper part of the picture. The composition is still constructed with clearly marked diagonals. In the following period, 1620-28, he was to regroup the figures in such a way as to achieve greater unity in the composition.*

effortless and harmonious, which the artist was striving to achieve. Contours still play their part in the working out of the composition, but they are less strongly accentuated; the solidity of the volumes is softened, so that the figures, instead of being individually outlined, are now fused by delightful gradations of tones and shades into a color chord of dazzling brilliance and richness. Pictorial values prevail over line and volume.

This very pronounced sense of the unity in composition and color, of harmonious transitions in form and tone, could already be seen in some of the smaller pictures painted before 1620. A comparison of the *Small Last Judgment* (1618-20) with the *Large Last Judgment* (1615–16) (Plate 22), both in the Alte Pinakothek, Munich,[18] clearly indicates the direction Rubens' art would take. *The Battle of the Amazons* (Plate 78)[19] is another example, for in it we find already that dynamic arrangement, linked and easy, that interplay of values, and the clear transparency of the flesh. We will see all these elements again, but on a much grander scale, in the altarpieces of the 1620s, together with a chromaticism that becomes always warmer and richer.

It goes without saying that the same characteristics are found in the numerous oil sketches of the period. We could select many examples from the preparatory studies for the series described above, but there are others too, such as *The Martyrdom of St. Ursula and Her Companions* (Fig. 101) which dates from about 1620.[20] It has been said, and not without reason, that these martyrs, perishing under the dagger or the sword, evoke the turbulence of waves whipped up by a storm.[21] In this tumultuous event the profusion of the whirling bodies joins into a flux whose drama is rendered with unforgettable brio.

Besides, we may wonder whether the many oil sketches that Rubens painted in the 1620s, in which he sometimes achieved a remarkable expressiveness simply by touches of blue, pink, tender blue, or yellow on an ivory or brownish ground, did not put their own stamp on the development of his style, as well as on that of the great altarpieces. Let us look, for example, at certain parts of that monumental work, *The Adoration of the Magi* in Antwerp (Plates 46, 47).[22] A few powerful strokes of the artist's broad brush sufficed to make the forms stand out from the brownish background, that unifying element which links them together. Here he applied the technique of the small oil sketch to the large format. It seems to us that the oil sketches for the church of the Jesuits were decisive in the development of this new style; the varied format and the exigencies of ceiling design required of the artist a more concentrated expression. The flowing garments and the poses and gestures of the figures are treated functionally in a dynamic ensemble that is characterized by tonalities which pass in value from light shades to warm. In his sketches for the ceiling paintings Rubens gave his figures an airy grace: something of this quality too can be found in most of the altarpieces.

To add to the effect of unity, the painter sometimes introduces into the compositions of his altarpieces a staircase on which the figures move about. This architectural motif is both a linking device and

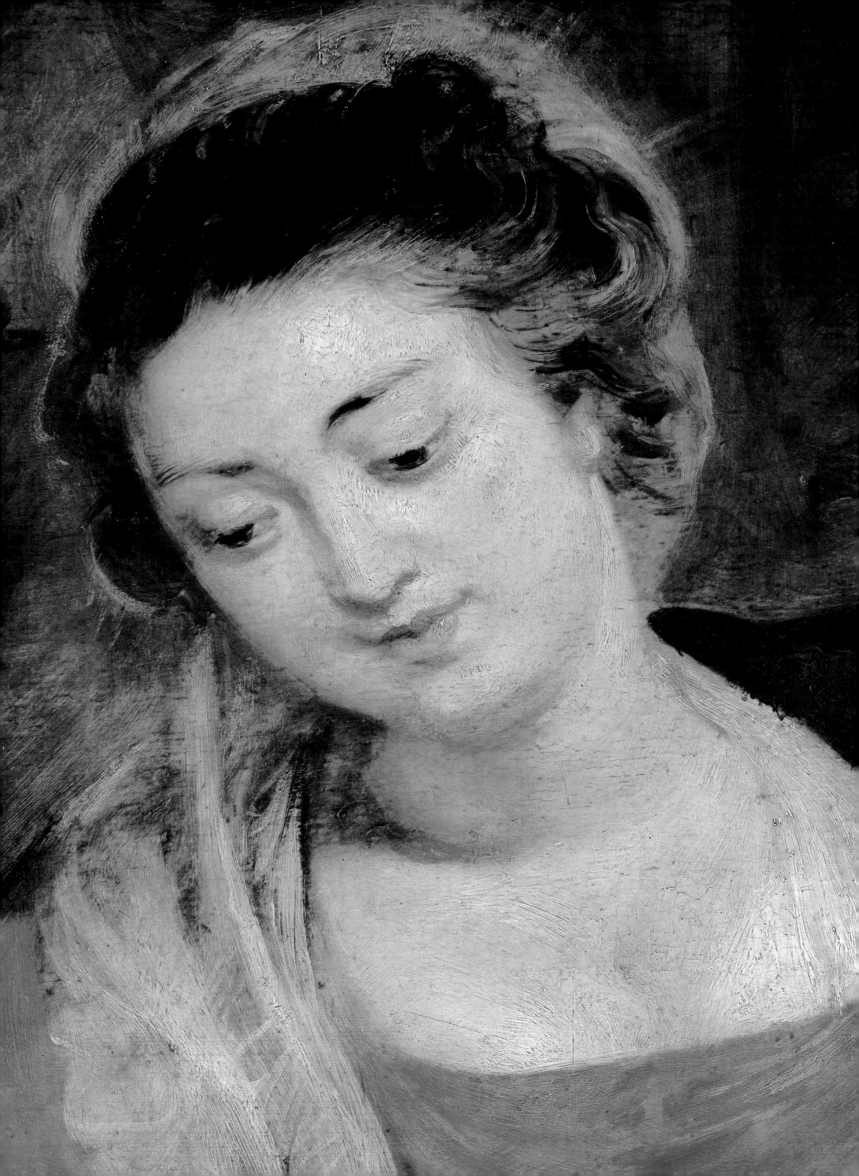

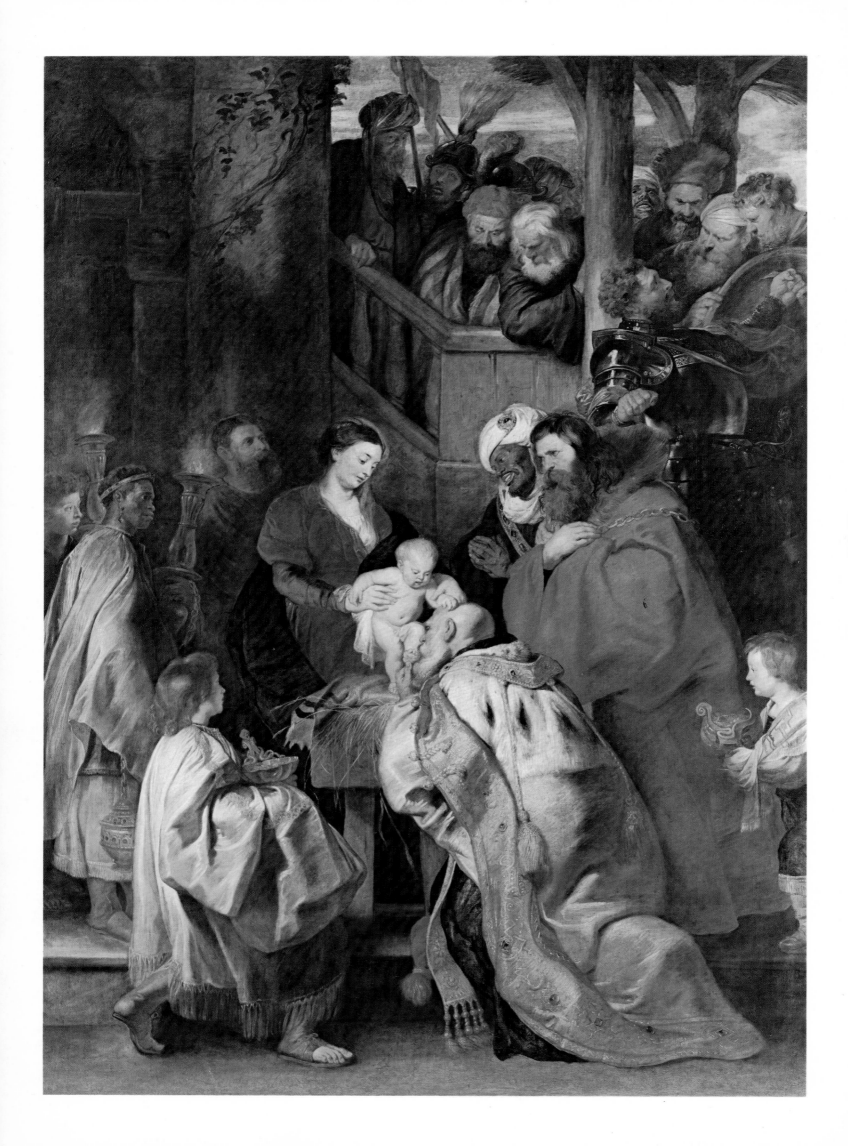

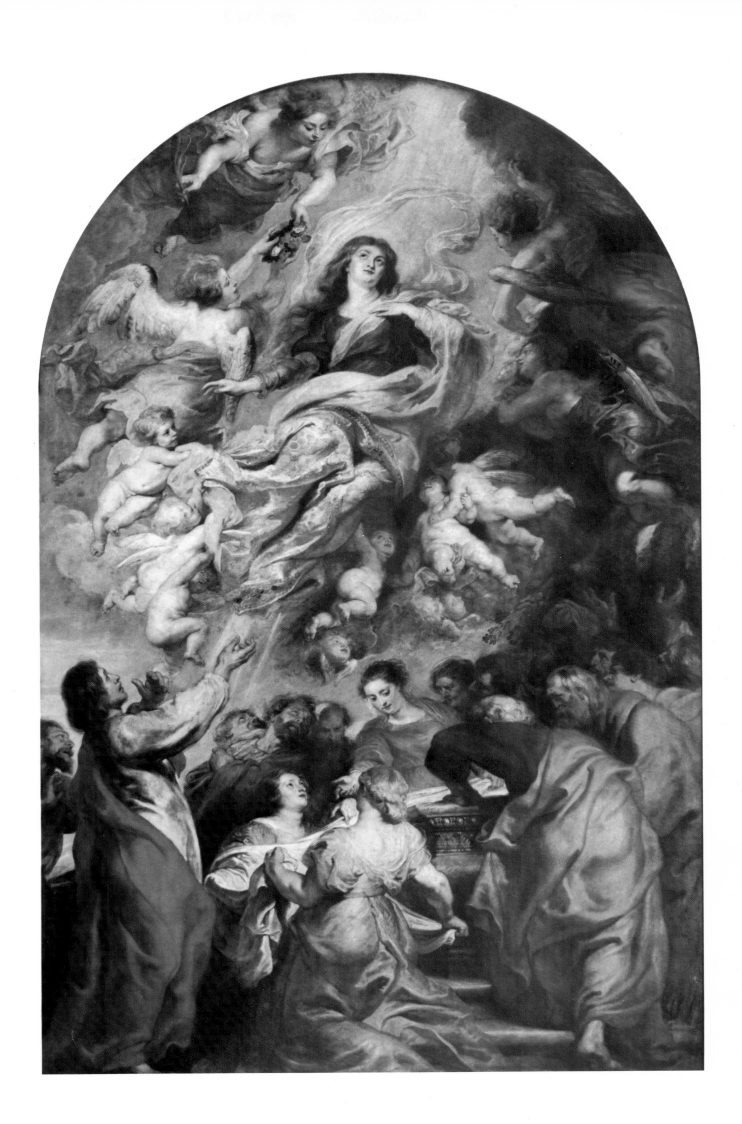

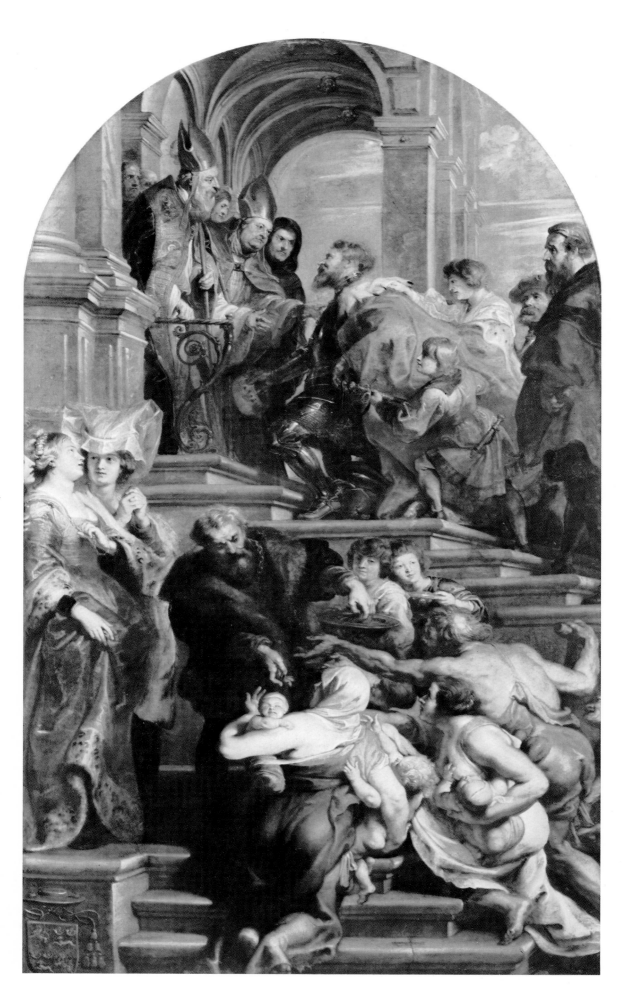

194

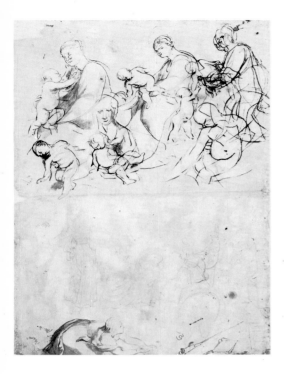

Figure 103
STUDIES FOR THE VIRGIN AND
CHILD
Drawing, 22⅛" × 16¼"
Verso, another STUDY FOR THE VIR-
GIN AND CHILD (see Fig. 107)
Stockholm, Nationalmuseum

*In this nervous scribble ("crabbelingh") as this type of sketch was called in the seventeenth century, the artist takes up the same motifs several times, seeking the best possible solution.*

*Preceding page*
Plate 49
THE ASSUMPTION OF THE VIRGIN
Panel, 16' × 10'8"
Antwerp, Cathedral of Our Lady

*Completed in 1626, this great altarpiece represents a stage of Rubens' artistic development in which the composition has become even more unified than before. The rich tonal values add to the elegant harmony that the painter achieves.*

Figure 102
THE CONVERSION OF ST. BAVO
Canvas, 15'6" × 9'2"
Ghent, Cathedral of St. Bavo

*In this altarpiece, painted in 1623–24, the stone staircase, starting from below to the right and then twisting around to the left as it moves upward, is an important element in the composition. Figure 44 shows Rubens' earlier rendering of this subject.*

a point of stability in the swirl of ascending and descending forms. In *The Adoration of the Magi* in Brussels (Plate 48),[23] painted about 1618–20 with the assistance of Van Dyck, Rubens puts in a wooden staircase as a means of filling the top part of the picture with figures. In the *Conversion of St. Bavo* (Fig. 102), in the cathedral of Ghent,[24] another staircase, this time a monumental one of stone, occupies a prominent position in the center of the composition. Rubens' *modello* for the altarpiece (Fig. 44), painted in 1611–12 but not executed in full until about fifteen years later, already contains a platform reached by two staircases and a landing,[25] but these serve mainly to accentuate a diagonal from upper left to lower right which seems to separate sharply the two groups of figures. All this is modified in the new composition; the figures are grouped according to oscillating lines which impose a vital, powerful pulsation to the scene.

There is no staircase in the altarpiece of 1624, *The Adoration of the Magi* in Antwerp (Plate 46), painted originally for the high altar of the abbey of St. Michael at Antwerp; everything moves with surprising freedom around the tall figure of the Moorish king. In contrast to the works with the same subject in the church of St. John at Malines and in the Brussels Museum (Plates 24, 48), this scene does not take place in the dark of night but is bathed evenly in the warm light of day and can freely display the iridescence of the colors and the infinite variety of tones in the chromatic scale. The marvels of the High Baroque emerge impressively from this dazzling symphony of colors.

In *The Assumption of the Virgin* in Antwerp Cathedral (Plate 49), an altarpiece finished two years later,[26] the whole composition pivots around the figure of Mary, who attracts immediate attention by the cool lapis-lazuli blue of her robe in strong contrast with the delicate tones dominating the whole. Around the Virgin crowds a suite of frolicsome putti, while graceful angels fly to meet her. The Virgin's figure rises in a delicate spiral through the slightly pivoting pose of her body, the elegant gestures of her hands, the flowing folds of her robe, and her loose, streaming scarf. The development of Rubens' art can best be measured by a comparison with the altarpiece in Düsseldorf of the same subject (Fig. 55), painted only eight years before. The composition has the same elements, but "what was once accentuated by means of a multitude of gestures, and by contrasts of light and shade, is here bound together into one harmonious pattern of movement, colour, and graceful attitudes. The Virgin is closer to mortals and yet upon a higher level."[27] We are fascinated once again by the tremendous variety of radiant colors, varied so richly and subtly graded, which give the whole a sumptuous and paradisiac appearence. The delicate pastel colors, in which shades of lilac predominate, anticipate the Rococo palette. No wonder that Watteau, Fragonard, and other masters of the "age of elegance" acknowledged their great admiration for Rubens.

A comparison of this work with *The Descent from the Cross* (Plate 16; Fig. 39), now installed in the same church of Our Lady in Antwerp, makes it easy for us to understand the nature of this

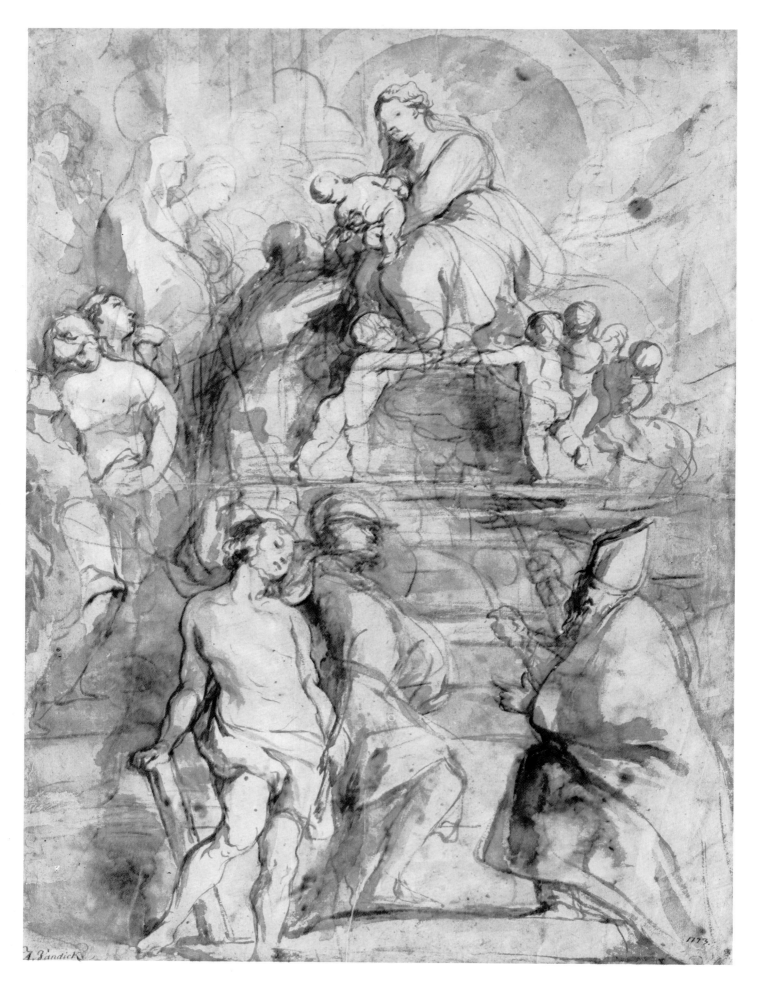

196

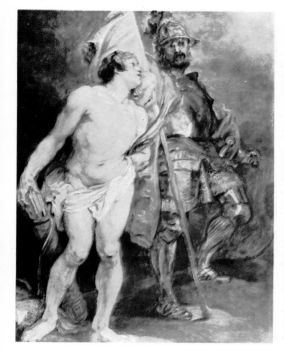

Figure 105
ST. SEBASTIAN AND ST. GEORGE
Oil sketch on panel, $16^1/_8'' \times 11^7/_8''$
Caen, Musée des Beaux-Arts

*Oil sketch for the two saints in the fore-
ground of the oil sketch for the* Virgin and
Child Adored by Saints *(Fig. 106). In
the finished altarpiece (Fig. 107), the figures
are reversed.*

Figure 106
VIRGIN AND CHILD ADORED BY
SAINTS
Oil sketch on panel, $25^1/_4'' \times 19^3/_4''$
Frankfurt, Städelsches Kunstinstitut

*The composition here is more elaborate than
it is in the drawing in Stockholm (Fig.
104).*

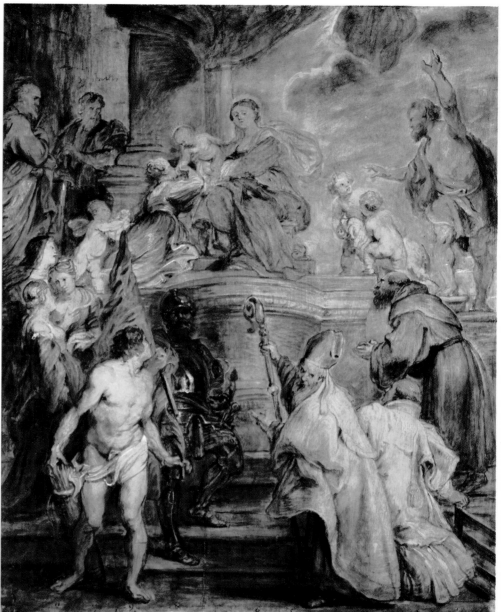

Figure 104
STUDY FOR THE "VIRGIN AND
CHILD ADORED BY SAINTS"
Drawing, $22^1/_8'' \times 16^1/_4''$
Recto: composition study
Stockholm, Nationalmuseum

*A quick drawing with several corrections
for the altarpiece of the church of St. Augustine. The composition was slightly altered
later, and worked out in more detail. Some
of the figures are fixed already in the position
they will assume in the painting, others will
be changed or will disappear.*

transformation. Pictorial values now predominate over sculptural
values. From this time onward color will no longer be "an
orchestration of tones, each maintaining in a very positive fashion its
own value in the total work, but a fusion and indivisible unity of
sumptuous and entrancing hues."[28]

In the altarpiece in the church of the Hermits of St. Augustine,
now the church of St. Augustine, in Antwerp (Fig. 107), Rubens again
uses an architectural element.[29] In the center of the composition he
places a high stone platform in the form of a Roman altar or pedestal,
a motif he had employed before, in a frontispiece (Fig. 136) among
other examples. He assembles the many saints on or near the flights
of steps leading to either side of the platform, and unites the composi-

197

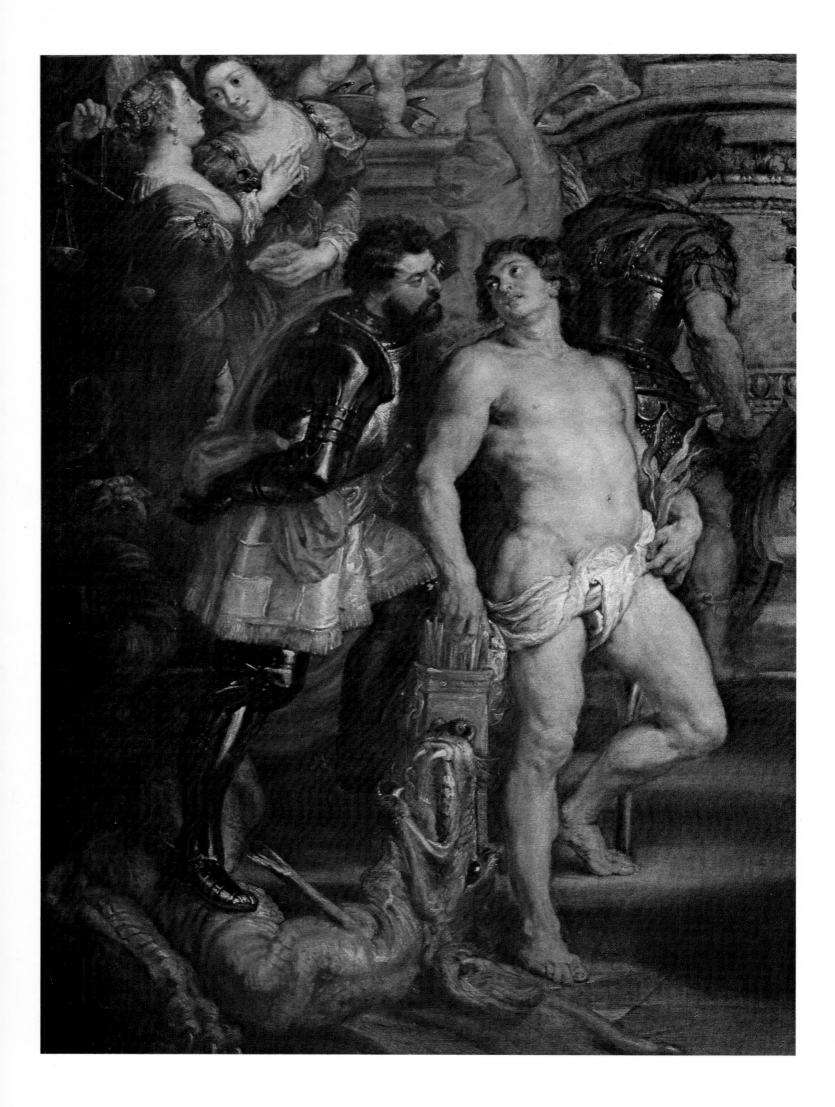

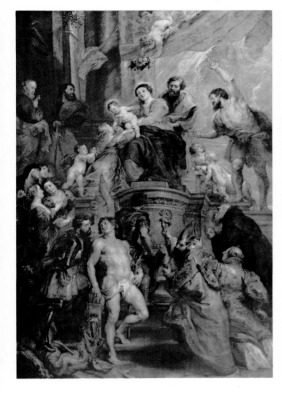

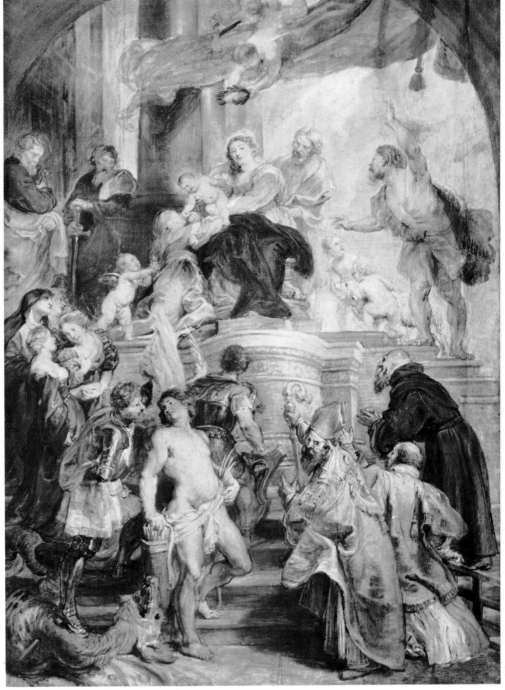

Plate 50
VIRGIN AND CHILD ADORED BY
SAINTS (detail; Fig. 107)
Antwerp, Church of St. Augustine

*The swift virtuosity of the execution of this altarpiece almost makes one forget the meticulous care that Rubens took with the preparation of his composition, by drawings and sketches. He even made a separate sketch for the group of St. George and St. Sebastian (Fig. 105), whose attitudes and gestures balance each other harmoniously.*

Figure 107
VIRGIN AND CHILD ADORED BY
SAINTS
Canvas, 18'5¹/₂'' × 13'1¹/₂''
Antwerp, Church of St. Augustine

*This grandiose altarpiece was completed in 1628. The oscillating compositional lines are remarkable: the figures seem to be swept along in a kind of "perpetuum mobile" around the elevated structure, a stable architectural element, on which are placed the Virgin, the Infant Jesus and St. Joseph.*

Figure 108
VIRGIN AND CHILD ADORED BY
SAINTS
Oil sketch on panel, 31'' × 21³/₄''
Berlin-Dahlem, Gemäldegalerie der Staatlichen Museen

*Compared to the Frankfurt sketch (Fig. 106), this oil sketch is proportionately higher; the composition, on the whole unchanged, is adapted to this modified format. The addition of St. Joseph above, the changed position of St. George below, on the left, and the presence of St. William of Aquitaine, armed and with his back to the spectator, are substantial differences.*

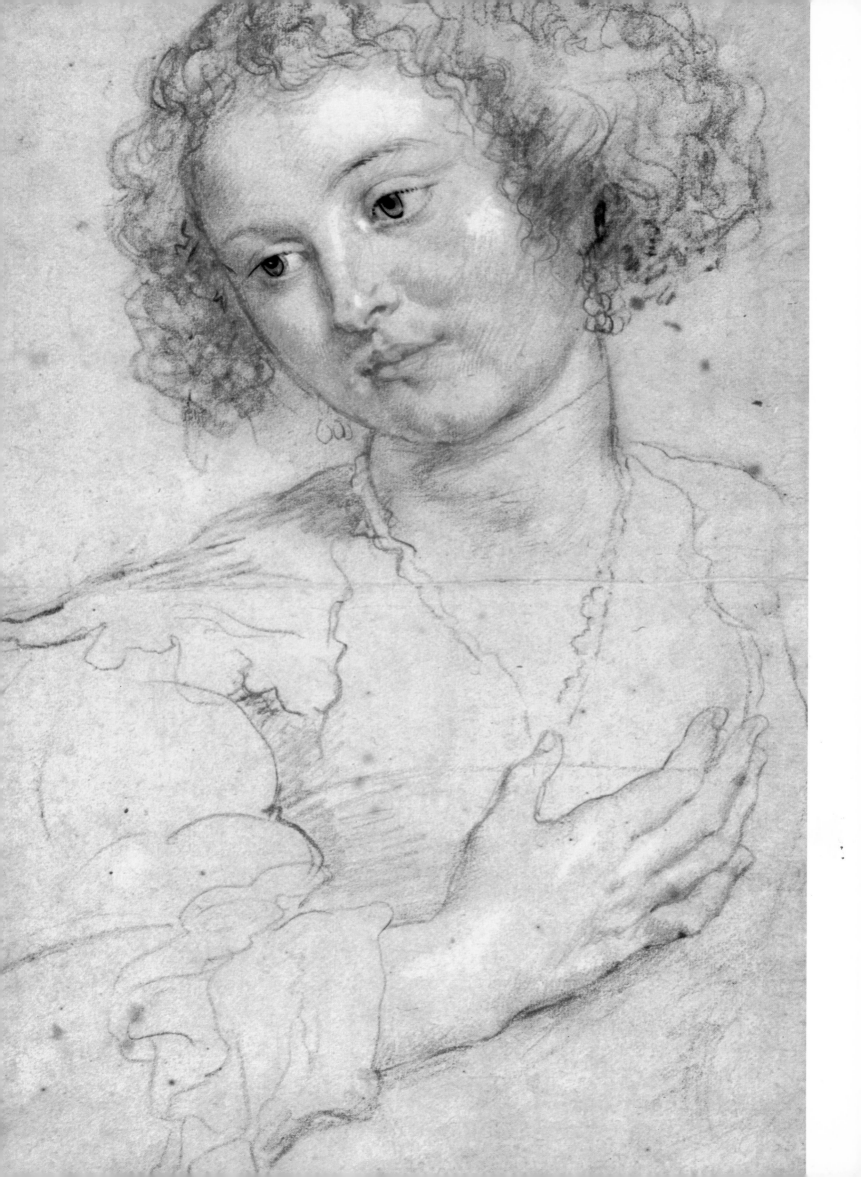

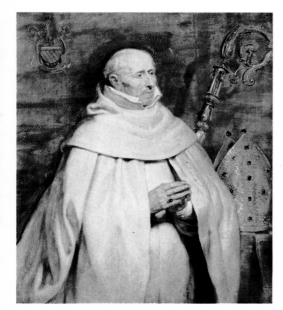

Figure 109
PORTRAIT OF MATTHEUS
YRSELIUS
Panel, 47$\frac{1}{4}$" × 40$\frac{1}{8}$"
Copenhagen, Statens Museum for Kunst

*The portrait of Mattheus van Yrsel or Yrselius (1541-1629), abbot of the Norbertine convent of St. Michael in Antwerp, was painted probably in 1624, when he commissioned Rubens to paint* The Adoration of the Magi *(Pl. 46) for the church of his convent.*

Plate 51
PORTRAIT STUDY (detail)
Drawing, over-all dimensions
16$\frac{1}{4}$" × 11$\frac{1}{4}$"
Florence, Uffizi Gallery

*Study from life; the clothing is only sketchily indicated. This study was used by Rubens for the figure of St. Apollonia in the* Virgin and Child Adored by Saints. *The artist used it a second time in* The Rape of the Sabine Women *(Fig. 128).*

tion by gracefully oscillating lines into a harmonious although asymmetrical whole.

This glorious masterpiece is frequently called *The Mystic Marriage of St. Catherine*, a title that covers only a part of what is represented; another title, *The Virgin and Child Enthroned with Saints*, is often used and seems more appropriate. The link between the subject of this picture and the dedication of the church—consecrated to Our Lady and all the Saints—for which it was painted has already been noticed by Peeters.[30] In this graceful *sacra conversazione*, on an unprecedentedly grandiose scale, "all the patches of color are set in motion by rapid transitions of tones, while the warmth of golden light, flowing from the celestial spheres above on the right, unifies the whole with a single vibrant emotion."[31] The gradations of color vie with this splendor, becoming brighter in the upper zone.

Looking at this picture, the spectator is once more amazed at the astonishing facility with which it seems to have been painted. Most of Rubens' works of the 1620s, moreover, will give him the same impression. Tradition has it that Rubens painted the large panel of the Antwerp *Adoration of the Magi* (Plate 46) in less than a week! Even if this is a strong exaggeration, it is no less true that this freedom and sureness of touch bear witness to his extremely effortless execution. This touch resulted, however, from a long period of incubation while the composition was pondered over before it became finally fixed. Drawings and oil sketches for the altarpiece in St. Augustine's church show admirably a number of stages in the preparatory work. A drawing in Stockholm (Fig. 104) gives in a few strokes a rough plan of the composition, which corresponds only in its general outlines to the finished picture;[32] on the verso of this sheet (Fig. 103) are studies of Mary and the Child side by side, and two of the Child alone.[33] In these rapid sketches, which Flemish seventeenth-century artists called "crabbelinge" ("scribblings"), Rubens takes up the same motif with several variants to achieve the most suitable representation. We also have two oil sketches of the whole composition: one is in Frankfurt (Fig. 106);[34] the other, the closest to the picture and perhaps the model for the final execution, is in the Dahlem Museum, Berlin (Fig. 108).[35] Between these sketches Rubens made a third, smaller one, showing only St. Sebastian and St. George (Fig. 105) in poses almost identical with those in the Stockholm drawing.[36] When the composition was at last clearly fixed, the artist made yet another very fine chalk study, now in the Uffizi Gallery, Florence,[37] of the young woman who served as the model for St. Apollonia in the final picture (Plate 51).

These preliminary studies—and doubtless others that have since disappeared—give evidence of how much thoughtful effort and study preceded the execution of a large canvas of this complexity. They also show us how Rubens succeeded in bringing order and balance into the impetuousness of his vision and the profusion of figures and motifs, thereby producing a composition which the eye takes in at a glance.

201

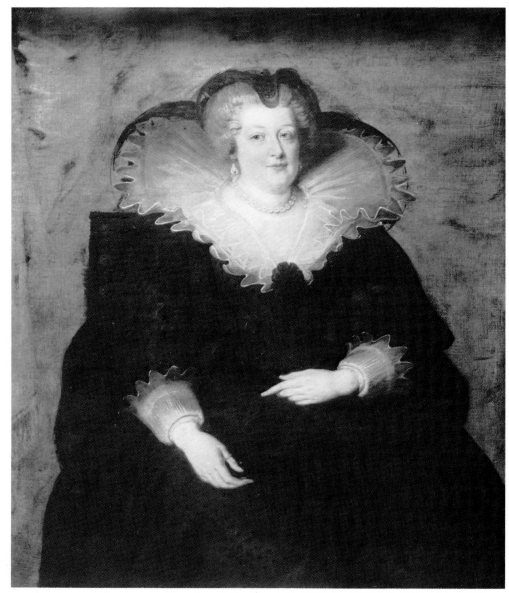

Figure 110
PORTRAIT OF MARIA DE' MEDICI
Panel, 51¹/₈" × 42¹/₂"
Madrid, Prado

*In this portrait of the queen-mother of France, painted in 1622, the conventional pose recalls sixteenth-century portraiture. The model was certainly not beautiful; Rubens has idealized her slightly.*

Rubens completed this magnificent altarpiece in 1628, shortly before his departure for Madrid at the end of August. It is one of the grandest and most beautiful he ever painted. In this work, and at this stage of Rubens' art, the grandiose hymn of the Baroque swells out to its fullest sonority. Rubens would never again conceive any religious picture so dynamic, so thrilling in its marvelously balanced counterpoint!

Plate 52
PORTRAIT OF ISABELLA BRANT
Panel, 22¹/₂" × 18⁷/₈"
The Cleveland Museum of Art

*This portrait of Rubens' first wife, painted around 1620, reveals an intelligent and lively personality. There is a hint of irony in the way she looks at the spectator.*

A final word on the quite numerous portraits which date from this period of the great series and altarpieces. Some of these also rank among the finest known by Rubens' hand and they follow the same development, from a strict classicism to a freer, more pictorial Baroque style. This change is not so apparent at first sight because the portraitist was obviously less free in depicting some of his models. Official

202

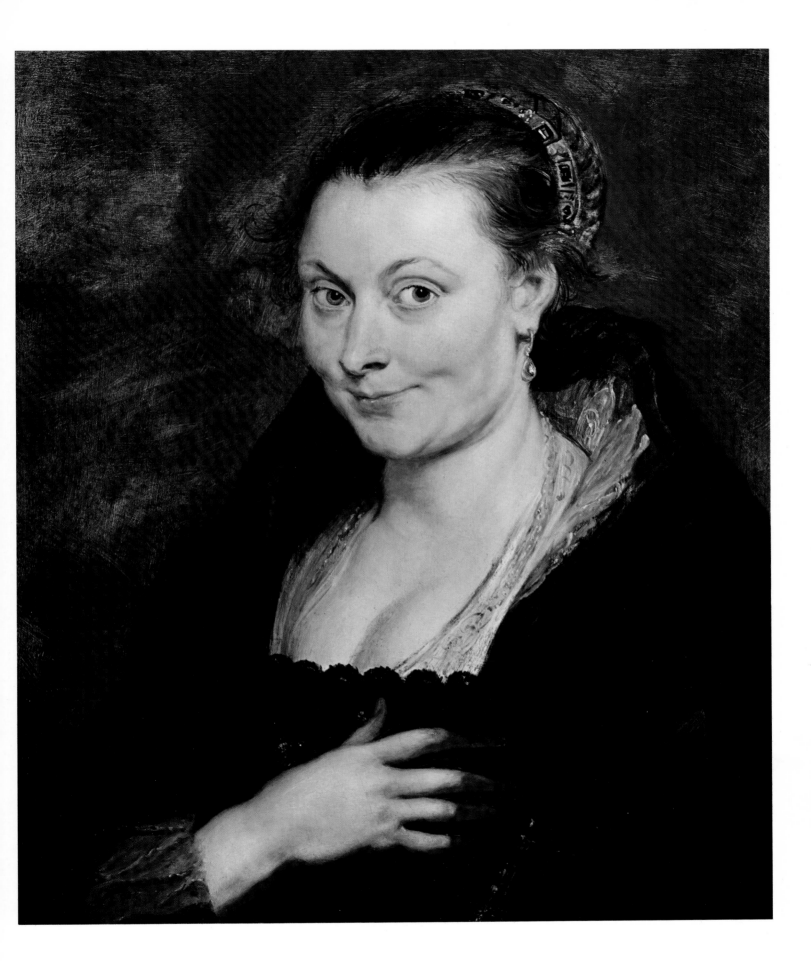

203

portraits, too, required him to take into account the conventional character of that genre.

Rubens painted some of these official portraits while executing the important royal commissions during that period. The *Portrait of Maria de' Medici* (Fig. 110) is a typical example.[38] The queen-mother's conventional seated pose recalls sixteenth-century portraiture, as in works by Anthonis Mor. One cannot say that the queen-mother of France was beautiful; one need only glance at Rubens' preparatory drawings of her (Fig. 120) for the Luxembourg Palace series:[39] the long, hooked nose, heavy chin, and plump, fleshy cheeks are not in harmony with the rather too-narrow forehead. In his painted portrait Rubens idealized the model: on the left the contours of her cheek and double chin are scarcely visible in the soft play of light, while the heavy volumes on the right are tactfully toned down by velvety shadows.

The *Portrait of the Abbot Matthäus Yrssel* or *Yrselius* (Fig. 109), painted in 1624, is also connected with an important commission: the *Adoration of the Magi*, which the abbot of St. Michael's ordered for the high altar of his church.[40] In his portrait the prelate is represented in prayer, in a conventional manner, with the insignia of his dignified office placed at his side. Nevertheless the portrait of the old churchman presents a realistic image of rare psychological penetration. The painter has boldly contrasted the austerity of the face—its hollow cheeks, its pinched, suffering mouth, and moist eyes—with the warmth of the crimson-lake background and with the monumental white robe, thereby giving the whole a Baroque sonority.

Other portraits had their origin in Rubens' diplomatic activities. Let us take as an example *Ambrogio Spinola* (Plate 59):[41] the general and statesman is also represented conventionally with one hand on his commander's baton and the other on the hilt of his sword, and with helmet and gauntlets on the table beside him. But the artist has succeeded in rendering masterfully the closed character of his model and his power of concentration. Rubens also made very fine chalk drawings of the marquis of Leganés (Plate 56)[42] and the duke of Buckingham (Plate 55),[43] with both of whom he had diplomatic contacts. These drawings were preliminary studies for the portraits he later painted of these statesmen.

Conventionalism gives way to a more direct and lively rendering when Rubens portrays his friends or members of his family. One or two examples will illustrate this. First, the engaging portrait of Isabella Brant, his first wife (Plate 58; see also Plate 52):[44] the Uffizi portrait, probably painted not long before Isabella died, is touching in the tender affection with which the features are depicted. The regular shape of the wide, almond-shaped eyes beneath high eyebrows, the spirited nose, the fine bow of the lips that turn up at the corners and extend like dimples onto the cheeks—all point to a vivacious personality: she looks at the spectator, and not without irony!

In another portrait Rubens represents his friend Jan Caspar Gevaerts or Gevartius (Plate 54),[45] the well-known humanist and a clerk of the

Plate 53
PORTRAIT OF SUSANNA FOURMENT
("LE CHAPEAU DE PAILLE")
(detail)
Panel, over-all dimensions 31" × 21³/₄"
London, National Gallery

*Susanna (1599–1643), the elder sister of Helena Fourment, married Arnold Lunden in 1622. She often posed as a model for Rubens. The layers of paint have been applied with such a fine and transparent effect that the face, despite its winsome reality, acquires an ethereal radiance. The traditional title of the picture goes back to an erroneous translation into French, for the young woman in fact wears a felt hat.*

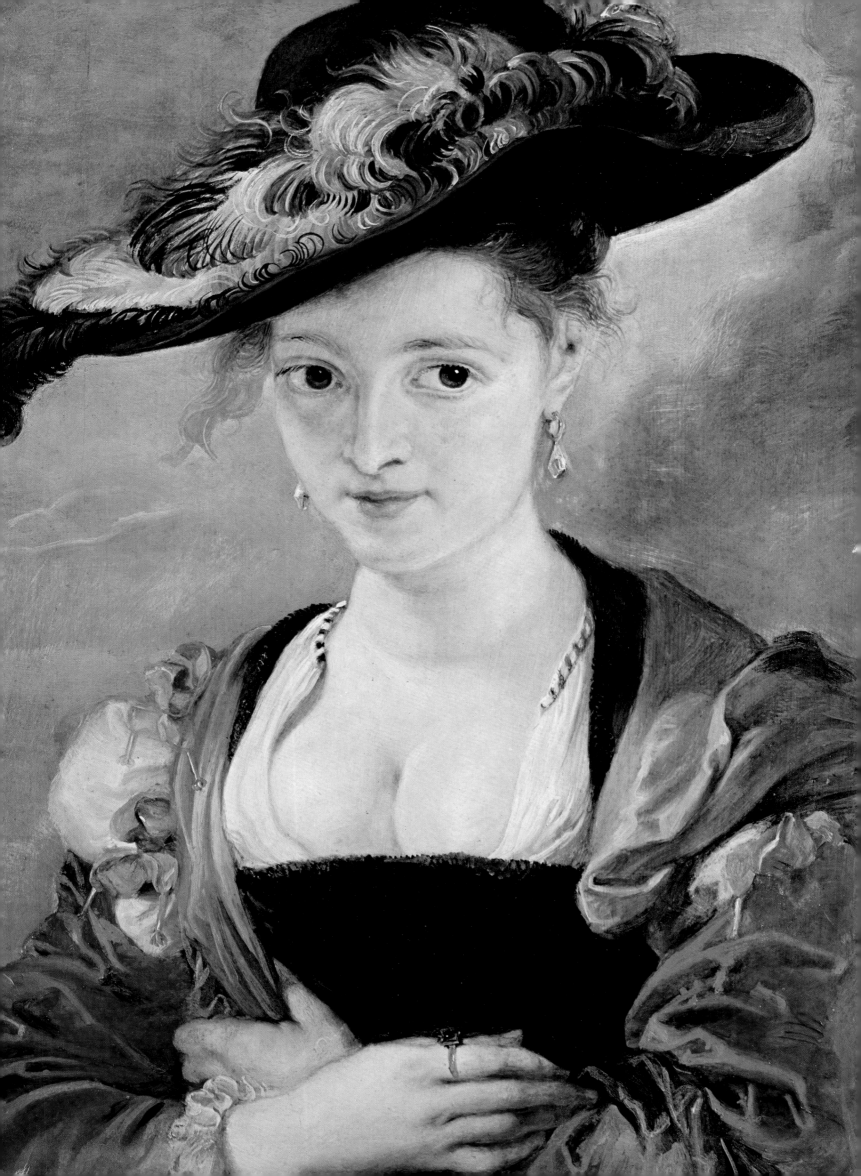

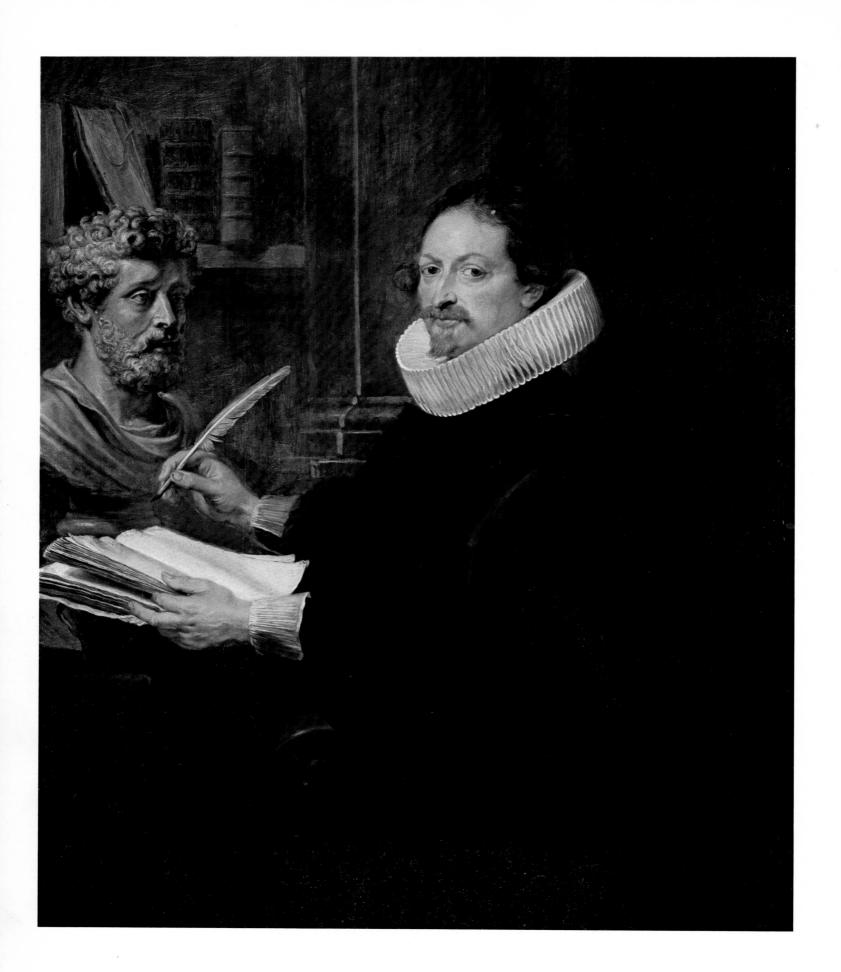

206

city of Antwerp, to whom Rubens entrusted the education of his son Albert when he was away in Madrid and London. The features of the face are delicately cut, and the head stands out most successfully against a brown-gray background. The clear skin, slightly ivory in its cast, is set off by the brilliant white ruff. This whiteness, repeated in the pages of the book on the table, cuts across the loose, black-silk magistrate's gown that the scholar wears. He has just dipped his quill pen in the inkwell, and the clear gaze of his brown eyes seems to turn for a moment toward the spectator before he goes back to his writing. By representing Gevaerts between two actions, so to speak, Rubens, the Baroque artist, breaks with the conventional character of the "posed" portrait. The bust of Marcus Aurelius on the table reminds us that Gevaerts was a Latin scholar who cherished a great admiration for the Roman philosopher-emperor.

The *Portrait of Ludovicus Nonnius* (Plate 71) also includes attributes that indicate the sitter's qualifications as scholar and doctor, but the artist's wish to represent an instantaneous action is more in evidence here. Nonnius' somewhat loose grip on the book in his lap, the gesture of his right hand, and the expression of his face make us feel that the doctor is somehow conversing with us. And more: he raises his eyes, pauses, and points with his right index finger to a passage he has just cited in the book. The static pose is counterbalanced by the slight fantasy of the contours of Nonnius' dark coat, the black cape falling from his shoulders, and the open book.

In Rubens' self-portrait in the Rubens House in Antwerp (Plate 70) the artist shows himself as if in a conversation, turning his face toward us and seeming to listen or reflect before speaking. He too is fixed in a transition between two actions. This fascinating portrait dates from about 1625–28, when Rubens was some fifty years old; in any event, it was painted before the end of August 1628, when he left Antwerp to carry out a diplomatic mission in Madrid.

His departure for Madrid closed the very rich period of 1620 to 1628, that of the "great series," the Baroque altarpieces, the fiery portraits, and of Rubens' artistic "break-through" in Europe. For the next two years he was again a diplomat, playing a leading part on the chessboard of European politics.

Plate 54
PORTRAIT OF CASPAR GEVAERTS
Panel, 47″ × 42³/₄″
Antwerp, Koninklijk Museum voor Schone Kunsten

*Humanist and clerk of the city of Antwerp, Caspar Gevaerts or Gevartius (1593–1666) was a close friend of Rubens. By catching him at a moment when he is looking up from his desk, Rubens gives the portrait a life-like quality which cuts across the convention of the pose.*

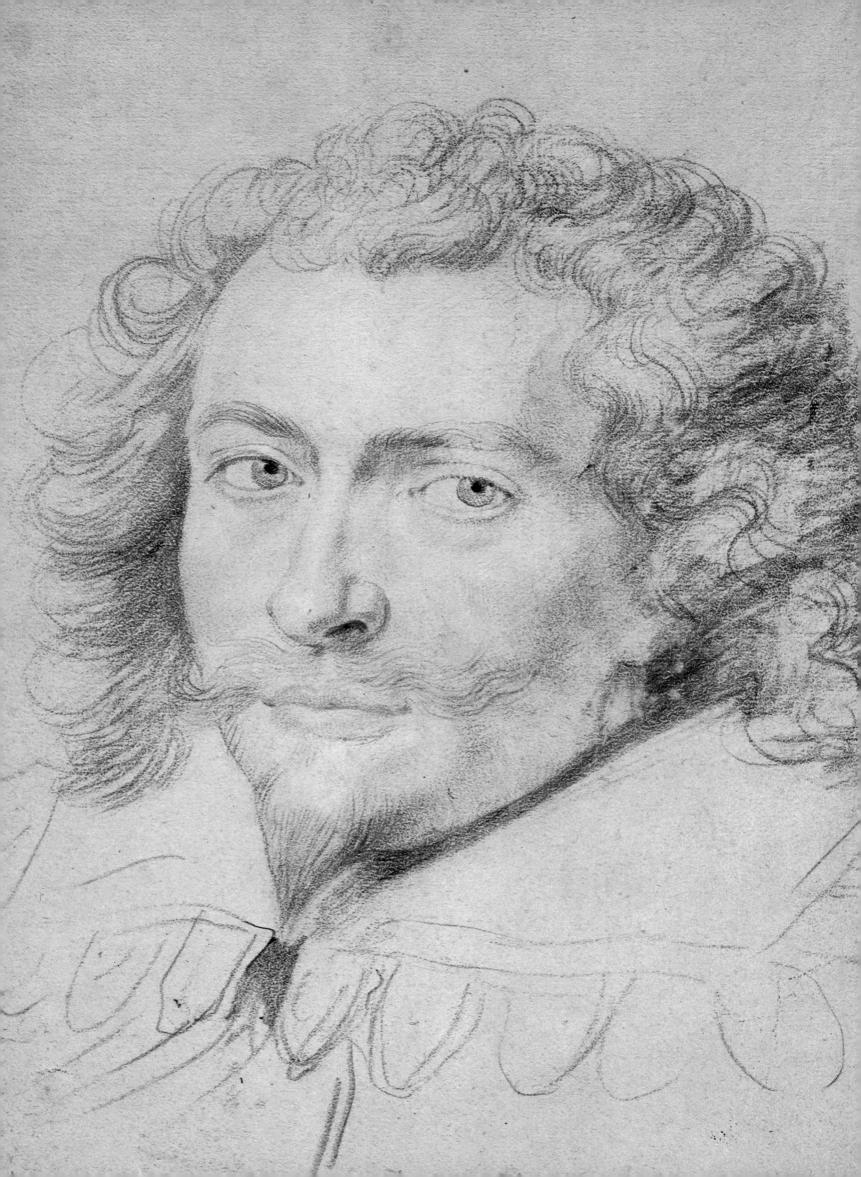

# Rubens the Diplomat

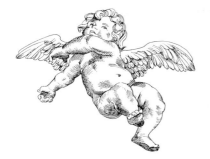

Plate 55
PORTRAIT OF GEORGE VILLIERS,
DUKE OF BUCKINGHAM
Drawing, 15$\frac{1}{8}$" × 10$\frac{1}{2}$"
Vienna, Graphische Sammlung Albertina

*Rubens made this chalk drawing of the head of the English statesman in the spring of 1625, in preparation for the portrait which the latter had commissioned. These contacts with Buckingham made possible, some years later, the beginning of negotiations between Spain and England, in which Rubens had a key role.*

In 1585 Alessandro Farnese reconquered the city of Antwerp for King Philip II of Spain and for the Catholic faith, and thereby made final the rift between the Northern and Southern Netherlands. Hostilities did not cease, however; quite the contrary, the king wished to reconquer *all* the hereditary territories which his father Emperor Charles V had bequeathed to him on his abdication in 1556. Thus Philip spared no effort to regain the Northern provinces, which had wrested their independence by armed force and proclaimed themselves the United Provinces. These "rebels" on their side wanted to consolidate their newly won liberty and still cherished the hope that the Southern provinces in their turn would free themselves from the Spanish yoke and join them.

When a series of vain attempts made the aging Philip II realize that neither force nor negotiation would succeed in winning back the United Provinces for the Spanish crown, he took a decision that was to have vital importance for the provinces. In 1598 he ceded the Netherlands to Archduke Albert and Archduchess Isabella—including *de jure* the provinces of the North, which in fact had broken away. Theoretically, the Netherlands no longer depended on Madrid, but now constituted an independent nation that was still bound by certain ties to Spain. Ties of blood, particularly: Archduke Albert, of the Austrian branch of the Hapsburgs, was the nephew of Philip II; Isabella was Philip's eldest daughter and also his favorite, "the apple of his eye."[1]

In signing this act of cession, Philip II was perhaps counting on the affection which the inhabitants of the Netherlands retained for their natural sovereigns, particularly if the regents came to live in the "country down there" ("Landen van herwaarts over"), and they were certainly welcomed triumphantly in the Spanish Netherlands. But the Northern "rebels" did not lay down their arms or renounce their dearly gained freedom—which, moreover, had brought them a number of economic advantages. Neither did they wish to abjure their Protestant faith. And in addition they possessed a great military leader in the person of Prince Maurice of Nassau, a son of William the Silent.

209

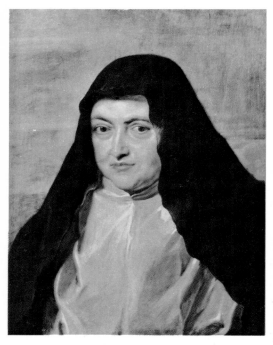

The document which settled the transfer of power to the regents contained certain provisions that were somewhat alarming. One stipulated that the Netherlands would return to the Spanish crown, should the regents die without issue; another, that a Spanish army would remain stationed in the Netherlands. A third article which aroused mistrust was the oath of eternal loyalty to Catholicism that the regents had to maintain; this provision applied only to the sovereigns' personal religious convictions, but, at a time when the principle of "cuius regio, eius religio" (the ruler's faith is the people's) was no idle phrase, it boded no good for the Northern Protestants.

Although Spain's cession of the Netherlands was restricted to certain conditions, it would be a mistake to declare the sovereignty of the regents a mere fiction. Lefèvre has proved that they truly reigned as autonomous sovereigns, within the limitations imposed upon them.[2]  For example, they appointed their own ambassadors to foreign countries, and diplomats from other countries were correspondingly accredited at the court at Brussels.  And the regents often pursued policies which were in no way those of Spain.  This fact is important in judging Rubens' activity as a diplomat; he has sometimes been regarded unjustly as an acolyte of the Spaniards, and certainly he did defend Spanish interests also, but only when these coincided with the policies of the Infanta.  Furthermore, he was obliged more than once to conduct secret negotiations, unknown to the Spaniards.

But let us not anticipate events.  The regents arrived in the Southern Netherlands on August 20, 1599; Rubens was then barely twenty-one years old.  The previous year he had completed his apprenticeship to the famous painter Otto van Veen,[3] who was commissioned late in 1599 to design triumphal arches celebrating the Entry of the Regents into Antwerp.  Rubens may have assisted him in the execution of this decoration; he could have had no inkling that one day he would be the Infanta's counsellor.  A few months later he left the Netherlands, in May 1600, to make his way to Italy.  And after his return, when he was made painter to the "household" of the regents on September 23, 1609,[4] he could not have expected that one day he would be entrusted with their political missions.  Yet this appointment—as well as the permission, rarely accorded, not to be obliged to live near the court—was later to prove decisive for Rubens' diplomatic activity.  In his capacity as a member of the regents' "household" he had easy access to the court, while secret diplomatic agents could approach him in his house in Antwerp without their visits arousing suspicion in political circles in Brussels.

In the first years after his return and for a long time thereafter, Rubens probably never dreamed of mixing in state affairs.  Painting monopolized his life.  When he made an occasional appearance at the court in Brussels it was in connection with some commission, or to give advice on some artistic matter for the regents.  Mostly he remained in Antwerp, where he kept up his astonishing artistic activity.  Not until some twelve years after his return, when his reputation as a painter had spread far beyond his own country, did he venture

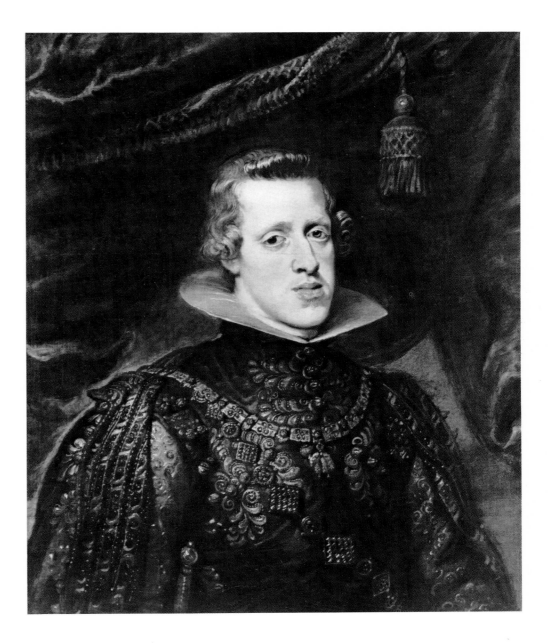

Figure 112
PORTRAIT OF PHILIP IV, KING OF
SPAIN
Canvas, 31″ × 28³/₄″
Zürich, Kunsthaus (Stiftung Ruzicka)

*This portrait of the king at the age of 23 was executed in 1628 in Madrid, during Rubens' stay in the Spanish capital.*

into the risky field of secret diplomacy—at first, it appears, in a casual manner, but later with the firm determination to achieve successful results in this area also.

Rubens entered the diplomatic scene about when the Twelve-Years' Truce expired on April 12, 1621. The regents were known to favor a prolongation of this truce. Before the expiration date they had already undertaken negotiations toward a lasting peace, or at least toward extending the truce. These negotiations failed, however. In Madrid, where the reluctant consent to sign an armistice had been given twelve years before, the government now wished to resume military operations against the North immediately. The Spanish rulers still regarded the inhabitants of the United Provinces as rebels, to be brought to obe-

211

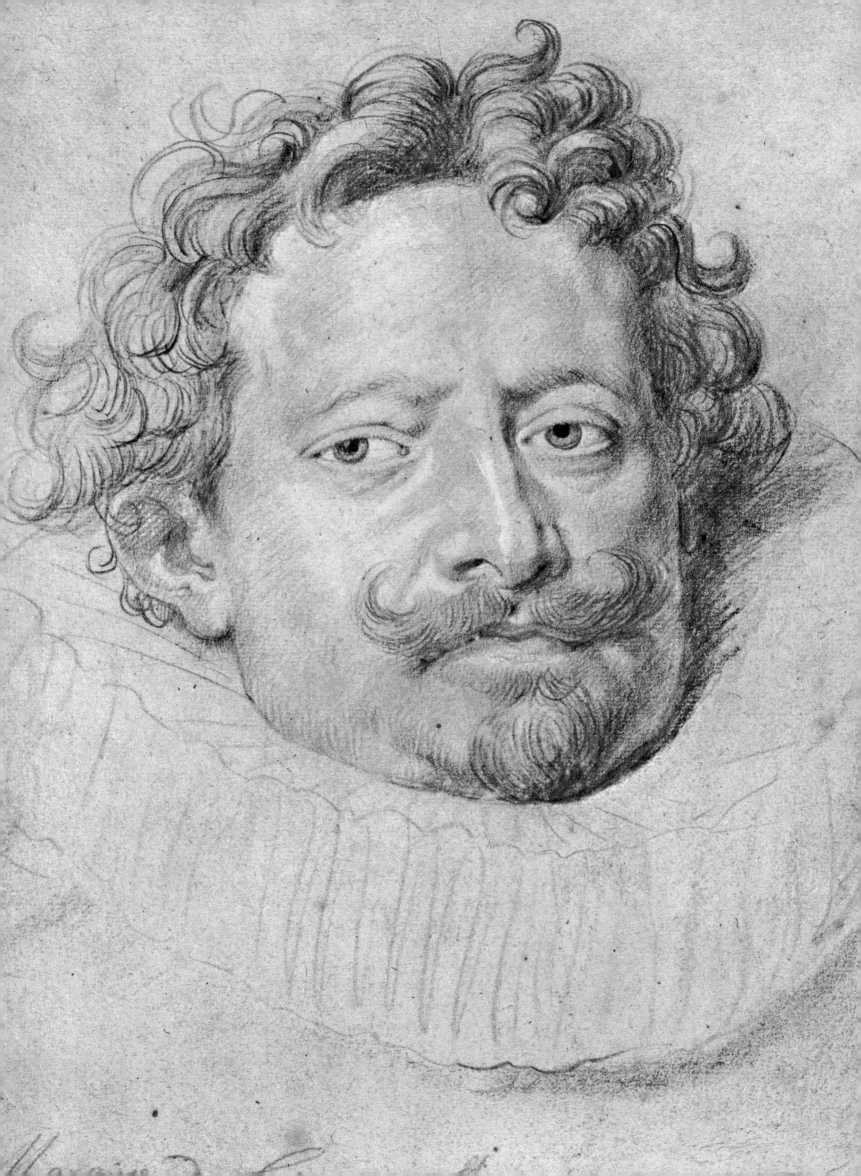

dience as soon as possible. The king of Spain, who had made himself the champion of Catholicism, could not tolerate the establishing of Protestantism in "his" territories; furthermore he was extremely vexed to see the growing maritime power of the Northern Provinces which threatened Spanish interests in the East and West Indies. Nevertheless at a given moment Philip IV declared himself ready to sign another truce, but on conditions then totally unacceptable to the United Provinces. The Northern Netherlands—particularly Amsterdam, whose progress was in full swing, and the trading towns of Zealand—were not inclined to conclude a peace treaty which would waste the economic advantage derived from the blockade of Antwerp. And finally there were France and England, both trying to oppose the worldwide hegemony of Spain, who would stop at nothing to keep in a minority the pacifist party in the Northern Provinces. Once again there was no recourse but to arms.

It did not improve matters for the Southern Netherlands that the Archduke Albert died on July 13, 1621, soon after the Twelve-Years' Truce expired. The Infanta now found herself alone, facing a situation full of danger and uncertainty. In the absence of an heir, the Netherlands reverted to the Spanish crown. The Infanta was "degraded," falling from the rank of sovereign to that of "governor" (Fig. 111). Her moral authority was such, however, that she continued to exercise the widest possible sovereignty, although in matters of war and peace she was compelled to follow the directives of her nephew Philip IV, the king of Spain (Fig. 112). Fortunately, in accomplishing her task she could always count on the faithful support of the Genoese marquis Ambrogio Spinola (Plate 59); since the first years of the regents' reign, this particularly intelligent and enterprising man had more or less combined the functions of marshal of the royal household, prime minister, general, and counsellor. Soon Rubens would also appear more and more frequently in the entourage of the Infanta and Spinola, whenever certain decisions pertaining to foreign policy had to be made.

The first extant letter by Rubens relating to his activities as a diplomat is dated September 30, 1623,[5] but its content justifies the conclusion that he had previously engaged in secret affairs of state. A decree of the Infanta Isabella confirms this—enacted, by coincidence, the same day—giving orders to the Spanish military authority of the citadel of Antwerp to pay the artist a monthly sum "by reasons of his merits and of services rendered to the king, and that he may continue to render them more easily."[6]

One may well be surprised that Rubens, an artist overburdened with commissions, should in addition be dabbling in matters of state. Obviously his sphere of interest extended beyond purely artistic concerns. Since early youth he had proved himself a perspicacious judge of character, and an acute observer of human actions and relationships as well. Nevertheless the circumstances were altogether fortuitous which led him to pursue actively the role of diplomat.

Relying on the meager data available to us, we can reconstruct these

Plate 56
PORTRAIT OF DON DIEGO MESSIA, MARQUIS OF LEGANÉS
Drawing, 15" × 10⅞"
Vienna, Graphische Sammlung Albertina

*Rubens met the marquis shortly after the latter's arrival in Brussels on September 9, 1627. Leganés was entrusted with a special message from Philip IV for the Infanta. On this occasion, the artist drew the portrait of the marquis in black, red, and white chalks.*

213

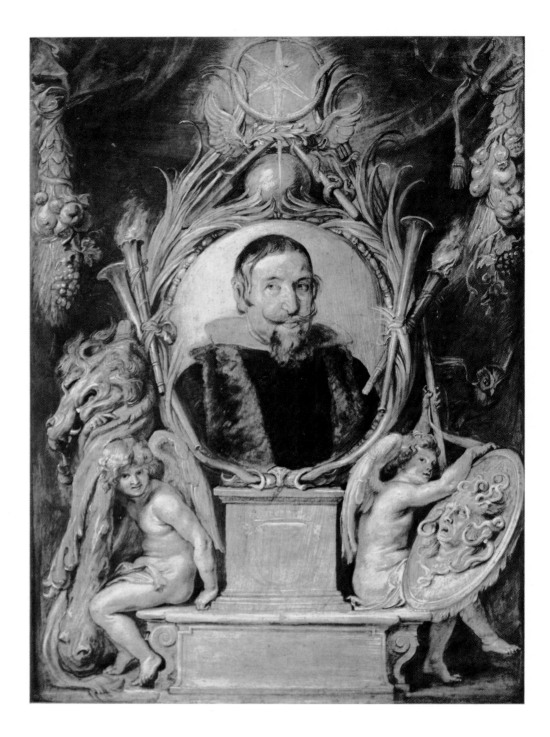

Figure 113
PORTRAIT OF THE COUNT DUKE
OLIVARES
Oil sketch on panel, 24³/₄″ × 17³/₈″
Brussels, Musées Royaux des Beaux-
Arts de Belgique

*Portrait in grisaille of Philip IV's influen-
tial chief minister, executed for an engraving
carried out by Paul Pontius and published
in 1627. The face is based on a drawing
by Velázquez, which the latter sent to
Rubens from Spain.*

circumstances as follows. When the Twelve-Years' Truce expired in
1621 Jan Brant, Rubens' first wife's nephew, who lived in The Hague,
tried to get in touch with the court of the regents in Brussels.[7] Brant
belonged to the Dutch branch of the family and bore the same name
as Rubens' father-in-law, with whom he should not be confused; he
was a trusted adherent of Maurice of Nassau, prince of Orange, and
was apparently one of the partisans of the truce who sought an agreement with the Spanish Netherlands. At a certain moment Prince
Maurice seemed inclined to sign a peace treaty, and Jan Brant wished

214

to pass this information on to the regents. He found Rubens to act as intermediary on this occasion. As painter to the regents' "household," he had easy access to the court in Brussels and could transmit secret information to influential persons without arousing suspicion. Rubens reported his conversations with Jan Brant to another distant relative of his family, Pierre Pecquius, or Peck (Fig. 116), the chancellor of Brabant and a trusted counsellor of the Infanta.[8] Rubens' first preserved diplomatic letter, mentioned above, is addressed to Pecquius and concerns the conditions for peace which he had discussed in Antwerp with Jan Brant, called by the pseudonym "El Catolico" in the correspondence. Thus it was two family relationships—one a nephew of his wife, the other an important civil servant at the Brussels court—that brought the artist into the capacity of a negotiator in state affairs.

It may seem strange that men like Jan Brant and Rubens, neither one a career diplomat in any way, should embark on negotiations in a matter so important as the peace treaty between the United Provinces and the Spanish Netherlands; the one having the sanction of the prince of Orange, the other by agreement with the Infanta's counsellor. But the reason is plain: although hostilities ceased during the Twelve-Years' Truce, continuous diplomatic relations between Brussels and The Hague had lapsed and neither side had appointed diplomatic agents, even unofficially.[9] When the truce expired there could obviously be no question of this, since the two sides were again at war. Diplomatic contact could thus be established only by the intervention of persons who, for family reasons, frequently crossed the frontier in both directions.

One such person was Bertholdis van Swieten, the widow of Florent T'Serclaes, whose journeys are well known. A native of Holland, she frequently came to Brussels to see her daughters, who were married to noblemen in the Spanish Netherlands. Although she was a Catholic convert she still enjoyed the confidence of Maurice of Nassau because her deceased husband had been a faithful companion of the prince's father. Between 1621 and 1624 she undertook no fewer than "thirty-eight journeys or more" to Brussels, and later this "mediator of peace" was at work again.[10] Another such person was Willem de Bie, secretary of the Council of Finance in Brussels; he was related to Constantine Huygens,[11] Prince Maurice's secretary, and under cover of family visits he went repeatedly to The Hague, though in reality he was acting on the Infanta's orders to exchange views of a political nature. Jan Brant too could invoke family reasons for coming to Antwerp, where he discussed with Rubens the conditions for a peace treaty or a truce.

The documents do not allow us to follow these conversations closely; their secret character probably caused a fair number of letters to be destroyed by the interested parties themselves. But in any case, Pecquius reported on the progress of his talks to the Infanta; she in turn informed her nephew, King Philip IV of Spain, about them in due course. On October 11, 1624, the king declared himself in agree-

*Following pages*
Plate 57
SELF-PORTRAIT
Panel, 33⁷/₈″ × 24⁷/₈″
Windsor Castle, Collection of Her Majesty Queen Elizabeth II

*This portrait, painted in 1622–23, was commissioned by the future king of England, Charles I. Rubens was then 45 years of age.*

Plate 58
PORTRAIT OF ISABELLA BRANT
Canvas, 33¹/₂″ × 24¹/₂″
Florence, Uffizi Gallery

*Rubens painted this portrait shortly before his wife's premature death on June 20, 1626. She was in her 35th year. Her bright, almond-shaped eyes, the arched eyebrows, the sensitive nose, the fine lips whose upward curve extends from the bow toward the cheeks into a charming dimple, point to a personality with an intense inner life.*

215

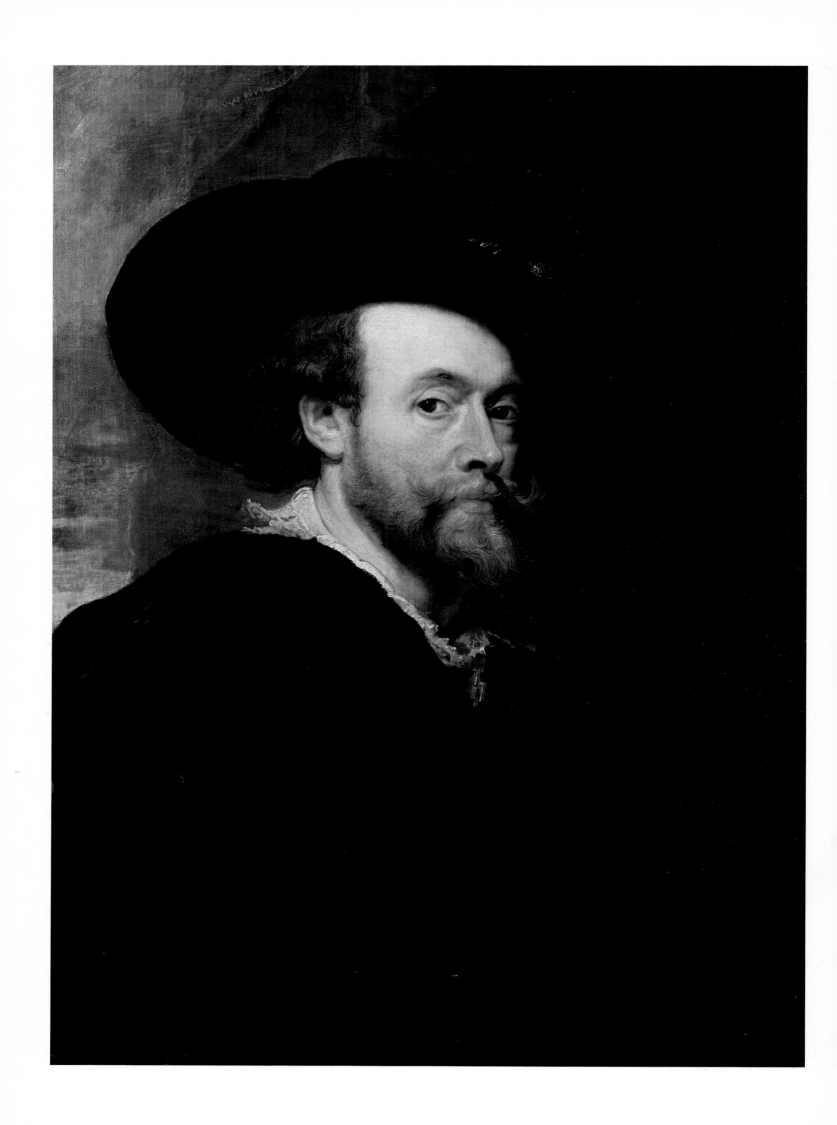

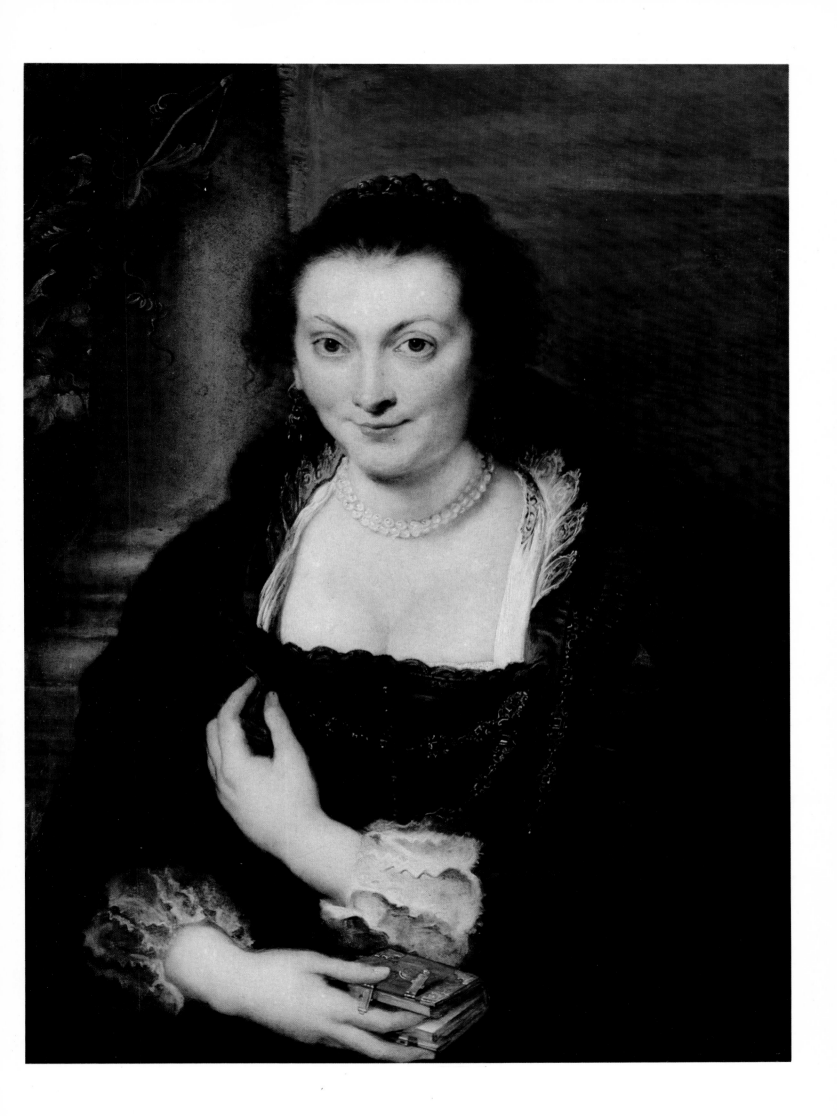

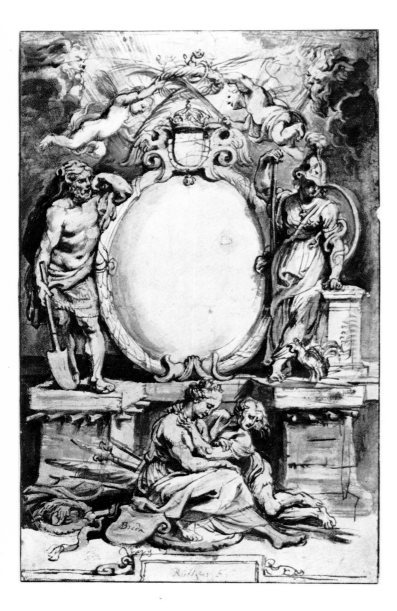

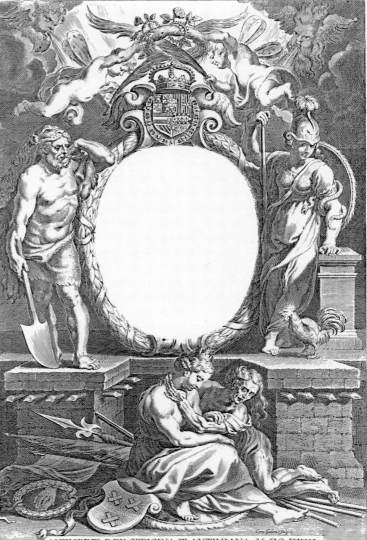

ANTVERPIÆ,EX OFFICINA PLANTINIANA, M.DC.XXXI.

Figure 114
PROJECT FOR FRONTISPIECE, HER-
MAN HUGO, OBSIDIO BREDANA
Drawing
London, British Museum

*On the left of the medallion is Hercules
with the spade, personifying Toil; on the
right, Wisdom-Vigilance with the cock and
serpent as her attributes; below, allegorical
figures representing Breda and Hunger.*

Figure 115
Cornelis Galle, after Rubens
FRONTISPIECE OF HERMAN HUGO,
OBSIDIO BREDANA
Antwerp, Officina Plantiniana, 1626
Engraving
Antwerp, Plantin-Moretus Museum

*This work was written by Herman Hugo,
S.J., and describes the siege and conquest
of Breda in 1625 by Spinola's troops.*

ment with a proposal by Jan Brant to bring together all parties concerned in a conference.[12]   The king's letter does not mention Rubens'
name but we can certainly assume that it was he who transmitted "El
Catolico's" proposal to the Brussels court.   In a letter of March 15,
1625, to the Infanta, Rubens refers again to these conversations, which
meanwhile had probably been cut off.[13]

The capture of Breda was finally accomplished on June 5, 1625,
by the Spanish, under the command of Spinola (Figs. 114, 115); this
gave rise to hopes that the North might now lean toward concluding
a peace with the South.   Two letters written by Rubens to Jan Brant
not long after this event express his wish to take advantage of the
favorable circumstances to reach the goal so long pursued in vain.[14]

While it was to Pecquius that Rubens reported his diplomatic conversations of 1623 with Jan Brant, he soon had the opportunity directly

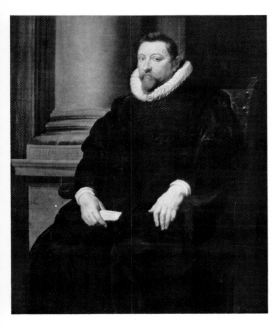

to inform the Infanta, and also Spinola, of their progress. On August 30, 1624, in fact, the French ambassador to Brussels, Nicolas de Baugy, notes that the Infanta granted Rubens several audiences; he discussed with her the chances of a truce, went back and forth frequently between the Brussels court and Spinola's camp, and let it be known that the prince of Orange was favorable to the "truce."[15] Furthermore Rubens' letter from Paris of March 15, 1625, to the Infanta[16] provides proof that he was held in sufficiently high esteem to address her directly on matters of state. Some months later the Infanta paid him a visit in his house in Antwerp, and on that occasion he painted her portrait (Fig. 111).

Rubens now found himself even closer to the court in Brussels. For six months (August 1625 to February 24, 1626) he stayed at an inn at Laeken, without however being there constantly: on some occasions we see him in Dunkirk, where the Infanta and Spinola were in residence for a time; another time he is at the German frontier, saluting Duke Wolfgang Wilhelm of Neuburg in the Infanta's name and conducting him through the Netherlands. We do not know precisely the missions he fulfilled during this period of intense diplomatic activity, but it is clear that the Infanta and Spinola had more and more frequent recourse to his services. Matters were also referred to Philip IV, of course, when this was judged necessary. On January 22, 1626, the king wrote that the Infanta could defer to Rubens' proposals, if she considered that the procedure recommended by the artist had some chance of success.[17] We do not know what these proposals were, but we can deduce from the king's letter that they referred to the peace negotiations discussed by Rubens and Jan Brant.

Isabella Brant, the artist's wife, died on June 20, 1626, perhaps in consequence of the plague.[18] A month later, Rubens wrote to a friend who had expressed sympathy that a journey might help him bear his grief.[19] We can gather that it was not pure chance that led him to become still more involved with state matters from this time forward. His diplomatic activity soon took a different direction. Whereas his interventions had all been aimed at bringing peace between the two separated sides of the Netherlands, he was to devote himself entirely, after the start of 1627, to the conclusion of a treaty between Spain and England.

Other fortuitous circumstances caused his intervention in European affairs, circumstances which had arisen two years previously. While Rubens was in Paris in the spring of 1625, completing the pictures of the cycle of the *Life of Maria de' Medici*, he had made the acquaintance of George Villiers, first Duke of Buckingham (Plate 55), an adventurous man who was a friend of the arts and the favorite of Charles I; he also met the duke's agent Balthasar Gerbier, who combined, like Rubens, the roles of painter and diplomat. In Paris Rubens painted the duke's portrait, which gave him the opportunity to know this important figure from close range. We must guess at the subjects —apart from artistic matters—of his conversations at that time with

Buckingham and Gerbier.　But there can be no doubt that their meeting in Paris explains why Buckingham, a few years later, called upon Rubens to mediate when he was trying to bring about a peace treaty between England and Spain; he dispatched Gerbier to the Netherlands to broach the negotiations on this subject with the Antwerp painter.

Here we should cast a glance at the rather involved political chessboard of Europe at this time.　In December 1625, Buckingham had formed a coalition among England, Denmark, and the United Provinces; this was aligned against Spain and the Austrian Hapsburgs, with the aim of winning back for the Elector Frederick V—the so-called Winter King, who was the brother-in-law of Charles I of England—the Palatinate, of which the Catholic League had robbed him.　The military operations of the coalition were a failure, however: the English fleet was sunk in the port of Cadiz; the army of 12,000 men commanded by the famous General Peter Ernst Mansfeld was driven back from the Palatinate.　Disappointed by this double defeat, which also caused mutterings in England, and fearing a coalition between Spain and France, Buckingham decided to reverse his policy completely and to seek a rapprochement between England and Spain.　One of his opening moves toward this objective was to instruct his confidential agent, Balthasar Gerbier, to renew contact with Rubens.

Gerbier and Rubens had in fact been carrying on a correspondence since their encounter in Paris, about, among other things, Buckingham's purchase of Rubens' collection of antique statues and a certain number of his pictures.　At the end of November 1626, Rubens made his way to Calais with a first consignment of these works of art, ostensibly to hand them over to Gerbier but in reality to have a meeting with him.　For three long weeks, however, he vainly waited for Buckingham's agent to arrive, and then he had the cases shipped to England unattended.

But Rubens and Gerbier did meet again a short time later in Paris. Rubens reported on their conversations to Spinola and the Infanta, and as a result Gerbier was invited to travel to Brussels to present Buckingham's proposal there.　Gerbier arrived in the second half of February 1627, bearing some letters from Buckingham addressed to Rubens that proposed opening negotiations for peace talks between Spain on the one hand, and England, the United Provinces, and Denmark on the other.　The Infanta held the opinion that the chances of success were greater if the talks were provisionally limited to England and Spain; Gerbier reported this to Buckingham.　As early as March 9, Buckingham let Rubens know that subject to certain conditions, he would accept the Infanta's proposal; when Isabella was informed of this by Rubens, she transmitted Buckingham's proposal to Philip IV and asked to be invested with the necessary full powers to conduct the negotiations.　A few weeks later Rubens received an unexpected visit in Antwerp from the abbé Cesare Scaglia, the astute diplomat in the service of the duke of Savoy; the abbé seemed not only fully acquainted with the plans for an alliance between England

Plate 59
PORTRAIT OF AMBROGIO SPINOLA
Panel, 46″ × 33¹/₂″
Brunswick, Herzog-Anton-Ulrich-Museum

*The Genoese general and statesman in the service of the Archduke Albert and the Infanta Isabella. His inscrutable character and powerful capacity for concentration are brilliantly rendered by Rubens. It emerges from their correspondence that Spinola and Rubens held each other in high mutual esteem for their respective talents.*

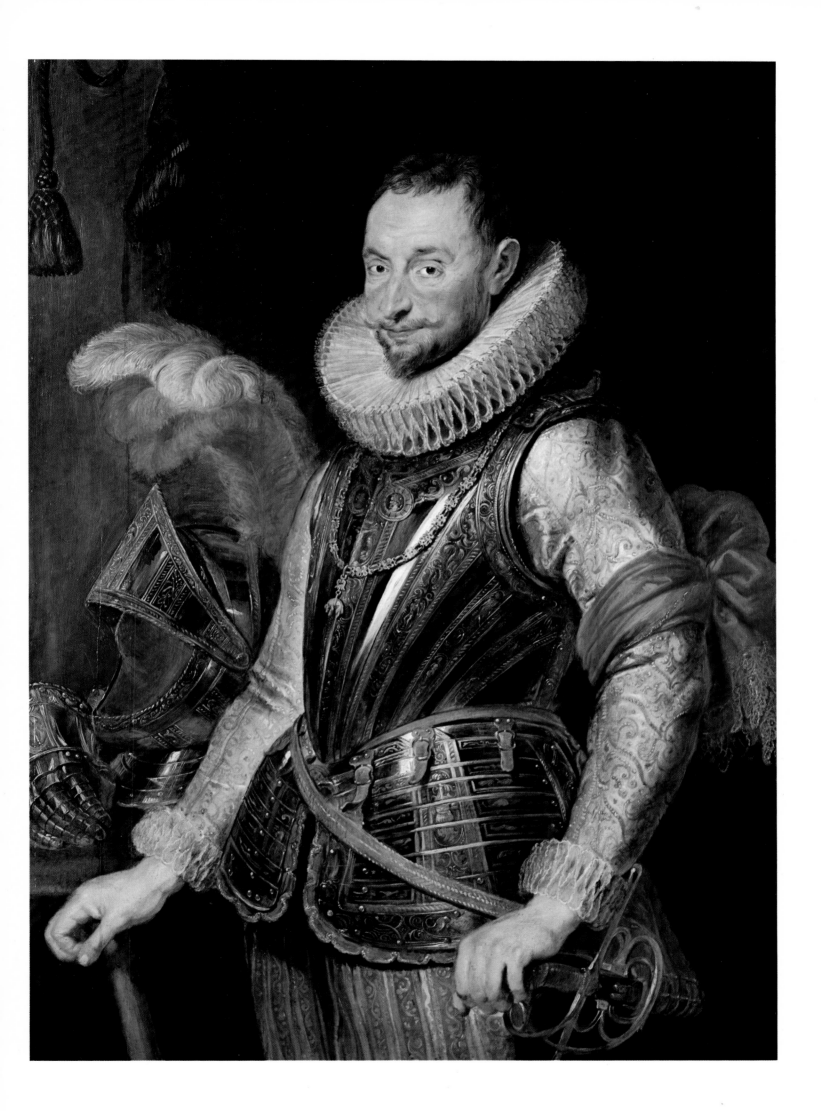

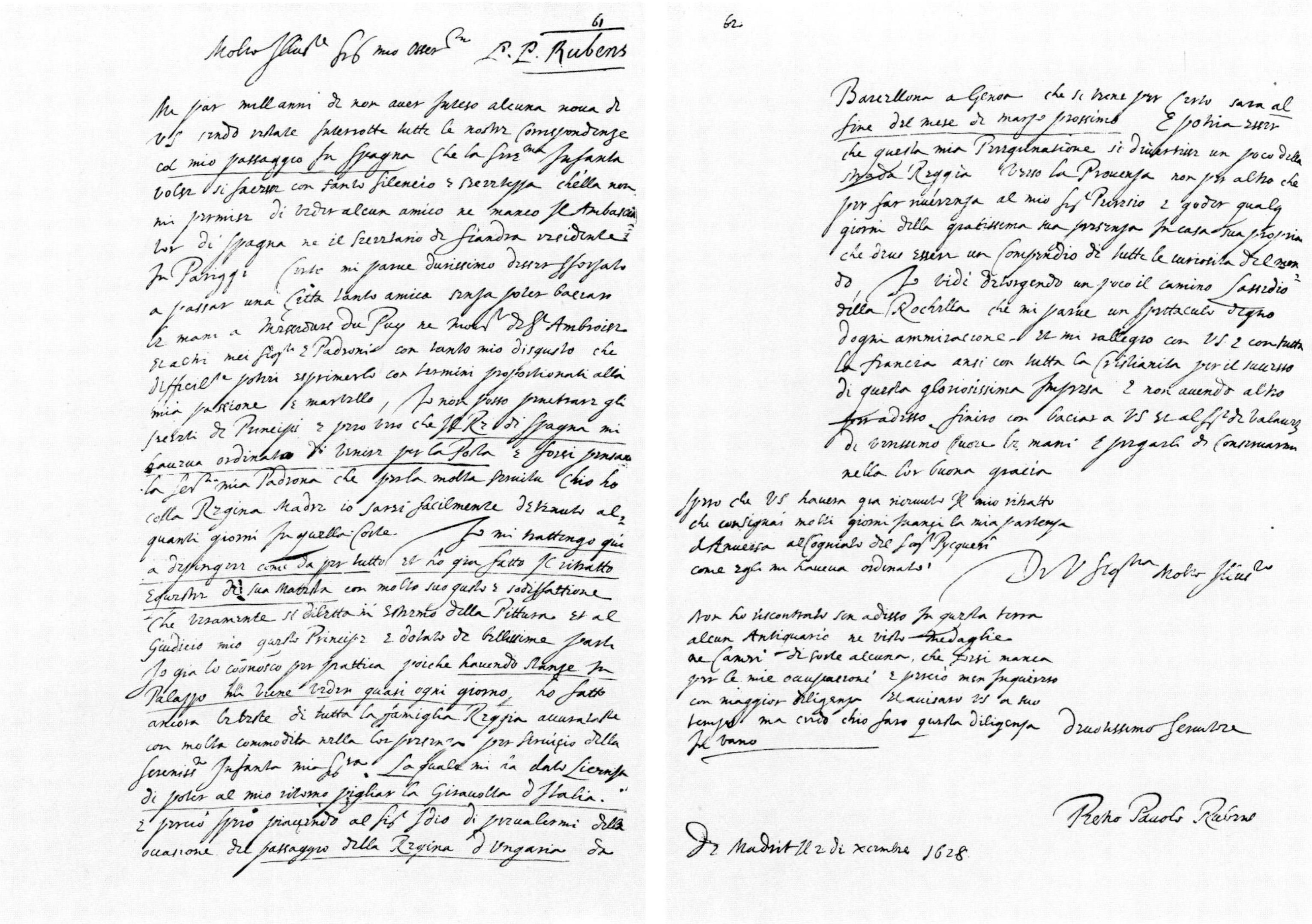

Figure 117
AUTOGRAPH LETTER BY RUBENS
TO PEIRESC
Madrid, December 2, 1628
The Hague, Royal Library

*Writing in Italian, Rubens sends to Peiresc news of his journey to Madrid. He was so "pressed" that he did not even have time to see his Parisian friends. In Madrid he is painting portraits, at the Infanta's request, of the king and the royal family; he does not mention his diplomatic mission. He is hoping to visit his friend Peiresc in Provence on his return in March (1629), while traveling home by way of Genoa.*

and Spain, but let it also be known that a certain faction in London leaned rather toward a possible alliance with France. Scaglia, accompanied by Rubens, went to communicate this message to the court in Brussels. The Infanta was so disturbed by the danger of a possible alliance between England and France—the Southern Netherlands would then be threatened from three sides—that she immediately wrote to Philip IV, again entreating him most urgently to give her full powers for conducting peace parleys.

It was only toward mid-June 1627 that a response came from Madrid. From it emerged the fact that on March 20 the Spanish prime minister, Olivares (Fig. 113), had already concluded a secret treaty with the French ambassador in Madrid. This document envisaged nothing less than the invasion and conquest of England, the partition of that country between the two crowns, and the establishment of Catholicism! Nevertheless Philip IV considered it prudent not to reject the offer of negotiations with England, and for this reason he granted the Infanta the necessary full powers, antedating them by

222

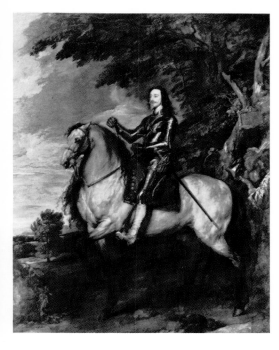

Figure 118
Anthony van Dyck
PORTRAIT OF CHARLES I, KING OF
ENGLAND
London, National Gallery

*This equestrian portrait was probably painted at the request of Charles I of England between 1632—the year Van Dyck was appointed painter to the king—and March 1638, the date of the registration of the picture in the inventory of the royal collection. Charles I was a great art-lover; it was with him that Rubens negotiated in 1629–30 toward a peace treaty between England and Spain.*

fifteen months. Furthermore he bound her to total secrecy on the subject of the treaty with France. It is very probable, therefore, that Rubens knew nothing of it.

Two weeks later the king of Spain wrote again to the Infanta, expressing his dissatisfaction on hearing that a painter had been entrusted with affairs of such importance.[20] Isabella immediately countered this reproach by pointing out that Gerbier too was only a painter, and that Buckingham had committed to his care a letter written in his own hand and addressed to Rubens, with orders to transmit the proposals to the latter. It was thus impossible for her to refuse to listen to him, and besides, she added, it little mattered who took the first steps in affairs of this sort, but if they were followed up, they should obviously be handled by persons of the highest rank.[21]

At this moment Rubens was preparing to travel to Holland for another meeting with Gerbier. It seems probable that Rubens had taken this initiative on his own during May, without asking permission of the Infanta or Spinola. Was he afraid that Madrid's delay in answering Buckingham's proposals might dampen the duke's interest in an alliance with Spain, or that the duke might initiate an agreement with France? Scaglia had hinted at this possibility. But to keep unspoiled the credit he enjoyed at the Brussels court, Rubens wanted to make it appear that the initiative for his meeting in Holland with Gerbier had come from Buckingham, and thus he wrote to Gerbier on May 19, 1627, asking that the duke send a letter inviting Rubens to go there.[22] Perhaps Rubens expected permission from the Infanta, thanks to this document, to undertake the trip, and perhaps he also hoped that Madrid would meanwhile give the green light for the planned negotiations.

The passport giving Rubens access to the territory of the United Provinces, ostensibly to talk with Gerbier about pictures and other rare objects, was sent to him early in June by Sir Dudley Carleton, the British ambassador in The Hague. Rubens did not meet his interlocutor in Delft until July 21. The interview, however, was not fruitful; Rubens had only the news that instructions from Philip IV, which would be transmitted by Don Diego Messia, marquis of Leganés (Plate 56), were still awaited in Brussels. The marquis, however, was delayed in Paris by the illness of Louis XIII—so ran the official version—and, pending his arrival, Rubens could promise nothing on behalf of his principals, either in writing or by word of mouth. After Rubens and Gerbier had traveled for a week in the United Provinces, visiting painters' workshops in Delft, Rotterdam, Amsterdam, and Utrecht, they agreed that Gerbier should remain in Holland for another month, waiting for the news that Rubens would bring him as soon as Don Diego de Messia had arrived.

But this "Messiah," as Gerbier ironically called him in his letters to Carleton, still did not appear, so Gerbier finally begged Rubens to send him at least a note in the Infanta's hand or in Spinola's to prove that their conversations rested on a serious basis. This would save his face with Buckingham. Gerbier also gave it to be understood

223

that Rubens would lose all credit at the English court if indisputable evidence did not establish it that the Infanta and Spinola were favorably disposed toward the peace talks.

Just about when Gerbier's letter arrived in Antwerp, Leganés at last made his appearance in Brussels. But far from bearing instructions for a possible peace, he brought instead a plan of campaign against England, worked out together by France and Spain. This meant the irremediable failure of the enterprise to which Rubens had harnessed himself with all his energy. The Infanta and Spinola, however, regarded the plan for invading England to be pure fancy, offering not the faintest chance of success, and instructed Rubens to keep in touch with Gerbier so that final agreements could be settled when the time was ripe. In one of his most confidential letters, written in Dutch to Gerbier, on September 18, Rubens does not hesitate to criticize Olivares, the Spanish prime minister, whom he considers mainly responsible for the treaty between Spain and France: "I beg you to believe that I am doing all I can, and that I find my masters very much agitated in this affair. They feel annoyed and affronted by Olivares, whose passion has prevailed over all reason and consideration..."[23] Bitter words indeed, from one who has sometimes been taken for a servant of Spain!

Fortunately it was understood in Londen that Rubens had acted in good faith. Only a few months later, in December 1627, he received letters from Gerbier and from Scaglia announcing that Buckingham wanted to try to reactivate the English negotiations with Spain. In her struggle with France, England had certainly not had much success, which strengthened Buckingham's conviction that an alliance with Spain was desirable; it had also been noted in Madrid that despite the most formal assurances, France continued to provide financial help for the United Provinces. In a few months the chances of an agreement between the kingdoms of Spain and England had considerably increased.

Thus Rubens was again authorized by Spinola to resume the talks; in Madrid, too, a livelier interest was now shown in this initiative. On May 1, 1628, Philip IV sent word to the Infanta that he wished to reach an agreement with London and that he desired to be informed of the written records of Rubens' negotiations. From all accounts, Rubens was quite prepared to comply with this request, but whether he feared that certain passages might be misinterpreted or even regarded as compromising, or did not wish to relinquish his role now that the negotiations were going favorably, he insisted on handing over the letters himself to some trustworthy person. Finally he was invited to report in person to Madrid with his dossier. After settling a few personal matters, he left for Spain late in August 1628, in great haste; his friends thought he had gone to Italy, and even at the Brussels court only a small circle knew of his real destination. The Infanta commissioned him to paint some portraits for her of members of her family in Spain, so the whole expedition was camouflaged fairly plausibly.

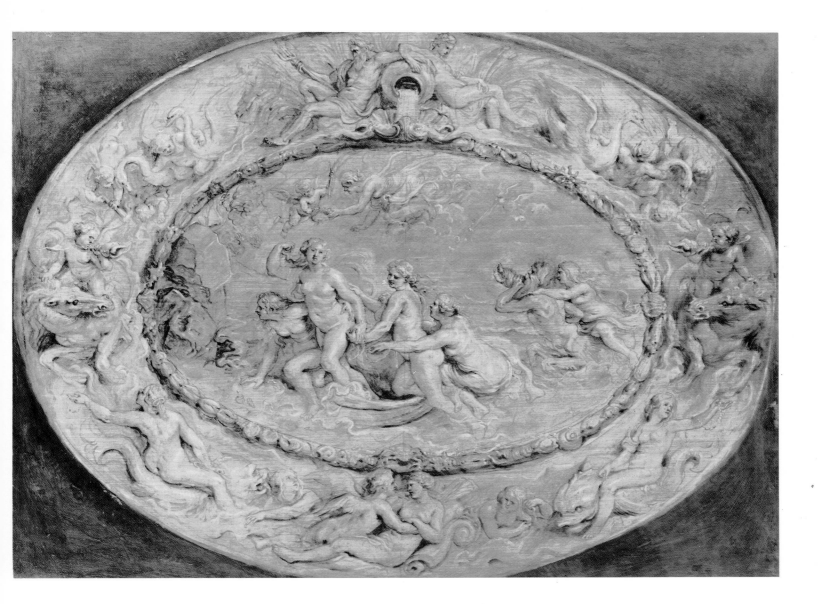

As soon as Rubens arrived in Madrid, the foreign ambassadors sent messages to their respective capitals that he was visiting Olivares frequently and that it was their impression that these numerous audiences had another explanation than mere painting. On September 28, 1628, the painter-diplomat reported on his negotiations with England; his account was favorably received; the king, of whom he painted no fewer than four portraits (Fig. 112), was very well disposed toward him, and Olivares, who was at first mistrustful, also showed great friendliness. The affair with England was thus presented in a good light, and Rubens began to hope that an alliance might soon crown his efforts when the news arrived in Madrid, early in October 1628, that Buckingham had been assassinated on August 23. From that moment, the ruling circles in Spain wished to await developments and see the course of events before taking any decisive steps themselves. Rubens was asked to remain in Madrid, where he mainly spent his time studying the royal collections and painting (Fig. 117);

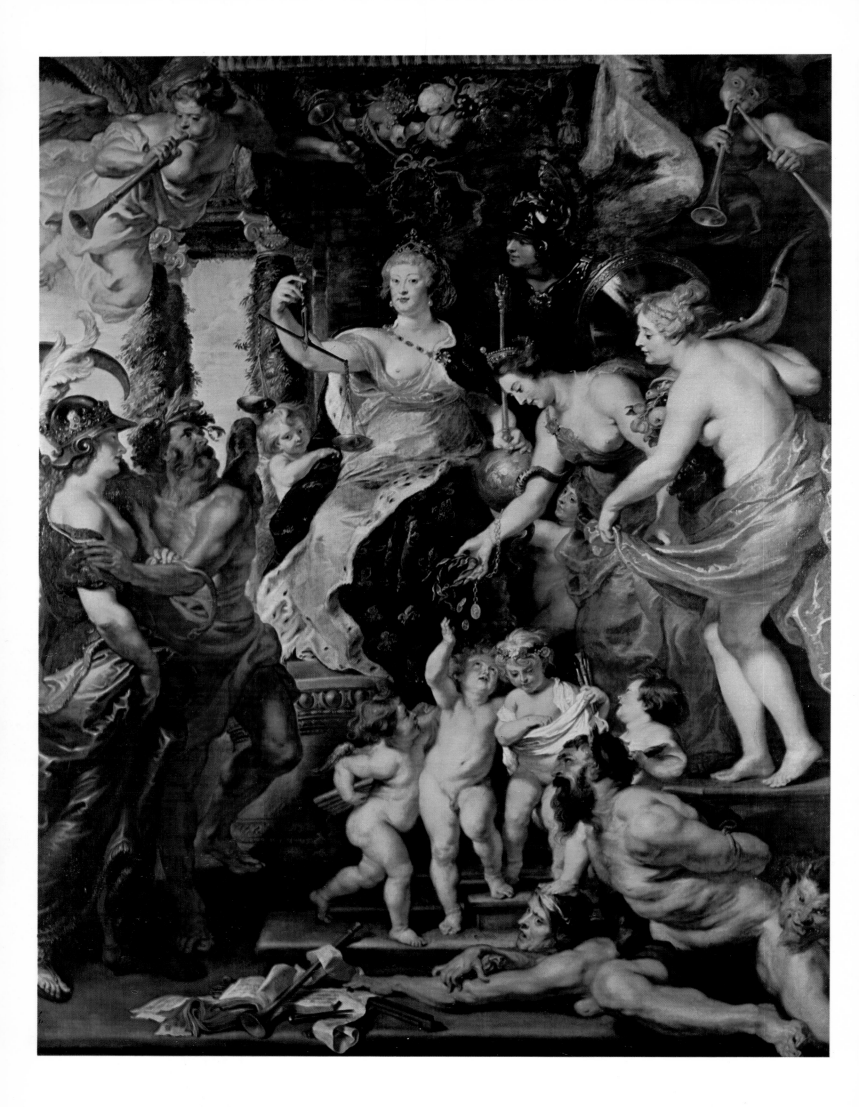

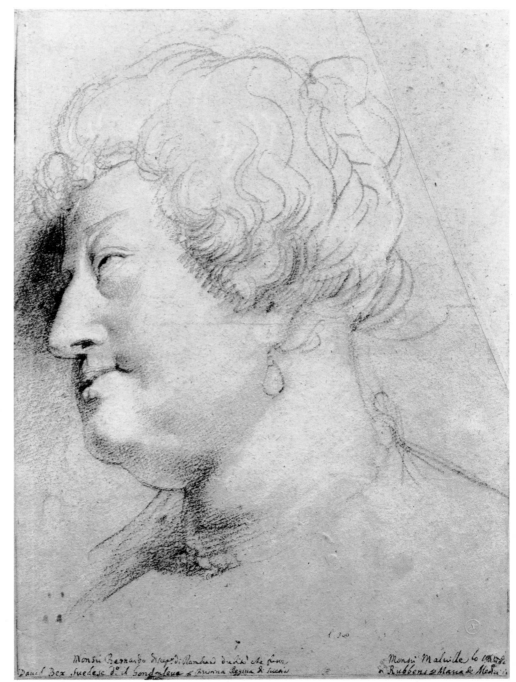

Figure 120
PORTRAIT OF MARIA DE' MEDICI
Drawing
London, Victoria and Albert Museum

*Study for the portrait of the queen-mother, seen from below and in three-quarter view toward the left. Rubens used this drawing in* The Coming of Age of Louis XIII, *one of the twenty-five pictures in the* Maria de' Medici *series carried out in 1622–25, today displayed in the Louvre.*

Plate 60
THE FELICITY OF THE REGENCY
Canvas, 12′11″ × 9′8″
Paris, Louvre

*Rubens has again introduced allegorical figures into the composition to give a special glamour to this episode in the life of Maria de' Medici. To the left of the enthroned queen-mother: Father Time and the personification of France; on her right: Minerva (Wisdom), Plenty, and Prosperity. Plenty is distributing laurel wreaths and gold coins among the four children, who symbolize the arts. In the lower right corner: Ignorance, Calumny (with asses' ears), and Envy.*

he became acquainted with the great Spanish painter Diego Velázquez, with whom he made excursions outside of Madrid. Apparently there had been no developments in England: Charles I even went so far as to propose an exchange of ambassadors between London and Madrid, toward a permanent peace settlement. But such haste was not to Spain's liking. Olivares, who had already devised a plan to send Rubens to England to sound out the situation, now suggested to Philip IV that he should entrust the painter with the preliminary talks. It should be pointed out, however, that Rubens was not sent in the ca-

227

pacity of ambassador—a rank which indeed he never had—but merely as a negotiator. "To give Mr. Rubens more standing, and to lend additional credit to his negotiations,"[24] Philip IV awarded him on April 27, 1629, the title of Secretary of the Privy Council of the Netherlands. Two days later Rubens left Madrid.

He went back to the Netherlands in as much haste as he had left. In Brussels he made his report to the Infanta; in Antwerp he went to see his two sons, whom he had entrusted to the care of his friend Caspar Gevaerts; then once again he was on the road, accompanied this time by a secretary, his brother-in-law, Hendrik Brant. He crossed the Channel on an English warship, sent to Dunkirk especially for him. On June 5 he arrived safe and sound in London, and settled in the house of Balthasar Gerbier.

In numerous detailed and lively letters to Olivares in Madrid, Rubens reported on the multifarious pitfalls he had to overcome to fulfill his mission. The principal and abiding difficulty was of course that he was not authorized to make the slightest concession to meet the wishes of Charles I, that the Palatinate be restored to his brother-in-law, Frederick V. Rubens was in no way empowered to discuss this problem, and had been instructed not to broach it. His talks were mainly with the king; a great friend of the arts, Charles I particularly appreciated the painter's presence. At the sovereign's request Rubens also had discussions with Sir Richard Weston, Lord High Treasurer and the king's most influential counsellor since the death of Buckingham, and also with Sir Francis Cottington, Chancellor of the Exchequer, and with William Herbert, Earl of Pembroke and Montgomery.

Rubens soon realized that Cottington was much in favor of peace with Spain. He could also count on the support of Sir Dudley Carleton, who had become Lord Dorchester in 1628 and occupied, in his capacity of Secretary of State, an important post in the king's entourage. Rubens had been in contact with Carleton when the latter was ambassador in The Hague, and had then exchanged pictures by his own hand or from his workshop for the diplomat's collection of antique statues. He was sorry to learn that another English gentleman he already knew, James Hay, first Earl of Carlisle, was kept out of the talks because, it was rumored, he could conceal nothing from his charming wife, who was herself a gossip. Nor could the art-lover Thomas Howard, Earl of Arundel, another acquaintance of Rubens—he had painted the portrait of the earl's wife, surrounded by her attendants, in Antwerp in 1620[25]—be of much help to him, for this nobleman did not enjoy the king's favor.

The results of Rubens' negotiations were not slow in coming. During a long private conversation which Charles I granted him on June 25, 1629, the king brought up again, as a precondition to any improvement in the relations between the two countries, the need for a solution to the problem of the Palatinate. The sovereign showed himself inclined to conciliation and proposed to summon all the interested parties to a conference in Madrid. Although Rubens

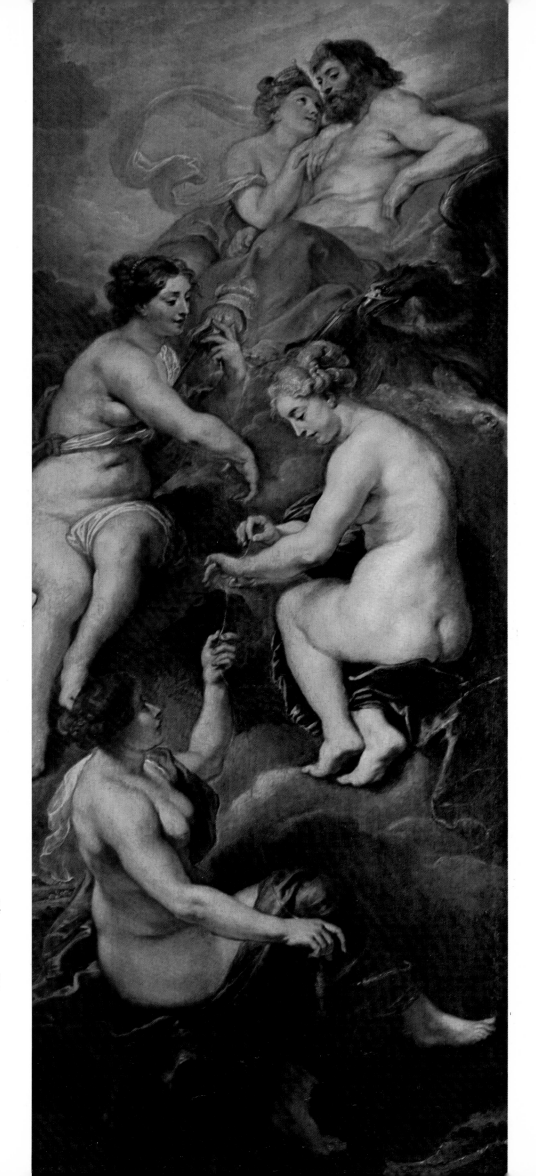

Plate 61
THE DESTINY OF MARIA DE'
MEDICI
Canvas, 12'11" × 5'1"
Paris, Louvre

*At the top, Juno is striving to attract the favor of her spouse, Jupiter; below, the three Fates spin out the thread of life of Maria de' Medici. Rubens executed this series of twenty-five paintings between 1622 and 1625 for the decoration of the "Grande Galerie" of the Luxembourg Palace. Gods, goddesses, and allegorical figures accompany the queen-mother through her life, conferring heroic and triumphal splendor on the rather ordinary events of her actual existence.*

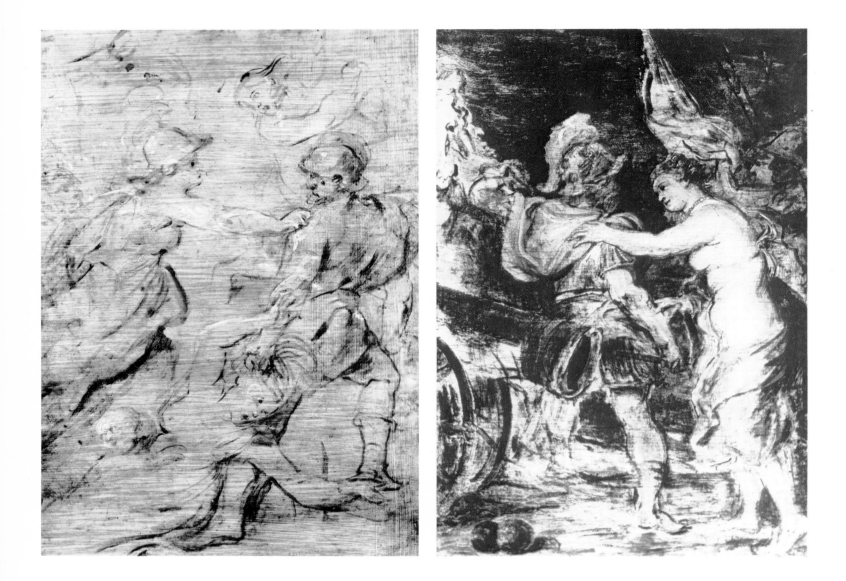

Figures 121, 122
MINERVA AND MARS (left)
VENUS AND MARS (right)
Oil sketches on panel: (left)
15³/₄″ × 10⁵/₈″, Rotterdam, Museum
Boymans-van Beuningen; (right)
15³/₄″ × 9¹/₂″, Paris, Louvre (Fondation
de France)

*These two sketches were conceived at a time
when Rubens was exerting every effort as
a diplomat for the cause of peace.*

exceeded at this point the instructions he had received, he agreed to
transmit this suggestion to Philip IV, provided the English sovereign
would meanwhile abstain from any alliance, offensive or defensive,
with France. This pledge was undertaken after lengthy discussions,
and the primary objective of Rubens' mission, namely, the conclusion
of an armistice, was thus realized *de facto*. The need for his precaution
soon became evident when an envoy from Cardinal Richelieu came
to London proposing a plan of campaign for a common military action
of France and England against the Palatinate.

The second result was that Charles I, as early as July 2, 1629,
appointed an ambassador to be resident in Madrid after August 1,
on condition that the Spanish government would give like powers
to a diplomat of equal rank in the British capital. With these achievements, Rubens could regard his mission as accomplished. He took
the further precaution of asking for and receiving written confirma-
tion of the king's promises, and dispatched it forthwith to Oli-

vares. However, it was only on August 17 that the Spanish ambassador to London was appointed. The choice fell on Don Carlos Coloma, who did not arrive in London until January 11, 1630. This meant that Rubens could not go home immediately, since he had to assist the new ambassador in his task. It was on April 6, 1630, that the artist arrived back in his house on the Wapper after an absence of nineteen months, except for the few days in May 1629.

Rubens' mission in London was certainly the summit of his diplomatic career. Great satisfaction was shown in Madrid for the part he had played in the English capital, and there were even plans to entrust him with other missions. But the artist, who had spent such a long time traveling abroad, now wished to lead a peaceful family life in Antwerp with his beautiful young wife, Helena Fourment, whom he married on December 6, 1630. Once again he hoped to devote himself completely to his art.

At the request of the Infanta, Rubens nevertheless accepted a few more diplomatic missions. In July 1631, when Maria de' Medici (Fig. 120) and her son, Gaston d'Orléans, took refuge in the Southern Netherlands, Rubens was appointed the regent's representative to the queen-mother of France, and in this capacity he accompanied her on a tour of the country. This was the occasion of Rubens' sole departure from his constant concern to work for peace. French emigrants had told him that if Spain gave military aid to France there would be an outbreak of riots against Richelieu's government. Rubens recommended that Olivares grant the requested aid; he was activated on the one hand by his sympathy for the queen-mother of France, whose life he had painted in the celebrated cycle of twenty-five pictures in 1622–25, and on the other hand by his aversion for the cunning policies of Richelieu, whom he saw as an enemy of Spain and a troublemaker in the Netherlands, through the French agreement with the United Provinces. But there was doubt in Madrid about the chances of success for so bold an enterprise. In any case Rubens himself had to yield to the evidence: Maria de' Medici was surrounded by a crew of suspect visionaries and schemers who put her, as well as the Infanta, in an embarrassing situation. He asked to be relieved of his mission.

Meanwhile the military and political situation in the Spanish Netherlands had become extremely critical. Frederick Henry, Prince of Orange, who succeeded Maurice of Nassau in 1625 as Stadholder, was taking city after city. A growing dissatisfaction with the Spanish administration prevailed everywhere among the nobility and the citizens; the general feeling was close to revolt. In these circumstances Rubens agreed, at the request of the Infanta, to go to the Stadholder for negotiations. He first met the prince in December 1631 and several times in 1632, but the fortunes of war were too favorable to Frederick Henry for the latter to think of talking peace.

Rubens met with the delegates of the Northern States General in Liège, but again with no result; they no longer wished to treat with Spain. No doubt they hoped that an inflexible attitude would induce

231

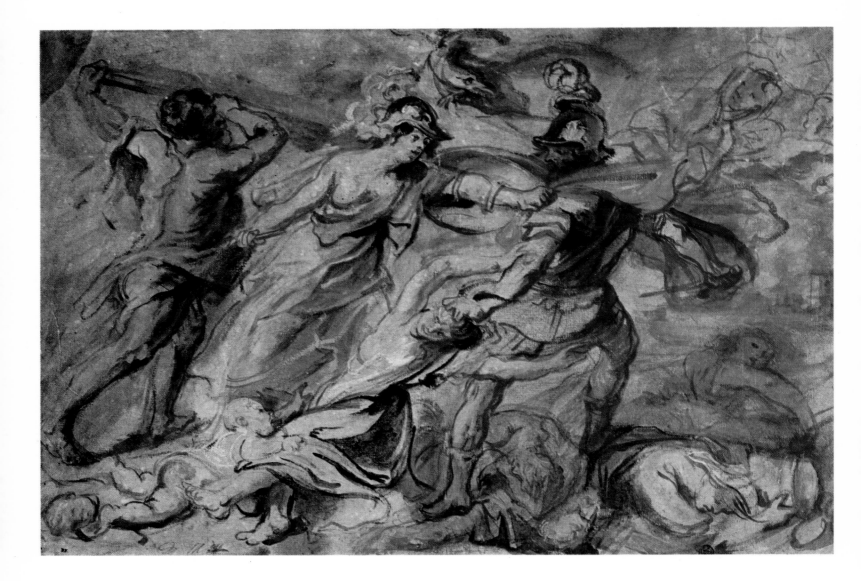

Plate 62

Hercules and Minerva Fighting Mars

Drawing, gouache over black chalk; $14^1/_2'' \times 21^1/_2''$

Paris, Louvre, Cabinet des Dessins

*Drawn about 1630, perhaps in connection with* Minerva Defending the Peace *(Pl. 63). "A profound striving for peace, that is the nucleus around which the edifice of Rubens' political conceptions is constructed. Whenever he intervened as a diplomat, it was always to contribute actively to the restoration of peace and prosperity in his country, so sorely tried" (Sabbe).*

232

the population of the "docile Netherlands" to recognize Spanish authority no longer and to join the Northern armies already on the march. The Infanta, despite Philip IV's opposition, now took the decision to convene the States General of the Spanish Netherlands, which had not met since 1600. These States begged her, considering that the United Provinces no longer wished to treat with Spain, to be allowed to treat directly with the States General in The Hague, in the hope of concluding a treaty or an armistice. Overriding renewed protests from Madrid, the Infanta consented. While these negotiations were making a painful start, Rubens was charged by the Infanta to go to The Hague, in December 1633, to assist the delegates in their task and no doubt also to see that Spanish interests were not neglected. The Infanta's decision aroused mistrust among the delegates, however, particularly with the duke of Aerschot, who, together with Jacques Boonen, archbishop of Malines, led the delegation; the conversations "between one States General and another" in The Hague had no more success than Rubens' own previous efforts had had. And with the Infanta's death on December 1, 1633, Rubens' diplomatic career came to an end.[26] Only once, in 1635, arose again the question of undertaking a mission in Holland at the request of Antoine Triest, bishop of Ghent, but Rubens did not make this journey. During the last years of his life, Rubens was no longer engaged in affairs of state.

The quintessence of Rubens' political conceptions, writes Sabbe, lies in an immense longing for peace. "Whenever he intervened as a diplomat, it was always to contribute actively to the restoration of peace and prosperity in his country, so sorely tried."[27] This assertion may sound like the official praise due to the memory of an illustrious man, rather than like an objective appreciation of the motives which inspired Rubens in his diplomatic activity; yet an analysis of the facts irrefutably confirms the accuracy of this opinion.

Rubens often described in his letters the desolation which reigned in his country. The following well-known passage from a letter of May 28, 1627, addressed from Antwerp to his friend Pierre Dupuy in Paris, deals with this subject: "This city, at least, languishes like a consumptive body, declining little by little. Every day sees a decrease in the number of inhabitants, for these unhappy people have no means of supporting themselves either by industrial skill or by trade."[28] On May 6 he tells of the political situation in these terms: "We are exhausted not so much by the trials of war as by the perpetual difficulty of obtaining necessary supplies from Spain, by the dire need in which we constantly find ourselves, and by the insults we must often endure through the spitefulness or ignorance of those ministers, and finally by the impossibility of acting otherwise."[29] Or again: "Here we remain inactive in a state midway between peace and war, but feeling all the hardships and violence resulting from war, without any of the benefits of peace. Our city is going step by step to ruin and lives only upon its savings; there remains not the slightest bit of trade to

233

support it. The Spanish imagine they are weakening the enemy by restricting commercial licence, but they are wrong, for all the loss falls upon the King's own subjects..."[30]

In these words there is direct criticism of the Spanish ministers who governed the country from Madrid without recognizing the actual situation in the Netherlands. They wanted at all costs to wage war against the "rebels" of the North and to force their submission, without providing the necessary financial means at the right moment and in sufficient quantity—which explains the frequent pillaging by mutinous troops.

At one point Rubens expressed doubts on the advisability of continuing the struggle, even if the needed money were available: "This is an intermediary state between inactivity and offensive warfare, which demands the greatest expenditure and labor, and shows slight results against people so powerful and so well defended by both the art of war and by nature."[31] The regents, too, had experienced these doubts many years before, when they had pushed for a settlement in the Twelve-Years' Truce in 1609; and after the death of Archduke Albert, the Infanta Isabella beyond all question continued to strive for peace.

Rubens' words of criticism for the Spanish administration are in strong contrast with his high praise for the Infanta. He wrote that her good health was very precious for the country, because she was irreplaceable; he counts it as a merit on her part that she remained indifferent to the "false theories" which "newcomers" brought from Spain: "I think," he writes, "that if Her Highness, with the help of the Marquis [Spinola], could govern in her own way and regulate affairs according to her wishes, everything would turn out very happily and one would soon see the greatest change, not only among us but everywhere."[32] More than once he expressed the assurance that she had no other desire than "the repose of the king, her nephew, and a good peace for the public welfare."[33]

Although her peaceful aspirations were unfortunately not shared by the King and his counsellors, this in no way prevented her from seeking secretly for soundings for peace. On this subject Rubens wrote: "Secret negotiations with the Hollanders are still maintained here, but you may be sure that Spain has not given orders to deal with them in any way, in spite of the fact that our Princess and the Marquis Spinola are very much in favor of it, both for the public welfare (which is dependent upon peace) and for their own peace of mind."[34]

We have already seen that Rubens' role was considerable in these soundings for peace. That we may appreciate the spirit of his interventions, let us quote the following passage from a letter to Jan Brant, written shortly after the capture of Breda in 1625: "Now is the time, as a good patriot, to offer every service to the general welfare, for which we have worked so hard that I hope, with God's help, our efforts will not be in vain."[35] It is clear that he saw his task as a patriotic duty, a service rendered to the public good. But do these words not also betray a certain feeling of solidarity with the separated provinces of the Northern Netherlands? The possibility cannot be

234

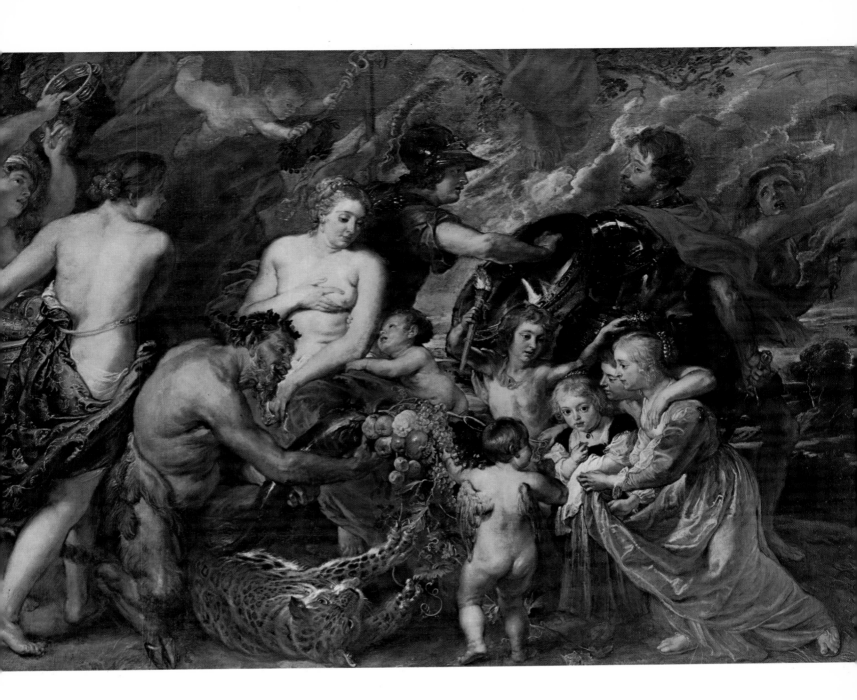

Plate 63
MINERVA DEFENDING THE PEACE
Canvas, 6′8¼″ × 9′9¼″
London, National Gallery .

*Rubens painted this Allegory of Peace in 1629–30 in London. He presented the picture to Charles I. There is no doubt that the artist is alluding here to the negotiations he conducted with the king of England, which led to a peace treaty between Spain and England.*

235

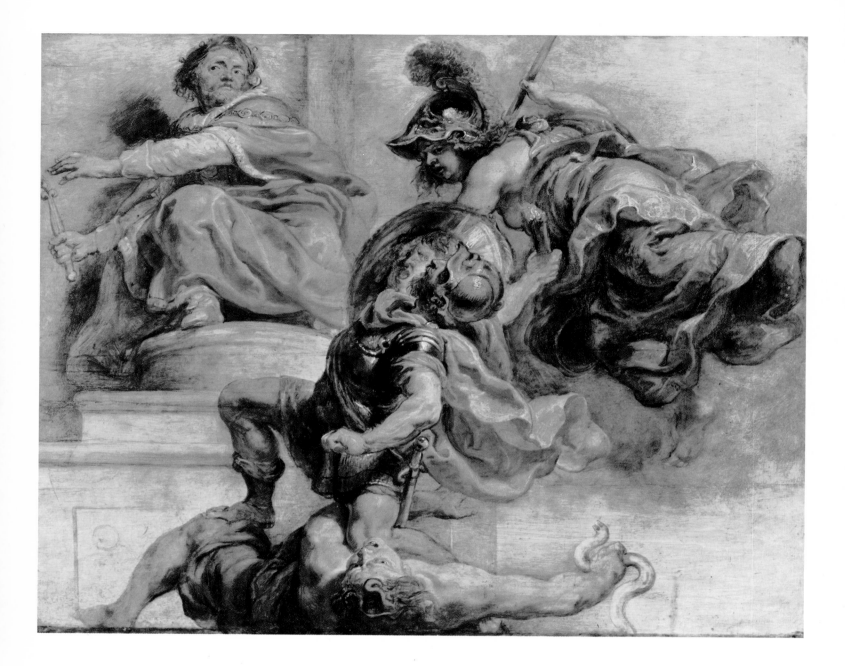

Figure 123
WISDOM TRIUMPHANT OVER WAR
AND DISCORD DURING THE REIGN
OF JAMES I OF ENGLAND
Oil sketch on panel, 27$\frac{1}{2}$" × 34"
Brussels, Musées Royaux des Beaux-
Arts de Belgique

Modello *for the lower right-hand part of
a large picture in the center of the ceiling
of the Banqueting Hall in Whitehall Palace,*
The Benefits of the Reign of James
I. *On the left can be seen James I; on
the right, Minerva (Wisdom) drives out
Mars (War), who kneels on the prostrate
body of Discord.*

ruled out.    In spite of their religious and political differences, the consciousness that both North and South belonged to one country was still
keenly felt in the intellectual circles in Antwerp which Rubens fre-
quented.[36]

When Rubens' activities shifted to the wider field of European relations and he worked for peace between Spain and England, he never
lost sight of the interests of the Netherlands.    On the contrary, he
considered that this treaty would serve his country better.    Gradually
recognizing the failure of direct negotiations between the Northern
and Southern Netherlands, he became convinced that if England, the
United Provinces' main ally, managed to reach an agreement with

236

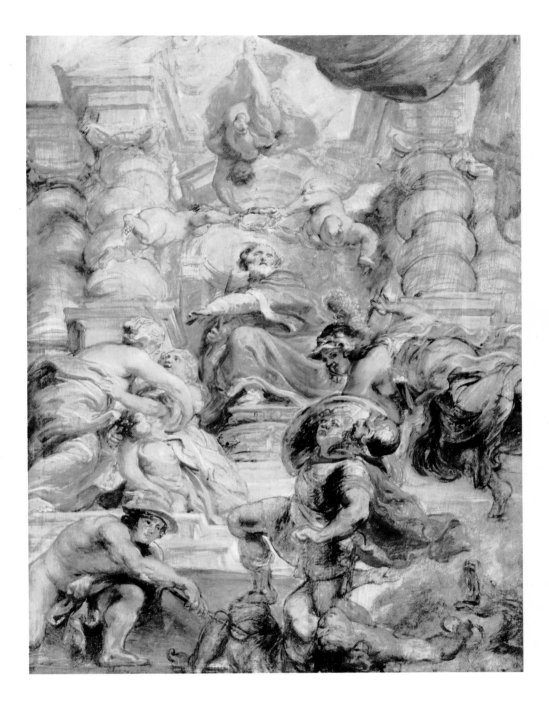

Figure 124
THE BENEFITS OF THE REIGN OF
JAMES I
Oil sketch on panel, $25^{3}/_{8}'' \times 18^{1}/_{4}''$
Vienna, Gemäldegalerie, Akademie der
bildenden Künste

*Final* modello *for one of the large paintings
for the ceiling of the Banqueting Hall in
Whitehall Palace, London. Charles I
entrusted Rubens with this commission in
1629–30, while the artist was in London
on his diplomatic mission, but he had to
wait until 1634 to see the finished work.*

Spain, then a settlement between Spain and the United Provinces would
become possible. His letters show that he cherished this hope. He
writes to the Infanta: "It is not to be thought that the United Provinces
will ever voluntarily yield a single point of their title as free states,
still less that they will ever recognize the King of Spain as sovereign,
be it only a title without substance; yet one may hope that by means
of the kings, their allies, rather than by force, the States General may
be made to feel the necessity of giving some satisfaction to the King
of Spain."[37] In the same vein he later wrote a letter to Olivares from
London which is remarkable in its frankness: "I have neither the talent
nor the position to give advice to Your Excellency. But I consider

237

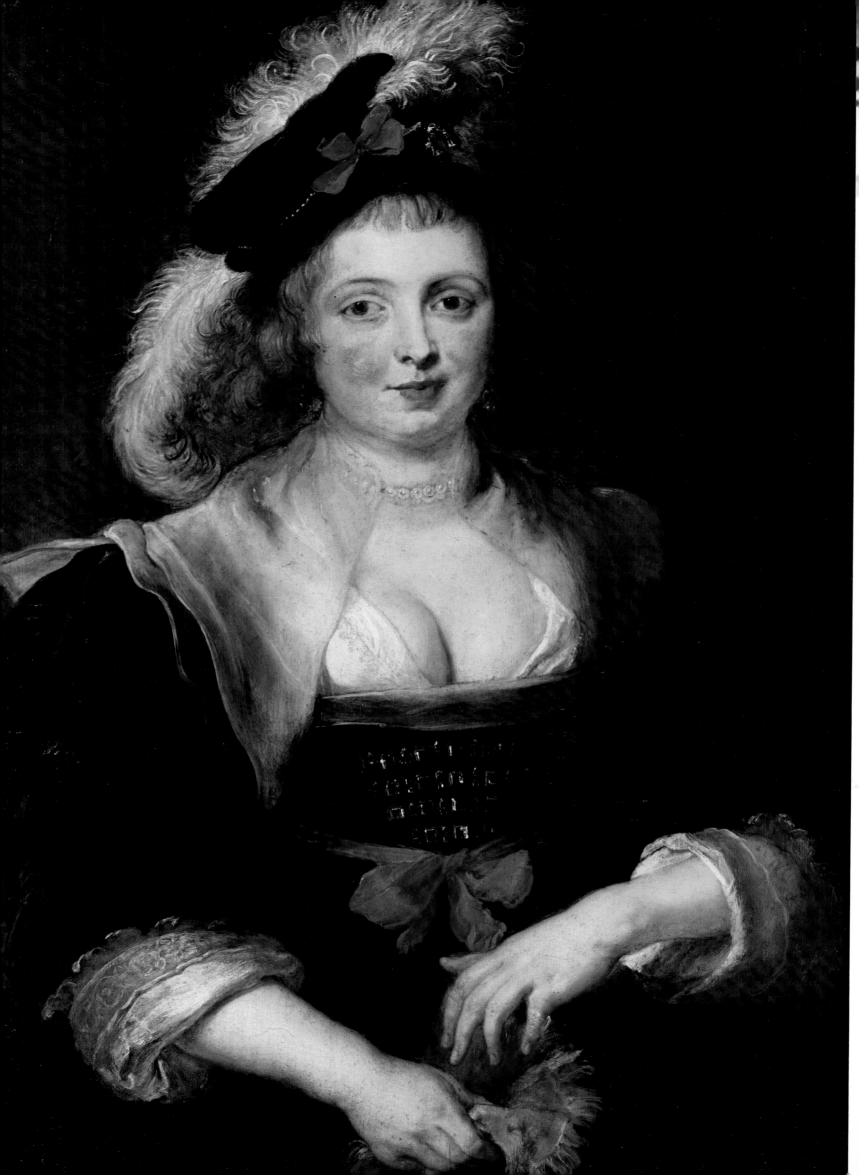

this peace [with England] to be of such consequence that it seems to me the connecting knot in the chain of all the confederations of Europe... I admit that for our King the peace with the Hollanders would be more important, but I doubt that this will ever come about without the intervention of the King of England. But perhaps this peace between Spain and England, made without the Hollanders, would give them something to think about, and make them decide upon peace also."[38]

In the light of these ideas we can explain an event which took place after Rubens had succeeded in his mission at the court of Charles I, shortly before he left London. Entirely on his own initiative and having been given no mandate he secretly visited Albert Joachimi, the ambassador of the United Provinces to the English capital. Using as his excuse an intervention in favor of Dunkirk sailors who had been taken prisoner, Rubens told the ambassador of his conviction that an agreement between England and Spain was at hand, and he discreetly suggested that the United Provinces might in their turn adopt a peaceful attitude.[39] As might have been expected, this attempt brought forth no results, but it does show Rubens' efforts to reach peace with the Northern Netherlands.

It has been claimed that Rubens, after his stay in Madrid and the honors he received for his successful English mission, put himself exclusively at the service of Spanish policy. Allegedly he became estranged from national concerns and the aspirations of his own people.[40] Supposedly this turnabout showed in the conflict in January 1633 between Rubens, the Infanta's confidential agent, on one side, and the duke of Aerschot, one of the delegation leaders of the States General of the Southern Netherlands, on the other: the latter was said to champion a national policy, while Rubens supposedly defended a policy obedient to government directives from Madrid. In default of adequate proof, it is not easy to judge Rubens' intervention during these talks in The Hague between the two States General. In support of Rubens' alleged change of heart, it is argued that no trace of his criticism of the Spanish administration is to be found after 1630. This is not true. Although fewer of Rubens' letters after this date are preserved, nevertheless two of these, and this is quite sufficient, contain severe criticism of the positions adopted by the Spanish court and of the actions of the Spanish officials.[41]

We must accept it that Rubens remained the Infanta's faithful servant, even at the most critical moments of her reign. He shared this attitude with the great majority of the inhabitants of his country, for whom the Infanta not only represented the king of Spain—the "natural sovereign" and the Defender of the Faith—but was also their governor, who cared for the needs of the people entrusted to her and shared their aspirations. No one knew this better than Rubens, her counsellor; had she not accomplished an act of sovereignty and also of understanding when, in opposition to Philip IV's orders, she allowed the States General to meet?

Rubens' loyalty, as we know, did not blind him to the shortcomings

Plate 64
PORTRAIT OF HELENA FOURMENT WITH GLOVES
Panel, $38^{1}/_{4}$" × $27^{1}/_{4}$"
Munich, Alte Pinakothek

*Painted in 1630–31, shortly after the marriage of Helena Fourment and Rubens on December 6, 1630. Rubens represents her as the wife of a well-to-do citizen, about to put on her gloves as she sets off on a visit.*

and mistakes of Spanish statesmen and officials. Consequently it is not fair to identify his opinions with those of an Antwerp citizen such as, for example, President Roose, who put himself entirely at the service of Spanish interests;[42] the difference between them emerges clearly from the fact that when, on Bishop Triest's insistence, Rubens again declared himself ready to attend the peace talks in Holland in 1635, every effort was made to keep Roose out of the affair![43] And here we cannot examine more closely the causes of the conflict that arose between the duke of Aerschot and Rubens, but its origin must apparently be sought as much in the personal ambition of the two men and their mutual distrust as in their differences of opinion on conducting negotiations with the North—and not in a more fundamental political incompatibility.[44]

We have traced rapidly the diplomatic career of Rubens and the motivations on which it rested. Now the question arises: was Rubens a good diplomat? Without doubt he was naturally endowed with certain qualities of the sort that gained him the confidence of his interlocutors. The scholar Gaspard Scioppius testifies that Rubens was "a man in whom he would find it difficult to know what to praise most, his skill as painter, his perfect knowledge of everything concerning belles-lettres, or his subtle judgment which was matched by such engaging powers of conversation."[45] The French humanist Peiresc writes that he cannot speak too highly of Rubens' integrity: "I have the warmest admiration for him and the greatest regret that he is leaving [Paris], for I am losing the sweetest and wisest conversation; on classical subjects especially, his knowledge is the most excellent and universal that I have ever come across."[46] Another time he writes that Rubens "was born to give pleasure and delight in everything he does or says."[47] These judgments and many other contemporary appreciations may contain a degree of rhetorical emphasis, but their unanimity is a guarantee of their truth.

As a boy, Rubens had been for a time a page in the service of Marguerite de Ligne-Arenberg, the widow of Philip, count of Lalaing, and had become familiar with the world of the aristocracy. On his travels he came to know the courts of Mantua and Madrid, and acquired experience which was certainly useful to him later in his diplomatic activity. His natural talents as much as his education and the memories of his youth prepared him to some extent for this task. In addition, when he began to concern himself in state affairs he enjoyed a European reputation as an artist; this stood him in very good stead in accomplishing his missions, just as, conversely, his stay as a diplomat in Madrid, where he studied the works of Titian in the royal collection, had great importance for the subsequent development of his art.

The fact that Rubens did not attain the goal he strove so long to reach—namely, peace with the United Provinces—should not make us judge him too severely. The same fate befell other negotiators: Bertholdis T'Serclaes van Swieten and Willem de Bie, whom we have already mentioned, and the competent Jan de Kesseler, who regularly

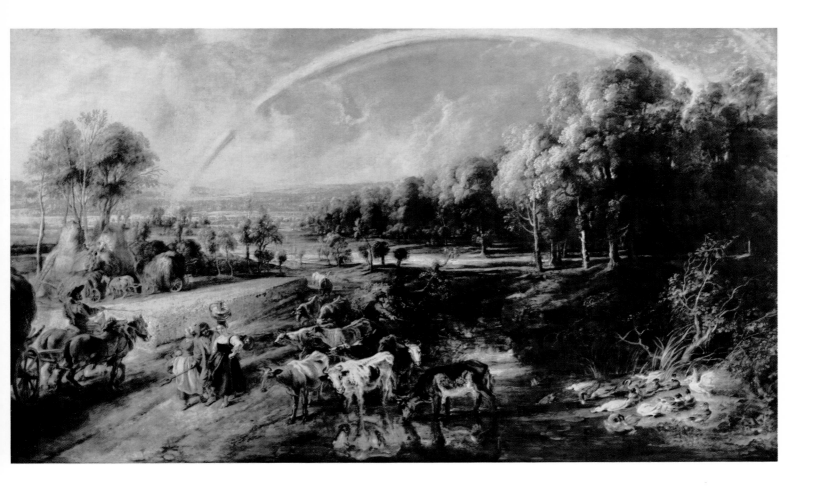

conducted talks at Roosendaal from 1627 to 1630.[48]   Circumstances
limited sharply the chances of success.   To maintain his prestige the
king of Spain often let slip very favorable opportunities, while showing
a more conciliatory face at times when his adversaries, intoxicated by
victory, would not hear of a truce or a treaty.   Even when he made
a concession the king insisted that his title of sovereign of all the Netherlands should be recognized by the "rebels," at least as a matter of
form; the United Provinces, on their part, demanded that no iota of
their title of Free State be changed.   If at times a political compromise
none the less offered some chance of success, it was destroyed by religious and economic opposition.   Furthermore European interests during the Thirty-Years' War were so inextricably intertwined, yet at the
same time so opposed, that within the multiple shifts of alliances, for
the most part unforeseen, no diplomat could boast of obtaining lasting
results.

One argument in favor of Rubens' talents as a diplomat is the fact
that in addition to the confidence of the Infanta, he also enjoyed that
of so circumspect a captain and statesman as Ambrogio Spinola; this
confidence was never disappointed.   Spinola had even declared that
he found so many conspicuous talents in Rubens that he considered

painting one of the least of his gifts. One can also put down to Rubens' credit that he won over the count of Olivares in Madrid, the man who held the real reins of power in Spain and apparently at first nourished prejudices against him. But the most eloquent proof of his talents as a diplomat was certainly the success of his mission at the English court. While in London he twice received congratulations from the Council of State in Madrid,[49] and his English interlocutors paid homage to his competence: Charles I showered gifts on him, and he was knighted on March 3, 1630.[50] On December 21, 1630, he was one of the three candidates for the post of Spanish ambassador to London whom Olivares presented to the Council of State. Rubens was not chosen because it was unsuitable that the title, Minister of the King, should be conferred on one who earned his living by the work of his hands;[51] Philip IV nevertheless thought of sending him to London as the close collaborator of the ambassador, "...because he is held in high esteem at the English court and because he is very suitable for negotiating all sorts of matters by reason of the discretion with which he handles them."[52] As we know, Rubens did not accept this offer.

Perhaps even more than the marks of honor bestowed on him by his masters, the testimony of his adversaries points to his high competence. The reactions of the ambassadors of France and Venice to The Hague are very characteristic in this respect, when they learned in 1635 that Rubens had asked for a passport to Holland. The war was going favorably for the South, following the victories of the Cardinal-Infante Ferdinand, who had succeeded the Infanta as regent; on the pressing advice of Bishop Triest, Rubens was asked once again to take soundings for peace. As soon as the diplomats of the countries at war with Spain heard of this mission, they tried in every way to prevent his arrival. The Venetian ambassador wrote in his dispatch to the Doge in Venice: "This Rubens is full of malice; he is very skillful in handling affairs and the Spaniards have already engaged him in other very important matters."[53] It would be difficult to find more flattering testimony than this description of Rubens as a formidable adversary!

On December 18, 1634, Rubens wrote to his friend Peiresc that three years before he had asked the Infanta to relieve him of "every sort of employment outside of my beloved profession." We can trace this request back to the spring of 1632, when he tired of serving as the mediator and traveling companion of Maria de' Medici. He took this decision, he continued, being conscious of the fact that one must "leave Fortune while she is still favorable, and not wait until she has turned her back." Kneeling at the Infanta's feet, he begged her "as the only reward for so much toil, to discharge me from such missions and to give me permission to serve her in my own house. I obtained this favor with more difficulty than any other she has ever granted me." During the critical period in the Infanta's last years, he did allow himself to be persuaded to carry out several missions, which moreover were less than successful. "Now," he added, "by God's

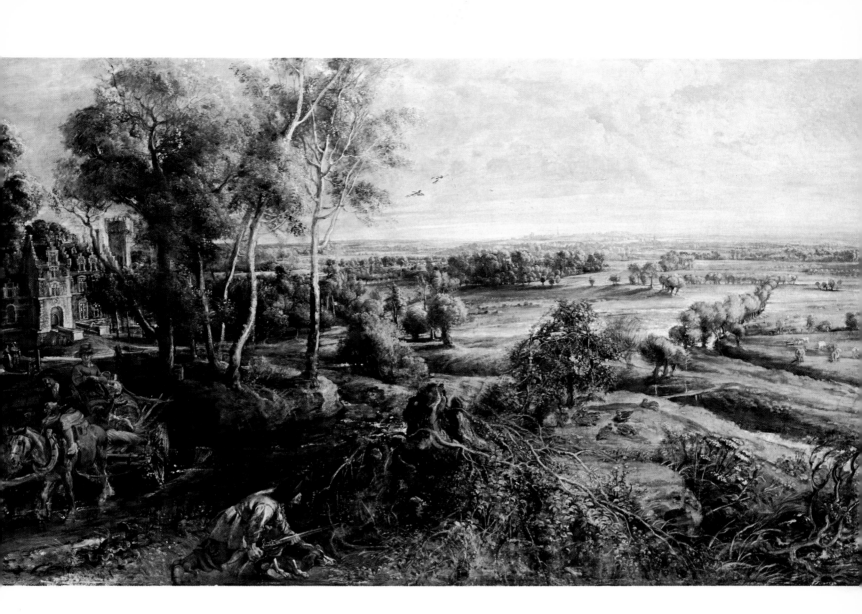

Plate 65
LANDSCAPE WITH THE CHÂTEAU
DE STEEN AT ELEWIJT
Panel, 4'5" × 7'9"
London, National Gallery

*Rubens painted this landscape after he had
purchased the Château de Steen at Elewijt
in May 1635. On the far left can be seen
the central part of the building with the
entrance; a little to the right of the château
is the tower, which is no longer standing.*

243

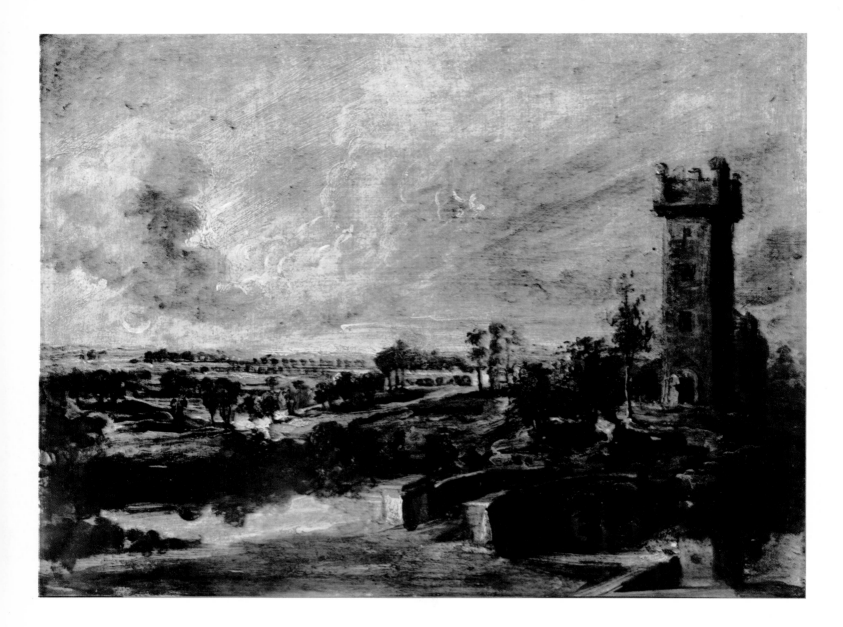

Figure 126
LANDSCAPE WITH A TOWER
Panel, 9″ × 11³/₄″
Berlin-Dahlem, Gemäldegalerie der
Staatlichen Museen

*The tower is that on Rubens' estate at Ele-*
*wijt (Pl. 65). Toward the end of his life*
*the artist spent the summer months there*
*with his family, and the countryside inspired*
*him to paint glorious landscapes.*

grace, ... I am leading a quiet life with my wife and children, and have no pretension in the world other than to live in peace" (Plate 88).[54]

In the year that he wrote this letter he bought the Château de Steen at Elewijt (Plate 65), where he henceforth spent the summer months with his family. On May 12, 1635, the Council of Brabant approved Rubens' purchase of the castle situated in the parish of Steen near Malines. From this time onward Philip IV was prepared to ennoble him, and Charles I had knighted him in 1630. Surely it was not without some vanity that Rubens bore the title of "Lord of Steen." This title was also engraved before all the others, on his tombstone.

The fertile land on a gentle slope which surrounded Rubens' domain,

244

the rows of waving trees along the fields and meadows, certainly contributed to the creation of his majestic and inspired landscape paintings of this period (Fig. 125). Rubens had painted landscapes before, but the softness, luxuriance, and charm of the countryside in these parts seemingly corresponded to his temperament more than any other. Rubens even represented features of his Steen in other landscapes, such as the square tower situated on the "motte" (mound), some traces of which were still visible in the nineteenth century (Fig. 126). Walking around this delightful estate, whose exuberant beauty he portrayed in joyful, lively landscapes (Plate 65; Fig. 126), he must have allowed his thoughts to fly back to the time when family relationships had drawn him into the field of diplomacy, and when, impelled by his talent and an undisputed ambition in his calling, he found himself in a sort of "labyrinth, beset night and day by a succession of urgent duties; away from my home ... and obliged to be present continually at Court ..." With sadness he must have evoked the figure of the Infanta, in whose service he had devoted his best powers to establishing peace in his own country and in Europe, which he was never to realize. With profound satisfaction he must have remembered his diplomatic missions crowned with success in Madrid and London. But he must have regretted that in spite of all his efforts and all his powers of persuasion, he did not succeed in bringing peace to the Netherlands, which had been the deep incentive for his activity as a diplomat.

He once wrote: "For my own part, I should like the whole world to be in peace, that we might live in a golden age instead of an age of iron."[55] But only in his pictures does the dawn of a golden century shine forth in the luminous brilliance of his colors, triumphant and unequaled.

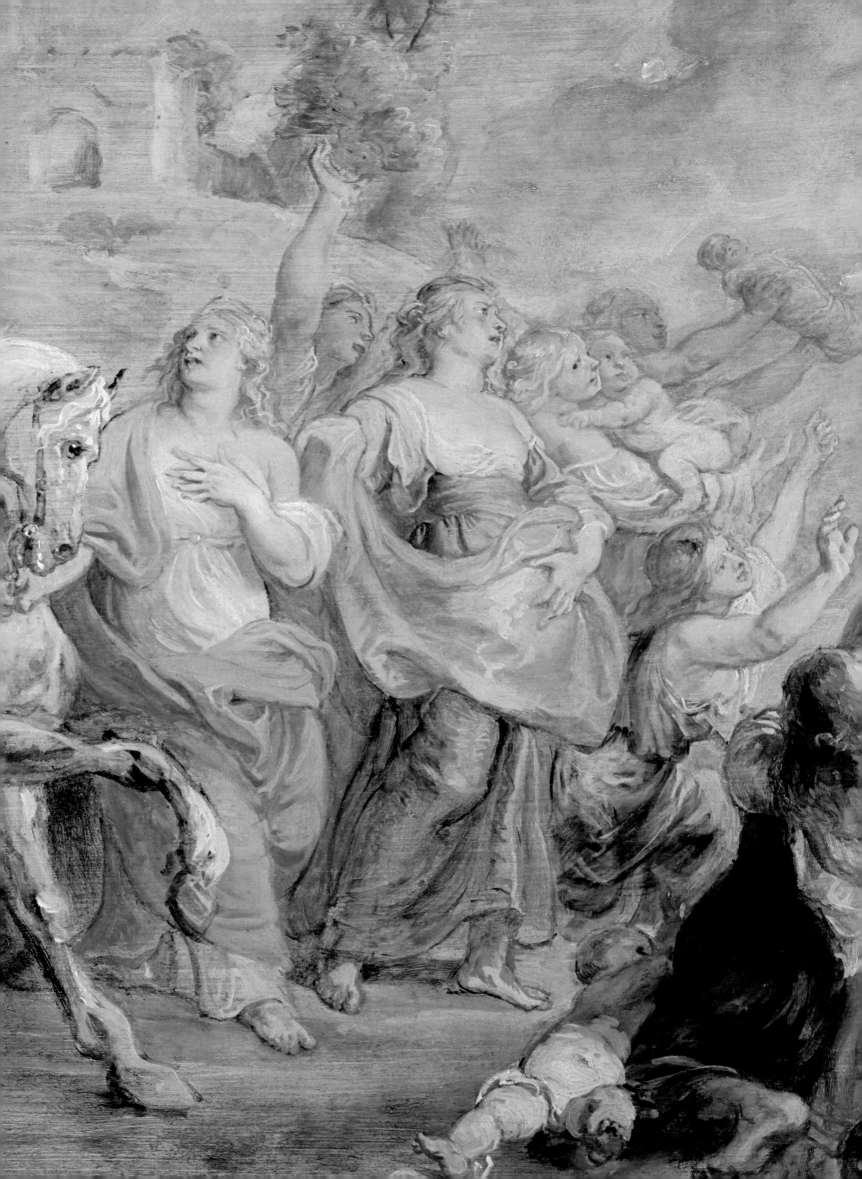

# CHAPTER 11

# War and Peace in Rubens' Works

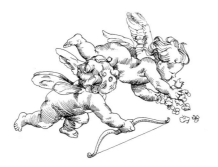

Plate 66
THE RECONCILIATION OF THE RO-
MANS AND THE SABINES (detail, Pl.
68)
Oil sketch
Antwerp, Osterrieth House

*Between the two opposing armies the Sabine women appear. In the center stands Hersilia; "chaster than any other Sabine woman, with wild hair, she puts an end to the war" (Juvenal).*

Contrary to the fate of many pendant works, Rubens' two sketches of *The Rape of the Sabine Women* (Plate 67)[1] and *The Reconciliation of the Romans and the Sabines* (Plate 68)[2] have never been separated throughout their long history. Quite recently they found their way, together, into the collection of the Bank van Parijs en de Nederlanden in Antwerp.

The first mention of the two panels is found in the catalogue of the auction of the Prince de Rubempré's collection, held in Brussels on April 11, 1765.[3] In the same year they passed into the collection of the Brussels banker Daniel Danoot. It was in his house that they were admired in 1781 by the well-known English painter and art theoretician Sir Joshua Reynolds, who noted that "few pictures of Rubens, even of his most finished works, give a higher idea of his genius."[4] We can still endorse this view, even though we do not share Reynolds' preference for the "finished" painting.

Both sketches left the Danoot collection, and the country, in 1828. For over one hundred and forty years they were in private possession in Great Britain, until they were purchased at a London auction in 1969[5] and brought back to their city of origin, where they were painted probably about 1635–40. They are displayed today in the Osterrieth House, a patrician dwelling in Antwerp, where as early as the seventeenth century a Rubens painting could be seen above a mantelpiece;[6] until the nineteenth century one of the drawing rooms was decorated with eight tapestries after cartoons by the artist, representing *The Story of Achilles*.[7] The acquisition of these sketches fills most felicitously a gap in our national heritage. Rubens is represented in Belgium primarily by large religious pictures, several of them still exhibited in the places for which they were intended; mythological and allegorical pictures are much fewer, and paintings of historical and classical subjects are rarer still. These two fine oil sketches thus illustrate an aspect of Rubens' art that is practically absent from Belgian collections.

247

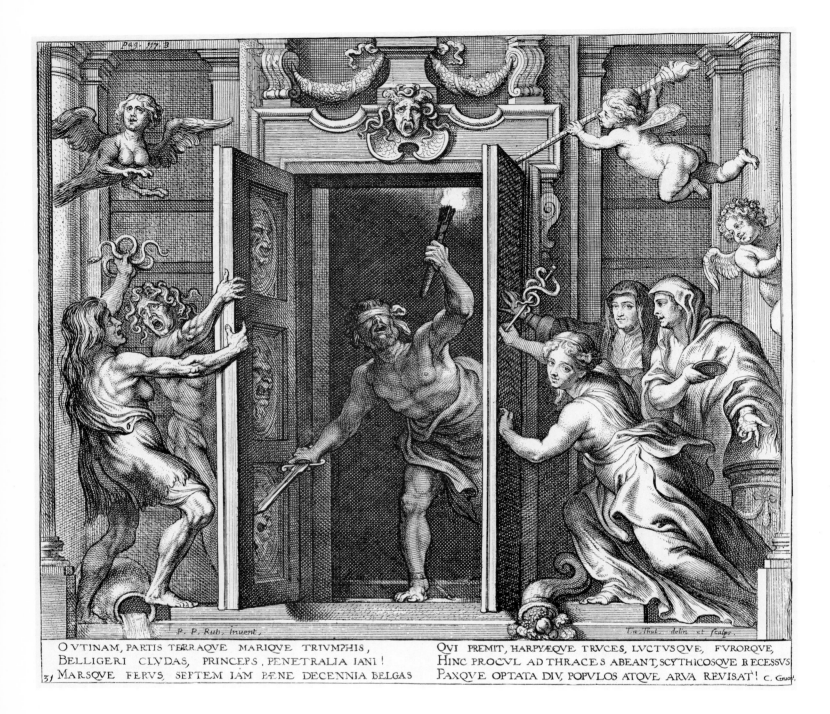

OVTINAM, PARTIS TERRAQVE MARIQVE TRIVMPHIS,
BELLIGERI CLVDAS, PRINCEPS, PENETRALIA IANI!
31 MARSQVE FERVS, SEPTEM IAM PÆNE DECENNIA BELGAS

QVI PREMIT, HARPYÆQVE TRVCES, LVCTVSQVE, FVRORQVE,
HINC PROCVL AD THRACES ABEANT, SCYTHICOSQVE RECESSVS
PAXQVE OPTATA DIV, POPVLOS ATQVE ARVA REVISAT! C. Geuot.

Figure 127
Theodore van Thulden, after Rubens
THE TEMPLE OF JANUS
Etching from POMPA INTROITUS
FERDINANDI, Antwerp, 1641

*The etching represents a "stage" built after a design by Rubens in the Melkmarkt in Antwerp in April 1635, on the occasion of the Entry of Cardinal Infante Ferdinand. The door is opened by Anger and Discord; the Infanta Isabella tries in vain, with the help of Peace, to shut it again.*

The themes depicted on these two panels take us back to the earliest legendary history of Rome, to the time of King Romulus. Livy, Cicero, Dionysius of Halicarnassus, Plutarch, and many other classical authors have told this legend, each of them in his own way and in various readings, without however changing the core of the story.[8] The first episode tells us how the Romans found a cunning solution to the dearth of women from which their country suffered: they invited their neighbors, the Sabines, to a festival in Rome and at a given sign abducted their guests' wives and daughters. This is depicted in the first sketch (Plate 67), in which four groups can be distinguished. There is first of all the compact group in the center: a horseman, who is helped by his groom holding the rearing horse by the reins, tries to lift a young woman in a brilliant white dress. To the left of this group a warrior flings his arm around the waist of a wailing young woman and with his left hand pushes aside an old woman, who bites him in the calf. A second group at the upper right consists of women who are driven together on a platform by armed soldiers. Below these an old woman grimly defends her daughter against a warrior and claws his cheeks with her nails. At the far left an old man assists his daughter in her attempt to escape a soldier who has seized her by the arm and by the skirt. Behind them can be seen a decorated triumphal arch, possibly representing a town-gate, and an imposing building with a dome, strongly reminiscent of the Pantheon in Rome.

The second oil sketch, which Reynolds thought had more novelty and was the more interesting of the two,[9] shows the following episode of the legend. Between the two hostile armies—on the left side the Romans, on the right the embittered Sabines—the Sabine women appear. Two of them try to hold back the Romans from the fight: the one on the left clutches a Roman soldier by the arm, while the other seizes the commander's horse by the reins. The rest of the women implore the Sabine men in order to move them into reconciliation. In the center of this group a woman sadly advances, noble in her controlled and majestic attitude: this is Hersilia, according to some authors the wife of Romulus, according to others the spokeswoman of the Sabines. Juvenal, who was Rubens' favorite poet, wrote of her that "chaster than any other Sabine woman, [appearing] with wild hair, she put an end to the war."[10] She is the woman who restores peace.

From these scenes emerges once more Rubens' familiarity with the world of the classics, to which he had been introduced in his youth by Rumoldus Verdonck, the headmaster of the Latin School ("papen-school") in the precinct of Antwerp Cathedral; he remained faithful to this world all his life. Evidence of this is found, among other instances, in Rubens' letters studded with quotations from Greek and Latin authors, some of whom are now known only to specialists.[11] Significant in this respect is the account given by a contemporary of his visit to Rubens in 1621: while he was at work, the master had a lector to read from Tacitus to him. Later the artist had his guests guided around the house to show them the antiquities and the Greek and Roman statues which he possessed in great number.[12] In this era of Christianized humanism, about which Sabbe has written in an illuminating way,[13] Rubens shared his passion for Antiquity with many of his learned contemporaries. But who among them could have called to people's minds with this colorful narrative power these events from the earliest history of the eternal city? The sketches are at the same time historically accurate, in representing the armors, and yet vivid in suggesting the emotions; utterly realistic in the horrors of some parts, and inspired in idealizing the vision of the whole; they

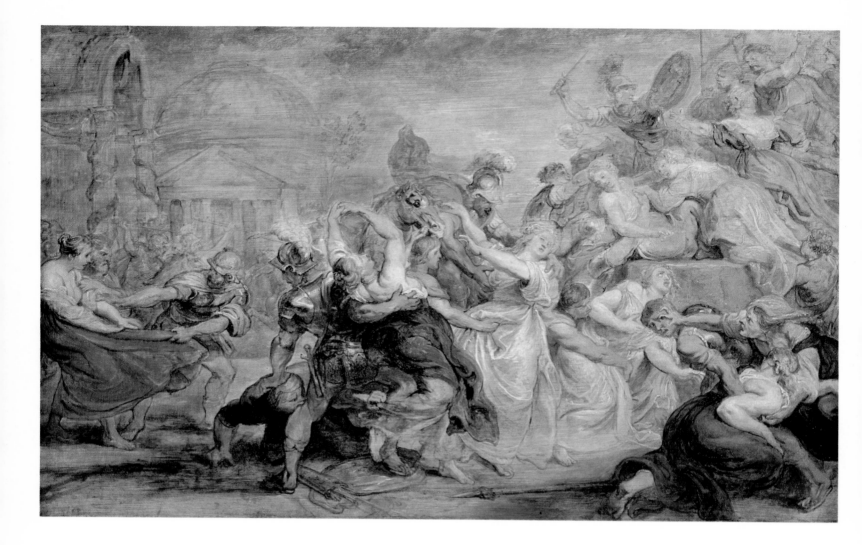

Plate 67
THE RAPE OF THE SABINE WOMEN
Oil sketch on panel, 22″ × 34¼″
Antwerp, Osterrieth House

*In his last years Rubens' consummate mastery and amazing sureness of touch enable him to sketch the boldest compositions from his creative imagination. With an unparalleled economy of means, he suggests the maximum of dramatic tension and dazzling beauty.*

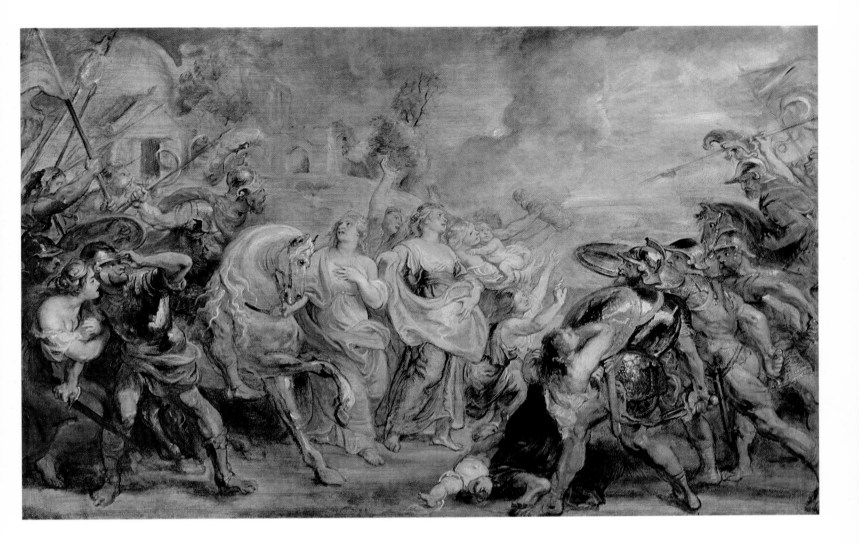

Plate 68
THE RECONCILIATION OF THE RO-
MANS AND THE SABINES
Oil sketch on panel, 22″ × 34¼″
Antwerp, Osterrieth House

*Rubens gives expression to his desire for
peace by contrasting here the fierce fight—the
Romans on the left, the provoked Sabine men
on the right—with the reconciliation in the
center. The same idea also inspired him
during this period to paint allegorical scenes
on the theme of war and peace.*

251

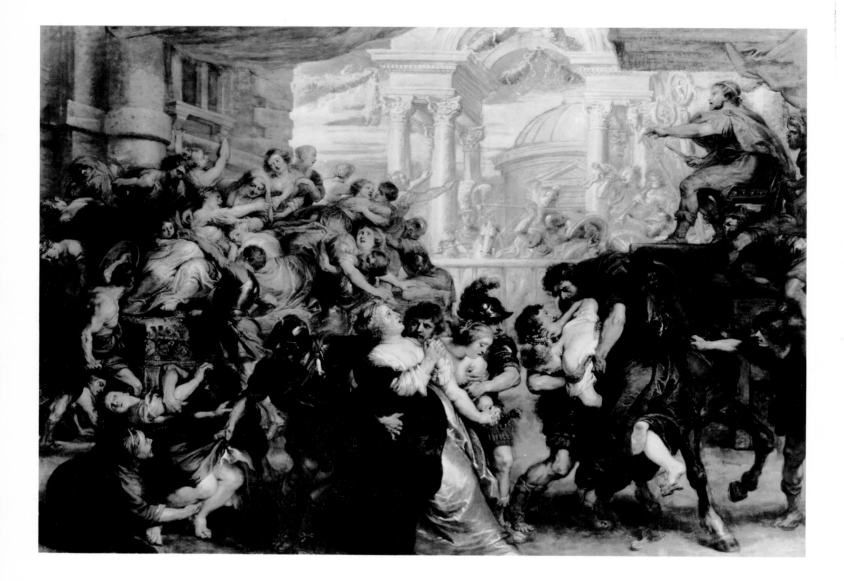

capture the turmoil of the story in a dashing rhythm of composition, which yet has been built up in a balanced and considered way, dramatic and at the same time exultant in its blazing colors.

Rubens painted the themes of *The Rape of the Sabine Women* and of *The Reconciliation of the Romans and the Sabines* more than once. The best-known example of the first subject is the large painting in the National Gallery in London, originating in the early 1630s (Fig. 128).[14] The Alte Pinakothek in Munich has a large canvas representing *The Reconciliation of the Romans and the Sabines*, which is clearly not by Rubens' hand (Fig. 129). It was painted in his studio, much earlier than the sketch at the Osterrieth House.[15] Wherever the latter shows a certain similarity in composition with the painting in Munich, this must be considered as a reworking of one of Rubens' earlier compositional ideas.

The question may be raised whether or not the artist painted the

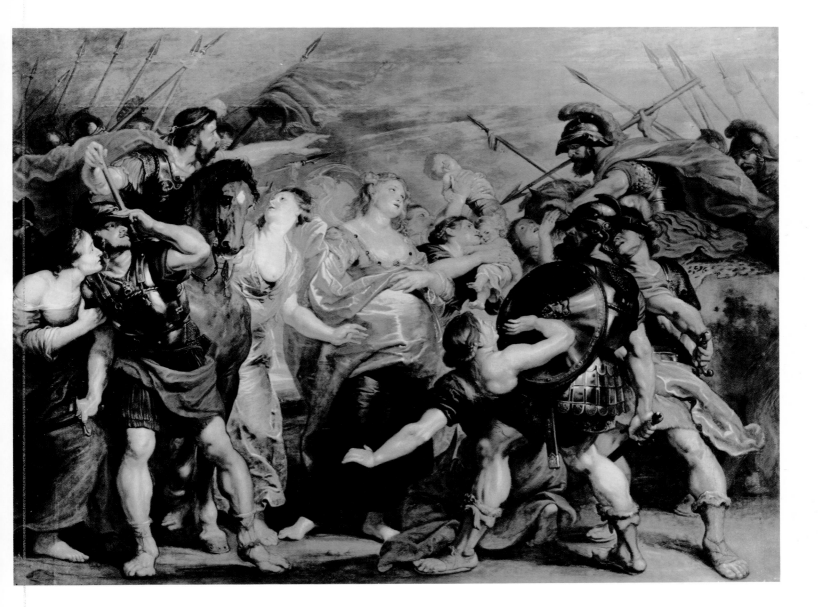

two sketches only with the aim of visualizing the old legend, out of pure pleasure in the narration. In the contrast between the first scene, a fierce fight, and the second, in which peace is restored, a deeper meaning may be hidden. For the idea of war and peace repeatedly inspired Rubens in the last ten years of his life, when these sketches were made, to works in which that very same deep-rooted desire for peace is expressed that is also revealed in several of his letters. We have in mind here in the first place the grandiose *Minerva Protects Pax from Mars* (Plate 63), painted in London in 1629–30 for Charles I,[16] with whom he had negotiated for the conclusion of a peace treaty between Spain and England.[17] In 1637 Rubens was commissioned by the Grand Duke of Tuscany to paint *The Horrors of War* (Fig. 130), a painting still at the Pitti Palace in Florence.[18]

Rubens wrote his own commentary on the content of the latter picture to Justus Sustermans on March 12, 1638: "The principal

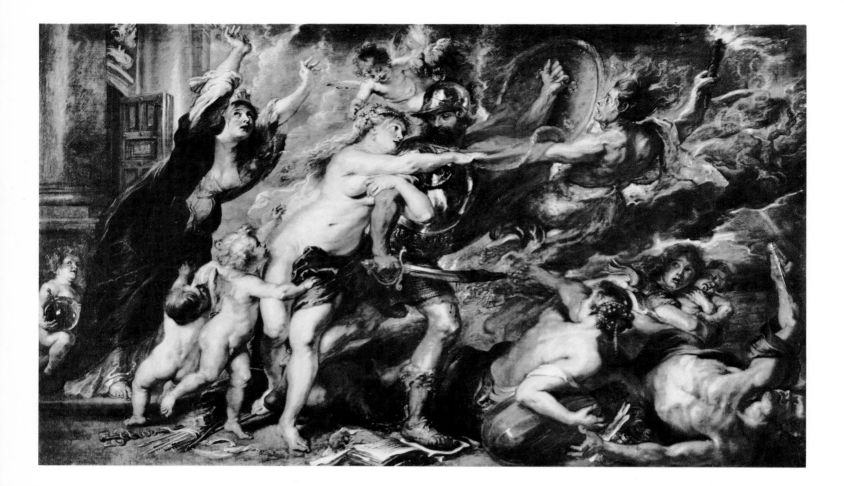

figure is Mars, who has left the open temple of Janus (which in time of peace, according to Roman custom, remained closed) and rushes forth with shield and blood-stained sword, threatening the people with great disaster. He pays little heed to Venus, his mistress, who, accompanied by her Amors and Cupids, strives with caresses and embraces to hold him. From the other side, Mars is dragged forward by the Fury Alekto, with a torch in her hand. Nearby are monsters personifying Pestilence and Famine, those inseparable partners of War. On the ground, turning her back, lies a woman with a broken lute, representing Harmony, which is incompatible with the discord of War. There is also a mother with her child in her arms, indicating that fecundity, procreation, and charity are thwarted by War, which corrupts and destroys everything. In addition, one sees an architect thrown on his back with his instruments in his hand, to show that that which in time of peace is constructed for the use and ornamentation of the City, is hurled to the ground by the force of arms and falls to ruin. I believe, if I remember rightly, that you will find on the ground under the feet of Mars a book as well as a drawing on paper, to imply that he treads underfoot all the arts and letters. There ought also to be a bundle of darts or arrows, with the band which held

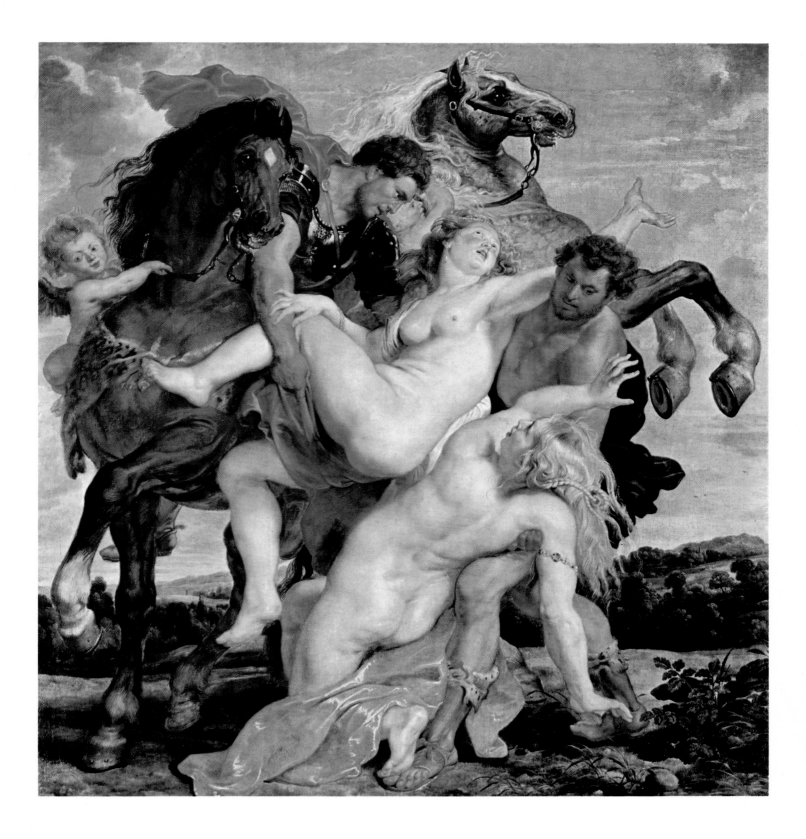

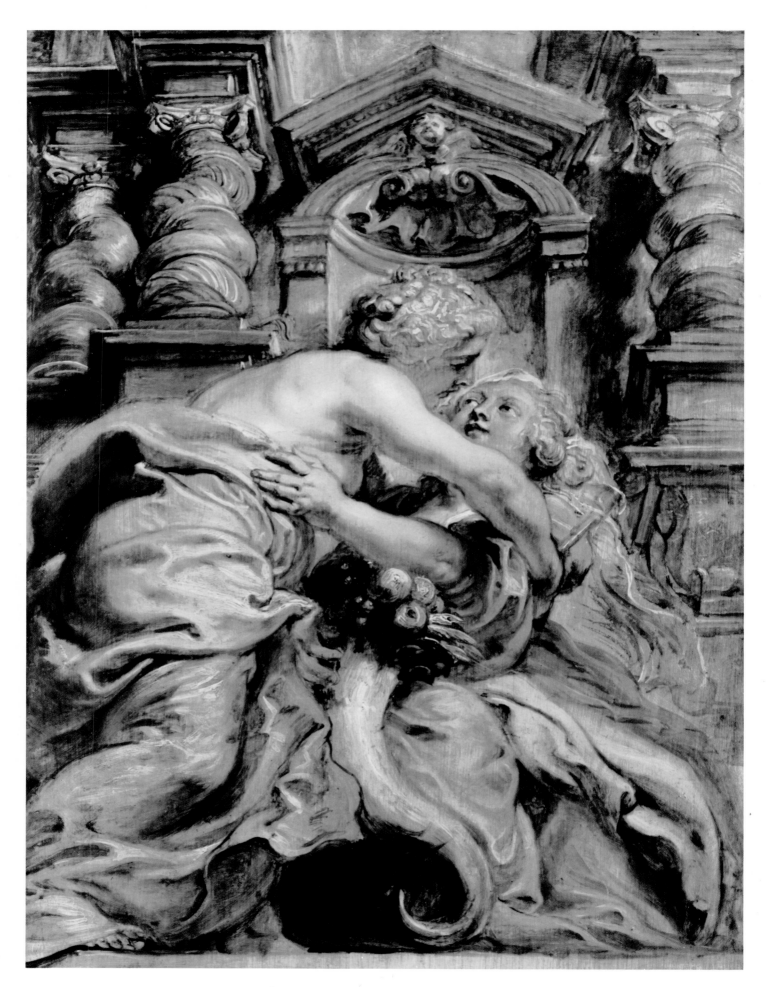

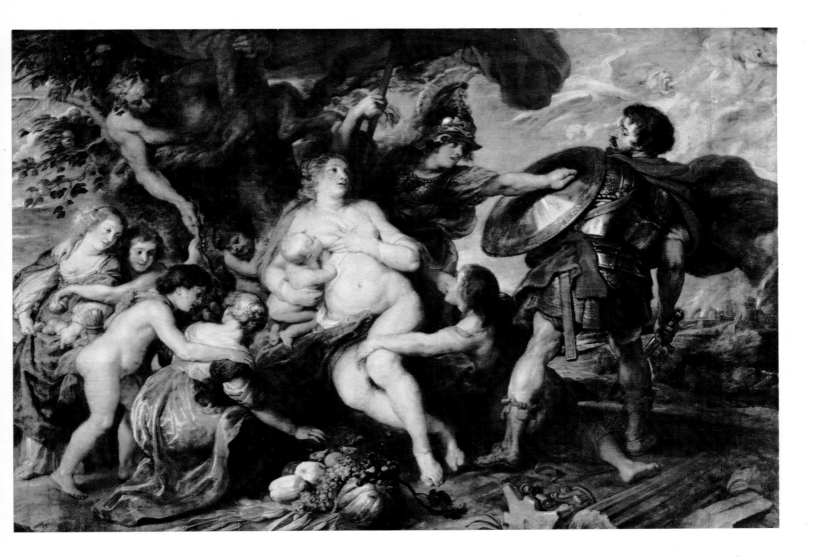

Figure 132
Workshop of Rubens
WAR AND PEACE
Canvas, $7'7\frac{1}{4}'' \times 11'1\frac{3}{4}''$
Munich, Alte Pinakothek

*Mars, the god of war, who menaces Peace and Fecundity, is being driven off by Minerva.*

Figure 131
PEACE AND ABUNDANCE EMBRAC-
ING
Oil sketch on panel, $24\frac{3}{8}'' \times 18\frac{1}{2}''$
Private Collection

*Modello for a part of the large picture The Benefits of the Reign of James I, which decorates the center of the ceiling of the Banqueting Hall in Whitehall Palace, London (see Fig. 124). The foreshortening of the architectural motifs can be observed, especially the heavy twisted columns.*

them together undone; these when bound form the symbol of Concord. Beside them is the caduceus and an olive-branch, attributes of Peace; these also are cast aside. That grief-stricken woman clothed in black, with torn veil, robbed of all her jewels and other ornaments, is the unfortunate Europe who, for so many years now, has suffered plunder, outrage, and misery, which are so injurious to everyone that it is unnecessary to go into detail. Europe's attribute is the globe, borne by a small angel or genius, and surmounted by the cross, to symbolize the Christian world."[19]

How clear and temperate is this description of the picture—and beside it, how lively is the picture itself! The symbols listed in the letter have here become a dynamic whole that is characterized, in form as in content, by an intense emotionalism. There is no doubt that Rubens is expressing his profound disappointment at the continuation of the war in spite of all the efforts to arrive at peace.[20]

Other works are equally revealing of Rubens' feelings toward war: the oil sketch of *Minerva and Mars*, fragmentarily preserved in the Boy-

257

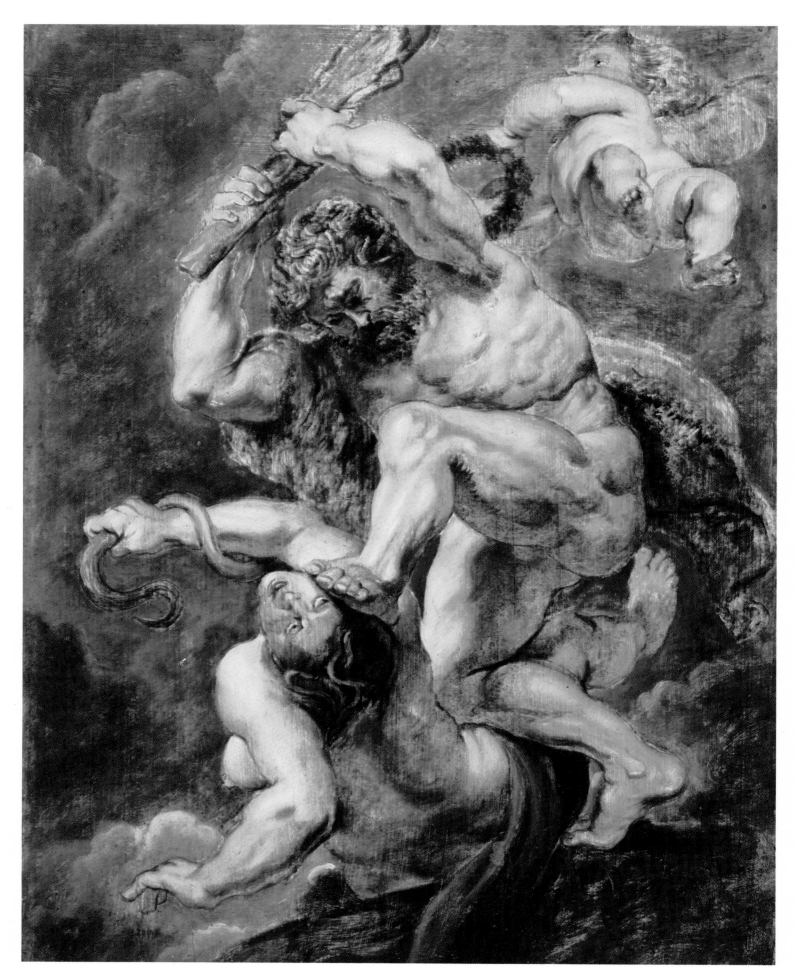

mans-van Beuningen Museum in Rotterdam;[21] *Minerva and Hercules Fighting Mars*, the oil sketch in the Cabinet des Dessins in the Louvre;[22] and the related oil sketch which appeared recently on the London art market.[23] And finally, the allegory of *War and Peace* in Munich (Fig. 132); this also dates from the 1630s, but it is more appropriately considered a studio work.[24]

War and peace appear in the guise of allegorical or mythological figures in all these works. Although these personifications are absent in the two oil sketches in the Osterrieth House, it should not be excluded that the historical themes had their place in Rubens' meditations on the miseries of war and the much-desired blessings of peace.

During his last ten years Rubens became less absorbed by large pictures, whether religious or secular.[25] For the important commissions he received he made extensive use of collaborators to execute the large-scale works after his sketches. This was his procedure for the series of mythological scenes commissioned shortly before November 1636 for the Torre de la Parada, Philip IV's new hunting lodge not far from Madrid.[26] On the basis of oil sketches by Rubens, many canvases in this cycle were painted by such artists as Jacob Jordaens, Cornelis de Vos, Theodore van Thulden, Erasmus Quellin, and Jan Cossiers, among others. For each subject Rubens put down the composition in an oil sketch, many of which we still possess: thus, *The Fall of Phaethon* (Plate 73).[27] Of the larger canvases in this series, Rubens executed only a small number himself.

It certainly seems that the artist wanted to free himself to paint at leisure the subjects that interested him or were dear to his heart. These works, small or medium in size, are among the most intimate he has left to us, with colors warmer and more radiant than ever before. Throughout his many-sided career Rubens had assembled a remarkable repertory of forms, and he could draw upon it at will. Marvelously trained, his hand effortlessly obeys his creative imagination, that now inspires him to the most audacious compositions. A few strokes of the brush suffice to render the contours of a figure; some touches of color give it full relief and expression. Even where the brush has only skimmed over the panel, forms take shape and a mood is summoned. With an extreme sparsity of means, Rubens creates a maximum of dramatic tension and dazzling beauty.

Figure 133
HERCULES SLAYING ENVY
Oil sketch on panel, 25″ × 19″
Boston, Museum of Fine Arts

Modello *for one of the smaller canvases decorating the ceiling of the Banqueting Hall in Whitehall Palace, London.*

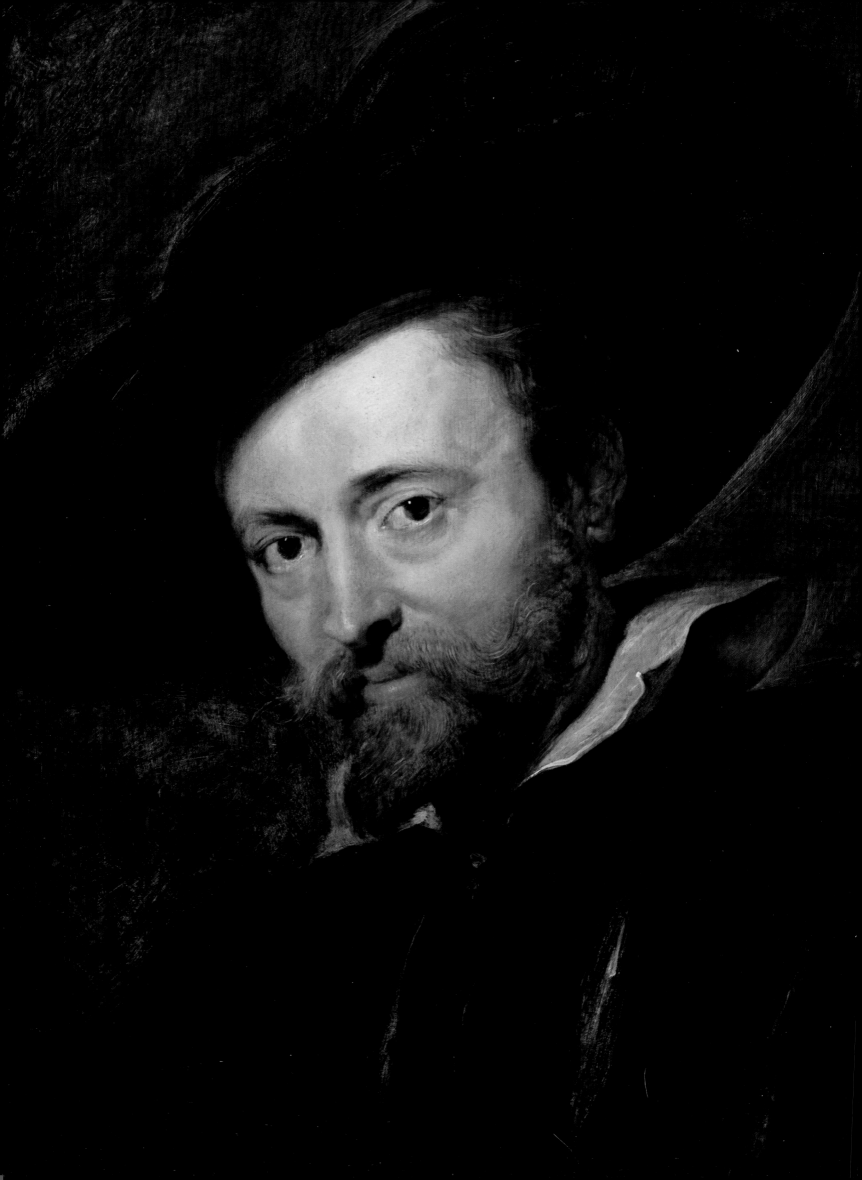

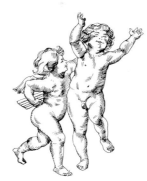

CHAPTER 12 Rubens and the Doctors

In 1606, while Rubens was visiting in Rome, we first read of a doctor as a member of his circle. It will be remembered that Rubens had set out for Italy in May 1600, and had shortly become court painter to the Duke of Mantua; his relations with the ducal house cooled somewhat when there were considerable delays in the payment of his wages, and thus he spent two years in Rome, where he received impor-tant commissions before he had to return to Antwerp.

The painter lived for some time in the Strada della Croce, not far from the Piazza di Spagna, with his brother Philip, who was secretary and librarian to Cardinal Ascanio Colonna. The two brothers had ample opportunity and leisure to study classical art and culture. The artist made drawings for a number of illustrations in the archaeological study which Philip Rubens was preparing: *Electorum libri duo*, which was published in 1608, by the Plantin Press in Antwerp.[1]

The brothers' interest in classical Antiquity must soon have brought them into contact with another connoisseur in Rome, Johannes Faber, the German doctor from Bamberg.[2] Faber was a remarkable man; his curiosity, far from being limited to medicine, extended to fauna and flora and the study of classical works. Attached to the hospital of Santo Spirito in Sassia, Faber taught at the Sapienza and also fulfilled the functions of curator of the botanic gardens of the Vatican. His reputation in scientific circles was such that in 1611, together with Galileo, he was made a member of the Accademia dei Lincei. He maintained friendly relations with several German, Flemish, and Dutch artists living in Rome, among them Adam Elsheimer, his compatriot from Frankfurt, and Paul Bril, the landscape painter from Antwerp. For several years Faber was also the purveyor of the Brotherhood of Santa Maria dell' Anima, a society to which belonged persons from Germany and the Netherlands who lived in Rome. In his will he left 250 scudi to this association for anniversary masses and services to be celebrated after his death, which occurred in Rome in 1629.

261

The Plantin-Moretus Museum in Antwerp preserves the correspondence between Balthasar Moretus I and Philip Rubens, which offers some information about the relationship of the Rubens brothers with Johannes Faber. Philip Rubens evidently used his good offices toward the publication by the Plantin Press of a book by the German scholar which appeared in 1606;[3] the book was in fact not entirely Faber's, but the fourth edition of the *Illustrium Imagines* of Fulvio Orsini (1529–1600), an archaeological study which had had great success throughout Europe in humanist circles. It contained one hundred and fifty-one portraits of famous men of Antiquity, engraved after ancient statues, coins, and cameos. Faber added another eighteen pieces, accompanied by a learned commentary; these were engraved in Antwerp by Theodore Galle, and in the opinion of some authors they are based on drawings made in Rome by Peter Paul Rubens.[4]

At the time this book was due to come out, in June or July 1606, Peter Paul Rubens fell seriously ill. On July 22, 1606, Philip Rubens wrote to the humanist Erycius Puteanus that he would have thanked him sooner for the present he had received "if the illness of my brother had permitted me to."[5] We learn more about the illness from the doctor who treated him, who was none other than Johannes Faber. In a writing of his, published in 1628, we read: "When, in Rome, I had cured him, with God's help, of a serious attack of pleurisy, he painted a cock for me under which he wrote these words, mocking but scholarly: 'In honor of the celebrated Johannes Faber, doctor of medicine, my Aesculapius, I gladly fulfill the promise I made when my life was despaired of.' He also painted my portrait in color, a very good likeness, on a large panel, which is highly praised by painters for its great artistic merit."[6] The idea of presenting his doctor with a picture of a cock proceeds from Rubens' knowledge of classical culture: was it not a custom of the Greeks to give a cock to Aesculapius, the god of medicine? Unfortunately we have no trace of either the picture of the cock[7] or of Faber's portrait.[8]

After his return to Antwerp late in 1608, Rubens remained for a time in correspondence with the German doctor who had cured him. The first letter, dated April 10, 1609, gives the news of his brother Philip's marriage and of the tribulations preceding it[9] (we shall return to these shortly). The painter continues by telling his friend that he has not yet decided whether to return to Rome or settle for good in Antwerp.[10] Although we can already read between the lines that the final choice will be for Antwerp, the letter reveals a lingering nostalgia for Rome that becomes definite in the last paragraph; Rubens asks Faber to pass on his greetings to the many friends in his circle: the humanist Gaspard Scioppius, converted into a virulent polemicist against Protestantism; Adam Elsheimer; the Dutch painter and draftsman, Hendrik Goudt; "and to the other friends whose good conversation makes me often long for Rome."[11] In a second letter, written in Antwerp on January 14, 1611, Rubens expresses his distress at the news of Elsheimer's death, which Faber had informed him of.[12]

Plate 71

PORTRAIT OF LUDOVICUS NONNIUS
Panel, 48½" × 39½"
London, National Gallery

*The aged doctor and numismatist, of Spanish "marrano" extraction, was Rubens' friend. This lively portrait was probably painted in 1627. A static pose has been avoided: the doctor holds his book in a somewhat uncertain way, and the gesture of his right hand and the expression on his face give the impression that he is speaking to someone.*

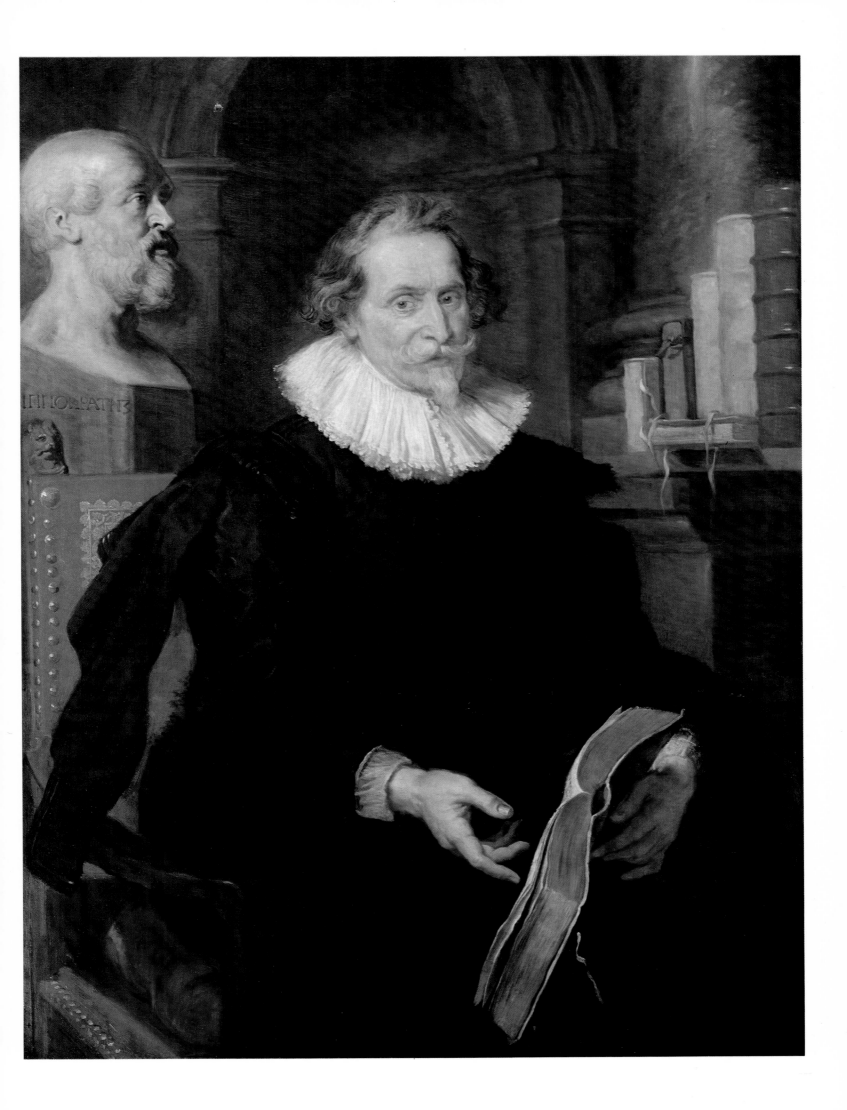

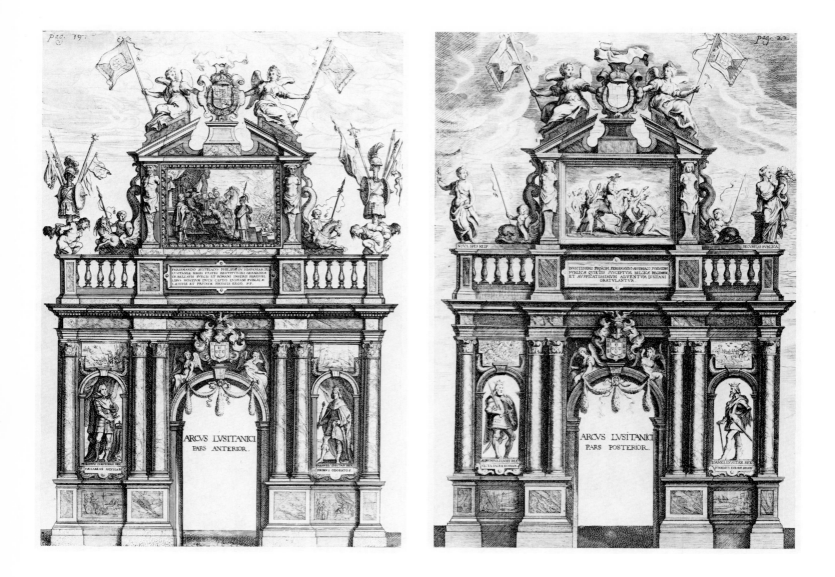

Figures 134, 135
Theodore van Thulden, after Ludovicus Nonnius
FRONT AND REAR FACES OF THE TRIUMPHAL ARCH OF THE PORTUGUESE MERCHANTS FOR THE ENTRY OF CARDINAL-INFANTE FERDINAND IN ANTWERP, 1635
Etching
Antwerp, Rubens House

*Nonnius' design for this triumphal arch was the only one built that did not follow Rubens' designs. These two etchings appear in the work entitled* Pompa Introitus Ferdinandi, *Antwerp, 1641 (published 1642).*

At the end of 1608 Rubens made the acquaintance of a completely different type of doctor, under circumstances that were rather unusual.[13] Master Guillielmus Verwilt or Verwiltius of Antwerp, doctor of medicine, seems to have come from a well-to-do background. His correspondence with the engraver Jacob de Bie allows us to guess that he was a good companion and a bon vivant—which in no way rules out an ability to exercise honorably the art of healing.

Guillielmus Verwilt was the son of an apothecary, also named Guillielmus, and of Laurentia Arlé; they lived in the Kipdorp in a house called "Den witten Engel" (The White Angel). He matriculated at the University of Padua on December 10, 1600, a university famous for its medical faculty. Returning to his native town in 1603, he fell in love with Maria de Moy, daughter of Hendrik de Moy, one of the Secretaries of Antwerp. The young lady, being very pretty and of a rich family, had many suitors, including Dr. Verwilt and Philip Rubens; the latter's courtship began after he returned from Rome in May 1607.

264

We cannot relate in detail the tricks devised by Verwilt to attract the attention of his beloved, or describe the evolution of the various wooers' chances; suffice it to say that after Peter Paul Rubens returned, the balance tipped in favor of Philip Rubens, to the great chagrin of Dr. Verwilt. On December 11, 1608, the doctor wrote to Jacob de Bie that his chances had been compromised "by the arrival of the painter, Rubens' brother; and that De Moy was strongly urged by the city authorities to sell his office to the city so that [Philip] Rubens could be discreetly given a post there; then, being Secretary, he will try once more to get the hand of the daughter; so I must get busy and keep an eye on things so that I can beat him to it for the last time (for the other pretenders are out of the running)."[14] On April 10, 1609, Peter Paul Rubens wrote to Faber on the subject of these trials: "I find by experience that such affairs [love and marriage] should not be carried on coolly but with great fervor. My brother has also proved this, for since my arrival he has changed his tactics, after pining for two years in vain."[15] There was no doubt in the minds of Dr. Verwilt nor of Rubens that Philip Rubens' victory was largely due to his brother. On February 12, 1609, the rejected suitor acknowledged defeat: "and as for the lady, it is clear that she thinks of no one but Rubens and that she absolutely must have him."[16] A month later, on March 26, Maria de Moy married Philip Rubens.

Later that year—in October 1609—Peter Paul also married, in his turn. His bride was Isabella Brant, daughter of the registrar of Antwerp, Jan Brant, and of Clara de Moy, the elder sister of Maria de Moy, his brother Philip's young wife. Meanwhile Dr. Verwilt had found a lady to console him: Hélène de Moulin, probably a native of Mons, with whom he contracted marriage. The ending of his bachelor days seems to have influenced his career beneficially, for he became one of the most prominent doctors in the Metropolis. On December 6, 1610, he and four colleagues signed a document that permitted doctors Godfried Vereycken and Lazarus Marcquis to found the "Collegium Medicum Antverpiense";[17] from 1612 onward Verwilt is frequently mentioned as official doctor of the City,[18] a function comparable to that of medical expert but entailing the duty to intervene in the event of epidemics, and in favor of needy patients. Although responsible for public health, the city doctors were authorized to have private practices as well.

In August 1617 Verwilt signed another petition, this time with twelve doctors, to found the "Collegium Medicum."[19] This body was not created until April 28, 1620, by decree of the Mayors and Aldermen;[20] the name of Guillielmus Verwilt occurs again in other documents concerning the "collegie der medecynen," as the citizens of Antwerp called it.[21]

The old rivalry of the doctor with Philip Rubens does not seem to have produced lasting rancor toward the Rubens family. In 1626, as we shall see later, Dr. Verwilt was called to the bedside of Isabella Brant in her last illness.

Rubens struck up an acquaintance with another doctor in Antwerp,

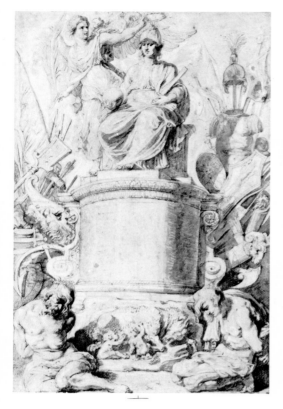

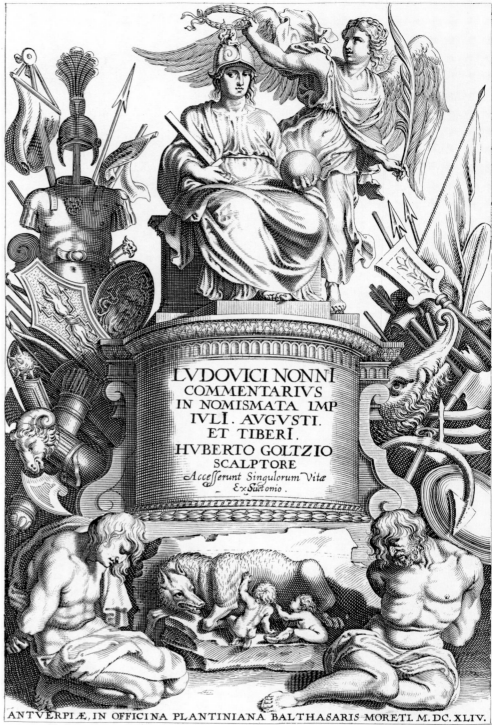

Figure 136

FRONTISPIECE (ROMA TRIUM-
PHANS) FOR LUDOVICUS
NONNIUS, COMMENTARIUS IN
NUMISMATA IMP. JULII,
AUGUSTI ET TIBERII
Drawing
London, British Museum

*Drawn as the design for the title page of
a book on numismatics published in
Antwerp in 1617 by Jacob de Bie,* Numismata Imperatorum Romanorum, *and reused subsequently as the title page for Nonnius'* Commentarius in Numismata *(first
published 1620).*

Figure 137

Michel Lasne, after Rubens
FRONTISPIECE FOR LUDOVICUS NONNIUS, COMMENTARIUS IN NUMISMATA
IMP. JULII, AUGUSTI ET TIBERII
Engraving
Antwerp, Plantin-Moretus Museum

*This engraving, first used in 1617 in the work by Jacob de Bie described in the previous caption,
was used again for the* Commentarius *by Nonnius already mentioned, which was published by
H. Verdussen in 1620 in Antwerp, and in the second edition, published by Balthasar Moretus I
in 1644 as the second volume of his edition of the numismatic works of Hubert Goltzius, accompanied
by commentaries by other authors.*

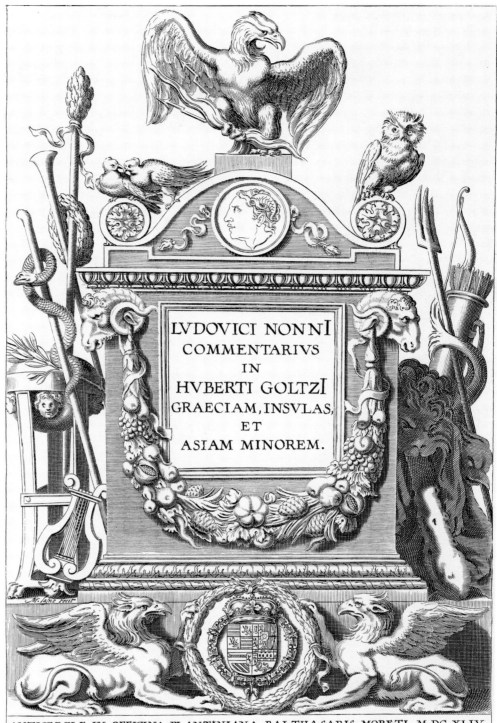

Figure 138

Michel Lasne, after Rubens

FRONTISPIECE FOR LUDOVICUS NONNIUS, COMMENTARIUS IN HUBERTI
GOLTZI GRAECIAM, INSULAS ET ASIAM MINOREM

Engraving

Antwerp, Plantin-Moretus Museum

*Engraved after a drawing by Rubens, now apparently lost, for the second edition of the portion of
Hubert Goltzius' works that deals with the coins of Greece, the Islands, and Asia Minor, published
in 1618 by Jacob de Bie. The engraving was used again in 1644 for Nonnius' commentaries on the
same subject, published as volume III of the Moretus edition of Goltzius' numismatic works.*

Ludovicus Nuñez (c. 1553–1645/46), better known under his latinized name Nonnius.[22] Like Johannes Faber, Nonnius was the type of doctor, scholar, and humanist whose interests went beyond medical science. Nonnius, in fact, concerned himself with numismatics, in which field another friend of Rubens, Nicolaas Rockox, also distinguished himself. Our painter, himself well versed in archaeology—Faber called him "an amateur scholar of bronze and marble antiquities"—must have met Nonnius soon after returning to Antwerp. Did they meet perhaps at the house of Rockox, Rubens' friend and patron? Or was it through Philip Rubens, Justus Lipsius' favorite pupil, who probably counted the doctor-numismatist among his friends?

It is not our purpose to sketch Nonnius' biography in full, we want only to throw light on his relations with Rubens, but certain biographical references should be mentioned. Ludovicus Nonnius was born in Antwerp in or about 1553; his father, Alvares Nonnius, also a well-known doctor, was born in Frarinale, Spain, probably of Portuguese parents. Ludovicus studied medicine at Louvain and settled later in Antwerp. His first work, *Hispania* (1607), is a synthesis of Spain, following the example of Francesco Guicciardini's *Descrittione di tutti i Paesi Bassi* of 1567. His next two books, *Ichtyophagia* (1616) and *Diaeteticon* (1627; enlarged edition 1645), are more in line with his medical practice. Doctor P. Boeynaems has pointed out that in the field of dietetics the *Diaeteticon* is one of the earliest publications to insist upon the importance of food hygiene for man's health.[23]

Rubens probably knew this work. He sent some books to Pierre Dupuy on August 12, 1627, "more for the sake of sending something, than because I consider them worthy of your curiosity," but he makes for Nonnius' book an exception to this by adding in the margin: "The little work of Ludovicus Nonnius is considered a good book, in the opinion of our physicists":[24] no doubt Rubens is referring to the *Diaeteticon*, which had come out that year.

We have mentioned Nonnius' activity in the field of numismatics. Two books that he published on this subject have frontispieces after designs by Rubens (Figs. 137, 138). The first is his *Commentarius in Nomismata Imp. Julii, Augusti et Tiberii*, published in 1620 by H. Verdussen, and reprinted in 1644 by Balthasar Moretus II, as the second part of his edition of the works of Hubert Goltzius; the second, *Commentarius in Huberti Goltzii Graeciam, Insulas, et Asiam Minorem*, was published in 1644 as Part III of the Moretus edition of Goltzius' *Opera Omnia*.[25] However, Rubens did not draw these frontispieces, engraved by Michel Lasne, at Nonnius' request: they had already served, the first in 1617 (Fig. 136), the other in 1618, for numismatic publications by Jacob de Bie, the correspondent of Dr. Verwilt! They were simply used a second time for Nonnius' books.

Rubens painted an impressive portrait of Ludovicus Nonnius on a panel that recently came to the National Gallery in London (Plate 71).[26] It shows the elderly doctor-numismatist seated in front of an alcove in a room, holding an open folio volume in his hand. In the

Plate 72
CHARLES I AS PRINCE OF WALES, CROWNED BY BRITANNIA
Oil sketch on panel, 33¼" × 27⅞"
The Minneapolis Institute of Arts

*Sketch executed about 1633–34 for a portion of the ceiling of the Banqueting Hall of Whitehall Palace, London. At right and left of the child are England and Scotland; with Britannia above, they hold the triple crown over his head.*

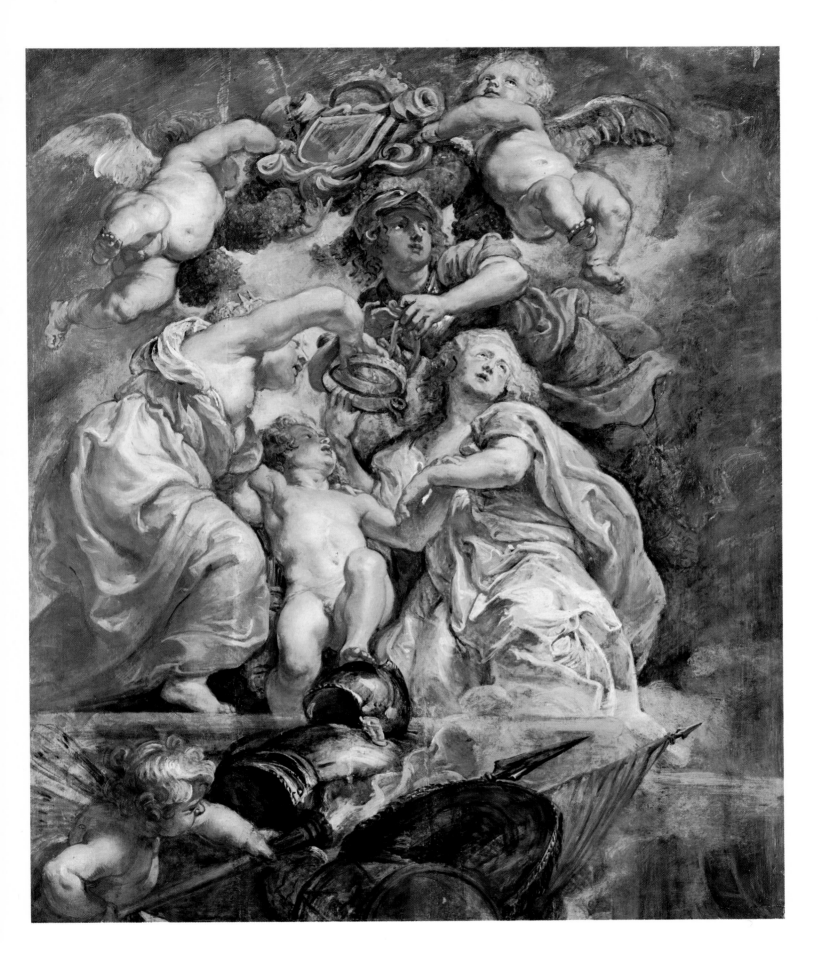

269

background several books are visible and on a pedestal there is a marble bust on which is carved, in Greek letters, the name Hippocrates. For a long time this portrait was not identified, though the bust of Hippocrates, "the father of medicine," indicated the sitter's profession. Several names of doctors were put forward but all proved inaccurate. Burchard succeeded in solving the enigma in 1950 when he noticed that the same person was represented in another portrait painted by Erasmus Quellin, preserved in the Plantin-Moretus Museum, of which documents had long since established that the sitter was Ludovicus Nonnius. Burchard showed at that time that Erasmus Quellin's portrait was only a partial copy of Rubens' original portrait of Nonnius, probably painted about 1627.[27]

To complete our knowledge of Nonnius' diverse talents, we should add that in 1634–35, for the Entry of Cardinal Infante Ferdinand into Antwerp, he drew the design for the Triumphal Arch of the Portuguese Merchants (Figs. 134, 135), the only decoration erected for this occasion after a design other than Rubens'.[28] He was certainly brave to set himself up against the "Apelles of his time"! Compared with the astounding vigor with which Rubens embellished the triumphal arches and stages of his own design (Fig. 17), Nonnius' talent appears rather conventional, but one must grant him nevertheless a sense of architectural design.

After the splendid display of the Entry the town counsellors of Antwerp decided to publish a richly illustrated book as a souvenir of the triumphal arches erected for this solemn occasion. This became the famous *Pompa Introitus Ferdinandi* of 1641: Theodore van Thulden, Rubens' assistant over a number of years, undertook to make the etchings, and Caspar Gevaerts, the scholarly municipal registrar and friend of the painter (Plate 54), to write a Latin commentary in elegant prose. The text was submitted for approval to a committee of three Latin scholars; Ludovicus Nonnius, one member of this triumvirate, received on January 26, 1639, a cask of French wine as his reward.[29] When the Dutch humanist Nicolaas Heinsius visited Antwerp five years later, in 1644, he noted the name of Ludovicus Nonnius as one of only three learned men he had discovered there;[30] the majority of those who had contributed only a few years before to the fame of the Metropolis were no longer alive, and Ludovicus Nonnius, an aged man himself, died shortly afterward, in 1645 or 1646.

Probably on the occasion of Nonnius' death, Balthasar Moretus II must have commissioned Erasmus Quellin to copy Rubens' portrait of Nonnius, painted a number of years previously. The payment of Quellin's fee was recorded on April 18, 1647.[31] His picture completes the series of portraits of eminent men that had been set up by Balthasar Moretus I, and in the Plantin-Moretus Museum it still perpetuates the memory of the friendship which linked Nonnius with the great Antwerp printers, Balthasar Moretus I and Balthasar II.[32]

It is known that the plague claimed many victims in Antwerp during the first decades of the seventeenth century. In 1625 Rubens found

Figure 139
Theodore van Thulden, after Rubens
FRONTISPIECE FOR POMPA INTROITUS FERDINANDI
Etching
Antwerp, Osterrieth House

*The oil sketch for this frontispiece is today in the Fitzwilliam Museum, Cambridge, England.*

270

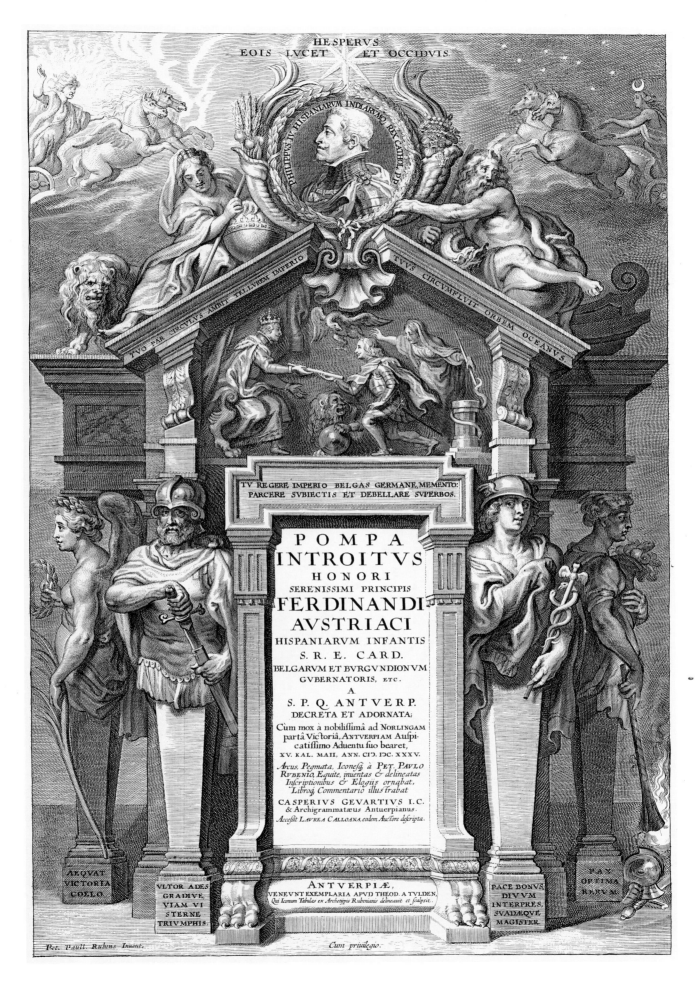

HESPERVS
EOIS LVCET ET OCCIDVIS

PHILIPPVS IV HISPANIARVM INDIARVMQ. REX CATHOL. P.P.

TVO PAR IVGVLVS AMBIT TELLVREM IMPERIO

IVVS CIRCVMFLVIT ORBEM OCEANVS

TV REGERE IMPERIO BELGAS GERMANE, MEMENTO:
PARCERE SVBIECTIS ET DEBELLARE SVPERBOS.

POMPA
INTROITVS
HONORI
SERENISSIMI PRINCIPIS
FERDINANDI
AVSTRIACI
HISPANIARVM INFANTIS
S.R.E. CARD.
BELGARVM ET BVRGVNDIONVM
GVBERNATORIS, ETC.
A
S.P.Q. ANTVERP.
DECRETA ET ADORNATA;
Cùm mox à nobilissimâ ad NORLINGAM
partâ Victoriâ, ANTVERPIAM Auspi-
catissimo Aduentu suo bearet,
XV. KAL. MAII. ANN. CIƆ IƆC. XXXV.
Arcus, Pegmata, Iconesq̃, à PET. PAVLO
RVBENIO, Equite, inuentas & delineatas
Inscriptionibus & Elogiis ornabat,
Libroq̃ Commentario illustrabat
CASPERIVS GEVARTIVS I.C.
& Archigrammatæus Antuerpianus.
Accessit LAVREA CALLOANA, eodem Auctore descripta.

ÆQVAT
VICTORIA
COELO.

VLTOR ADES
GRADIVE,
VIAM VI
STERNE
TRIVMPHIS.

ANTVERPIÆ,
VENEVNT EXEMPLARIA APVD THEOD. A TVLDEN,
Qui Iconum Tabulas ex Archetipis Rubenianis delineauit et sculpsit.

PACE BONVS
DIVVM
INTERPRES,
SVADÆQVE
MAGISTER.

PAX
OPTIMA
RERVM.

Pet. Paull. Rubens Inuent.                    Cum priuilegio.

271

himself obliged to leave the Metropolis. He settled with his family in an inn at Laeken, not far from Brussels; between August 25, 1625, and February 20, 1626, he wrote letters that are still extant from this village, or from the capital nearby. On November 28, 1625, he announced to Valavez in Paris: "I am thinking of returning very soon to Antwerp. The plague, thank God, is diminishing day by day, and I am tired of remaining so long away from home."[33] But he had to be patient until late in February 1626, before getting back to his own fireside.

Would he not have done better to stay in Laeken? It is a fact that on June 20, 1626, four months after returning to Antwerp, Isabella Brant died, probably a victim of the plague. She was only thirty-four. Listed in the "Personal Estate in the House of the Deceased Isabella Brant" we find the names of the doctors summoned to her bedside: "Nuñes, Verwilt, Lazarus and Vereycken."[34] We already know the first two, Nonnius[35] and Guillielmus Verwilt, the rejected suitor of Maria de Moy. The third doctor, "Lazarus," can be no other than the famous Doctor Lazarus Marcquis; together with the fourth, Dr. Godfried Vereycken, he was the principal promoter of the "Collegium Medicum Antverpiense."

If the fee paid to each of these is a good criterion, Dr. Godfried Vereycken was the patient's principal doctor. He was then already an elderly man,[36] for he was born in Antwerp in 1558. He had lived in France and studied medicine at different universities there, particularly at Toulouse, where he obtained his doctorate on June 13, 1586; he later returned to Antwerp, and in 1591 he was sworn in as a doctor of the City. In 1625 he published his *Tractatus de cognitione et conservatione sui*, a book concerned mainly with precepts of hygiene, with the firm of Henricus Haye, in Malines, which brought out a second edition in 1633. His last years were spent in Malines, where his son was a member of the Grand Council; he died there on December 2, 1635.

Dr. Lazarus Marcquis received thirty florins for his medical care of Isabella Brant. This doctor was an intelligent, competent, and energetic man,[37] of the same generation as Rubens. He was baptized in Antwerp on January 7, 1574, the son of a Walloon merchant who specialized in the diamond trade; he studied first at the Jesuit College in Antwerp and medicine at Louvain with the famous Thomas Feyens (1567–1631), physician to the Archduke Albert and the Archduchess Isabella. He completed his medical studies at the University of Padua, taking his doctor's degree at twenty-four in 1598. In Antwerp, he became a practicing doctor on January 28, 1599, and that year married Maria van den Broeck, the daughter of an apothecary. In 1606 he became attached to the hospital of Saint Elisabeth and in 1611 was appointed teacher in the school of surgeons. Doctors Lazaras Marcquis and Vereycken had been charged by their colleagues the year before to found a "Collegium Medicum."

Lazarus Marcquis needs no complete biography here, but we must mention that the frequent epidemics of plague which ravaged these regions gave him the opportunity to study that terrible illness and

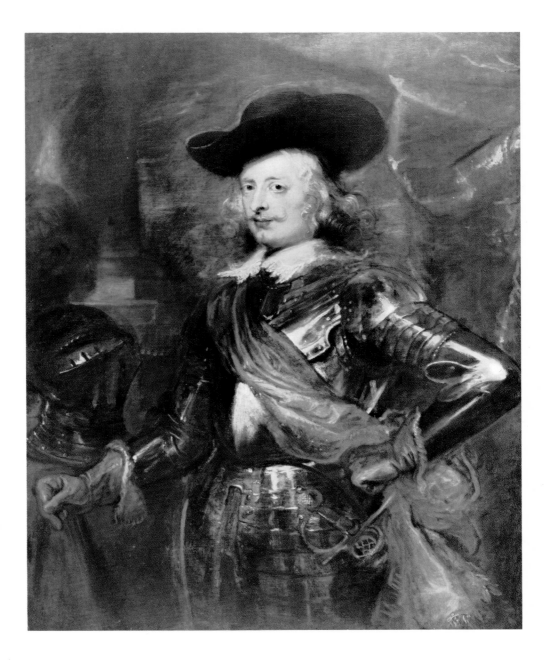

the remedies prescribed to the afflicted patients. The results of his research were published in his *Volcomen tractaet van de peste* (Complete treatise on the plague) in 1634, with a second edition two years later. An active practitioner all his life, Dr. Lazarus Marcquis died in Antwerp on December 20, 1647. Seven years earlier he had attended Rubens in his last illness.

Shortly after Rubens' first wife died, he himself required medical help.[38] On October 15, 1626, he wrote to Jacques Dupuy in Paris that a high fever kept him confined to bed:[39] "I feel languid both in body and spirit, because even though the fever is going down, you know that the intermittent days have been occupied by doctors with

273

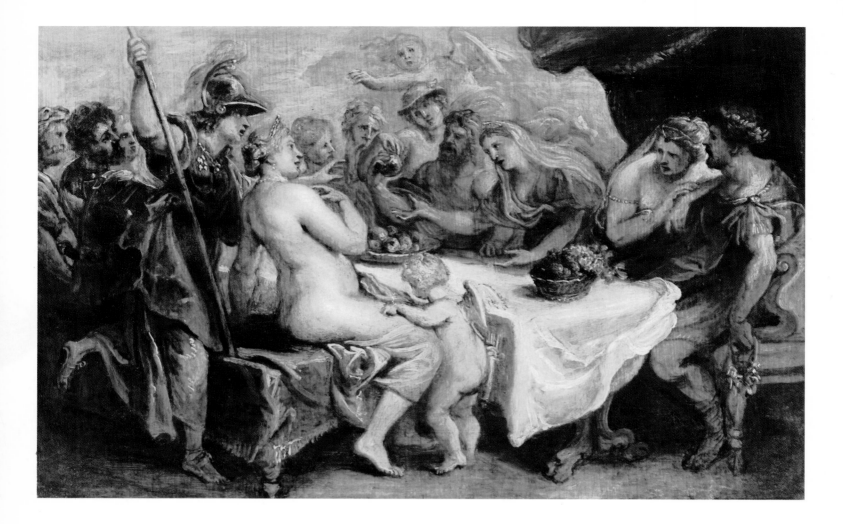

Figure 141
THE MARRIAGE OF PELEUS AND
THETIS
Oil sketch on panel, 11¾″ × 17″
The Art Institute of Chicago

*The wedding of Peleus and the sea-nymph
Thetis is interrupted by the goddess Eris
or Discord, who was not invited and who
throws her golden apple among the
gods.  Oil sketch for one of the mythological
paintings of the series executed in 1636–38
for the decoration of the Torre de la Parada,
the hunting lodge of Philip IV near Madrid.*

purges, bloodletting, and similar remedies often more grave than the illness itself."[40]   Does the last part of the sentence not betray Rubens' skepticism about what were then common practices?   He was not the only one to doubt the value of these procedures: Dr. Lazarus Marcquis, for example, was far from agreeing with these treatments, at least to combat the plague.

The following week, on October 22, 1626, Rubens wrote again to Dupuy: "Although the fever has left me, I still feel the effects of my recent illness.   Just as the sea, after a great tempest, does not subside at once, but retains a certain agitation before becoming calm, so do I find myself in an intermediary state—out of danger, but not entirely free from illness."[41]   But Rubens soon recovered and even undertook a journey to Paris.   After his return, however, he wrote to Dupuy on January 22, 1627, that from the time he left Paris until he reached Péronne, he had suffered pain in his foot.[42]   This is our first information about his experience of gout, the illness that frequently attacked him afterward.

Two years later, while detained in Madrid by a lengthy diplomatic

274

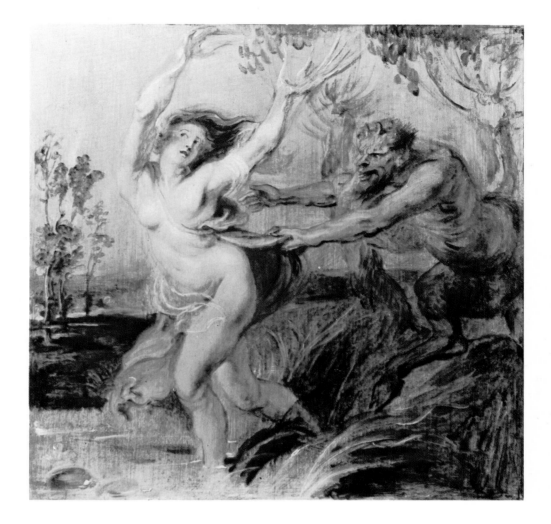

mission, Rubens wrote to his friend Caspar Gevaerts on December
29, 1628, starting in Dutch and writing the remainder in Latin: "These
last few days I have been very sick with gout and fever, and to tell
the truth, I could hardly draw a breath between groans and sighs. But
now, thank God, I am better."[43] Other sources inform us that at
that time he was going for treatment to a somewhat reckless personage,
Don Fabrizio Valguarnera, a native of Palermo, a doctor of laws, and
a friend of the arts who also boasted that "he possessed the secret
of curing certain diseases such as gout and pleurisy."[44] Clearly Valguarnera had no medical diploma and was a charlatan; indeed we draw
our data about him from documents relating to a judicial enquiry against
him in Rome in 1631, concerning a diamond theft in Madrid in which
he was implicated.[45] But at any rate in 1628 Valguarnera put Rubens
back on his feet, in Madrid. In reward for this care and attention
Rubens promised his doctor a canvas painted by his own hand, yet
as late as June 20, 1631, he writes to Valguarnera from Antwerp
expressing surprise that he has received no information about the subject and dimensions of the work which it had been his pleasure to

275

promise him. Perhaps he would like to accept an *Adoration of the Magi*, then unfinished in his workshop: a picture "seven to eight feet in height and almost square, which could serve as an altarpiece at some private chapel or to adorn the chimney piece of a large salon."[46] Rubens probably received no reply, for the reckless Valguarnera was arrested soon afterward in Rome, and died a few months later in the Carcere dei Sei.

After Rubens' recovery in Madrid, he did not continue to complain about his health. Is this pure chance? or could it be because the correspondence he has left us is incomplete? The artist did indeed write to Pierre Dupuy from London on August 8, 1629: "To see so many varied countries and courts, in so short a time, would have been more fitting and useful to me in my youth than at my present age. My body would have been stronger, to endure the hardships of travel, and my mind would have been able to prepare itself, by experience and familiarity with the most diverse peoples, for greater things in the future. Now, however, I am expending my declining strength, and no time remains to enjoy the fruits of so many labors, unless thereby I shall succeed in dying a wiser man."[47] Rubens was then fifty-two. This did not prevent him, more than a year later, from marrying Helena Fourment, a pretty sixteen-year-old who subsequently gave him five children.

In the following years he was frequently troubled by attacks of gout. That the disease kept him in bed in April 1635, at the moment when Cardinal Infante Ferdinand made his Entry into Antwerp, may be only an eighteenth-century legend,[48] but it is an established fact, on the other hand, that in October of that year, when he was about to set out for London to deliver the ceiling paintings commissioned by Charles I for Whitehall Palace, he had to cancel the journey because he was "desperately ill."

Rubens does not seem to have had to complain of his general health in the following years, although Balthasar Moretus II informed his nephew Frans van Ravelingen on April 8, 1638, that Rubens' hand pained him so much that he was unable to draw the small designs for the engravers or to retouch the engraved plates; thus the gout was now in the artist's hand also, though the attack must have been brief, since we know that Rubens produced a great deal of work in that year. But we infer that the artist frequently suffered short attacks after this time. One instance was shortly before October 24, 1638, when Mathieu de Morgues reports to Philippe Chifflet that "Mr. Rubens is better, we are expecting him here";[49] in February 1639, the painter sends his oldest son Albert to Brussels, "since, in view of the attack of gout he is at present suffering from, he cannot appear in person";[50] on April 6 the illness was so much worse that the notary Henry Cantelbeek, when he signed for Rubens on a document, added a note: "As proxy for the gentleman, who, having gout in his right hand, has declared he can neither write nor sign his name."[51]

Rubens nevertheless spent the summer of 1639 at the château of Steen, his estate at Elewijt, though during his stay he summoned two

Plate 73
THE FALL OF PHAETHON
Oil sketch on panel, 11″ × 11″
Brussels, Musées Royaux des Beaux-Arts de Belgique

*Phaethon, the son of Apollo, is driving his father's sun-chariot. When he cannot control the horses, Jupiter hurls him down into the abyss. Design for one of the paintings for the Torre de la Parada, the hunting lodge of Philip IV. The series was executed to a large extent by several Antwerp artists in 1636–38, after designs by Rubens.*

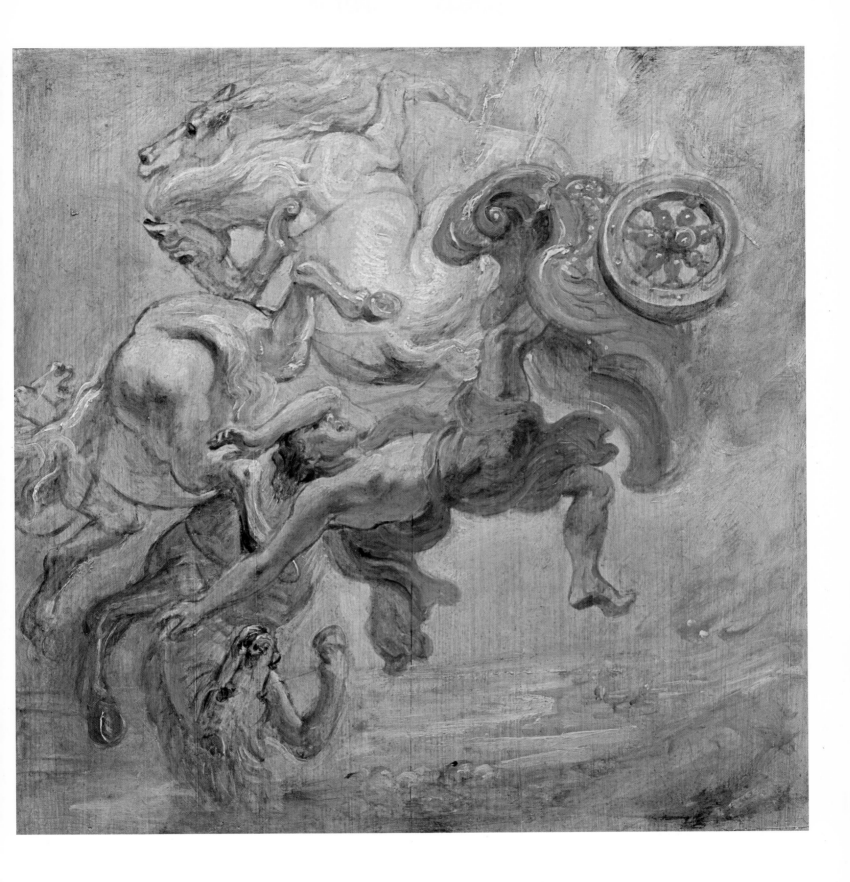

277

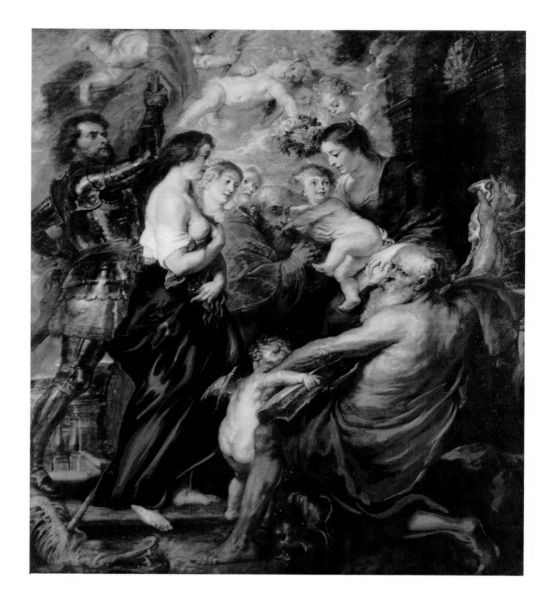

Figure 143
VIRGIN AND CHILD WITH SAINTS
Panel, 6′11″ × 6′4³/₄″
Antwerp, Church of St. Jacques

*This superb* sacra conversazione *was painted during Rubens' last years and is a magnificent example of the lyrical style of this period. Rubens himself chose this panel to be put on the altar of his funeral chapel.*

Plate 74
VIRGIN AND CHILD WITH SAINTS
(detail)
Antwerp, Church of St. Jacques

*The face of the child resembles that of Frans Rubens, the eldest child of Rubens' second wife, Helena Fourment.*

doctors from Malines to attend him. He must have sensed that the end was near, since he called in a notary to Elewijt, and to Antwerp after he returned in September, to add codicils to the will that he and his wife had drawn up the day after their marriage in 1631.

Then his condition improved, and during the winter he negotiated for several months about an important commission he had received from Charles I of England. But the end drew near, and on April 5, 1640, Cardinal Infante Ferdinand informed the king of Spain that there was little hope that Rubens would ever take up his brush again. Yet a week later Gerbier wrote the artist that he was glad to have received his long letter in which the words were penned as if he no longer had any pain in his hand.[52]

The patient had his ups and downs, and the news of him was contradictory. Thus Gerbier wrote to Charles I on April 21 that Rubens

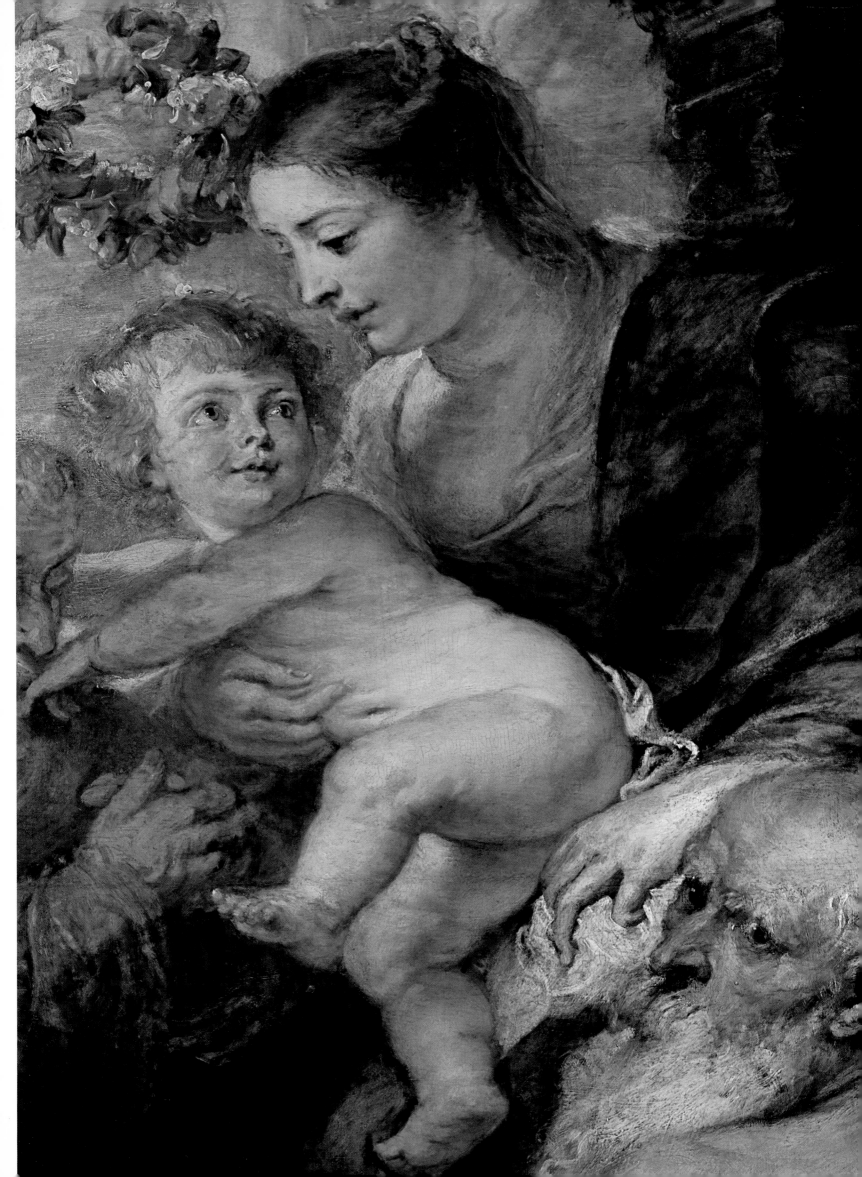

was paralyzed. A few days later, the Cardinal Infante stated that Rubens had promised to finish "the large canvas and the ten small canvases for him before Easter." On May 9 Rubens himself writes a letter full of zest to the sculptor from Malines, Lucas Fayd'herbe, congratulating him on his marriage. He adds that "in a few days" his wife, Helena Fourment, will leave for Elewijt and that she will stop by Malines on the way to wish good fortune to the newlyweds in person. These plans seem to indicate that Rubens' health was sufficiently good that his wife could leave him for a time. We do not know if she actually set out; but it is certain that her husband's condition rapidly deteriorated. On May 27 he dictated his last will and testament and three days later, on May 30, toward mid-day, he died in his house on the Wapper.

From a letter written by Gerbier on May 31, we know that the news of Rubens' death had not yet reached Brussels: "Sr. Peter Paul Rubens is deadly sick. The Physicians of this Towne being sent unto him to trye their best skill on him."[53] Alas, they arrived too late. Later that day Gerbier learned of Rubens' death; on June 2 he wrote: "Sr. Peeter Rubens, whoe deceased three dayes past off a deflaction which fell on his heart, after some dayes indisposition of ague and goutte."[54] The malady had reached the heart, and after that the outcome was inevitable. The accounts mentioned in the inventory of Rubens' estate give us the names of the doctors who attended him. There were two: "Dr. Lazarus and Dr. Spinosa."[55]

So Lazarus Marcquis was again in the house on the Wapper, where he had been before at the bedside of Isabella Brant. As for Dr. Spinosa, or Spinossa as he is sometimes called, he seems to have been a younger colleague. Like Ludovicus Nonnius or Nuñez, he was from Spain or Portugal, of a Jewish family which, together with many others during the persecutions in the Iberian peninsula, abjured their faith and became Christian converts. These Jews, whose conversion was usually forced and who often practiced their own religion in secret, were colloquially called "marranos." Dr. Antonio Spinosa first appears in the Netherlands about 1628, in Malines, as a doctor in the hospital of the Spanish garrison; in 1631 he is mentioned in that capacity in Antwerp, and he married Sara de Aguilar, also of a "marrano" family of Spanish origin.[56] In 1633 Spinosa was registered as an official doctor of the city of Antwerp, an office he still held in 1660.[57] According to Dr. J. Pines, he then joined his family in Amsterdam, where he died at an advanced age.[58]

It is surprising that the fee of these two doctors, Lazarus Marcquis and Antonio Spinosa, for their attendance on the dying Rubens—they received only six florins between them—is very much less than that paid to the surgeons: Master Hendrick the barber, and Master Hans Daepe, barber, who were paid the sizable sums of sixty and forty florins, respectively.[59] The medical treatments and surgery ultimately could not prevent the artist's death. Balthasar Moretus I informed a Parisian correspondent a few days later of his passing: "In truth our city has lost a great deal by the death of Monseigneur Rubens, and I in particular one of my best friends." [60]

Rubens was buried in Antwerp on June 2, 1640, in the church of St. Jacques. He was asked a few days before his death if a chapel could be erected for him, and he replied "with his innate modesty": "that if his widow, his grown son, and the guardians of his children who were not yet of age considered that he had deserved such a monument, they could have the said chapel built without any further authorization on his part, and that they could use for this a picture of the Holy Virgin." [61] His heirs respected these wishes. Since 1644, the altar built by the Fourment family has been adorned by *The Virgin and Child with Saints* (Plate 74; Fig. 143). In this superb *sacra conversazione*, on which Rubens was still working shortly before his death, we find again that lyric ardor, that astounding virtuosity, and that warm splendor of color that mark the painting of his last years. Happy years from the point of view of art, in spite of the pain he endured and his approaching death.

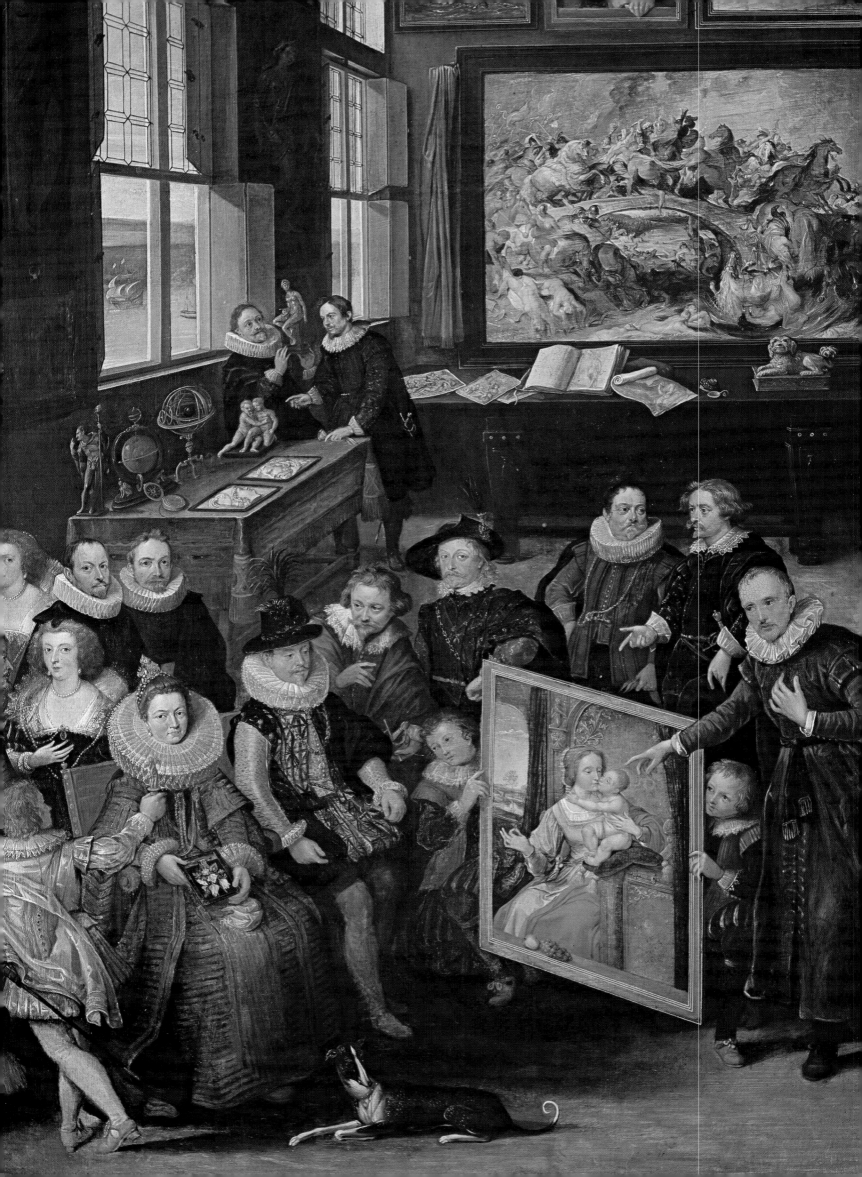

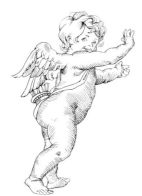

CHAPTER 13   "The Picture Gallery"
of Cornelis van der Geest

by Willem van Haecht

During the first decades of the seventeenth century a new subject of painting makes its appearance in Antwerp: the "Constkamer" or "picture gallery."  Nowhere else, not in the Netherlands nor in any other part of Europe—not even in Italy—had this genre been cultivated before.  It consists of the representation of pictures and art objects that decorated the halls, generally quite spacious ones, where amateurs displayed their collections, or at least their most noteworthy pieces.  In these "picture galleries" there are often persons as well, but the full attention of every spectator is claimed by the wonderful works of art which embellish the interiors.  These representations, then, are of "pictures within a picture."  Since most of these "galleries" reproduce works that belong to a specific collector, or appear in a dealer's shop, they usually have great documentary value to offer.  They show us the artistic riches contained in certain Antwerp dwellings at that time, and allow us also to appreciate visually, so to speak, the taste of their inhabitants.  The art historian moreover finds in them a precious source of information; whenever he recognizes a work that is still preserved today, he has evidence he can use toward establishing its provenance and date.  This genre of art, which, as we have said, seems to be an Antwerp invention, was cultivated extensively in the Metropolis until the eighteenth century, when it became imitated in France by Antoine Watteau, in Italy by Giovanni Pannini, and in England by Johann Zoffany.

Among the many Antwerp "picture galleries" of the seventeenth century that of Cornelis van der Geest, as painted by Willem van Haecht (Plate 76), occupies a high place,[1] and Held even speaks of the work as unique in the history of the genre.[2]  This picture deserves his flattering evaluation.  Not only is it an important and very rare work, painted by an artist who was without question the best and also one of the first to practice this genre, but it also shows one of the most important art collections ever built up within Antwerp's walls.  In no other picture can one find so many personages who played leading roles in the art history of Antwerp and the Nether-

283

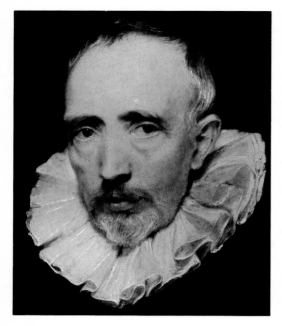

lands. Thus it is a masterpiece in its genre, and also an invaluable document of the period when Antwerp set the tone, on its side of the Alps, in the domain of the arts. This explains why no other Flemish picture of the seventeenth century—except, of course, for the masterworks by Rubens, Van Dyck, and Jordaens—has been the object of so many publications.[3]

In the sales catalogue of Sotheby's, from which the Rubens House acquired the picture in 1969, it was entitled "The Spanish Regents Visiting the Picture Gallery of Cornelis van der Geest,"[4] and this designation can be found more than once in art literature. Certainly it is the Archduke and the Archduchess who are represented in the foreground on the left, with two kneeling pages holding a painting (Plate 75); within this group Cornelis van der Geest stands at the right, pointing to the painting. The canvas in its entirety recalls an actual event: the visit of the sovereigns to the house of Cornelis van der Geest, situated in the Mattenstraat (no longer extant), in the neighborhood of the church of St. Walburga and of the Steen. From this house the company had a splendid view of the river Scheldt, and they watched a water tournament—and of course took advantage of the occasion to admire their host's famous art collection. All this occurred on August 23, 1615.[5]

Willem van Haecht finished his picture thirteen years after this event—the date 1628 beside his signature proves it—and therefore we cannot expect a strictly faithful account of the visit. Such was certainly not the artist's intention, since he includes in his picture persons who quite evidently were not present, as we shall see; moreover it has been pointed out that the artist has also reproduced pictures which were not painted until after 1615 and thus were not part of Van der Geest's collection at the time of the august visit. It has also been suggested that the gallery was in reality less spacious than the canvas indicates, this change made because Willem van Haecht must have been trying to include the greatest number of pictures that the collection ever contained. It thus becomes justifiable to put the question, whether the visit of the Archduke and the Archduchess should be considered the real subject of the picture. There is no doubt that the painter wished to recall that event, for it added importance to the collection of Cornelis van der Geest: did not the interest shown by the sovereigns in a way consecrate, almost officially, the fame which the collection already enjoyed? Yet the regents' visit in this picture gallery is only a detail, though not an unimportant one, in the total composition; it provided an excellent opportunity to bring together in the gallery a group of eminent persons, particularly artists with whom Cornelis van der Geest had bonds of friendship, and to represent them amid a great number of the works of art which were the object of his artistic interest and his legitimate pride. In short, the artist's aim is to give us neither a perfect historical reconstruction nor an "occasional" picture; he is trying to achieve, in one evocative synthesis, a triple goal: to give us an idea of the content and significance of an exceptionally rich collection; to introduce us to the circle of acquaint-

284

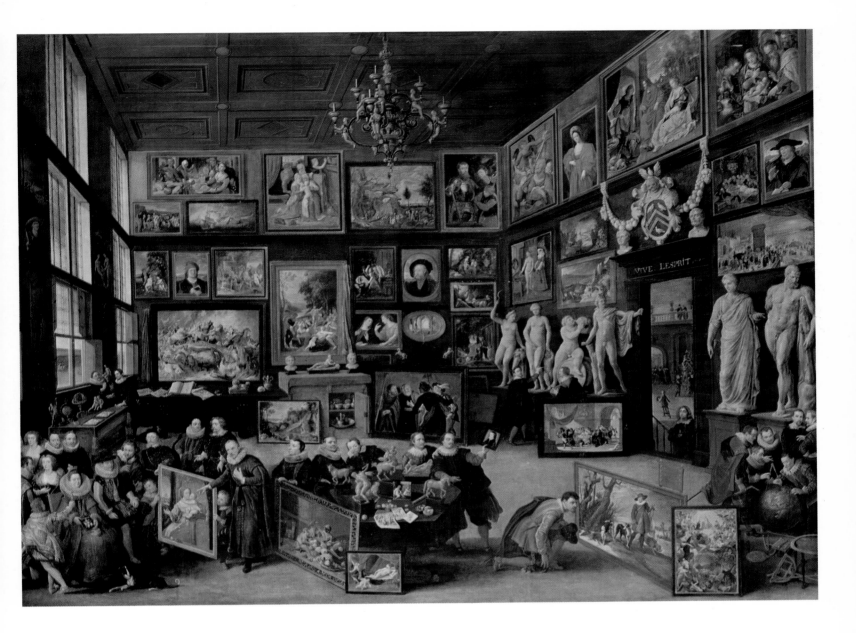

Plate 76
Willem van Haecht
"THE PICTURE GALLERY" OF
CORNELIS VAN DER GEEST, 1628
Antwerp, Rubens House

*Among the numerous seventeenth-century representations of Antwerp collections, this panel occupies a unique place. Not only does it represent one of the most important collections, but in it are also assembled the most famous artists and art-lovers of Rubens' time.*

285

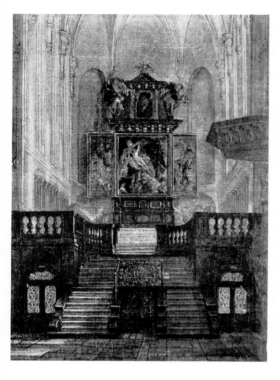

Figure 145
Anthoon Gheringh
THE INTERIOR OF THE CHURCH OF
ST. WALBURGA (detail: the high altar
with Rubens' THE RAISING OF THE
CROSS)
Antwerp, Church of St. Paul

*Here we see the triptych, preserved today
in Antwerp Cathedral, as it was formerly
placed in the choir of St. Walburga's
Church, which no longer exists. The panels
on top of the high altar were also painted
by Rubens.*

ances surrounding Cornelis van der Geest in his capacity of friend of the arts; and to present to us the influential persons who honored that collection by their visit. The fusion of these three themes into a single motif is consummated, so to speak, in a play on words on the name of the collector: on top of the door the words *Vive l'Esprit* (Long Live the Spirit; "geest" means spirit) appear beneath his coat of arms. In addition, the scene symbolizes—as we will show below—a homage to Pictura, "the noble and free art of Painting," whom the patron Van der Geest protected with such generosity.

The rather extensive biography of Cornelis van der Geest, drawn up by Delen, makes it sufficient for us to recall that he was born in Antwerp in 1575, two years before his friend Rubens. He became a rich merchant and was, from 1609 to 1615, the dean of the Guild of Haberdashers ("Meerseniers"). After he had resigned that office the merchants frequently appealed to his wisdom and sense of justice to arbitrate in complicated commercial or trade-guild litigation. Moreover, his charity and piety were outstanding. But it was especially for his quality of "gentle friend and connoisseur of the noble art of painting" (as his contemporary Frans Fickaert called him), or again as *Artis pictoriae amator Antverpiae* (the dedication on his portrait engraved by Paul Pontius after Van Dyck), that his name was entered in the history of the city of Antwerp. To give an idea of his role as patron one could enumerate the goodly number of pictures and sculptures adorning the churches or public buildings of Antwerp of which he was the sole or main donor, if not indeed the initiator. His collection, as Willem van Haecht depicts it, is certainly the most eloquent illustration of the contemporary titles, "friend of the arts" and "connoisseur." It contained many paintings by older as well as contemporary masters, monumental statues, and a quantity of smaller objects which in Van Haecht's picture are displayed on tables and cabinets: bronze statuettes, miniatures, medals, pottery, engravings, and drawings. The sculptures included "modern" works and large-size copies of famous antique statues, such as the *Farnese Hercules* and the *Apollo Belvedere*. Van der Geest died at Antwerp on March 10, 1638. Unfortunately no written inventory of his collection is known, nor do we possess information on its fate after the collector's death.

We know the features of Cornelis van der Geest from his portrait by Anthony van Dyck (Fig. 144).[6] This picture ranks among the masterpieces of the Flemish portraitist, for indeed he not only reproduces most strikingly the sitter's physical appearance, but also reveals his character with penetrating insight. Delen well describes the portrait: "This intelligent head with the pale and emaciated features, the high forehead fringed with fine grey hair, the straight nose, the thoughtful eyes, slightly tired and at the same time melancholy; the skeptical air, kind and resigned, which drifts around the bluish lips of a cardiac—all this points to an unhealthy man, who laughs only rarely, who speaks slowly in a soft and hesitant voice. Against a dark background, emerging from the black of the gown and the white of the ruff, this

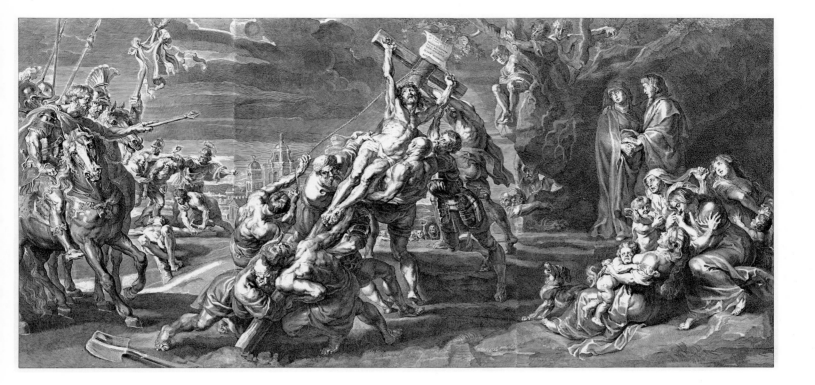

Figure 146
Hans Witdoeck, after Rubens
THE RAISING OF THE CROSS
Engraving
Antwerp, Stedelijk Prentenkabinet

*Beneath this engraving, dated 1638, there is a dedication by Rubens to Cornelis van der Geest in which the latter is called "the principal author and promotor of this altar-piece."*

sympathetic face stands out, spiritual and otherworldly, as that of a noble and refined man for whom the only remaining joys are those of beauty and the spirit."[7]   In Van Dyck's portrait drawing of him in the Nationalmuseum, Stockholm,[8] a certain firmness is added to the melancholy expression, a quality that we know in him from other witnesses of his appearance: Frans Francken the Younger also represented Van der Geest, as the patron, on the outer side of one wing of a triptych (in the church of St. Gommaire, at Lierre) for which he gave the funds.   A comparison of these portraits clearly shows that Willem van Haecht drew on Van Dyck's painting for this *"Picture Gallery."*

It will remain the principal and most lasting merit of Van der Geest that he recognized very early the masterly talent of Rubens.   Thanks to him the young artist obtained in 1610 the commission for the great triptych *The Raising of the Cross* (Plate 15; Figs. 37, 145) for the high altar of the church of St. Walburga, Van der Geest's parish church.   It is even not unlikely—although difficult to prove, for want of documentation—that the year before he had contributed to Rubens' obtaining the commission for *The Glorification of the Holy Eucharist* (Fig. 36) for the Brotherhood of the "Holy Sweet Name of Jesus" in the Dominican Church, now St. Paul's, where it still adorns the altar of this community.   The hypothesis is certainly not without foundation, since Van der Geest made a financial contribution to the marble enclo-

287

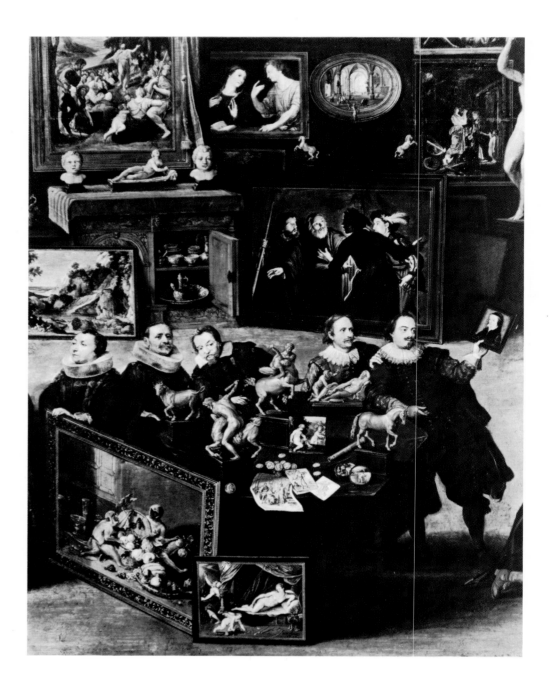

Figure 147
Willem van Haecht
"THE PICTURE GALLERY" OF
CORNELIS VAN DER GEEST (detail,
center)
Antwerp, Rubens House

*A group of art-lovers stands behind a table
on which are displayed drawings, small pictures, and small bronze sculptures. The
woman on the left is Catherine van Mockenborch, the collector's housekeeper. The man
leaning on the right-hand side of the table,
holding the little portrait of a lady, is Peter
Stevens, painter and art dealer.*

sure around this altar, the work of Hans van Mildert.[9] However this
may be, it stands that he placed his trust in Rubens at a time when
the latter, scarcely back from Italy, had still to paint the masterpieces
which would make his name.

This confidence was acknowledged in the dedication in Latin below
the large copperplate made after *The Raising of the Cross* (Fig. 146) which
was engraved for Rubens by Hans Witdoeck in 1638, shortly after
the death of Cornelis van der Geest. The dedication could be translated thus: "To Mr. Cornelis van der Geest, the best of men and my
oldest friend, who, since my youth, has been my never-failing patron,
whose whole life showed a love and admiration of painting, I offer

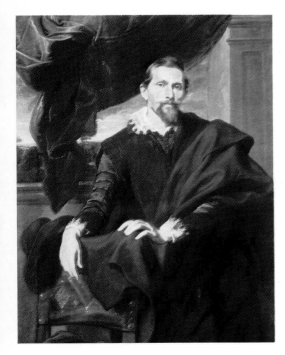

Figure 148
Anthony van Dyck
PORTRAIT OF FRANS SNYDERS
New York, The Frick Collection

*Willem van Haecht used this incredibly refined portrait for representing the features of the celebrated animalist and still-life painter in the "Picture Gallery" of Cornelis van der Geest.*

with all my heart and dedicate to him posthumously the well-deserved token of my eternal friendship.   Made after the picture in the church of St. Walburga, of which he was the chief promoter and sponsor."[10]   The friendship between Rubens and the great patron is also confirmed by a declaration, made in 1630 before the aldermen of the city of Antwerp and signed by the two friends, that contains this clause: "... the friendly relationship which he [i.e., Van der Geest] has had and still maintains with Mr. Peter Paul Rubens."[11]

So Cornelis van der Geest was pleased to add works by Rubens to his collection.   The *"Picture Gallery"* by Willem van Haecht contains two of these: *The Battle of the Amazons* (Plate 78) occupies a place of honor, being hung just beside the window, well lit, and in full view above the figures grouped around the regents.   It is still regarded today as one of Rubens' masterpieces.   The other painting, showing a captain being helped by two pages to don his armor (Fig. 150), hangs at the top of this broad wall, far to the right; until recently it has meanwhile been in the collection of Earl Spencer at Althorp.[12]   The style of this picture indicates to us that it was painted immediately after Rubens' return from Italy, and therefore it may have been the first work Van der Geest acquired by the artist.

After this account of the bonds of friendship uniting the two men, the presence of Rubens himself in the gallery of Cornelis van der Geest appears quite natural.   We recognize him next to the Archduke Albert, leaning slightly toward him and evidently commenting on the picture which is displayed to the sovereigns.   Rubens' role as court painter accounts for the place that Willem van Haecht gives him, so close to his host and providing commentaries during the regents' visit.   One of the most important tasks of this office was, as has been pointed out by De Maeyer, that of advising on all matters connected with art.[13]

Held has suggested that Willem van Haecht grouped all of these persons according to their social rank and professions: near the Archduke and Archduchess are the nobles, court dignitaries, and persons who exercise important functions; around the table in the center are collectors, colleagues of Cornelis van der Geest; on the right, the painters; sculptors in the back, at right and left.   The concept of hierarchy is appropriate to the mentality of the time, so that in principle this grouping is perfectly acceptable.   Nevertheless, several persons have not yet been identified with absolute certainty, and we are of the opinion that for the time being this classification can be applied only as a working hypothesis.   It is nevertheless undeniable—and thus speaks in some measure for Held's supposition—that those represented on the left, near the sovereigns, are indeed all persons of high rank and dignitaries (Plate 75).

The following have been identified thus far: the woman immediately behind the Infanta is Geneviève d'Urfé, duchess of Croy; the man in profile beside her is probably Ambrogio Spinola, the general and counsellor of the regents;[14] the woman behind them, at the far left,

289

is probably the countess of Arenberg; beside her is Nicolaas Rockox, mayor of Antwerp, who, like Van der Geest, was one of Rubens' first patrons (Fig. 45); he is accompanied by another friend of Rubens, Jan van de Wouwer, humanist and counsellor at the Court of Finance in Brussels. To Rubens' right, wearing a hat (which, as a sovereign, was permitted him), is Prince Ladislaus Sigismund, the future king of Poland, who was certainly not present at the visit of the regents in 1615 for he did not come to Antwerp until 1624; the portrait Rubens painted of the prince at that time has clearly inspired Van Haecht. To the right of the future king we recognize an influential person at the court of the regents, Jan van Montfort, director of the Mint, also a friend of Rubens; his likeness is after a portrait by Van Dyck and here he is seen chatting with that artist, whom Van Haecht has represented in turn from a portrait by Rubens, to be seen today in Windsor Castle (Fig. 149).

It will surprise nobody that Rubens is among the group of visitors of high rank when we remember that he had received the title of "painter to the Household of their Royal Highnesses" as early as 1609, and that he was raised to the nobility with the title of knight on June 1, 1624. But does this also hold for Van Dyck? Held explains Van Dyck's presence among the gentlefolk by the fact that the likenesses of the majority of persons in the picture were taken from Van Dyck's portraits of them; this would explain why Van Dyck stands near Cornelis van der Geest, of whom he was certainly a good friend, and also why he would belong, as something of an exception, to the first group. There is however a simpler explanation: Van Dyck, too, received the title of court painter! Indeed there is good reason to believe that this dignity was conferred on him in 1628,[15] the same year that Willem van Haecht finished the "*Picture Gallery.*"

The figure of Van der Geest himself links the group we have described to the group that stands behind the central table (Fig. 147). From the left, the first of these is a woman, formerly thought to be the collector's wife. Held has correctly pointed out, however, that Van der Geest apparently never married; basing his statements on solid arguments, he has convincingly identified this "formidable woman" (his words) as Catherine van Mockenborch, the sister of Willem van Haecht's mother, Susanna van Mockenborch; she was also Cornelis van der Geest's housekeeper, a function that gives her her important place in the center of the picture, just behind the master.

Of the four men standing to the right of Catherine van Mockenborch, only one has yet been identified for certain. The man leaning on the right corner of the table, holding a small portrait of a lady, is Pieter Stevens, another owner of a rich collection of pictures. Various authors have advanced names for the other three figures, but do not agree on their identifications.[16] Further research is necessary; perhaps it will establish the presence of other collectors.

The same observation applies for the young man kneeling in the right foreground, who gazes attentively at a wintry landscape with

PORTRAIT OF PARACELSUS
Panel, 30$^1/_2$″ × 21$^1/_2$″
Brussels, Musées Royaux des Beaux-Arts de Belgique

*Rubens made a copy of the so-called* Paracelsus *by Quentin Matsys that is today in the Louvre. In the "Picture Gallery" it is difficult to determine whether Cornelis van der Geest possessed the Matsys original or Rubens' copy of it.*

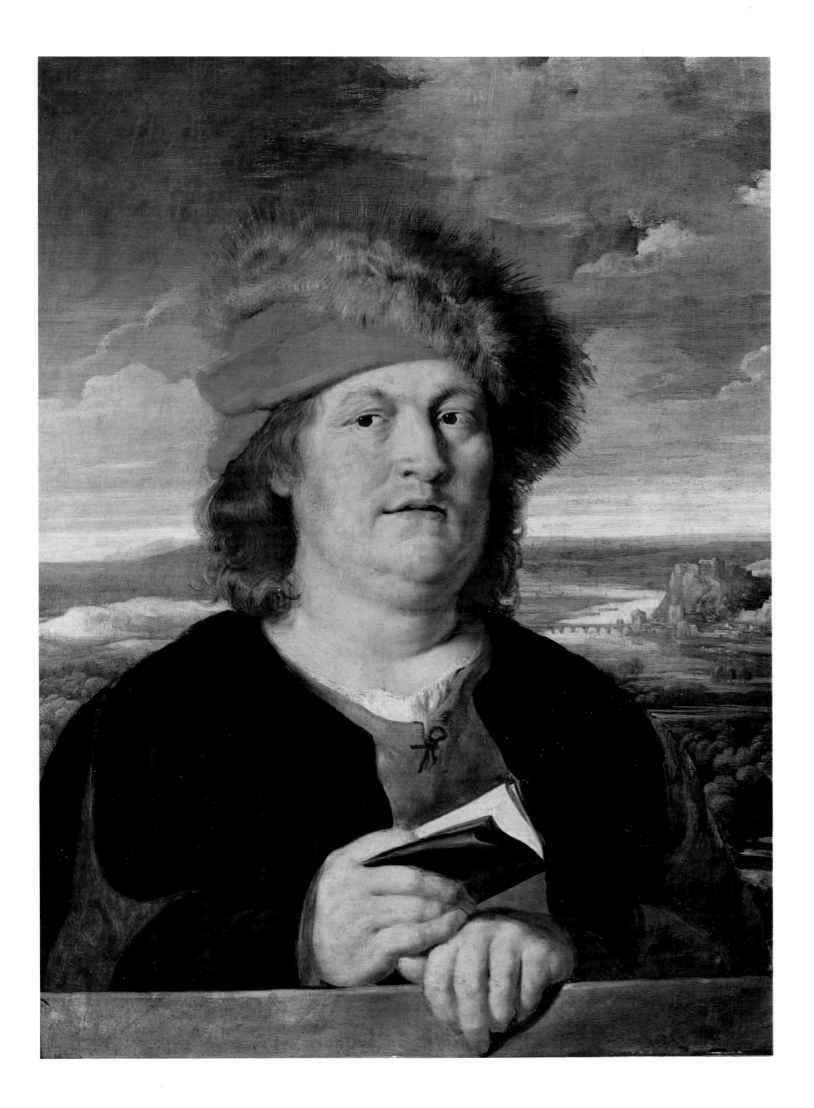

a hunter and three dogs by Jan Wildens (now in Dresden).[17]   In the composition he serves to link the men behind the table with the third group (Fig. 153), which would include the painters, although probably geographers are also among them.   That Van der Geest, like many merchants of his time, was interested in geography is indicated by the globe and cartographers' instruments.   The man we recognize at once in this group of six is the great animalist and still-life painter, Frans Snyders, standing just beneath the large cast of the *Farnese Hercules*; Van Dyck's marvelous portrait of him (Fig. 148) served here as the model.   To the right of Snyders is Hendrik van Balen; Jan Wildens, painter of the *Winter Landscape with Huntsman* just mentioned, is to the left, leaning slightly forward; Willem van Haecht's inspiration came this time from a portrait by Rubens.   No one, as far as I know, has yet suggested names for the other three men.

Farther back, a few more persons stand at the left and right.   They may indeed be sculptors, as has been suggested, although we must remember that Willem van Haecht may not have grouped his figures in such a rigid sequence, that perhaps he merely wanted to establish the distinction between persons of high rank and those who did not claim that level.   In any case the members of this group seem to have eyes only for the statues, large and small, which abound in the collection.   Only one of these persons has thus far been identified with some degree of probability: the man who points to the over life-size *Venus and Cupid* could be Jörg Petel, the German sculptor and friend of Rubens who was certainly the author of this statue.[18]   One would also expect to find Rubens' friend Hans van Mildert, who seems to have been a friend also of Van der Geest.   One may wonder if he is not to be recognized in the stout man with the black moustache who stands near the window, on the left, raising a statuette in his hand to study it in better light.

In the doorway on the far right there is an unobtrusive figure with a rather sickly appearance who leans against the stair railing.   It has already been plausibly suggested that this is the author of the "*Picture Gallery*," Willem van Haecht himself.   He seems to be keeping his distance, as it were, and his position, beneath the coat of arms and the motto of Cornelis van der Geest, also argues in favor of this supposition.   He worked for the collector, and had the care of his pictures; in this capacity he lived in Van der Geest's house and was part of the domestic staff, although in a somewhat exceptional position.   Furthermore he was related to both the collector and Rubens!

Willem van Haecht was baptized on November 7, 1593, the son of Tobias Verhaecht, Rubens' first master.   According to Van den Branden, he left Antwerp for Paris on August 24, 1615 (he could, just barely, have been present the previous day for the regents' visit); in 1619 he was on the road again, this time to Italy.   But in any case he had returned to Antwerp in 1626 or 1627, because at that time he was received as master in the Guild of St. Luke, and thereafter resided in the house of Cornelis van der Geest until he died, on July 12, 1637.[19]

292

Let us now return to his picture, painted shortly after he was received
into the Antwerp guild. We do not propose to comment on all the
panels and canvases that Willem van Haecht has reported upon with
such scrupulous accuracy. They number no fewer than forty-three,
and we shall examine only some of them here. The majority clearly
belong to the Flemish school, although Italian and German painters
are also represented.[20]

The oldest piece is an extremely rare secular painting by Jan van
Eyck showing a nude woman standing in a room, in the company
of a very well-dressed lady. The picture hangs deep on the side wall,

very near the far corner (Fig. 153). Held has proved that this subject is connected with the ritual bath to which the bride was submitted on her wedding day.[21] The clothed woman may be the painter's wife, Marguerite van Eyck, and the bride Giovanna Cenami, the wife of Giovanni Arnolfini, with whom she appears in the marriage picture, the unique and marvelous double portrait of *Arnolfini and His Wife* in the National Gallery at London. Comparable works by the founder of early Flemish painting are known to us only from documents; thanks to the representation in Van Haecht's "*Picture Gallery*," we are able to form a clearer idea of how they looked.

Many of the pictures are by Flemish painters of the sixteenth century. At least three are by Quentin Matsys; these will be discussed at greater length below. Without claiming to be exhaustive, we can mention, among others: at the top left, between the windows (hardly visible on the photograph), a representation of a picture by Pieter Bruegel the Elder showing a landscape with a cart, known to us today only through one of the master's drawings. Above Rubens' *Battle of the Amazons* (Plate 78), near the ceiling, is Pieter Aertsen's *The Pancake Makers*, now in the Boymans-van Beuningen Museum in Rotterdam. To the right of it hangs a *Holy Family* by Frans Floris. Between the latter and Rubens' youthful picture, *Captain in Armor with Two Pages*, hangs a *Landscape with Nomads* by the rarely encountered master Cornelis van Dalem; this picture was subsequently cut into four parts, now scattered in different collections.

Bridging the sixteenth and seventeenth centuries is Otto van Veen, Rubens' principal master, represented by a small panel depicting *The Last Supper*, with the disciples lying on couches at the meal in the ancient Roman manner. The panel is above the door, at the right of Cornelis van der Geest's escutcheon.

There is also a fair number of works by seventeenth-century Antwerp masters. I have already indicated that Rubens is well represented, not only by the two pictures by his hand, but also indirectly, by his portraits that Willem van Haecht has used to reproduce the features of several persons here. No picture by Van Dyck hangs on these walls but he is nevertheless present everywhere, for the features of the majority of these persons—including some not yet identified—are reproduced from his portraits of them. We draw attention also to the following works: a *Still Life with Monkeys* attributed to Frans Snyders, on the floor, behind Van der Geest (Fig. 147); Jan Wildens' *Winter Landscape with Huntsman* on the floor at the right; and *The Denial of Peter* by Gerard Seghers, against the back wall, next to the small open cupboard. No less interesting is Sebastiaan Vrancx' *View of Antwerp Harbor* (now in the Rijksmuseum, Amsterdam), which dates from 1622, at the right of the door, above the two classical statues. At the left of the door, below the statues, is a *Merry Company* by Simon de Vos. And, leaning directly in the center foreground is a small picture representing *Danae*; signed at the bottom by Willem van Haecht, it must be a work by his own hand.

Italian art is represented, among other works, by a *Portrait of Albrecht*

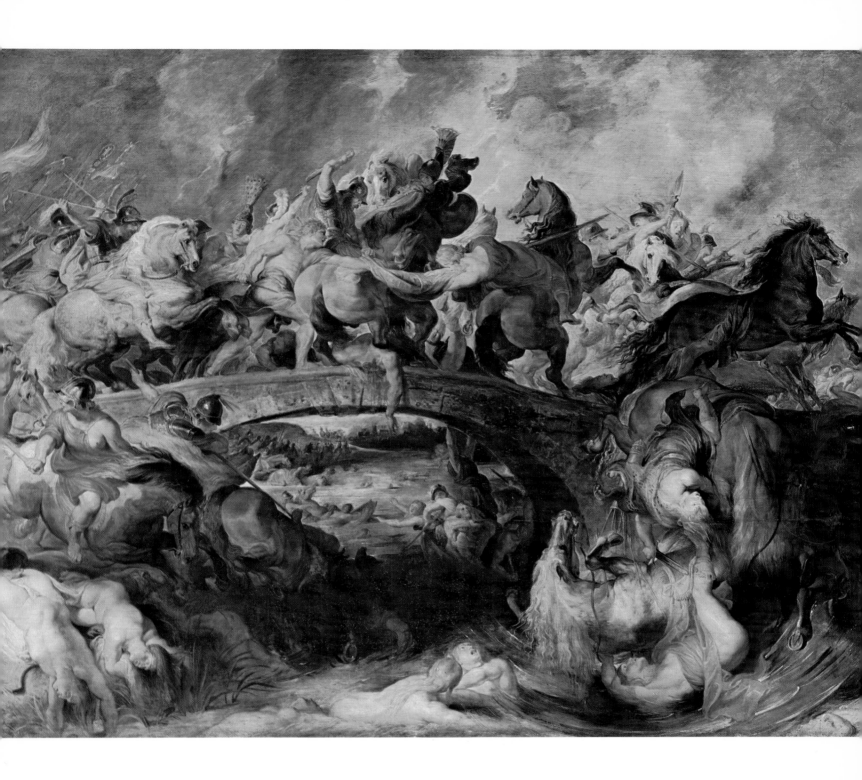

Plate 78
THE BATTLE OF THE AMAZONS
Panel, $47^{1}/_{2}'' \times 65''$
Munich, Alte Pinakothek

*Rubens probably painted this panel about 1618. It illustrates strikingly the artist's daring and inexhaustible imagination, ordered by a vigorous spirit and finally transformed into a work of paramount beauty and harmony. Willem van Haecht's copy of it is fully detailed.*

295

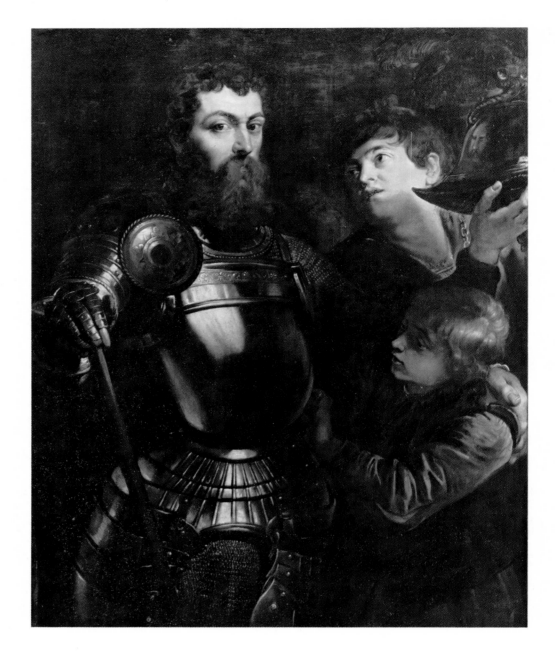

*Dürer* by—or after—Tommaso Vincidor of Bologna (below the land-scape by Van Dalem), and a portrait of a woman in a red gown, probably by Bernardino Licinio (on the upper right wall). German painting has its place also. In the right foreground, leaning against Wildens' *Landscape*, is a *Last Judgment* by Hans Rottenhammer, now in the Alte Pinakothek, Munich. There are two small panels by Adam Elsheimer: *Judith Cutting off the Head of Holofernes* (between the picture by Adam van Noort and the *Portrait of Dürer*) and *The Mocking of Ceres* (on the back wall, just to the left of the statue in the corner). It is possible that these last two pictures were bought by Cornelis van der Geest at Rubens' suggestion, for Rubens was a friend and admirer of Elsheimer, whose acquaintance he had made in Rome. The painter died young, at thirty-two years, and Rubens' letters make clear his great efforts to place works by Elsheimer into Antwerp collections.[22]

296

Some authors have emphasized the evident predominance of the Antwerp School in the collection of Cornelis van der Geest. The spectator will also note that there are no fewer than three pictures by Quentin Matsys, the "father" of this school. One is vividly conspicuous, the *Virgin and Child* which the collector, helped by two pages, is showing to the regents; obviously, this shows the special significance that was given to this work. In his short book on Quentin Matsys, published in 1648, Frans Fickaert claims that the Archduke and Archduchess tried to obtain this picture during their visit to Cornelis van der Geest. He speaks of their entreaty, gracious yet pressing, made almost publicly but rejected by the silent ardor of the owner, who preferred his prize possession to the sovereigns' favors.[23] Although it is asserted that the regents greatly appreciated the art of Matsys—a *Virgin and Child* hung in the Infanta's Oratory, and they possessed several other works by him[24]—one may reasonably wonder, with Held, whether this account was not thought up after the event that inspired this painting by Willem van Haecht. In any case, Matsys' *Virgin and Child* makes very clear the high esteem in which Van der Geest held the "father" of the Antwerp School. It was certainly by no mere stroke of chance that the collector, one hand to his breast, presents it to the regents. How better could he explain than by this gesture his preference both for the work and for the artist who painted it?

This is further marked in the *"Picture Gallery"* by the presence of two other works by Matsys: his *Man with the Spectacles* (now in the Städelsches Kunstinstitut, Frankfurt) hangs on the upper wall, near the edge of our picture; and just above Rubens' *Battle of the Amazons* is found the second, the so-called *Portrait of Paracelsus* (now in the Louvre), a picture of which Rubens painted a copy (Plate 77).[25] Van der Geest eloquently expressed his admiration for Matsys in 1629, the centenary of the artist's death, when he had the artist's tombstone put on the façade of Antwerp Cathedral, because, he wrote, "it is important that the memory of so illustrious a master should not fade."[26] Mathias Winner, the author of a very sound study on the sources of the Antwerp "picture galleries," insists that it is no coincidence that in 1628—exactly a year before Matsys' tombstone was installed—Willem van Haecht brought together a number of well-known Antwerp artists in Cornelis van der Geest's gallery, forming what could be called a circle around the master's *Virgin*, placed in the center.[27] Indeed it is these artists who must count as Matsys' successors in the illustrious Antwerp School, of which he was the first great representative. Van Haecht's picture can thus be interpreted as a homage to the Antwerp School of painting, where the present now joins the past.

Two other elements in this picture extend this link across the centuries, connecting, one might say, the Antwerp School with a still broader tradition. First of all, there is that unique work already discussed, the secular picture by Jan van Eyck, the great fifteenth-century painter who was also the "founder" of the early Flemish school. Second, there is the drawing that lies on the front of the table in the center of the composition; although it does not immediately

297

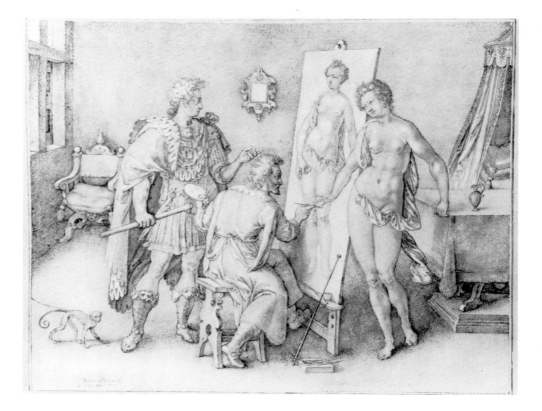

attract the spectator's eye, it is so placed that its subject can be distinguished without difficulty: Apelles, the most illustrious painter of classical Antiquity, painting Campaspe, the mistress of Alexander the Great, who stands at the artist's left, admiring the work (Fig. 152). Independently of one another, Winner and De Coo have drawn attention to the significance of this motif in the *"Picture Gallery."* To quote the latter: "To represent the greatest painter of antiquity at work—and what a work!—was an act of homage to painting, homage that was justified and clearly expressed in this representation of a collection of pictures. Painting was thereby not only honored, but also rewarded and laureated; does not the story go, in fact, that Alexander—who appears in the drawing—felt such passionate admiration for the portrait that he surrendered his beloved to the painter ...?"[28] Using evidence from texts and works of art, Winner clearly explains the symbolism of this motif: He shows that since the beginning of the sixteenth century, and especially through the writings of Ariosto and Vasari, Apelles came to be considered *the* perfect painter, and soon became the symbol of Pictura itself—"the Apellean art"—just as Apollo had long been the symbol of the art of Poesia.[29] Those who cultivated the art of painting could thus be regarded as pupils and followers of Apelles: "The dear, faithful students of Apelles," was the greeting used by Sebastiaan Vrancx, painter and poet, to the members of the Guild of St. Luke in Antwerp in 1619.[30] This appellation adds another dimension to Willem van Haecht's picture. Have not some of these faithful "students" of Apelles been gathered together with these dis-

298

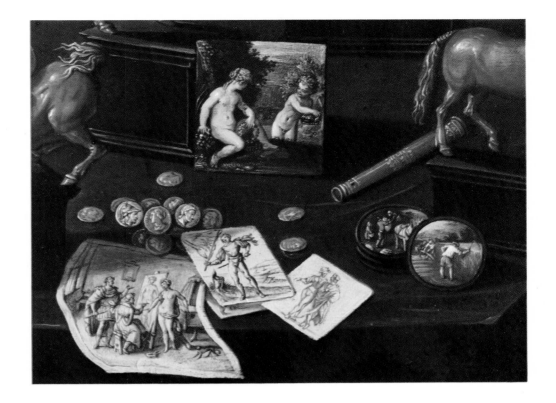

tinguished amateurs—and, I was going to write, "gathered for pleasure" ("Wt jonsten versaemt"), like the device of the Antwerp Guild of St. Luke?[31]    And does one not find Rubens among them, soon to be called the "Apelles of his century" by his contemporaries?    And Cornelis van der Geest, although not a painter, must also be counted among the disciples of Apelles, for he was indeed a member of the Guild of St. Luke, inscribed in its register in the capacity of amateur.[32]

The drawing of *Apelles and Campaspe* can, as Winner has already pointed out, also be interpreted as disguised homage to Cornelis van der Geest himself.   Did he not protect Painting with a generosity equal to that of Alexander the Great?—although in a different manner, no doubt, from his illustrious predecessor!   Perhaps the drawing alludes to the regents' love of art, for just as Alexander came to see the painter in his workshop, they have come to visit the great Antwerp collector in order to honor Pictura.   Thus this drawing, placed so near the edge of the table, signifies the homage rendered both to Pictura and to those who protect her, for without patrons, painting cannot blossom fully: the artist and the amateur cannot live without one another.[33]

This symbolism, with its several converging meanings, is appropriate to the writers contemporary with the painter of this *"Picture Gallery"*; steeped as they were in humanism and rhetoric, the meanings and veiled allusions in this picture would not have escaped them.

The drawing in Cornelis van der Geest's collection which holds such interest for the interpretation of the picture is fortunately still in Antwerp, in the Mayer van den Bergh Museum (Fig. 151), where the

Figure 152
Willem van Haecht
"THE PICTURE GALLERY" OF
CORNELIS VAN DER GEEST (detail)

*The drawing in the foreground, near the edge of the table, is by Jan Wierix (Fig. 151); it gives the key to the allegorical interpretation of the whole picture, a tribute to Pictura.*

299

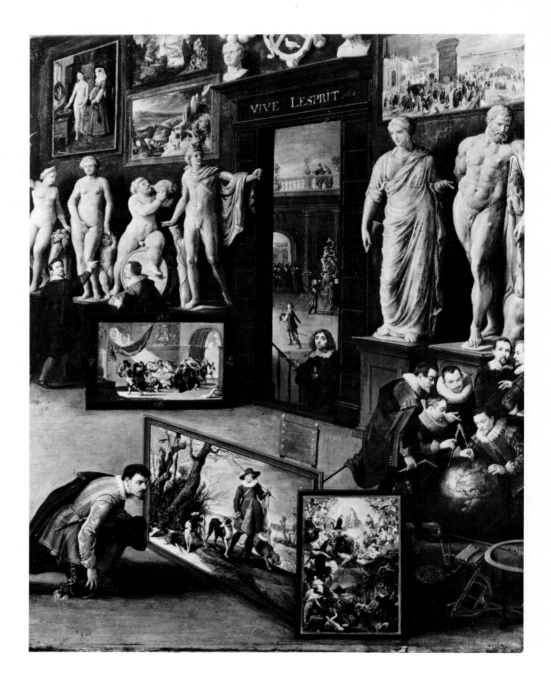

Figure 153
Willem van Haecht
"THE PICTURE GALLERY" OF
CORNELIS VAN DER GEEST (detail,
right side)
Antwerp, Rubens House

*At the upper left, the man pointing to the statue* Venus and Cupid *is the German sculptor Jörg Petel. Below on the right, standing, are Frans Snyders and, at the edge of the picture, Hendrik van Balen. On the left of Snyders, leaning slightly forward, is the landscape painter Jan Wildens. The three other figures around the globe are probably geographers. It is thought that the man in the doorway is probably Willem van Haecht, the painter of this "Picture Gallery."*

presentation of the collected precious objects has some of the character and charm of a seventeenth-century collector's gallery. As De Coo has informed us, it was Held who identified the symbolic drawing. It is signed "Johan Wiricx + inventor 1600."[34]

We venture to think that this explanation has demonstrated adequately that the *"Picture Gallery" of Cornelis van der Geest,* painted by Willem van Haecht with so refined an artistic sense and such care for detail, signifies more than the mere representation of a historic event. The painting is a marvelous illustration of the distinguished role played by this great art lover, collector, and patron in the life of Antwerp

300

of his time. It is testimony of his admiration for Quentin Matsys, "father" of the Antwerp School, and it shows some illustrious representatives from his own time, among them Rubens, the new "Apelles," and his chief disciple, Van Dyck. The majority of the artists here, such as Snyders and Wildens, were, moreover, occasional collaborators of Rubens.

And the painting also gives us a precise image of what was contained in the collection of Cornelis van der Geest. It is a valuable document for the works of art that constituted its richness, some of them now in foreign museums. It is also a document for the presence and appearance of numerous persons who were prominent in the history of the nation and the city. Furthermore it can be seen as an act of homage paid to the great collector and art lover and to the Antwerp School of painting, to Apelles-Pictura, and to patronage, that indispensable support of all the arts. Finally, the work was painted by one who lived in Cornelis van der Geest's house and took care of his pictures, this Willem van Haecht who was also a relative of Rubens and the son of his first master. Van Haecht the artist deserves to be known as the most remarkable painter of the genre of "picture galleries," an "invention" which can be declared typically Antwerpian.

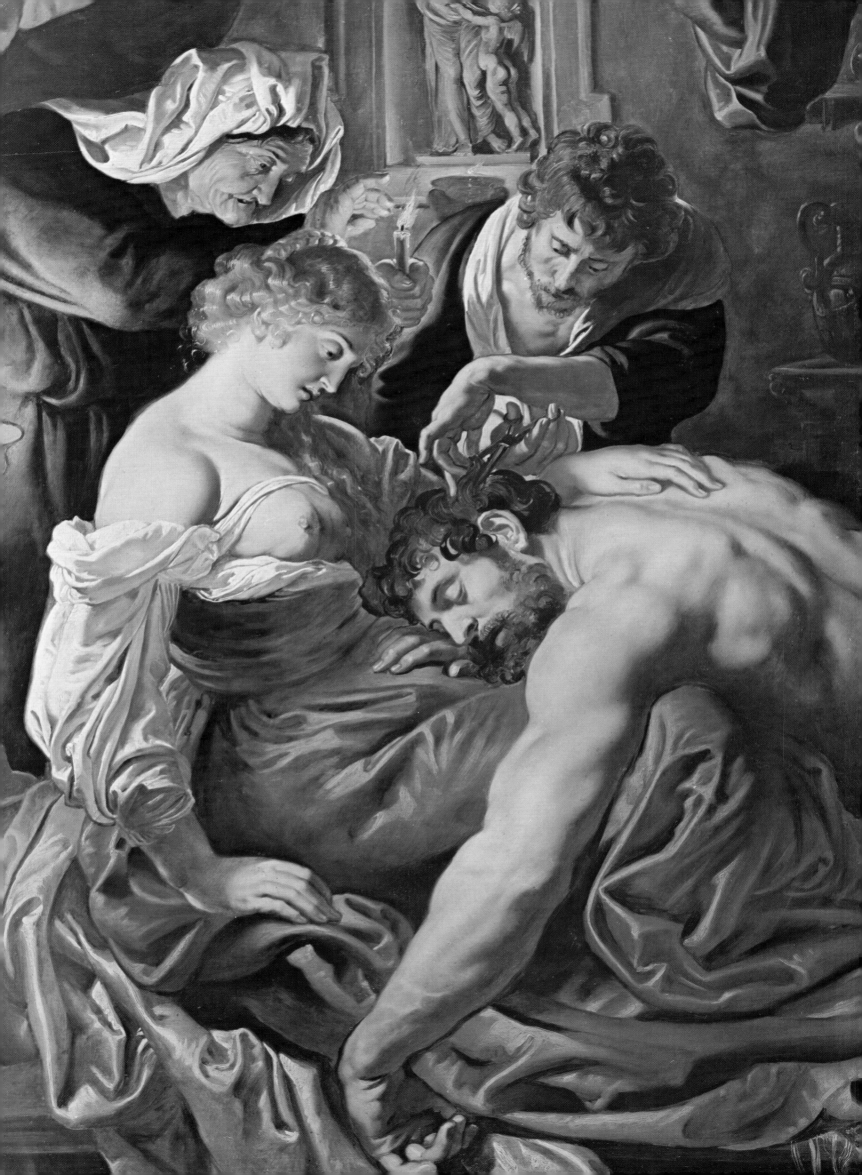

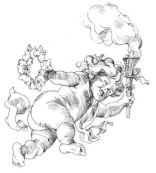

CHAPTER 14  # Rubens and His Social
and Cultural Background

It is generally agreed that before 1600 no essential difference separates the art of the Northern from that of the Southern Netherlands. Until then, or perhaps somewhat earlier, one school of painting embraced all the provinces of North and South. Regional characteristics that can be distinguished are of only minor importance. After 1600, however, the differences become so evident that two distinct schools must be recognized: the Dutch School and the Flemish School.

This distinction has long been established as the result of the military, religious, economic, and social circumstances which proceeded from the rupture of the Netherlands. It has been pointed out that in the United Provinces the social situation engendered a truly democratic art, in striking contrast to the art of the Spanish Netherlands which was dependent on the court of the Archduke Albert and the Infanta Isabella and on the Catholic Church as regenerated by the Counter-Reformation. Hauser goes so far as to cite this antithesis in the sphere of the plastic arts as a "supreme test case for the sociology of art," since, according to him, only social factors furnish a satisfactory explanation of this phenomenon.[1]

Apart from slight variations in their formulations, art historians who have treated this problem have found this same sociological explanation for it. A few examples must suffice. First of all a passage by Friedländer on Flemish and Dutch art in the seventeenth century: "The Northern states broke away from Catholic Europe as a whole and founded a middle-class democratic society, while the Southern states, under the Hapsburg dynasty which had become more flexible and forbearing, and under the Catholic Church, developed a different form of freedom, open to the world around it, so that different tasks were presented in the two areas to the common gifts and talents."[2]

The contrast between "democratic" on the one hand and "dynastic" and "Catholic" on the other is also discernible in a book by W. Martin which has become a classic in the history of Dutch seventeenth-century painting: "The primary characteristic of Dutch painting that a foreigner would pick out would be its *middle-class* character. We accept this characterization inasmuch as it expresses a contrast to an art entirely

Plate 79
SAMSON AND DELILAH (detail, Fig. 156)
Private Collection

*This detail represents Samson resting his head on the knees of Delilah at the moment that she is betraying him. In her face can be seen both triumph and dread.*

303

devoted to the Church and the Crown. Such an attitude was repugnant to our great masters and, considered from this standpoint, their art is, contrary to that of Rubens and Van Dyck, a definitely middle-class art, if one interprets this term as democratic. It is a popular art, of the people and for the people."[3]

Martin considers the problem only as it bears on Dutch art. Michel, however, in his essay on Flemish painting in the seventeenth century, also maintains that in the Southern Netherlands the form of the works of art was largely determined by the fact that the artists were working for the aristocracy and the Church: "In the South the artists were to work for princes, for a church service which sought to be pompous, attractive, and if need be gracious. Thus the native gifts of this school which had already asserted themselves in the fifteenth century were to be amplified and magnified; these gifts were: a taste for color and a taste for the beauty of the materials. Circumstances were to add to these ostentation, epic grandeur, brilliance, and movement. From this time on, the Flemish school was to contrast with the Dutch school, where the predominant feature was to be a love of light in conflict with shade, the pursuit of intimacy and realistic simplicity, the joy in catching small details with great accuracy, and in rendering the humbler and innermost recesses of life."[4]

In his famous and illuminating *Social History of Art*, Hauser arrives at the same conclusion. After a brief analysis of the social background of Flemish art in the seventeenth century, he writes: "Even if all the circumstances do not explain the artistic genius of a Rubens, they make it clear that it was in the courtly and ecclesiastical milieu of Flanders that he found the form peculiar to his art."[5]

For a long time this widespread view concerning Rubens' social milieu met no serious opposition. A more searching study of the Antwerp master, however, raises certain doubts as to the accuracy of this thesis. We propose to explain that one must review the problem of the social context in which Flemish art developed in the seventeenth century. Here we will limit our task to the case of Rubens, without investigating whether our considerations hold true for the whole sphere of Flemish art at this period. It is appropriate to remember first that we possess interesting studies concerning social movements in Dutch art, among others those written by Huizinga,[6] Brom,[7] De Vrankrijker,[8] and Presser.[9] For the Flemish side of the problem we have as yet no definitive studies, although a great number of documents have been published which permit close and detailed study.[10]

The first problem to be solved concerns the origin of the commissions carried out by Rubens. In the quotations above, which emphasize that Flemish artists worked for "princes" or for the "Royal House," the Archduke Albert and the Infanta Isabella are assumed to have been the painter's main clients. Terlinden, in his remarkable monograph on the Infanta Isabella, points to the same conclusions on this subject: "Nothing is fine enough to give back to our churches the splendor due to them and *the indefatigable Rubens turns out masterpiece after master-*

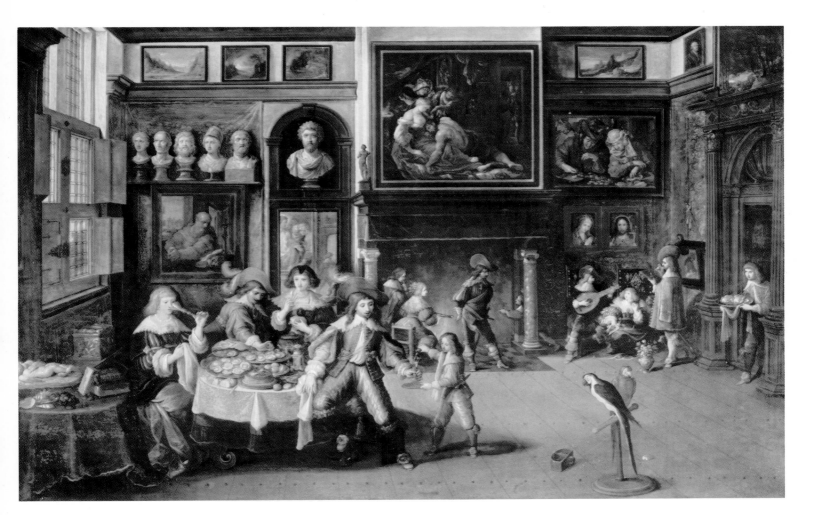

Figure 154
Frans Francken the Younger
THE "PICTURE GALLERY" OF NICO-
LAAS ROCKOX
Munich, Alte Pinakothek

*In this representation of the Antwerp burgo-
master's large drawing-room the artist has
depicted a company of people celebrating a
festival. Above the mantelpiece can be seen
Rubens' Samson and Delilah (Fig.
156). The many classical busts indicate the
owner's interest in classical Antiquity.*

*piece in compliance with the commands of the devout princess."* [11]    The same
opinion is also to be found in the words of Lambotte: "Everywhere
new churches and monasteries are built and ancient temples are
restored.    Thanks to the generosity of the sovereigns, altars are richly
decorated and Rubens is overwhelmed with commissions." [12]

Now that we have at our disposal De Maeyer's excellent monograph
on the regents of the Spanish Netherlands, it has become evident that
their commissions to Rubens were smaller in number than used to
be thought.    For them he mostly painted their portraits as well as
those of foreign princes, several mythological subjects, and something
like ten or twelve religious pictures.    De Maeyer was no doubt right
in concluding, after a scrupulous examination of all the available documents (some never published before), that "His relations with the Archduke and the Infanta were certainly not decisive for Rubens'
career.    Independently of them he was unanimously acclaimed as the
leading painter of his time, independently he had seen the growth of
his circle of friends and acquaintances, and the number of his international contacts." [13]

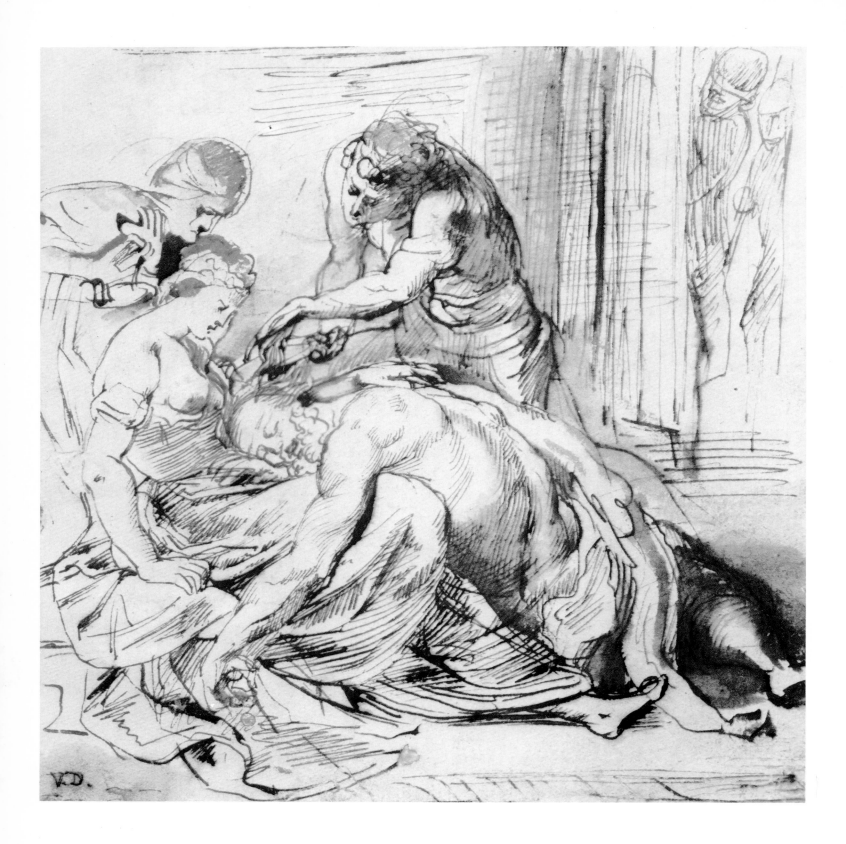

Figure 155
SAMSON AND DELILAH
Drawing, $6^1/_2'' \times 6^3/_8''$
Amsterdam, Collection Prof. Dr. I.Q.
van Regteren Altena

*Project in pen and wash for the painting*
Samson and Delilah *belonging to Nicolaas*
*Rockox, Rubens' friend. In the finished*
*painting a numer of details have been*
*modified.*

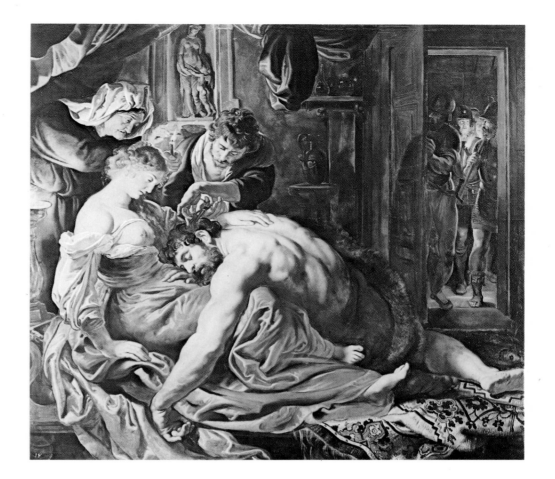

While the Archduke and the Infanta certainly played a part in the
artistic life of their realm, it seems that their influence, never clearly
established until now, was mostly exerted in an indirect
manner.   Their names appear in documents referring to the restoration
and construction of churches and monasteries; stained-glass windows
are a frequent testimony to their generosity in this area.[14]   Because
the regents encouraged the building and restoration of churches, and
because these churches, whether new or restored, had to be decorated,
the regents indirectly stimulated painting and sculpture.

In considering the social background of Dutch art, art historians attach
great importance to the fact that the Northern provinces, in contrast
to those of the South, possessed neither a real court nor an aristocracy
which loved and favored the arts.   Yet if one examines the commissions Rubens received, those coming from the aristocracy prove to
represent only a very small part of these.[15]

During the first years after his return to Antwerp, the commissions
Rubens received from Antwerp's upper middle class were particularly
decisive for his career.   The reputation which he acquired throughout
western Europe was determined in large measure by his first great

altarpieces, carried out for prosperous merchants, rich magistrates, and the guilds and corporations of the Metropolis on the Scheldt.

Indeed Rubens was commissioned by the city authorities, only a few months after his arrival, to paint a huge *Adoration of the Magi* (Fig. 35) for the Hall of the States in the Town Hall.[16]  Probably about that time he painted, at the request of the Brotherhood of the Holy Sacrament, the altar painting *The Glorification of the Holy Eucharist* (Fig. 36) in the church of the Dominicans, now St. Paul's, in Antwerp.[17]  Another huge canvas in that church, *The Adoration of the Shepherds* (Plate 14), dates from the same period, but we do not know who commissioned it.[18]

Even more important were the commissions by the churchwardens of St. Walburga for *The Raising of the Cross* (Fig. 37) in 1610,[19] and in 1611 by the guild of the Arquebusiers, for the *Descent from the Cross* (Fig. 39) for their altar in the cathedral of Notre-Dame.[20]  It is reasonable to assume that during these first years several canvases by Rubens already found their way into the dwellings of rich merchants in Antwerp.  Among these, for example, are *Samson and Delilah*, which decorated the house of Nicolaas Rockox (Plate 79; Fig. 156) (now in a private collection in Hamburg[21]) and *The Battle of the Amazons* (Plate 78), which enriched the art gallery of Cornelis van der Geest and is today in the Alte Pinakothek, Munich.[22]

The first works that Rubens painted in Antwerp certainly made a great impression on the connoisseurs in the Metropolis itself, as well as those in other towns in the Southern Netherlands.  After 1612 the young master received commissions for altarpieces from churches in Brussels, Ghent, Lille, Malines, and Lierre, among others.[23]  Dutch collectors also became interested very soon in Rubens' canvases.  Van Gelder has shown that there were at least two of the painter's works in Holland as early as the period 1610–12,[24] probably bought in Antwerp by visiting Dutch travelers.  Such visits became very numerous as soon as the Twelve-Years' Truce was signed in April 1609.[25]

Several years later, Rubens received some very important commissions from abroad; among these the *Large Last Judgment* (Plate 22), apparently ordered by Duke Wolfgang Wilhelm von Neuburg in 1615,[26] remains his most impressive achievement.  It was soon followed by cartoons representing scenes from the *Life of Decius Mus*, designed for tapestries made to order for "certain Genoese gentlemen."[27]

But for a long time the commissions from his fellow citizens and compatriots were to remain by far the most numerous.  To name all of them goes beyond our present scope, but what should be recalled here is the set of thirty-nine ceiling paintings for the church of the Jesuits in Antwerp in 1620.[28]  These works can be said to herald the great series of canvases and cartoons for tapestries which Rubens executed later for foreign sovereigns: Maria de' Medici (1622-25), Louis XIII (1622), Charles I of England (1629/30–1634), and Philip IV of Spain (1636–37). For Rubens to become the "painter of princes," it

Plate 80
JUSTUS LIPSIUS AND HIS STUDENTS (THE FOUR PHILOSOPHERS)
Panel, 65³/₄" × 56¹/₄"
Florence, Palazzo Pitti

*Justus Lipsius, the famous humanist and philologist, is seated among his disciples at a table on which lie heavy folios.  Behind him, in a niche, is a classical bust, at that time thought to represent Seneca (see Fig. 163), the Roman Stoic philosopher whose complete works had been published by Lipsius, the philologist at the University of Louvain.  On the right, Jan van den Wouwer or Woverius, a disciple of Justus Lipsius; likewise Philip Rubens, seen here on the left holding a quill pen.  Behind Philip is Peter Paul Rubens, who painted this work about 1610.*

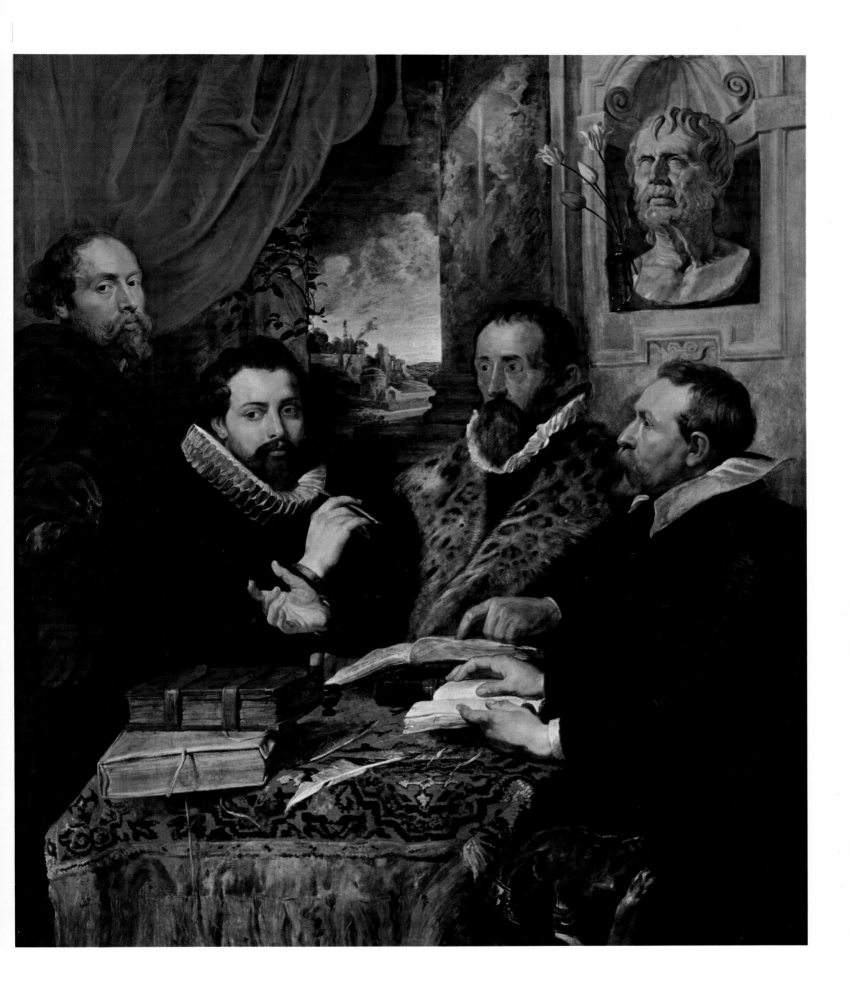

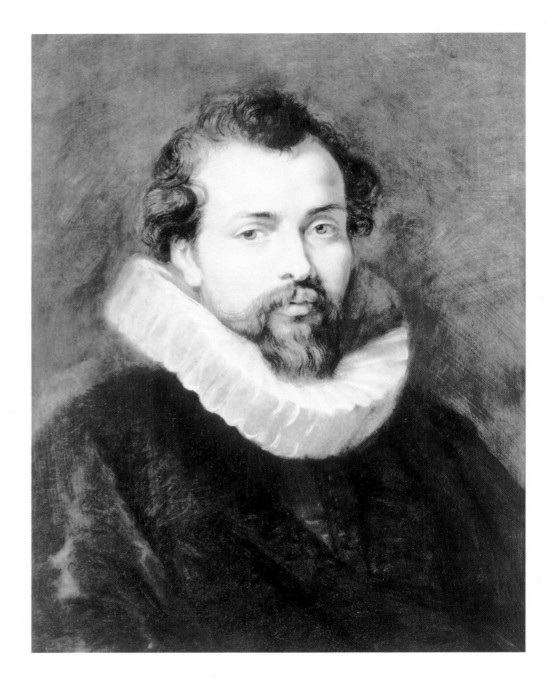

was important for him to become first the "prince of painters." The numerous and significant commissions which fell to his lot in Antwerp in the decisive years after his return from Italy allowed him to create for himself a reputation extending far beyond the frontiers of the Southern Netherlands.

Rubens seems to have more or less foreseen the possibilities that Antwerp could offer for a successful artistic career. A letter of April 10, 1609 (when he had been back in Antwerp about five months), to his friend Johannes Faber, the German doctor living in Rome, tells us that the painter was weighing his chances most carefully before deciding on the place where he would live: "But to come to my own

310

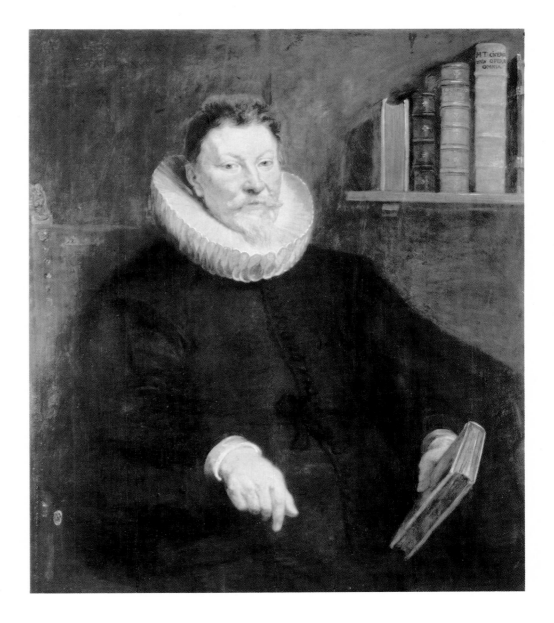

affairs, I have not yet made up my mind whether to remain in my own country or to return forever to Rome, where I am invited on the most favorable terms. Here also they do not fail to make every effort to keep me, by every sort of compliment. The Archduke and the Most Serene Infanta have had letters written urging me to remain in their service. Their offers are very generous, but I have little desire to become a courtier again. Antwerp and its citizens would satisfy me, if I could say farewell to Rome. The peace, or rather, the truce for many years will be ratified, and during this period it is believed that without doubt our country will flourish again. It is thought that by next week it will be proclaimed through all these provinces." [29]

In this letter Rubens examines the opportunities offered to him at a moment when, like Hercules at the crossroads, he has to make a crucial decision for his future career. While he does not exclude a possible return to Rome, where indeed he could count on such influential people as cardinals Scipione Borghese, Ascanio Colonna, and Jacomo Serra,[30] he puts forward such pertinent arguments for settling in Antwerp that we have the impression that he wants to prepare his friend for a possibly unexpected decision. He first mentions the efforts of the Archduke and his spouse to bind him to the court;[31] yet, despite the excellent conditions they offer, he has no desire to become again a "corteggiano" after his disappointing experiences at the court of Mantua.

Thus it seems unlikely that the intervention of the Archduke and the Infanta was the decisive argument in Rubens' choice to remain in the Southern Netherlands. In this regard it should also be emphasized that Rubens was not appointed court painter until several months after the letter of April 10, 1609. Furthermore it is significant that he apparently accepted it only on condition that he would not be obliged to reside at the court in Brussels.[32] By having a free choice of domicile he could benefit from the great advantages connected with his duties—such as an annual salary of 500 florins, exemption from certain taxes, and freedom from the rules of the guild—while avoiding the disadvantages of a courtier's life.

In the Twelve-Years' Truce Rubens found another argument in favor of his settling in Antwerp. Like the majority of his fellow citizens, he foresaw that the end of hostilities would mark the beginning of a considerable economic resurgence for the Southern Netherlands, and that good prospects would soon open up for the flourishing of the arts and the circumstances of artists. Rubens certainly realized that the advent of peace would bring the repair and furnishing of many churches and other buildings which had been damaged during the interminable war years. It is not impossible that when Rubens wrote to Faber he already had knowledge of plans that would be executed as soon as the political and economic situation allowed major enterprises to be undertaken. Perhaps he knew that certain religious orders, such as the Jesuits, intended to build "modern" churches and religious houses, and also that the guilds and religious brotherhoods were only waiting for the return of peace to set up new altars in the churches of Antwerp.

To Rubens' eyes these prospects probably looked more important than the attempts of the Archduke and the Infanta to engage him as court painter. A shrewd businessman, he weighed the advantages which would proceed from their offer and accepted it only after first obtaining all the freedom he needed to carry on his career in his own way. And indeed, as we have seen, events proved Rubens' expectations correct. After the Twelve-Years' Truce was signed it became possible that "Antwerp and its citizens would satisfy [him]." This remark in his letter to Faber deserves more attention than it has received up to now, and we note that it immediately follows Rubens' expression of distaste for the courtier's state!

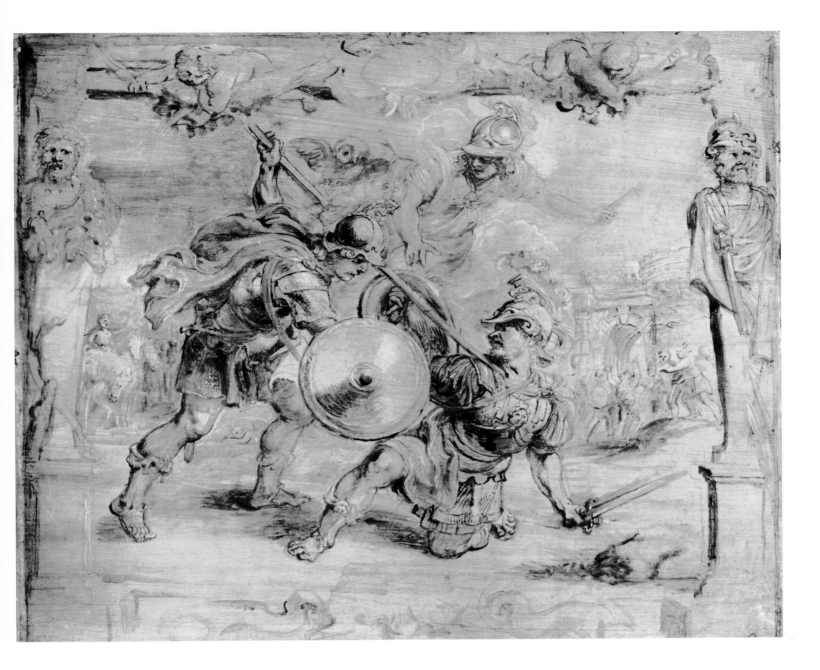

But to return to social conditions in the Netherlands which gave rise
to the artistic differentiation of North from South; now that we know
the situation confronting Rubens, perhaps it is relevant to compare
it with that in Holland and to indicate its consequences in the sphere
of the arts.

In the North, the court of the Stadholder exerted practically no influence on artistic development. There was no aristocracy to encourage
artists. The Protestant clergy, being opposed on principle to the decoration of churches, scarcely played the role of patron. The main
centers of cultural life in the Northern provinces were in the patrician
houses and the country estates of rich merchants. In these, and to

313

a lesser extent in the houses of small shopkeepers and artisans, we find those whom Huizinga has called "the consumers of civilization."[33]

As for those who produced art, "they did not become grands seigneurs like Rubens, Van Dyck, and Velázquez."[34] Dutch painting "found its raison d'être in the wealth and joy of living of the well-to-do middle class; it was in this milieu that it found its inspiration, its patrons, and its customers. Here there were no great Maecenas figures but an infinite number of art-lovers."[35]

Was the situation so different in the South? It seems to us that from a strictly sociological point of view, the Southern "consumers of civilization" scarcely differed from those in the North. One cannot say that the court and the aristocracy played the part of great patrons and sponsors of the arts. In the South, no less than in the North, this role was taken by the rich middle class.

Nevertheless we should make one distinction: the clergy of the Southern provinces, far from banning art, had a marked preference for sumptuously decorated churches; and in this magnificence the paintings, with their impressive dimensions and brilliant colors, constituted an element of first importance. But it is our opinion that even the role of the clergy was not as considerable as it would appear at first sight. It is true that examples are known of church councils and religious communities that ordered works of art directly from the artists, and also of rich members of the clergy who remunerated the makers of altarpieces out of their own purses. Canon Del Rio, for example, paid Rubens for *The Assumption of the Virgin* (Plate 49), destined for the high altar presented by the Archduke and Archduchess to Antwerp Cathedral.[36] It is no less true, however, that in large measure the decoration of the churches and religious houses seems to have been due to the generosity of the middle class and sometimes even of the entire population.

With regard to church pictures, several categories of gifts must be distinguished:

1. Personal gifts, such as the pictures presented to the Franciscans of Antwerp, among them the *Coup de Lance* (Fig. 57) given by Nicolaas Rockox, a magistrate and several times mayor of the city.[37] Or *The Last Communion of St. Francis of Assisi* (Plate 25; Fig 53), presented to the Minorites by the merchant Jaspar Charles,[38] or again *The Flagellation of Christ* (Plate 27) which the merchant Louis Clarisse presented to the church of the Dominicans.[39]

2. Collective donations, of two sorts: those from church councils, and those from guilds and religious brotherhoods.

a. Church councils: we cite as an example *The Raising of the Cross* (Plate 15; Fig. 37), now in Antwerp Cathedral but painted by Rubens in 1610 for the high altar of the church of St. Walburga.[40] It is probable, however, that the rich merchant Cornelis van der Geest contributed in large measure toward the payment for this masterpiece. Another example is the triptych of *The Adoration of the Magi* (1617–19) in the church of St. John at Malines (Plate 24); here the

Plate 81

THE TRIUMPH OF THE EUCHARIST
Oil sketch on panel, 12⅝" × 12⅝"
The Art Institute of Chicago (Mr. and Mrs. Martin A. Ryerson Collection)

*Rubens made this oil sketch for a velum, or hanging placed in front of the altar during Holy Week, for the church of the Descalzas Reales in Madrid. It is part of the series of designs for the tapestries in the* Triumph of the Eucharist *series. Using this all-over design, five tapestries were executed; their compositions can be found in the sketch, with slight modifications and in reverse. The Eucharist series is a brilliant testimony to the spirit of the Counter-Reformation.*

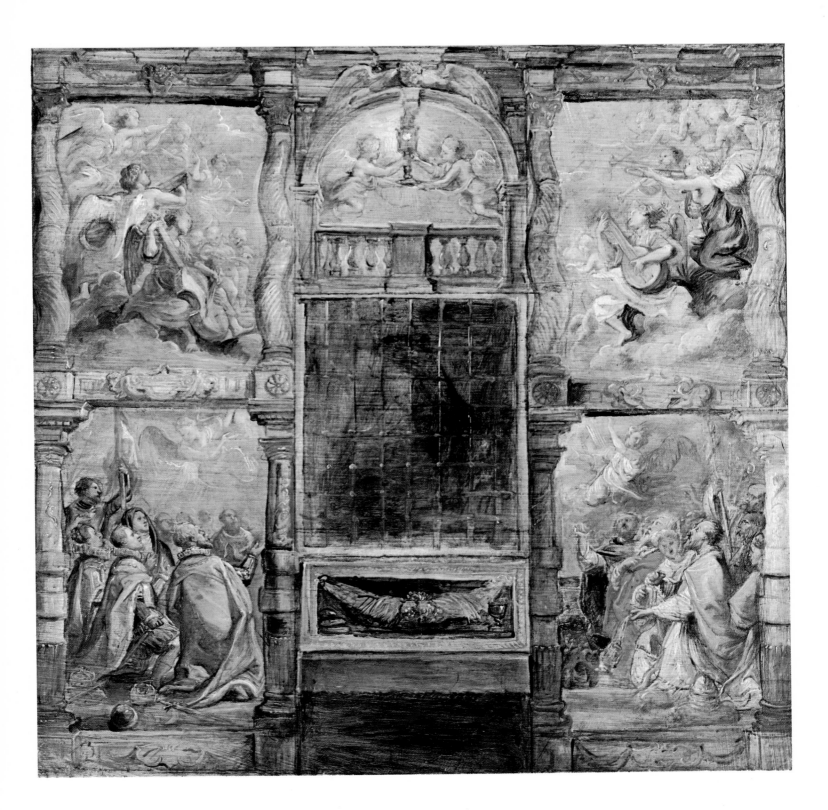

315

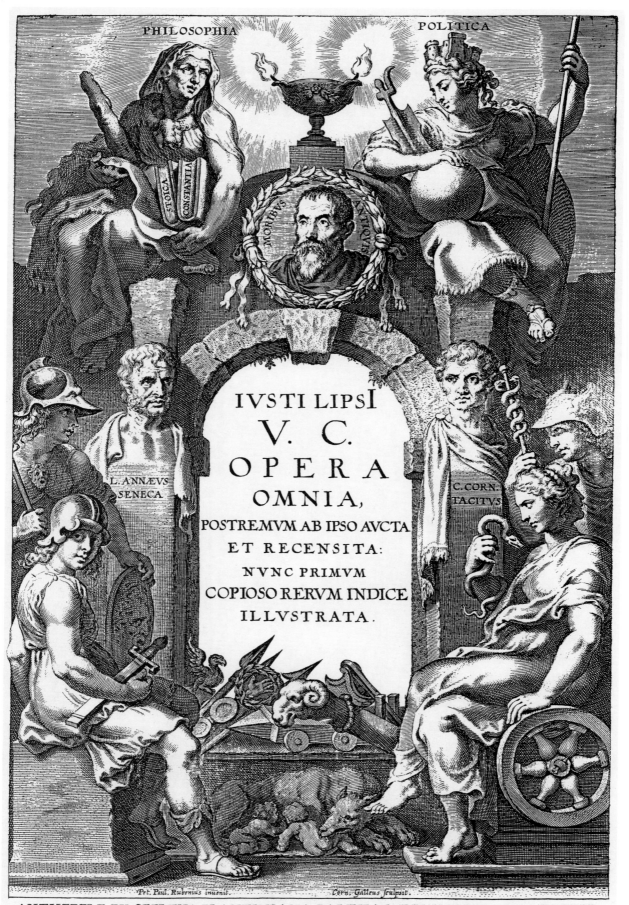

PHILOSOPHIA

POLITICA

IVSTI LIPSI
V. C.
OPERA
OMNIA,
POSTREMVM AB IPSO AVCTA
ET RECENSITA:
NVNC PRIMVM
COPIOSO RERVM INDICE
ILLVSTRATA.

L. ANNÆVS
SENECA

C. CORN.
TACITVS

Prt. Paul. Rubenius inuenit.    Corn. Gallæus sculpsit.

ANTVERPIÆ EX OFFICINA PLANTINIANA BALTHASARIS MORETI. M. DC. XXXVII.
CVM PRIVILEGIIS CÆSAREO ET PRINCIPVM BELGARVM.

funds seem to have been collected from the offerings in church services, which means that the whole parish paid for the altarpiece.[41]

b. Guilds and religious brotherhoods: these probably underwrote the greatest number of gifts of church pictures. We know that each guild and each brotherhood had its own church altar. *The Descent from the Cross* for which Rubens received the commission in 1611 from the Guild of the Arquebusiers, for their new altar in Antwerp Cathedral, is typical of the donation specified here (Plate 16; Fig. 39).[42] A few years ago a document was discovered which tells us that this admirable triptych was paid for not only out of the funds at the disposal of the guild, but also by sums obtained from rich Antwerp merchants such as the already-mentioned Louis Clarisse.

Such examples as these—and many others could be cited—permit the conclusion that the majority of church pictures also owe their existence to the generosity of the middle class. One may naturally suppose that the clergy encouraged this form of donation. But the fact is that piety and ambition incited wealthy individuals as well as middle class associations to contribute substantially, by the donation of paintings and statues, to the marvelous decoration of the churches in the Southern Netherlands.

One wonders if any great difference *from the sociological point of view* separates the Guild of Arquebusiers in Amsterdam, for instance, from that in Antwerp. Yet the fact is striking that the Dutch guilds commissioned group portraits[43] to decorate their buildings and perpetuate their union of fraternity and the pride of their members, whereas the Flemish guilds, and the religious brotherhoods as well, considered that a superb altarpiece in their particular chapel in a church represented the highest affirmation of their existence. This shows clearly that the obvious contrast between artistic conceptions in the Northern and Southern Netherlands was probably not determined by social factors.

Other elements in this area must have played a more fundamental part—religious and cultural factors, and differences in mentality, education, and outlook. We cannot enter deeply into this question here.[44] Let us limit ourselves to the following observations: in the North in the early seventeenth century we find a young, enterprising, not very traditionalistic middle class which had quickly raised itself above the social strata from which it had sprung. Its interest in business was clearly greater than its desire for culture, and it did not yet aspire to the aristocratic style of living which would characterize the next generation.[45] In the South, on the contrary, the life of the middle-class citizen was intrinsically attached to three traditions.

First and foremost was the cosmopolitan tradition, largely due to the presence in the Metropolis of Genoese, Florentine, Spanish, and Portuguese merchants and bankers since the beginning of the sixteenth century. Although their number decreased during the desolate period of religious strife, contacts were maintained thanks not only to commercial relations but also through intermarriage.[46] Thus the Southern Netherlands, contrary to the North, were associated with

Figure 160
Cornelis Galle, after Rubens
FRONTISPIECE FOR JUSTUS LIPSIUS, OPERA OMNIA,
Antwerp, 1637
Antwerp, Plantin-Moretus Museum

*In the medallion can be read the device of Justus Lipsius,* Moribus Antiquis. *The allegorical figures represent Philosophy and Politics, two disciplines in which the humanist excelled. The two busts are of Seneca and Tacitus, Lipsius' two favorite authors, whose works he published. On the left, Minerva and Virtus (Virtue); on the right, Mercury and Prudentia (Wise Government). The content of the works of the well-known humanist, who exerted a profound influence on his time, is illustrated in this allegorical fashion.*

317

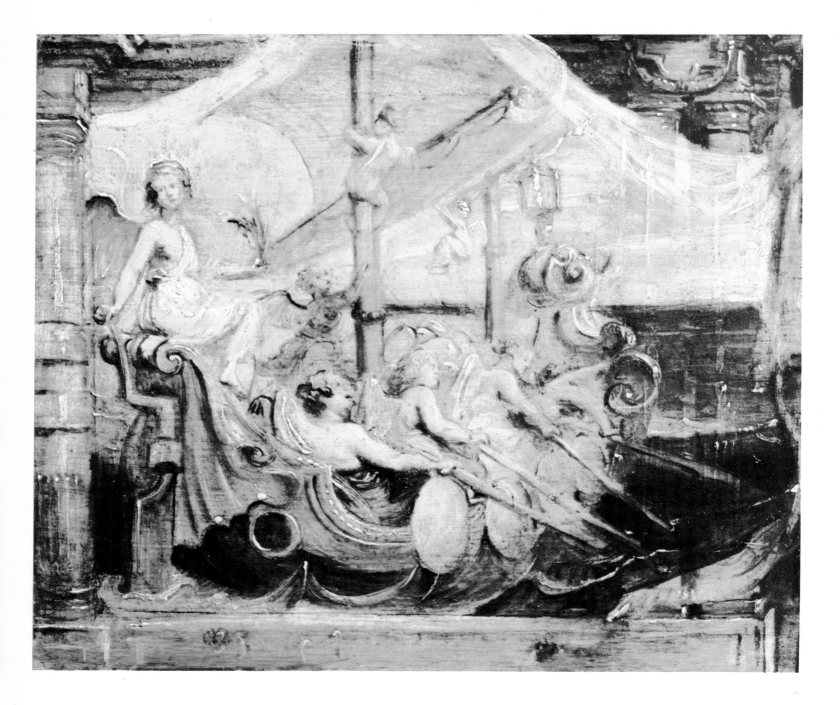

Figure 161
THE TRIUMPH OF HOPE
Oil sketch on panel, 6¼″ × 7½″
New York, Collection Richard L.
Feigen and Co.

*Small sketch for a tapestry in the* Triumph
of the Eucharist *series; this one was, however, never executed.*

the European Baroque; surely this also explains the kind of decoration
reflected in the arts of the South.

Secondly it is appropriate to mention the humanist tradition which,
in its Christian guise, experienced an ever greater expansion, mainly
through the Jesuit, Augustinian, and Dominican schools. Not only
magistrates and scholars, but businessmen also, such as François Sweertius, the noted writer and publisher, acquired a very thorough training
in these schools through the study of classical literature and culture.

The third and probably the strongest tradition that we will cite was
that of Roman Catholicism, which had found new life and strength

in the fervor of the Counter-Reformation. Here one must emphasize the influence that the clergy exercised on intellectual life. It was their ambition to illustrate religious doctrine through ardent works of art and to make the churches seem to echo the celestial Paradise.

In the mere choice of subjects a difference is revealed between North and South with regard to the spiritual background of each region. The artists of the Southern Netherlands treat religious and mythological themes; their Northern fellows paint landscapes, interiors, and still lifes of fairly modest dimensions, and large-scale group portraits. Only in a country whose cultural life had been molded by the triumphant Counter-Reformation could Rubens have carried out his impressive altarpieces; only in a city and country where humanist culture, together with a cosmopolitan outlook, led to an association with the European Baroque could Rubens have conceived and produced those mythological and allegorical paintings, frontispieces, and illustrations in which abound motifs inspired by classical Antiquity and the Italian Renaissance.

How Rubens came to terms with these three cultural elements in the Southern Netherlands, and how these components are manifested in his works, could be the subject of a further study. We hope it has been shown that neither the court of the Archduke, nor the nobility, nor the Church as an institution had decisive importance for the career of the master, but that the well-to-do middle class did; and it follows that social circumstances cannot furnish an adequate explanation of the artistic differences between the two parts of the Netherlands. If the "consumers of civilization" differ little from one another from a sociological point of view, they nevertheless diverge greatly on the spiritual and cultural levels. These contrasts, which we believe should be examined more closely, seem to us more important than the mere social framework of civilization in the Northern and Southern Netherlands in the seventeenth century.

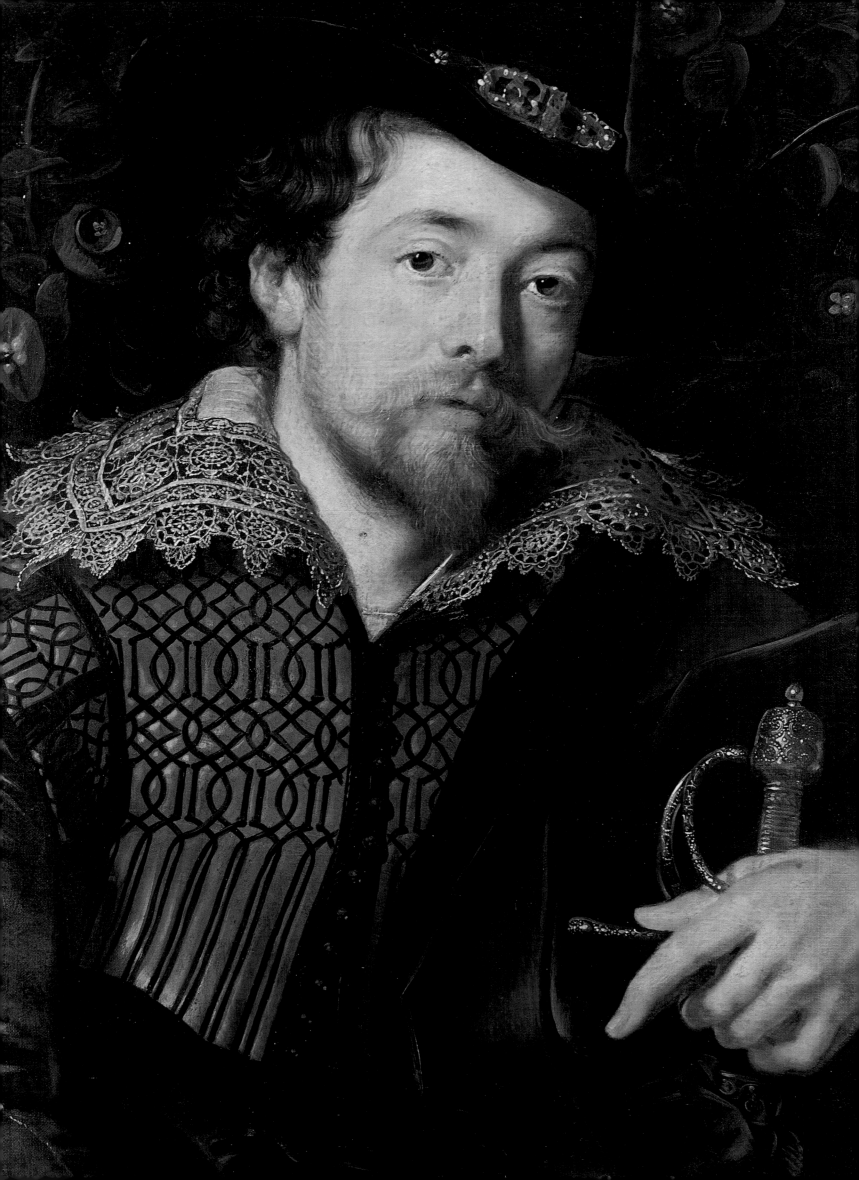

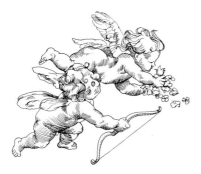

# CHAPTER 15

Rubens' Personality

Who was Rubens really? What were the character traits of this man who is unanimously ranked among the greatest artists who ever lived? These questions inevitably arise for anyone who studies Rubens' work. And there is another one: does his personality account for his incomparable creativity, for the artistic heights he attained, and for his astonishing productivity?[1]

To answer these questions seems all the more difficult today inasmuch as neither Rubens' attitude in the society of his time nor his life itself corresponds at all to the image we usually have formed of the life and behavior of an artist. In his case there is indeed nothing of egotism or of a forced isolation in the margin of society; still less can we see him taking up a deliberately critical position against society, although his criticism of persons and situations is by no means absent in his correspondence. With Rubens there was no "ivory tower" mentality, no cult of "art for art's sake," no tendency to "épater le bourgeois," and not a trace of leading a Bohemian life, which for many people are still the undeniable, distinctive marks of the "artist." Rubens led the ordered life of a well-to-do citizen and sometimes took on the air and style of a lord; at his death he left a considerable fortune; all this is incompatible with the kind of behavior that has usually been attributed to artists since the Romantic period. From this point of view, Rembrandt's life seems to correspond better to the general expectation of an artist.

The deciphering of Rubens' personality has been rendered even more difficult by the artist's being a skillful diplomat, and regarded by his contemporaries as one of the best connoisseurs of classical Antiquity; also he was obviously interested in the literature and philosophy of his time as well as in many of the theories and experiments that made the seventeenth century a turning point in the history of science. Like Leonardo da Vinci, Rubens is among those few artists who played a part in other fields of action and human thought. Contrary to certain artists of genius such as Titian, Frans Hals, and Anthony van Dyck, whose lives were solely devoted to painting, Rubens' name would have survived—albeit with less glory—if he had never painted anything. It

Plate 82
RUBENS AND ISABELLA BRANT (detail: self-portrait of Rubens)
Munich, Alte Pinakothek

*Rubens represents himself here at the age of about 32, almost a year after his return from Italy.*

321

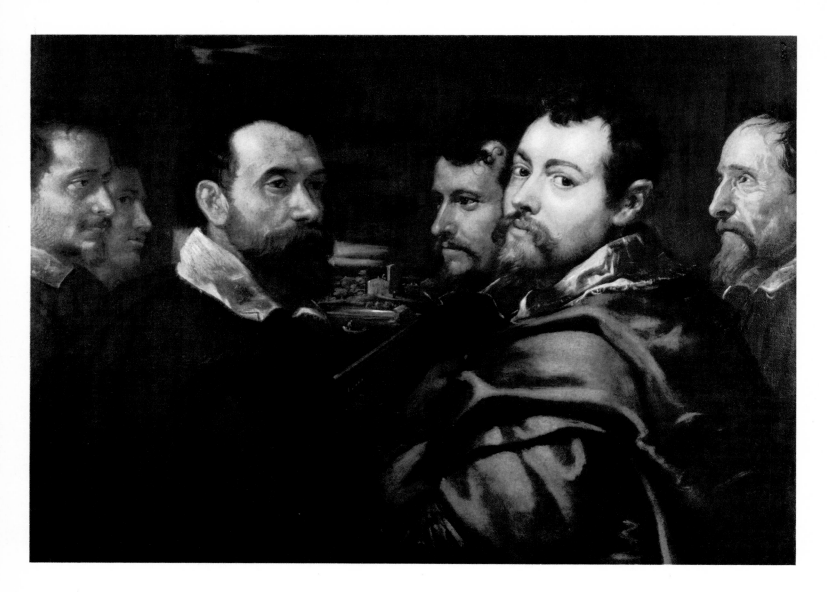

Figure 162
RUBENS AND HIS MANTUAN
FRIENDS (see Pl. 10 for detail in color)
Canvas, $30^3/_4'' \times 39^3/_4''$
Cologne, Wallraf-Richartz-Museum

*The young man who looks toward the specta-*
*tor is indisputably Rubens. A number of*
*widely divergent identifications for the other*
*figures have been put forward. There is also*
*little unanimity about the date of the pic-*
*ture; according to some it was painted in*
*Mantua in 1602, others suggest 1606, in*
*Rome. In the background of the picture,*
*however, the city of Mantua seems to be*
*represented.*

Figure 163
PORTRAIT BUST OF SENECA
Drawing, $10^1/_8'' \times 7^1/_2''$
New York, The Metropolitan Museum
of Art. The Robert Lehman Collec-
tion

*This drawing was executed after a classical*
*bust that belonged to Rubens and was consid-*
*ered at that time to represent the Stoic*
*philosopher. The graphic character of the*
*drawing suggests that it was made in prepa-*
*ration for an engraving, and, indeed, it was*
*engraved by Lucas Vorsterman.*

is his many-sided personality that makes his biography extremely fascinating, more so than that of the majority of his fellow artists.

Nevertheless, Rubens was primarily a painter, even more so than
Leonardo, and it is in his painting—his *dolcissima professione*—that his
personality reveals itself in full majesty. How then to solve the enigma
of the personality that hides behind this glorious art?

To accomplish this, we have several sources at our disposal. His
few self-portraits allow us to become familiar with his physical appearance and to come closer to his inner life. We have also some two
hundred and fifty handwritten letters, although these must be only
a small percentage of the very numerous letters he certainly
wrote. Rubens was a great letter-writer, not only in the large quantity
of his letters on the most varied subjects, but also by reason of his
particularly lively style.[2] There is the additional evidence provided
by his contemporaries. And finally there are his works which tell

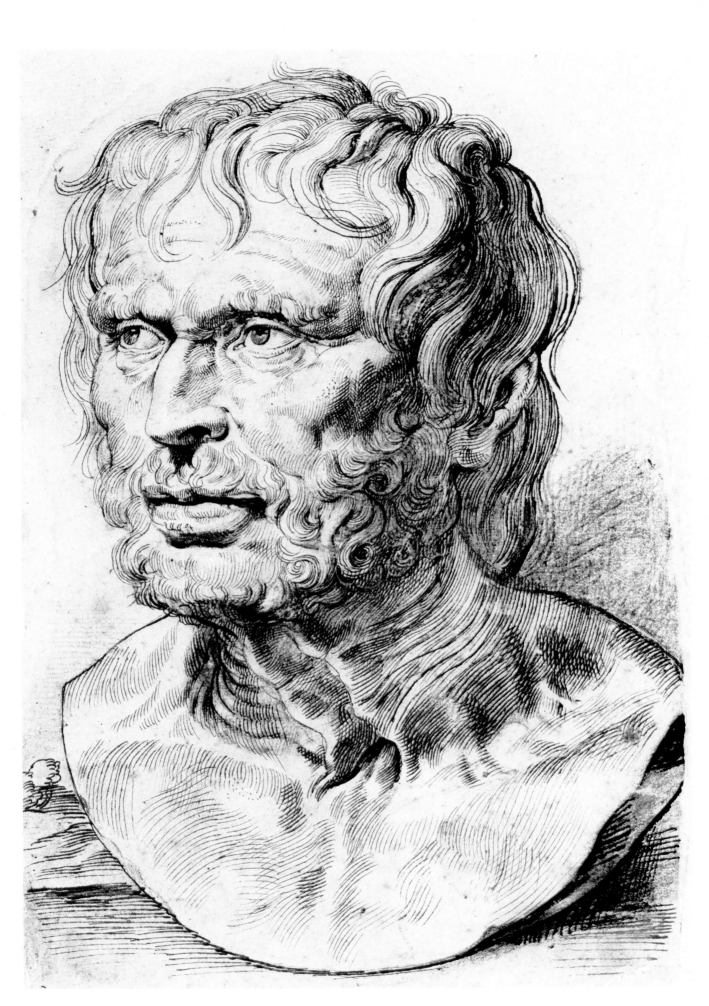

323

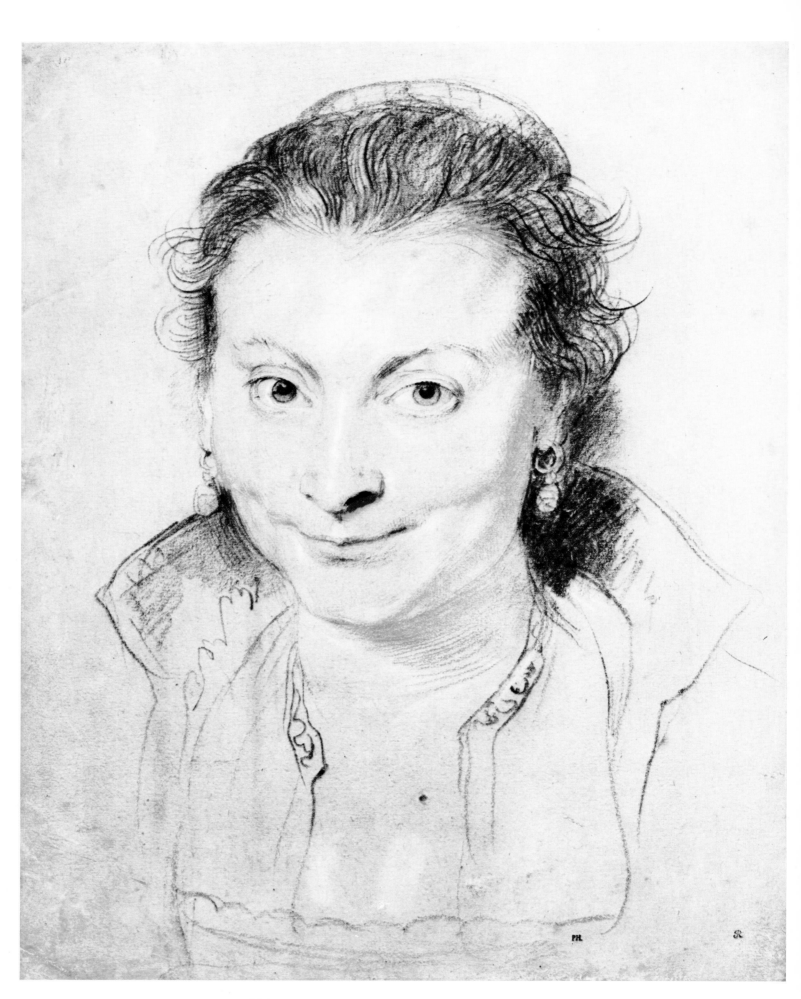

324

us about his vision of the subjects he painted, his temperament, and his emotional make-up, revealed through his workmanship and style.

But as a starting point for my thoughts on Rubens' personality, I would rather choose a different source. Among the biographies written on Rubens in the seventeenth century, the *Vie de Rubens* by the French aesthetician Roger de Piles, which forms part of his *Conversations sur la connaissance de la Peinture* (Paris, 1677), is unquestionably the most important.[3] The author himself tells us that his sketch of Rubens' life is based on data passed on to him by Philip Rubens, the artist's nephew, the son of his brother Philip. The correspondence between Philip Rubens and Roger de Piles, a copy of which is preserved in the Royal Library in Brussels, shows that this nephew obtained for his correspondent a "summary which I extracted and formulated from the memoir about him left by his eldest son [Albert Rubens]," as well as some supplementary information.[4] Thus the French author's *Vie de Rubens* is largely based on information supplied by persons in Rubens' immediate circle.

This circumstance makes Roger de Piles' account particularly precious. It might, however, also give rise to a degree of mistrust, for it often happens that the close relatives of a great man will tend to overestimate his qualities. Fortunately such suspicion does not seem to be justified in this case, because the French author gives us rather concrete information which is, moreover, mostly confirmed by other sources. The *Vie de Rubens* contains the only physical description of the artist which has come down to us: "He was of tall stature, of stately bearing, with a regularly shaped face, rosy cheeks, light-brown hair, eyes bright but with restrained passion, a pleasant expression, gentle and courteous."[5] We are not able to verify beyond question the "tall stature" and "stately bearing," since the majority of Rubens' self-portraits that we know are only half-length figures. However, we do find these physical characteristics present to some extent in the picture *Rubens and Isabella Brant* (Fig. 165), that poem of tender love, in which he represented himself in a honeysuckle bower beside his first wife, Isabella Brant, like "a young man still looking somewhat bewildered; the expression on his face is barely beginning to break away from the charming insignificance peculiar to youth, although he is already thirty-two. Isabella, seated beside him, already seems to be awakening gently to inner doubts and certainties" (Maurice Gilliams). The tall stature and stately bearing seem to be found again in the self-portrait in Windsor Castle (Plate 57), painted in 1622–23 at the request of the future Charles I, then still Prince of Wales; in this portrait Rubens depicts himself as a self-assured, distinguished, and strong-willed gentleman.

The other features of Rubens' physical appearance mentioned by Roger de Piles—the regular features of his face, rosy cheeks, brown hair, the eyes bright but with restrained passion—are apparent in virtually all the self-portraits, from the first, in Cologne (Plate 10; Fig. 162), in which he shows himself as a man of about twenty-five, accom-

Figure 164
PORTRAIT OF ISABELLA BRANT
Drawing, 15″ × 11½″
London, British Museum

*Study in black, red, and white chalks for the portrait of Isabella Brant in the Uffizi Gallery (Pl. 58), probably executed shortly before her death in 1626.*

325

panied by his "Mantuan" friends, to the last one, in Vienna (Plate 92), painted shortly before his death, where he appears "already in physical decline and with a touch of suffering, but with a far deeper appeal than before."[6]

The "pleasant expression, gentle and courteous" which Roger de Piles mentioned on the strength of the testimony of Philip Rubens, seems at its best in the most intimate self-portrait preserved in his own house, the Rubens House in Antwerp (Plate 70). Here he seems to be turning his face somewhat pensively toward the spectator as if he were quietly and attentively listening to conversation.[7]

Rubens usually represented himself wearing a black, wide-brimmed hat. The few portraits in which he is bareheaded show his premature baldness, a feature that is not mentioned by Roger de Piles. If we do not notice this in the earliest known portrait, it is unmistakable in the famous group portrait known by the title of *The Four Philosophers* (Plate 80), painted about 1610, at the age of thirty-three. The same is true of another self-portrait (Fig. 168) executed a few years later, no doubt, where the bald area above the forehead shows up in contrast to the thick curls at the sides and the back of the head. In the self-portrait which he integrated into the extreme right of the *Adoration of the Magi* (Fig. 35), a picture painted in 1609 but enlarged precisely on the right some twenty years later by Rubens himself, in 1628–29 during his stay in Madrid, one can observe that he has combed his hair toward the front to cover his baldness.

Different from Rembrandt, who painted some sixty or more self-portraits, Rubens painted only a small number of himself. Apart from the few pictures where he is accompanied by Isabella Brant or Helena Fourment, or by some friends, he represented himself alone in only four self-portraits. In contrast to the great Dutch master, Rubens does not seem to have had the constant need for confrontation with himself, for continuous introspection, and this in itself reveals one of the traits of the personality of Rubens, who did not feel constrained to fathom persistently the mystery of his inner life. Or should this rather be explained by insufficient time, the result of the numerous commissions? Did he not describe himself as "the busiest and most harassed man in the world"?[8]

What strikes us in Rubens' self-portraits, especially those painted at an advanced age, are the eyes, which Roger de Piles said were "bright but with restrained passion." An excellent observation, which, it seems, could apply to the whole inner life of Rubens: intense passion moderated by energetic control. This balance is also manifested in his art, where an overflowing imagination is transformed by a regulating intelligence into scenes of exultant beauty. Harmonious compositions control the most dramatic, passionate, and lively representations. His intelligence imposes structures appropriate for a torrent of shapes and masses, born from an inexhaustible imagination, which are intertwined in confusion. This impetuosity is bridled with the help of diagonals and geometrical constructions which give a stable framework to the composition. Rays of light and alternately shad-

Figure 165
RUBENS AND ISABELLA BRANT
Canvas, 70" × 53½"
Munich, Alte Pinakothek

*Rubens and his wife, Isabella Brant, are sitting in front of a honeysuckle bower. Their marriage took place on October 8, 1609; this double portrait was no doubt painted about the same time.*

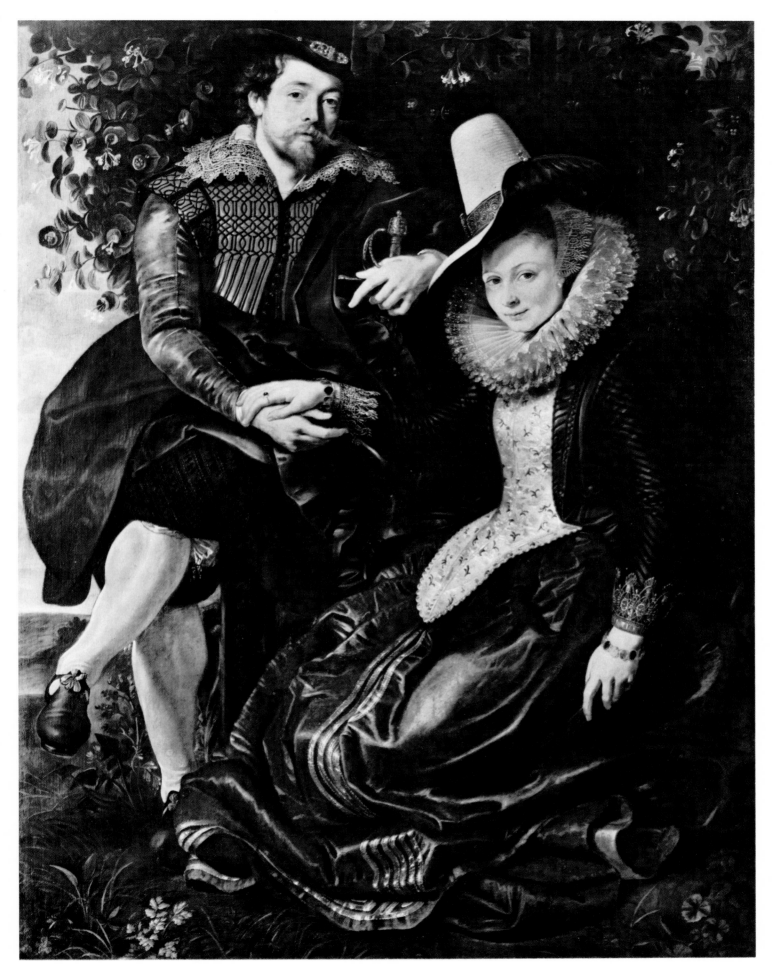

327

owed areas contribute to the achievement of this balance. What is most astonishing is that the poses, movements, and gestures of the figures do not seem in any way to be constrained by this intervening regulation, and the impetus of the imagination loses none of its initial force.

One's first impression of Rubens' personality through his self-portraits is that of strong will power and self-control, behind which is almost hidden a burning fire of intense life. In addition, the artist appears also to be a gentle man from whom emanates a natural distinction, someone who scrutinizes the world and his contemporaries with a calm but penetrating gaze. In this respect, our impression corresponds to the description by Roger de Piles. It is certain also that Rubens was conscious of his own value, but without self-conceit.

Portraits tell us not only about the sitter's physical appearance, but also bring to us something of his inner being. The impressions we derive from observing them, however, must be checked against the testimony of those who actually knew the person. Roger de Piles, again relying on information furnished by Philip Rubens, provides a useful starting point for such a comparison. He writes: "His approach was engaging, his temper was easy, his conversation pleasant, his wit lively and penetrating, his way of speaking calm and steady, and the tone of his voice pleasing; all this made him naturally eloquent and persuasive."[9] In a word, an intelligent personality, affable and engaging. One might nevertheless again wonder whether Philip Rubens did not give too flattering a description of his uncle's character to Roger de Piles, who was already a great admirer of Rubens. But on the other hand a fair number of Rubens' contemporaries also mention the very special charm which emanated from his personality. As early as November 1600—when the artist had only been in Italy six months—an old schoolmate, Balthasar Moretus I, wrote to Rubens' brother: "I knew your brother at school, when he was still a child, and I liked the boy, who was very good-natured and most likable."[10]

In 1607 Gaspard Scioppius (Schoppe), a scholar and theologian from Bavaria (1576–1646), noted in his book *Hyperbolimaeus:* "Mr. Rubens, a man in whom I would find it difficult to know what to praise most, his skill as a painter, an art in which, according to the connoisseurs, he has reached perfection—if anybody can perform this today—or that fine judgment, which in him goes together with a special charm in conversation, or his knowledge of literature."[11] Rubens had met Scioppius in Rome in the years 1605–6, perhaps even earlier, in the circle of scholars and artists who were gathered around Johannes Faber, the German doctor who was also a great connoisseur of Antiquity.

A few years after Rubens' return to Antwerp, the Leyden humanist Dominicus Baudius dedicated a poem to him in which, having praised the painter and connoisseur of Antiquity, he writes: "In kindness you are second to none. You are always ready to pursue the Good."[12] Baudius also emphasizes the painter's cultured distinction, which stands out markedly from the coarseness and rough manners

Plate 83
RUBENS AND ISABELLA BRANT (detail: portrait of Isabella Brant) Munich, Alte Pinakothek

*When this portrait was painted, Isabella Brant was 18 or 19 years old. Her beauty was "like that of the noble beauty of a fervent handshake, of a look full of gratitude" (Gilliams).*

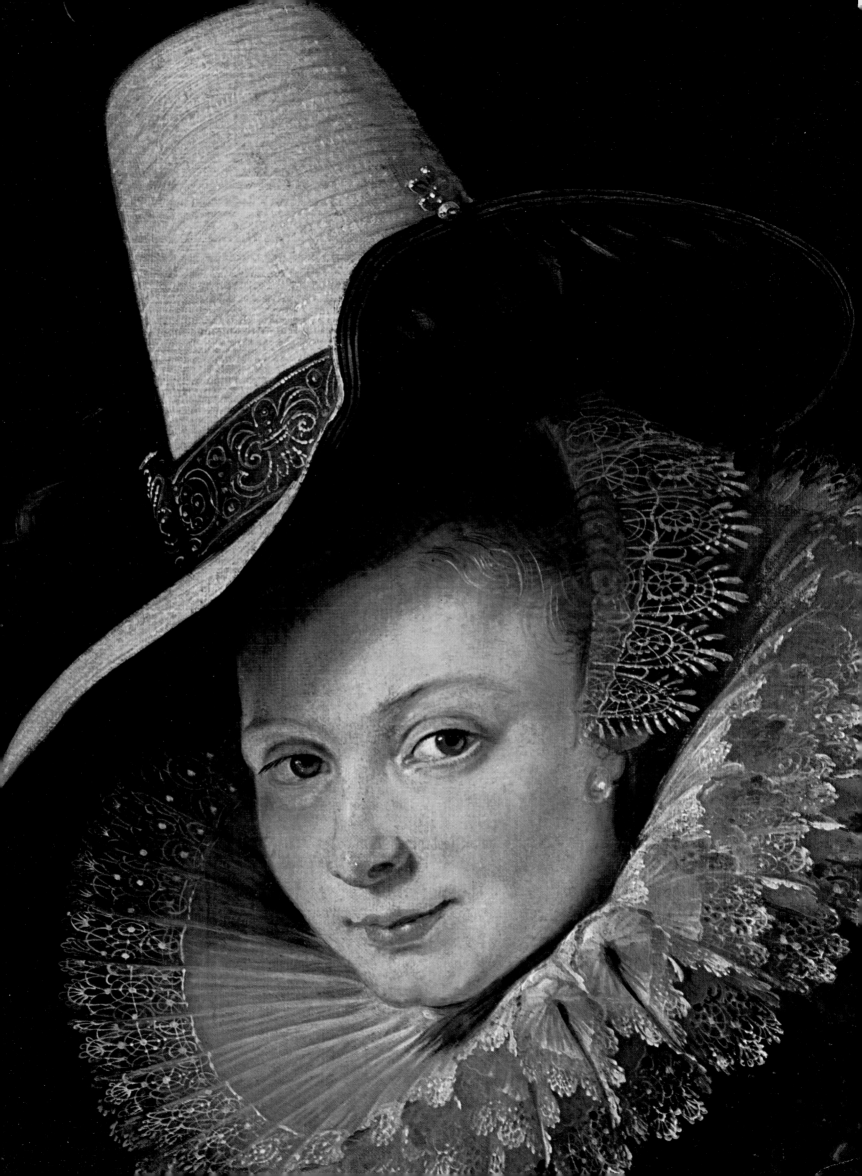

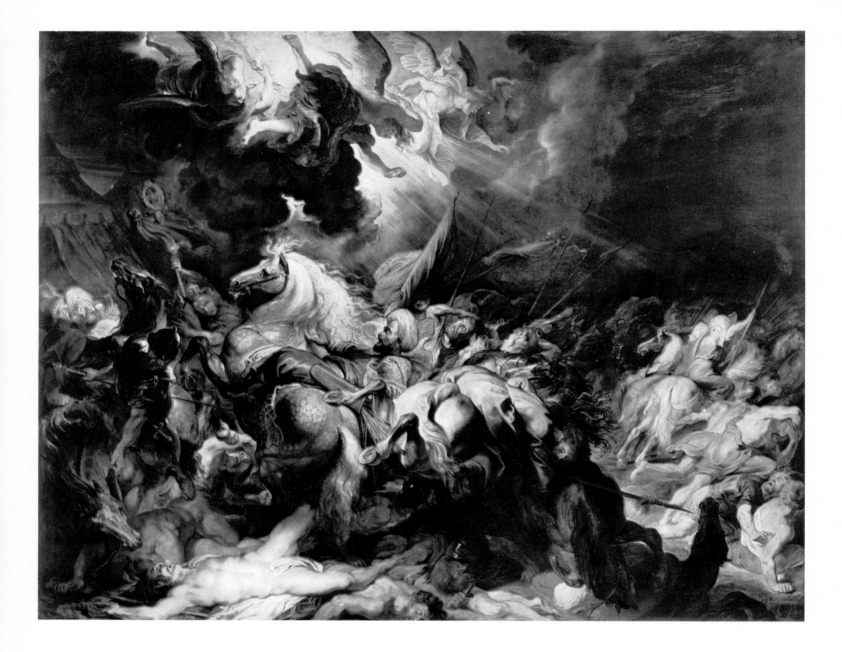

Figure 166
THE DEFEAT OF SENNACHERIB
Panel, $38\frac{1}{2}''\times 48\frac{1}{2}''$
Munich, Alte Pinakothek

*This picture dates from about 1615, a time when dynamic elements were asserting themselves once again in Rubens' style. It was also the period of very animated hunting pictures. The treatment in this work is brilliant; Rubens succeeds in harmonizing bold impulsive movements into an ordered composition. He uses judicious contrasts between light and dark areas.*

of many other artists. Nevertheless one should attach not too much importance to Baudius' testimony; he wrote his poem in the hope of receiving a painting from the artist in return, hence it is appropriate that we measure the implications of the praise.

The opinion of Nicolas Claude Fabri de Peiresc, the French humanist and scholar whom Rubens met on several occasions in Paris in 1622, takes on more significance for the sincerity of its tone. When the artist was on the point of leaving the French capital, Peiresc handed him a letter destined for Guidi di Bagno, the papal nuncio in Brussels, in which he wrote: "Although I already wrote to you yesterday as usual, I did not want to let that kind Mr. Rubens leave without giving with him a few lines to tell you that if I already esteemed his talents

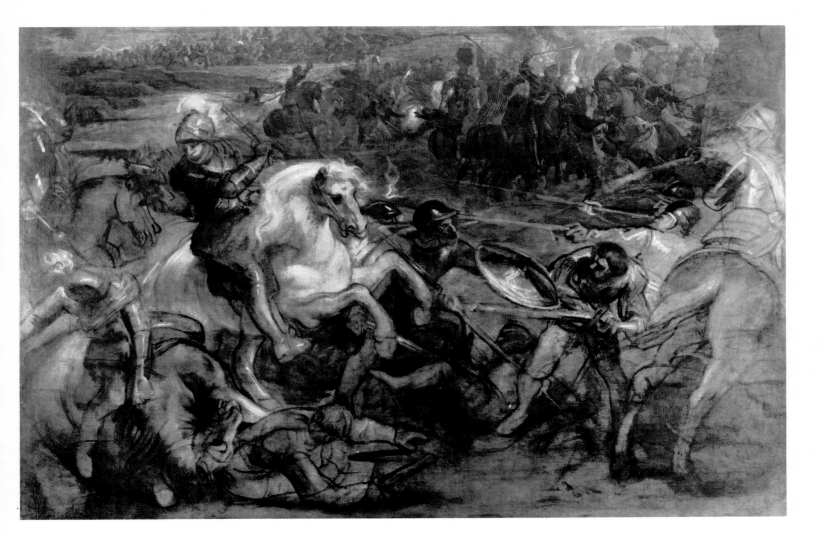

Figure 167
THE BATTLE OF HENRY IV FOR
THE OUTSKIRTS OF PARIS
Canvas, 22'8" × 12'5"
Private Collection

*This unfinished work for the cycle* The Life
of Henry IV, *which Rubens never completed, shows with what gusto the artist could
render the movement of men and horses in
dramatic scenes.*

because of his fame and reputation, I have now been able to judge
for myself his exceptional merit and knowledge, not to speak of the
perfection of his art. I cannot but admire him exceedingly and I cannot let him go without regretting the loss of the most scholarly and
pleasing conversation that I have ever enjoyed. Especially in matters
concerning antiquity, he has the most universal and outstanding knowledge that I have ever come across."[13]

That same day Peiresc wrote another letter, this time to Caspar
Gevartius, the young humanist and registrar from Antwerp through
whom Peiresc had met Rubens: "The good will of Mr. Rubens, which
you have procured for me, has filled me with such happiness and contentment that I shall be indebted to you all my life, for I cannot praise
too highly his courtesy, nor extol adequately his virtue and great qualities, both in the domain of profound scholarship and marvelous knowledge of antiquity, and in his rare and skillful conduct of business
affairs, as well as his excellence as an artist and the infinite sweetness
of his conversation."[14]

Shortly afterward, on March 7, 1622, he wrote to an Italian named

331

Aleandro that Rubens was "of such gentle manners that it would be impossible to find a pleasanter man." [15]  Fifteen years later, on August 1, 1637, Peiresc uses the phrase: "Mr. Rubens, who was born to please and give delight in all that he does and says." [16]

Ambrogio Spinola, the Genoese general in the service of the regents Albert and Isabella, is said to have declared one day that he saw so many brilliant talents in Rubens that his painting seemed to him the least of these.  Rubens himself had a great liking for the statesman, whom he as a diplomat had come to know well, and he noted in his turn that the great Spinola "understood no more about art than his stable-boy." [17]  De le Serre, the confessor of Maria de' Medici, testifies on the subject of Rubens in the same vein as Spinola: "He is a man whose industriousness, although rare and marvelous, is the least of his qualities: his judgment in matters of state, and his spirit and behavior raise him so high above the estate he professes, that the works of his wisdom are as remarkable as those of his brush," [18] this judgment referring both to Rubens' knowledge of affairs of state and to his qualities as a diplomat.  No one rendered him more homage in this field than one of his political adversaries, the Venetian legate to The Hague, who wrote home to Venice: "This Rubens is full of malice; he is very skillful in handling affairs and the Spaniards have already engaged him in other very important matters." [19]

It was especially the amiability that emanated from Rubens' physical appearance, his conduct, and "the very special charm" and "the gentleness of his conversation," which struck his contemporaries, in addition to his talents as a painter, his knowledge of Antiquity, and his skill as a diplomat.  His own letters bear witness to these qualities.  As Delen has pointed out, "everywhere we find this courteous tone, this gracious civility, this almost exaggerated politeness, which we might call by the name of flattery if we did not know that it was peculiar to the Flemish Renaissance, influenced by the Spanish and the Italians." [20]

Kaufmann, for his part, was of the opinion that from Rubens' correspondence emanates "a virile and human nobility, a heart overflowing with frankness." [21]  It is obvious that these characteristics of Rubens were greatly useful in his dealings with everyone, and in particular with his sponsors, the sovereigns, and with statesmen and diplomats.  We should mention, in this connection, that Olivares, who had been prejudiced against the artist-diplomat, completely changed his attitude after he came to know him in person.

In reviewing the life and work of Rubens, one is struck first and foremost by his tremendous capacity for work; this remained unimpaired throughout, thanks to a well-regulated life.  The organization of his days included long hours of assiduous work, but also allowed him time to devote to physical exercise and mental relaxation.  Roger de Piles writes: "He got up every day at four in the morning, and made it a rule to begin his day by hearing mass, unless he was prevented by the gout, by which he was extremely troubled; after which he set

Plate 84
THE CORONATION OF ST. CATHERINE
Canvas, 8'6" × 6'10"
Toledo, Ohio, The Toledo Museum of Art

*A magnificent picture, painted in 1633 for the altar of St. Barbara in the church of the Augustines in Malines; it is characteristic of Rubens' art in the last ten years of his life. The pictorial refinement and the idyllic, heavenly atmosphere are typical of this phase, which has sometimes been called his "lyrical" period. Helena Fourment was the model for St. Catherine, kneeling on the right.*

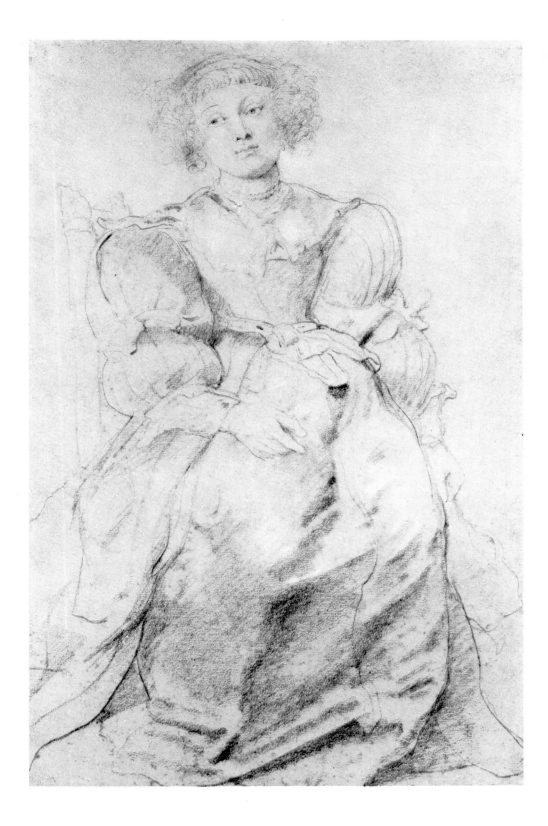

Figure 169
PORTRAIT OF HELENA FOURMENT
Drawing, $19\frac{1}{4}'' \times 12\frac{5}{8}''$
Rotterdam, Boymans-van Beuningen
Museum

*Study in black, white, and red chalks for
the portrait of Helena Fourment in her wedding dress (Fig. 170).*

biological explanation, because we are unable to grasp the essence of
this phenomenon. At best we can point out a few factors which
account to some extent for Rubens' prodigious productivity.

Rubens did a great deal of drawing, from his early youth onward;
first he imitated the works of other artists, especially engravings after

335

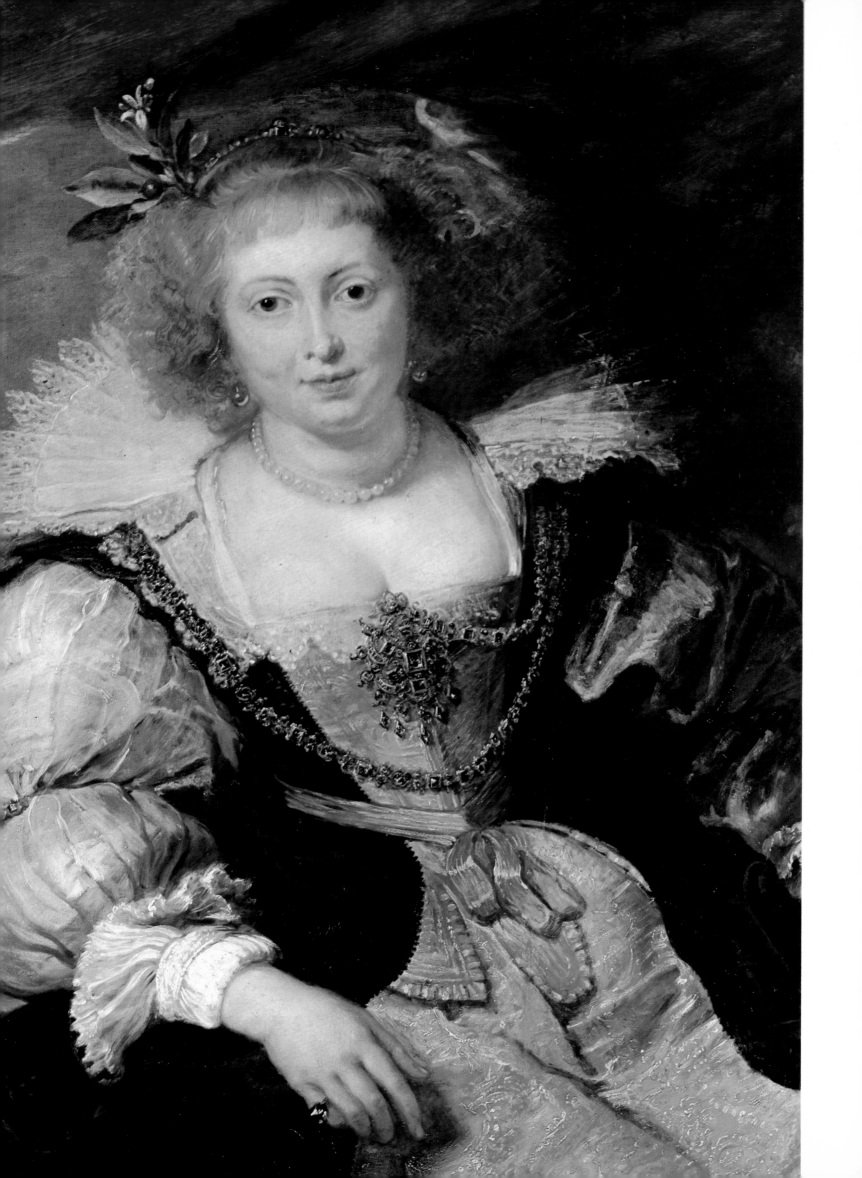

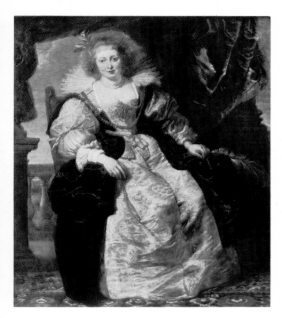

Figure 170
HELENA FOURMENT IN HER WED-
DING DRESS
Panel, 64½" × 53½"
Munich, Alte Pinakothek

*Rubens married Helena Fourment on December 6, 1630. She was not yet 17 years old. This magnificent portrait was executed about that time.*

Plate 85
HELENA FOURMENT IN HER WED-
DING DRESS (detail)
Munich, Alte Pinakothek

*In the portraits of Helena Fourment, Rubens' second wife, one can feel "a breath of prayer-like veneration. The adornment, the face, the hands, all sing like the music of strings and cymbals" (Gilliams).*

them; later he also copied antique sculptures, often more than once and from different angles, and masterpieces of the Italian Renaissance; and he also drew from life. Throughout his whole life he practiced drawing: an illuminating example of this are his studies in the 1630s of details for *The Garden of Love* (Plate 87; Figs. 171–74). In this way he built up an extensive repertory of forms to which he could refer at will. If, in a composition, he wanted to represent a man crouching toward the right or left, or a woman looking upward, he usually found what he needed at that moment in his store of drawings. By this uninterrupted exercise of perception and drawing, he acquired a skill which allowed him to work quickly and efficiently.

Certain eighteenth-century authors claimed that Rubens needed only a week to paint an altarpiece such as *The Adoration of the Magi*, now in the Koninklijk Museum voor Schone Kunsten in Antwerp (Plate 46). This is without any doubt an exaggeration, as becomes clear in his letters—the successive layers of paint required that a painting had to dry several times before it was finished. The assertion need not, however, be totally discounted for this reason. A study of the brush strokes shows that at his peak Rubens must have worked with such facility, such virtuosity, such "furia del penello" that the execution of similar pictures of large format probably took him in fact only a relatively short time. Nevertheless this final stage of achievement was preceded by very extensive preliminary work, so that the accomplishment of the work could go smoothly. Drawings and sketches done in advance provide ample proof of this method, the "scribbles" by means of which he rapidly noted his first findings; sketches in grisaille, often followed by others in color, allowed him to fix a composition at a more advanced stage; later came the chalk drawings after nature for figures planned in the composition, unless he was using his own repertory of drawings after already existing forms.

It is certain that Rubens, whose daily program was orderly and regulated, also organized his workshop in such a way that a fair number of minor or material tasks were entrusted to his assistants. However, even if we take into account the help he received in the studio, his enormous output and the superior quality of his workmanship present perhaps the greatest and most impenetrable mystery of his artistic personality.

Rubens must have possessed a capacity for concentration almost beyond comprehension. Everyone who visited him was astonished by the intensity with which he worked and by his ability to attend to several things at a time. Already in Mantua, Vincenzo Gonzaga, whose official painter Rubens was, once took the young artist by surprise in his workshop and found him scanning lines of Virgil aloud as he was painting, because their rhythm stimulated him as he worked. Even more remarkable is the account of Otto Sperling, general physician to the king of Denmark, who went to see the master in 1621: "We visited the very famous and eminent painter Rubens, whom we found at work. While he was painting he was having

337

Tacitus read to him and at the same time he was dictating a letter. We remained silent, for fear of disturbing him, but he spoke to us without thereby interrupting his work, and allowing the reading to continue, he went on with the dictation of the letter and replied to our questions at the same time, as if he wanted to furnish proofs of his great gifts."[23]   No doubt the claim is overemphasized that all these activities were simultaneous, making the story seem improbable to us, but this does not necessarily mean that it is pure invention.   Roger de Piles, too, tells us that Rubens had a "reader" at his disposal who, while he was painting, read from some good book, most often from Plutarch, Livy, or Seneca.   Furthermore he adds that Rubens had no difficulty in keeping up a conversation while he was painting.   When he was finishing the pictures which were part of the series of the life of Maria de' Medici in Paris, the queen-mother used to sit behind him, and she experienced as much pleasure listening to him as in watching him paint.[24]

"Much as we admire his keen perception and intelligence," writes Valentiner, "it cannot be denied that we can observe a slight inclination to dramatize himself.   One has the impression that Rubens found it necessary to have this bustle and stir around him, this audience, as it were, to enhance the "nearness-to-life" of his works.   Not that he tried to impress his public—he was too great a man for this—but that his creative faculties were stimulated by the dramatic character of his surroundings.   One can scarcely imagine that Rembrandt, when depicting his deep and intimate representations, had onlookers around him or that he dictated letters while painting.   In this Rubens was like Leonardo, who liked to have musicians and actors nearby when he worked; in both an astonishing intellect prevailed over the power of feeling.   Rubens' *forte* was the dramatization of life."

This tendency toward "dramatization" is already apparent in the earliest figures drawn after engravings, which he endowed with greater expressiveness than was shown in the works he copied.   It is manifest in his subsequent work, especially in the vigorous contours or in the strokes of color with which he accentuated movements.   This very pronounced taste for violent, dramatic expression, which is peculiar to Baroque feeling in general, must be accounted for primarily by Rubens' special talent for evoking people and events in a very precise and lively fashion in his imagination, as well as by the miraculous power of his hand which allowed him to render, on paper, wood, or canvas, forms that were adequate to his vision.

Other factors may also have contributed to this sense of drama: we might think particularly of his first childhood years spent in exile, under circumstances which were certainly dramatic from his parents' point of view.   His father and mother lived, indeed, at a time which has generally been regarded as one of the most troubled in the history of the old Netherlands.   Perhaps these early memories made a strong impression on him, or it is even possible that the reprehensible facts of his father's life were kept hidden from him.   Stories of the adventures of a good many men in those troubled times must have seemed

Plate 86
STUDY OF A WOMAN WITH
CROSSED HANDS (detail)
Drawing, 18⅝" × 14"
Rotterdam, Boymans-van Beuningen
Museum

*During his last ten years Rubens executed, with warm tenderness, enchanting portraits in black, red, and white chalks of Helena Fourment and of other young women also, such as the one represented here. The head and hands are usually rendered with more detail than the costume, which is mostly indicated by a few soft, evocative strokes of unerring accuracy. The facial expressions are nearly always a little dreamy.*

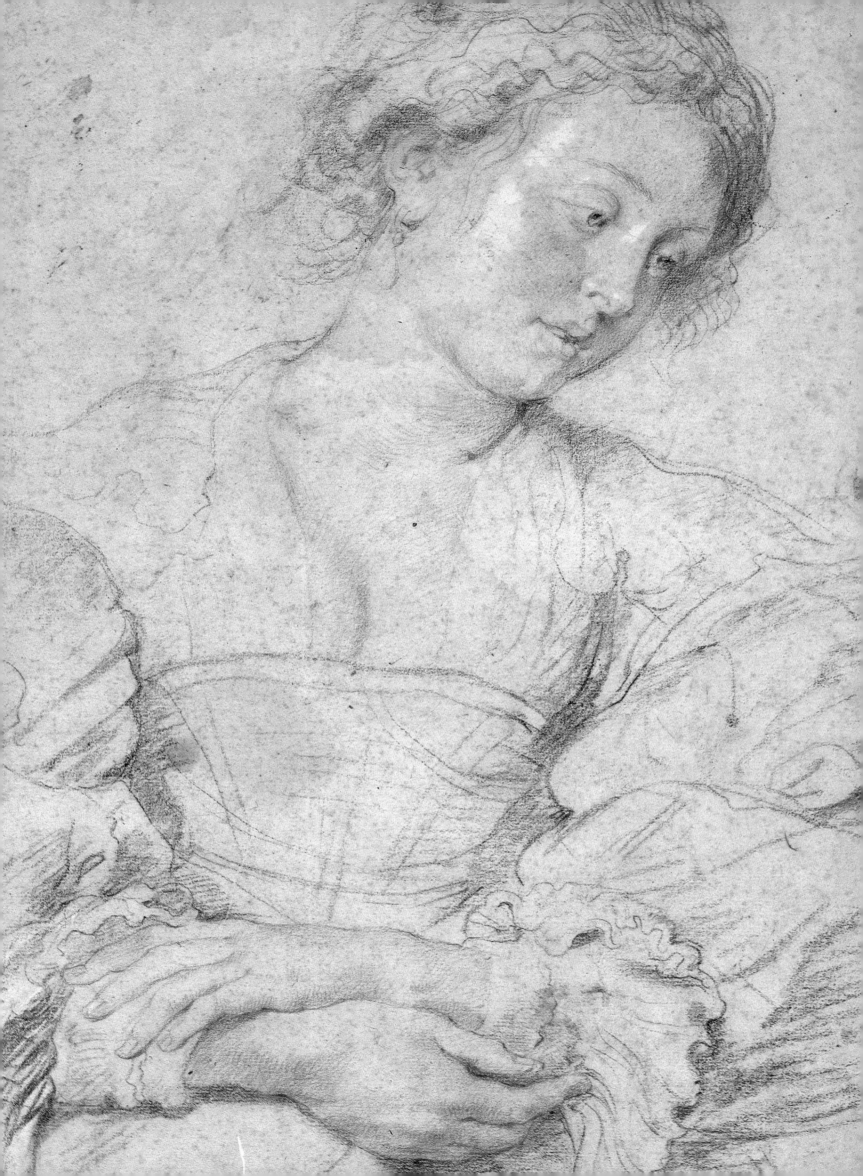

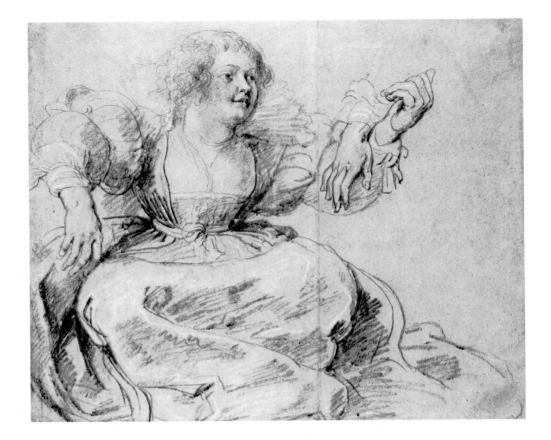

as bewildering to him as some of the thrilling epics of the heroes or gods of Antiquity which he became familiar with during his boyhood at the Latin School in Antwerp, under his teacher, Rumoldus Verdonck. Then again there were the vicissitudes of political life; wartime situations were familiar to him all through his life (except during the Twelve-Years' Truce of 1609–21), and he was fascinated to observe a great many tragic episodes. More than once the noise of cannon was heard at the gates of Antwerp.

His correspondence bears witness to the curiosity that he showed about everything that was going on in the world scene. Rubens traveled in many countries and he observed the actions of the people wherever he went. On returning home, he always liked to be informed about what had been going on meanwhile. As an artist and diplomat, he met personally, as a privileged witness, many leading figures in political life. Passages in his letters frequently provide evidence that his critical eye scrutinized their qualities and defects, and also that he followed their destiny with close attention. Irony and humor are moreover by no means absent; how could this be otherwise, when we remember that his favorite poet was the satirist Juvenal. Rubens shared his curiosity about world events with some of his learned friends, both in his own country and in France, and this formed a positive chain along which news could pass. Jan van de Wouwer (Woverius) wrote to Balthasar Moretus—both were

340

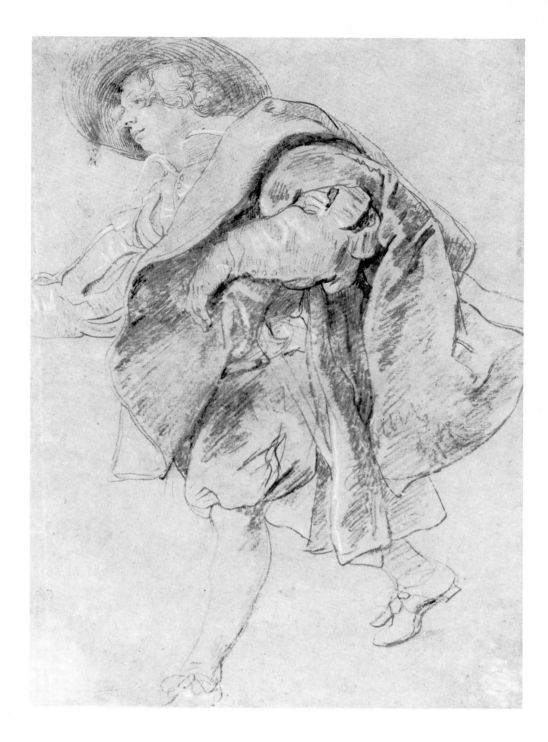

Rubens' childhood friends—about 1623: "I am sending you news of
the last few months, not just of one town but the whole world.   What
a pleasure to see unfolding itself, so to speak, the theater of the whole
world.   In future you will receive news of our Rubens regularly.   I
ask you to send me back news by return."[25]

Rubens no doubt regarded the tragic events of his time as part of
the eternal drama of human life.   Fidelity and treason, moral greatness
and baseness, uprightness and duplicity, generosity and selfishness,
good and bad fortune—in brief, all the virtues and human passions,

341

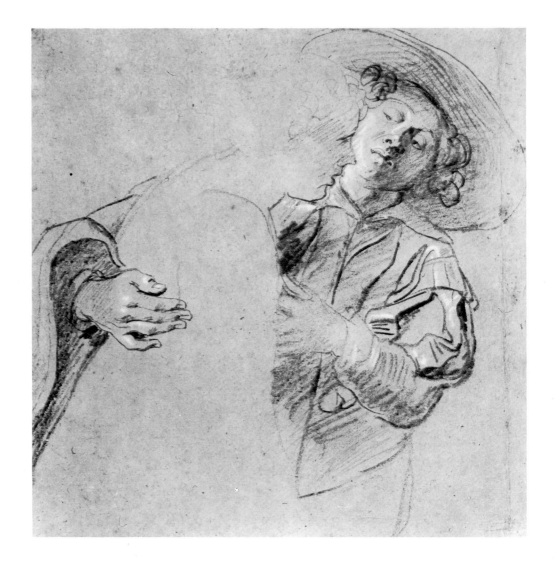

and the fatality which determines our destiny—all this was known to
him from the writings of the Greeks and Romans.

These authors had already given such powerful expression to human
joy and suffering that they became irreplaceable models for Rubens
and for his humanist friends, just as classical statues served as artistic
models. It has been emphasized that Rubens endowed his gods and
heroes—draped in their tunics and peplums or wearing shining armor
and feathered helmets, attributes which were familiar to him through
his study of Antiquity—with the feelings and passions common to
ordinary mortals. He humanized them, so to speak, and their adventures are those experienced by all men through the ages. Conversely,
the actions of the men and the events of his time call up associations
in his mind with Antiquity. Thus, by using many quotations from
Latin authors, he connects the present with the past.

The "dramatization of life" of which Valentiner speaks was certainly
promoted by Rubens' classical culture. It was no mere whim on his
part to have works by Latin authors read to him while he was

342

painting. Nor is it a coincidence that Eugène Delacroix and Jacob Burckhardt later linked his name with that of Homer, the greatest epic poet of all times.

Rubens' conception of life was influenced by classical antiquity. It is certain that the Stoicism of Seneca made a strong impression on him. There was great interest in the doctrine of the Stoa (the Stoic group) throughout Europe among intellectuals under the influence of Justus Lipsius, who edited the complete works of the Roman philosopher Seneca and propagated a synthesis of Christianity and Stoicism in his own writings (Fig. 160). Against the uncertainty which characterized much of the sixteenth century, the troubles and wars which were still going on in Rubens' time, the Stoic dispassion, in the slightly varied form of Justus Lipsius' *De Constantia*, appeared to be the only anchor in the midst of a stormy sea (Plate 80; Fig. 163).

Lipsius gave the following definition of this *constantia*: "The sure and unshakable strength of the soul, which does not extol itself with the external matters of Fortune, and also does not succumb to them." This Stoic constancy appears in the inscriptions which Rubens had engraved on panels on the portico which leads to the inner courtyard of his house. Above the left arch can be read "Let us leave to the Gods the task of granting to us what is good and useful; man is dearer to them than to himself." Above the right arch he had engraved: "We must pray for a healthy spirit in a healthy body, for a courageous soul which fears not death, which is free of anger and which covets nothing." These two maxims are taken from the *Satires* by the Latin poet Juvenal, and express a serene acceptance of destiny.

Without any doubt, Rubens' self-mastery, which is confirmed in his self-portraits and in his letters, can be linked with the exercise of the Stoic virtues.

It is nonetheless true that Rubens, at a certain moment of his life, took a very relative view of Stoicism. In his thanks addressed to Pierre Dupuy for his message of sympathy on the death of Isabella Brant, he wrote: "You do well to remind me of the necessity of Fate, which does not comply with our passions, and which, as an expression of the Supreme Power, is not obliged to render us an account of its actions. It has absolute dominion over all things, and we have only to serve and obey. There is nothing to do, in my opinion, but to make this servitude more honorable and less painful by submitting willingly ..."[26]

Up to this point the words are a confession of Stoic faith, which Rubens accepts on a rational basis. He goes on to say: "... but at present such a duty seems neither easy, nor even possible. You are very prudent in commending me to Time, and I hope this will do for me what Reason ought to do. For I have no pretentions about ever attaining a stoic equanimity; I do not believe that human feelings so closely in accord with their object are unbecoming to man's nature, or that one can be equally indifferent to all things in this world. *Sed aliqua esse quae potius sunt extra vitia quam cum virtutibus* (There are certain things which are rather outside the vices than with the virtues [Tacitus,

343

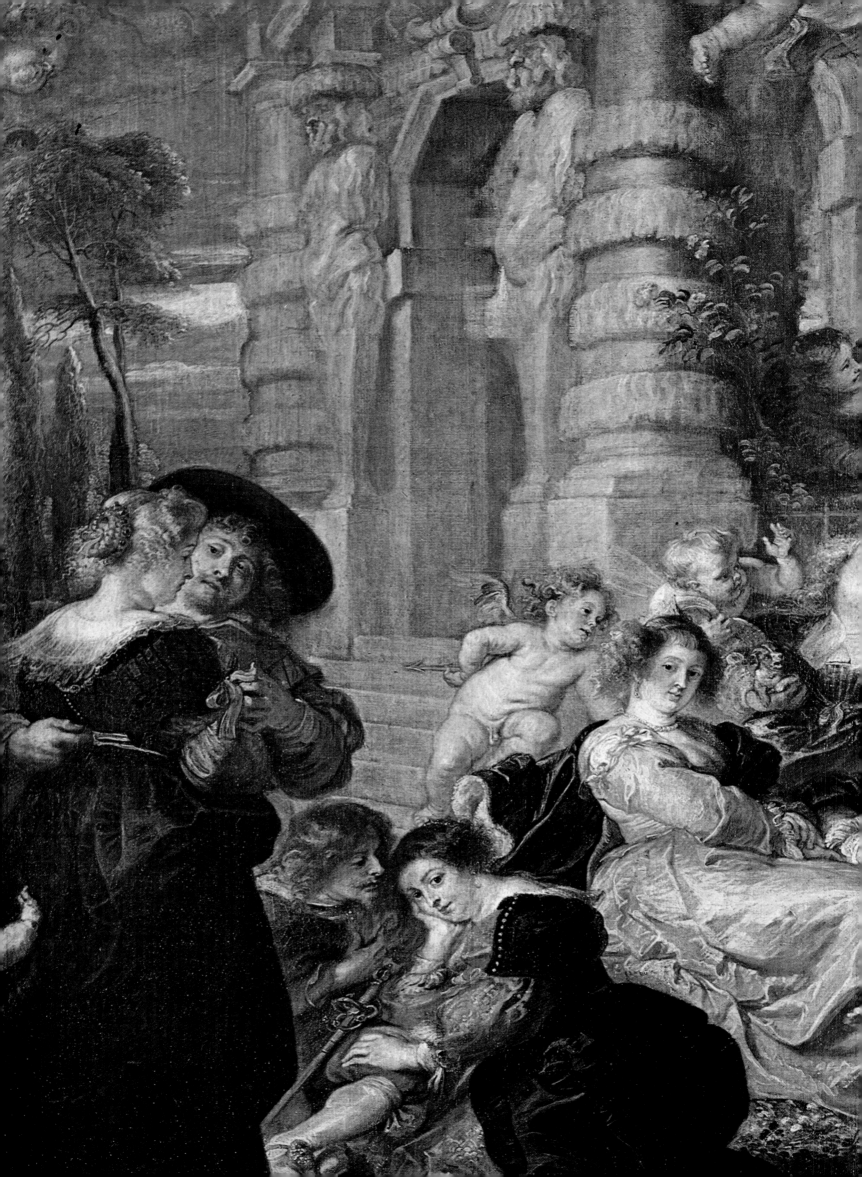

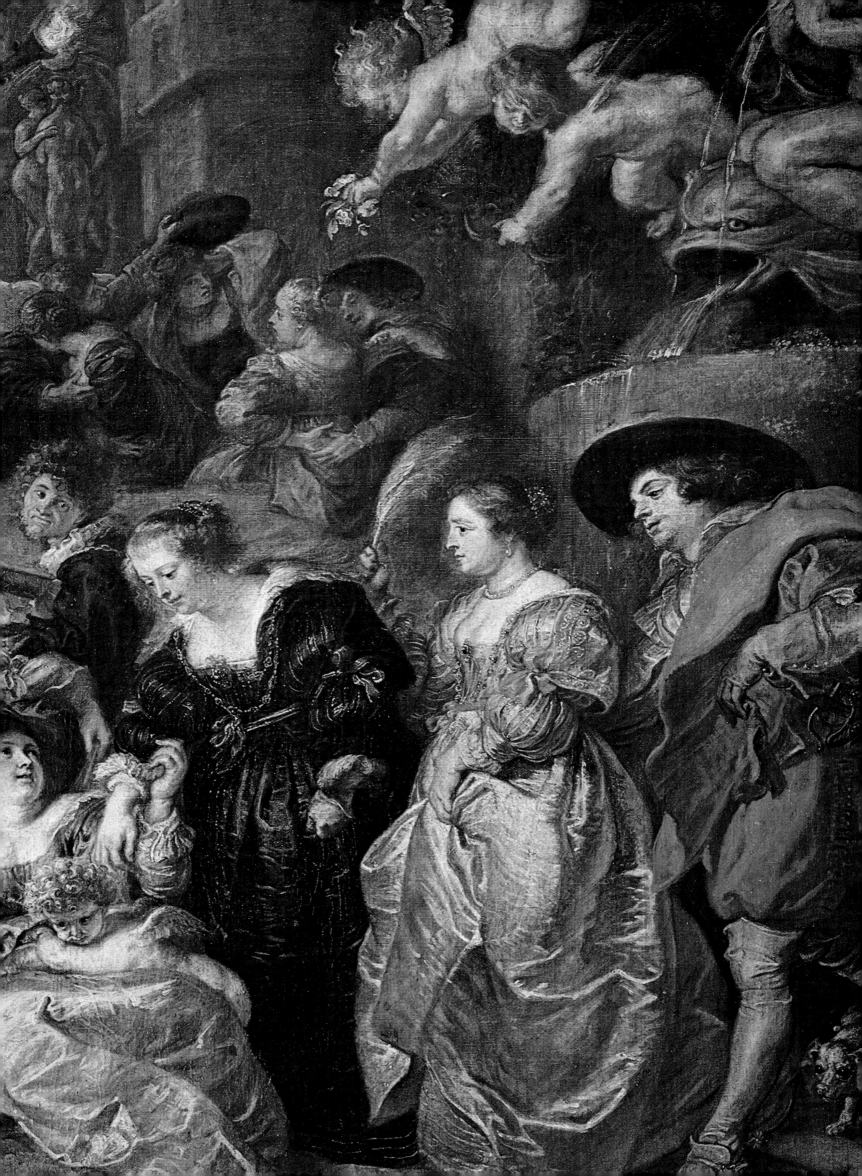

*Historiae* 1.49]), and they arouse in our souls a kind of sentiment *citra reprehensionem* (beyond censure) ..."

This criticism of Stoic dispassion is followed by a touching "in memoriam" to his wife Isabella Brant; it is restrained, and at the same time he reacts in it against this apathy which seems to him totally unbecoming: "... Truly I have lost an excellent companion, whom one could love—indeed had to love, with good reason—as having none of the faults of her sex. She had no capricious moods, and no feminine weakness, but was all goodness and honesty. And because of her virtues she was loved during her lifetime, and mourned by all at her death. Such a loss seems to me worthy of deep feeling, and since the true remedy for all ills is Forgetfulness, daughter of Time, I must without doubt look to her for help. But I find it very hard to separate grief for this loss from the memory of a person whom I must love and cherish as long as I live ..." To this Rubens adds that it would do him good to get away, for everything in his house brings back memories of his beloved wife.

Up to a point, true Stoic dispassion can perhaps be reconciled with the Catholicism which Rubens professed and practiced faithfully, but in no case can it be assimilated to it. Catholicism also knows asceticism, and detachment which renders relative the things of this world, but what is of primary importance is love of one's neighbor, alongside and on the same level as the love of God. Suffering and compassion are certainly not rejected as blameworthy. There is no doubt that Rubens professed the Christian faith: not only was he present every day at the celebration of mass, he was also a member of a fellowship founded by the Jesuits of Antwerp whose purpose was to deepen the devotional life of its members. His religious pictures likewise testify to a fervor inspired by the spirit of the Counter-Reformation. Rubens' Catholicism, however, has given rise to questions on the part of believers as well as unbelievers. Delen wrote that "his Catholic religious works had a pagan, classical resonance," and he wondered whether "this humanist, educated in the pagan school, was not sometimes, in his heart of hearts, skeptical with regard to Catholic dogma." That does not prevent him from going on to assert: "It is certain that he accepted Catholic doctrine unconditionally for his private and public life ... But as a cultured man he is less Christian than pagan."[27]

Stubbe has pronounced judgment even more categorically: "*As an artist*, Rubens was an exemplary pagan, his art provided a new incarnation, the most perfect after that of the classical Renaissance, of the Greek artistic ideal. Rubens was a Catholic but his religion did not influence him at all in his art."[28] Must one conclude that there was a kind of schizophrenia between Rubens' private religious convictions and his art? One may wonder whether this approach to the problem is not too much influenced by "modern" conceptions of Christian religiosity. A searching study of religiosity in the seventeenth century might lead to a better understanding of the symbiosis of Antiquity and Christianity that is so characteristic of Rubens' time.

346

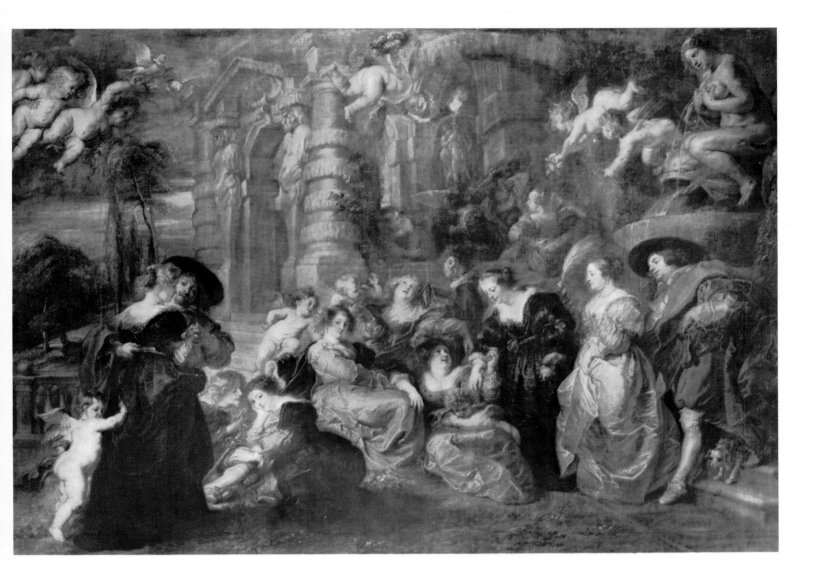

Figure 174
THE GARDEN OF LOVE
Canvas, 6'6" × 9'3½"
Madrid, Prado

*This marvelous picture dates from the beginning of the 1630s, shortly after Rubens' marriage to Helena Fourment.*

*Following page*
Plate 88
HELENA FOURMENT WITH HER EL-
DEST SON, FRANS
Panel, 57" × 40⅛"
Munich, Alte Pinakothek

*Frans was born on July 12, 1633. Nude except for the feathered beret he wears on his head, he is seated on his mother's knee. The age of the child indicates that the picture must have been painted late in 1634 or in 1635.*

Rubens' adherence to Catholicism did not prevent him from evincing a lively interest in other religious and philosophical convictions. With equal curiosity, he tried to obtain the poems of the libertine Théophile Viau, the Remonstrant writings of the Arminians, and books dealing with the movement of the Rosicrucians, and he read the *Mémoires* of the Huguenot theologian Duplessis-Mornay.

Together with his self-control and his sense of the relativity of earthly things, reinforced no doubt by the practice of the Stoic and Christian virtues; and together with his natural affability, so much praised by his contemporaries; there remains to be mentioned another characteristic of Rubens which we have already thought to discern in the self-portraits, namely, the consciousness of his own value. This was not a matter of conceit, but of a self-respect claiming its due rights. Rubens knew his value and wished it to be recognized; this trait is clearly evident in some of his letters. Moreover, it manifests

347

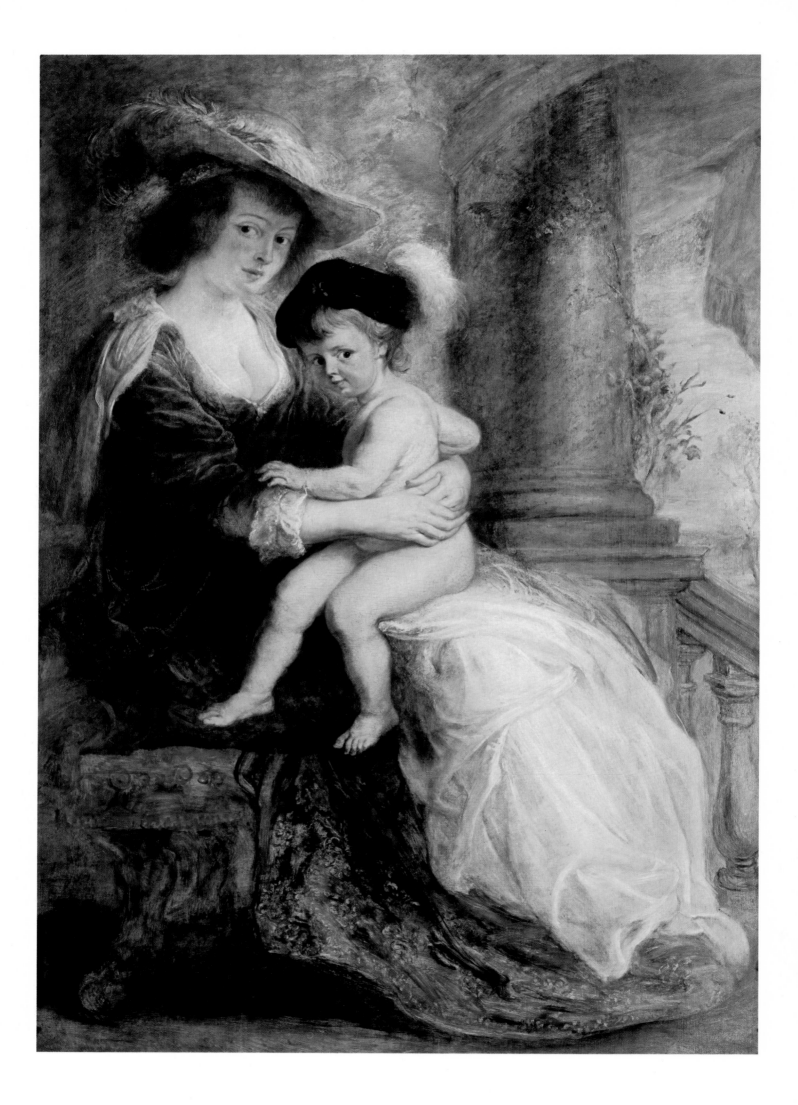

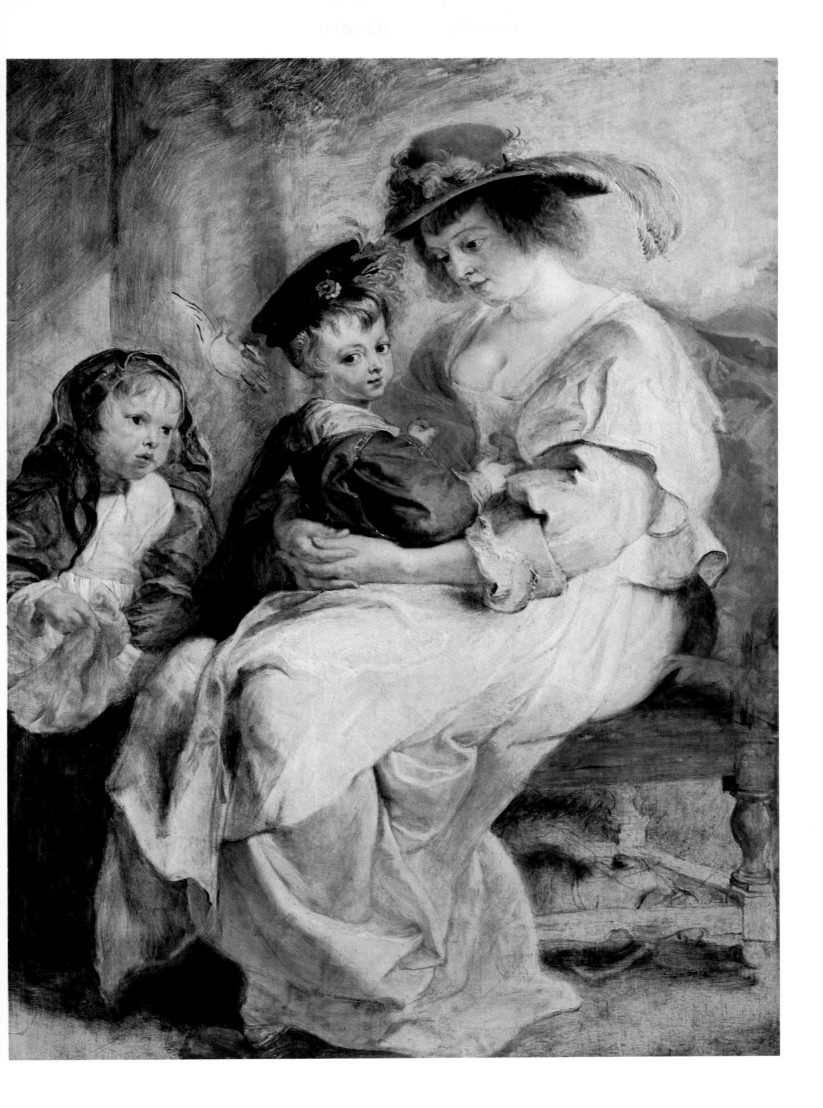

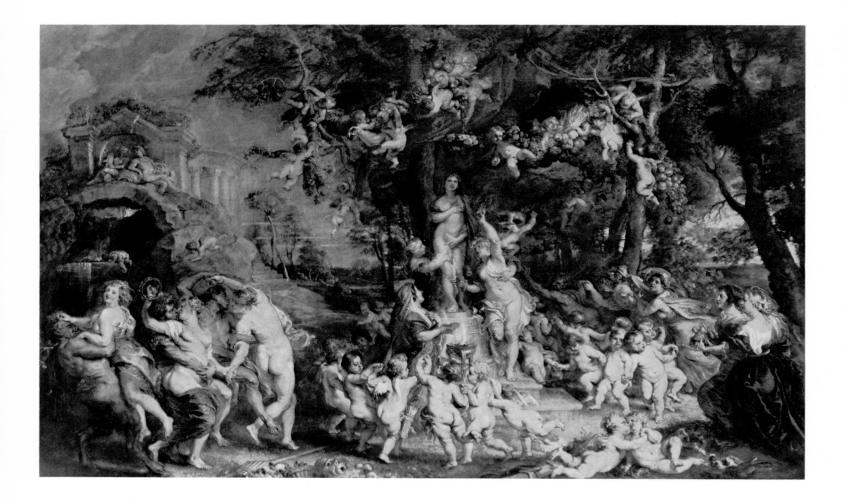

Figure 175
THE FEAST OF VENUS
Canvas, 7'1" × 11'6"
Vienna, Gemäldegalerie, Kunsthistorisches Museum

*Painted about 1630, a multiplicity of motifs drawn from the artist's inexhaustible imagination are ordered into a eurythmically balanced composition of radiant beauty.*

*Preceding page*
Plate 89
HELENA FOURMENT WITH HER CHILDREN
Panel, 44½" × 32¼"
Paris, Louvre

*Little Frans is sitting on his mother's knee and she clasps him around the waist. On the left is the eldest of the Rubens-Fourment children, Clara Johanna, born on January 18, 1632. On the right, half-way up the chair, is faintly sketched the hand of the third child clutching at its mother's dress: this is Isabella Helena, born on May 3, 1635, and doubtless taking her first steps at the time the picture was painted, about 1636. Although unfinished, this work testifies to an almost inconceivable artistry, so complete is its beauty.*

itself comparatively early, already in 1603 when he was twenty-six, in his manner of refusing a commission which he considers beneath his dignity: the duke of Mantua having directed Rubens, who was at that time in his service in Spain, to go to Paris to paint there more portraits of beautiful women for the duke's "Gallery of Beauties," Rubens wrote to Annibale Chieppio, on whom he relied as intermediary, to be exonerated from this task. He tells Chieppio that the duke would save time and money if he entrusted this commission to a painter attached to the French court; that if he obeyed his master's wishes, he would find himself obliged "to waste more time, travel, expenses, salaries (even the munificence of His Highness will not repay all this) upon works unworthy of me, and which anyone can do to the Duke's taste. Nevertheless I submit myself, like a good servant, completely to the decision and to the slightest command of my patron, but I beg him earnestly to employ me, at home or abroad, in works more appropriate to my talent ..."[29]

On another occasion Rubens wrote to an intermediary in the service of the king of England, when the king approached him on the subject of possibly undertaking the painting of frescoes for the ceiling of the Banqueting Hall in Whitehall Palace—an enterprise which was not ac-

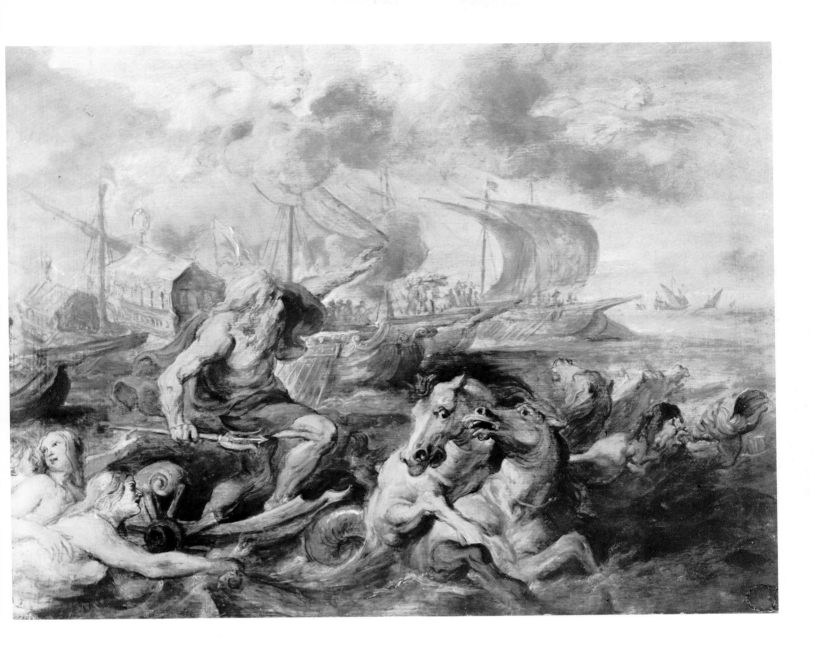

complished until about ten years later——: "... I confess that I am, by
natural instinct, better fitted to execute very large works than small
curiosities [as might have applied to his good friends Adam Elsheimer
and Jan "Velvet" Brueghel]. Everyone according to his gifts; my
talent is such that no undertaking, however vast in size or diversified
in subject, has ever surpassed my courage."[30] This last remark may
seem rather presumptuous, but we must not forget that Rubens wrote
it in 1621, that is, shortly after carrying out successfully a huge commission, the painting of thirty-nine pictures for the ceiling of the church
of the Jesuits in Antwerp; thus it must be accepted that his expression
of his own value was entirely justified. Rubens knew what he was
capable of.

His awareness of his own value also played an important part in
his business relationships. Rubens saw to it that he was well paid

351

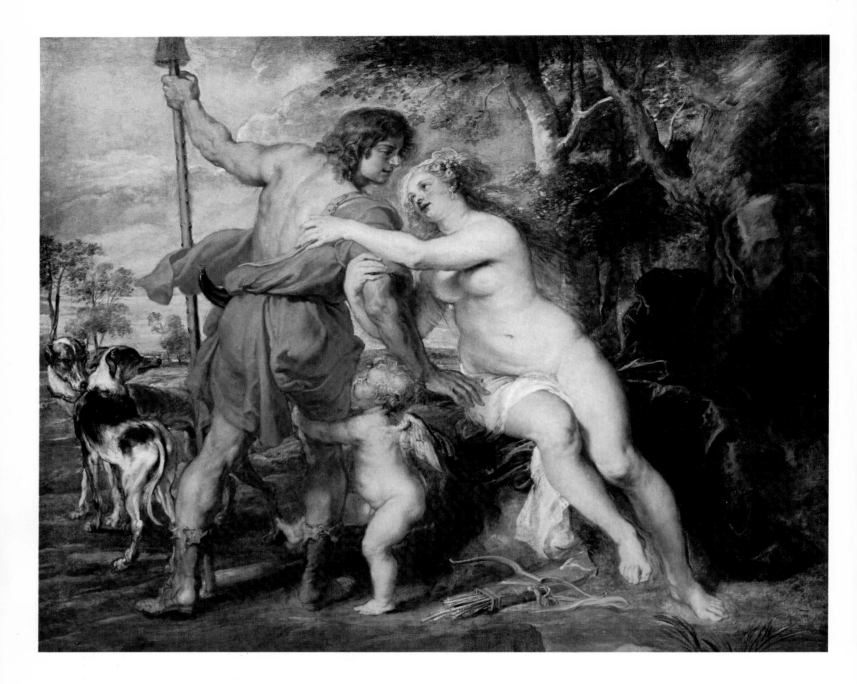

Plate 90
VENUS AND ADONIS
Canvas, 6′5½″ × 7′10½″
New York, The Metropolitan Museum
of Art

*Venus strives to divert Adonis from the
hunting party which will prove fatal to him;
Cupid is helping by holding the hero's
leg. This is a typical work of Rubens' late,
"lyrical" period.*

Figure 177
BELLEROPHON SLAYS CHIMERA
Oil sketch on panel, 15½″ × 10⅝″
Bayonne, Musée Bonnat

*Bellerophon, the national hero of Corinth,
is astride the winged horse Pegasus and he
crushes with his spear the monstrous chimera
spitting flames. Oil sketch for a painting
decorating the back of a triumphal arch
erected in 1635 near the abbey of St.
Michael, for the Entry of the Cardinal-Infante Ferdinand.*

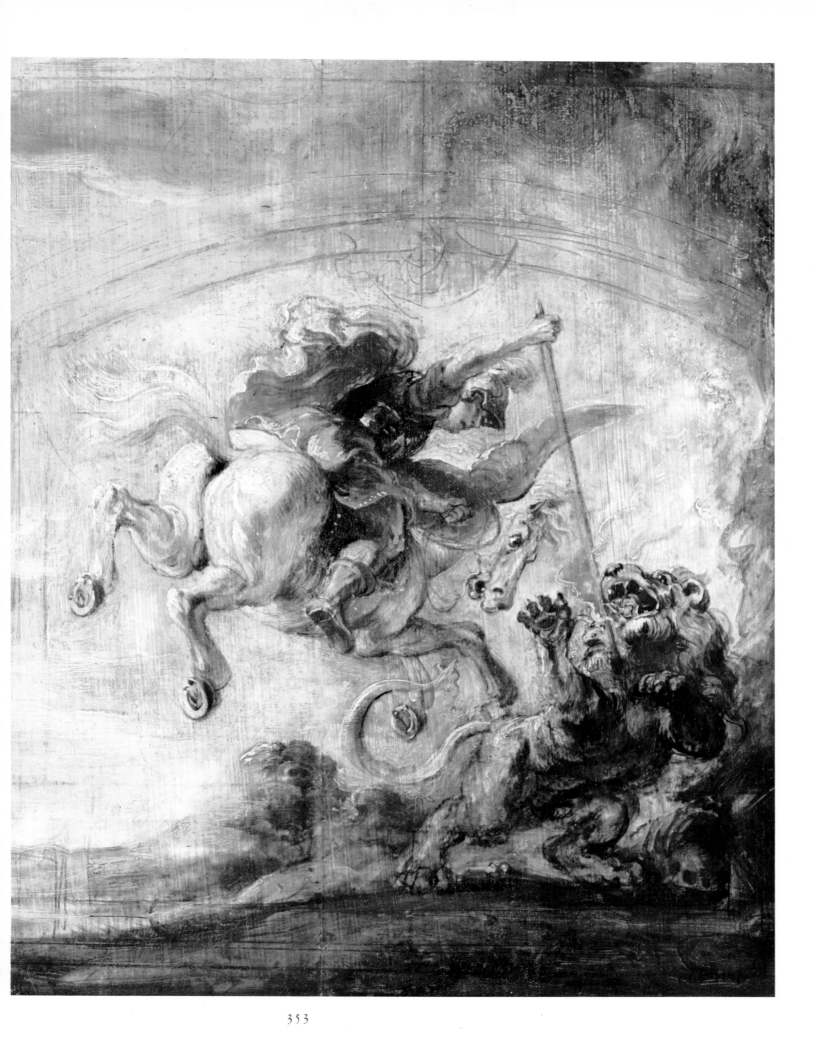

353

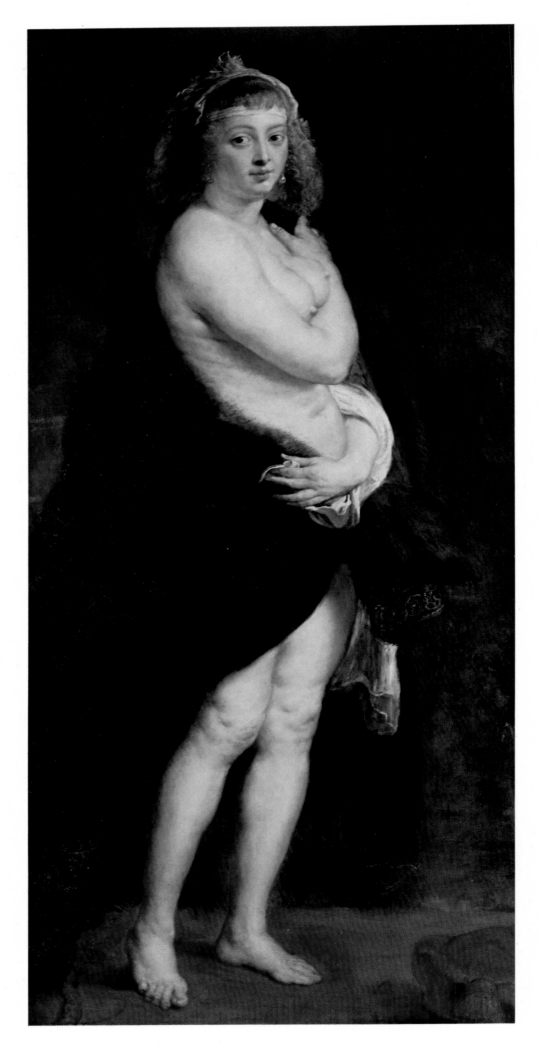

Plate 91
HELENA FOURMENT IN A FUR COAT
Panel, 69″ × 38″

Vienna, Gemäldegalerie, Kunsthistorisches Museum

*When this life-size portrait was executed,
that is to say, about 1638–40, Helena
Fourment was 25 or 26 years old and the
mother of four children. Rubens chose to
paint her in a pose derived from a classical
statue of Venus. The title "Het Pelsken"
(the little fur) was probably given by
Rubens himself, for the picture appeared
under this name in the inventory after his
death; there it is indicated that the artist
bequeathed it to his wife.*

Plate 92
SELF-PORTRAIT
Canvas, 43″ × 32³⁄₄″
Vienna, Gemäldegalerie, Kunsthisto-
risches Museum

*In this self-portrait, painted at the end of
his life, Rubens preserves the bearing of a
man conscious of his own value. His slightly
drawn face, however, and the circles around
the eyes and the somewhat tense appearance
reveal the weakening of his physical
state. Rubens suffered from gout. The
sword he wears is not merely a symbol of
his belonging to the nobility, but also a support for his stiff, tired hand.*

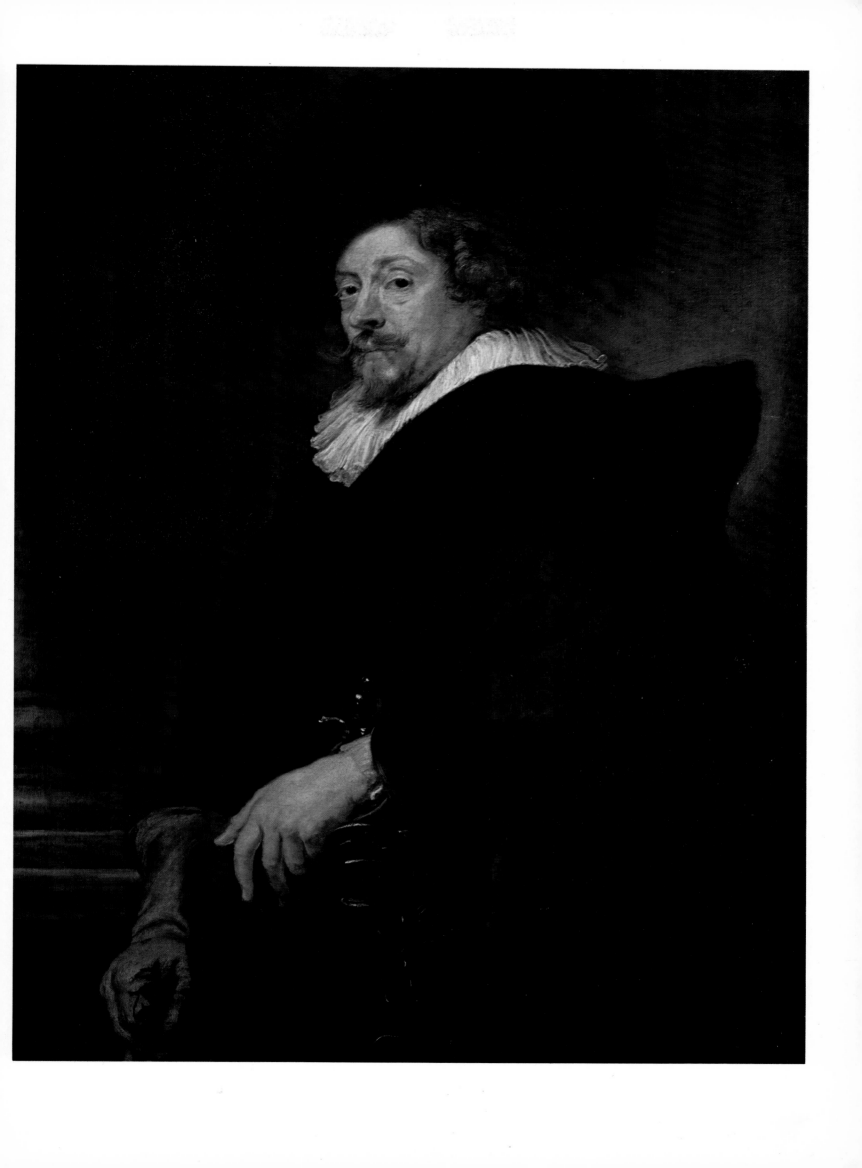

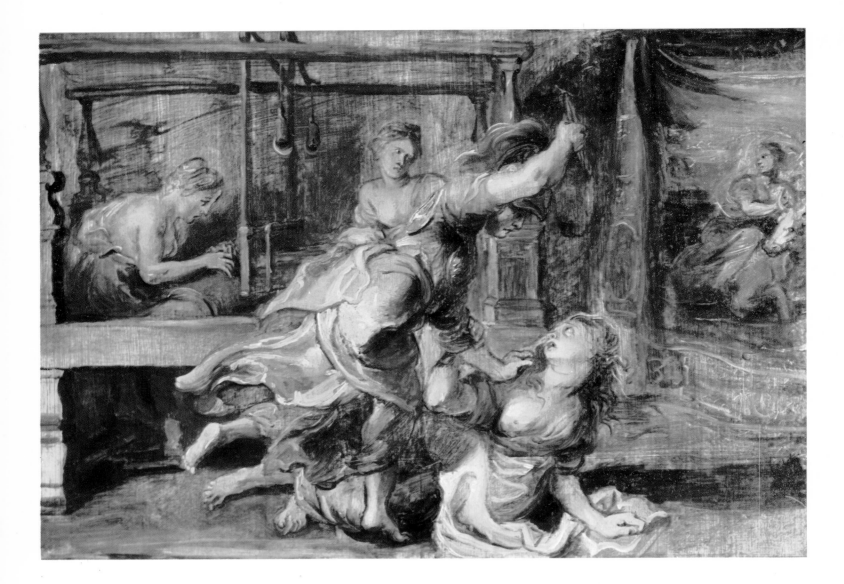

for his work and stood his ground when it was a question of defending his own interests. Among other documents, this appears in his correspondence of the years 1618–19 with Sir Dudley Carleton, the English ambassador in The Hague, who wished to exchange his collection of ancient statues for paintings from Rubens' workshop. In accepting this proposition, the artist wrote: "... I like brief negotiations, where each party gives and receives his share at once"; [31] nevertheless the affair dragged on, and proposals and counterproposals succeeded each other before any exchange took place. From this transaction one can observe with what realistic business sense the artist looked after his own interests, "but not without dignity," as Delen justly pointed out. A short time later another English intermediary sought to negotiate a different exchange with Rubens, and wrote after their meeting: "I did, with all ye discretion I had, deale with him about ye price, but his demands ar like ye lawes of Medes and Persians, which may not be altered." [32]

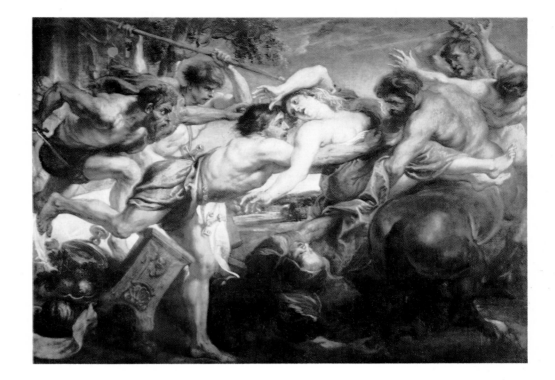

Figure 179
THE ABDUCTION OF HIPPODAMEIA
Canvas, 6′ × 9′6″
Madrid, Prado

*This painting is part of the series of more than sixty large mythological scenes that were painted between 1636 and 1638 for the Torre de la Parada, the hunting lodge of Philip IV near Madrid. Most of the canvases were executed in large format by other Antwerp artists; The Abduction of Hippodameia is one of the rare scenes painted by Rubens' own hand. Along with a number of other canvases, it was sent from Brussels to Madrid on May 11, 1638. The bold dynamism of the inspiration is held in check by the mastery of the composition, from which stems this impression of harmonious beauty.*

It was about this time that Rubens tried to sell a *Lion Hunt* painted by one of his assistants, which he had scarcely retouched, as one by his own hand. He did not succeed, and had to take back the picture in question. Undeniably, it was love of money that was operating; if any mitigating circumstances can be found it was possibly in the nature of the transaction presented by the other party. But no doubt even Rubens had his weakness. On the other hand, his uncontested and rapidly recognized mastery as a painter, his great energy, his realistic business sense, as well as the exemptions from taxes and other obligations which came to him from his position as court painter, all these account for the fortune which made him one of the most well-to-do citizens of Antwerp.

Although Rubens spoke several languages, had the style of an aristocrat, and possessed all the requisite qualities to frequent royal courts with ease, his life from the social point of view was essentially that of a citizen living by the work of his own hands. The relatively small rooms of his house are certainly not comparable to the spacious halls of a palace, but the inner courtyard with its impressive portico and the elegant pavilion in the garden testify in their way to the *grandezza* which would be presentable in a palace (Plate 1; Fig. 8). So much for his aristocratic style. The portico inscriptions mentioned above as well as the decoration of the house bear further witness that its owner was a man imbued with humanism.

As a result of his experiences, while still young, at the court of the Gonzagas in Mantua, Rubens had soon become weary of court

357

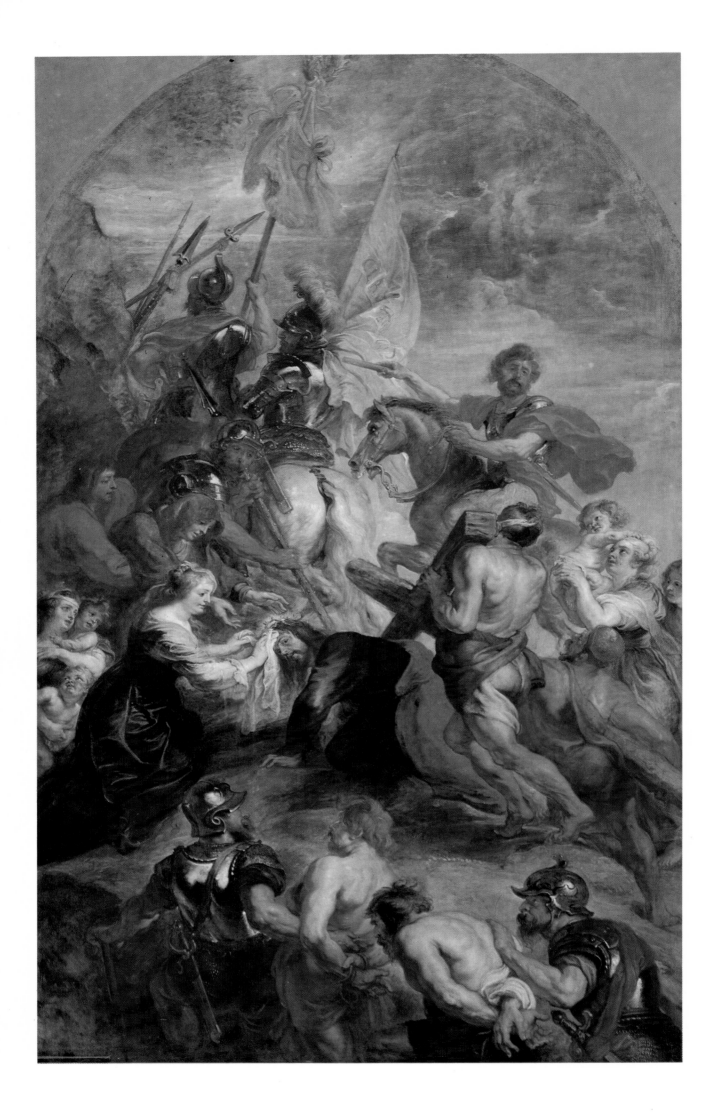

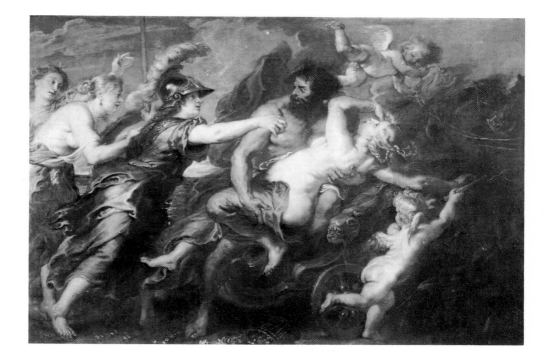

life. When Archduke Albert and the Infanta Isabella wished to appoint him their official court painter, he accepted this honor only on condition that he would not be tied to their entourage, a concession which was granted. By this arrangement, he gained the advantages connected with the said office—exemption from taxes and other civil obligations such as the function of alderman, civil guard, and almonership—without thereby losing any part of his freedom. Later the great royal commissions, as well as his diplomatic activity, led him to renew his contact with a fair number of royal courts, where he sometimes spent long periods of time. But he always yearned to return home as quickly as possible, to be once more completely himself.

Several years after he had retired from diplomacy Rubens wrote to Peiresc that he had had to decide to force himself to turn away from "ambition" in order to regain his freedom. Knowing "that one must leave Fortune while she is still favorable, and not wait until she has turned her back on us," he had asked the Infanta to absolve him from all obligations except those for which he need not leave his house: "This favor I obtained with more difficulty than any other ... Now [he adds], by God's grace, I am leading a quiet life with my wife and children, and have no pretension in the world other than to live in peace."[33]

Rubens was first married in 1609, at the age of thirty-two, to Isabella Brant (Plates 52, 58, 83; Figs. 164, 168). She bore him three children, a daughter who died in infancy and two sons (Plates 4, 39, 95). She died in 1626 at thirty-four years of age, after sharing his life for seven-

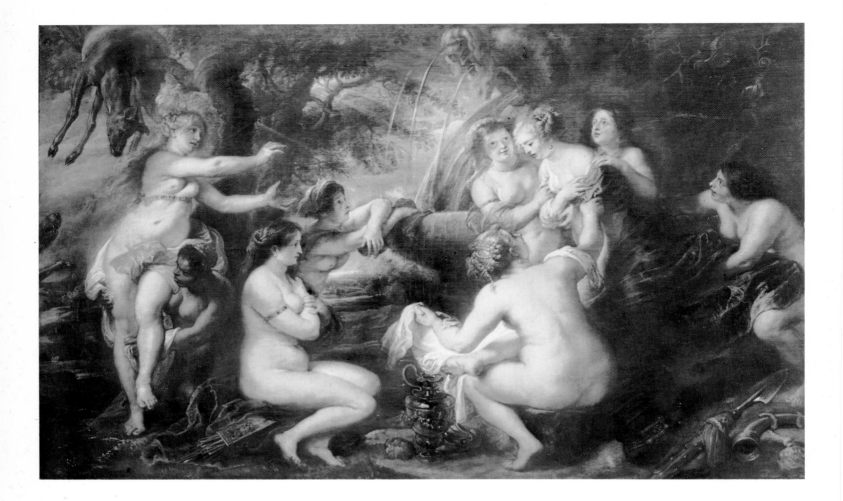

Figure 181
DIANA AND CALLISTO
Canvas, 6'7½" × 10'7"
Madrid, Prado

*In the last ten years of his life, Rubens
paints mythological works which are, so to
speak, hymns to the beauty of woman; the
figures are placed in magnificent landscapes.*

Plate 94
THE THREE GRACES
Panel, 7'3" × 5'11"
Madrid, Prado

*Painted in 1638–40, this picture is one of
the artist's finest representations of the
female nude, inspired by the radiant beauty
of Helena Fourment.*

teen years. The words that Rubens wrote shortly after her death have
already been quoted: one could not help loving her because she was
kind and good. The portraits which Rubens painted of her indeed
show her as a likable woman. She was as beautiful "as the noble
beauty of a warm handshake, of a look expressing gratitude"
(Gilliams). Bright, almond-shaped eyes, arching eyebrows, thin lips
ending in dimples, these features add up to a picture of a lively personality who approached life with a hint of irony.

When she died, in the prime of life, perhaps a victim of the plague,
Rubens wept greatly for her and his Stoicism was powerless against
the grief that took possession of him.

Four years later—two of these divided between Madrid and
London—Rubens remarried, in 1630, at the age of fifty-three, this time
to Helena Fourment, who was still only sixteen (Plates 64, 85, 86,
91; Figs. 169, 170). "I made up my mind to marry again, since I
was not yet inclined to live the abstinent life of the celibate, thinking
that, if we must give the first place to continence, *fruimur licita voluptate
cum gratiarum actione* (we may enjoy licit pleasures with thankfulness). I
have taken a young wife of honest but middle-class family, although
everyone tried to persuade me to make a Court marriage. But I feared

360

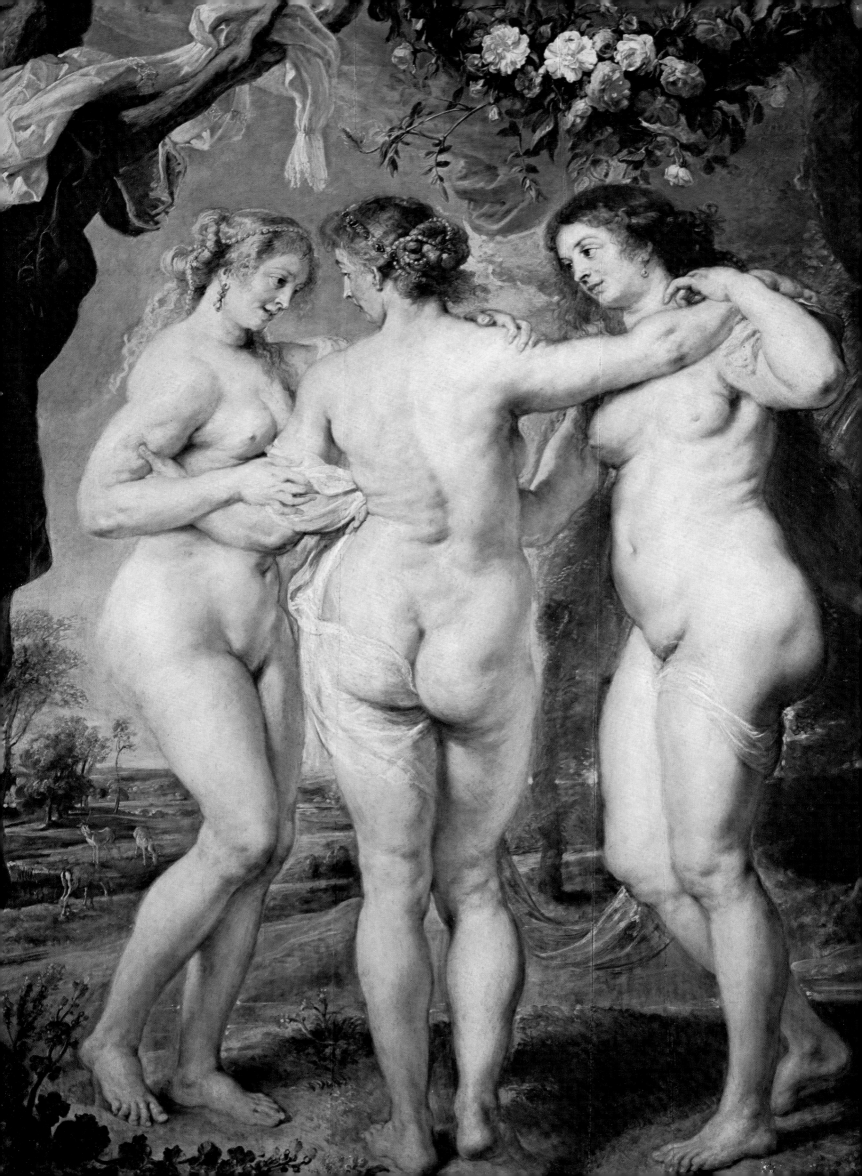

*commune illud nobilitatis malum superbiam praesertim in illo sexu* (pride, that inherent vice of the nobility, particularly in that sex [cf. Sallust, *Jugurtha*, 68]), and that is why I chose one who would not blush to see me take my brushes in hand. And to tell the truth, it would have been hard for me to exchange the priceless treasure of liberty for the embraces of an old woman."[34] Gilliams has observed that a "breath of adoration" could be felt in the portraits of Helena Fourment. "The adornment, the face, the hands, all sing like the music of the hurdy-gurdy and cymbals. And when he painted her with her children, he did not see in her the female-mother who pets and suckles her children, but the woman-child whom one welcomes with cries of admiration." During his last ten years she bore him five children (Plates 88, 89), the fifth born only after the great painter's death.

These two women, each beautiful and attractive but very different in temperament and disposition, both inspired him to paint scenes of earthly and heavenly joy—reflections, without any doubt, of his own love and happiness.

To the outside observer Rubens lived with his family the life of a successful man who devoted himself to his art with great energy, just as others devote themselves totally to business affairs, to their trade or office. But in his art he unveils a universe of stormy emotions, of triumphant exaltation—an inner fire.

Nor was Rubens' great interest in literature and the sciences, his knowledge of people and things, limited to the frontiers of his own country. In his conception of the world he was indeed anything but "middle-class."

In several of his letters he demonstrates his fondness for Antwerp and his native land; in addition, his activity as a diplomat shaping peace tended to strengthen the flowering of his country, *La Fiandra, nostra carissima patria.*[35] But he also wrote: "I consider the whole world my country and I think that I should be welcome everywhere."[36] He rightly called himself a cosmopolitan: he had traveled a great deal, he was aware that through his works his reputation was spreading to practically every capital of Europe, and that he had played a part in European diplomacy.

How should we now present a picture of Rubens' full personality, of which we have, so far, attempted to indicate a few features? To sum up, his contemporaries were struck above all by his sweetness of temper, the unaffectedness of his approach to people, and his natural distinction. They were likewise impressed by his great talent as an artist, his lively and penetrating mind, his competence in the field of classical Antiquity, and his wisdom and skill as a diplomat and "man of the world."

Along with these characteristics, we have observed a great self-mastery which enabled Rubens to curb his exuberant imagination and tame the violent passions of his existence. This natural gift was also reinforced by his vision of the world, influenced by the philosophy of

Stoicism. His great capacity for concentration and the facility with which he applied himself to different tasks are directly connected with this self-control, as is the precision with which he fixed what he saw and what he imagined. Without this precision and these powers of concentration Rubens could never have summoned the energy necessary to produce so many masterpieces. The well-ordered planning of his day and his talent for organization certainly contributed to this astonishing productivity. A justified awareness of his own value can also be read in the features of his face, and verified by certain passages in his letters. It is known that he profited from his artistic superiority and that on at least one occasion he showed greed for gain; Rubens was persevering when it came to defending his own interests. He showed this quality in his diplomatic capacity also.

Altogether, Rubens appears to us as an exceptionally talented man, who balanced with equal success the conflicting elements in his life as in his art. He could be a court painter without for that reason losing his freedom as a man and as an artist. His standard of living appeared to be that of a well-to-do middle-class citizen, but one endowed with an intense inner life that was in no way bourgeois.

In his art he attained a harmony between his exuberant, dramatic imagination and the energetic intelligence which he used to temper this impetuosity into measured composition. Passionate ardor and command of execution are the two inseparable components of this triumphant harmony.

At the beginning of this chapter we posed the following question: does his personality account for his incomparable creativity, for the peaks he attained as well as his astonishing productivity? We believe that it does, that this is true to some extent. His qualities of character as well as his mode of life can explain this productivity. His ideas, his vision of the world, and the general sensibilities of his epoch can account for his choosing certain subjects and for the way in which he interprets them. It is also possible, although this goes beyond the aim of our present work, to follow the different stages of his development step by step; to establish the tradition to which he was originally linked and what he learned from other artists and applied in his own works; and finally, to determine the solutions that he found on his own to give form to his vision. But does this enable us to elucidate the essence of his style, the undeniable and peculiarly individual stamp of his artistic personality?

In posing this question, we approach the limits of what can be explained. Beyond them lies the impenetrable mystery of Rubens' genius.

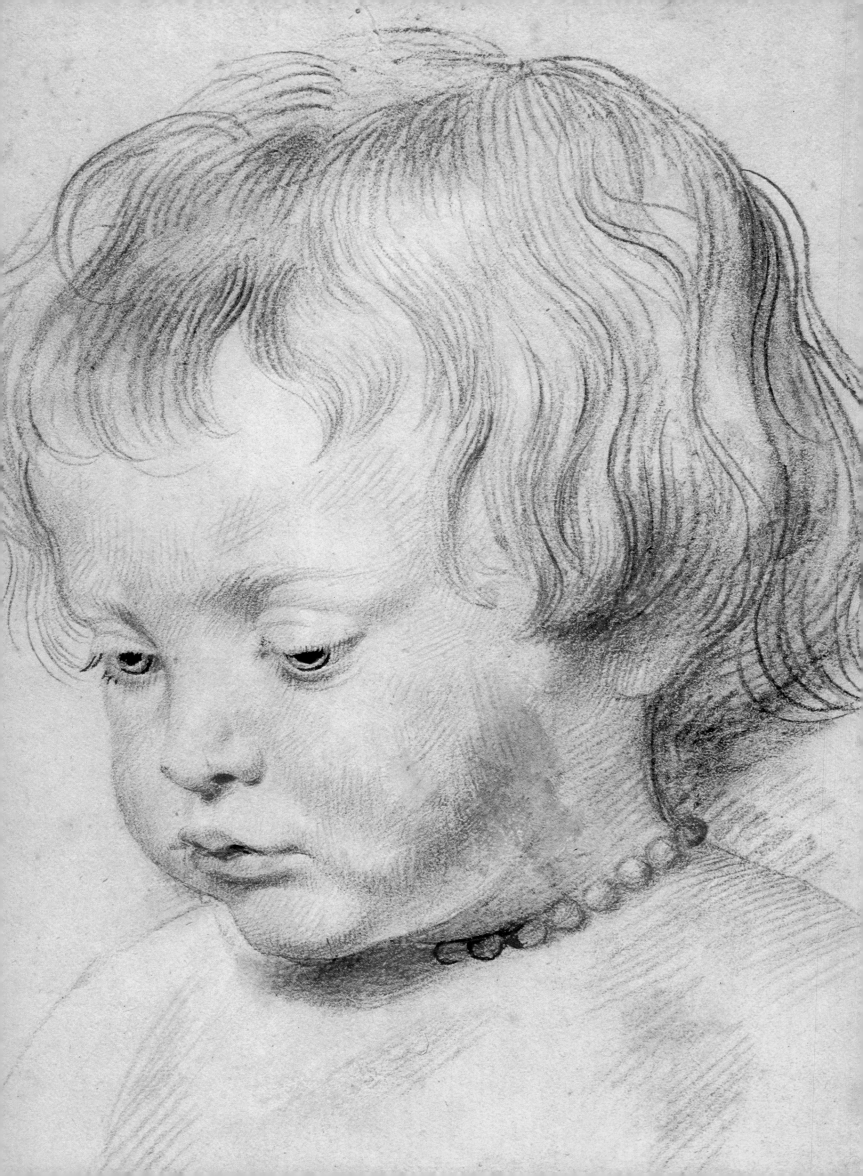

# Notes

## Abbreviations

BURCHARD-D'HULST: LUDWIG BURCHARD and ROGER-ADOLF D'HULST, *Rubens Drawings,* I–II, Brussels, 1963.

DE MAEYER: MARCEL DE MAEYER, *Albrecht en Isabella en de Schilderkunst,* Brussels, 1955.

GACHARD: LOUIS PROSPER GACHARD, *Histoire politique et diplomatique de Rubens,* Brussels, 1877.

GLÜCK-HABERDITZL: GUSTAV GLÜCK and FRANZ MARTIN HABERDITZL, *Die Handzeichnungen von Peter Paul Rubens,* Berlin, 1928.

HELD: JULIUS S. HELD, *Rubens, Selected Drawings,* I–II, London, 1959.

LEYSSENS: ISIDORE LEYSSENS, "Hans van Mildert," *Gentsche Bijdragen tot de Kunstgeschiedenis,* VII, 1941, pp. 73–136.

MARTIN: JOHN RUPERT MARTIN, *The Ceiling Paintings for the Jesuit Church in Antwerp (Corpus Rubenianum Ludwig Burchard,* I), Brussels, 1968.

OLDENBOURG: RUDOLF OLDENBOURG, *P.P. Rubens, Des Meisters Gemälde (Klassiker der Kunst,* V), 4th ed., Stuttgart-Berlin, 1921.

PONCELET: ALFRED PONCELET, *Histoire de la Compagnie de Jésus dans les anciens Pays-Bas,* I–II, Brussels, 1927.

PRIMS: FLORIS PRIMS and others, *Rubens en zijne Eeuw,* Antwerp, 1927.

ROMBOUTS-VAN LERIUS: PHILIPPE ROMBOUTS and THÉODORE VAN LERIUS, *De Liggeren,* I–II, Antwerp, 1872.

ROOSES: MAX ROOSES, *L'Oeuvre de P.P. Rubens, histoire et description de ses tableaux et dessins,* I–V, Antwerp, 1886–92.

ROOSES, *Leven:* MAX ROOSES, *Rubens' Leven en Werken,* Amsterdam-Antwerp-Ghent, 1903.

ROOSES-RUELENS: MAX ROOSES and CHARLES RUELENS, *Correspondance de Rubens et documents épistolaires concernant sa vie et ses oeuvres,* I–VI, Antwerp, 1887–1909.

ROSENBERG: ADOLF ROSENBERG, *P. P. Rubens, Des Meisters Gemälde (Klassiker der Kunst,* V), 1st ed., Stuttgart-Leipzig, 1906.

VAN DEN BRANDEN: FRANZ JOSEF VAN DEN BRANDEN, *Geschiedenis der Antwerpse Schilderschool,* Antwerp, 1883.

VLIEGHE: HANS VLIEGHE, *Saints,* I–II (*Corpus Rubenianum Ludwig Burchard,* VIII), Brussels, 1972–73.

*Nicolaas Rubens, born in 1618, is here 2 or 3 years of age. Rubens made several drawings of this child of his first marriage and used them repeatedly in his pictures.*

## 1. The Portraits of Rubens' Grandparents

First published in *Antwerpen,* XI, 1965, pp. 12–25.

1. Panel, each 22½" × 15" (57 × 38 cm); Inv. no. S. 156/1 and S. 156/2.

2. F. DE JONGHE D'ARDOYE and L. ROBYNS DE SCHNEIDAUER, "Une curieuse découverte. Les portraits (datés 1530 et armoriés) de Barthélémy Rubens et de son épouse Barbe Arents dit Spierinck, grands-parents paternels de Pierre-Paul Rubens," *Revue belge d'archéologie et d'histoire de l'art,* XXXVIII, 1959, pp. 175–203 (published in 1961); M. J. FRIEDLÄNDER, *Early Netherlandish Painting,* Leyden-Brussels, 1975, p. 142.

3. See note 2.

4. F. VERACHTER, *Généalogie de Pierre-Paul Rubens et de sa famille,* Antwerp, 1840, p. 10. It should be noted in passing that the patronymic of Bartholomeus Rubens is usually spelled with two b's in the documents of his time.

5. F. VERACHTER, *op. cit.,* pp. 10, 32, 33, docs. XII, XIII.

6. F. VERACHTER, *op. cit.,* p. 10; P. GÉNARD, "De Kwartieren van P.P. Rubens," *Rubens-Bulletijn,* IV, 1896, p. 144.

7. F. VERACHTER, *op. cit.,* pp. 10, 32–34, docs. XI, XV; P. GÉNARD, *op. cit.,* pp. 144, 145.

8. F. VERACHTER, *op. cit.,* p. 10; P. GÉNARD, *op. cit.,* p. 146.

9. F. VERACHTER, *op. cit.,* p. 34, doc. XVI.

10. F. VERACHTER, *op. cit.,* p. 10; P. GÉNARD, *op. cit.,* pp. 146–48; but especially F. DE JONGHE D'ARDOYE and L. ROBYNS DE SCHNEIDAUER, *op. cit.,* pp. 196, 197.

11. F. VERACHTER, *op. cit.,* p. 10.

12. F. DE JONGHE D'ARDOYE and L. ROBYNS DE SCHNEIDAUER, *op. cit.,* pp. 191, 197.

13. F. VERACHTER, *op. cit.,* p. 32, doc. XIII; P. GÉNARD, *op. cit.,* p. 145.

14. F. VERACHTER, *op. cit.,* p. 35, doc. XVIII.

15. E. SERGYSELS, *Chronycke der Antwerpsche Apothecarissen, 1422–1835,* Antwerp, 1935, pp. 3–12. This study is mainly based on older publications such as E. GEUDENS, *Het Hoofdambacht der Meerseniers,* I–IV, Antwerp, 1891–1904, and C. BROECKX, *Histoire du Collegium Medicum Antverpiense,* Antwerp, 1858.

16. E. SERGYSELS, *op. cit.,* p. 4.

17. E. SERGYSELS, *op. cit.,* p. 6.

18. E. GEUDENS, *op. cit.,* III, Antwerp, 1903, p. 19.

19. E. SERGYSELS, *op. cit.,* pp. 10, 11. For the complete text of the decree, see C. BROECKX, *op. cit.,* pp. 10–13.

20. F. DE JONGHE D'ARDOYE and L. ROBYNS DE SCHNEIDAUER, *op. cit.,* p. 196.

21. M. J. FRIEDLÄNDER, "Neues über Jacob van Utrecht," *Oud-Holland*, LVIII, 1941, pp. 7, 8, nos. 17 and 18. The facts which follow were taken mainly from this article (pp. 6–17); those in connection with the artist's stay in Lübeck were taken from J. J. DE MESQUITA, "Nog meer nieuw werk van Jacob van Utrecht," *Oud-Holland*, LVIII, 1941, pp. 59–75 and 135–47.

22. M. J. FRIEDLÄNDER, *op. cit.*, p. 15.

23. M. J. FRIEDLÄNDER, *op. cit.*, p. 8.

24. For this information, as well as for that derived from the sale catalogue of 1913, we are indebted to the Rijksbureau voor Kunsthistorische Documentatie in The Hague, where the documentation bequeathed by M. J. FRIEDLÄNDER is housed.

25. F. VERACHTER, *op. cit.*, p. 7.

26. This was communicated to us by Mr. Foster of Wildenstein & Co. in London. This restoration was done for the exhibition *Fleurs et Jardins dans l'Art Flamand*, Musée des Beaux-Arts, Ghent, 1960, nos. 150, 151. Previously the portraits had been displayed in the following exhibitions: *Five Centuries of European Painting*, Los Angeles, 1933, no. 11; *Paintings by Rembrandt and Others*, Wildenstein & Co., London, 1959, no. 26. They were mentioned by G. MARLIER (*Die Weltkunst*, May 15, 1960, p. 13) and A. BURY (*The Connoisseur*, May 1961, p. 207, ill.).

## 2. An Early Work, *Adam and Eve in Paradise*, and the Relationship of Rubens and Otto van Veen

First published in *Antwerpen*, XIV, 1968, pp. 45–61.

1. Panel, 71″ × 62¼″ (180 × 158 cm); Inv. no. S. 164.

2. For more detailed information on Otto van Veen, see P. VISSCHERS, *Iets over Jacob Jonghelinck, metaalgieter en penningsnijder, Octavio van Veen, schilder, in de XVIde eeuw; en de gebroeders Collijns de Nole, beeldhouwers, in de XVde, XVIde en XVIIde eeuw*, Antwerp, 1853, pp. 15–50; F.M. HABERDITZL, "Die Lehrer des Rubens," *Jahrbuch der Kunsthistorischen Sammlungen des allerhöchsten Kaiserhauses*, XXVII, 1908, pp. 191–235; J. MÜLLER HOFSTEDE, "Zum Werke des Otto van Veen 1590–1600," *Bulletin des Musées Royaux des Beaux-Arts*, VI, 1957, pp. 127–74; I. GERARDS-NELISSEN, "Otto van Veen's Emblemata Horatiana," *Simiolus*, V, 1971, pp. 20–63; L. VAN LOOVEREN, "'Venationum novum Archetypa,' negen allegorische jachttaferelen door Otto van Veen," in *Bijdragen tot de Geschiedenis van de Grafische Kunst, opgedragen aan Prof. Dr. Louis Lebeer, ter gelegenheid van zijn tachtigste verjaardag*, Antwerp, 1975, pp. 151–75.

3. See J. PURAYE, *Dominique Lampson, humaniste, 1532–1599*, Bruges–Paris, 1950.

4. "Ego de te Veni idem dico te primum in nostro Orbe qui litteras liberaliores cum hac arte iunxisti" (J. VAN DEN GHEYN, *Album Amicorum de Otto Venius*, Brussels, 1911, p. 47).

5. R. DE PILES, *Conversations sur la Connaissance de la Peinture, et sur le Jugement qu'on doit faire des tableaux. Où par occasion il est parlé de la vie de Rubens, et de quelques-uns de ses plus beaux Ouvrages*, Paris, 1677, p. 185. For more detailed information on Roger de Piles, see B. TEYSSÈDRE, *Roger de Piles et les débats sur le coloris au siècle de Louis XIV*, Paris, 1957.

6. "La mesme inclination qu'ils avoient tous deux pour les lettres, les ayant liéz d'amitié, ce Maistre n'oublia rien de ce qu'il sçavoit pour en faire part à son Disciple, il luy découvrit librement tous les secrets de son Art, & luy apprit sur tout à disposer les Figures, & à distribuer les lumieres avantageusement. Enfin l'ayant fort avancé en peu de temps, & la répu-

tation de cet illustre Disciple estant venue à tel point, qu'on doutoit lequel estoit le plus habile de luy ou de son Maistre; Rubens prit resolution de passer en Italie . . ." (R. DE PILES, *op. cit.*, p. 185).

7. "Amicus quidem meus Petrus Paulus Rubenius, in quo utrum commendem magis nescio, pingendi ne artificium, ad cujus ipse summam, si aetatis hujus quisquam pervenisse intelligentibus videtur, an omnis humanioris litteraturae peritiam politumque judicium cum singulari sermonis et convictus suavitate conjunctum" (G. SCIOPPIUS, *Hyperbolimaeus*, Mainz, 1607, p. 110; quoted by C. RUELENS, "Un témoignage relatif à P. P. Rubens en Italie," *Rubens-Bulletijn*, IV, 1896, p. 115, and by ROOSES-RUELENS, II, p. 4).

8. "Avant son voyage d'Italie, ils avoient quelque ressemblance avec ceux d'Octave van Veen, son maistre" (extract from a letter to Roger de Piles, written in 1676; see C. RUELENS, "La vie de Rubens, par Roger de Piles," *Rubens-Bulletijn*, II, 1883, p. 166).

9. VAN DEN BRANDEN, p. 409.

10. C. NORRIS, "Rubens Before Italy," *The Burlington Magazine*, LXXVI, 1940, p. 193, pl. II B.

11. See J. MÜLLER HOFSTEDE, "Zur Antwerpener Frühzeit von Peter Paul Rubens," *Münchner Jahrbuch der bildenden Kunst*, XIII, 1962, pp. 179–216; *Idem*, "Zur frühen Bildnismalerei von Peter Paul Rubens," *Pantheon*, XX, 1962, pp. 279–90.

12. M. JAFFÉ, "Rubens and Raphael," in *Studies in Renaissance and Baroque Art Presented to Anthony Blunt*, London, 1967, p. 98; I. Q. VAN REGTEREN ALTENA, "Het vroegste Werk van Rubens," *Mededelingen van de Koninklijke Vlaamse Academie voor Wetenschappen, Letteren en Schone Kunsten, Klasse der Schone Kunsten*, XXXIV, 1972, no. 2, Brussels, 1972, p. 5, ill. 7; J. Müller Hofstede also attributes the work to Rubens (written communication).

13. A. BARTSCH, *Le peintre graveur*, XIV, Leipzig, 1867, p. 3, no. 1.

14. All of them associated the name of Rubens with Homer. Eugène Delacroix calls Rubens "this Homer of painting" (A. JOUBIN, *Journal de Eugène Delacroix*, II, Paris, 1900, p. 95); Jacob Burckhardt writes: "die beiden grössten Erzähler, welche unser Erdball bis heute getragen hat, Homer und Rubens" (J. BURCKHARDT, *Erinnerungen aus Rubens*, Vienna, 1938, p. 193; 1st ed., Basle, 1898).

15. In a manuscript report dated February 17, 1967.

16. K. A. KNAPPE, *Dürer, das graphische Werk*, Vienna–Munich, 1964, pl. 43. In this print, also, a parrot is represented.

17. Our thanks are due to Mr. J. Carpentier, director of the bird section of the Antwerp Zoological Garden, who helped us to identify the birds in this picture.

18. G. DE TERVARENT, *Attributs et symboles dans l'art profane 1450–1600*, II, Geneva, 1959, cols. 231, 241, 242.

19. G. DE TERVARENT, *op. cit.*, II, cols. 352–55, with reference to H. W. JANSON, *Apes and Ape Lore in the Middle Ages and the Renaissance*, London, 1952.

20. G. DE TERVARENT, *op. cit.*, II, cols. 303, 304.

21. G. DE TERVARENT, *op. cit.*, I, Geneva, 1958, cols. 97, 98.

22. R. OLDENBOURG, "Beiträge zu Rubens als Bildnismaler," in *Peter Paul Rubens*, Munich, 1922, pp. 136, 137, fig. 78; J.-A. GORIS and J. S. HELD, *Rubens in America*, New York–Antwerp, 1947, p. 29, no. 19, pl. 1; [*Exh. Cat.*] *Le Siècle de Rubens*, Musées Royaux des Beaux-Arts de Belgique, Brussels, 1965, no. 205, ill.

23. We are indebted to Mr. F. Van den Heuvel, inspector of parks in Antwerp, for his help in the identification of plants.

24. F. BAUDOUIN, "Deux tableaux de Rubens de la collection de la reine Christine: 'Hercule et Omphale' et 'La Mort d'Adonis,'" in *Queen Christina of Sweden. Documents and Studies* (*Analecta Reginensia*, I), Stockholm, 1966, pp. 20–32, fig. 1.

25. OLDENBOURG, p. 1; M. DE MAEYER, "Rubens en de altaar-

stukken in het hospitaal te Grasse," *Gentse Bijdrage tot de Kunstgeschiedenis,* XIV, 1953, pp. 75–87.

26. M. JAFFÉ, *op. cit.,* p. 100.

27. We find it again in the top right corner of *The Glorification of the Holy Eucharist* in St. Paul's Church in Antwerp. (fig. 36). This picture was executed in 1609, shortly after his return from Italy.

28. J. NEUMANN, "Z Mladých let Petra Pavla Rubense. Shromázdeni olympských bohu (Aus den jungen Jahren des Peter Paul Rubens. Die Versammlung der Olympischen Götter)," *Umeni,* XIII, 1965, pp. 547–606; J. NEUMANN, *La galerie de tableaux du château de Prague,* Prague, 1967, pp. 242–50, no. 54; I. Q. VAN REGTEREN ALTENA, *op. cit.,* p. 8, fig. 12.

29. F. M. HABERDITZL, *op. cit.,* p. 202, pl. 32; J. MÜLLER HOFSTEDE, *op. cit.,* pp. 127–30, pl. 1.

30. F. M. HABERDITZL, *op. cit.,* pp. 206, 207, pl. 35.

31. F. M. HABERDITZL, *op. cit.,* p. 220, pl. 48.

32. F. M. HABERDITZL, *op. cit.,* p. 208, pl. 38; J. MÜLLER HOFSTEDE, *op. cit.,* pp. 142–51, fig. 11.

33. F. BAUDOUIN, *op. cit.,* p. 28, pl. 5.

34. Canvas, 9'5 1/2" × 6'8 1/2" (283 × 200 cm). Signed and dated *P. P. Rubens fecit 16(03?).* M. DIAZ PADRON, *Museo del Prado. Catálogo de Pinturas,* I: *Escuola Flamenca Siglo XVII,* Madrid, 1975, pp. 311–13, no. 3137, fig. 198.

35. P. VISSCHERS, *op. cit.,* pp. 30, 31; F. M. HABERDITZL, *op. cit.,* p. 206.

36. F. J. VAN DEN BRANDEN, *op. cit.,* p. 407; F. M. HABERDITZL, *op. cit.,* p. 220.

37. In fact, on September 21 and 24, a large number of pictures which had come from the Town Hall in Antwerp were put up for auction. Among them was the one "that is thought to be the altarpiece of the former altar of the chapel of the said college" ("hetwelk men denkt het autaerstuk van den ouden autaer der capelle in voorseide collegie geweest te zijn"; J. F. and J. B. VAN DER STRAELEN, *De Kronijk van Antwerpen 1770–1817,* VII, Antwerp, 1935, p. 102). See also F. PRIMS, "De plundering van het Stadhuis," *Antwerpiensia,* IX, 1935, p. 251. My attention was drawn to this by Dr. C. Van de Velde.

38. P. VISSCHERS, *op. cit.,* pp. 38 ff.; F. M. HABERDITZL, *op. cit.,* p. 220, pl. 46.

39. F. M. HABERDITZL, *op. cit.,* p. 207, pl. 37; E. DHANENS, *Sint-Baafs-kathedraal Gent (Inventaris van het Kunstpatrimonium van Oost-Vlaanderen,* V), Ghent, 1965, p. 204, no. 454, pl. 190.

40. See C. RUELENS on the conjugal tribulations of Philip Rubens, "Le mariage des frères Rubens," *Rubens-Bulletijn,* III, 1888, pp. 145–88, in which is printed a letter of December 11, 1608, from Guillielmus Verwilt in Antwerp to Jacob de Bie in Brussels, announcing the arrival of Rubens' brother ("dat den scilder comen is Rubbens broeder"; p. 186).

41. See Chapter 14.

42. DE MAEYER, *op. cit.,* pp. 293, 294.

43. F. PRIMS, "Rubens in de Kloosterstraat," *Antwerpiensia,* I, 1927, p. 21.

44. A. J. J. DELEN, *Het huis van Pieter Pauwel Rubens. Wat het was, wat het werd, wat het worden kan,* Brussels, 1933; A. J. J. DELEN, *Het huis van P. P. Rubens. De invloed van Rubens op de Vlaamsche barokarchitectuur,* Diest, 1940.

45. See Chapter 3.

46. DE MAEYER, pp. 68, 69.

47. "Intendo chel Sigr Ottavio Veen suo Fratello ha messo in stampa un operetta Anonima della Teoria universale o simil cosa, il quale io desidererei summamente di vedere e se V.S. fosse servita di communicarmelà dovendo lei senza dubbio haver un essemplare io lhaverei sum caro et l'accettarei sotto parola di huomo da bene di tenere questo suo favore secretissimo senza parlarne con huomo vivente se cosi e necessario" (ROOSES–RUELENS, II, pp. 444, 445). This letter is preserved in the Rubens House in Antwerp (inv. no. D. 28; F. BAUDOUIN, "Recente aanwinsten van het Rubenshuis," II, *Antwerpen,* XI, 1965, pp. 66, 67).

48. "P. P. Rubenium urbis nostrae, paene dixeram Orbis Apellem discipulum habuit" (quoted by F. M. HABERDITZL, *op. cit.,* p. 191).

## 3. Altarpieces from the Period 1609 to 1620

1. The reader will find an outline of the economic situation in J. A. VAN HOUTTE, *Economische en Sociale Geschiedenis van de Lage Landen,* Zeist, 1964, pp. 137 ff.

2. Quoted by F. PRIMS, "Rubens' Antwerpen, Geschiedkundig en economisch geschetst," in *Rubens en zijne Eeuw,* p. 18.

3. F. PRIMS, *op. cit.,* pp. 19, 20; F. PRIMS, "Altaarstudiën," *Antwerpiensia,* XII, 1938, pp. 286–339, and *Antwerpiensia,* XIII, 1939, pp. 300–447. This last-mentioned work tells us that certain guilds and trades, which had had a new altar built shortly after 1585 to replace the former one that was destroyed or damaged in the troubled times, had yet another new one built after 1610, more in keeping with the artistic conceptions of the time. The same thing was to happen in the second half of the 17th century.

4. "... je confesse d'estre par un instinct naturel plus propre à faire des ouvrages bien grandes que des petites curiositez" (ROOSES–RUELENS, II, p. 286).

5. A. MONBALLIEU, "P. P. Rubens en het 'Nachtmael' voor St.-Winoksbergen (1611), een niet uitgevoerd schilderij van de meester," *Jaarboek Koninklijk Museum voor Schone Kunsten Antwerpen,* 1965, pp. 183–205.

6. A. MONBALLIEU, *op. cit.,* pp. 195, 196, doc. 2.

7. ROOSES, I, p. 273; II, pp. 273–75, no. 441; OLDENBOURG, p. 23; a more recent work, which takes account of new documents: M. JAFFÉ, "Peter Paul Rubens and the Oratorian Fathers," *Proporzioni,* IV, 1963, pp. 209–41; and, with additions and corrections: G. INCISA DELLA ROCCHETTA, "Documenti editi e inediti sui Quadri del Rubens nella Chiesa Nuova," *Atti della Pontificia Accademia Romana di Archeologia,* III, *Rendiconti,* XXXV, 1963, pp. 161–83. See also J. MÜLLER HOFSTEDE, "Rubens' first bozzetto for Sta. Maria in Vallicella," *The Burlington Magazine,* CVI, 1964, pp. 442–50 and, by the same author, "Zu Rubens' zweitem Altarwerk für Sta. Maria in Vallicella," *Nederlands Kunsthistorisch Jaarboek,* XVII, 1966, pp. 1–78.

8. F. SWEERTIUS, *Monumenta Sepulchralia et inscriptiones publicae privataeq. Ducatus Brabantiae,* Antwerp, 1613, pp. 143, 144; quoted by A. MONBALLIEU, *op. cit.,* pp. 186, 187.

9. For a recent survey of these contemporaries of Rubens, see H. GERSON and E. H. TER KUILE, *Art and Architecture in Belgium 1600 to 1800,* Harmondsworth, 1960.

10. ROOSES, I, pp. 203–7, no. 157; OLDENBOURG, p. 26; C. NORRIS, "Rubens' Adoration of the Kings of 1609," *Nederlands Kunsthistorisch Jaarboek,* XIV, 1963, pp. 129–136; M. DÍAZ PADRÓN, *Museo del Prado, Catálogo de Pinturas,* I: *Escuela Flamenca Siglo XVII,* Madrid, 1975, pp. 226–29, no. 1638, fig. 163. Already in 1612 the picture was presented by the magistrates to Don Rodrigo Calderon, Conde d'Oliva; from 1623 on, it was part of the king of Spain's collection. During his stay in Madrid in 1629–30, Rubens enlarged the canvas and partly reworked it.

11. H. G. EVERS (*Peter Paul Rubens,* Munich, 1942, pp. 67, 486, no. 66), referring to *Antwerpsch Archievenblad,* VI, n.d., pp. 260, 300 ff.

12. "Boven aen den Muur, *nevens den autaer van den roosen crans,* hangt een fraye schilderye, synde eenen *kersnacht* ofte Christi Geboorte, door P. P. Rubens geschildert, seer Capitael en Schoon geordonneert. De Belden syn meer als Levens groo-

te" (J. DE WIT, *De kerken van Antwerpen,* ed. by J. de Bos-schere (*Uitgaven der Antwerpse Bibliophilen,* no. 25), Antwerp-The Hague, 1910, p. 58.

13. See J. DE WIT, *op. cit.,* p. 58.

14. L. VAN PUYVELDE, "Rubens' Aanbidding door de Herders te Antwerpen," *Jaarboek van het Koninklijk Museum voor Schone Kunsten te Antwerpen,* 1942–47, pp. 83–87.

15. "In San Domenico nell'altare del Sacramento li quattro Dottori che parlano del Divino pane" (G. P. BELLORI, *Le Vite de' Pittori, Scultori et Architetti Moderni,* Rome, 1672, p. 223).

16. ROMBOUTS-VAN LERIUS, I, p. 402, n. 1; ROOSES, II, pp. 196–99, no. 376; VLIEGHE, I, no. 56, fig. 90.

17. This emerges from the fact that Van der Geest paid, on behalf of the Brotherhood, the balance of the sum still owed to Hans van Mildert for making an enclosure for the choir of the Holy Sacrament; the payment was made in the form of a delivery of alabaster, with a value equal to the last three items due (LEYSSENS, p. 100).

18. ROOSES, II, pp. 68–84, nos. 275–85; OLDENBOURG, pp. 36, 37. The most recent study on this work, giving a detailed bibliography and a number of literary quotations, is by J. R. MARTIN, *Rubens: The Antwerp Alterpieces, The Raising of the Cross / The Descent from the Cross,* New York, 1969.

19. ROOSES, II, pp. 79, 80; see also J. VAN BRABANT, *Onze-Lieve-Vrouwekathedraal van Antwerpen, grootste gotische kerk der Nederlanden,* Antwerp, 1972, pp. 260–68.

20. ROOSES, II, p. 83; J. S. HELD, "Artis Pictoriae Amator. An Antwerp Art Patron and his Collection," *Gazette des Beaux-Arts,* 1957, pp. 54, 55. See also Chapter 13.

21. R. OLDENBOURG, *Peter Paul Rubens,* Munich–Berlin, 1922, p. 73.

22. J. R. MARTIN, *op. cit.,* p. 48. See also the recent publications of M. JAFFÉ, "Un Chef-d'œuvre mieux connu," *L'Œil,* 43–44, 1958, pp. 14–21, 80; E. HUBALA, "Rubens und Michelangelo; eine Bemerkung zum Christus der Antwerpener Kreuzabnahme von 1611–1612" (offprint from *Nordelbingen,* Heide in Holstein, XL, 1971, pp. 64–76).

23. Most recently by J. VAN DEN NIEUWENHUIZEN, "Histoire matérielle de la Descente de Croix de Rubens," *Bulletin de l'Institut Royal du Patrimoine Artistique,* V, 1962, pp. 40–44.

24. Antwerp, City Archives, *Privilegie Kamer, 700 (Rekwestboek 1611)* fol. 95 v°, fol. 96 r°. No doubt this request was drawn up after a meeting of the "Camer" on March 13, 1611, when there were discussions about the building of the new altar (J. VAN DEN NIEUWENHUIZEN, *op. cit.,* p. 40, appendix I).

25. Antwerp, City Archives, *Gilden en Ambachten, 4665* (Accounts of the Arquebusiers Guild, 1604–1630), fol. 88 v°, fol. 98 v°, fol. 100 v°, fol. 102 r°, fol. 104 r°, fol. 109 v°, fol. 113 v°, fol. 117, etc.

26. J. VAN DEN NIEUWENHUIZEN, *op. cit.,* p. 40, appendix 2.

27. J. VAN DEN NIEUWENHUIZEN, *op. cit.,* p. 40, appendix 4.

28. J. VAN DEN NIEUWENHUIZEN, *op. cit.,* p. 41, appendix 7.

29. J. VAN DEN NIEUWENHUIZEN, *op. cit.,* p. 41, appendices 5 and 6.

30. After noting, on fol. 100 v°, the sums received from those exempted from services for the expenses for the altar ("ontfanck vande Wepelaers innegenomen om te vervallen de oncosten van den aultaer"), and after mentioning, on fol. 101, that the total of these sums, together with the money from Dean Oistendoren (less 35 florins) amounted to 3,900 florins, the accountant noted: "De Betaelingen bijden Rendant aenden schilder, beeltsnyders, ende taeffereelmaecker daermede gedaen, bedragen luijt de specificatie ende quittancien daer aen gehecht tot no. 5 ... IIIm VIIIc XXXVIII gul. VIst" [in the margin]: "bij de particuliere specificatien ende quittancien" (The payments made by the accountant to the painter, to the sculptors, and to the panelmaker, with this sum, came to IIIm VIIIc XXXVIII fl. VIst, according to the specification

and receipts no. 5 attached to it [in the margin] special specifications and receipts; Antwerp, City Archives, *Gilden en Ambachten,* 4665, fol. 101 r°). Since these entries are mentioned in the accounts from December 25, 1611, to December 25, 1612, it is certain that Rubens received an initial payment before the last-mentioned date, probably after the central panel was completed and at the latest on September 17, 1612, when the panel was taken to the cathedral.

31. J. VAN DEN NIEUWENHUIZEN, *op. cit.,* p. 43, appendices 10 and 12.

32. J. VAN DEN NIEUWENHUIZEN, *op. cit.,* p. 43, appendix 14.

33. N. VERHAEGEN, "Iconographie," *Bulletin de l'Institut Royal du Patrimoine Artistique,* V, 1962, p. 22, and no. 5; A. and P. PHILIPPOT, "Examen stylistique," (*Ibidem,* pp. 94, 95).

34. "24 Martii 1611 Comparuit D. Octavio, pictor istius civitatis, et exhibuit dominis projectum sive modellum certae picturae et historiae (quae Dominum nostrum Sponsam suam de Libano provocantem ad coronam continet) in summo altari chori nostri ponendae, et placuit dominis idem projectum et historiae, et deputatus est cum Domino decano dominus thesaurarius ad agendum desuper cum aedituis istius ecclesiae, acturi insuper super electione pictoris dictam tabulam picturi" (Archives of the cathedral of Our Lady in Antwerp, *Acta Capitularia,* III, pp. 71, 72; published by L. PHILIPPEN, "Le Culte de Notre Dame 'op 't Stocxken' à Anvers 1474–1580," *Annales de l'Académie royale d'Archéologie de Bruxelles,* LXXII, 1924, p. 324 and by P. J. GOETSCHALCKX, *Geschiedenis der Kanunniken van O.L.V. Kapittel te Antwerpen 1585–1700,* Antwerp, 1929, p. 76).

35. "22 Aprilis 1611. Exhibita sunt a N. Vriendts Aedituo ecclesiae nostrae Petri Rubenii pictoris (qui etiam postea in capitulo comparuit) duo modella continentia historiam Assumptionis B. Mariae Virginis, diverso modo depicta, quae tanquam nihil inhonestatis aut ecclesiae traditionibus continentia, placuerunt dominis, mansuris nihilominus in optione eligendi praestantissimum pictorum" (Archives of the cathedral of Our Lady in Antwerp, *Acta Capitularia,* III, p. 75; published by L. PHILIPPEN, *op. cit.,* p. 324 and by P. J. GOETSCHALCKX, *op. cit.,* p. 77; the texts were checked and corrected by Dr. C. Van de Velde).

36. ROOSES, II, p. 189, no. 364.

37. M. V. DOBROKLONSKI, "The 'Coronation of the Virgin' by Rubens in the Hermitage," *Hermitage Studies,* III, Leningrad, 1949, pp. 17–24 (in Russian); M. VARSHAVSKAYA, *Rubens' Paintings in the Hermitage Museum,* Leningrad, 1975, pp. 63–68, no. 3, repr. [in Russian, with titles and summaries in English].

38. See n. 34.

39. Usually the altar is crowned with a representation, most often a sculpture, of God the Father or God the Son. An engraving by Adriaan Lommelin, dating from 1631, shows how the high altar of the cathedral of Our Lady was constructed (see reproductions of this engraving in ROOSES, II, pl. 124, K. FREMANTLE, *The Baroque Town Hall of Amsterdam,* Utrecht, 1959, pl. 146, and M. CASTEELS, *De beeldhouwers De Nole te Kamerijk, te Utrecht en te Antwerpen,* Brussels, 1961, fig. 65). One may wonder whether the sketch *Christ Descending on the World with the Crown of Glory,* from the collection of E. Schwartz, New York (ROSENBERG, p. 57; [*Exh. Cat.*] *Paintings by Rubens and Van Dyck,* Los Angeles County Museum, 1946, no. 19, ill.; J.-A. GORIS and J. S. HELD, *Rubens in America,* Antwerp–New York, 1947, p. 52, no. A. 63) was not conceived as a project for a similar representation in the form of a statue or, which would be more plausible, for a large picture to be placed on the high altar. The angels above *The Raising of the Cross* on the high altar of St. Walburga's is an example of this. See a picture of this altar in the painting by Anthoon Gheringh, *The Interior of St. Walburga's Church,* preserved in St. Paul's Church in Antwerp

([*Exh. Cat.*] *Herinneringen aan P. P. Rubens,* Rubens House, Antwerp, 1958, no. 65; J. R. MARTIN, *The Antwerp Altarpieces, op. cit.,* fig. 2) and in the drawing of P. Verhaert after the picture reproduced in ROOSES, *Leven,* p. 129. Held (J.-A. GORIS and J. S. HELD, *op. cit.,* p. 52) does not consider the sketch to be an original work by Rubens.

40. OLDENBOURG, p. 206.

41. HELD (I, pp. 108, 109, no. 35; II, pl. 38) suggests the date 1614–15 for this drawing; according to BURCHARD-D'HULST (I, pp. 121, 122, no. 73; II, pl. 73), it is a drawing for the upper part of the *Assumption of the Virgin* in Vienna, based on a *modello* in Buckingham Palace that was executed before 1615, and perhaps even in 1611. This last date seems too early to us, however.

42. PONCELET, I, p. 475.

43. See, for example, OLDENBOURG, p. 206.

44. Communicated to S. T. Madsen, December 1952 (S. T. MADSEN, "Some Recently Discovered Drawings by Rubens," *The Burlington Magazine,* XCV, 1953, p. 304); see also BURCHARD-D'HULST, I, p. 121.

45. Panel, $8^1/_2'' \times 6'4''$ (249 × 193 cm); C. VAN DE VELDE, "De Aanbidding der Herders van Frans Floris," *Jaarboek Koninklijk Museum voor Schone Kunsten Antwerpen,* 1961, pp. 59–73, fig. 1.

46. "Ad lectum libellum supplicem porrectum ex parte Magistratorum Altaris hortulanorum in ista ecclesia quo petierunt quod tabulam hactenus in summo altari pretendentes illam spectare ex donatione Francisci du Terne, quondam thesaurarii ad altare B. Mariae quod vocant op stocxen in quo ipsi nunc suum servant altaris officium, ..." (Archives of the cathedral of Our Lady in Antwerp, *Acta Capitularia,* III, p. 183; published by L. PHILIPPEN, *op. cit.,* pp. 324, 325 and C. VAN DE VELDE, *op. cit.,* p. 70).

47. Antwerp, Rubens House, Inv. no. D. 23; [*Exh. Cat.*] *Herinneringen aan P. P. Rubens,* Rubens House, Antwerp, 1958, no. 49; published by M. ROOSES, "L'Assomption de la Vierge. Tableau du Maître-Autel de la Cathédrale d'Anvers," *Rubens-Bulletijn,* I, 1882, pp. 70, 71; ROOSES, II, p. 175, 176; reproduced in C. VAN DE VELDE, "Rubens' Hemelvaart van Maria in de kathedraal te Antwerpen," in *Jaarboek 1975, Koninklijk Museum voor Schone Kunsten, Antwerpen,* p. 248, fig. 2.

48. M. ROOSES, in *Rubens-Bulletijn,* I, 1882, pp. 68, 69; ROOSES, II, p. 175; L. PHILIPPEN, *op. cit.,* p. 325; P. J. GOETSCHALCKX, *op. cit.,* p. 77; M. CASTEELS, *op. cit.,* p. 122.

49. "Exhibita per Notarium publicum Supplicatione Hortulanorum petentium suo altari restitui tabulam quae nunc est in summo altari, tridem eorum altari per D. du Terne concessam et (non concesso quod tabula praefata pertineat ad hortulanos, sed potius ad fabricam ecclesiae) placuit ordinari aedituis ecclesiae ut proximo opere curent fieri novum altare maius et deinde praefata tabula dimittatur ad opus jus habentium" (Archives of the cathedral of Our Lady in Antwerp, *Acta Capitularia,* III, pp. 367, 368; published by L. PHILIPPEN, *op. cit.,* p. 325 and C. VAN DE VELDE, *op. cit.,* p. 71).

50. ROOSES, II, pp. 173–80, and M. CASTEELS, *op. cit.,* pp. 122–24.

51. A sketch for this altarpiece is preserved in the National Gallery of Art, Washington (Cat. 1965, no. 1393; *Paintings and Sculpture from the Samuel H. Kress Collection,* Washington, 1959, p. 293, repr.). The finished *modello,* formerly in the collection of Colonel F. T. Davies ([*Exh. Cat.*] *P. P. Rubens,* Wildenstein & Co., London, 1951, no. 2; [*Exh. Cat.*] *Olieverfschetsen van Rubens,* Museum Boymans, Rotterdam, 1953–54, no. 51) has been in the Mauritshuis since 1957 (Cat. 1958, no. 926).

52. CARL VAN DE VELDE (*op. cit.,* pp. 245–77) has devoted a study to the complicated origin of the *Assumption of the Virgin*

in Antwerp Cathedral. He rightly draws attention to the fact that Rubens, by presenting two sketches, proposed two solutions to the Chapter: either a *Coronation of the Virgin,* or an *Assumption.* In accepting the second alternative, the Chapter still had to provide for a representation of the Holy Trinity above the altar. By 1618 the choice between the two proposed solutions had not been made. Van de Velde's stylistic comparison of the Vienna picture with the side panels of *The Descent from the Cross* seems to me less convincing. The lower part of the Vienna picture must rather be dated before 1613 or, at the latest, in that year.

53. A. MONBALLIEU, *op. cit.,* p. 190.

54. The most recent publication on this subject, taking into account the available material in great detail, is G. MARTIN, *National Gallery Catalogues, The Flemish School circa 1600–circa 1900,* London, 1970, pp. 126–33, no. 57.

55. ROOSES, I, pp. 159–62, no. 129; V. DENIS, "Saint Job, patron des musiciens," *Revue Belge d'Archéologie et d'Histoire de l'Art,* XXI, 1952, pp. 285–87; BURCHARD-D'HULST, I, pp. 120, 171, 172.

56. Inasmuch as it is possible to judge this altarpiece on the basis of stylistic criticism—the picture is hung rather high and seems to have been damaged—it appears to have been executed later, although the dating suggested by Jan Bialostocki (about 1620) is too late. ROOSES (II, p. 128) quoted a passage from a chronicle preserved in the Bibliothèque Nationale de St.-Omer (Ms. 808, II, p. 433), which mentions that in December 1612 the altar of the chapel of St. John the Evangelist was restored and decorated with a picture representing *The Descent from the Cross,* for which 250 florins were paid in Antwerp. As Rooses was not fully convinced of the reliability of this text, J. Bialostocki checked it and established its accuracy. He adds that the 18th-century manuscript is based on a text written about 1640 by Jean Hendricq (J. BIALOSTOCKI, "The Descent from the Cross in Works by Peter Paul Rubens and his Studio," *The Art Bulletin,* XLVI, 1964, pp. 522, 523, notes 46 and 47). It should be noted here that the date of December 1612 perhaps refers to the contracts or to the first mention in the books of accounts of the altar in question. It may be that Rubens accepted this commission about this time, and that he did not execute it until later, as frequently happened. If the sum of 250 florins is correct, it must have been the intention from the beginning to purchase a work not by the hand of Rubens alone. But it is nevertheless possible that a zero was left out when the sum was transcribed and that the actual sum was 2,500 florins, which would correspond more closely to the fees usually fixed by Rubens.

57. Preserved in the Strasbourg museum and in the collection of Count Seilern in London ([Count Antoine Seilern], *Flemish Paintings and Drawings at 56 Princes Gate, London, SW 7,* I, London, 1955, pp. 28, 29, nos. 16, 17; II, pl. XXXIX).

58. Painted to decorate the tomb of Rockox and his wife in the chapel behind the high altar of the church of the Minorites in Antwerp; ROOSES, II, pp. 157–60, nos. 346–50; OLDENBOURG, pp. 84, 85; A. MONBALLIEU, "Bij de iconografie van Rubens' Rockox-epitafium," *Jaarboek Koninklijk Museum voor Schone Kunsten Antwerpen,* 1970, pp. 133–51. This author emphasizes that it is probably not the Doubting Thomas that is represented here but the appearance of the risen Christ to his disciples, and, more generally, the theme of *Christum videre.* The date 1615 appears on the left side panel, but the last digit has been painted over the original 3.

59. OLDENBOURG, p. 62.

60. OLDENBOURG, p. 70, on the left.

61. ROOSES, II, pp. 245–48, nos. 410–13; OLDENBOURG, pp. 158, 159; BURCHARD-D'HULST, I, p. 147, dates this work not later than 1615–16; VLIEGHE, II, no. 146, dates it 1615–20, which seems too late to me.

62. ROOSES, II, pp. 164–67, no. 355; OLDENBOURG, p. 120; BURCHARD–D'HULST (I, p. 120): 1615–16. J. F. M. MICHEL (*Histoire de la Vie de Rubens*, Brussels, 1771, p. 67) tells us that the Archduke and the Infanta were present on October 15, 1614, the day of the beatification of St. Teresa of Avila, at mass in the church of the Barefoot Carmelites in Brussels and that when they noticed that the altar had not been decorated, they decided to commission a large picture from Rubens. The author adds that the regents also asked him to paint a simulated altar on wood with architecture similar to that of the other altars. In the accounts no mention is made of the expenses relating to the works of art commissioned by the Archduke and Duchess (cf. DE MAEYER, p. 120). On the other hand, we know that the Archduke and Duchess were the patrons of the community of the Barefoot Carmelites, and that their architect, Wenceslas Coebergher, drew the designs for the church which was destined for them. The first stone was laid on March 15, 1607, and the building was finished in 1611. The work of interior decoration went on until 1613 and the cross was not placed on the pediment until 1615. It is thus probable that the altar picture was painted around 1613–15 by Rubens. That the altar was in existence in 1613 is clear from an account of that year in which it is mentioned that Coebergher was paid for the painting of the ceiling in oil paint, for the picture on canvas of the high altar, and for those of the other four side altars, etc. (J. H. PLANTENGA, *L'Architecture religieuse du Brabant au 17e siècle*, The Hague, 1926, pp. 19, 20). This payment may refer to the "simulated altar" mentioned by J. F. M. MICHEL, which might therefore have been painted by Coebergher and not by Rubens. (For the sculptures of the façade of the same church, the work of Robert Colyns de Nole that was supplied in 1613–14, see M. CASTEELS, *op. cit.*, pp. 148, 149, 316–19, 328–31). The dating "about 1619" of Rooses, accepted by VAN PUYVELDE ([*Exh. Cat.*] *Le Siècle de Rubens*, Musées Royaux des Beaux-Arts de Belgique, Brussels, 1965, no. 193), is at all events too late.

63. ROOSES–RUELENS, II, p.35.

64. OLDENBOURG, p. 94; H. VEY and A. KESTING, *Katalog der Niederländischen Gemälde von 1550 bis 1800 im Wallraf-Richartz-Museum und im öffentlichen Besitz der Stadt Köln*, Cologne, 1967, pp. 99, 100, no. 1043, fig. 133 (with detailed references to previous literature). J. MÜLLER HOFSTEDE writes that H. Vey has pointed out to him that according to a recently discovered archive, the picture decorated the altar at the time of the consecration of the church in October 1616 ("Neue Ölskizzen von Rubens," *Städel Jahrbuch*, II, 1969, p. 28, n. 113); VLIEGHE, I, no. 90.

65. *Antwerpsch Archievenblad*, VI, n.d., p. 352; H. G. EVERS, *Rubens und sein Werk. Neue Forschungen*, Brussels, 1943, p. 42.

66. According to the chronicle of the Council of Neuberg, mentioned in *Aeltere Pinakothek München. Amtlicher Katalog*, Munich, 1936, p. 214, under no. 890.

67. A. H. CORNETTE, *Petrus Paulus Rubens*, Antwerp, 1940, p. 58.

68. R.-A. D'HULST, *Rubens en de Barokschilderkunst* (*Kunst in België*, VI, published by 'Cultura'), Brussels, n.d., p. 4.

69. H. GERSON, (*op. cit.*, p. 81) draws attention to this.

70. HELD, I, pp. 99, 110, 134, fig. 34; the article of E. DEVAL, "Le Rubens de l'Eglise Saint-Géry à Cambrai," *Mémoires de la Société d'Emulation de Cambrai*, 1927, pp. 271–94 seems to have been ignored up to now.

71. BURCHARD–D'HULST (I, p. 149, with reference to P. HILDEBRAND, "Rubens chez les Capucins. Un témoignage de 1617," *Etudes franciscaines*, XLVII, Paris, 1935, pp. 726–29).

72. ROOSES, II, pp. 123, 124, no. 311; OLDENBOURG, p. 89; BURCHARD–D'HULST, I, p. 118, referring to P. HILDEBRAND, *op. cit.*, pp. 727, 728; see also VLIEGHE, I, pp. 146–47.

73. BURCHARD–D'HULST, I, pp. 118, 119, no. 71. It seems not impossible that this drawing, with its contrasts of light and shade that are typical of the beginning of the Antwerp period, may have been another preliminary study for *The Descent from the Cross* in Antwerp Cathedral. The attitude of John corresponds fairly closely to that of the executioner, seen to the left of Christ and holding the cross, in *The Raising of the Cross* now also in Antwerp Cathedral.

74. ROOSES, II, pp. 104, 105, no. 306; OLDENBOURG, p. 88.

75. ROOSES, II, pp. 140–43, no. 327–31; OLDENBOURG, pp. 160, 161.

76. ROOSES, I, pp. 89–91, no. 82; OLDENBOURG, p. 91.

77. ROOSES, I, pp. 214–23, nos. 162–69; OLDENBOURG, pp. 164, 665; F. BAUDOUIN, "De restauratie van het Drieluik van P. P. Rubens in de St.-Janskerk te Mechelen," *Handelingen van de Kon. Kring voor Oudheidkunde, Letteren en Kunst van Mechelen*, LX, 1956, pp. 206–8.

78. ROOSES, II, pp. 259–62, no. 429; OLDENBOURG, p. 190; J. B. KNIPPING, *De Laatste Communie van Sint-Franciscus van Assisië*, Leiden, 1949; VLIEGHE, I, no. 102; II, p. 180, no. 102 (mentions the place where the receipt for this picture is preserved: the Castle of Hovorst, in Viersel, province of Antwerp).

79. "Tutto il gruppo in umbra et una luce vehemente del sole bastenda per la finestra." For the communication of the precise text of this inscription, I thank Dr. H. Vlieghe, who has been the first to read it correctly (VLIEGHE, I, no. 102).

80. In the large Rubens room in the Antwerp Museum, if one looks at the picture from the entrance opposite it and thus at a distance (as it was most often seen by the faithful in the church of the Minorites), it will be seen that only the body of St. Francis stands out clearly, while the rest of the composition fades almost completely into the background.

81. See chapter 6.

82. ROOSES, III, pp. 183–86, no. 700; OLDENBOURG, p. 137, on the right.

83. See Chapter 8.

84. ROOSES, II, pp. 170–72, no. 358; OLDENBOURG, p. 193.

85. "Anno 1618. Erigitur in choro altare marmorum juxta prototytam Rubenianum, in quo exponitur Assumpta Virgo depicta a praefato famoso pictore." This altar has been in the church of St. Josse-ten-Noode since 1870 (I. LEYSSENS, *op. cit.*, p. 117). To H. Peters' question as to whether the picture was originally higher and semicircular in shape (H. PETERS, *Meisterwerke der Düsseldorfer Galerie*, Honnef/Rhein, 1955, p. 32, under no. 19), a negative answer must be given, considering the shape of the altar. See: F. BAUDOUIN, "Altars and Altarpieces," in *Rubens Before 1620*, ed. by J. R. Martin, Princeton, N. J., 1972, pp. 80–82, fig. 38.

86. ROOSES, II, pp. 19–28, nos. 245–52; OLDENBOURG, p. 172.

87. The same opinion was previously expressed by G. Glück, who thought he recognized the hand of Frans Snyders in the representations of the fish and shells in the foreground (G. GLÜCK, *Rubens, Van Dyck und ihr Kreis*, Vienna, 1933, pp. 185, 358).

88. The work was commissioned by Marquis Niccolo Pallavicini, who had previously entrusted Rubens with a painting of the *Circumcision* for the same church at the time when the latter was living in Italy (ROOSES, I, pp. 201–3, no. 156; OLDENBOURG, p. 21). According to an unpublished document, it seems that from 1612 on, the decoration of the chapel of St. Ignatius, where this altarpiece would be displayed, had been conceived of (M. JAFFÉ, "Rediscovered Oil Sketches by Rubens, II," *The Burlington Magazine*, CXI, 1969, pp. 529, 530). The archives of Carrega in Genoa tell us that the picture arrived in this town in 1620 (A. BASCHET, "Pierre-Paul Rubens, peintre de Vincent Ier, duc de Mantoue," *Gazette des Beaux-Arts*, XXIV, 1868, p. 334). Niccolo Pallavicini was

certainly in the circle of Rubens' friends: this Genoese gentleman was the godfather of the painter's second son, baptised Nicolaas, on March 23, 1618 (ROOSES, *Leven*, p. 660).

89. OLDENBOURG, p. 202.

## 4. *The Flagellation of Christ* in the Church of St. Paul in Antwerp

1. Panel, 6'10" × 5'3" (219 × 161 cm); OLDENBOURG, p. 147. For a study of the series as a whole: M. ROBBROECKX, *De Vijftien Rozenkransschilderijen in de Sint-Pauluskerk te Antwerpen*, diss., Ghent, 1972. For the paintings of Van Dyck and Jordaens, see M. ROOSES, *Jordaens' Leven en Werken*, Antwerp–Amsterdam, 1906, p. 10; H. VEY, *Van Dyck-Studien*, diss., Cologne, 1958, pp. 13, 14; H. VEY, *Die Zeichnungen Anton van Dycks*, I, Brussels, 1962, pp. 84, 85. A succinct summary of the series, in which special attention is paid to the iconography (L. WUYTS, *De Vijftien Schilderijen van de Rozenkrans*), can be found in the leaflet which accompanies the record *Meesterwerken der religieuze Muziek* (S. Pauli 020468), in which the first version of our chapter 4 also appeared.

2. Amsterdam, Rijksmuseum; panel, 26³/₄" × 41¹/₂" (68 × 105.5 cm), signed and dated *anno 1.6.3.6. Peeter Nefs* (Cat. 1934, no. 1715).

3. Now in the Kunsthistorisches Museum in Vienna; canvas, 11'11¹/₄" × 8'2" (364 × 249 cm); Cat. 1965, I, no. 483; for the early history of this canvas, see W. FRIEDLAENDER, *Caravaggio Studies*, Princeton, N.J., 1955, pp. 198–202, and D. BODART, *Louis Finson (Bruges, avant 1580–Amsterdam, 1617)*, Brussels, 1970, pp. 132–36.

4. J. DE COO, "Een Wondere Kerk," *Antwerpen*, IV, 1958, p. 133.

5. J. DE COO, *op. cit.*, p. 131. The copy of A. van Yzendyck (1801–1875), which for a long time occupied the place of the original picture, is now hanging elsewhere in the church.

6. S. ZAJADACZ-HASTENRATH, *Das Beichtgestühl der Antwerpener St. Pauluskirche und der Barockbeichtstuhl in den Südlichen Niederlanden*, Brussels, 1970, pp. 33–43.

7. See E. MÂLE, *L'Art religieux après le Concile de Trente*, 2nd ed., Paris, 1951, pp. 465–70; L. RÉAU, *Iconographie de l'art chrétien*, II, 2, Paris, 1957, pp. 120–22.

8. First published by M. ROOSES, *op. cit.*, pp. 10, 11; see also F. PRIMS, "De Antwerpsche Predikheeren en hun Archief," *Antwerpsch Archievenblad*, 1928, pp. 61–63.

9. "door verscheyde aelmoessen."

10. See Chapter 3.

11. H. VLIEGHE has recently attributed a few works to this little-known master ("Artus of Antoni de Bruyn?," *Jaarboek Koninklijk Museum voor Schone Kunsten*, 1969, pp. 169–80); H. VLIEGHE, "De boedelinventaris van Artus de Bruyn," *ibid.*, 1973, pp. 213–31. On another painter with a picture in the series under discussion, see E. DUVERGER, "Arnout Vinckenborch," *ibid.*, 1973, pp. 233–46.

12. This hypothesis was advanced by M. ROOSES (*op. cit.*, p. 10).

13. This is true, among others, in the case of Van Dyck (H. VEY, *Die Zeichnungen Anton van Dycks*, I, Brussels, 1962, p. 85) and Jordaens (R.-A. D'HULST, *De Tekeningen van Jakob Jordaens*, Brussels, 1956, p. 19).

14. Ghent, Museum voor Schone Kunsten; Cat. 1938, no. 1910-Z; L. VAN PUYVELDE, *Les Esquisses de Rubens*, Basle, 1948, p. 68, no. 15, pl. 15; R.-A. D'HULST, *Olieverfschetsen van Rubens uit Nederlands en Belgisch Openbaar Bezit*, n.p., 1968, p. 91, no. 4, pl. 2.

## 5. *The Prodigal Son* in the Koninklijk Museum voor Schone Kunsten in Antwerp

First published in *Openbaar Kunstbezit in Vlaanderen*, II, 1964, no. 15.

1. Panel, 42" × 61" (107 × 155 cm).

2. Cat. 1959, p. 213, no. 781; ROOSES, II, pp. 38, 39, no. 260; OLDENBOURG, p. 182; G. GLÜCK, *Die Landschaften von Peter Paul Rubens*, 2nd ed., Vienna, 1945, p. 54, no. 3, pl. 3.

3. A.H. CORNETTE, *Inleiding tot de Oude Meesters van het Koninklijk Museum te Antwerpen*, Antwerp, 1939, p. 69.

4. BURCHARD-D'HULST, I, pp. 162, 163, no. 98; II, pl. 98.

5. OLDENBOURG, p. 166.

6. L. BURCHARD, "Die Neuerworbene Landschaft von Rubens im Kaiser-Friedrich Museum," *Jahrbuch der Preussischen Kunstsammlungen*, XLIX, 1928, pp. 62–68.

7. BURCHARD-D'HULST, I, p. 164, no. 99; II, pl. 99.

8. OLDENBOURG, p. 186.

9. BURCHARD-D'HULST, I, pp. 165, 166, no. 101; II, pl. 101.

10. OLDENBOURG, p. 238; for the painting in the Hermitage, see M. VARSHAWSKAYA, *Rubens Paintings in the Hermitage Museum*, Leningrad, 1975, pp. 63–68, no. 3 (text in Russian, with English titles).

11. BURCHARD-D'HULST, I, pp. 166, 167, no. 102; II, pl. 102.

12. J. THEUWISSEN, "De kar en de wagen in het werk van Rubens," *Jaarboek Koninklijk Museum voor Schone Kunsten Antwerpen*, 1964, p. 199.

## 6. *The Adoration of the Shepherds,* an Oil Sketch by Rubens

First published in *Antwerpen*, I, 1955, pp. 144–50.

1. Panel, 18" × 17" (46 × 34 cm); inv. no. S. 123.

2. [*Exp. Cat.*] *P.-P. Rubens. Luonnoksia ja piirustuksia sekä Graffiikkaa mestarin teosten mukaan (P.-P. Rubens, Sketches, drawings, and engravings)*, Ateneum, Helsinki, 1952–53, no. 1, ill. (private collection, London).

3. [*Exp. Cat.*] *Rubens, Esquisses et dessins*, Musée d'art ancien, Brussels, 1953, no. 1, ill. (private collection, London).

4. J.S. HELD, "A propos de l'exposition Rubens à Bruxelles," *Les Arts Plastiques*, VI, 1953, p. 113, fig. 57.

5. F. BAUDOUIN, "Nota's bij de tentoonstelling 'Schetsen en Tekeningen van P.P. Rubens,'" *Bulletin des Musées Royaux des Beaux-Arts*, I, 1953, p. 50.

6. [*Exh. Cat.*] *Olieverfschetsen van Rubens*, Museum Boymans, Rotterdam, 1953–54, no. 20, pl. 19 (collection Dr. F.H. Rothmann, London).

7. R. LONGHI, "La 'Notte' del Rubens a Fermo," *Vita Artistica*, II, 1927, pp. 191–97; L. BURCHARD, "Alcuni Dipinti del Rubens nel periodo italiano," *Pinacoteca*, I, 1928–29, pp. 1, 2; M. JAFFÉ, "Rubens and the Oratorian Fathers," *Proporzioni*, VI, 1963, pp. 209 ff.

8. Reproduced in G. GRONAU, *Correggio. Des Meisters Gemälde (Klassiker der Kunst, X)*, Stuttgart–Berlin, 1907, p. 131.

9. See Chapter 3.

10. [*Exh. Cat.*] *Drawings by Old Masters*, Diploma Gallery of the Royal Academy of Arts, London, 1953, no. 292.

11. H. G. EVERS, *Rubens und sein Werk. Neue Forschungen*, Brussels, 1943, p. 195, with bibliography.

12. OLDENBOURG, p. 116.

13. ROOSES, I, no. 150. See also in the Louvre the drawing for an engraving of L. Vorsterman in which the composition is almost identical to that of the Rouen picture (F. LUGT, *Inventaire général des dessins de l'Ecole du Nord, Ecole flamande*, II, Paris, 1949, p. 38, no. 1134, pl. LXI).

14. OLDENBOURG, p. 198.
15. C. VAN HASSELT, [*Exh. Cat.*] *Vlaamse Tekeningen uit de zeventiende eeuw, verzameling Frits Lugt, Institut Néerlandais, Parijs,* London, Paris, Bern, Brussels, 1972, pp. 116–17, no. 79, pl. 41.
16. MARTIN, pp. 60–62, no. 2, pl. 17.
17. OLDENBOURG, p. 186.
18. OLDENBOURG, p. 290. See also the sketch for this picture, which was part of the collection of Sir Felix Cassel, Bart., Luton, Bedfordshire (L. VAN PUYVELDE, *Les esquisses de Rubens,* Basle, 1940, pl. 21).
19. OLDENBOURG, p. 127.
20. OLDENBOURG, p. 105; J.-A. GORIS and J. S. HELD, *Rubens in America,* New York–Antwerp, 1947, pl. 38.
21. OLDENBOURG, p. 166.
22. OLDENBOURG, p. 164.
23. OLDENBOURG, p. 124.
24. OLDENBOURG, p. 177.
25. Lille, Musée des Beaux-Arts; Cat. 1893, no. 213; canvas, $21^1/_4'' \times 16^1/_8''$ (57 × 44.5 cm). See: L. RÉAU, "Les influences flamandes et hollandaises dans l'œuvre de Fragonard," *Revue belge d'archéologie et d'histoire de l'art,* II, 1932, pp. 97–104. Attention was drawn to this article by L. BURCHARD, [*Exh. Cat.*] *Olieverfschetsen van Rubens,* Museum Boymans, Rotterdam, 1953–54, p. 50, under no. 20. See also: A. CHÂTELET, *Cent Chefs-d'œuvre du Musée de Lille,* n.d., p. 150, no. 67, with ill.

## 7. Rubens and the Church of the Jesuits in Antwerp

First published in *Openbaar Kunstbezit in Vlaanderen,* IX, 1971, no. 9.

1. PONCELET, I, pp. 451–84; L. BROUWERS, *Het Hof van Lierre,* Antwerp, 1976, pp. 25–29.
2. M. SABBE, "Het Geestesleven te Antwerpen in Rubens' Tijd," in PRIMS, *Rubens en zijne Eeuw,* p. 97.
3. J. VALLERY-RADOT, *Le recueil de plans d'édifices de la Compagnie de Jésus conservé à la Bibliothèque Nationale de Paris,* Rome, 1960, pp. 287–91.
4. G. MÖRSCH, *Der Zentralbaugedanke im Belgischen Kirchenbau des 17. Jahrhunderts,* diss., Bonn, 1965.
5. For the architecture of the church, see, among others, J. BRAUN, *Die belgischen Jesuitenkirchen,* Freiburg, 1907, pp. 151–71; J. H. PLANTENGA, *L'architecture religieuse du Brabant au XVII^e siècle,* The Hague, 1926; S. BRIGODE, "Les projets de construction de l'église des jésuites à Anvers d'après les plans conservés à la Bibliothèque Nationale de Paris," *Bulletin de l'Institut historique belge de Rome,* XIV, 1934, pp. 157–73; THIBAUT DE MAISIÈRES, *L'architecture religieuse à l'époque de Rubens,* Brussels, 1943, pp. 30–32; S. LEURS, *Geschiedenis van de Bouwkunst in Vlaanderen van de Xde tot het einde der XVIIIde eeuw,* Antwerp, 1946, pp. 99, 100.
6. J. EVELYN, *Memoirs of . . . comprising his diary from 1641 to 1705–6 and a selection of his familiar letters,* ed. by W. Bray, London, 1879; quoted by J.-A. GORIS, *Lof van Antwerpen,* Brussels, 1940, p. 82.
7. A. S. HARTMANN, "Tagebuch Adam Samuel Hartmann über seine Kollektenreise im Jahre 1657–1659," *Zeitschrift des Historischen Gesellschaft für die Provinz Posen,* XIV, 1899, and XV, 1900; quoted by J.-A. GORIS, *op. cit.,* p. 79. Extracts from other accounts of journeys can be found here.
8. A. JANSEN and C. VAN HERCK, "J. P. van Baurscheit I en J. P. van Baurscheit II, Antwerpsche beeldhouwers uit de 18de eeuw," *Koninklijke Oudheidkundige Kring van Antwerpen. Jaarboek,* XVIII, 1942, pp. 56, 80.

9. On this point see MARTIN.
10. S. LEURS, *op. cit.,* p. 100.
11. *Ibidem.*
12. GLÜCK–HABERDITZL, p. 46, no. 128, ill.; L. BURCHARD and R.-A. D'HULST, [*Exh. Cat.*] *Tekeningen van P.P. Rubens,* Rubens House, Antwerp, 1956, p. 68, no. 67, pl. XXVIII; HELD, I, pp. 149, 150, nos. 144, 145; II, pls. 149, 150; BURCHARD–D'HULST, I, p. 185, under no. 116.
13. HELD, I, p. 165, no. Add. 172, fig. 58; BURCHARD–D'HULST, I, pp. 186, 187, no. 117.
14. L. BURCHARD and R.-A. D'HULST, [*Exh. Cat.*] *Tekeningen van P. P. Rubens,* Rubens House, Antwerp, 1956, p. 69, no. 69; BURCHARD–D'HULST, I, p. 186, under no. 116.
15. See Chapter 8, note 68.
16. See Chapter 8.
17. GLÜCK–HABERDITZL, p. 46, no. 129, ill.; L. BURCHARD and R.-A. D'HULST, *op. cit.,* 1956, pp. 69, 70, no. 70.
18. See, for example, M. JAFFÉ, "Rubens' Drawings at Antwerp," *The Burlington Magazine,* XCVIII, 1956, p. 314, note 5 (in this article, the author attributes to Rubens a certain number of drawings preserved in the archives of St. Charles Borromeo in Antwerp); BURCHARD–D'HULST, I, pp. 185, 186, under no. 116.
19. GLÜCK–HABERDITZL, p. 37, no. 37, ill.; H. BOUCHERY and F. VAN DEN WIJNGAERT, *Rubens en het Plantijnsche Huis,* pp. 59, 60, 131, 132, pls. 27–30; M. JAFFÉ, "Rubens and Optics: Some Fresh Evidence," *Journal of the Warburg and Courtauld Institutes,* XXXIV, 1971, pp. 360–66.

## 8. The Date of Two Pictures for the High Altar of the Church of the Jesuits in Antwerp, and Some Notes on Hans van Mildert

First published in *Miscellanea Jozef Duverger,* I, Ghent, 1968, pp. 301–22.

1. Canvas: *The Miracles of St. Ignatius of Loyola,* $17'6^1/_2'' \times 12'11^1/_2''$ (536.5 × 396.5 cm); *The Miracles of St. Francis Xavier,* $17'6'' \times 12'11''$ (535 × 395 cm); ROOSES, II, pp. 264–66, no. 432; pp. 289–91, no. 454; PONCELET, I, pp. 570, 571; MARTIN, pp. 29–32, pls. 4, 5.
2. F. PEETERS, *Une visite à l'église Saint-Charles d'Anvers,* Antwerp, 1924, pp. 27, 28; F. HUYBRECHTS, *Kunst in St.-Caroluskerk te Antwerpen,* Antwerp, 1974, p. 12.
3. F. PEETERS, *op. cit.,* pp. 28, 29; D. PAPEBROCHIUS, *Annales Antverpienses,* V, Antwerp, 1848, p. 44.
In 1840 still another painting was commissioned from G. Wappers by M. Key, the prefect of the Archconfraternity of Our Lady of Carmel. Since then it has been shown on the high altar in alternation with the altarpieces by Schut and Seghers (F. PEETERS, *op. cit.,* pp. 29, 30; F. HUYBRECHTS, *op. cit.,* p. 12).
4. *Kunsthistorisches Museum. Katalog der Gemäldegalerie,* II, Vienna, 1963, pp. 108, 109, no. 311; p. 110, no. 313; VLIEGHE, II, nos. 115 and 104.
5. *Kunsthistorisches Museum. Katalog der Gemäldegalerie,* II, p. 108, no. 310; pp. 109, 110, no. 312; VLIEGHE, II, nos. 115ᵃ et 104ᵃ. Both on panel; *The Miracles of St. Ignatius of Loyola,* $41^3/_4'' \times 29^1/_8''$ (105.5 × 74 cm), *The Miracles of St. Francis Xavier,* $41^1/_4'' \times 28^3/_4''$ (104.5 × 72.5 cm).
6. J. C. DIERCXSENS, *Antverpia Christo nascens et crescens,* VII, Antwerp, 1773, p. 145; PONCELET, I, p. 461.
7. L. RÉAU, *Iconographie de l'art chrétien,* III, 2, Paris, 1958, p. 673.
8. J. BRODRICK, *De Heilige Franciscus Xaverius* (translated from the English), Antwerp, 1953, p. 381.
9. PONCELET, I, p. 461.

10. L. RÉAU, *op. cit.*, III, 2, p. 673; PONCELET, I, p. 463, n. 1; see also (pp. 463–70) the description of the enthusiastic festivities organized by the Antwerp Jesuits on July 23 and 24, 1622.

11. "twee groote Schilderien van onze Heylige Vaders Ignatio ende Xaverio, alreede door den selven Sr. Rubbens opgemaeckt voor de hoochsale van de voors. Nieuwe Kercke" (MARTIN, p. 214).

12. ROOSES, II, pp. 265, 290.

13. M. ROOSES, in *Rubens-Bulletijn*, V, 1910, p. 298, nos. 432–54.

14. ROOSES-RUELENS, II, pp. 199–212; F. BAUDOUIN, "Recente aanwinsten van het Rubenshuis, II," Antwerpen, XI, 1965, pp. 66, 67.

15. ROOSES-RUELENS, II, pp. 194–98.

16. "Un pezzo delle Gesti d'Ignazio" and "Un altro di Xaviero" (ROOSES-RUELENS, II, p. 200; see also the commentary, p. 207).

17. See note 13. Some years earlier, Rooses still maintained his opinion on the subject of the dating of the altarpieces. He knew the letter of January 23, 1619, but since Rubens himself stated in it that some of the engravings, although he had applied for the privilege to publish them, were not yet finished, Rooses did not think it necessary to modify his opinion (Rooses, *Leven*, p. 242).

18. For example, OLDENBOURG, pp. 204, 205; HELD, I, pp. 136, 161 (nos. 100, 165); of the Kunsthistorisches Museum, Vienna (see note 4).

19. H. G. EVERS, *Peter Paul Rubens*, Munich, 1942, p. 493, n. 191.

20. L. VAN PUYVELDE, *Rubens*, Paris–Brussels, 1952, pp. 127, 206, n. 90.

21. H. GERSON and E. H. TER KUILE, *Art and Architecture in Belgium 1600 to 1800*, Harmondsworth, 1960, p. 88. Gerson cites (p. 186, n. 89) an oral communication of L. Burchard, according to which the sketches of the altar pictures had been done about 1614–16, i.e., much earlier than is generally believed. Burchard no doubt made a mistake in interpreting what we had told him about the cash-book kept by the Jesuits for the church building; this cash-book is discussed at greater length below.

22. BURCHARD-D'HULST, I, p. 184. A drawing in the Louvre is referred to here, executed for a print after the painting *The Miracles of St. Francis Xavier*. The authors consider that this was drawn by Lucas Vorsterman (the engraver who worked for Rubens at this time) and retouched by Rubens himself. Lugt, on the other hand, was inclined to attribute this drawing to Van Dyck (F. LUGT, *Musée du Louvre. Inventaire général des dessins des écoles du Nord. École flamande*, II, Paris, 1949, p. 42, no. 1149, pl. LXV). A similar drawing after *The Miracles of St. Ignatius of Loyola*, also preserved in the Louvre, is attributed to Van Dyck by H. Vey (H. VEY, *Die Zeichnungen Anton van Dycks*, I, Brussels, 1962, pp. 232, 233, no. 162). On the basis of the letter of January 23, 1619, this author is also of the opinion that the two pictures had been completed by that date. It can be noted in passing that Lucas Vorsterman, because of his rupture with Rubens, certainly did not engrave the two compositions. It was Marinus van Goes who took charge of them in the 1630s.

23. MILTON J. LEWINE, "The Source of Rubens' *Miracles of St. Ignatius*," *The Art Bulletin*, XLV, 1963, p. 147, n. 18.

24. See note 22. According to Lewine, J. S. Held would now date the two altarpieces about 1615–17.

25. ROOSES, IV, p. 25, no. 809, pl. 257.

26. J. S. HELD, *op. cit.*, I, p. 110, nos. 38, 39; II, pls. 40, 41.

27. "Ten sesden ist by aldien dat voor den hoogen autaer van de voorseide kercke eene nieuwe schilderie sal moeten gemaeckt worden soo en sal P. Praepositus die selve door niemant anders dan door den voors. Rubbens doen maken,

behoudens redelycke conditie ende accoort met malcanderen" (MARTIN, p. 215).

28. "Dans la suite, on doit s'être servi, au maitre-autel, des deux grands tableaux terminés et que leurs dimensions empêchaient de placer aux murs ou sur les deux petits autels latéraux" (L. VAN PUYVELDE, *op. cit.*, p. 127). Later the same author was to develop an opinion (L. VAN PUYVELDE, "Le 'Saint Ignace' et 'Saint François Xavier' de Rubens," *Gazette des Beaux-Arts*, 1959, pp. 227, 228) which seems to us less acceptable.

29. F. PEETERS, *op. cit.*, pp. 27–29.

30. A register of 145 folios of $12^1/_4'' \times 7^3/_4''$ ($31 \times 19.5$ cm), 245 pages of which are covered with writing, in a modern binding; inv. no. Hs D. 31. See F. BAUDOUIN, [*Exh. Cat.*] *Herinneringen aan P.P. Rubens*, Rubens House, Antwerp, 1958, no. 48.

31. Charles Droeshout (Merchtem 1824–Antwerp 1908) entered the Society of Jesus in 1843. He devoted the last fifteen years of his life to the writing of the history of the Jesuit houses in Antwerp (PONCELET, I, p. IX; L. BROUWERS, *Carolus Scribanus S. J., 1561–1629*, Antwerp, 1961, p. VII). The manuscripts of his unpublished works constitute the *Fonds Droeshout* and are preserved in the archives of the order. The *Fonds* is now in the Residence of the R. P. Jesuits at Egenhoven, near Louvain.

32. On the first page of his copy (Egenhoven, *Fonds Droeshout*), Father Droeshout writes; "Note. This register is an exact copy of the account book of the building of the church of the Professed House of the Society of Jesus in Antwerp (for the years 1614–1628), today the church of St. Charles. The original is in the church of that parish and was made available to me by the kindness of the vicar, le Curé Corluy. Sept. 1897. Droeshout S. J." (Note. Ce registre est une copie exacte du livre de comptes de la bâtisse de l'église de la Maison Professe de la Compagnie de Jésus à Anvers [Années 1614–1628] aujourd'hui église St. Charles. L'original repose dans les Archives de la Fabrique de cette Paroisse et m'a été communiqué par l'obligeance du P. Mr. le Curé Corluy. Sept. 1897. Droeshout S. J.). This note thus tells us that in 1897 the account book was in the archives of St. Charles Borromeo.

33. This author quotes as one of his manuscript sources a register entitled "Bouw der Kercke van Professen S. J. Antwerpen" ("Accounts for the building of the church, 1614–1628, in the archives of the parish church of St. Charles in Antwerp") [PONCELET, I, p. 450, n. 1]. He mentions this cash-book several times, but whether it was the original or the copy that he consulted never emerges clearly.

34. *Bouw der Kercke van Professen S. J. Antwerpen/Oncostboeck 1614–1628.*

35. It is not certain that these marks on the first page represent an obliterated text; they could as well be blots of ink.

36. The subtitle "Oncostboeck 1614–1628" (Expenditure Book 1614–1628) on the back of the volume seems somewhat suspect to us, because in this cash-book, one finds frequent references precisely to an "oncostboeck," or expenditure book.

37. "Oncostboeck" mentioned for the first time in June 1614 (Cash-book, p. 6) and *passim*.

38. In July 1615, one can read the following: "Betaelt aan diversche oncosten als v. memoriaelboeck int lange gespecifieert … 1580–13–$^1/_2$" (Paid, various expenses detailed in the "memorial book," etc.) [Cash-book, p. 35]. It is probable that this "memoriaelboeck," mentioned only once, is none other than the "oncostboeck" (the Expenditures Book).

39. This book is referred to when there is mention of money being borrowed (Cash-book, pp. 76, 102, 109, etc.).

40. "Aen schulden vant huys overgenomen als by den staet gemaeckt by Lib. expositorum … 54.190.16 (Fl.)" (Debts taken

over from the house, as in the state of accounts in the *Liber expositorum*) [Cash-book, p. 208].

41. Such tallies were made in June 1616 (pp. 56, 57), April 13, 1617 (pp. 78–80), June 1, 1617 (pp. 94–96), July 1, 1619 (pp. 148–157), February 13, 1621 (p. 186), and finally on November 10, 1621 (pp. 196–209). In the final balance one finds the working out of charges with the Residence (pp. 200, 201), and a general tally of the income and outgo from 1616 onward as well as a statement of unpaid debts (pp. 202–9). One can find other recapitulatory statements on April 15, 1623 (pp. 216–24), and on December 31, 1623 (pp. 228–35). The last entry in the cash-book (p. 245) is dated December 31, 1628. Several times one finds signatures of people who approved the accounts, that of Carolus Scribanus, the Provincial of the "Provincia Flandro–Belgica" (pp. 152, 157), that of Gualterius Clericus (p. 188), and that of Johannes de Tollenaere (p. 235).

42. "Aen Cornelis Lanslodt tot voldoeninge van sijn overgegeven memorie van de marber ... 631.12.$^1$/$_2$ (Fl.)" [Cash-book, p. 83].

43. "Aen diverse materialen als andere oncosten, oock de wercklieden betaelt als p. den oncostboeck ... 2781.2 (Fl.)" [Cash-book, p. 83].

44. PONCELET, I, p. 454.

45. "Casse debet aende Kerck" and "De kerck debet aen de Casse".

46. PONCELET, I, pp. 452–54.

47. PONCELET, I, 479–82.

48. "Generale afrekinghe *(sic)* tuschen de nieu kerck ende het huys van Professen" (Cash-book, pp. 200, 201).

49. K. Droeshout, *Histoire de la Compagnie de Jésus à Anvers. B. La Maison Professe, I, Années 1607–1621* (ms. at Egenhoven, *Fonds Droeshout*), pp. 167, 236, 237.

50. Cash-book, pp. 135, 137, 169, and *passim*.

51. "Schulden bevonden tot laste vande nieu kerck": "Leeninghe sonder interest"; "Leeninghe met interest" and "Aende de ondergenoemde personen."

52. "Petro Paulo Rubbens ... 3000.– (Fl.)" [Cash-book, p. 80; see MARTIN, p. 220].

53. K. DROESHOUT, *op. cit.*, p. 297.

54. At least, if we compare this sum with the 667 florins which the Plantin firm paid Rubens for the numerous frontispieces and illustrations which he had executed during the long period from 1610 to 1640 (H. BOUCHERY and F. VAN DEN WIJNGAERT, *P. P. Rubens en het Plantijnsche huis,* Antwerp, 1941, p. 49). It should be noted here that Rubens' name does not figure in the cash-book in the list of persons who contributed to the construction of the new church. Other artists however dit not lag behind in this respect: Johan Ruckers, the maker of harpsichords, gave 28 florins when there was a collection in the parish of Our Lady in May 1617 (p. 89); Anthony van Dyck donated ten florins that same month and 16 sous in a collection in the parish of St. Walburga (p. 90), and "Brueghel the painter" gave 12 florins in July 1618 (p. 124). It is possible that Rubens thought he had contributed sufficiently to the enterprise by his advice and by the drafts and sketches carried out by him for the sculptured decoration of the church (unless he made an anonymous donations.)

55. J. R. Martin also admits this possibility, contrary to Jaffé, who seems to regard the 3,000 florins as representing Rubens' fees for his collaboration in the construction of the new church (MARTIN, p. 220). It may seem surprising that the sum does not appear again in the balance sheet of July 1, 1619, but the latter covers only the financial transactions after June 1, 1617, so that the item in question would not have been mentioned again.

56. J. BRANDS, article *Boekhouden, Grote Winkler Prins,* IV, Amsterdam–Brussels, 1967, pp. 190–93.

57. OLDENBOURG, p. 118.

58. OLDENBOURG, p. 158.

59. BURCHARD–D'HULST, I, p. 147.

60. OLDENBOURG, pp. 142–47.

61. BURCHARD–D'HULST, I, p. 135.

62. "Petro Paulo Rubens schilder ... 10,000.– (Fl.)" [Cash-book, p. 187; MARTIN, p. 221].

63. For the dating of the ceiling paintings, see MARTIN, p. 40.

64. Cash-book, p. 205; MARTIN, p. 221.

65. Here is the text of the contract: "ende sal den voors. P. Praepositus van dien voorseyden dage—voor de voorseyde f. 10,000 aan den voorseyden Sr Rubbens Jaerlycx Rentswys tot 6$^1$/$_4$p.c$^{to}$ betalen f. 625, totten tyd toe hem gelieven sal de voors. somme ten geheelen oft ten deel afteleggen" (and the above-mentioned P. Praepositus will pay, on the agreed date [i.e., the day of delivery of the 39 ceiling pictures], for the aforesaid 10,000 florins, to Sr. Rubens, an annual income of 625 florins, at the interest of 6$^1$/$_4$%, until such time as he decides to pay the entire sum mentioned above, or a part of the same). [MARTIN, p. 214].

66. "Pedro Paulo Rubbens ... 10000.– (Fl.)" [Cash-book, pp. 219, 231; MARTIN, p. 221].

67. PONCELET, I, pp. 479–82.

68. A drawing by Rubens for the high altar is preserved in the Albertina in Vienna (GLÜCK–HABERDITZL, p. 46, no. 130, ill.; L. BURCHARD et R. A. D'HULST, [*Exh. Cat.*] *Dessins de Rubens,* Rubens House, Antwerp, 1956, no. 69). In the Kupferstichkabinett of the Dahlem Museum, Berlin, one can see a page of studies for one of the angels which crown the altar (GLÜCK–HABERDITZL, p. 46, no. 132, ill.). Jacob de Wit points out that a sketch on wood that Rubens made for the statues which crown the altar was in the Residence. In 1748, however, it was part of the collection of A. de Groot in The Hague (J. DE WIT, *De Kerken van Antwerpen,* ed. J. de Bosschere, Antwerp–The Hague, 1910, p. 60). A few years ago, the sketch was to be found on the London art market ([*Exh. Cat.*] *Oil Sketches and Small Pictures by Sir Peter Paul Rubens,* King's Lynn, 1960, no. 10; [*Exh. Cat.*] *Oil Sketches and Smaller Pictures by Sir Peter Paul Rubens,* Agnew, London, 1961, no. 15). A contemporary source, namely, a leaflet written by Father Michiel de Gryse, on the occasion of the festivities organized in Antwerp for the canonization of Ignatius of Loyola and Francis Xavier, mentions Rubens as the author of the high altar. This little volume was published by the Plantin Press in 1622, without the author's name, under the title: *Honor D. Ignatio de Loyola... habitus a Patribus S. J. domus professae ex collegii Soc. Jesu Antverpiae* (Rubens is named on p. 18; cited by K. DROESHOUT, *op. cit.,* pp. 464, 465).

69. P. VISSCHERS, *Iets over Jacob Jonghelinck, metaalgieter en penningsnijder, Octavio van Veen, schilder in de XVI$^e$ eeuw; en de gebroeders Collijns de Nole, beeldhouwers in de XV$^e$, XVI$^e$ en XVII$^e$ eeuw,* Antwerp, 1853, p. 100.

70. M. KONRAD, "Antwerpener Binnenräume im Zeitalter des Rubens," in P. CLEMEN and others, *Belgische Kunstdenkmäler,* II, Munich, 1923, pp. 210, 211.

71. Konrad uses the small head of the Jesus on the statue of the Virgin which can be seen on the façade of the church of St. Charles Borromeo as a basis to attribute the *Virgin and Child* of the high altar to Van Mildert. This argument can hardly be valid, since the small head was sculptured in 1820 by J. B. van Hool, who later restored the damaged statue. (LEYSSENS, p. 30). According to Visschers, F. Peeters (*op. cit.,* p. 27) attributes the high altar to Andries Colijns de Nole. A. Jansen et C. Van Herck ("De Antwerpsche beeldhouwers Collijns de Nole," *Jaarboek Kon. Oudheidkundige Kring van Antwerpen,* XIX, 1944, p. 76, 77, no. 61) do the same, while also mentioning the alternative of Nole–Van Mildert. Cas-

teels (*De beeldhouwers de Nole te Kamerijk, te Utrecht en te Antwerpen*, Brussels, 1961, pp. 134) sees in the high altar a relatively early work of Andries Colijns de Nole. Burchard and R. A. d'Hulst consider Hans van Mildert to be the author of the work (BURCHARD–D'HULST, I, p. 186).

72. "... is waarschijnelijck gevrogt door Johannes van Mildert" (J. VAN DER SANDEN, *Oud Konst-Toneel van Antwerpen*, ms. now in the City Archives, Antwerp, *Privilegie Kamer*, 173, II, f. 128/18).

73. "Mr. Hans van Mildert beelsnyder ... 700,– (Fl.)" (Cash-book, p. 56). It may be, of course, that an earlier payment to Van Mildert is contained in one of the entries for which the cash-book refers to the "expenditures book." Immediately below Van Mildert one finds a colleague of his: "Mr. Melchior beelsnyder ... 100,– (Fl.)." This could be Melchior van Beveren, a pupil of Robert Colijns de Nole, who became a master in 1615 (ROMBOUTS–VAN LERIUS, I, p. 514) and who probably died as early as 1620 (M. CASTEELS, *op. cit.*, pp. 48, 126, 269).

74. "Mr. Hans van Mildert beelsnyder ... 2 688.10 (Fl.)" [Cash-book, p. 187].

75. "200.– (Fl.) Mr. Hans van Mildert ... 3 200.– (Fl.)" [Cash-book, p. 204]. The 200 florins which precede the name represent the annual payment at $6^1/_4\%$, which, as in the case of Rubens, had to be paid as long as the main sum was not entirely paid off.

76. "Item noch aen dese naer volgende loopende schulden: Aen Mr. Hans van Mildert beelsnyder ... 4 234.8 (Fl.)" [Item, for the following debts not yet paid: to Mr. Hans van Mildert, sculptor, etc.]. (Cash-book, p. 208).

77. For the sculptures ornamenting the main façade, see, among others, P. VISSCHERS, *op. cit.*, pp. 93, 94 (with mention of numerous restorations), LEYSSENS, pp. 128–30, and A. JANSEN and C. VAN HERCK, *op. cit.*, pp. 65, 66, no. 42 (with detailed bibliography). One can read interesting observations on the sculptures decorating the interior of the church in: K. FREMANTLE, *The Baroque Town Hall of Amsterdam*, Utrecht, 1959, pp. 128 ff.

78. The tower was certainly completed on July 23, 1622, if not earlier, for on that day it was brilliantly illuminated for the celebrations in honor of the canonization of Ignatius and Francis Xavier (PONCELET, I, p. 465).

79. "... voor vercochte materialen als tgeene t'over betaelt was aent houdt van den daecke ... 1 249.10 (Fl.)" [Cash-book, p. 187].

80. "alreede opgemaeckt" (MARTIN, p. 214).

81. "... et la trova cosa mariviglioosa" (M. F. S. HERVEY, *The Life, Correspondence and Collection of Thomas Howard, Earl of Arundel*, Cambridge, England, 1921, p. 175).

82. "van Baele schilder ... 500 (Fl.)" [Cash-book, p. 187].

83. For the description of these pictures, see T. VAN LERIUS, *Biographies d'artistes anversois*, II, Antwerp–Ghent, 1881, pp. 283, 284. It is possible, but far from having been proved, that in this sum of 500 florins was included the fees for two small pictures painted by Van Balen in the little niches near the altar, dedicated to St. Joseph (T. VAN LERIUS, *op. cit.*, pp. 284, 285). The scenes that this artist represented on the marble of the altar of the Chapel of the Virgin are certainly of a later date (J. H. PLANTENGA, *L'architecture religieuse dans l'ancien Duché de Brabant*, The Hague, 1926, p. 91). This item of expenditure of February 13, 1621, contradicts the opinion put forward by VAN LERIUS (*op. cit.*, pp. 282, 283), namely, that makeshift altars had been put up for the benediction of the church and that Hendrik van Balen had therefore not executed the small pictures until after 1621.

84. On November 10, 1621, the sum due to Van Balen had diminished to 334 florins ("aen Hendrick van Bael schilder ... 334.– (Fl.)" [Cash-book, p. 209]. In the meantime, a first

payment had no doubt taken place. When on December 31, 1623, a fresh tally of debts was drawn up, the painter's name no longer figures in it: his work had probably been remunerated in full.

85. "Mr. Hans van Mildert beelsnyder ... 957.4 (Fl.)" [Cash-book, p. 224]. On the Van Mildert family, see: J. VAN ROEY, "De Antwerpse Herkomst van Hans van Mildert, beeldsnijder," in *Jaarboek, Antwerpen, Koninklijk Museum voor Schone Kunsten*, 1966, pp. 181–92; on the place of the altar in the development of the portico-altar in the Southern Netherlands, see: F. BAUDOUIN, "Altars and Altarpieces before 1620," in *Rubens Before 1620*, ed. John Rupert Martin, Princeton, N. J., 1972, pp. 85–91.

## 9. An Outline of Works by Rubens in the Period 1620 to 1628

1. H. G. EVERS, *Rubens und sein Werk. Neue Forschungen*, Brussels, 1943, pp. 28–55. For Rubens' journey to Bois-le-Duc, see E. GEUDENS, *Het Hoofdambacht der Meerseniers (Godsdienst en Kunstzin)*, Antwerp, 1891, p. 136. We hope to return to this subject in a later study.

2. J. G. VAN GELDER, "Rubens in Holland in de zeventiende eeuw," *Nederlands Kunsthistorisch Jaarboek*, II, 1950–1951, pp. 119, 120.

3. See Chapter 10.

4. MARTIN, pp. 213–15.

5. "... mitsgaders sommige andere syne disipelen"; "... 't gene men bevinden sal daer aen te gebreken" (*Ibidem*, p. 214).

6. From a letter of April 28, 1618, to Sir Dudley Carleton, in which there is a list of canvases which Rubens had at that time and was counting on handing over to Carleton in exchange for his collection of classical statues. One of the pictures is described in these terms: "Un quadro di un Achille vestito di donna fatto del meglior mio discepolo, i tutto ritocco de mia mano, quadro vagliissimo e pieno de molte fanciulle bellissime" (ROOSES–RUELENS, II, p. 137). This "meglior discepolo" can be none other than Van Dyck, according to the commentators of Rubens' correspondence.

7. See Chapter 3.

8. H. VEY, *Die Zeichnungen Anton van Dycks*, I, Brussels, 1962, pp. 61–63.

9. O. MILLAR, *Rubens: The Whitehall Ceiling (Charlton Lectures on Art)*, London–New York–Toronto, 1958, p. 5; see also on this series, which was executed only in 1630–1634: P. PALME, *Triumph of Peace*, Stockholm, 1956; J. S. HELD, in *The Burlington Magazine*, CXII, 1970, pp. 274–81; O. MILLAR, [*Exh. Cat.*] *The Age of Charles I, Painting in England 1620–1649*, London, Tate Gallery, 1972, pp. 37–41, no. 39–41.

10. J. THUILLIER and J. FOUCART, *Rubens' Life of Marie de' Medici*, New York, 1969. See also J. THUILLIER, "La 'Galerie de Médicis' de Rubens et sa genèse: un document inédit," *Revue de l'Art*, 4, 1969, pp. 52–62.

11. D. DUBON, *Tapestries from the Samuel H. Kress Collection at the Philadelphia Museum of Art. The History of Constantine the Great designed by Peter Paul Rubens and Pietro da Cortona*, n.p., 1964.

12. See Chapter 3.

13. ROOSES, I, pp. 53–78, no. 41–55; E. TORMO Y MONZÓ, "La Apoteosis eucaristica de Rubens," *Archivo español de arte*, XV, 1942, pp. 1–26, 117–31, 291–315; V. H. ELBERN, [*Exh. Cat.*] *Peter Paul Rubens, Triomph der Eucharistie, Wandteppiche aus dem Kölner Dom*, Villa Hügel, Essen, 1954–1955; G. SCRIBNER III, "Sacred Architecture, Rubens' Eucharist Series," *The Art Bulletin*, LVII, 1975, pp. 519–28; N. DE POORTER, *The Eucharist Series (Corpus Rubenianum Ludwig Burchard*, II), Brussels, 1977.

14. "Hier viert de *Fides Catholica* triomf over Nijd en Twee-dracht, die onder den forschen tred van haar fiere rossen en de wielen van haar wagen vermorzeld worden, niettegenstaande het machteloos geweld van hun Rubeniaansche spierenoverdadigheid. Tevens zegepraalt zij over Verblindheid en Onwetendheid, die nu hun licht gaan ontvangen van de katholieke leer, opstralend uit den Sacramentskelk, dien de *Fides Catholica* als een zon over de wereld laat gloren" (M. SABBE, "Het Geestesleven in Rubens' Tijd," in PRIMS, *Rubens en zijne Eeuw,* p. 64).

15. ROOSES-RUELENS, III, p. 319.

16. I. JOST, "Bemerkungen zur Heinrichsgalerie des P. P. Rubens," *Nederlands Kunsthistorisch Jaarboek,* XV, 1964, pp. 175–219.

17. OLDENBOURG, pp. 316, 317; I. JOST, *op. cit.,* pp. 196 ff., figs. 5, 6.

18. *Large Last Judgment,* panel, 19'9³/₄" × 15'6¹/₄" (605 × 474 cm); *Small Last Judgment,* panel, 70¹/₄" × 46⁷/₈" (183.5 × 119 cm); Cat. 1957, no. 611; ROOSES, I, pp. 103–5, no. 91; OLDENBOURG, p. 195.

19. Panel, 47¹/₂" × 65" (121 × 165.5 cm); Cat. 1957, no. 324; ROOSES, III, pp. 51–54, no. 570; OLDENBOURG, p. 196; L. VAN PUYVELDE, *Peter Paul Rubens, Die Amazonenschlacht,* Amsterdam, 1950.

20. Panel, 19¹/₄" × 15³/₈" (49 × 39 cm); Cat. 1959, no. 393; ROOSES, II, pp. 359, 360, no. 499; OLDENBOURG, p. 234.

21. A. H. CORNETTE, *Petrus Paulus Rubens,* Antwerp, 1940, p. 84.

22. Panel, 14'8" × 11' (447 × 336 cm); Cat. 1959, no. 298; ROOSES, I, pp. 227–30, no. 174; OLDENBOURG, p. 277.

23. Canvas, 12'7" × 9'2" (384 × 280 cm); Cat. 1959, no. 377; ROOSES, I, pp. 207–10, no. 158; OLDENBOURG, p. 192; [*Exh. Cat.*] *Le Siècle de Rubens,* Musées Royaux des Beaux-Arts de Belgique, Brussels, 1965, no. 187, ill.

24. Canvas, 15'6" × 9'2" (475 × 280 cm); ROOSES, II, pp. 222–30, no. 396; E. DHANENS, *Sint-Baafskathedraal Gent (Inventaris van het Kunstpatrimonium Oostvlaanderen,* V), Ghent, 1965, pp. 206, 208, no. 460, figs. 204, 205.

25. See Chapter 3.

26. ROOSES, II, pp. 173–80, no. 359; OLDENBOURG, p. 301; J. DE COO, *Rubens-Gids voor de Antwerpse Kerken,* II, Antwerp, 1947, pl. 5; recently: C. VAN DE VELDE, "Rubens' Hemelvaart van Maria in de Kathedraal te Antwerpen," in *Jaarboek, Kon. Museum voor Schone Kunsten, Antwerpen,* 1975, pp. 245–77.

27. H. GERSON and E. H. TER KUILE, *Art and Architecture in Belgium 1600 to 1800,* Harmondsworth, 1960, p. 95.

28. "... een orchestratie van tonen, die op een zeer positieve wijze hun eigen waarde in het geheel handhaven, maar een ondeelbare versmeltende eenheid van verrukkend weelderige kleuren" (A. STUBBE, *Het zien en genieten van schilderkunst. Aesthetische beschouwingen,* Antwerp, 1942, p. 44).

29. ROOSES, I, pp. 285–88, no. 214; OLDENBOURG, p. 305; J. DE COO, *op. cit.,* II, pl. 10.

30. F. PEETERS, *L'église Saint-Augustin à Anvers,* Antwerp, 1930, p. 99.

31. A. STUBBE, *op. cit.,* p. 45.

32. P. BJURSTRÖM, "Rubens' *St. George and the Dragon,*" *The Art Quarterly, XVIII,* 1955, p. 28, fig. 1; F. GROSSMANN, "Notes on some Dutch and Flemish Paintings at Rotterdam," *The Burlington Magazine,* XCVII, 1955, p. 337; HELD, I, p. 117, no. 53 °; II, pl. 59; BURCHARD-D'HULST, I, pp. 225–27, no. 145; II, pl. 145 °.

33. P. BJURSTRÖM, *op. cit.,* fig. 2; HELD, II, pl. 58; BURCHARD-D'HULST, II, pl. 145 v°.

34. Panel, 25¹/₄" × 19³/₄" (63.5 × 49.5 cm); inv. no. 464; ROOSES, I, p. 289, no. 214³; OLDENBOURG, p. 303, on the right; L. VAN PUYVELDE, *Les esquisses de Rubens,* Basle, 1948, pp. 82, 83, no. 57, pl. 57; P. BJURSTRÖM, *op. cit.,* p. 31; F. GROSSMANN, *op. cit.,* p. 337.

35. Panel, 31" × 21³/₄" (79 × 55 cm); Cat. 1963, no. 780; ROOSES, I, p. 289, no. 214²; L. VAN PUYVELDE, *op. cit.,* p. 83, no. 58, pl. 58; P. BJURSTRÖM, *op. cit.,* p. 31; F. GROSSMANN, *op. cit.,* p. 337.

36. Caen, Musée des Beaux-Arts; panel, 16¹/₈" × 11³/₄" (41 × 30 cm); P. BJURSTRÖM, *op. cit.,* pp. 31, 41, fig. 4; F. GROSSMANN, *op. cit.,* p. 337.

37. Inv. no. 1043 E; GLÜCK-HABERDITZL, p. 53, no. 173, ill.; HELD, I, p. 140, no. 113; II, pl. 122; BURCHARD-D'HULST, I, pp. 232, 233, no. 148; II, pl. 148.

38. Panel, 51¹/₈" × 42¹/₂" (130 × 108 cm); Cat. 1963, no. 1685; ROOSES, IV, pp. 215, 216, no. 997; OLDENBOURG, p. 268; J. THUILLIER and J. FOUCART, *op. cit.,* pl. 1.

39. London, Victoria and Albert Museum; inv. no. D 906–1900; GLÜCK-HABERDITZL, pp. 49, 50, no. 151, repr.; F. BAUDOUIN, [*Exh. Cat.*] *Rubens Diplomaat,* Rubenskasteel, Elewijt, 1962, pp. 119, 120, no. 36, fig. 21; BURCHARD-D'HULST, I, pp. 203, 204, no. 130; II, pl. 130.

40. Copenhagen, Statens Museum for Kunst; panel, 47¹/₄" × 40¹/₈" (120 × 102.5 cm); Cat. 1951, no. 613; ROOSES, IV, pp. 285, 286, no. 1081; OLDENBOURG, p. 276.

41. Panel, 46" × 33¹/₂" (117 × 85 cm); ROOSES, IV, pp. 270, 271, no. 1059; OLDENBOURG, p. 289; F. BAUDOUIN, *op. cit.,* pp. 107, 108, no. 7, fig. 7.

42. Inv. no. 8258; GLÜCK-HABERDITZL, p. 51, no. 164, ill.; F. BAUDOUIN, *op. cit.,* pp. 124, 125, no. 42, fig. 8.

43. Inv. no. 8256; GLÜCK-HABERDITZL, p. 50, no. 156, ill.; HELD, I, p. 138, no. 107; II, pl. 119; F. BAUDOUIN, *op. cit.,* pp. 120, 121, no. 37, fig. 15.

44. The portrait in Cleveland: J.-A. GORIS-J. S. HELD, *Rubens in America,* Antwerp, 1947, p. 26, no. 1, pl. II; the portrait in Florence: panel, 33¹/₂" × 24¹/₂" (86 × 62 cm); Cat. 1952, no. 779; ROOSES, IV, p. 133, no. 896; OLDENBOURG, p. 282, on the right.

45. Panel, 47" × 42³/₄" (119 × 98 cm); Cat. 1959, no. 706; ROOSES, IV, pp. 186, 187, no. 958; OLDENBOURG, p. 304.

## 10. Rubens the Diplomat

1. J. LEFÈVRE, *La Politique des Archiducs Albert et Isabelle 1598–1633,* [*Exh. Cat.*] *Rubens Diplomate,* Elewijt, 1962, p. 9.

2. J. LEFÈVRE, "Het Zuiden tijdens het Bestand," *Algemene Geschiedenis der Nederlanden,* VI, Utrecht, 1953, pp. 288–304.

3. See Chapter 12.

4. DE MAEYER, pp. 96, 293, 294.

5. ROOSES-RUELENS, III, pp. 253–60.

6. "... teniendo consideracion á las buenas partes de Pedro Paulo Rubens y á lo que ha servido á su Magestad, para que pueda continuarlo con mas comodidad ..." (GACHARD, pp. 6, 265; this work is still the authority concerning Rubens' role as a diplomat, although one can add the odd detail discovered in subsequently found letters. We would mention as a recent publication: C. V. WEDGWOOD, *The Political Career of Rubens,* London, 1975. The importance of Rubens' relationship with Jan Brant is scarcely mentioned here.

7. It seems that the initiative came from Jan Brant (GACHARD, pp. 21, 22, note 1).

8. For the biography of Pecquius (1562–1625) see V. BRANTS in *Biographie nationale de Belgique,* XVI, Brussels, 1901, cols. 784–92, and L. P. L. PIRENNE, "Petrus Peckius, dienaar der Aartshertogen," *Voor Rogier,* Hilversum, 1964, pp. 81–96. He was related to Rubens through his mother, Catharina Gillis, the sister of Jan Gillis, pensioner of the city of Antwerp. The latter was addressed as cousin ("mon cousin") by Jan Rubens, the painter's father (ROOSES-RUELENS, I, p. 387). Pecquius acted as legal adviser of Maria Pijpelinckx, Rubens' mother, in 1591 (ROOSES-RUELENS, I,

p. 400). Philip Rubens, the artist's brother, who wrote in a letter on June 11, 1607, that he only knew Pecquius by name, but that he also knew that he was connected with his father "by ties of friendship and of blood" ("mihi quidem de fama notum, patri vero quondam meo tum amicitia sanguinis nexu junctum"; ROOSES-RUELENS, I, pp. 384, 385), soon started a correspondence with him (*Ibidem*, I, p. 396; II, pp. 14 ff.). A portrait of Pecquius by Rubens formed part of a private English collection in 1953 ([*Exh. Cat. Flemish Art 1300–1700*, Royal Academy, London, 1953–54, no. 208). Another version of this portrait is preserved in the Musées Royaux des Beaux-Arts de Belgique, Brussels (Cat. 1959, no. 968).

9. J. LEFÈVRE, "Het Zuiden tijdens het Bestand," *op. cit.*, p. 217. In the 17th century, the career of diplomat was still not a very clearly defined office. "During the first half of the century, negotiators in no way constituted a special class of official in any country; to mention only a few names well known to everybody: president Jeannin was a judge; Rubens and Gerbier were painters" (GEORGE CLARK, *De Zeventiende Eeuw (Aula-Boeken)*, Utrecht–Antwerp, 1959, p. 125).

10. GACHARD, pp. 19, n. 2; 184, n. 2; A. HALLEMA, *Prins Maurits*, Assen, 1949, pp. 181, 182.

11. On the role of Willem de Bie, see GACHARD, p. 19; *Correspondance de la Cour d'Espagne*, II, ed. H. Lonchay, J. Cuvelier, and J. Lefèvre, Brussels, 1927, pp. 2, 9, 13, 205; for his relationship to Constantine Huygens, see P. GEYL, *Kernproblemen van onze geschiedenis*, Utrecht, 1937, p. 64.

12. GACHARD, p. 21, n. 1; *Correspondance de la Cour d'Espagne*, *op. cit.*, II, pp. 181, 182.

13. ROOSES-RUELENS, III, p. 335.

14. ROOSES-RUELENS, III, pp. 378–80, 385.

15. GACHARD, p. 26.

16. ROOSES-RUELLENS, III, pp. 335–40.

17. *Correspondance de la Cour d'Espagne, op. cit.*, II, p. 250.

18. See Chapter 12.

19. "Io crederei un viaggio esser proprio per levarmi dinansi molti oggietti, che necessariamente mi raffrescono il dolore …" (ROOSES-RUELENS, III, p. 445).

20. "… he sentido mucho que se halle introducido por ministro de materias tan grandes un pintor" (GACHARD, p. 55; ROOSES-RUELENS, IV, p. 82).

21. "Gerbier es pintor como Rubens, y el duque de Bocquingan le embió aqui con carta de su mano propria para el d^ho Rubens a hacer la propusicion: con que no se podia dexar de oyrle. Y estas propusiciones, aunque se comienzen por uno ó otro, haviendo despues de passar adelante, cosa clara es que se harian por personas gravas" (GACHARD, p. 56; ROOSES-RUELENS, IV, p. 85, n. 1).

22. "C'est pourquoy je vous prie de trouver moyen q[ue] cela se face à requisition de [Buckingham] m'escrivant une lettre à cest effect disant qu'il vous envoye celle part, vous enchargeant de beaucoup de choses qui ne se peuvent seurement ny aisément fier à papier. Et qu'il ne vous ose renvoyer de nouveau à [Bruxelles] pour ce que cela causeroit trop de bruict, comme il fit l'autre fois …" (GACHARD, p. 58; ROOSES-RUELENS, IV, pp. 71, 72).

23. "Ick bidde U.E. te ghelooven dat ick doen al wat ick can, ende dat ick vinde mijne meesters seer gheappassioneert in de saecke, haer vindende ghepicqueert ende gheaffronteert van Olivares, wiens passie prevaleert ende gheaffronteert van Olivares, wiens passie prevaleert aan alle redenen ende consideratien, …" (ROOSES-RUELENS, IV, p. 125).

24. DE MAEYER, p. 105.

25. Now in the Alte Pinakothek in Munich (canvas, 8'6³/₄" × 8'8¹/₈"; 261 × 265 cm; OLDENBOURG, p. 200).

26. M. G. DE BOER, *Die Friedensunterhandlungen zwischen Spanien und die Niederlanden in den Jahren 1632 und 1633*, Groningen, 1898.

27. M. SABBE, "Het geestesleven in Rubens' tijd," in PRIMS, *Rubens en zijne Eeuw*, p. 110.

28. "Questa citta va languendo come un corpo ethico che si consume poco a poco. Ogni di vediamo mancar il numero degli habitanti, non havendo questo misero populo alcun mezzo da sostentarsi colla industria degli suoi arteficii o traffichi" (ROOSES-RUELENS, IV, p. 265).

29. "Gia si trovano stracchi, non tanto per gli travagli della guerra quanto delle perpetue difficulta a cavar le provisioni necessarie da Spagna e le necessita estreme nelle quali quasi di continuo si ritrovano, e per le indignità che soffriscono ben spesso per la malignita o ignoranza di quei ministri ò della impossibilita di far altrimenti" (ROOSES-RUELENS, IV, p. 252).

30. "Qui siamo in ocio et in un stato mezzano tra Pace e Guerra sentendo però tutte le incommodita di violenza in fuori della Guerra senza alcun beneficio de Pace. Questa citta si perde à poco et suo jam succo vivit non avendo alcun resto di traffico per sostentarsi. Gli Spagnoli pensano col serrar le licenze indebbolire il nemico e s'ingannano redondando tutto il danno sopra gli vassalli del Re" (ROOSES-RUELENS, IV, p. 452).

31. "Questo è un temperamento fra l'ocio y la guerra offensiva, la qual è di grandissima spesa y fatica et di poco frutto contro populi tanto potenti e ben muniti per arte e natura" (ROOSES-RUELENS, IV, p. 30). Balthasar Moretus I shared this opinion (M. SABBE, *op. cit.*, p. 213).

32. "Di maniera chio non penso se S.A. insieme col Sig^r Marchese potessero disporre del publico a suo modo et sponte sua componere curas, che le cose passerebbono felicis^te et si vederebbe ben presto una grandissima mutatione non solamente appresso di noi ma da per tutto" (ROOSES-RUELENS, IV, pp. 446, 447).

33. ROOSES-RUELENS, IV, p. 124.

34. "Qui si mantengono ancora vive alcune prattiche secrete con Ollandesi ma sappia V.S. e creda di certo, che non cè ordine alcuno da Spagna da trattar con essi in alcuna forma non ostante che la nostra Principessa et il sig. marchese Spinola siano inclinatissimi al bene publico (che despende della pace) et la reposo proprio" (ROOSES-RUELENS, IV, p. 252).

35. "… adresso il tempo di far ogni opera da buon Patriotto per il ben commune il quale habbiamo travagliato tanto che spero col aiuto di Dio non sarà in vano" (ROOSES-RUELENS, IV, p. 252).

35. "… adresso il tempo di far ogni opera da buon Patriotto per il ben commune il quale habbiamo travagliato tanto che spero col aiuto di Dio non sarà in vano" (ROOSES-RUELENS, III, p. 379).

36. See, among others, M. Sabbe, "Betrekkingen tussen Noord en Zuid in de XVII^e eeuw," *Verslagen en Mededeelingen van de Kon. Vlaamsche Academie voor Taal- en Letterkunde*, Ghent, 1933, p. 561–79; L. VAN DER ESSEN, *De historische Gebondenheid der Nederlanden*, Brussels, 1944, pp. 46–48.

37. "… no se deve pensar que jamás aquellos estados cederán un punto de su titulo de estados libres, ni menos reconocerán al rey de España por su soberano, ni tampoco con eltitulo solo sin otra sustancia, de su propria voluntad; pero si se deve esperar que tal cosa no se hará mas que por el medio de los reyes sus confederados que acaso podrán apretarlos, aunque no forzarlos, à dat alguna satisfacion al rey de España" (ROOSES-RUELENS, IV, p. 165). There is no doubt that Rubens is putting forward here the opinion of Josias Vosberghen, a Dutchman who was the Danish ambassador in The Hague, but it is clear that he shared the point of view. An interesting detail: when Vosberghen arrived in London, shortly after his meeting with Rubens, he was accompanied by Jan Brant, the Catolico (GACHARD, p. 21).

38. "Yo non ho talento ne qualità de dar consiglio à V. Ex^a,

ma ben considero de quanta consequenza sia questa pace, che mi pare il nodo della catena de tutte le confederacioni d'Europa, ... et ancor ch'io confesso che per il Rey nostro signor saria piu importante la paz con Holandesi, mi dubito che non si fara giamai quella senza l'intervencione del Rey de Inghilterra, ma forse questa fra España et Inglaterra senza gli Ollandesi che daria da pensar et faria risolvere ancora gli altri" (ROOSES-RUELENS, V, p. 177).

39. GACHARD, pp. 312–15. See also H. G. EVERS, "Der Besuch von Rubens beim holländischen Gesandten Albrecht Joachim am 5. März 1630," *Rubens und sein Werk, Neue Forschungen,* Brussels, 1943, pp. 289–97.

40. R. VAN ROOSBROECK, "De diplomaat Rubens," *De Vlaamsche Gids,* 1940, pp. 460–68; see also by the same author; "Rubens als diplomaat," *Dietsche Warande en Belfort,* 1939, pp. 729–46, and "Bij de briefwisseling van Peter Rubens," *Nederlandsche Historiebladen,* III, 1940, pp. 136–49. It seems to me that this author is presenting us with a one-sided judgment on Rubens' political opinions. Nevertheless, one must recognize that, contrary to certain critical literature which is both superficial and fulsome, concerning Rubens' role as a diplomat, he has studied this aspect of the painter's career with a keener critical sense.

41. A. PAZYMELIA, *Serie de los mas importantes documentos del Archivo y Biblioteca del Ex.<sup>mo</sup>. Senor Duque de Medinaceli, I<sup>a</sup> Serie,* Madrid, 1915, pp. 395, 396. (English translation: RUTH S. MAGURN, *The Letters of Peter Paul Rubens,* Cambridge, Mass., 1955, pp. 370, 371).

42. DE MAEYER (p. 107) already indicated this.

43. GACHARD, pp. 258, 341, 342.

44. See, among other things, the report of the duke of Arschot himself (P. L. GACHARD, *Actes des Etats-Généraux de 1632,* II, Brussels, 1866, p. 993).

45. See Chapter 2, note 7.

46. "Io non posso se non amirarlo sommamente et lasciarlo tornare de se con grando dispiacere di perdere la piu dolce e piu erudita conversatione ch'io habbia mai havuto; in materia dell'antiquita principalmente, egli ha una notitia la piu universale e la piu esquisita ch'io viddi mai" (ROOSES-RUELENS, II, p. 336).

47. ROOSES-RUELENS, IV, p. 290.

48. J. CUVELIER, "Les négociations diplomatiques de Roosendael (1607–1630)," *Mélanges d'Histoire offerts à Henri Pirenne,* I, Brussels, 1926, pp. 73–80.

49. GACHARD, pp. 156, 157, 176.

50. GACHARD, p. 187.

51. GACHARD, pp. 195, 196.

52. GACHARD, p. 198.

53. GACHARD, pp. 259, 342, 343.

54. "ad ogni sorte d'impiegi fuori della mia dolcissima professione"; "... e lasciar la fortuna mentre che vi applaude senza aspettar chella da se vi volti la schena ..."; "... per mercede di tante fatiche la sola essentione di tali impiegi e permissione di servirla in casa mia. La qual gracia ottenni con molto maggior difficulta ch'alcuna altra chella mi habbia giamai concessa" (ROOSES-RUELENS, VI, pp. 81, 82). "Hora mi trovo per la gracia divina... colla mia moglie e figliuoli in riposo, e senza alcuna pretensione al mondo che di vivere in pace" (ROOSES-RUELENS, VI, p. 82).

55. "Io per me vorrei che tutto il mondo stesse in pace, et potessimo vivere un secolo d'oro in vece di ferro" (ROOSES-RUELENS, VI, p. 246).

## 11. War and Peace in Rubens' Works

First published in *The Connoisseur,* April, 1977, pp. 261–65.

1. Panel, 22″ × 34¹/₄″ (56 × 87 cm).

2. Panel, 21⁷/₈″ × 34″ (55.5 × 86.5 cm).

3. "62. Twee stukken, zynde nette Schetzen, waar van een verbeeldt: de Roof der Sabynen; en d'ander, den Oorlog der Sabynen tegen de Romeinen; zynde in allen deelen zeer schoon, door *Pieter Paulus Rubbens,* op *paneelen,* hoog 21, breet 32 duimen."

4. "... few pictures of Rubens, even of his most finished works, give a higher idea of his genius" (J. REYNOLDS, "A Journey to Flanders and Holland in the year 1781," in *The Literary Works of Sir Joshua Reynolds,* ed. by H. W. Beechey, II, London, 1852, pp. 149, 150).

5. Sale at Sotheby's, London, December 3, 1969, nos. 7, 8.

6. A. THYS, *Historiek der Straten en openbare Plaatsen van Antwerpen,* 2nd ed., Antwerp, 1893, p. 405; cited in R. AVERMAETE, *Jan-Peter van Baurscheit de jonge en het Huis Osterrieth,* Antwerp, 1956, pp. 35, 36.

7. *Notice sur les riches tapisseries flamandes provenant de l'Hôtel van Susteren-du Bois, dont la vente aura lieu ... à Anvers, Lundi 18 Janvier 1875,* Antwerp, 1875 (with notes by A. Siret and P. Génard). The tapestries were bought for the Museum of la Porte de Hal, in Brussels.

8. J. POUCET, *Recherches sur la légende sabine des origines de Rome,* Louvain, 1967.

9. "... this last has more novelty, and is the most interesting of the two" (REYNOLDS, *op. cit.,* p. 149).

10. JUVENAL, *Satires,* VI, pp. 240, 241.

11. W. STECHOW, *Rubens and the Classical Tradition (Martin Classical Lectures,* XXI), Cambridge, Mass., 1968, p. 6.

12. See ROOSES, *Leven,* pp. 315, 316.

13. M. SABBE, "Het Geestesleven te Antwerpen in Rubens' Tijd," in PRIMS, *Rubens en zijne Eeuw,* pp. 63–172.

14. Panel, 5′7″ × 7′9″ (170 × 236 cm); OLDENBOURG, p. 379; G. MARTIN, *National Gallery Catalogues. The Flemish School circa 1600–circa 1900,* London, 1970, pp. 109–16, no. 38.

15. Canvas, 8′4″ × 11′2″ (254 × 341 cm); Cat. 1958, no. 350; OLDENBOURG, p. 149.

16. Canvas, 6′8¹/₄″ × 9′9¹/₄″ (203.5 × 298 cm); G. MARTIN, *op. cit.,* pp. 116–25, no. 46.

17. See Chapter 10.

18. Canvas, 6′9″ × 11′3″ (206 × 342 cm); OLDENBOURG, p. 428; H. VON EINEM, *"Die Folgen des Krieges," Ein Alterswerk von Peter Paul Rubens* (offprint from *Vorträge, Rheinisch-Westfalische Akademie der Wissenschaften* [1975], pp. 1–20).

19. "La principal figura è Marte, che lasciando il tempio di Jano aperto (il quale in tempo di pace, secondo gli costumi romani, stava serrato) va collo scudo e la spada insanguinata minacciando ai popoli qualche gran ruina, curandosi poco di Venere sua dama, che si sforza con carezze ed abbracciamenti a ritenerlo, accompagnata dalli suoi Amori e Cupidini. Dall' altra banda Marte vien tirato dalla furia Aletto, con una face in mano. Mostri acconto, che significano la Peste e la Fame, compagni inseparabili della Guerra. Nel suolo giace rivolta una donna con un liuto rotto, che denota l'armonia, laquale è incompatibile colla discordia della guerra; siccome ancora una madre col bambino in braccio, dimostrando che la fecondita, generazione e carità vengono traversate dalla guerra, che corrompe e distrugge ogni cosa. Ci è di più un architetto sottosopra colli suoi strumenti in mano, per dire, che ciò che in tempo di pace vien fabbricato per la comodita e ornamento delle citta, si manda in ruina e gettasi per terra per la violenza dell' armi. Credo, sebben mi ricordo, che V. S. trovera ancora nel suolo, di sotto i piedi di Marte, un libro, e qualche disegno in carta, per inferire che egli calca le belle lettere ed altre galanterie. Vi deve esser di più un mazzo di frezze o saette col laccio, che le stringeva insieme, sciolto; che era, stando unite, l'emblema della Concordia, siccome ancora il caduceo e l'ulivo, simbolo della pace, che finsi giacerli a canto. Quella matrona lugubre, vestita di negro e col velo stracciato, e

378

spogliata delle sue gioie e d'ogni sorte d'ornamenti, è l'infelice Europa, la quale già per tanti anni soffre le rapine, gli oltraggi e le miserie, che sono tanto novice ad ognuno, che non occorre specificarle. La sua marca è quel globo, sostenuto da un angeletto o genio, con la croce in cima, che denota l'orbe cristiano" (ROOSES-RUELENS, VI, p. 208; letter of March 12, 1638).

20. Panel, 16″ × 10⁷/₈″ (40.5 × 27.5 cm); HELD, I, p. 124, under no. 66, fig. 4.

21. HELD, I, p. 124, no. 66; II, pl. 74; BURCHARD-D'HULST, I, pp. 260–63, no. 169; II, pl. 169.

22. *Brod Catalogue 1976*, London, 1976, p. 42, no. 19, ill.

23. Canvas, 7′7¹/₄″ × 11′1³/₄″ (232 × 340 cm); Cat. 1958, no. 343; OLDENBOURG, p. 313.

24. There are a few exceptions, however, such as *La Montée au Calvaire* (canvas, 18′8″ × 11′8″; 560 × 350 cm), in the Musées Royaux des Beaux-Arts in Brussels (OLDENBOURG, p. 419).

25. S. ALPERS, *The Decoration of the Torre de la Parada (Corpus Rubenianum Ludwig Burchard, IX)*, Brussels, 1971.

26. S. ALPERS, *op. cit.*, pp. 231, 232, no. 37b, fig. 138.

## 12. Rubens and the Doctors

First published in *Liber Memoralis. 350 jaar Collegium Medicum Antverpiense. 25 jaar Geneeskundige Dagen van Antwerpen*, Antwerp, 1970, pp. 55–75.

1. H. BOUCHERY and F. VAN DEN WIJNGAERT, *P. P. Rubens en het Plantijnsche Huis*, Antwerp, 1940, pp. 57, 58, 131, pls. 25, 26.

2. On Johannes Faber, see K. GERSTENBERG, "Rubens im Kreise seiner Römischen Gefährten, *Zeitschrift für Kunstgeschichte*, I, 1932, pp. 100–104, and H. WEISZÄCKER, *Adam Elsheimer der Maler von Frankfurt*, I, Berlin, 1936, pp. 82–85.

3. ROOSES-RUELENS, II, p. 465.

4. K. GERSTENBERG (*op. cit.*, pp. 107, 108) was the first to draw attention to this possibility, followed here by H. G. EVERS (*Rubens und sein Werk. Neue Forschungen*, Brussels, 1943, pp. 117, 118). The attribution to Rubens of these projects for illustrations, mostly preserved in the Louvre, is refuted, however, by F. Lugt, except for one drawing. (*Musée du Louvre, Inventaire général des dessins des écoles du Nord, Ecole Flamande*, II, Paris, 1949, pp. 30–32, nos. 1086–1102). According to H. M. VAN DER MEULEN-SCHREGARDUS (*Petrus Paulus Rubens Antiquarius, Collector and Copyist of Antique Gems*, Diss., Utrecht, 1975, pp. 64 ff.) a second drawing of this series could also be by the hand of Rubens. She also points out that the 17 drawings in the Louvre are copies after drawings of Theodore Galle and that they were not used to illustrate Faber's book.

5. "... egissem jam pridem, si per fratris morbum licuisset" (ROOSES-RUELENS, I, p. 338).

6. "Hunc cum olim Romae pleuritide graviter laborantem, per Dei gratiam, sanitati restituissem, Gallum mihi depinxit gallinaceum, cum iocosa haec verba, erudita tamen subscripsit. Pro Salute V.C. (Viro clarissimo) Joanni Fabro M.D. (medico doctori) Aesculapio meo, olim damnatus L. M. (Libens merito) votum solvo. Verum quoque effigium meam simillimam, in magna tabula, coloribus expressit, quae ob artis praestantiam magni a pictoribus aestimatur" (K. GERSTENBERG, *op. cit.*, p. 101).

7. Rooses thought he could recognize this representation of a cock, given as a present by Rubens to Faber, in a picture in the Musée Suermondt in Aachen. Today, however, there is general agreement that this work should be attributed to Frans Snyders (see K. ARNDT, "De gallo et jaspide. Ein Fabelmotiv bei Frans Snyders," in *Argo. Festschrift für Kurt Badt*,

Cologne, 1970, pp. 290–96 and in *Aachener Kunstblätter*, XL, 1971, pp. 186–93).

8. Unless one wants to identify this picture, as K. Gerstenberg did (*op. cit.*, p. 104), with the group portrait preserved in the Wallraf-Richartz-Museum, Cologne, which seems to us very risky (see the *status quaestionis* in H. VEY and A. M. KESTING, *Katalog der niederländischen Gemälde von 1550 bis 1800 im Wallraf-Richartz-Museum*, Cologne, 1967, pp. 94, 95, no. Dep. 248).

9. ROOSES-RUELENS, VI, pp. 323, 324.

10. See Chapter 1.

11. "Supplico V.S. al arivo del Sgr. Scippio in Roma a voler me li tener in Gratia e quella del Sig. Adamo mio compare, il Sigr. Enrico et altri boni amici la cui bona conversatione mi fara venire talvolta martello di Roma" (ROOSES-RUELENS, VI, p. 324).

12. ROOSES-RUELENS, VI, pp. 327, 328.

13. Our account of Doctor Verwilt is based mainly on C. RUELENS, "Le mariage des frères Rubens," *Rubens-Bulletijn*, III, 1888, pp. 145–88.

14. "... doer dien dat den scilder comen is, Rubbens broeder, ende men tracteert geweldich van stadtswegen dat de Moy soude syn officie willen vercoopen aan de stadt om alsoo stillekens Rubbens in officie te stellen, en als dan met volle machte ende secretaris wesende, de dochter weder te comen pretenderen, soo dat ic dapper in de weer syn ende toe sien, dat ic noch omstoote (want de ander al afgeseten sancten syn) voor de laatste reyse" (C. RUELENS, *op. cit.*, p. 186).

15. "Io trovo per esperienza che simil negocii non vogliono esser trattati freddamente ma con ogni fervore, come ancora ha provato mio fratello doppo il mio arrivo con cangiar stilo, havendo penato duoi anni in vano" (ROOSES-RUELENS, VI, p. 323).

16. "Voorts van de Matresse, het is claer sy is nu heel Rubbens versint, ende wilt hem nu per fortse hebben" (C. RUELENS, *op. cit.*, p. 187).

17. C. BROECKX, *Histoire du Collegium Medicum Antverpiense*, Antwerp, 1858, p. 25.

18. C. BROECKX, *Galerie médicale anversoise*, Antwerp, 1866, p. 74; in 1630 his name is met for the last time on a list of official doctors of the city of Antwerp.

19. C. BROECKX, *Histoire du Collegium Medicum Antverpiense*, Antwerp, 1858, p. 26.

20. *Ibidem*, p. 41.

21. *Ibidem*, pp. 44, 51, 71, 72.

22. P. BOEYMANS, "Les Nuñez, famille d'illustres médecins d'origine espagnole à Anvers aux XVIᵉ et XVIIᵉ siècle," *Actas del XV Congreso Internacional de Historia de la Medecina*, I, Madrid, 1958, pp. 229–33. See also: J. PINES, "Les médecins marranes espagnols et portuguais à Anvers au XVIᵉ et XVIIᵉ siècles" (offprint from *Le Scalpel* [Brussels], no. 26, June 29, 1963, pp. 4–5); E. SCHMIDT, *Geschiedenis van de Joden te Antwerpen*, Antwerp, 1963, p. 40.

23. P. BOEYMANS, *loc. cit.*; see by the same author: *De Geneeskunde te Antwerpen in de 17de eeuw*, in *Liber Memorialis. 350 jaar Collegium Medicum Antverpiense. 25 jaar Geneeskundige Dagen van Antwerpen*, pp. 89–102.

24. "L'operetta di Ludovico Nunnio si trova buona in quella materia secondo il giudicio de nostri Phisici" (ROOSES-RUELENS, IV, p. 291).

25. H. BOUCHERY and F. VAN DEN WIJNGAERT, *op. cit.*, pp. 92, 145, pls. 100, 101.

26. Panel, 48¹/₂″ × 39¹/₂″ (123 × 100 cm). Formerly in the collection of Lady Lucas (L. BURCHARD, [*Exh. Cat.*] *Works by Peter Paul Rubens, Kt.*, Wildenstein & Co., London, 1950, p. 46, no. 26).

27. L. BURCHARD, *loc. cit.*

28. ROOSES, III, pp. 299, 300; J. R. MARTIN, *The Decorations for*

the *Pompa Introitus Ferdinandi* (*Corpus Rubenianum Ludwig Burchard*, XVI), Brussels, 1971, pp. 64–66, fig. 15.

29. ROOSES, *Leven*, p. 569.

30. L. VOET, *The Golden Compasses*, I, Amsterdam, 1969, p. 394, no. 4.

31. L. VOET, *op. cit.*, pp. 319, 330.

32. It was also Nonnius who treated Moretus I (d. July 8, 1641) in his last illness (L. VOET, *op. cit.*, p. 211).

33. "Io penso di ritornare presto in Anversea, poiche per la gratia divina, la peste se va scemando di giorno in giorno, et io sono stuffo di star tanto tempo fuor di casa mia" (ROOSES-RUELENS, III, p. 399).

34. "Item betaelt aen versceyden visiten over d'afflyvighe in heur ziecke gedaen namentlyck aen doctor Nunes guldens XVI-XVI st.; Aen doctor Verwilt gelycke guldens XVI-XVI st.; Aen doctor Lazarus guld. XXX,–; Ende aen doctor Vereycken guld. XL" (Gaasbeek, Archives of the Estate, no. Ae. 123; published by ROOSES "Staat van goederen in het sterfhuis van Isabella Brant," *Rubens-Bulletijn*, IV, 1896, p. 177).

35. ROOSES *(loc. cit.)* reads here "Unnis" and is mistaken in transcribing the fees of "Dr. Vereycken" as amounting to XI florins.

36. C. BROECKX, *Notice sur Godefroid Vereycken*, Malines, 1850.

37. C. BROECKX, "Levensschets van Doctor Lazarus Marcquis, geneesheer en vriend van Rubens," *Taelverbond*, X, 1854, pp. 17–44; C. BROECKX, *Histoire du Collegium Medicum Antverpiense*, Antwerp, 1858, pp. 24–69; C. BROECKX, *Galerie médicale anversoise*, Antwerp, 1866, pp. 33–41; A. GOOVAERTS, *Biographie nationale de Belgique*, XIII, 1894–95, pp. 562–75.

38. The following outline is based mainly on ROOSES, *Leven*.

39. "trovando mi simil^te al letto con una terziana molto gagliarda" (RUTH S. MAGURN, *The letters of Peter Paul Rubens*, Cambridge, Mass., 1955, p. 422). "Una terziana" corresponds to the illness mentioned in Cornelis Galle's letter to Balthasar Moretus I as "eene tertiaire ofte derdendaegsche coortse" (tertiary or three-day fever), which had troubled the former for five or six weeks (H. BOUCHERY and F. VAN DEN WIJNGAERT, *op. cit.*, p. 92, no. 2).

40. "Io mi trovo languido di corpo et animo perche non ostante la remission de la febre V.S. sa che gli giorni intermittenti vengono occupati da medici con purge e sangrie e simil rimedij più gravi tal volta che il male istesso" (MAGURN, *loc. cit.*).

41. "Ancor che la febbre mi ha lasciato mi trovo ancora con qualche rissentimento del male passato si come il mare doppo gran fortuna no s'acquieta al instante ma con qualche agitatione si dispone alla bonaccia, cosi mi ritrovo in un stato mezzano, piutosti fuori di pericolo che senza male" (ROOSES-RUELENS, III, pp. 479, 480).

42. "L'accidente del piede m'accompagnó sino a Peronna et di poi si e diminuito poco a poco et al mio arrivo a Brusseles svanito total^te y per la gracia divina mene trovo adesso libero affatta" (ROOSES-RUEENS, IV, pp. 27, 28).

43. "Ick ben dese voorleden daeghen seer sieck gheweest van fleccyn en cortsen, et ut vere fatear quod erat, aegre spiritum duxi inter gemitus et suspiria, sed jam Deo volente respiravi" (ROOSES-RUELENS, V, p. 15). In the same letter one also reads *(ibidem)*: "scribo de lectulo inter dolores podagricos."

44. A. BERTOLOTTI, "P. P. Rubens, Corneille de Wael, Jean Roos, Antoine van Dyck. Lettres et renseignements inédits," *Rubens-Bulletijn*, III, 1888, p. 203.

45. A. BERTOLOTTI, *op. cit.*, pp. 198–206.

46. ROOSES-RUELENS, V, p. 382.

47. "Il veder tanta varieta de paesi e corti in si poco mi sarebbe stato piu proprio et utila nella mia gioventù che nella eta presente perche il corpo sarebbe più robusto per tolerar gli disaggi della posta e l'animo colla esperienza et uso de diversissime nationi si poteria rendere idoneo per l'avenire a cose maggiori, ma adesso io consumo le forze corporali che da se

vanno declinando ne mi resta tempo da cavar il frutto di tante fatiche, nisi ut, cum hoc resciero doctior moriar" (ROOSES-RUELENS, V, p. 147).

48. J. R. MARTIN (*op. cit.*, p. 33) believes that this anecdote was thought up by Rubens' biographer, J. F. M. Michel.

49. ROOSES, *Leven*, p. 618.

50. "… mits sijn jegenwoordich gebreck van flercijn nijet en connende compareren in persoone" (VAN DEN BRANDEN, p. 578).

51. "… Alsoo den Heer constituant 't flercijn was hebbende in zijn rechte handt verclaerde nijet te connen scrijven noch teeckenen" *(ibidem)*.

52. "Ick hebbe met groote vreughde ghesien Ul. langhen brief den welcken my versekert dat het noch soe qualick met U.E. niet ghestellt is als men my heeft gheseit het was, want de caracteren syn alsoo goet al ofte Ul. gheen pyne aende handt en hadde" (ROOSES-RUELENS, VI, p. 263).

53. "Sr. Peter Rubens is deadly sick. The Physicians of this Towne being sent unto him for to trye their best skill on him" (ROOSES-RUELENS, VI, p. 296).

54. "… Sr. Peeter Rubens, who deceased three dayes past off a deflaction w^ch fell on his heart, after some dayes indisposition of ague and goutte" (ROOSES-RUELENS, VI, p. 300).

55. "… Aen doctor Lazarus ende doctor Spinosa voor hunne gedaene visitatie … (Fl.) 6,–" (P. GÉNARD, "De nalatenschap van Rubens," *Antwerpsch Archievenblad*, II, 1865, p. 122).

56. J. PINES, *op. cit.*, p. 7; E. Schmidt, *op. cit.*, p. 58.

57. C. BROECKX, *Galerie médicale anversoise*, Antwerp, 1866, pp. 76–78 (according to the list of sworn doctors drawn up in accordance with the archives by P. GÉNARD).

58. J. PINES, *op. cit.*, p. 7.

59. "Aen Mr. Hendrick den barbier, voor het meesteren ende cureren vanden voet des heeren afflijvigens … 60,–" "Aen mees ter Hans Daepe, barbier, ter saecken als vore 40,–" (P. GÉNARD, *op. cit.*, p. 122).

60. "Vrayment nostre ville a beaucoup perdu par la mort de Mons^r Rubens, et moy en particulier un de mes meilleurs amis" (ROOSES-RUELENS, VI, p. 308).

61. "… dat vindende syne weduwe, meerderjarige sone ende de momboiren van syne minderjarige kinderen, dat hy soodanige gedenckenisse soude verdiendt hebben, sy de voorseyde cappelle souden doen bouwen, sonder andere syne schilderye van Onse Lieve Vrouwe met het kindeken Jhesu op haren arm, vergeselschapt met verscheyden Heyligen etc.; ende noch een beldt van Onse Lieve Vrouwe van marmeren steen" (P. GÉNARD, *op. cit.*, p. 168; ROOSES, I, p. 279, no. 1; J. VAN HERCK, *De Rubenskapel in de Sint-Jacobskerk te Antwerpen, Historisch-Archaeologische Studie*, Antwerp, 1927; H. VLIEGHE, in *Openbaar Kunstbezit in Vlaanderen*, 1971, 28a–28b, pl. 28).

## 13. *"The Picture Gallery" of Cornelis van der Geest* by Willem van Haecht

First published in *Antwerpen*, XV, 1969, pp. 158–173.

1. Antwerp, Rubens House, inv. no. S. 171. Provenance: Lord Huntingfield, Birmingham; The Hon. Esmond C. Harmsworth, London; S. Hartveld, Antwerp; S. van Berg, New York; sale at Sotheby's, London, June 25, 1969, no. 104 (bought for the Rubens House). Exhibitions: *Winter Exhibition*, Royal Academy of Arts, London, 1907, no. 52; *La Toison d'Or*, Bruges, 1907, no. 173; *Flemish and Belgian Art 1300–1900*, Royal Academy of Arts, London, 1927, no. 298; *Pictures within Pictures*, Wadsworth Atheneum, Hartford, Conn., 1949, no. 22.

2. "a unique place in the history of gallery pictures"; J.S. HELD,

"*Artis Pictoriae Amator.* An Antwerp Art Patron and his Collection," *Gazette des Beaux-Arts,* 1957, p. 84.

3. H. HYMANS, *Une galerie anversoise au XVII<sup>e</sup> siècle, La Chronique des Arts et des Curiosités,* 1907, p. 99; E. DILLON, in *Atheneum,* London, 1907, p. 109; W. MARTIN, in *Bulletin van den Oudheidkundigen Bond,* 1908, p. 33; K. ZOEGE VON MANTEUFFEL, in *Allgemeines Künstlerlexikon,* XV, Leipzig, 1922, p. 424; J. DENUCÉ, *De Antwerpse "Konstkamers" in de 16de en 17de eeuwen. Inventarissen van Kunstverzamelingen (Bronnen voor de Geschiedenis van de Vlaamsche Kunst,* II), Antwerp, 1932, p. 53, pl. 6; [M. VAN BERG], *The Van Berg Collection of Paintings,* New York, 1947, pp. 14 ff.; L. VAN PUYVELDE, "Willem van Haecht en zijn '*Galerij van Cornelis van der Geest*'," *Revue belge d'archéologie et d'histoire de l'art,* XXIV, 1955, pp. 159–63; J. S. HELD, *op. cit.,* pp. 53–84; S. SPETH-HOLTERHOFF, *Les Peintres flamands de Cabinets d'Amateurs au XVII<sup>e</sup> siècle,* Brussels, 1957, pp. 98–104; M. WINNER, *Die Quellen der Pictura-Allegorien in gemalten Bildergalerien des 17. Jahrhunderts zu Antwerpen,* diss. Cologne, 1957, pp. 35–40; A. J. J. DELEN, "Cornelis van der Geest, een groot figuur in de geschiedenis," *Antwerpen,* V, 1959, pp. 57–71; J. DECOO, "Nog Cornelis van der Geest. Een tekening uit zijn verzamelingen, thans in het Museum Mayer van den Bergh," *Antwerpen,* V, 1959, pp. 196–99; N. DE POORTER, *Willem van Haecht, De kunstkamer van Cornelis van der Geest, Openbaar Kunstbezit in Vlaanderen,* IX, 1971, no. 16; M. J. FRIEDLÄNDER, *Quentin Massys (Early Netherlandish Painting,* VII), Leyden–Brussels, 1971, p. 69, pl. 135. We have not attempted here to include every reference by systematic notes. The majority of the items have already been published many times. Furthermore, they can easily be found in the more detailed sources mentioned above, namely, the contributions of J. S. Held and A. J. J. Delen. We have only departed from this rule in the case of publications which have appeared since these, and also whenever it seemed necessary to elucidate a less well-known point.

4. "The Spanish Regents visiting the Picture Gallery of Cornelis van der Geest" (*Catalogue of Old Master Paintings,* London, Sotheby & Co, June 25, 1969, p. 60, no. 104, ill.).

5. This date is given by F. FICKAERT (*Metamorphosis, ofte Wonderbaere Veranderingh' ende Leven vanden vermaerden Mr. Quinten Metsys Constigh Graf-Smit, ende Schilder binnen Antwerpen,* Antwerp, 1648, p. 15) and A. VAN FORNENBERCH (*Den Antwerpschen Protheus, ofte Cyclopsken* [sic] *Apelles,* Antwerp, 1658, p. 25). VAN DEN BRANDEN (p. 650) is mistaken, on the contrary, in quoting the date August 15, 1615. See the arguments concerning the exact date in DE MAEYER, p. 57.

6. Panel, 38⅞″ × 36⅞″ (37.5 × 32.5 cm); G. MARTIN, *National Gallery Catalogues. The Flemish School circa 1600–circa 1900,* London, 1970, pp. 34–37.

7. A. J. J. DELEN, *op. cit.,* p. 58.

8. H. VEY, *Die Zeichnungen Anton van Dycks,* I, Brussels, 1962, p. 327, no. 262; II, pl. 314.

9. LEYSSENS, pp. 100, 101.

10. "D. Cornelio van der Geest virorum optimo et amicorum vetustissimo suoque ab adulescentia perpetuo Fautori Artisque pictoriae summo dum vixit admiratori monumentum hoc aeternae amicitiae quod supersiti destinarat defuncto L.M.D.D.Q. Ex tabula Walburgensis Ecclesiae cuius ipse praecipuus Author et promotor fuit" (J. S. HELD, *op. cit.,* pp. 54, 55).

11. "... ex summa familiaritate quae cum praedicto domino Petro Paulo Rubens usus est in diesque utitur" (ROOSES-RUELENS, V, p. 296).

12. Another copy, the property of Julius H. Weitzner, London, was exhibited in Cologne in 1968 (*Weltkunst aus Privatbezitz,* Kunsthalle, Cologne, 1968, no. F 25). See also J. MÜLLER-HOFSTEDE, "Rubens und Tizian. Das bild Karls V.," *Münchner Jahrbuch der bildenden Künste,* XVIII, 1967, pp. 67–71.

13. DE MAEYER, pp. 96, 97.

14. The young page in the foreground on the left is borrowed by Willem van Haecht from Rubens' picture *The Coronation of Maria de' Medici* in the Louvre, Paris (OLDENBOURG, p. 252).

15. DE MAEYER, pp. 193–95.

16. Similarly, suggestions for the man standing on the right of Catherine van Mockenborch are the art-lover Anthony Cornelissen (M. WINNER, *op. cit.,* p. 37), the collector Adriaan Stevens (S. SPETH-HOLTERHOFF, *op. cit.,* p. 101), and the painter Gerhard Seghers (A. J. J. DELEN, *op. cit.,* p. 65); the second man from the left has been thought to be the collector Jacob de Cachiopin (J. S. HELD, *op. cit.,* p. 69) or Jacob Jordaens (A. J. J. DELEN, *op. cit.,* p. 65; M. WINNER, *loc. cit.,* with some restriction); G. Glück has identified the third man as the animal painter Paul de Vos (quoted by J. S. HELD, *loc. cit.,* who at the same time draws attention to a facial resemblance to the portrait of the unidentified man, painted by Van Dyck, in Windsor Castle); but M. WINNER *(loc. cit.)* thought it more likely to be Peter Snayers and S. SPETH-HOLTERHOFF *(loc. cit.)* Caspar Gevartius.

17. For this man the following names have been suggested: Jan Wildens (S. SPETH-HOLTERHOFF, *op. cit.,* p. 101) and Paul de Vos (A. J. J. DELEN, *op. cit.,* p. 65); J. S. HELD (*op. cit.,* p. 69) points out a certain resemblance to the portrait called *The Man in Fur Coat* in Vienna (ROSENBERG, p. 58).

18. A small version of this composition in ivory, signed Iörg Petle. F. is to be found in the Ashmolean Museum, Oxford ([*Exh. Cat.*] *Georg Petel 1601–1634,* Munich, 1964, pp. 20, 21, no. 5, pl. 9). The physiognomy of Petel is known, among others, from his portrait by Van Dyck in Munich and from a *Double-Portrait of two Sculptors* (probably François Duquesnoy and Petel) by an anonymous master, in Copenhagen (*Ibidem,* p. 18, nos. A and B, pls. 1 and 2).

19. For biographical details of the Van Haecht family, see J. VAN ROEY, *Het Antwerpse geslacht van Haecht (Verhaecht), tafereelmakers, schilders en kunstenaars, Miscellanea Jozef Duverger,* I, Ghent, 1968, pp. 226–28 (especially on Willem van Haecht: p. 226).

20. VAN DEN BRANDEN, p. 650. Only a few pictures by Willem van Haecht are known. Taking stylistic critical elements as a basis, two "picture galleries" have been attributed to him: *The Studio of Apelles* in the Mauritshuis in The Hague (no. 226), and a second version of the picture, formerly in the Cremer Collection in Düsseldorf (J. DENUCÉ, *op. cit.,* fig. 2) and at present in the collection Charles de Beïstegui in Montfort-l'Amauray (S. SPETH-HOLTERHOFF, *op. cit.,* pp. 107, 108, pl. IV). A fourth "picture gallery," in the collection of Mrs. Hardcastle at Hawkhurst in Kent, is attributed to him by S. SPETH-HOLTERHOFF *(op. cit.,* p. 108, figs. 39–41). The same author believes she has recognized a fifth work by the artist in the "*Picture Gallery*" *with the story of Joseph and the Wife of Potiphar,* which was formerly in the art trade in Berlin (Sale, Berlin, Lepke, June 11–12, 1936, no. 183, as *K. E. Biset*). She identifies it with a "schilderije van Joseph ende huysvrouwe van Putufer wesende een constkamerken" (a painting of Joseph and the wife of Potiphar, being a small picture gallery) which Van Haecht bequeathed, on the eve of his death, to Joris van Mockenborch (S. SPETH-HOLTERHOFF, *op. cit.,* pp. 110, 111, 201, 212). In this same will, dated July 11, 1637, Van Haecht bequeathed to Cornelis van der Geest "de grootste constkamere by den testateur geschildert" (the largest picture gallery painted by the testator) (*Ibidem,* p. 201). H. GERSON (in H. GERSON and E. H. TER KUILE, *Art and Architecture in Belgium 1600–1800,* Harmondsworth, 1960, p. 195) and S. SPETH-HOLTERHOFF (*op. cit.,* p. 100) assume that this refers to the picture which is at present preserved in the Rubens House. Nevertheless

J. S. Held (*op. cit.,* p. 84) has pointed out quite rightly that the *Studio of Apelles* in The Hague is in any case of larger format, and that very probably Cornelis van der Geest had already, at an earlier date, acquired the picture which represents his art gallery.

21. J. S. HELD, *op. cit.,* pp. 74–83, with detailed biography; an old copy after the same composition by Jan van Eyck is in the Fogg Art Museum, Harvard University, Cambridge, Mass.

22. See for example his letter to Johannes Faber, in Rome, of January 14, 1611 (ROOSES-RUELENS, VI, pp. 307–11). Later, the two small pictures by Elsheimer became part of Rubens' personal collection (J. DENUCÉ, *op. cit.,* p. 58, nos. 32, 35); no doubt they found their way there after the death of Cornelis van der Geest.

23. "een stille groote half openbare vrijagie: maar wiert afgheslaghen door eenen stilswijghenden yver van den eyghenaer, den welcken groote gunsten door eyghen liefde liet passeren" (F. FICKAERT, *op. cit.,* p. 15). For panels by Quentin Metsys which resemble the *Virgin and Child* in Cornelis van der Geest's collection, see M. J. FRIEDLÄNDER, *Early Netherlandish Painting,* VII, Leyden–Brussels, 1971, p. 68, no. 67, but especially W. E. SUIDA, *A Catalogue of Paintings in the John and Mable Ringling Museum of Art,* Sarasota, Fla., 1949, p. 69, no. 200, ill. on page 168.

24. M. SMEYERS, "Schilderijen van Kwinten Metsijs in het bezit der aartshertogen Albrecht en Isabella," *Miscellanea Jozef Duverger,* I, Ghent, 1969, pp. 139–52.

25. According to GERT VON DER OSTEN "*Paracelsus,* ein verlorenes Bild von Wolf Huber?" *Wallraf-Richartz Jahrbuch,* XXX, 1968, pp. 201–14, the original picture is not by the hand of Matsys, but by the German painter Wolf Huber. W. STECHOW ("Some Thoughts on Rubens as a Copyist of Portraits 1610–1620," in *Rubens before 1620,* ed. by J. R. Martin, Princeton, N.J., 1972, p. 24, n. 7) is of the opinion that the *Paracelsus* reproduced in Van Haecht's picture is certainly not Rubens' copy.

26. "van sulcken fameusen meester de memorie niet en behoort te versterven."

27. M. WINNER, *op. cit.,* p. 40.

28. "De beroemdste schilder van de Oudheid voor te stellen aan de arbeid – en welke! – was zoveel als een hulde aan de Schilderkunst, een hulde die wel op haar plaats was en tot haar recht kwam op de weergave van een schilderijenverzameling. De Schilderkunst werd er niet alleen door gehuldigd, maar tegelijk beloond, gelauwerd, want het verhaal geldt toch dat Alexander – hij is op de tekening present – zozeer door het portret ingenomen was, dat hij zijn geliefde zelf aan de schilder afstond…" (J. DE COO, *op. cit.,* p. 197).

29. M. WINNER, *op. cit.,* pp. 3–40.

30. "Apelles costbaer trou scholieren" (F. DONNET, *Het Jonstig Versaem der Violieren. Geschiedenis der Rederijkkamer De Olijftak sedert 1480,* Antwerp, 1907, p. 40; M. WINNER, *op. cit.,* p. 31).

31. "Uyt Jonsten versaemt!"

32. ROMBOUTS-VAN LERIUS, I, p. 579.

33. M. WINNER, *op. cit.,* p. 40.

34. J. DE COO, *op. cit.,* pp. 196–99.

## 14. Rubens and His Social and Cultural Background

First published in *Stil und Ueberlieferung in der Kunst des Abendlandes,* III, Berlin, 1967, pp. 9–19.

1. ARNOLD HAUSER, *Sozialgeschichte der Kunst und Literatur,* I, Munich, 1953, p. 494. See also: ARNOLD HAUSER, *Philosophie der Kunstgeschichte,* Munich, 1958, pp. 16, 17.

2. "Die Nordstaaten sonderten sich ab gegen die allgemein europäische katolische Welt und bildeten eine bürgerliche demokratische Gemeinschaft aus, während die Südstaaten unter der habsburgischen Dynastie, die milde und nachgiebig wurde, und unter der katholischen Kirche eine andere Art von Freiheit, bei offenen Türen gegen die Umwelt entwickelten, so dass der gemeinsamen Anlage und Begabung dort andere Aufgaben zufielen als hier…" (M. J. FRIEDLÄNDER, *Die Niederländischen Maler des 17. Jahrhunderts (Propyläen-Kunstgeschichte,* XII), 2nd ed., Berlin, 1927, p. 25).

3. "De eerste eigenschap der Nationale Hollandsche schilderkunst, die een buitenlander u zal noemen, is dat zij *burgerlijk* is … Wij onderschrijven die eigenschap als tegenstelling tot die van een kunst, die de kerk of de vorsten naar de oogen ziet. Van dit laatste waren onze groote meesters afkeerig en aldus bezien is hun kunst, in tegenstelling b.v. tot die van Rubens en Van Dyck, in hooge mate burgerlijk, in den zin van democratisch. Het is een volkskunst, uit de bevolking gesproten en daarvoor bedoeld" (W. MARTIN, *De Hollandsche Schilderkunst in de Zeventiende Eeuw,* I, Amsterdam, 1935, p. 68).

4. E. MICHEL, *La peinture flamande au XVIIe siècle,* Paris, 1939, p. 7.

5. "Wenn nun alle diese Umstände das künstlerische Genie eines Rubens nicht erklären, so machen sie es doch verständlich, dass er in dem *höfisch-kirchlichen Milieu Flanderns* die Form fand, die seiner Kunst eigen war" (A. HAUSER, *Sozialgeschichte der Kunst und Literatur,* I, Munich, 1953, p. 993).

6. J. HUIZINGA, *Nederland's Beschaving in de Zeventiende Eeuw. Een Schets,* Haarlem, 1941. This essay is in Dutch, adapted and developed from a series of talks which Huizinga gave in Cologne in 1932. They were first published under the title: *Holländische Kultur des siebzehnten Jahrhunderts. Ihre sozialen Grundlagen und nationale Eigenart,* Iena, 1933.

7. G. BROM, *Schilderkunst en Litteratuur in de 16de en 17de Eeuw,* Utrecht-Antwerp, 1957, pp. 162–205.

8. A. C. J. DE VRANKRIJKER, *Het Maatschappelijk Leven in Nederland in de Gouden Eeuw,* Amsterdam, 1937. See also by the same author: *Neerlands volk in oorlogstijd,* in J. PRESSER and others, *De Tachtigjarige Oorlog,* II, 4th ed., Amsterdam–Brussels, 1963, pp. 294–320.

9. J. PRESSER, *op. cit.,* pp. 321–76.

10. Apart from DE MAEYER, we can also mention: H. FLOERKE, *Studien zur niederländischen Kunst- und Kulturgeschichte,* Leipzig, 1905; the five volumes of J. DENUCÉ in the collection *Bronnen voor de Geschiedenis van de Vlaamsche Kunst,* Antwerp, 1931–1949. See also the pages on Rubens (pp. 33–45) in G. THIEME, *Kunsthandel in den Niederlanden im 17. Jahrhundert,* Cologne, 1959.

11. VICOMTE C. TERLINDEN, *L'Archiduchesse Isabelle (Collection "Notre Passé"),* Brussels, 1943, p. 85.

12. "Overal bouwde men nieuwe kerken en kloosters en de oude tempels werden hersteld. Dank zij de vrijgevigheid van de vorsten waren de altaren rijk versierd en Rubens werd met bestellingen overstelpt" (P. LAMBOTTE, "Rubens' Leven en Werk," in *Rubens en zijne Eeuw,* p. 479).

13. "Decisief voor zijn carrière is Rubens' verhouding tot de Aartshertogen nochtans zeker niet geweest. Onafhankelijk van hen was hij algemeen erkend geworden als de eerste schilder van zijn tijd; waren zijn kring van vrienden en bekenden, zijn internationale vriendschappen gegroeid" (DE MAEYER, p. 129). The author observes (pp. 126, 127), on the subject of the triptych of St. Ildefonso in the church of St. Jacques-on-Caudenberg, that this altarpiece was probably not commissioned by the Infanta. The idea of having the picture painted came presumably from her major-domo Ferdinand d'Andelot. However, the work seems to have been paid for by the Infanta.

14. Several interventions on the part of the Archduke and the

Infanta with regard to the building of the church are mentioned by J. H. PLANTENGA, *L'Architecture religieuse du Brabant au XVIIᵉ siècle*, The Hague, 1926, pp. 19, 20, 295, 297. For their financial help to the Jesuits toward the construction of the churches, see, for example: J. ANDRIESEN, *De Jezuïeten en het samenhorigheidsgevoel der Nederlanden, 1585–1648*, Antwerp, p. 115, notes 25 and 26. No detailed study exists of their generosity in this domain. For the stained-glass windows presented by the regents, see: J. HELBIG, *De Glasschilderkunst in België. Repertorium en Documenten*, I, Antwerp, 1943, nos. 95, 770, 413, 446, 725, 868, 914, 915, 919, 960, 989, 1022, 1083, 1093, 1094, 1095, 1368, 1379, 1545, 6648, 1669, 1689, 1833, 1869, 1871, 1889, 2079; II (in collaboration with R. VAN STEENBERGHE DE GOURMONT), Antwerp, 1951, nos. 2142, 2218.

15. It is known that Rubens declined the offer of Jacob de Bie who wanted to buy from him, for the duc de Croy, the picture *Juno and Argus,* today in the Wallraf-Richartz-Museum in Cologne (ROOSES, *Leven,* p. 42). It is possible, moreover, that Prince Charles of Arenberg presented to the church of the Capuchin Friars in Brussels, about 1620, an altarpiece of *The Lamentation of Christ,* now in the Musées Royaux des Beaux-Arts de Belgique in Brussels (*Ibidem,* p. 229). About 1616, Rubens sold a large hunting scene to the Duke of Aerschot (*Ibid.,* p. 253). Furthermore, it is possible that Rubens painted a certain number of portraits for the nobility which have not been identified to this day. Speaking of the inventory of the collection of Alexaander of Arenberg, SPETH-HOLTERHOFF makes the following observation on the artistic tastes of the aristocracy of the Spanish Netherlands: "[they were] anxious to honor the memory of their ancestors, to show their attachment to the Church, to adorn the vast halls of their castles. They did not always demand high standards in the quality of the pictures they had collected and they possessed neither the competence nor the sensitivity of true connoisseurs of art" (S. SPETH-HOLTERHOFF, *Les peintres flamands de cabinets d'amateur au XVIIᵉ siècle,* Brussels, 1957, p. 40).

16. OLDENBOURG, p. 26. See also C. NORRIS, "Rubens' *Adoration of the Kings* of 1609," *Nederlands Kunsthistorisch Jaarboek, XIV,* 1963, pp. 129–136.

17. J. DE COO, *Rubens-Gids voor de Antwerpse Kerken,* II, Antwerp, 1947, pl. 9.

18. See Chapter 3.

19. OLDENBOURG, p. 36.

20. OLDENBOURG, p. 52.

21. H. G. EVERS, *Rubens und sein Werk. Neue Forschungen,* Brussels, 1943, pp. 151–66, pl. 54.

22. See Chapter 13.

23. See, for example, ROOSES, *Leven,* pp. 171–189.

24. J. G. VAN GELDER, "Rubens in Holland in de zeventiende eeuw," *Nederlands Kunsthistorisch Jaarboek,* III, 1950–51, pp. 118, 119.

25. J. ANDRIESSEN, *op. cit.,* pp. 112–83.

26. OLDENBOURG, p. 118.

27. OLDENBOURG, pp. 142–47.

28. See MARTIN.

29. "Ma per venire alle cose mie sappia V.S. chio non saprei in adresso che resolutione pigliarmi che fermarmi nella Patria o di ritornare per sempre in Roma donde vengo sollecitato con buonissime conditione; qui ancora non mancano di far ogni sforzo a ritenermi con ogni sorta di carezze. L'arciduca, e l'Infante serenissima mi hanno fatto scrivere facendo instanza di rimanere al loro servizio con grandissime offerte, benché ho poca volontà di rifarmi corteggiano. Anversa mi bastarà colli suoi cittadini, quando potessi dir a Dio a Roma. La pace o per dir meglio tregua per molti anni si fa di sicuro mediante la quale si crede che questi paesi rifioriranno et si crede che per la settimana si publicarà per tutte queste provincie"

ROOSES-RUELENS, VI, pp. 323, 324).

30. M. JAFFÉ, "Peter Paul Rubens and the Oratorian Fathers," *Proporzioni,* VI, 1963, pp. 217, 218, 221, 222. For Ascanio Colonna, see ROOSES-RUELENS, I, p. 275; E. HAVERKAMP-BEGEMAN, [*Exh. Cat.*] *Olieverfschetsen van Rubens,* Rotterdam, 1953, no. 2.

31. M. DE MAEYER, "Rubens' terugkeer uit Italië naar Antwerpen," *Gentse Bijdragen tot de Kunstgeschiedenis,* XI, 1945–48, pp. 147–665. In this article the author wished to prove that the regents had already tried in 1607 to engage Rubens in their service. The arguments do not seem completely convincing, however.

32. It is worth pointing out that in the letters patent conferring on Wenzel Coebergher the title of court architect, it is expressly stipulated that the advantages and exemptions will only be granted to him on condition "that he is bound to reside in our city of Brussels" ("qu'il sera tenu de faire sa résidence en ceste notre ville de Bruxelles"; DE MAEYER, p. 280, doc. 40), while no similar condition figures in Rubens' patent (*Ibidem,* pp. 293, 294, doc. 62).

33. J. HUIZINGA, *op. cit.,* pp. 59–68; the term "consumers of civilization" ("consumenten der beschaving") is found on pp. 64–65.

34. "...zij werden geen heeren als Rubens, Van Dyck of Velazquez" (J. HUIZINGA, *op. cit.,* p. 71).

35. "...vond in den rijkdom en den levenslust der welgestelde burgerkringen haar reden van bestaan; zij vond in die kringen haar inspiratie en haar beschermers en opdrachtgevers. Hier geen grote Maecenaten, maar een onbeperkt getal van kunstliefhebbers" (J. HUIZINGA, *op. cit.,* p. 127; in this connection, especially, his Chapter V (pp. 127–62) is important.

36. See Chapter 3.

37. ROOSES, II, pp. 96, 97.

38. ROOSES, II, p. 261.

39. See Chapter 4.

40. ROOSES, II, pp. 79–81.

41. See Chapter 13.

42. ROOSES, II, pp. 219–21.
ROOSES, II, pp. 113–18; M. ROOSES, "De Afdoening van het Kruis. Uit het rekeningboek der Antwerpsche Kolveniersgilde," *Rubens-Bulletijn,* V, 1910, pp. 230–33; J. VAN DEN NIEUWENHUIZEN, *Histoire matérielle, Bulletin de l'Institut Royal du Patrimoine Artistique,* V, 1962, pp. 27–85.

43. Thus, for example, Frans Hals, *The Banquet of the Officers of the Cluveniersdoelen of Haarlem* and *The Reunion of the Officers of the Cluveniersdoelen of Haarlem* (both in the Frans Halsmuseum at Haarlem), and *The Night Watch* by Rembrandt (Rijksmuseum, Amsterdam).

44. An excellent outline is given in M. SABBE, "Het Geestesleven te Antwerpen in Rubens' Tijd," in *Rubens en zijne Eeuw,* pp. 63–172.

45. J. HUIZINGA, *op. cit.,* pp. 28 ff., 66–68.

46. J. LEFEVRE, "La compénétration hispano-belge dans les Pays-Bas catholiques pendant le XVIIᵉ siècle," *Revue belge de philologie et d'histoire,* XVI, 1937, pp. 599–621; J. DENUCÉ, *Italiaansche koopmansgeslachten te Antwerpen in de XVIde–XVIIde eeuwen,* Malines–Amsterdam, n.d.

## 15. Rubens' Personality

1. Consult on this subject: M. ROOSES, "Rubens jugé par sa correspondance," in: ROOSES-RUELENS, VI, p. V–XVI; W.-R. VALENTINER, in [*Exh. Cat.*] *Sixty Paintings and Some Drawings by Peter Paul Rubens,* The Detroit Institute of Arts, 1936, 2 p. [18 pp.]; A. J. J. DELEN, "Rubens als Mensch," in *Oude Kunst en Graphiek, Verzamelde Opstellen,* Antwerp, 1943; M. GILLIAMS, *Rubens en zijn beide Vrouwen,* Antwerp [1947]; H.

KAUFMANN, "Peter Paul Rubens im Licht seiner Selbstbekenntnisse," *Wallraf-Richartz Jahrbuch,* XVII, 1955, pp. 181–88; M. WARNKE, *Kommentare zu Rubens,* Berlin, 1965.

2. On Rubens as a letter-writer and the style of his letters: *The Letters of Peter Paul Rubens,* translated and edited by Ruth S. Magurn, Cambridge, Mass., 1955, pp. 1–18.

3. R. DE PILES, *Conversations sur la Connaissance de la Peinture,* Paris, 1677. On the author: B. TEYSSÈDRE, *Roger de Piles et les débats sur le coloris au Siècle de Louis* XIV, Paris, 1957.

4. "...abrégé que j'ai tiré et dressé du mémoire que son fils aisné en a laissé" (CH. RUELENS, "La Vie de Rubens" par Roger de Piles," *Rubens-Bulletijn,* II, 1885, pp. 157–75, particularly p. 163.)

5. "Il avoit la taille grande, le port majestueux, le tour du visage régulièrement formé, les joues vermeilles, les cheveux châtains, les yeux brillans, mais d'un feu tempéré, l'air riant, doux et honneste" (R. DE PILES, *op. cit.,* pp. 211, 212).

6. "... schon in physischer Abnahme und mit einem Zuge des Leidens, aber wundersam und anders sympathisch als früher dargestellt" (J. BURCKHARDT, *Erinnerungen aus Rubens,* Basle, 1898, p. 274). On the portrait of Rubens and his "Mantuan friends," see H. VEY and A. M. KESTING, *Katalog der niederländischen Gemälde von 1500 bis 1800 im Wallraf-Richartz-Museum Köln,* Cologne, 1967, pp. 94, 95, no. Dep. 248; I. BINI, "Un Rubens del Periodo Mantovano a Colonia," *Civiltà Mantovano,* VIII, 1974, pp. 293–303. On the last self-portrait: J. BURCKHARDT, *Erinnerungen aus Rubens,* Bâle, 1898, p. 274.

7. F. BAUDOUIN, ·*Kunstwerken tentoongesteld in het Rubenshuis,* Antwerp, 1974, no. 10 (with bibliography).

8. "... Je suis l'homme le plus occupé et oppressé du monde" (ROOSES-RUELENS, III, p. 319, letter of January 10, 1625, to Valavez).

9. "Son abord était engageant, son humeur commode, sa conversation aisée, son esprit vif et pénétrant, sa manière de parler posée et le ton de sa voix agréable; tout cela le rendoit naturellement éloquent et persuasif" (R. DE PILES, *op. cit.,* p. 212).

10. "Fratrum tuum jam a puero cognovi in scholis, et amavi lectissimi ac suavissimi ingenii juvenum" (ROOSES-RUELENS, I, p. 1).

11. ROOSES-RUELENS, II, p. 4. Text quoted in note 7, Chapter 2.

12. "Sed comitatis laude cedis nemini, sed promptus et paratus adspiras bonis: Virtus reperta rara nostris moribus in arte vostra..." (ROOSES-RUELENS, II, p. 57).

13. "Se ben le scrissi hieri per l'ordinario non pero ho dovuto lasciar partire il gentilissimo signor Rubens senza accompagnarlo di queste due righe e dirle che si io haveva in grand[a] stima il valore di questo personnaggio senz' altro fondamente che della fama et voco publica del suo merito, hora dico son teste oculato della sua virtu et singolare eruditione oltre la destrezza et eccelenza della mano. Io non posso se non amirarlo sommamente e lasciarlo tornare da se con grando dispiacere di perdere la piu dolce e piu erudita conversatione ch'io habbia mai havuta; in materia dell' antiquita principalmente, egli ha una notitia la piu universale et la piu esquisita ch'io viddi mai" (ROOSES-RUELENS, II, p. 336).

14. "La bienveuillance de Monsieur Rubens que vous m'avez prucurée, m'a comblé de tant de bonheur et de contentement, que je vous en debvray des remerciments tout le temps de ma vie, ne pouvant assez me louer de son honnesteté, ne célébrer assez dignement l'éminence de sa vertu et de ses grandes parties, tant en l'érudition profonde et cognoissance merveilleuse de la bonne antiquité, qu'en la dextérité et rare conduitte dans les affaires du monde, non plus que l'excellence de sa main et la grande doulceur de sa conversation" (ROOSES-RUELENS, II, p. 337).

15. "Egli e versatissimo in ogni genere di antiquà, et di tanta dolcezza di costumi, che non si pero vedere niente di piu amorevole" (ROOSES-RUELENS, II, p. 340, letter from Peiresc to Aleandro).

16. "Mr Rubens, qui est né pour plairre et délecter en tout ce qu'il faict ou dict" (ROOSES-RUELENS, IV, p. 290, letter of August I, 1627).

17. "... perche non si diletta ne s'intende piu di Pittura, che un facchino..." (ROOSES-RUELENS, IV, p. 357).

18. DE LA SERRE, *Histoire curieuse de ce qui s'est passé à l'entree de la Reyne Mere du roy tres chretien dans les villes des Pays-Bas,* Antwerp, 1632, pp. 49, 68; cited in ROOSES, *Leven,* p. 513.

19. "Questo tale è pieno d'artificj, molto atto a trattar negocj, ed in altre occasioni ben gravi da Spagnoli impiegato" (GACHARD, p. 342).

20. A. J. J. DELEN, *op. cit.,* p. 23.

21. H. KAUFMANN, *op. cit.,* p. 181.

22. "Il se levoit tous les jours à quatre heures du matin, et se faisoit une loy de commencer sa journée par entendre la Messe, à moins qu'il ne fut empesché par la goutte dont il estoit fort incommodé; apres quoy il se mettoit à l'ouvrage, ayant tousiours auprès de luy un Lecteur qui estoit à ses gages, et qui lisoit à haute voix quelque bon livre; mais ordinairement Plutarque, Tite-Live, ou Seneque. Comme il se plaisoit extremement à l'ouvrage, il vivait d'une maniere a pouvoir travailler facilement et sans incommoder sa santé; et c'est pour cela qu'il mangeoit fort peu à disner, de peur que la vapeur des viandes ne l'empeschast de s'appliquer, et que venant à s'appliquer, il n'empeschast la digestion des viandes. Il travailloit ainsi jusqu'à cinq heures du soir, qu'il montoit à cheval pour aller prendre l'air hors de la ville ou sur les remparts, ou il faisoit quelqu'autre chose pour se delasser l'esprit. A son retour de la promenàde il trouvoit ordinairement quelques-uns de ses amis qui venoient souper avec luy, et qui contribuoient au plaisir de la table. Il avoit neantmoins une grande aversion pour les excés du vin et de la bonne chere, aussi bien que du jeu. Son plus grand plaisir estoit de montrer quelque beau cheval d'Espagne, de lire quelque livre, ou de voir et considérer ses medailles, ses agates, ses cornalines et autres pierres gravées dont il avoit un tresbeau recueil" (R. DE PILES, *op. cit.,* pp. 213–15).

23. H. HYMANS, "Une visite chez Rubens racontée par un contemporain," *Bulletin de l'Académie de Belgique,* 56e année, 3e série, XIII, 1887, p. 150.

24. "En peignant il parlait sans freine, et sans quitter son ouvrage, il entretenoit facilement ceux qui le venoient voir. La Reyne Marie de Medicis prenoit un si grand plaisir en sa conversation que pendant tout le temps qu'il travailla aux deux Tableaux qu'il a faits à Paris, de ceux qui sont dans la gallerie de Luxembourg, sa Majesté estoit tousiours derriere luy, autant charmée de l'entendre discourir que de le voir peindre" (R. DE PILES, *op. cit.,* p. 212).

25. "Ecce ad te mitto, retro exactorum mensium non unius urbis sed orbis res gestas ... A Rubenio nostro deinceps hebdomatim accipies quod legas et ad me remittas" (ROOSES-RUELENS, III, p. 111).

26. "V.S. fa bene di rimettermi alla necessità del fato che non si piega alle nostre passioni, y come un effetto della suprema potenza non è obligato di render conto né ragione à noi delle sue attioni. Tocca a lui il dominio assoluto d'ogni cosa, et a noi il servire et ubidire; né resta altro, al parer mio, che di rendere questa servitù più honesta y manco servibile col assenso volontario; ma non mi pare negocio tanta leggiero ne pratticabile al instanto et perciò V.S. prudentissamente sui recommanda il tempio, il quali, spero, farà in me quello que deverebbe far la ragione; perchè io non ho pretensioni d'arrivar giamai alla impassibilità stoica ne penso d'esser impropria all' huomo alcuna qualità humana congrua al suo oggetto, né

tutte le cose di questo mondo esser ugualmente indifferenti, *sed aliqua esse quae potius sunt extra vitia quam cum virtutibus,* et che si vindicamo mentalmente qualcunque sentimento nel animo nostro *citra reprehensionem.* Io veramente ho perso una buonissima compagna, che si poteva anzi doveva amar con raggione, non havendo alcum vicio proprio del suo sesso; senza morosità y senza impotenza donnesca, ma tutta buona, tutta honnesta y per sue virtù amata in vita y dopo morte pianta universalmente da tutti. Et un tal danno mi par degno di gran sentimento, et perché la vera medicina di tutti mala è l'oblivione figlia del Tempo, bisogna senza dubbio sperarne soccorso: ma trove ben difficile la distintione del dolore per la perdita, dalla memoria d'una persona che devo riverire et onorare mentre averò vita" (ROOSES-RUELENS, III, pp. 444–445, letter of July 15, 1626 to Pierre Dupuy).

27. A. J. J. DELEN, *op. cit.,* pp. 53–55.

28. A. STUBBE, *Rubens (Palet serie),* Amsterdam, n. d., p. 57.

29. "... senza ch'io butti a perdere più tempo, viaggij, spese, salarij ancora ch'el splendore di S.A. non ripara in cotesto, in opere vili a mio gusto et communi a tutti nel gusto del Sign.r Ducca. Con tutto ciò mi rimitto totalmente come buon servitore nel arbitrio d'ogni minime cenno del Padrone, supplicando però volersi servire di me in casa o fuori, de cose più appropriate al genio mio et al bisogno de l'opere sue incominciate" (ROOSES-RUELENS, I, p. 226).

30. "... je confesse d'estre par un instinct naturel plus propre à faire des ouvrages bien grandes que des petites curiositez. Chacun a sa grâce; mon talent est tel que jamais entreprise encore quelle fust desmesurée en quantité et diversité de suggests a surmonté mon courage" (ROOSES-RUELENS, II, pp. 286–287, letter of September 13, 1621, to William Trumbull).

31. "... mi piacçiono li negotij brevi dando i recevendo ciascuno il suo in un tratto" (ROOSES-RUELENS, II, p. 136).

32. ROOSES-RUELENS, II, pp. 261.

33. "... e considerando che bisogna par tal retirata nel erto e non nella scesa, e lasciar la fortuna mentre chella vi applaude senza aspettar chella da se vi volti da schema mi gettai (colla occasione di un viaggietto secreto) alli piedi di S.A. pregandola per mercede di tanta fatiche la sola essentione di tali impiegi e permissione di servirla in casa mia. La qual gracia ottienni con molto maggior difficulta ch'alcuna altra chella mi habbia giamai con riserva però di alcune intelligense e prattiche secrete di stato che si potevano continuare con minor scommodo. Hora mi trovo per la gracia divina come V.S. ha inteso del Sign.r Picquery colla mia moglie e figliuoli in riposo, e senza alcuna pretensione al mondo che di vivere in pace" (ROOSES-RUELENS, VI, pp. 81–82, Letter to Peiresc of December 18, 1634).

34. "Io mi risolsi al matrimonio non trovandomi anchora atto alla abstinenza del celibato et si come prima damus alla mortificatione fruimur liçita voluptate cum gratiarum actione etc.ª, e presi una moglie giovine di parenti honesti pero cittadini benche tutti volevano persuadermi di casarme in corte ma io temeva commune illud nobilitatis malum superbiam praesertim in illo sexu, et percio mi piacque une che non 'sarrosserebbe vedendomi pigliar gli penelli in mano e a dire al vero il tesoro della pretiosa libertà mi parve duro di perdere col cambio delli abracciamenti di una vecchia" (ROOSES-RUELENS, VI, p. 82, letter to Peiresc of December 18, 1634).

35. ROOSES-RUELENS, VI, p. 271.

36. "J'estime tout le monde pour ma patrie; aussy je croys que je serais le tres bien venu partout" (ROOSES-RUELENS, III, p. 320).

# List of Illustrations

387

# Index of Proper Names

397

# Index of Subjects of Rubens' Works

The following abbreviations are used:
P: Painting
OS: Oil Sketch
D: Drawing
PR: Print
S: Sculpture
T: Tapestry

# Photographic Credits

Amsterdam, Gemeentemusea  Figs. 172, 173
———, Rijksmuseum  Fig. 58
Antwerp, De Schutter  Plates 14, 18, 20, 23, 46, 49, 50, 54, 70, 74
———, 't Felt  Fig. 137
———, Rubenianum  Plates 39, 51, 79; Figs. 2–10, 13, 14, 18, 19, 21–27, 47, 48, 55, 56, 61, 67, 69, 70, 72, 74–76, 79, 82, 84, 87, 89–91, 94, 95, 97, 101, 111, 114, 115, 117, 122, 134, 135, 146, 147, 153, 155–157, 160, 161, 164, 167, 179, 180
———, R. Van Den Boom  Plates 77, 78, 80
Berlin-Dahlem, Gemäldegalerie der Staatlichen Museen  Figs. 65, 108, 126
———, Kupferstichkabinett der Staatlichen Museen  Figs. 92, 171
Boston, Museum of Fine Arts  Fig. 133
Brunswick, Herzog-Anton-Ulrich-Museum  Plate 59
Brussels, A.C.L.  Plate 93; Figs. 31, 32, 37, 39, 40, 45, 46, 52–54, 57, 59, 60, 62, 102, 107, 113, 116, 120, 123, 143, 145, 151, 152
———, Musées Royaux des Beaux-Arts de Belgique  Plates 21, 73, 77
———, Royal Library  Figs. 1, 11, 138
Buffalo, Albright-Knox Art Gallery  Plate 41
Cambridge, Mass., Harvard University, The Fogg Art Museum  Fig. 176
Chicago, The Art Institute of Chicago  Plate 81; Fig. 141
Cleveland, Ohio, The Cleveland Museum of Art  Plate 52

Cologne, Wallraf-Richartz Museum  Plate 10; Figs. 49, 162
Copenhagen, Statens Museum for Kunst  Fig. 109
Florence, Fratelli Alinari  Figs. 30, 68
———, Giacomo Brogi  Fig. 168
———, Scala Istituto Fotografico Editoriale  Plates 43–45, 58, 60, 61, 80; Fig. 130
Frankfurt, Städelsches Kunstinstitut  Fig. 106
Grenoble, Musée des Beaux-Arts  Plate 12
Groningen, Groninger Museum voor Stad en Lande  Fig. 34
Haarlem, Teylers Stichting  Fig. 136
The Hague, A. Dingjan  Fig. 98
———, A. Frequin  Figs. 121, 124, 159, 169
Hendon, A. C. Cooper  Fig. 150
Leningrad, Hermitage  43, 63, 93
London, National Gallery  Plates 57, 63, 65, 71; Figs. 44, 66, 118, 119, 128, 144, 149
———, The Wallace Collection  Figs. 100, 125
Madrid, Museo de las Descalzas Reales  Fig. 96
———, Museo del Prado  Plates 13, 87, 94; Figs. 33, 35, 110, 174, 181
Marseilles, L. Borel  Fig. 73
Minneapolis, The Minneapolis Institute of Arts  Plate 72
Munich, Alte Pinakothek  Plates 22, 64, 69, 78, 82, 83, 85, 88; Figs. 129, 132, 154, 158, 165, 166, 170

Naples, Museo Archeologico Nazionale  Figs. 41a, b
New York, The Frick Collection  Fig. 148
———, The Metropolitan Museum of Art  Plate 90; Fig. 163
———, Eugene Victor Thaw  Fig. 131
Paris, Archives Photographiques  Figs. 50, 51, 105
———, Bulloz  Fig. 86
———, Giraudon  Fig. 177
———, Service de Documentation Photographique—Réunion des Musées Nationaux  Plates 42, 62, 89; Fig. 142
Philadelphia, Johnson Art Collection  Fig. 99
———, Philadelphia College of Art  Fig. 38
Prague, Hradsin  Figs. 28, 29
Richmond, Va., The Virginia Museum of Art  Fig. 178
Sarasota, Fla., John and Mable Ringling Museum of Art  Fig. 140
Stockholm, Nationalmuseum  Figs. 103, 104
Toledo, Ohio, The Toledo Museum of Art  Plate 84
Vienna, Gemäldegalerie, Kunsthistorisches Museum  Plates 17, 35–37, 91, 92; Figs. 85, 88, 175
———, Graphische Sammlung Albertina  Plates 3–5, 55, 56; Figs. 15, 16, 20, 42, 81, 83
———, Mandl  Plates 32, 38; Fig. 71
Zurich, Kunsthaus  Fig. 112

405

Official UNESCO medal,
issued on the occasion of the 400th anniversary
of the birth of Peter Paul Rubens.
Engraved by S. Santucci; struck by the Paris Mint

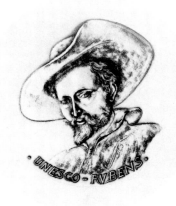 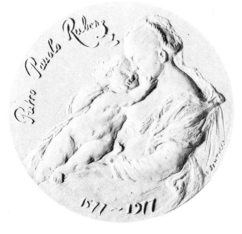

*recto:*
SELF-PORTRAIT
Antwerp, Rubens House

*verso:*
MATERNITY
Paris, Louvre

Designed by Louis Van den Eede. Text composed in Garamond 12/14 by Brufizet S. A., Bruges. Printed by Lannoo, Tielt, on paper by Cartiere Italiane Riunite, Rome. Illustrations by Photogravure De Schutter, Antwerp. Binding by Van Rijmenam, The Hague

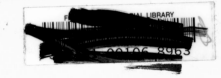
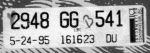